SOLD AMERICAN

CONSUMPTION AND

CITIZENSHIP, 1890–1945

CHARLES F. MCGOVERN

Sold American

The University of North Carolina Press   CHAPEL HILL

Set in Scala and Berliner types
by Keystone Typesetting, Inc.

This book was published with the assistance of
the Thornton H. Brooks Fund of the University of
North Carolina Press.

The paper in this book meets the guidelines for permanence
and durability of the Committee on Production Guidelines for
Book Longevity of the Council on Library Resources.

Frontispiece: "Votes for Women." (*Woman's Home Companion*,
November 1914, cover III)

Library of Congress Cataloging-in-Publication Data
McGovern, Charles.
Sold American : consumption and citizenship, 1890–1945 /
Charles F. McGovern.
    p. cm.
Includes bibliographical references and index.
ISBN-13: 978-0-8078-3033-8 (cloth : alk. paper)
ISBN-10: 0-8078-3033-x (cloth : alk. paper)
ISBN-13: 978-0-8078-5676-5 (pbk. : alk. paper)
ISBN-10: 0-8078-5676-2 (pbk. : alk. paper)
    1. Consumption (Economics)—Political aspects—United States—
History. 2. Consumer behavior—Political aspects—United States—
History. I. Title.
HC110.C6M35 2006
339.4′7097309041—dc22   2006010728

cloth   10 09 08 07 06   5 4 3 2 1
paper   10 09 08 07 06   5 4 3 2 1

CONTENTS

FIGURES

ACKNOWLEDGMENTS

Finishing any large project offers a sense of elation and loss. The best compensation for this is the pleasure in thanking at long last the many colleagues, teachers, and loved ones who offered their encouragement, critical wisdom, and assistance. Due to the demands of working in an institution not explicitly committed to monographic research, *Sold American* had a very long gestation, but at last I'm delighted to thank all those who have aided the book and its author along the way. I alone am responsible for its flaws.

Research for this book was partially supported by the Smithsonian Institution and Harvard University's Program in the History of American Civilization. I have presented portions of this work as papers at conferences and colloquia over the years. My warm thanks to Susan Douglas, Sut Jhally, John Kasson, Roland Marchand, Kathy Peiss, and Robert Westbrook for their comments and helpful criticisms.

When this project was just beginning, I was fortunate to meet F. J. Schlink and spend several days with him out at the Consumers' Research facilities in Washington, New Jersey. Mr. Schlink was unfailingly gracious and helpful, welcoming me without condition or constraint. He showered me with books, papers, and clippings from his own personal files while answering endless and what to him must have seemed obvious questions about the organization's history. He also understood when my views of the project's direction and intent inevitably strayed from his. Although his story did not become the focus of this book, I trust that readers will see that he was a key figure in articulating both the potential of a consumer movement and its limitations in a U.S. context. Mr. Reginald Joyce, Schlink's longtime neighbor and co-worker, joined us one day as well to recall the early history of Consumers' Research both in New York and later at its "country quarters" in New Jersey. The late Carroll Wilson of the Hills Bros. coffee company graciously answered my questions about his company and its longtime relationship with the N. W. Ayer agency. My grateful thanks to Albert Berger and the late Richard Kiernan for informative conversations about the agency business in the 1950s.

This work took initial shape in the History of American Civilization Program at Harvard. I thank Daniel Aaron, Bernard Bailyn, David Donald, and Stephan Thernstrom for their encouragement and genial skepticism; each has been equally important to me over the years. I especially wish to thank the late Judith Shklar, Jon Roberts, and Alan Brinkley for inspiring me as both teachers and scholars; they demonstrated every day the intimate connections of pedagogy, research, and humane decency in a setting sometimes hostile to all three. Finally, it is a great pleasure at last to thank Donald Fleming for his faith and support. He believed in this project and its author from the first, and I am one of a legion of scholars indebted to his wide-ranging curiosity and rigorous standards.

In Cambridge, Chandos Brown, Gordon Hylton, Richard John, Neil Jumonville, Greg Pfitzer, Tom Siegel, and most of all Dave Samson and Fred Marchant shared ideas and pushed me as the first outlines of this project took shape. Peter Berkowitz, Sam and Lynn Beshers, Temple Dickenson, Jeff Lubin, Henry Murphy, Beth Saxon, Lalitha Vaidyanathan, Jonathan Willens, and Jan Wussow comprised a community that made graduate school more pleasurable. I cannot thank all the members of HLSDS but must especially shout out to Dale Cendali, Becky Dao, Rosemary Fei, Lou Ann Fields, Francis Fitzpatrick, Gary Harrington, Lori Laubich, William James, Jan Miller, Ruben Perlmutter, Andrea Stang, and Marlene Wittman for sustaining me personally over five years and giving me an ancillary education in American law that has come in handy ever since.

A Smithsonian predoctoral fellowship enabled me to research much of this book. I would like to thank the great community of fellows and researchers who shared ideas and resources and made my fellowship year exciting and productive. My thanks to Colleen Dunlavy, Wayne Durrill, Karen Lynn Femia, Joni Kinsey, Mike O'Malley, Grace Palladino, Mary Panzer, Ron Radano, David Reid, Francie Robb, Julie Weiss, John Wetenhall, Rebecca Zurier, and most prominently, Lynne Kirby. I owe the late Mary Dyer so much. Her subversive wisdom, good cheer, and passionate commitment to education taught me wonderful life lessons and made the Fellows Program a special place.

Susan Strasser, Mattias Judt, and I organized a 1995 conference on consumption, cosponsored by the German Historical Institute and the National Museum of American History. My thanks to the twenty-nine participants in the conference, and contributors to the subsequent book *Getting and Spending*, who spent three days and many subsequent e-mails exchanging ideas, approaches, and methods. My thanks especially go to Susie, whose pioneering work and steadfast commitment to writing everyday life history have been a model and inspiration for me.

The National Museum of American History Archives Center was my home for a year, and much of the work for this book was done there. I thank the archivists, past and present, who helped me: Stacy Flaherty, David Haberstich, Rob Harding, Reuben Jackson, Cathy Keen, Lorene Mayo, Mimi Minnick, Craig Orr, Kay Peterson, Deborra Richardson, Wendy Shay, Vanessa Simmons, and most of all, John Fleckner. I became interested in Consumers' Research as Rutgers University was beginning to take possession of the archive. Bill Miller welcomed and enlisted me in organizing and culling the collection, and he made sure I could access the parts most useful to me. Once the collection was at Rutgers, Ron Becker always went out of his way to assist me every way he could. The Center for the Study of the Consumer Movement at Consumers Union, Inc., gave me complete access to its archive. I am very grateful. At the J. Walter Thompson Archives, Cynthia Swank in New York and then Ellen Gartrell at Duke University were models of helpfulness and insight. Anna Marie Sandecki at the Ayer Archives in New York extended herself above and beyond the call. Paula Brown at BBDO in New York enabled me to spend several very fruitful days in its archives. Catherine Heinz opened the riches of the Broadcast Pioneers Library (now the Library of American Broadcasting) and made her own vast knowledge available to me. My thanks as well to the staffs at the State Historical Society of Wisconsin and the Western Reserve Historical Society in Cleveland.

Rick Prelinger has been a friend to this project and to scholars everywhere who work in the intersection of commercial culture and everyday life for many years. He opened his unequaled archive of commercial and sponsored films to me and spent a number of hours discussing this project. His own work in collecting, preserving, and making available precious historical resources embodies a different lesson than the ones most often taught in consumer culture: wealth increases not by hoarding but by giving away.

I owe a great deal to the librarians at the National Museum of American History. Amy Begg, Brigid Burke, Chris Cottrell, Helen Holley, and especially Jim Roan and Stephanie Thomas unfailingly ferreted out fugitive materials and made researching this book infinitely easier. In the final stages the great staff at Swem Library at William and Mary handled every loan request with efficiency and humor. I must add particular thanks to Suzanne Shook of the Richmond Public Library, who arranged access to the library's run of *Printers' Ink*. At a time when major repositories have been throwing out perfectly sound journals and substituting poorly done microfilm, I greatly appreciated her example and kindness. The unparalleled collections of the Baker and Widener Libraries at Harvard and the Library of Congress were indispensable.

I was blessed to work with some terrific interns and assistants: Beth Broadrup, Dominique Bregunt, Amy Dixon, Paula Kaczor, and Rebecca Van Dyk. Special everlasting thanks to Lauren Brown.

I was privileged to work at the National Museum of American History for fifteen years. During that time this project was most often on hold, but over the years numerous fellows and researchers there shared common interests in questions of consumption and culture with me. Working with so many creative minds was a great gift. Their ideas and suggestions have shaped this project in innumerable ways. My thanks to Kevin Armitage, Jane Becker, Cynthia Blair, Angie Blake, Elspeth Brown, Oscar Campomanes, John Cheng, Alison Clarke, Catherine Cocks, Joe Corn, Sharon Corwin, Tracey Deutsch, Elissa Engleman, Katy Fenn, Benjamin Filene, Miriam Forman-Brunell, David Freund, Paul Gardullo, John Gennari, Caroline Goldstein, Elise Goldwasser, Janet Green, Philip Gruen, Catherine Gudis, Bob Haddow, Grace Hale, Marybeth Hamilton, John Hartigan, Kristin Hass, Amy Howard, Vicky Howard, Michael Jo, Colin Johnson, Alison Kibler, Arlene Kriv, Jeanne Lawrence, Tina Manko, Jean Mansavage, Amy Marver, Denise Meringolo, Anna McCarthy, Eliza McFeely, Julia Mickenberg, Karl Miller, Elizabeth White Nelson, Ruth Oldenziel, Cecilia O'Leary, Charlie Ponce de Leon, Chris Rasmussen, Nicolas Sammond, Lawrence Samuel, Scott Sandage, Linda Scott, Dawn Schmitz, Marlis Schweitzer, Peggy Shaffer, Helen Sheumaker, Lauren Sklaroff, Katherine Smith, Tim Spears, Randy Stearns, Jonathan Sterne, Todd Uhlmann, Robin Veder, Shirley Wadja, Matt Wray, and Marilyn Zoidis. I want specially to thank Lonnie Bunch, Spencer Crew, and Jim Weaver for support and encouragement over the years.

My colleagues past and present at the National Museum of American History have been an exemplary group of teachers and coworkers. They accepted a nonmuseum person such as myself into their midst without question and patiently taught me about material culture and museum practice. Their fierce dedication to their collections, and to the integrity of history and material culture independent of market and political pressures, has shaped my work permanently. I cannot name them all but want to thank Richard Ahlborn, Sheila Alexander, Joyce Bedi, Dwight Bowers, Camy Clough, Maggie Dennis, Richard Doty, Barney Finn, Anne Golovin, Hank Grasso, John Hasse, Elizabeth Harris, Ellen Hughes, Claudia Kidwell, Stacey Kluck, Gary Kulik, Steve Lubar, Edie Mayo, John Meehan, Art Molella, Shannon Perich, the late Rodris Roth, Harry Rubenstein, the late Carl Scheele, David Shayt, Monica Smith, Carlene Stephens, Gary Sturm, Deborah Warner, and Helena

Wright for teaching me so much. I thank Pete Daniel, Katherine Ott, Marvette Perez, Fath Ruffins, and Barbara Clark Smith all for inspiring me with their scholarship and teaching me so much about collaboration. For fifteen years Larry Bird and I have discussed consumption, business culture, and politics. I thank him for those many conversations and more to come; his enthusiasm and willingness to share ideas have shaped this work on practically every page.

A number of colleagues took time from their own work to read drafts of this project and provide thoughtful comments and suggestions for its improvement. I am really grateful to Alan Berolzheimer, Larry Bird, Ian Gordon, Matt Guterl, Jeanne Houck, Jerma Jackson, Alexis MacCrossen, Patrick Miller, Shelley Nickles, Mike O'Malley, Elena Razlogova, and Alex Russo. For this and much more besides, I owe a special debt to Barry Shank for a penetrating reading that reshaped this book so much for the better.

I cannot thank JoAnne Brown enough. Her ideas and encouragement have been invaluable at every step.

Several people have gone well above the call of collegiality in their efforts and encouragement. Dan Horowitz and the late Roland Marchand read early versions of this study, and their wise comments greatly shaped its subsequent form. Casey Blake did all that and much more. I couldn't have a better reader or a better friend. Nadine Cohodas lavished unwavering attention on my prose and worked tirelessly to make this a clearer and more useful book. Laura Helper has become a sister as well as one of the best teachers and readers I will ever have. Thanks for everything.

For their inspiring scholarship and their friendship, I thank Beth Bailey, Casey Blake, Michele Bogart, and David Scobey. They supported me through finishing this book and offered priceless perspectives as I moved from the museum to the university. From very early on in this project Jackson Lears has offered wonderful feedback, unfailing support, and shrewd practical suggestions. He helped me see the big picture of this book when it was still only a chapter, and it is much the better today for his advice and critical acumen.

To Jean-Christophe Agnew and George Lipsitz, I owe great thanks for their readings of this book for the University of North Carolina Press. They both set standards in their scholarship and teaching that I try to honor. Their interest in and encouragement of my work have sustained me through times of great doubt and uncertainty. After many years I thank Lewis Bateman for his commitment to quality, his astute observations about writing, and his faith in this project. Chuck Grench cheerfully took on the project from Lew and has worked hard to make this the book it should be. I hope their faith has been repaid. Paula Wald has expertly shepherded the book and made it better at every step. I thank Bethany Johnson for heroic, masterful copy-editing.

My bandmates in both The B Sides and The Pretensions—Larry Bird, Mark Hirsch, Matt Karush, and Mike O'Malley—have sustained me for the better part of a decade now. Whether discussing Gramsci or Grand Funk, they are a constant source of delight and learning. Mike selflessly contributed an endless stream of fabulous insights and encouragement over many years, and I thank him as well for securing several key images for this book. Mark has given me wise editorial council on more occasions than either of us remember.

My new colleagues in American Studies and in History at William and Mary have been welcoming and generous. I am proud to be part of their communities. I am especially indebted to Chandos Brown, Barbara Carson, Maureen Fitzgerald, Grey Gundaker, Arthur Knight, Leisa Meyer, Scott Nelson, Carol Sheriff, Alan Wallach, and Lynn Weiss. For many kindnesses and help with the transition, I thank Betty Flanagan, Roz Stearns, and Jean Brown. Finally, my deep thanks to Jim McCord, Jim Whittenburg, Kim Phillips, and Rich Lowry. Thanks to all my students at William and Mary but especially the graduate students in my seminars, whose tough questions and enthusiastic interest in consumption and culture have energized my spirits and messed with my head!

Like most scholars, I am indebted to a cavalcade of wonderful teachers. At Swarthmore College Jim Field and Bob Bannister saw the makings of a scholar and pushed me to see them, too. I owe Bob Sabbatelli and John Connelly at Regis High School, along with Bob VerEecke SJ, Jack McSherry SJ, Bob Voelkle, and the late Stephen Duffy SJ, a lifetime of thanks for giving me good training and most of all for pushing me to open my horizons and my mind. The late Warren Susman will inspire me always.

Old friends Alan Abramson, Leslie Berger, Peter Honchaurk, Lou Jerome, Chris Lowney, Chris Lynch, and Nina Morais have seen this project from its beginnings, and I thank them for their support and insights over the years. Paul Yamada has talked over just about every aspect of this book with me and pushed me to explore its deepest implications for American history and contemporary politics. To Paul Kiernan, I can only offer my thanks for taking the whole journey with me and caring about it at every step.

My family has sustained this project—and its author—for its whole life. My sister Elissa has been a source of infinite good cheer and perceptive practical questions that admit no easy answers or weasel language. My brother John also has offered critical support and encouragement all the way while reminding me that ideas that cannot be translated into the plainest everyday language will not mean much. My parents, Jack and Mary Jane McGovern, first put a book in my hand and instilled a desire in me for learning and teaching. All their lives they have shown me the stakes of the moral questions that *Sold American* addresses. They taught me that there were things more important than getting and spending and showed me that citizenship in the United States entailed more than low taxes, new cars, or the large economy size.

Mary McGovern has lived with this book I suspect longer than she can believe. She has read countless drafts, seen deadlines come and go, and endured innumerable discussions about consumers, always with enthusiasm and great insight. So much smarter than I, she has improved this book in countless ways and inspired me to improve it even further. More important, she has taught me what I know of the many differences between goods and the good. She enriches me beyond measure in her loving wisdom, good humor, and inspiration to do my best. My sons, Tom and Nat, are of course avid consumers, but more important, they remind me every day of the limits of markets and of things, and of the power of those things that are not commodities. It is to my parents and my family that this book is dedicated.

The American citizen's first importance to his country is no longer that of citizen but that of consumer. Consumption is a new necessity.[1]

We are all Alices in a Wonderland of conflicting claims, bright promises, fancy packages, soaring words, and almost impenetrable ignorance.[2]

We begin with a story. It is spring of 1929, the high tide of an unprecedented prosperity in American life. In a small upstate New York community, the local savings and loan faces closure and liquidation. The board of directors remains skeptical that, despite its solvency, the bank can survive on its current business plan. Its young manager appeals to these executives—all local merchants and businessmen—to keep the bank open to serve its needy clientele: working people, those on fixed incomes, small wage-earners. These depositors and workers, he argues, need an institution to extend them credit, an institution that takes into account character as well as material assets, one that offers them a welcome home for their dreams along with their few dollars. Many board members remain opposed, arguing that small institutions especially cannot afford such customers. After all, without collateral, such borrowers are bad risks for the bank and the town as a whole. Easy access to credit, even for a home, will only make them "a discontented rabble instead of a thrifty working class." The young banker reminds them that his is the only institution that serves these members of the community. Then he counters with an impassioned second argument:

> You're all businessmen here. Doesn't it [credit and property] make them better customers, better citizens? You said . . . that they had to wait and save their money . . . wait? Wait for what? Until their children grow up and leave them or until they get so old and broken down that . . . ? Just remember this . . . this rabble you're talking about—they do most of the working and paying and living and dying in this community. Is it too much to ask to have them work and pay and live and die in a couple of decent rooms and a bath?

Where his moral argument fails, the appeal to civics and economic self-interest wins out. Acknowledging that being a consumer made one a better citizen, the board members (who, indeed, are merchants in the business of selling to these same people) fold their opposition; the bank and the banker stay in business. This scene took place at a now familiar American institution —the Bailey Building and Loan in Bedford Falls, New York. The idealistic young executive was George Bailey, hero of Frank Capra's 1946 film *It's a Wonderful Life*.[3] The film has since passed into common American lore, endlessly referenced, often remade, and ritually repeated at that most sacred feast of consumption, Christmas.

THE HEARTBEAT OF AMERICA

Americans are consumers. Their prodigious buying appetite is the life-blood of the United States's economy and a major force worldwide. Material abundance, realized in thousands of goods, services, and experiences, symbolizes the United States around the world and is the hallmark of American everyday life. That life powerfully attracts the millions who today comprise a new immigration wave as socially transformative as its counterpart one hundred years ago. With the collapse of most socialist regimes, advanced capitalism—global and indifferent to the nation's borders and interests, state-supported but advocating free markets—reigns for now and indeed the foreseeable future.[4] No form of socioeconomic organization as yet has challenged its pervasive presence or legitimacy.

In the wake of the September 11, 2001, attacks on the World Trade Center and the Pentagon, President George W. Bush and his cabinet called for Americans to attend to life as normal—to shop, spend money, and consume for the good of the nation.[5] Soon after, numerous marketing campaigns appeared trumpeting patriotic themes. While such pleas met mixed success at best in a recession economy, few questioned the idea that increased consumption benefited the nation. The president's political message also was clear: the citizen's duty was not mandatory military service to combat terrorism (although the rate of volunteers rose), or civic engagement to strengthen social bonds in the wake of national disaster and shock. The citizen's duty certainly did not include sincere questioning or reexamination of national security and diplomacy, although millions of Americans did just that. Instead, the president urged everyone to resume business as usual: individual, atomized consumption was best for the nation as a whole. Americans faced trauma, doubt, and fear; the White House directed them to the nearest mall. Although they generally turned a deaf ear to the subsequent sales campaigns that associated spending with patriotism or brands with national glory, such appeals surprised no one.[6]

Americans have long recognized that being consumers is central to their shared experiences as Americans. Getting and spending to acquire more, newer, and better things has become lived ideology, a deeply held common sense that shapes the ways we understand culture and social difference. Economists, critics, marketers, designers, and everyday citizens routinely examine tastes and spending patterns as indices of American life, from the quality of its collective civilization to the strength of its diversity and to its entrenched inequality.[7] While the aspirations evoked by phrases like "the American dream" and "the American way of life" are numberless, common versions highlight worldly goods and the wealth to acquire them.[8] Even so, since World War II a growing gulf has separated the worlds of George Bailey and George Bush, a gap between one world where consuming made better citizens and another where consumption supersedes other civic duties.

This common sense was forged between the late nineteenth century and the Depression, decades when the U.S. economy came to rest decisively on consuming. *Sold American* argues that in those years Americans came to understand spending as a form of citizenship, an important ritual of national identity in daily life. Explicit political and civic language, images, and practices that equated voting with buying shaped common understandings of consumption. In entertainment and public discourse Americans saw their common heritage defined as much by goods and leisure as by political abstractions or historical figures. Through prosperity, depression, and war, an ideology emerged naming plenty as the distinctive feature of an exceptional American history and culture. As the nation evolved from isolated country to imperial power, from rural republic to industrial giant, Americans embraced a material nationalism that placed goods and spending at the center of social life.

Between 1890 and 1945 the United States became a consumer society whose inhabitants used the mass market to make their daily lives, from personal hygiene to communal leisure. People learned to buy brand-name, trademarked commodities and to adopt new products and behaviors sold through a dizzying array of emporia and media. That brand system was largely in place by 1910; during the economic boom of the 1920s, the so-called New Era saw brand goods embraced throughout the American middle class and make inroads in the working class as well.[9] The crisis of capitalism in the Depression revealed the consumer-voter's centrality to the political and social order. The economy, in turn, depended on workers' producing goods at adequate wages and sufficiently low prices to enable them to purchase what they made.[10] To combat the economic crisis, New Deal remedies tacked from state economic centralization to buttress profits, to fiscal policies to shore up the buying power of the citizen-voter, the consumer.[11] During World War II, national commitments to consumption only increased. Like George Bailey, home-front citizens would struggle against fascism and the Axis in their roles as consumers. They fulfilled civic obligations in war work and war bonds and through patriotic, frugal consuming. Both servicemen and civilians perceived the war as a struggle to defend freedom, defined not as intellectual abstractions but in the quotidian realm of family, home, and community. That realm prominently featured consumer products, entertainment, and rituals.[12] Postwar policies further extended state promotion of individual consumption; from fiscal programs to social benefits, the American government subsidized and encouraged certain forms of consumption and spending.[13] The Cold War focused attention on the contrasting consumer regimes of capitalism and communism. U.S. policies deployed consumer plenty as an ideological and economic weapon against communism, both abroad and at home.[14] Unprecedented economic expansion only reinforced this transformation from the dark Depression days. In the sunny postwar moment of unchallenged economic dominance and growth, the United States was unmistakably a society defined by and dedicated to consumer plenty for all. Being an American meant being a consumer.

Where did such languages, images, and beliefs originate? Classical liberalism locates individual freedom, as an economic as well as political right, deep in inherited political beliefs and practices. Yet there have been more specific origins of the now common associations of consuming with American freedom and citizenship. *Sold American* argues that professionals who studied and addressed buyers made civic language and ideas a centerpiece of common discourse about consumers. Such experts, most notably advertising agents and those whom I call consumerists, helped invent modern consumption. Advertising agents worked with business enterprises to sell goods by developing and placing sales messages throughout the landscape, the media, and numerous institutions. Consumerists were the social scientists, engineers, and bureaucrats who contested advertising's influence and fought for regulation and information on behalf of ultimate buyers. These two groups of professionals created powerful, pervasive prescriptions for acquiring and using goods, along with models of proper appetites and aptitudes. As experts they cultivated specific relationships with consumers, representing them in large-scale institutions. By examining these professionals' activities and ideas, we can trace the complex embrace of consumption in the twentieth century.[15] Decades before the Cold War explicitly linked consumption with an aggressive nationalism, Americans learned to associate both their national identity and political order with spending. Such ideas firmly cast American citizenship as consumption; they are the focus of this book.

Advertisers and consumerists both were part of the "new class" of professionals that came to influence in the late nineteenth century. Performing the white-collar work of an emerging corporate order, they have long been identified as an advance guard of modernity.[16] I argue that such professionals helped bring about a mass consumer society by facilitating the spread of corporate influence in daily life and serving as intermediaries between everyday people and corporate commerce. They developed direct relationships with buyers, claimed consumers as their constituency, and claimed to be consumers' best spokesmen. As self-conscious professionals, they purveyed "scientific" expertise. Such advice would enable consumers to evaluate an ever-increasing myriad of products and services and make sound decisions based on their needs. From their very different perspectives, advertisers and consumerists each viewed themselves as consumers' natural ally in choosing and using goods. Of course, other professionals worked with consumers as well. Home economists, reformers, and lawyers worked to improve goods and purchasing skills and represented consumer interests in public debates.[17] Industrial designers, marketers, and pollsters all surveyed buying publics.[18] But advertisers and product-testing professionals represent a useful focus for the study: their divergent views, bitter debates, and surprisingly shared assumptions illuminate broad conflicts over the emerging consumer culture. Each group left important institutional and cultural legacies that to this day influence debate on the nature and ends of consumption and the market in daily life.

These professionals drew on American political traditions and languages to socialize Americans and to shape popular understanding of consumption. Such language and concepts cast spending as a specifically *American* social practice, an important element of distinct national identity. Adapting "American" ideals, cultural icons, traditions, and languages, they framed consuming as the basis of a reconstituted modern citizenship. Market replaced polis in a new communal public life characterized not by geography, religion, or politics, but by spending. Although these professionals differed profoundly over specifics of proper consumption, they nonetheless shared similar views on consumers. Whatever the results of their work in selling products, educating consumers, or testing goods, they helped make consuming a centerpiece of American life and the foundation of civic identity.

This shift could only occur because meanings and experiences of American citizenship themselves were changing dramatically through the combined influences of urbanization, modernization, and immigration. During the Progressive Era, reformers struggled to make government more directly responsive to popular will; American women fought for and won the vote. But as popular interest in expanding democracy increased, rates of voting participation fell sharply in the years between 1880 and 1920. Political parties grew more centralized and developed an educational style that emphasized distant, top-down direction at the expense of mass participation.[19] The massive European migrations of these years stirred xenophobic and racist fears that were exacerbated in World War I and channeled in the eugenics movement. The result was a series of congressional restrictions that effectively halted immigration for more than a generation and, more important, created pressures on nonnatives to conform to specific prescriptions of Americanism and citizenship.[20] Changing ideas of human psychology, new scientific theories of behavior, and social science interest in mass society gravely undermined long-held Jeffersonian assumptions of the common person's competence to participate effectively in democracy and public affairs.[21] Lastly, urban commercial culture, with its basis in spectacle and frank allusions to sex and sensory gratification, disturbed traditional ideals of popular diversions and moral order. Cultural dimensions of citizenship emerged to reinforce or challenge explicitly legal and ascriptive definitions. Clearly, citizenship had changed under the centralization of politics, the fragmentation of urban society, and new experiences of public life. That new public life was characterized as much by entertainment and commodities as by the immigrants and mass audiences associated with them. Any new political or civic order would have to contend with these emerging cultural forms. The professionals involved in promoting and reforming consumption envisioned consumers—middle and working class, native and immigrant, urban and rural—as a prominent part of a new public culture. They used American national symbols and political language not only to legitimize their work, but also to unite a nation in a citizenship based on purchasing, ownership, entertainment, and display.[22]

Advertisers and consumerists shared overlapping audiences, but they disagreed markedly in their ideas of a consumer-centered common interest. Advertisers claimed to serve consumers best through products they promoted; they brought the public good news and news of goods that would improve people's lives by increasing their everyday freedom.[23] On the other hand, the first consumer products-testing organization, Consumers' Research (CR), originated specifically and directly in opposition to advertising. The organization propagated a populist science over salesmanship and a republican vision of consumption for the common good. Consumers' Research inspired a web of Depression-era organizations and activists—the consumer movement— that criticized business and lobbied the federal government to protect retail purchasers. This study cannot address the consumer movement's history, but Consumers' Research's own story illustrates the movement's ideas and limitations.[24] Most organizations drew from CR's advocacy of practical and uncensored science for the consumer. The tensions between these two commitments to increasing "freedoms" or enhancing "protection" remain evident today.

In outlining hopes and fears for the consumer culture, advertisers and consumerists alike drew on differing political traditions, dating back to antiquity, to frame their descriptions of consumption. Competing ideologies of liberalism and republicanism held contrasting visions of society and commerce in debating the national direction. The republican faithful feared concentrated economic power and its alliances with the state. They placed their trust instead in a producer-oriented economy undergirding a stable society of communally minded, independent, freeholding citizens, workers, and farmers. This republic relied on expansion in space to safeguard national stability and fought the growth of commercial practices and institutions. By contrast, liberal ideology emphasized individualism, the contractual basis of society, and an activist state to promote commerce. Liberalism's adherents envisioned society's expansion over time rather than space. Seeking growth of commerce and markets, they embraced social change and courted technological advancement. They accepted as inevitable that a class system would accompany trade and economic growth.[25] Advertisers generally held these liberal beliefs to argue that private enterprise and personal wealth defined the American pursuit of happiness. Many consumerists, in turn, fashioned a republican-inspired vision that distrusted the marketplace and viewed material goods as only one element of the pursuit of happiness. Advertisers appropriated the metaphors of voting, elections, and representation, while consumerists adapted a republican civic language of virtuous independence and hostility to moneyed corruption to contest corporate authority.

These two groups drew on cultural commentary as well, adapting nationalist and patriotic iconography. They celebrated mass-produced goods as the basis of a distinct American culture, yet these well-educated, affluent professionals were ambivalent about the material abundance they publicly praised. In private, their responses ranged from guarded endorsement to uneasy dismissal and contempt, especially among advertisers. Behind the scenes, advertisers ridiculed consumers and cultivated a distinct sense of difference from them. Consumerists fought for more educated consumers, but they criticized popular tastes as banal and debased. Beneath this disaffection we can detect more than the familiar class and cultural disparities of elites and masses. I argue that studying consumers led the professionals literally to objectify consumers, to understand them primarily in terms of the goods they sold or critiqued. They judged social class and caste through the material framework of taste and acquisition. They categorized consumers by the things they bought. Ultimately, they blurred classes of goods with social class.[26]

The consequences of such objectification have been far-reaching. The scale of mass society eludes easy description, and using goods to symbolize groups is both convenient and evocative. But such objectification prevented a better appreciation of the complex attitudes of people toward their things. Paradoxically, it may have overemphasized the attachments of Americans to their commodities and obscured the ways in which Americans placed limits on the marketplace in their lives. A century ago, German sociologist Georg Simmel noted that money was a symbol that was also a solvent; representing the potential for all things to be understood through its value, money eroded specific values in any particular thing. Money also established impersonal relations that allowed classes to interact. Yet by making goods equally fungible, he might have added, the money economy prevented people from understanding or deciding on meaningful differences between things or among values.[27] Similarly, by categorizing people in terms of commodities, consumer professionals often lost sight of the startling complexity and diversity among Americans. They encouraged Americans to view consumer goods and entertainment as the common culture and unifying bonds of their society. Muted social and cultural conflict would yield a consensual nation in which the quest for the good became the pursuit of goods.

What was at stake in the decades-long struggle to train consumers and define consumption? The fusion of consumption, nationalism, and citizenship today is commonplace, if contested. While consuming dominates many national economies, Americans particularly maintain a fierce commitment to spending that is deep-seated, perhaps defining. The professionals who claimed consumption as citizenship and who used political language to depict market behavior tapped enduring and sacred political ideals. But consumption's importance in American life also has clear nationalist dimensions. Although Americans have only ambivalently embraced economic nationalism, they nonetheless view consumption as central to their national identity.[28] Critic Lisa Lowe has noted, "It is through the terrain of national culture that the individual subject is politically formed as the American citizen."[29] In the consumer era, that national culture assumed the form of commercial entertainment and consumer goods. Citizenship does not depend on laws alone, as many scholars have noted.[30] The law defines political status, but customs, beliefs and the material world all shape affiliation and meaning. It is indeed in culture—in symbols, language, rituals, and forms of expression—that nationality is made and redefined. In consumption, generations of migrants and natives both have become "American," even as the markers of national origin, race, class, or gender limited full political citizenship for many. An episode in Abraham Cahan's 1917 novel *The Rise of David Levinsky* shows how Russian immigrant Levinsky's new suit of ready-made clothing not only removed the appearance of the newly arrived greenhorn but made him over: "It was as though the hair-cut and the American clothes had changed my identity."[31] For countless real-life Levinskys, shopping, spending, and acquiring mass-manufactured goods confirmed their identities as Americans.[32]

Through the work of Benedict Anderson, Eric Hobsbawm, and others, we know that nationalism rests on a cultural foundation.[33] One historian has claimed that "cultural elements have been indispensable in the rise of modern nations and states." Echoing Lisa Lowe, David Lloyd and Paul Thomas have recently argued that ideas of the modern state and of culture are inseparable; training in "culture" was a tool used by states to manufacture citizens.[34] In the simultaneous emergence of the modern state and the mass market at the turn of the twentieth century, consumption and nationalism were cast in mutual terms. In their decades-long campaigns, advertisers and consumer scientists engaged in the same training. They promoted consumption as citizenship and trained consumers to be citizens. In this sense, consumption became a core element of the American nation-state.

MAKING AMERICAN CONSUMPTION:
CULTURE, COMMERCE, SOCIETY, AND STATE

Historians have come to understand the half century after 1880 as the time when the United States became a consumer society. Rapid demographic, economic, and institutional growth, along with technological, intellectual, and material changes, fueled the United States's transition to a complex bureaucratic state, an advanced industrial economy, and a modern consumer culture. Briefly, the most important factors in this history include a widespread, rationalized system of industrial production and labor controlled by managerial capital; new technologies and goods adapted to household uses; national media, including mass-circulation magazines, radio, film, sound recordings, electrical signs, and billboards; new institutions of national distribution; and new modes of thought about the self—all contributed to the emergence of mass consumption.[35] By 1930, the American economic system had undergone a tremendous evolution, which made a staggering variety of goods available for purchase. Though much of the populace still lived in small villages and towns and made a living from the land, the agrarian republic of local preindustrial economies had given way to an urban nation of new values, experiences, and institutions. These all were bound up intimately in a commercial system where anything—not only food, clothing, and furniture but ideas, perceptions, and emotions themselves—could and did become a commodity.[36] The United States became a consumer society, its economy one of mass consumption, its culture deeply influenced by commodities and spending.

Why did this happen in this particular period? Beginning with Charles and Mary Beard in 1927, historians have noted the United States's transformation from a society of rural farms to one of city-based industries—American-style modernization—as the driving change of the nation's history.[37] Some observers in the 1920s directly connected this transformation to the consumer order.[38] When did the United States become a consumer society? Numerous historians today claim consumer society had emerged in Europe as early as the seventeenth and eighteenth centuries.[39] T. H. Breen argues that the colonists who rebelled against England and fought the Revolution had been made into a proto-nation by being consumers for English goods. Americans certainly had been purchasing ready-made consumer goods for decades.[40] However, it seems clear that only between 1880 and 1930 did Americans come to depend on the commercial marketplace, with few feasible alternatives, for the necessities of daily life. Moreover, manufacturing and selling consumer goods occupied a significant sector of the economy. The United States fully and markedly became a consumer society when its economy produced, and most Americans purchased, the things used to serve material needs and shape daily experience.[41] While pockets of the poor and of rural America, especially in the South, came only later to the full dependence on these commodities, by 1930 the United States, for better or ill, was a consumer society.

In the past two decades we have seen a remarkable outpouring of literature on the advent of consumer society, and much of it has been devoted to the implications of this transition in the late nineteenth century. Led by Richard Fox, Jackson Lears, and William Leach, scholars who view consumer society as an outgrowth of long-term capitalist modernization have focused on its cultural consequences.[42] Lears has asserted that mass consumption signaled a "disenchantment of the world," an incomplete but devastating detachment of people from direct connection to their material environment. Redefining abundance—the measure of wealth—businesses substituted products for well-being and encouraged people to define themselves through commodities. Advertising promulgated an "ethos of personal efficiency," which both nurtured and required a strictly disciplined self. In consumer society, work and leisure were now routinized, rationalized, and stripped of spiritual compensations and sensual appeals. Yet Lears notes that this process was necessarily incomplete. The corporate-driven consumer regime could eclipse and dilute but never fully erase traditional folkways. Advertising might have debased the sacred and spiritual, but Americans still grounded themselves in "in an animated universe." While the new culture hinged on a compulsion to rationalize and commodify all experience, Lears notes that Americans generated numerous strategies to resist and evade that impulse.[43] But if Lears finds the persistence of animism, William Leach finds only displacement and debility. He argues that a grand commercial entente—department store merchants, professionals, therapeutic faith mongers, and the state—created a new "culture of desire." Here money and accumulation, novelty, and change itself determined the good. People came to view accumulation rather than labor, art, or love as the true basis for human dignity and happiness. Leach does contend that for women, consumption offered certain opportunities and a public life beyond the precepts of Victorian domesticity.[44] Yet he concludes that consumption could neither liberate nor offer any transcendent meaning. The culture of desire denied the reality of death and eroded the sense of collective obligation in a society already under the fissive pressures of immigration and urbanization.[45] The consumer regime was indeed a bill of goods.

Not all historians have agreed. James Livingston has challenged Leach and Lears by arguing that the new consumer order entailed more than the destruction of local society and traditional cultures by bureaucratic corporate capital and industry. Displacing the nineteenth-century ideal of the white male laborer as the citizen, the consumer world ushered in new possibilities for self-fashioning and agency. Consumption enshrined the New Woman as citizen, according to Livingston, a status that ensured a public prominence for women even as they won the vote in the political sphere. Philosophical pragmatism's emphasis on experimentation and engagement with the material world typified the new consumer regime. Consumption allowed people pragmatically to fashion themselves with their things.[46]

Powerful institutions built and maintained such a culture, but everyday people challenged its influence with new values fashioned from their own circumstances. Not all groups accepted the consumer regime or followed the dictates of advertisers and marketers. Accordingly, social historians have investigated the roles of groups, particularly the working class, in consumer society. Though struggling and often impoverished, workers strategically adopted goods, styles, and entertainment to serve their own needs. The free labor ideology of the mid-nineteenth century had portrayed consuming as the antithesis of honest labor: producing nothing, consumers were economic and social parasites.[47] Yet even as industrialization ultimately eroded laborers' control and autonomy within the workplace, they turned to consumption, not as a pathetic substitute for, but as a logical fulfillment of their desires for autonomy, on or off the job. According to Lawrence Glickman, even as they struggled to control work processes, workers also fought for "a living wage" based on a consumption standard of living. In doing so, they reversed their own long-standing animus against consumption to seek full participation in the economy as consumers.[48] The labor movement similarly took part in boycotts and buyers' strikes, protested high prices and costs of living, and demanded government regulation of goods and markets.[49] In many instances, workers drew no meaningful distinction between their interests as workers and as consumers.

Following British scholars E. P. Thompson and Raymond Williams, many more historians have looked to working-class leisure pursuits, communal practices, and everyday life to argue that culture was an indispensable, inevitable site where working-class people struggled to secure freedom and justice. Battling with cultural, civic, and religious authorities over commercial entertainment and leisure, workers fought to define and control their recreation and time outside of work.[50] These struggles inevitably drew on the commodity system, as more and more leisure practices and rituals themselves became commercialized experiences for sale.[51] Lizabeth Cohen argues that between 1920 and 1940 workers used the material resources of consumer plenty, along with their local and ethnic traditions and communities, to fashion a distinct workers' consciousness that underpinned their emerging union and political activism. At the same time, she shows that marginalized groups within the working class, especially African Americans, adapted specific strategies to attain their own equality as consumers. White workers supplemented, but did not abandon, traditional ethnic communities and folkways with a newer culture—forged from the rituals and expectations of consumption—that bridged traditional ethnic divisions. Even as the Depression and New Deal revived and strengthened the labor movement, workers drew on the new consumer economy and culture to ground their claims for economic equity and social justice.[52] There was no single model for the consumer; despite authorities' attempts to contest or shape popular consumption, American workers pursued their own distinct agendas and made their own versions of consumer culture.

While these groups fought to define consumption against capital and other powerful institutions, what was the relationship of the state to consumption? As part of a broad but diffuse critique of capitalism, citizens first organized as consumers for political and regulatory reform in the Progressive Era. From the Pure Food Act of 1906 to middle-class buyers' movements against living costs and utility companies, consumers gained crucial victories in stronger governmental regulation and hard-won but fragmentary concessions from business.[53] During the 1930s the state assumed a much broader and seemingly permanent role in both regulating and facilitating consumption. The New Deal's social contract not only guaranteed the rights of industrial labor to organize for economic security and social justice, but over time it also included consumer interests within the federal government's purview.[54] Alan Brinkley has argued most prominently that New Deal liberalism's lasting legacy was neither labor protection nor a true welfare state, but a diminished form of Keynesian economic regulation. In the mild redistributive guise of deficit spending and tax policy, New Deal Keynesianism cast the national interest (at least for a time) as enhancing purchasing power.[55]

Such policies often masked their own implications. In a provocative essay George Lipsitz has argued that, following World War II, federal officials built a series of consumer entitlements into major legislative initiatives on suburban housing, lending, and education. Such initiatives normalized middle-class family spending patterns as universal standards and subsidized the growth of atomized suburbs, detached one-family dwellings, and decentralized communities. The urban culture of working people built around public amusements and dense residential patterns gave way to increasingly privatized realms where consumption and shopping defined leisure and sociability. Policymakers hid transfers of subsidies from common public assets to private middle-class amenities and entitlements (such as the virtual abandonment of public transit for highway spending), thus impoverishing Americans' collective resources.[56] Most recently, Lizabeth Cohen has offered a sweeping and compelling interpretation of mid-twentieth century American political and social history along similar lines. She locates the rise of a "consumers' republic," rooted in the Depression and coming to fruition after World War II. The American government identified citizens as consumers, who in turn demanded effective product regulation, subsidies, and continued federal interventions in the price and market systems. Federal policies sought to increase aggregate consumer demand; such programs created entitlements for the middle class that ultimately disguised the social costs of subsidizing private consumption. From the design of suburban malls and subdivisions to civil rights battles over access to goods, shopping, banking, and public accommodations, consumers' needs and desires shaped culture and environment, as well as policy and politics.[57] But not without cost: in the consumers' republic, federal policies in effect replaced civic-minded consumers with customer-citizens, most valuable to society as spenders. At the same time, the new republic established a model of government as commodity and service in place of governance as a social process.

"SOLD AMERICAN!": NATIONALIZING CONSUMERS AND CONSUMPTION

This literature reveals how consumption became the linchpin of the economy and of state economic policy; it further indicates how people made their own lives and identities with things. The United States has long been identified abroad with goods and entertainment, even as many nations have developed similar forms of material modernity.[58] While we understand the origins of consumer institutions, we have little understanding of its commonsense dominance. Thus, I argue that we need to study consumption nationally. Understanding consumption's connections with citizenship might explain its tenacity over time and illuminate the gaps between the broad context of state policies and experience of everyday life. *Sold American* takes up this story. Part I outlines advertising's invention of consumers as naturalized citizens, while Part II traces the origins of a consumer public interest and the consumerists' civic approach to spending and goods. Part III concludes with the story of the open conflict of these two groups during the Depression and World War II.

Chapter 1 examines national advertisers' invention of the consumer in crucial episodes: their prescriptions for women as consumers, and their encounters with the mass audience of broadcast radio. Advertisers conceived of women as incompetent yet sovereign consumers. They located women's agency and public power in consumption, substituting it for political suffrage as the best means to secure women's rights. Advertisers' relationship with the sponsored radio audience in turn reveals a corporate sociology in which they categorized social classes and groups simply in terms of their propensity to consume. Even as advertisers worked to make the audience a reliable commodity, they strove to separate themselves from the masses. The political language of national advertising is the subject of chapter 2. I argue that advertisers constructed consumers as citizens through political metaphors and language. While the larger project of product advertising offered self-transformation through purchasing, advertisers consistently rendered such self-determination in political and nationalist terms. Chapter 3 explores how advertisers "naturalized" consumers as Americans, by portraying consumption as the adhesive of a common shared culture. Madison Avenue copywriters celebrated spending as the symbolic heritage of a white, de-ethnicized nation, the badge of Americanness. Here, national history and culture arose from a set of market-friendly traits and behaviors deemed distinctly "American."

Part II introduces the scientific and critical roots of consumer advocacy and research. Chapter 4 focuses on three critical social scientists whose writings influenced the emergence of Consumers' Research and shaped professional discourse on consumers: Thorstein Veblen, Wesley Mitchell, and Hazel Kyrk. These critics all argued that consumers were women, that consumption was shaped largely by cultural forces more than economic reasoning, and that business deliberately opposed and even sabotaged satisfactory consumption. Rejecting abstract economic formalism, these thinkers hinted but did not conclude that consumption made possible the pragmatic making of individual identity on a daily basis.[59] Chapter 5 sketches the emergence of an aggressive voice of the consumer's interest, chronicled in Stuart Chase and F. J. Schlink's 1927 best seller, *Your Money's Worth*. The full-blown analysis of the consumer's helplessness against deception and waste in advertising and sales inspired the many grassroots organizations that would coalesce as the consumer movement. The ideas offered by Chase and Schlink and adopted by their followers ultimately challenged the liberal individualist vision of consumption offered by corporate advertisers and their clients. Consumers' Research, the product-testing and advocacy organization that arose from *Your Money's Worth*, redefined consumption in the late 1920s and early Depression years. In chapter 6 I show that the group offered its own political language of consumption, drawing on republican traditions of hostility to concentrated power and commerce, along with Jeffersonian ideals of citizen independence, now updated to industrial realities. I argue that CR advocated a "consumer republicanism," a citizen activism that integrated machine discipline with the antebellum republic's craft and producer ethos.

Part III shows these starkly differing visions erupting in open conflict and reaching an uneasy truce. Chapter 7 outlines how advertisers and consumerist reformers fought over regulatory proposals, the right to represent consumers, and the direction of mass consumption. Consumers' Research became a national spearhead of antimarket sentiment and challenges to business prerogatives, while advertisers became vocal leaders of business efforts to fight New Deal regulation and to discredit the emergent consumer movement. The corporate counteroffensive against the New Deal, labor, and consumer activism is presented in chapter 8. Advertisers and public relations experts sought to replace regulation with symbols; they crafted a series of nationalist visions of "the American Way of Life" that placed consumption and private enterprise squarely at the heart of citizenship and social identity. Chapter 9 traces the partial resolution of these different visions in the merging of Americanism and consumption before and during World War II. On the home front, spending became a site of struggle over meanings of nation, patriotism, and citizenship. Madison Avenue aided the war effort through dozens of government programs while portraying the war effort as a product of corporate America, not government or nation. In their lived experience of scarcity and thrift, citizens enacted a version of the rational behaviors long advocated by Consumers' Research. They might have yearned for the limitless material abundance that advertisers promised to deliver after the war, but Americans instead consumed for the greater good. Although they temporarily endorsed a consumerist commitment to efficiency, thrift, and reuse, consumers ultimately embraced a vision of American life characterized by goods and abundance as the measure of private happiness.

American citizenship thus has been shaped by these long-opposed traditions. The postwar restoration of prosperity, long-term rollbacks of regulation, and the erosion of collectivist sentiments and spaces have resulted in the seeming triumph of private consumption and greatly expanded business prerogatives. Yet the morality of private thrift and collective demands for government vigilance and corporate responsibility endure as well, as the resurgent consumer movement and allied crusades proved in the 1960s and after.[60] The obsolescence and disposable ease of postwar life seem the antithesis of thrift or functionalism, yet Americans have continued to practice both. After World War II, the privatized, possessive individualism of modern consumption would gradually erode collective approaches to common concerns, not least in business interests' consistent attempts to define democracy in material terms. Yet social movements and critics have continually refused to view consumers' interests solely in strict individualist terms or to define freedom simply as freedom of choice.[61]

MORE FOR THE MONEY:
THE NATIONAL STAKES OF CONSUMPTION

The specific nationalist and cultural history of consumption traced in this study held significant consequences for the long-range development of politics, culture, and civics. First of all, the protracted debate of advertisers and consumerists marked critical episodes in the struggle for moral leadership in American life.[62] Consumer advocates' challenges to corporate enterprise concerned the location of authority: who would influence Americans in their relationship with goods and the marketplace? Would a corporate or civic vision shape the relationship of abundance and the national interest? Who would control the information and ideas about the goods that Americans would use? As the voice of capitalism, advertisers generally addressed their markets with few restrictions and little oversight. Moreover, they claimed a mandate to monopolize channels of common public discourse, including the built environment of signs, billboards, and commercial architecture, mass-circulation magazines, newspapers, and the airwaves, even at times schools and pulpits.[63] Casting consumption as American citizenship, advertisers clearly placed their wares and clients at the center of the common culture emerging in this era. Aligning their interests with historic figures and the nation itself, advertisers claimed the right to rule. They created a vision of American experience and placed consumption at its core. Consumerists, with their insolent critique of advertising and New Era consumption, questioned not just sales practices and business ethics but also the ends and meanings of consumption itself. They denied business's claims of authority and asserted that commercial interests should not be the sole arbiter of common concerns or the public good. Demanding scientific information about and higher-quality performance from goods, consumer critics pushed Americans to take explicit responsibility for their own consumption habits and activities, even as they called American business to account.

Second, the persistent use of political languages, images, and concepts illuminates the ways in which consumption became a right and entitlement. Both sides believed that spending money was, in effect, voting. Adopting a language of consent, however, blurred the critical differences between these two experiences. Markets were not communities; consumers indeed were not voters.[64] The democratic language of consumption diluted the crucial distinctions of public, market, and citizenry. In his famed account of the bourgeois public sphere, Jurgen Habermas argues that the eighteenth century's rational communal sphere of interested citizens had given way to a commercial order where "publics" were indistinguishable from markets. Factions led by commercial interests, Habermas charges, came to dominate public discourse, rendering impossible the independent rational deliberation of the common good. While Habermas's analysis has rightly been challenged and revised, his main point remains valid and indeed critical. Markets have never been the sole means of defining the common weal or the sole arena in which people organize or act. A system in which commerce becomes synonymous with the "public good" loses its claim to safeguard the interests of all within that society.[65]

Moreover, the conflation of democracy with spending had social consequences as well, as advertisers and marketers remade the conditions of community by redefining social organizations according to commercial needs. They took the lead in measuring and mapping the tastes, habits, and locations of their customers, and such efforts influenced the origins of both political polling and market analysis.[66] Today, commercial consultants have minutely partitioned the United States into a series of commercial zones, where Americans are categorized, sorted, and profiled as markets.[67] This activity rests on the semantic and cultural foundations that advertisers used till it became common sense decades ago. But as a result, it has now become difficult to disassociate values of public sanction and democratic choice from the individual pursuit of private gain. Moreover, American political operatives themselves have long used the techniques of product sales to promote candidates and issues. That significantly affects Americans' experience and understanding of the political system. Selling a candidate might be like selling soap, but the sales resistance and brand preference behaviors that product advertisers routinely encounter and reinforce have much more serious consequences in the political realm.[68]

Additionally, the democratic language of commerce limited understandings of common and publicly sanctioned welfare. Advertisers' longest-running campaign in these years was essentially political—the convincing portrayal of spending and acquiring goods as the center of American life. They substituted the private interests of corporations and consumers as the transcendent civic good of the nation while downplaying common causes worked out in a democratic process. The public emergencies of depression and war brought commercial critics to the fore, but during the war corporate enterprise succeeded in casting the common civic weal as the private pursuit of individual interest. In this business-friendly narrative, consumer abundance became the symbol of freedom, the ultimate goal of a war fought against fascism. This story contended that the corporation, more than the government, carried the nation to victory. The postwar consumer order that emerged in the Cold War era was built on consumer subsidies as entitlements for the white middle class and enshrined individualism and abundance against totalitarianism and scarcity. In that setting it often became difficult to call for communal civic action, especially when it involved material sacrifice. Attacks on government, on labor, and on other social programs or collective ideologies surfaced in waves from the Cold War to the present, from the powerful mainstream as well as the lunatic fringe. That environment has often rendered invisible or unheard any vision of a common good cast in terms other than the overall success of the market. Even while it was proclaimed a civic virtue, consumption foremost served private interests.

Finally, the professionals' democratic pretensions and political language occluded a central outgrowth of consumer abundance. Focusing so much on goods as arbiters and elements of a common culture has made it difficult to see what goods cannot do. They do not speak for themselves, but only as people interpret them. A culture fixed on the importance of cars, appliances, celebrity, and entertainment, within limits, might bind diverse peoples through common experience. But such adhesions can only be successful and long lasting if they accompany a commitment to direct communication among people and not just through possessions. Advertisers' skill in fashioning images does not easily transfer to discourse among people or between drastically different values. A truly democratic culture of abundance can only exist when people look beyond goods to one another.

Let it be clear: material abundance in itself does not erode civic bonds or lessen Americans' abilities to form meaningful communities. Nor in itself does it threaten freedom, at least for those who live in lands of plenty. Indeed, I argue that one of the reasons that advertisers' political language has endured has been its ability to make sense of, justify, and even naturalize material conditions and the relationships of everyday life. Abstractions such as liberty and freedom assumed immediate and powerful meanings in the arena of goods and leisure. The "lived theory" of consumption has allowed several generations of citizens to discern enduring links between material abundance and leisure on the one hand and a political-economic system on the other that presents these things as the birthright of U.S. citizens. It is, of course, undeniable that such abundance has been realized in an unequal and discriminatory social and economic system. Like citizenship and freedom, abundance for many has been built on its denial for many others; whether in federal policies, local laws and customs, or the actual experience of goods, Americans learned to consume in a social system that discriminated on the basis of gender and race, class and age. Markets may represent freedom and equality to many, but to many more they simply enact anew old inequities or oppression.

These debates remain with us today. Proponents of unfettered commerce still use political language to justify their goals, while critics of commercial exploitation look to civic and moral virtue to redirect their society's concerns to equity and stewardship. Neoliberal proponents of an "ownership society" seek a private system with unequal social benefits under the cope of freedom, growth, and efficiency; haunted by fears of stagnation, recession, and a decline in American economic power, they seek endless growth. Today's moral consumers boycott products and businesses corporations, protest labor exploitation, and spend according to moral as much as commercial criteria. Today's battles take place in a world economy in which the United States is dominant but no longer all-supreme. For all their resemblance to past struggles, the crusades of culture jammers and "no logo" adherents and the campaigns of antiglobalization activists have transcended the parochial past quarrels between those in lab coats and gray flannel suits, between Mrs. Consumer and Mr. Advertiser.[69] However different, these present movements are nevertheless rooted in the past, and today we are caught up in the continuation of conflicts between proponents of a boundless market and advocates of collective civic responsibility. This is one consumer choice we must decide.

ADVERTISERS

CHAPTER 1
ADVERTISERS
AND
CONSUMERS,
1890–1930

Modern advertising is part and parcel of the whole set of thought movements and mechanical techniques which changed the medieval into the modern world.[1]

What a nation eats and wears—its pleasures, comforts and home conditions—these questions are being settled by the modern economic force called Advertising.[2]

Mr. James Ultimate Consumer is the most famous man in the world. He has to wear all the Knox hats, eat all the Premium bacon, listen to all the Victrolas and Panatropes, wear all the Fashion Park clothes, monkey with all the Radiolas, wind all the New Haven Clocks, roll over sleepy-eyed to shut off all the Big Bens in the morning, plod his way to work in all the Regals, poke his fingers through all the Adler gloves, step on all the Texaco, wear out all the Goodrich Cords, eat up all the Bean Hole beans, cram down his hungry neck all the Fifty-Seven varieties, find some reason for drinking all the Canada Dry, and take care of all the Camels in the world. James Ultimate Consumer—he's the Man! He is "It" in every sense of the word. He is the destination of all made things.[3]

Advertisers should never forget that they are addressing stupid people—one of which I am whom.[4]

The American advertising business evolved to sell goods. From shadowy origins on the fringes of respectable bourgeois society before the Civil War, advertising became an important element of American culture in the half century after 1880. In those years advertisers defined themselves as a unique, influential profession to serve the industrial capitalism then revolutionizing daily life.[5] Seemingly ubiquitous, advertising dominated both the structure and content of mass communications, assuming an unmistakable prominence in the built environment. Just as important, advertisers claimed for themselves the critical task of defining identity for Americans. Advertisements encouraged people to purchase a plethora of products to meet the material needs of their everyday lives. In conveying information about goods and ideal living, advertisers also provided images and prescriptions for the self.[6] They encouraged consumers to understand themselves through their possessions and to fabricate their identities in and through things. In that process, advertising became "the privileged discourse for the circulation of messages and social cues about the interplay between persons and objects."[7] The late nineteenth-century experience of modernity in its many guises showed

that the individual was not a fixed and stable character but a complex, changing entity shaped by the external world. Advertising encouraged customers—
now increasingly termed "consumers" by the national corporations that were
supplanting the face-to-face relationships of local commerce—literally to
make themselves from their things.[8] In this capacity, advertising shaped
modern culture. This was achieved haltingly over many years and seldom
with conscious purpose: after all, advertisers sold goods, not symbols. Yet they
trafficked in images and ideals, and they educated consumers to interpret
goods totemically as intimate, even animate, parts of their lives. As consumption helped define the self, advertisers taught Americans to view themselves
as consumers.

Over its long history, critics have castigated advertising for encouraging
demeaning behavior and crass concerns. They have charged that advertising
fosters greed and insecurity and diverts us from humane values. Detractors
assert that advertising's depictions of social life insult our intelligence and
strain our credulity. Such criticisms were leveled in 1904 as well as 2004. Yet
however distorted their depictions of American life, advertising campaigns, I
argue, served as social and political representations. Advertisers crafted and
purveyed a vision of social life in the United States that highlighted consumption as the key not only to individual happiness but also to the health of
American society. National media advertising presented a social order in
which the consumer held a central place as both free individual and ideal
citizen. Depicting the good life, the distribution of wealth, and a class system
enforced though goods, advertisements worked as political documents. They
intervened in broad economic and political discussions along with other
forms of popular culture: the movies, periodical fiction, popular songs, the
comics, theater. In company with editorialists, critics, and statesmen, advertisers interrogated politics and economics. The social world as seen in advertisements no doubt struck many as false and irrelevant, and we should on no
account mistake them as transparent or reliable renderings of social experience. Yet advertising proved no more distorted than representations made by
party politicians, self-help writers, or businessmen. As the voice of corporate
capital, advertisers' visions of wealth and the social order likely enjoyed an
equal or greater popular appeal than others offered in entertainment, the
press, or the pulpit. Throughout this study, the passionate critiques and de-
fenses of mass-produced goods and culture reveal Americans' investment in
consumption's manifold possibilities.[9] By 1930, advertising was ingrained in
American everyday life, not only as a thoroughly integrated tool of industrial
capitalism, but also as a widely accepted cultural influence. By 1930, for better

or worse, the United States was a consumer society. In order for that to have happened, advertisers first had to establish their authority with both business and the public.

SERVANTS AND SALESMEN:
ADVERTISING PROFESSIONALISM AND IDEOLOGY

Early in 1909, the legendary Claude C. Hopkins, copy chief of Chicago advertising agency Lord & Thomas, addressed the Sphinx Club, a New York organization of advertisers, agents, and publishers:

> From our desks we sway millions. We change the currents of trade. We populate new empires, build up new industries and create customs and fashions. We dictate the food that the baby shall eat, the clothes the mother shall wear, the way in which the home shall be furnished. We are clothed with no authority. Our very names are unknown. But there is scarcely a home, in city or hamlet, where some human being is not doing what we demand. The good advertising man comes pretty close to being an absolute czar.[10]

Hopkins's self-satisfied oration sums up the contemporary claims of his profession. Between 1880 and 1930 advertising agents became indispensable to marketing goods. When Hopkins spoke, advertisers already worked for hundreds of businesses and influenced millions of purchasing decisions.[11]

Advertising men gained their influence because they developed specific expertise: publicizing information about goods to prospective buyers and conveying detailed information about retail customers to those with goods to sell. They became professionals, cultivating their expertise and selling it as a specialized, exclusive commodity. Veteran agent C. E. Raymond said bluntly, "The 'goods' an agency produces is service." Advertising agents developed a professional ethos, based on their skills and alleged independence in judgment.[12] Like other professionals, advertisers organized to promote their expertise and to serve as gatekeepers to professional practice. In addition, they mounted sporadic reform efforts and self-regulation of standards and practices.[13] Ideals of service to both business and consumers undergirded the profession's legitimacy and hastened its ascendance as a commercial and cultural institution.[14] To understand fully advertising's role in inventing the modern consumer requires an exploration of the service commodity advertisers sold to business and the consuming public.

The advertising business underwent a significant transformation after

1880. Challenged by industry's needs to expand and rationalize markets, advertising agents changed their methods and redefined their functions. They had originally been speculative brokers in advertising space (newspapers, magazines, signage), but they now turned to preparing and placing advertising artwork and copy in that space for business clients.[15] Ultimately, advertising agents helped invent marketing by identifying and analyzing appropriate segments of the populace who could buy their clients' wares.[16] Advertisers critically enabled the rise to national dominance of branded goods, which were mass-produced and sold under copyrighted and trademarked names. As historian Susan Strasser has shown, the branded goods system assumed its characteristic form by 1920, after a fierce thirty-year struggle over patterns and control of retail distribution. By pinpointing and fostering demand in the retail market for specific brands, advertising tipped the balance of power away from wholesale distributors and retail merchants, who had previously controlled the flow of goods to store shelves and influenced consumers' selections. As Daniel Pope has observed, an advertiser "had to persuade consumers to buy his brand at the same time he convinced dealers that they could profit by stocking it." Manufacturers increasingly used advertising to bypass wholesalers and retailers alike, ultimately winning the struggle to determine which goods made it to the shelves, the market basket, and ultimately the home.[17] In this process advertising emerged as a beneficiary of as well as principal agent in the new distribution.[18]

Advertising's primary service to business, then, was creating, maintaining, and increasing demand for goods. To foster demand, advertisers developed expertise in locating, addressing, and ultimately persuading consumers. By 1920, a number of agencies had become involved in their clients' overall business operations. Led by the nation's largest agency, J. Walter Thompson, advertisers routinely researched competitors and distribution conditions. Less frequently, they conducted investigations into markets, gathering information ranging from demographic data to taste preferences.[19] They implemented a range of ancillary services for clients, such as devising brand names (such long-lived brands as Uneeda Biscuit, Karo Syrup, Yuban Coffee, and Kelvinator were all coined by advertising agents), preempting competitors' entry into markets, designing packaging, and originating what eventually became corporate public relations.[20] Yet advertisers always accompanied this vision of business acumen by portraying themselves as public servants with information about commodities and values that would enhance the public welfare.[21] Identifying their clients' interests with the general good of the public and the state, advertisers adopted a stance of enlightened stewardship. They accomplished this largely by portraying products as offering solutions to otherwise baffling personal difficulties.[22] Advertisements depicted products as the means to self-transformation, and ad men held themselves out as the dispensers of happiness and enlightenment. The material modernity offered in advertising placed America at the pinnacle of world civilizations.

Like many different elites, advertisers viewed themselves as guardians of greater values. They linked consumption to national progress, one of the most cherished core beliefs about American life.[23] For advertisers, progress entailed the forward advance of higher civilization through goods; as agents of commerce, advertisers were fundamentally servants of civilization, the sum total of human achievement (fig. 1.1). "Yours is the profession of enlightenment," one advocate wrote. "A promoter of commerce? Yes. An instrument of distribution? Assuredly. But you think too meanly of advertising if you confine it to these terms. It is an agency of civilization."[24] The trade journal *Printers' Ink* claimed in 1889 that advertising "is a test of the increasing wants of the people . . . a sign of civilization." According to advertising writer Edwin Balmer, "The rapidity of our progress as a nation is determined very largely by the efficiency and effectiveness of our advertising . . . . Individuals, communities and races are progressive as they acquire new needs—as they learn to make things and to use them."[25] Ad men interpreted the variety and numbers of goods they sold as the raw evidence of the quality of civilization itself. "Look for a nation whose people are not advertisers and you will find a country whose inhabitants are either semi-civilized or savages," announced one advertising writer.[26] "Give me a list of a nation's wants and I can tell you of the state of that nation's civilization," claimed the president of the Alexander Hamilton Institute, a correspondence school. "If their wants are increasing in number and quality, we know that the nation is alive, that it is not decadent. The man whose wants are those of his forefathers [is] making no progress." The extent of advertising thus reflected a nation's progress.[27] Perhaps the pinnacle of such advertising puffery and self-congratulation was reached in this pious sentiment: "The creator, in his infinite wisdom, could confer no greater benefaction upon an increasing population than that which we find in the one word 'advertising.'"[28]

Spreading civilization meant deploying advertising throughout the world. Ad men contrasted the United States's leadership in advertising and consumption to nascent commerce in other countries.[29] Long before the Cold War's contrasts of capitalism and communism made "underdeveloped" synonymous with "underconsuming," China and Russia frequently served as

PROGRESS

THE Soul of the world has found a new desire. Out of the wreck of war a new branch appears on the tree of life,—world-progress. We have fought, and learned more of both friends and foes than a century of peace had taught us. Through helping others we have helped ourselves.

Peace is here, but no unintelligent peace will satisfy us. The good of human nature requires constructive peace. Out of the eternal past into the eternal future Progress leads on, or casts aside.

Business for man; not man for business, is the watchword of progress. Service to mankind must be our standard of judgment.

What is true of our social and industrial life is true of advertising. The advertising ways of yesterday are not the ways of today or tomorrow. Here also enters the problem of service to mankind.

We of N. W. Ayer & Son believe our work must be an acceptable contribution to society if it would serve commerce; for commerce must serve society or it is not commerce, but piracy. To make our advertising service true to the spirit of Progress, we must keep our finger on the pulse of humanity and diagnose desire while it is in the very process of development.

Our organization is trained to meet changing conditions. This elasticity accounts for our known ability to increase trade for both the large and small house, the old and the new business. Perhaps these are the reasons why we are this year celebrating our Fiftieth Anniversary.

N . W . A Y E R & S O N

ADVERTISING HEADQUARTERS

PHILADELPHIA

NEW YORK   BOSTON   CLEVELAND   CHICAGO

FIGURE 1.1. "Progress." (N. W. Ayer Collection, Archives Center,
National Museum of American History, Smithsonian Institution, Washington, D.C.)

Madison Avenue's examples of nations whose ignorance of advertising and material desire kept them in semibarbarity.[30] Implicit in these views was a corporate anthropology of mass consumption, no less articulate, if much more simplistic, than the complex taxonomies produced in the academy. Advertisers judged civilizations by the number and complexity of their material artifacts. Only the mass-produced goods of industrialism ranked as the highest forms of civilized attainment.[31]

Not surprisingly, advertisers flattered themselves by continually contrasting their wares with the goods of so-called primitive peoples. In a particularly telling example, O'Sullivan's Rubber Heels in 1908 claimed to "bridge the chasm between the barefooted savage and the civilized man." The advertisement demonstrated the instantaneous transition from savagery to civilization with the proper product. The O'Sullivan workman strides purposefully across the frame, the menacing crowd behind him embodying the march of civilization upon a prone Indian's doomed wilderness (fig. 1.2).[32] Consumption separated modern nations from decay and decline. "A world without advertising" as one critic wrote in 1907, would resemble nothing so much as "the primitive past, or the undeveloped savagery of the present."[33] In 1927 executive and popular writer Bruce Barton summarized three decades of such thinking:

> You go into a savage tribe and what do you find? You find men who have no wants. You find that the savage is perfectly content if he has a skin to wrap around his loins, another skin to keep off the rain, a skin to lie on, and a little food and a fire . . . . But suppose that out of an airplane an advertising man dropped into that tribe and brought with him pictures of red neckties and tan shoes, and underwear and new hats, and automobiles and bicycles, and feathers and strings of beads. Instantly there would be in that tribe a transformation. Wants would be kindled, and the desire to satisfy those wants would overcome all other desires, and in obedience to them even a savage is willing to abandon his life of leisure and voluntarily enlist himself in servitude to the creation of civilization.[34]

The enthusiastic embrace of instant transformation through the talismans of tan shoes and neckties represented the profession's grandest fantasies of influence. Barton's was a corporate anthropology, where primitives still existed in the twentieth century, scarcely removed from their ancestors millions of years before, whose ascent into civilization and true happiness awaited only the timely arrival of Madison Avenue missionaries.[35] Himself a preacher's son, Barton later made a specialty of convincing the most powerful corpo-

FIGURE 1.2. "O'Sullivan's Heels."

(*Munsey's Magazine*, April 1908, Advertising Section, n.p.)

rate executives to advertise their contributions to civilization and progress as much as a particular product.[36]

Advertisers thus viewed their work as a benevolent process of destabilization.[37] In no uncertain terms, the J. Walter Thompson agency proclaimed, "Advertising is revolutionary. Its tendency is to overturn the preconceived notions, to set new ideas spinning through the reader's brain, to induce something that they [sic] never did before. It is a form of progress, and interests only progressive people." Agency executive James Webb Young told his University of Chicago advertising classes, "The purpose of advertising is to disturb the status quo." Advertising served as the "energizing power" of American society, which not only propelled the engines of commerce but also "implanted the modern man's mind with thousands of desires his great-grandfather knew not of."[38] Advertising's ultimate boon was its initiation of new desires, which led to greater freedom and unprecedented happiness. Advertising seemed revolutionary because it promised more opportunities for self-cultivation, leisure, and escape from toil.

Copywriters propelled civilization by imparting new knowledge to the citizenry. Advertisers viewed themselves as teaching the public what it wished to know.[39] If consumer demand was the focus of the economy, advertisers showed consumers how to develop more intelligent desires. By serving as "the school where consumers are trained to know the true value of commodities," advertising "has educated the consumer into being a connoisseur." Advertising was "the most potent educator in regard to the standard of living" and "the schoolmaster of the human race."[40] Thus advertisers characterized their sales work as education in the public interest. As the chairman of the Standard Sanitary Manufacturing Company told an advertising writer, "People subconsciously crave knowledge. Advertising that points a way to improve our homes and our health, that assists us to dress better, to live better and to think better, or that helps us in any way, is the advertising that is vital." Its educational value appeared not only in shaping buying habits for advertised brands but also in encouraging the public's extensive curiosity and willingness to adopt the new ideas and values proposed in advertising.[41]

MASSES AND MARKETS: ADVERTISING SOCIOLOGY

Never at a loss for stating their own importance, advertisers eagerly interpreted their pervasiveness as power. The N. W. Ayer agency's 1912 claim—"It is difficult for one not associated with the advertising business to correctly measure the influence of advertising upon the very existence of the average man"—echoed the sentiments of most agents and numerous clients.[42] J. George Frederick crowed that an ad man

> can put an argument for his product in the newspaper at the breakfast tables of most of the comfortable families in all the cities of the country inside of twenty-four hours. He can now even flash across the continent an illustrated ad via radio. He can put a message in a single periodical which reaches practically every village and town in the whole of the United States and Canada. . . . He can make the very rail fences along the farm roads speak to the passers-by; he can mass the one thousand and one methods of advertising into a concentrated volume of appeal which will make people absorb his thought as through the air they breathe, and as naturally.[43]

Yet this routine boasting barely concealed ad men's frustration that their persuasive powers had distinct limits. Professionals often expressed displeasure at their inability to predict, guide, or control consumer spending. One disgruntled executive complained, "If you were able to present Jesus Christ giving the Sermon on the Mount, and said it was sponsored by Chase and Sanborn Coffee, no one would buy any coffee as a result of that favor."[44] Consumers did not purchase simply as advertisers exhorted. Sales resistance was the first refuge of the consumer and every advertiser's bane.

Pressed to develop ever more elaborate and effective sales campaigns, by the 1910s advertisers began studying consumers themselves. As one professional claimed, "Advertising men everywhere are vitally interested in the life of the people, in the conditions under which the common people are obliged to live and the chances that are accorded them for their advancements, their convenience and their pleasure."[45] Led especially by J. Walter Thompson, agencies theorized, located, surveyed, and interpreted consumers. Ad men reasoned that they would only achieve greater powers of persuasion through more extensive and specific knowledge of consumers. Speaking effectively to consumers required advertisers to observe and engage consumers in public, in the marketplace, and in the home. Agencies here were joined by others in allied industries, most notably leading national magazines, newspapers, and eventually radio, and the manufacturing corporations themselves. Yet advertisers staked out for themselves a particular expertise in this process. Advertisements sold goods, but advertising agents sold *markets*—ever-changing aggregate representations of consumers distinguished by specific demographic and cultural attributes. Success in advertising came to mean increasing the client's sales by connecting goods with buyers. The push to sell markets led advertisers in effect to invent "the consumer." As markets, consumers became advertisers' stock in trade, commodities continually redesigned and tailored explicitly to individual corporate clients. Having thus identified markets, advertisers sold them to clients and the media. Similarly, the great national magazines, newspapers, and ultimately radio and television did the same. The consumer became the commodity sold by advertising. Advertisers created abstract aggregates (people who bought oatmeal, or middle-class buyers in Cincinnati, for example), representations of buyers; they in turn developed and sold specific traits of those aggregates, the "characteristics" of a desirable market, to businesses. And then, advertisers sold those same attributes to their target markets in the form of specific products. The result was a continuous process of producing not sales but customers. The largest advertising agencies, national media, and manufacturers all collaborated in developing marketing concepts, techniques, and practices. Along with the business academics who established marketing as a field of study, advertisers made clear connections between the rationalization of industrial production and the rationalization of consumption.[46]

In observing marketplace behavior, surveying popular tastes, and testing buyers' aptitudes, advertisers invoked the aura of science in their labors, thus offering clients a shimmering promise of certainty. Advertisers treated different social strata as typified by specific goods and spending habits.[47] Psychologist Walter Dill Scott asserted, "It is a well-observed fact that different classes of society think differently and that arguments which would appeal to one class would be worthless to another."[48] In this spirit, advertisers continually sought to classify people by income levels, occupations, regions, and tastes and to correlate such observations with markets. Their many attempts to understand and gauge consumers' tastes, habits, and behavior led ad men to a specific, if crude sociology. In their understandings of the "classes" and "masses," elites and commoners, advertisers created an American society symbolized and compartmentalized by income, tastes, and propensities to spend. Marketers specified basic income brackets: A ($5,000–10,000 per year); BB ($3,000–5,000); B ($2,000–3,000); C ($1,000–2,000); and D (less than $1,000).[49] These categories and divisions persisted with surprising resilience from the Progressive Era through World War II. In most cases, advertisers catered to the comparatively fewer families in the upper BB and B brackets, even though by most calculations, the majority of Americans lived at best at the B level or below. Critical to these designations was the potential for spending; the income brackets represented not only incomes but also the ability to spend.

In this sociology advertisers told themselves that they were distinctly superior to the common people; the great mass of consumers did not view or experience the world as ad men did. Copywriters tailored arguments and imagery to an audience they believed to be far inferior in income, cultivation, and aspirations.[50] As one wag put it, "The masses . . . the words should be spelled them asses." Another summed up the feelings of the profession: "the great buying public of the United States is composed of morons . . . whose intelligence has stopped development."[51] The images of America that advertisers presented in their work and in their deliberations on consumers reflected their own class interests and experiences as much as any scientific knowledge about their "public."[52] While the rudimentary "class" and "mass" distinctions withered easily under scrutiny, in fact advertisers applied pejorative beliefs about mass tastes to those of middle-class status, as well as to working people. However sophisticated their understanding of incomes, advertisers conceived of most consumers, from factory worker to office worker, cleaning woman to clubwoman, as belonging to an amorphous aggregate in need of uplift and incorrigibly beneath the standards of sophistication they held out for themselves. As one writer solemnly reminded colleagues, "The general knowledge of the average individual is quite astonishingly limited, and it is far easier to shoot over the heads of an audience than to be too elementary."[53]

The Madison Avenue elite were acutely aware of differences between themselves and the consuming public, and even as they painstakingly parsed the telling differences among income groups, they still held themselves to differ markedly from most consumers. A Thompson man proudly laid out the facts for his colleagues:

> None of our writers belongs to a lodge or a civic club; only one in twenty-five ever attends a political meeting; not one ever goes to a public picnic. Only one out of five ever goes to church except on rare occasions. Half never go to Coney Island or to a similar resort; the other half go once in one or two years. This—in a nation that can almost be described by such experiences. Considerably *over* half our writers have never had the experience of living within the average national income of $1580 a year, and half can't even remember any *relatives* or *friends* who live on that figure! While 5% of all homes have servants, 66% of our writers are blessed with domestics. Only one in eight does his or her own grocery shopping; half buy their own drug supplies and 60% shop in department stores. The men writers are virtually unanimous in their agreement that shopping is something to be avoided entirely. All this in an agency that depends on the retail sale of staple consumer goods to the masses for its principal income!

Although their income depended on the ability to manipulate the public's sense of class distinctions, in private advertisers clung to their difference from all but the most sophisticated and educated buyers. Advertising humor columnist, "Groucho," spoke for many: "I haven't got near enough the consumer yet to know whether he's got me licked or not."[54]

Data from other sources only confirmed advertisers' beliefs about consumers' low tastes and limited intelligence. During World War I the U.S. Army conducted intelligence tests to screen inductees and volunteers to the American Expeditionary Force. Based on dubious assumptions, the test results led to shocking conclusions that immediately sparked heated debate and anxious hand-wringing. Directed by Brahmin psychologist Robert Yerkes, the tests found that the majority of male adult American citizens were illiterate and that 60–70 percent of Americans had levels of intelligence as low as that of a twelve year old. Though these claims were widely contested and ultimately discredited, they temporarily offered significant scientific support for the prejudice that the majority of adult Americans were without basic mental competence and fueled enthusiasm for the emerging eugenics movement.[55] Significantly, the "twelve-year-old mentality" had a lasting commercial afterlife. Advertisers and media executives adopted it when discussing customers and audiences behind closed doors. Moreover, it became the benchmark for conceptualizing markets and addressing consumers.

Paradoxically, the closer advertisers drew to consumers and the greater the success they achieved in effective communication, the more they were determined to uphold cultural barriers between the masses and themselves. The tension between embracing the daily culture of plain people—the consuming public—and distancing itself from the common folk's habits and tastes underlay the profession's development until well after World War II. Moreover, that tension shaped advertising's depictions of personal transformation through commodities. Whatever the democratic justification for mass consumption, in fact ad men sorted consumers into different hierarchical markets. Yet fundamental to advertising sociology was a characterization of social groups *simply* by their possessions; in advertisers' minds consumers were symbolized by the goods they owned. Even as ad men tried to educate consumers to think of themselves in terms of certain products, the inhabitants of Madison Avenue were caught up in this same process, mistaking persons for products. Despite their many field trips to mingle with the masses at Coney Island, to meet Mrs. Consumer by ringing doorbells or passing out samples in groceries, and to practice sales techniques behind the counters of department, chain, and drug stores, ad men felt ill equipped to understand fully the daily lives of consumers.[56] This myopia not only informed but ultimately shaped the most influential aspects of advertising sociology: its portrait of American women as the ideal consumer and its construction of the lower-middle and working classes as a mass audience.

COURTING MRS. CONSUMER:
ADVERTISERS AND WOMEN, 1890–1930

The Charles Daniel Frey advertising agency summarized what was by 1930 long-standing and conventional advertising wisdom:

> She is 16; she is 30; she is 65. She sells eggs in the country, notions in a department store, bonds on Wall Street. She is a graduate of the fourth grade, high school, or occasionally Smith. She wears $15 frocks, home-sewn dresses, Chanel gowns. She is a drudge, a hoyden, a help-mate, a lady; she is the aggregate American woman . . . and, in her various ways, she is the spender of the nation. Deciding how the bulk of her family's money shall be divided, she controls the profits of many manufacturers. Extravagant, frugal; wise, foolish; fickle, dependable; she holds your business, in all likelihood, in the hollow of her hand.[57]

As spenders, women composed the market for virtually all forms of household goods. James Collins in 1901 neatly summed up a fundamental industry tenet: "The advertiser talks vaguely of a creature which he calls, variously, 'he,' 'it,' 'clientele,' and 'the public,' yet that creature is woman, pure and simple."[58] Through their responsibilities for homemaking and spending, women constituted the vast majority of the consuming public. From the late 1880s till after World War II, it was a commercial commonplace (admittedly overblown) that women were responsible for 85 percent of all purchasing decisions, with influence over all the rest.[59] Only that advertising which effectively addressed women would successfully sell goods. Roland Marchand has observed, "No facet of the advertiser-audience relationship held such consequence for advertising content as the perception by the overwhelmingly male elite that it was engaged primarily in talking to masses of women."[60] Not only did male advertisers believe that their audience was predominantly composed of women, but the result of their work was the creation of powerful gender prescriptions and images. It would be impossible to understand the history of mass consumption fully without acknowledging the centrality of men writing to women.[61] The pervasive images of ideal spending and women's roles that made a profound impact on women's lives were shaped according to advertisers' perspectives as corporate businessmen.[62] Agency sage Earnest Elmo Calkins intoned in 1930, "Woman has recreated merchandising in her own image." While he undoubtedly meant to compliment women on their lasting beneficial impact on marketing and design, more often the opposite was true.[63] Advertisers envisioned women according to business interests, recasting women's work in male terms while promulgating an ethos of consumption as a natural female trait.

The focus on women shaped the use of early consumer "psychology," principles of copywriting, development of marketing plans, and product design. In an early formulation of advertising psychology, Walter Dill Scott in 1903 claimed that the key to effective advertising was suggestion. By implanting an idea in the consumer's memory through repetition and saturation of the visual environment, rather than attempting overtly to compel or persuade prospects with logic, advertising could gain sales.[64] Consumers responded to suggestion because human beings did not act according to strict rationality. "It was once supposed that suggestion was something abnormal and that reason was the common attribute of men," Scott contended. "Today we are finding that suggestion is of universal application to all persons, while reasoning is a process that is exceptional, even among the wisest. We reason rarely, but act under suggestion constantly."[65] Suggestion and primal emotion were keys to opening consumers' hearts and wallets.

Others connected the notion to long-standing associations of the feminine with the irrational: women responded principally to emotional, irrational appeals. Most male advertisers believed that women were less capable of "reason" than men, and therefore, successful advertising to women would have to be based on suggestion and sentimental depictions, images that aroused feeling without inducing a conscious chain of reasoning. "Men as a class are not as much influenced by advertising as women are. Men are more philosophical and do not yield as readily to outside influences. They are 'on to the game,' as it were," one expert told the advertising journal *Mahin's Magazine* in 1903.[66] By contrast, women allegedly were more emotional, more open to the subconscious influences of beautiful illustrations or helpful hints and the blandishments of sales voices. "Woman is more artistic, more influenced by sentiment, and cares more for details than men. . . . Generally speaking, she reads more advertising than men, and believes more," observed expert copywriter S. Roland Hall. "The minute a woman reads an advertisement, by her actions she brings to mind that rare melodious air written ages ago to commemorate the love of a maiden fair, and how her first glance toward her favorite swain surprised her, entitled, 'I Was Happy 'Till I

Met You, But I'm All Excited Now.'"[67] Such facetious commentary indicated advertisers' ambivalence about the use of suggestion. Ad men found suggestion very appealing, but they were troubled by its implications for human self-control. For one thing, suggestion worked most effectively through unconscious means: consumers balked at admitting advertising's overt influence on their actions. Scott cautioned, "Although we do obey commands, we are unwilling to admit it. We like to think of ourselves as independent beings, who act only because it is the reasonable thing to do and because we want to." The effect of suggestion on the subconscious challenged advertisers' notions of autonomy; although there was nothing inherently gendered in such theories, advertisers generally referred only to women when speaking of the malleability of human minds through suggestion.[68] Mrs. Consumer would take suggestion, while Mr. Consumer stood firm. To admit differently would erode the crucial barrier advertisers maintained between their female audience and themselves.

Advertisers further enhanced their notions of women consumers with the contemporary advent of the "reason-why" style of advertising, which emphasized appeals to self-interest. Copywriters assembled a sequential logical argument built around key attributes of the product's service to the consumer. First associated with Chicago's Lord & Thomas agency and advertising agent Albert Lasker, the style's adherents asserted that although most consumers were unsophisticated, naive, and ignorant, they did possess "common sense," a practical point of view grounded firmly in their own self-interest. The female consumer was unintelligent but still had the necessary smarts to make informed decisions. Reason-why copy thus deployed fact-laden, simple argumentation, unadorned by artifice or even illustrations. Copywriter John E. Kennedy's phrase "salesmanship in print" typified this approach; the most successful advertising would resemble the manner and voice of a good drummer persuading the consumer in plain language with his or her needs foremost in mind.[69]

Although most advertisers viewed women as more susceptible to emotion in selling, reason-why advocates claimed that their approach to copy was especially effective in selling Mrs. Consumer. That such leading brands of domestic wares as Ivory Soap, Campbell's Soup, Uneeda Biscuit, Old Dutch Cleanser, Cream of Wheat, and Kellogg's Corn Flakes all utilized sentimental or pictorial advertising—all based on suggestion—did not deter reason-why partisans. They viewed women as busy and shrewd shoppers who responded to a convincing sales argument, not subtle suggestion or attractive illustrations. One woman advertiser commented, "A woman today doesn't buy things as blindly as the funny papers would have us believe. She reads and forms her own opinions. She looks for proof of the claims made for a thing, and before an advertisement can induce her to spend her money, it must first convince her that the proposition is worth while; for the woman of today has a pretty keen sense of values, and it is getting good values that pleases her, not the mere spending of money, as a great many advertisers seem to imagine." Women consumers in fact approached their spending in a businesslike fashion. Another advocate stated this view even more explicitly: "Women are not to be made buyers by pretty-polly talk . . . . If there is a hollow ring to your advertisement, if the coin of your logic be spurious, she will detect it . . . . Despite all the sarcastic reflections upon women's reasoning owners, they enjoy reasoning—sound reasoning—and they are willing to pay close attention to it, and be convinced by it."[70]

The struggle of reason-why and suggestion dominated the trade for nearly a generation after 1900, as agencies fiercely competed for business and struggled to convert new clients to advertising. Yet these debates proved inconclusive. Advertisers on both sides of the battle believed that women did not simply use a cold-blooded economic calculus in making purchasing decisions. Moreover, they agreed that ad men had to present their appeals in simple terms, without relying heavily on elaborate reasoning: Mrs. Consumer could not pass the army intelligence tests any more than her husband. As Christine Frederick, a commercial home economist and marketing consultant, put the matter, "I really believe that the average woman's vocabulary would be only 1200 words . . . . Mrs. Average Consumer does not know more, intellectually, than the present 14-year old adolescent, if as much."[71] Agency experts urged the heavy use of sentiment. Advertisers courted resentment and resistance if they presented consumption simply as a matter of logic, or talked above their prospects' heads. A female commentator cautioned reason-why adherents: "For centuries women have been struggling to establish the fact that they are the intellectual equals of their brothers . . . . if the use of his [the ad man's] product is simply a matter of intelligence, I must give it due attention—I must either buy it and use it, or be able to give reasons for not wanting it, reasons so forcibly logical that they will have weight against his . . . . [The] ad man has taken a mean advantage of me."[72] Logic was a primary tool of business, but of much less use at home. Helen Woodward, one of the most famous copywriters at this time, recalled, "We learned that women seldom buy anything through logical reasoning, not even for their babies. When you are selling a product to millions, you must present even its facts to the average mind and the average mind has nothing to do with reason." She added, "To sell articles to men it is often wise to appear to reason with them, but you must be careful merely to appear to do so—never actually to be logical. Or you will sell no goods."[73] Yet the prolonged debate between suggestion and reason-why hid advertisers' shared assumptions about women. Since women were more susceptible to emotional appeals than men, advertising could persuade women by first addressing their sentiments to attract their interest.[74] Ad men thus addressed the consumer's self-interest, preferably through a combination of appeals to their emotions and the reason-why "facts" about the product that associated it with those feelings.

However, advertisers fretted that as men, they were at a pronounced disadvantage in addressing women. Effective copywriting depended on advertisers' finding women to provide "the feminine viewpoint" for their products or cultivating it in themselves.[75] "There are too many advertisements written by men and not enough by women," claimed a leading stove manufacturer in 1909. "The woman knows where lies the human element of the thing that goes into the home, better than any man that lives." Women could speak with women more easily; most men, no matter how knowledgeable, simply did not possess adequate experience with goods and women's work. "As a general rule, a woman knows much more about a garment than the most loquacious salesman can tell her," another writer observed. "Anyhow, he can't fool her very much about it. She could give a much more intelligent description of it than he could; that is, her description would be more lucidly given, and be more easily understood by women than would his."[76] Although the profession largely remained closed to women, especially in its management and business sectors, some women did find great success in the creative aspects of advertising, writing to women or consulting on the "women's viewpoint," from the earliest days of the business. Women prepared artwork and wrote copy, and in Boston, Kate Griswold published one of the earliest trade journals, *Profitable Advertising*, which highlighted women in advertising.[77] Women ran agencies and managed accounts. In large agencies they almost exclusively staffed the all-important "checking" departments, monitoring published advertisements and ensuring that clients were properly billed for them. Perhaps most famously, at J. Walter Thompson co-owner Helen Resor founded and ran the "women's" department, which trained women as copywriters and executives to specialize in the household and beauty products that were the agency's staple accounts.[78] Nevertheless, the business overall remained a male domain.

Advertisers developed two major strategies to portray women as consumers. The first was to describe spending as an inborn skill or sensibility. Hence, consuming was women's labor as ordained by nature. Women were not only superior but natural consumers, better than men by birth. Shopping and spending came easily to women in this view, and advertisers accordingly portrayed brand preferences and taste as signs of innate instinct. Cadillac announced, "American women have a sort of sixth sense, by which they know the best in everything . . . . An American woman usually knows, unerringly, the one product in its particular field in which she can properly feel pride of possession."[79] Whether celebrating women for their choice in goods, encouraging them in the selection of specific brand-name products, or simply urging them to consume more, advertisers claimed that women were the natural and proper sovereigns of spending. Women "knew" values in goods, whereas men did not.[80] Women were attentive to practical details of housekeeping, dress, and social position.[81] Even as advertisers celebrated women's increasingly public roles by linking suffrage, careers, and personal independence to the marketplace, the underlying assumption was that women were innately suited to consumption.[82]

Yet if women were by nature better consumers, why would they need advertisers? If executives celebrated women in public, in private they often argued that women in reality were ignorant and incompetent shoppers. Many women, they contended, were scarcely able to cope with the difficulties of homemaking or even to identify brand names for popular products. Mildred Holmes of J. Walter Thompson described the discouraging results of door-to-door housewife surveys where canvassers struggled to elicit from ignorant and distracted homemakers the brand names they used: "The routine of housekeeping forces the many untrained women who follow it, daily to act upon ideas they do not formulate. So it is that the average housewife, pressed for answers and reasons becomes inarticulate." The consumer, reminded Claude Hopkins, "cannot judge values. Nor can you and I."[83] Advertisers told themselves that the housewife was virtually helpless in her work without advertising's education, which paradoxically taught women how to fulfill their nature as consumers. "Is there one of us," asked Louise Davis, "who, in her earliest housekeeping days, hasn't faltered, almost panic-stricken, in a crowded grocery store, confronted by some bustling, pencil-poising clerk; who hasn't glanced wildly about at shelves and counters seeking help; who hasn't gasped, at last, 'Yes, that's the kind I want!' feeling unalterably reassured at the sight of a friendly, familiar advertised package or label?"[84] Advertising enabled women to do their work more easily and thereby realize their true selves. If domesticity was still accorded to women as "natural," ad men worked to enforce consuming as women's role.

Advertisers' second strategy was to portray consumption in business terms, often drawing on scientific management and the efficiency movement popularized by Frederick W. Taylor and others, along with home economists. Uncomfortable writing about products used by women, they found it convenient to recast spending in male terms. Advertisers described housework as a business and urged women to acquire business methods and equipment in their homes.[85] "A good workman needs good tools," pronounced one ad for the Florence cookstove. The Nepanee Dutch Kitchenet firm hired an efficiency engineer to analyze the work of meal preparation. Conserving time and steps, eliminating wasteful motions, and saving the worker labor and energy—all part of the agenda of industrial scientific management—lent legitimacy to kitchen and household products.[86] These strategies were well illustrated in the marketing of the Hoosier Kitchen Cabinet. Combining cupboard, food storage, and work space in one central area, the Hoosier could save steps, energy, and time; it challenged conventional kitchen arrangements, and its design became the centerpiece of Christine Frederick's popular 1912 articles on household efficiency. A one-dollar-down installment plan brought the Hoosier within easy reach of thousands. The ads equated housework with other professions and with a social movement of national import: "You will get the same enjoyment out of owning a Hoosier Cabinet that an efficient engineer gets from a perfect new tool. You will find delight in your own greater efficiency; in your ability to do better work with less effort; in the easy system which suddenly makes itself part of your kitchen work." Hoosier consumers formed a national "club" led by a "Council of Kitchen Scientists." By 1916, the company could claim, "A million women have realized their right to a Hoosier. Are their time and health worth more consideration than yours?"[87] Thus individual interest, political entitlement, and social welfare all combined in the equation of housework with industrial and managerial efficiency (fig. 1.3).

Men were also encouraged to view their wives' work as on par with their own. Invoking Uncle Sam, Hoosier invited men to "become a self-appointed efficiency engineer. Rule against time and energy wasters. Provide the labor-saving equipment your 'home superintendent' should have—the conveniences she deserves." Hoover vacuum cleaners urged male consumers to view housework "from her point of view" and to provide their wives the same modern technologies that led to success in men's businesses. A happy young couple in a Campbell's Soup ad counted the blessings provided by the already familiar red and white cans—economy, nutrition, convenience. The husband's last word was the capstone: "That's sense. That's business."[88]

FIGURE 1.3. "Why 700,000 American Women Use Hoosier Cabinets." (*Saturday Evening Post*, October 24, 1914, 44)

The best thing advertisers could say about housework was that it was "The World's Greatest Business". The *Ladies' Home Journal* described the home as "The First Factory" and the housewife as plant manager: "There raw materials are being converted into finished products, flour into pastry, cloth into clothes. There she competes with other men's wives in the dressing of her children, in the dainties on her table, in the tasty arrangement of the living-room. And she reads her own trade journal, in which she studies the market for the purchase of her raw materials, and learns the alchemy of her own cooking."[89] In purchasing guided by the ads in mass-circulation magazines, middle-class professionalism and women's natural traits converged. No greater compliment did Mr. Advertiser pay Mrs. Consumer than to equate her work with his.

Among themselves, advertisers admitted their unfamiliarity with housework and their inability to describe it convincingly. Such unease encouraged their tendency to demean housework even while praising it. Writer Amos Bradbury kept house for his wife to generate fresh copy ideas. "It was surprising to me what a very different picture I got of the housekeeper's job, down there on my knees on the bathroom floor. . . . I began to think of the need for new household appliances to banish still more of the drudgery of housework. And I began to have a greater appreciation for existing labor-saving devices. I wondered as I worked if my wife or our ex-maid thought as much about this while she worked at the same old routine jobs day after day as I was thinking."[90] This patronizing or joking tone often surfaced when discussing homemakers. Advertisers admonished themselves to maintain a realistic picture of women's work and their low mental aptitude. "It is all very well to idealize the consumer in our advertising illustrations—to picture the housewife at her five o'clock potato peeling, clad in a two-hundred dollar Lanvin model in a spotless kitchen, immaculate, unhurried, unflustered—but there is no need to deceive ourselves," cautioned hard-sell specialists Ruthrauff and Ryan.[91] Mrs. Consumer had to be both gifted and savvy enough to earn praise but incompetent enough to require Mr. Advertiser's help.

If they privately derided women's housework, ad men quickly acknowledged her purchasing power. A standard ad industry cliché, again borrowed from business, viewed the housewife as the home executive or general purchasing agent (GPA):

Businesses may have their treasurers, . . . but homes have their wives who do the same work in 25 million independent businesses, the households of America. Without elaborate research, without the counsel and conferences of big business, *these* executives spend annually 40 billion dollars. They spend it amazingly well, too, though they are not specialized purchasing agents any more than they are specialized cooks, or interior decorators, or educators, or furnace tenders.

Thus N. W. Ayer described "The Little Woman, GPA" (fig 1.4). While this image was favorable, it still allowed ad men the superior edge. Even if the homemaker were a skilled purchasing agent, she was not a professional, such as advertisers, engineers, or scientists. If actual business purchasing agents utilized graphs, figures, and specifications, the Little Woman had to rely on the manufacturer of advertised goods. Her success embodied another's expertise and not her own. She needed no tedious technical data (nor could she use it) but only an advertised trademarked name.[92] Christine Frederick expressed this trusting partnership between women and business, made possible by advertising. "The printed page acts as a constant inter-communicating telephone or radio between manufacturer and Mrs. Consumer," Frederick contended. "They were strangers before this was the fact, but are in effect now co-partners in advancing American standards of living."[93] In her great home office Mrs. Consumer was sovereign, but she unavoidably depended on advertisers to do her work.

The contradictions of an instinctive yet incompetent consumer blossomed in a 1928 Thompson series for the Piggly Wiggly grocery chain, which pioneered self-service in grocery retailing.[94] "And Now . . . Even Husbands Can See What Their Wives Have Accomplished!" one ad proclaimed. "In their own domain of shopping for food stuffs wives are regularly doing the very thing that makes husbands feel a little cocky, when they achieve it in *their* business. Week in and week out many women are today using the business method of buying that men call ideal" (fig. 1.5). "Is She a Better Business Man Than Her Husband?" another ad needled. Self-service was not presented merely as a shopping convenience but as "a nation-wide movement sponsored by modern women." Freedom of choice, unassisted by clerks, was not only liberation but also total autonomy: "At last she is entirely free to choose for herself. Through this new plan of buying foods, she can make her own knowledge pay full dividends." But this movement was grounded in the mutual trust of consumer and manufacturer and not in her own innate skills. "From the vast number of brands and grades of foods offered for sale today," the ads promised, "the able men in charge of Piggly Wiggly have sifted out the few very best of each kind." The consumer thus depended on male experts' doing the *real* choosing to make her a better businessman than her hus-

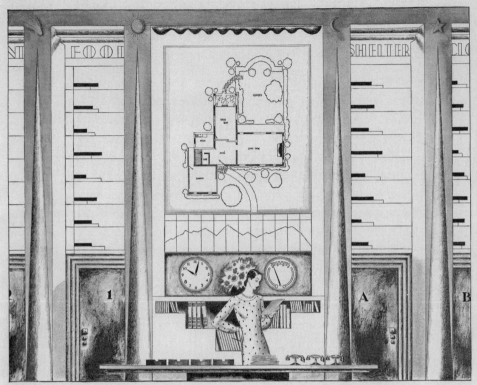

The Little Woman, G·P·A·

BUSINESSES may have their treasurers, their comptrollers, even their boards of directors who watch expenditures. By careful perusal of charts and graphs, by weighty conferences, they determine how annual income is to be spent.

But homes have their wives who do the same work in 25 million independent businesses, the households of America. Without elaborate research, without the counsel and the conferences of big business, *these* executives spend annually 40 billion dollars. They spend it amazingly well, too, though they are not specialized purchasing agents any more than they are specialized cooks, or interior decorators, or educators, or furnace tenders.

Their decisions are governed by the welfare of their families. "Is this breakfast food better for my children to eat?" . . . "Will this davenport and these curtains, this lamp and this piano, make my home a pleasanter place to be?" . . . "Will this school give my daughter what I know she needs?" . . . "Would another kind of heating equipment make our home more comfortable, more healthful next winter?" These are samples of the questions they ask.

Always they visualize the ideal, these wives and mothers, before they consider economies. But they watch for economies as few business men do. By aptitude and training they are excellent shoppers. The

competition for their attention, the courting of their favor, is tremendous. The way to their hearts and their purses is not easy, but it is clear. These general purchasing agents are readers of advertising, consistent, critical readers of advertising. It has been estimated that they buy more than eighty per cent of all advertised merchandise.

Addressing the women of America on the printed page is an art, but an art that can be applied with almost the exactitude of a science. Already it has meant the growth and continued success of many concerns who manufacture products useful in the business of making a home and rearing a family.

N. W. AYER & SON   *ADVERTISING HEADQUARTERS* PHILADELPHIA
NEW YORK   BOSTON   CHICAGO   SAN FRANCISCO

FIGURE 1.4. "The Little Woman, GPA." (N. W. Ayer Collection, Series 6, Box 14, Archives Center, National Museum of American History, Smithsonian Institution, Washington, D.C.)

FIGURE 1.5. "And Now . . . Even Husbands Can See What Their Wives Have Accomplished." (*Good Housekeeping*, March 1928, 185)

band.[95] The Thompson ads hedged their bets as well; in addition to the copy's emphasis on the consumer's competence and independence, illustrations showed her chicly attired, attended by maids and chauffeurs. The ads also did not reveal that the Piggly Wiggly "system" strictly limited the number of brands and items on the shelves, reducing the "very best of each kind" to the product lines that were most profitable for the retailer.[96] This, then, was the vision of women consumers at the height of 1920s prosperity: women were independent, sure of their skills, and willing participants in the adventure of shopping, but always the junior partners of the male domains of production and publicity.[97] Underneath, the female consumer was still in need of others to help. Women would realize their freedom only as freedom of choice.

By 1930, advertisers' collective vision of women was clear: behind every successful homemaker was a man from Madison Avenue. The imagery of smart, modern sophistication concealed incompetence and juvenile intelligence. Advertisers were beholden to millions of women whom they considered their inferiors in every conceivable standard—knowledge, cultivation, aspirations. These professionals thus were compelled to profess loyalty and dedication to women while feeling at every turn superior to them. Such dependence on the habits, interests, budgets, and attention of supposedly emotive and illogical women fostered resentment that would emerge fully when the economy ran aground. That same alienation colored advertisers' relationships and perceptions of the mass public of consumers. Advertising's construction of "the masses" can best be seen in its relationship with radio listeners, the most spectacular grouping of the American public the profession had yet encountered.

"THE PEOPLE WHO BUY TOOTHPASTE": ADVERTISERS AND THE RADIO AUDIENCE, 1920–1935

Although advertisers had addressed large aggregates for decades, their conquest of broadcast radio as an advertising medium gave them audiences of millions, far outstripping anything they had ever achieved in print. With radio came spectacular commercial success. Yet the successful, even intimate contact with listener-consumers threatened the barriers that advertisers carefully maintained between themselves and the masses. As a result, advertisers' opinions of consumers fell much further. The more successful the selling, the greater the contempt advertisers had for the consuming public. Radio's democratic cultural promise and demographic access blurred the cultural divisions between Madison Avenue and Main Street. The closer they came to consumers, the more fiercely advertisers maintained the gulf between themselves and the masses in radio-land.

Radio's status as an advertising-based medium was neither inevitable nor expected in 1920 when KDKA's broadcast of the Warren G. Harding–James M. Cox election demonstrated broadcasting's viability. Yet by the decade's end, broadcasting had become thoroughly commercialized. Scores of advertisers placed millions of dollars of business on national networks to broadcast "entertainment" containing some commercial message. Using broadcast radio to convey their clients' sales messages prompted advertising agencies to become producers of entertainment (the programs), as well as the commercial announcements that were their stock in trade. The medium produced vast sums for agencies and clients, often beyond all expectations. "The people— the advertising people—during the eighteen years or so of radio's rise and decline were like children turned loose in a candy store," remembered one writer.[98] As they developed radio departments to produce programming, advertisers not only built highly lucrative businesses but also found their ideas about consumers transformed. For radio not only gave national ad men a greater audience, but by its very nature as aural communication, radio also changed advertisers' ideas about their audiences.

Radio was not inevitably a commercial enterprise, and many early listeners, broadcasters, and advocates passionately opposed any commercialization of the medium. Indeed, as Susan Douglas astutely observes, "More than the movies, mass magazines, or television (and up until the Internet) radio has been the mass medium through which the struggles between rampant commercialism and a loathing of that commercialism have been fought out over and over again."[99] Although some broadcasters viewed radio as a commercial proposition from the first, most advertising agents opposed the commercialization of radio for many years. At best, they were ambivalent, perceiving that audiences expected "free entertainment" and resented commercial interruptions of their listening enjoyment. Often radio enthusiasts themselves, ad men of the early 1920s protested against commercial broadcasting as vehemently as other audience members. In 1925 a commentator who had examined hundreds of letters from listeners to the government Radio Division concluded:

There is a strong public sentiment against those stations which go in for advertising too strongly and the direct advertising now being broadcast is rapidly building up a strong prejudice against all forms of advertising over the radio. . . . In the minds of intelligent radio fans, broadcast advertising of all kinds is considered a destructive influence closely allied with trickery and deceit. . . . An army of fans, perhaps a majority, looks upon broadcasting as an advertising medium with antagonistic disfavor, and bitterly resents the increasing attempts of stations to make broadcasting profitable by means of paid publicity.[100]

The chairman of the Federal Radio Division even more emphatically stated the case against direct radio advertising in 1927. "The business man who employs direct radio advertising as a selling force is working against himself. . . . I know from the many letters we receive that he makes numerous enemies."[101] Although advertising programs for such early sponsors as Happiness Candy, A&P, and Goodrich seemingly brought about increased sales to those sponsors, so-called direct advertising (messages exceeding a brief mention of a sponsor's name and product) continually provoked sharp protest against the invasion of what one listener called "God's free air." This resentment was best captured by a listener writing in 1925 to Louisville's WHAS, "If it's the last act of my life, I'm going to invent something to turn off my radio during those advertising talks, and turn it on again when the music starts!"[102]

Ad men shied away from using radio as well due to its ephemeral messages. Accustomed to print, they disdained a medium of uncertain range and temporary duration, and they remained loath to spend clients' money for mere "publicity," the brief sponsor mentions of so-called indirect advertising. Barred from offering full-fledged sales messages, and with few reliable means to check radio circulation, ad men deemed broadcasting a foolish investment.[103] Only with RCA's heavily capitalized launching of the National Broadcasting Company (NBC) in 1926 on an explicit advertising basis, and the subsequent successes of advertised popular programs (most notably, *Amos 'n' Andy*), did advertising executives overcome their resistance.[104] Not until late 1928 did most major agencies establish their own fledgling radio departments and encourage clients to add broadcasting to their marketing plans.[105]

What brought ad agencies and their clients to radio and kept them there was simple: it moved goods. The influential George Washington Hill, president of American Tobacco Company, told both his ad agency and NBC that radio boosted Lucky Strike sales over 47 percent in 1928. Similarly, products such as Pepsodent (*Amos 'n' Andy*), Ipana Toothpaste (*The Ipana Troubadors*) and Vaseline (*Real Folks*) enjoyed vastly expanded markets as a result of radio exposure.[106] By 1930, one agency executive could claim, "We have had several cases of where our clients were asked to go before meetings for example, to tell about the results of their radio advertising and they have refused to do so because they did not want their competitors to know just how good it was . . . . Most everybody on the air does his best to keep the facts from getting to anybody in tangible form."[107] That nearly 12 million homes possessed radios (about 40 percent of the total) by 1930 convinced advertisers that radio was a permanent addition to American social life. More important, as one executive noted, radio homes comprised "the cream of the middle class market of the country."[108] By 1940 a veteran NBC executive could frankly admit, "It's very hard to use radio and not make a success of it. . . . The kind of results we get just read, I admit, something like a fairy tale."[109]

Why was radio so powerful as a sales medium? Its aural element, the sound of the human voice, promised to reconstitute the ideal face-to-face relationship of consumer and vendor, which print advertising lacked.[110] Copywriters had long labored to create sales arguments from the consumer's point of view, written in simple, unintimidating language. For ad writers, the ideal copy evoked the friendly manner and personal authority of a good salesman, who could persuade the most uninterested or resistant consumer.[111] Radio promised to restore that personal element of salesmanship—intimacy—that had been lost in the print medium, to national advertising. Speech would collect a much larger and more responsive audience than the printed page. Although radio did not, of course, entail actual face-to-face contacts, the fiction of a direct conversation was cited repeatedly as the source of its hypnotic charm. "The radio message comes through the medium of an announcer's voice," one advocate explained, "[which is] naturally more interesting than cold, silent, type characters."[112] One commentator noted that "broadcasting most closely resembles personal salesmanship in that the spoken message goes directly into the ears of the radio audience." Another radio executive made the link explicit between radio's aural delivery and salesmen, observing, "Unquestionably that is the explanation of the success of radio—it is the familiar voice in the home by invitation."[113] The restoration—indeed a remaking—of personal intimacy was the key to radio's success with listeners. Broadcasting provided the equivalent of the salesman's "foot in the door," as illustrated by a Thompson executive: "Now, if you start out to sell aluminum, the first thing you are given is a little maroon book. And one chapter of the book tells you how to get into houses where you are not invited. . . . You do something, you give something [a sample pie-pan] to get in Mrs. Albright's door but after you are inside you forget about the pie-pan and so does she. Your job is then to sell her your wares just as convincingly as you can. We believe that an advertiser should follow the same course with radio advertising."[114] Radio provided an entering wedge into the home, which would facilitate delivery of persuasive sales talk.

Writing for radio and the extended contact with radio audiences lowered advertisers' opinions of their listeners' intelligence levels still further, however. Biased in favor of the written word, some advertisers considered writing an effective print ad more difficult than a radio commercial.[115] Radio writing seemed irredeemably unintelligent and lowbrow since its aural characteristics demanded that ad men overthrow the rules of composition, rhetoric, and grammar fundamental to their training as writers. As one radio writer advised, "Keep your sentences short. Forget all you ever learned about the rules of syntax. You don't have to be able to diagram a radio announcement for it to be effective. Pile phrase upon phrase and forget a verb in a sentence now and then. Remember that a series of high-priced adjectives means nothing when it is heard over the air."[116] Accustomed to the freedom to set forth long blocks of text to elaborate their arguments, ad men chafed at the limits of writing for radio and concluded that their audiences were even less intelligent than Madison Avenue had customarily believed. The content of radio—both programs and sales messages—was proof positive that consumers were little more than children.

Still, in radio's capacity for particularly direct communication, and in the audience's seeming unlimited hunger for intimacy, advertisers believed they had discovered a foolproof source of sales. Students of radio generally agreed that aural communication was more effective than writing. Network publicists and radio researchers maintained that most listeners could remember broadcast advertising much better than print ads.[117] Listening apparently was less taxing than reading. But the medium's great advantage lay in the familiarity of an attractive human voice emanating in the home. "Not only is radio easy to listen to, it is likewise more personal than the printed word," Hadley Cantril and Gordon Allport observed in *The Psychology of Radio*. "A voice belongs to a living person, and living people arrest our attention and sustain our interest better than do printed words."[118] Consumers responded to the suggestions of the announcer's voice, friendly and persuasive. Familiarity bred authority. "Think how natural it is to hear the friendly things, the intimate things and the authoritative things of life spoken to us by a human voice," a network brochure gushed. The spoken word was radio's "supple power to move people and mold them, to enlist them and command them. For people do what they're told."[119] The spoken word provided both intimacy and influence.[120]

The human voice in the home gave listeners a point of emotional contact with the programming. In radio's early years especially, listeners often re-sponded to broadcasts in highly personal ways that revealed strong and last-ing identification with performers or proceedings.[121] Advertisers learned from the floods of letters and postcards that many listeners felt convinced that the radio shows seemed broadcast expressly for them. Martin Block, a sensa-tionally successful radio salesman and pioneering disc jockey, exploited this phenomenon, directing his sign-off "to you, to you and especially *you*."[122] Observers of broadcasting often noted the heartfelt comments from listeners grateful for the contact with the outside world. One executive commented, "I have read hundreds, perhaps thousands of letters from men and women who find diversion, not to say needed cheer and companionship from their radio sets . . . . It is by no means rare for radio stations to find a hoarded dollar bill among the day's mail. 'I felt so grateful for my radio set last night that I just had to send you something.' "[123] Although skeptics doubted that many people engaged in such single-minded listening, especially to commercials, most advertisers felt that listeners maintained a personalized relationship with broadcasts.[124]

The audience's seeming delight in the intimate contact of radio convinced ad men that consumers craved authentic emotional experience and contacts outside the narrow sphere of their everyday lives. In Kenneth Goode's acute observation, radio functioned "primarily as a medium of self-expression by the audience." Radio advertisers thus came quickly believe that a program, "if it is to make effectual contact with the listener at all, . . . must appeal to the listener's feelings." The spoken word addressed the emotions more power-fully than print. For ad men, "The emotional reaction makes the audience responsive to an amazing degree."[125] No rationality was necessary; sales ap-peals based on emotion and simplistic ideas became radio advertisers' pre-ferred type of commercial message. Broadcasting brought to life Walter Dill Scott's process theory of suggestion and amplified it exponentially.

No other vision of the audience proved more appealing to ad men than that of the family gathered around the set, expectant, impressionable, and above all receptive to the ad messages along with the entertainment (fig. 1.6). NBC executive Frank Arnold described the archetypal radio audience: "Never visu-alize it as a tremendous number of people seated in an audience hall listening to a performance. Instead, visualize a family group about the receiving set. . . . Here you have the advertiser's ideal—the family group in its moments of relaxation awaiting your message. Nothing like this has ever been dreamed of by the advertising man."[126] Only a few publications had previously promised advertisers credible access to an entire family; radio promised them maxi-

FIGURE 1.6. The Advertiser's Dream: The Expectant Family Ready to Listen.
(George H. Clark Collection of Radioana, Series A, Subseries 6, Box 417, File 1988-2077,
Archives Center, National Museum of American History, Smithsonian Institution,
Washington, D.C.)

mum and effective exposure, especially at times when the prospects were susceptible to an advertising message. By 1934 one network executive would claim, "When you use radio . . . you are dealing with something that has become an integral part of the life of the average family."[127]

Broadcasting not only reached families, but it also promised to penetrate the lower-middle and working class much more than advertisers had ever hoped to do with print. The greatest attraction of radio was that it would deliver to clients the families beneath the reach of national mass periodicals and beneath the A and B levels of income that occupied much of advertisers' attention. Radio reached those characterized by one ad man as the "great number of illiterates who could never read your printed advertising copy, or who would never take the trouble to decipher it."[128] Radio was likely to be a principal form of entertainment for the mass audience. As one writer declared in 1929, "You will find the workman and his family much more faithful to the loudspeaker than those who forsake the radio for golf, tennis, yachting, theaters, motoring, swimming and fishing." Most important, radio simultaneously reached an affluent "class" audience and the "masses," the large strata of working and lower-middle class—in advertisers' terms, the Sweeneys as well as the Stuyvesants, the Clancys along with the Delanceys.[129]

Of course, consumers did not simply respond whenever the advertiser broadcast a sales appeal. As one copywriter reminded his colleagues, "When '20,000,000 families buy the things they're told to buy,' radio will be a miracle, not a medium. A radio set, as such, has no more moral influence than a telephone. Less perhaps."[130] The prospect of an eager and responsive audience of millions, responding to the merest hint from an announcer, was at best an ad man's fantasy. Yet the powerful emotional responses that radio evoked from listeners, as well as its ability to gather unprecedented numbers of consumers, made advertisers reconsider their relationships with the lonely masses who could respond so emotionally to voices from the ether.

For one thing, the fervent and often painfully heartfelt responses from listeners elated, disturbed, and sometimes just overwhelmed ad men. Over 200,000 families wrote regarding one early hit program, *Main Street Sketches*. One agency alone received more than 600,000 pieces of mail between mid-1929 and 1930. NBC claimed to pull in 5.5 million letters in 1936 and nearly 23 million over its first nine years.[131] Such claims were difficult to prove or evaluate, since most mail contained premium requests or contest entries. Even so, broadcasters were impressed at the flood of earnest personal confidences in the mail. One radio department head noted, "It is simply amazing the way the radio audience opens its heart to the broadcasting stations and to the advertisers who are providing them with entertainment." However, the public's personal revelation of radio's importance in their lives discomfited more than it impressed advertisers. Madison Avenue professionals were openly dismissive of listeners who claimed emotional relationships with these obviously fabricated and disembodied broadcasts. One letter shared by a radio chief with his colleagues indicates both radio's capacity to evoke such intimate responses and professionals' ambivalent attitudes toward them. Wrote one mother of her daughter's love for Cream of Wheat, "I am very grateful to you and your programs, as it has been hard to get her to eat any hot cereal . . . . She eats it daily and is gaining in weight and health . . . thanking you, in the name of all the underweight children who may benefit as my little girl has from your programs." The scornful executive concluded,

"This is not an unusual letter, in fact *there are lots worse than that.*"[132] That the mass audience responded to distant and disembodied voices with such openness indicated a childlike credulity and simple-mindedness, which for ad men verged on the fantastic. The sales manager of *Amos 'n' Andy*'s sponsor Pepsodent recalled with disbelief that listeners sent in hundreds of dollar bills when the two characters started a bank on the program. Marveling at the hundreds of personal items sent by listeners to these fictional characters, executive Harlow Roberts declared, "I at one time studied psychology . . . but our radio experiences have made me give up trying to understand the workings of the human mind."[133]

Similarly, advertisers found the mass audience unsophisticated and ignorant. Radio listeners' tastes provoked snickers in the conference rooms of metropolitan agencies. Advertisers disdainfully noted the difference between their own preferences and the public's appetite for "entertainment spread with a thick, gooey coating of sentiment."[134] J. Walter Thompson writer Carroll Carroll recalled that "it was generally conceded by the 'sophisticates' of the day that only morons listened to radio and that only the dopiest of those tuned in pure corn like Eddie Cantor's show." A typical attitude emerged in one executive's description of a popular program, *Thirty Minutes of Sunshine*: "The radio program was entirely handled by one man, a Mr. Hamp, who sang, played instruments, cracked jokes and otherwise stirred up the air . . . . His program is just terrible, awful. None of us would listen to it, but the people who buy toothpaste like it. . . . It is a sort of silly stuff for grownups." As NBC programming head Bertha Brainard cautioned, "It may be, for example, that you do not like a corny program, but if it is good corn, it will in all probability attract a large audience."[135]

Clients often shared advertisers' views of the audience's tastes. Embracing an admittedly elite sensibility, clients and ad men both denigrated "jazz" on the air instead of classical music and preferred the urbane wit and wordplay of comedians Fred Allen or Ray Perkins to the broad humor and folksy platitudes of an Eddie Cantor. Such strong tastes often made sponsors and agents reluctant to offer lowbrow entertainment, even if it was lucrative. As the J. Walter Thompson radio chief John Reber noted:

> Even if it were true that the Stebbins Boys would have trebled the sales of Chase and Sanborn's Coffee, we could not have used them. Every night nine or ten of the officials at Standard Brands regularly broke their ankles rushing to the radio to turn off the Stebbins Boys. You couldn't possibly

sell it to them. If someone were to suggest [vaudeville comics] Olsen and Johnson for Pond's Cold Cream, [Thompson executives] Dr. Watson, Mrs. Resor, [and Pond's owners] Mr. Lamont and Mr. Corliss would all scream and die immediately.[136]

Corn might have been popular, but some advertisers preferred to remain silent on the air than present corn.

Copywriters lampooned the benighted public's lowbrow appetite, but in practice agents had to satisfy it. This led to a self-protective cynicism about programs, clients, network executives, performers, and especially the audience. Their physical distance from listeners here again allowed ad men to indulge in abstractions, thinking once more of markets rather than people. Commentator Kenneth Goode chided, "All of us have come more or less recklessly to reckon radio listeners—human beings—with the same statistical detachment with which we reckon radio sets. 'Listeners' come thus to be visualized as squadrons of soldiers on parade . . . reporting, let us say, for a daily period of three hours."[137] Moreover, their cultural distance allowed advertisers to indulge in some abstract and condescending notions about their listeners. The mass audience seemed a huge nation of children perfectly unconcerned with advertising but willing in self-interest to adopt new behaviors or products.[138] "The great mass has never had an idea," agency sage William Day proclaimed. "It has no ideas about government, it has no ideas about religion, it has no ideas about biology; it is purely and simply a vast shapeless force which is led in one direction or another by leaders."[139] Radio's spectacular success, ad men repeated to themselves, was due to the people's boundless susceptibility to suggestion and their willingness to respond to authority. Consumers not only had the intelligence level of fourteen year olds, but they were also children in their attitudes and behavior.

Advertisers nevertheless made numerous attempts to compensate for their separation from the world of the mass audience. Most important was the ongoing discussion of the "average listener." Some ad men believed that the average listener was "actually no more than a hypothetical concept, but he is extremely important for the advertiser to know." Even with this complication, many throughout the industry adopted such a model in writing for the masses.[140] Agency head and radio producer Roy Durstine described the advertising agent's informed sense of his audience:

The typical listening audience for a radio program is a tired, bored, middle-aged man and woman whose lives are empty and who have exhausted their sources of amusement when they have taken a quick look at the evening paper. They are utterly unlike those who are most vocal in their criticism of radio programs—people with full lives, with books to read, with parties to attend, with theaters to visit, with friends whose conversational powers are stimulating. Radio provides a vast source of delight and entertainment for the barren lives of the millions.[141]

In contrasting the masses with urbane sophisticates, Durstine's portrait openly confirmed that ad men conceived of the consumer-masses as everything which they themselves were not.

Although they polled listeners, gave away premiums, and held contests to gauge consumers' income levels, family composition, and social status, ad men were still at a great distance from ongoing personal contact with consumers. In fact, they relied on that gulf to distinguish themselves from their audiences, as radio itself seemed to erode other barriers that separated elite and mass. Ad men conceived of their mass audience of "typical listeners" as everyone outside their own sphere. In one executive's words, "If your office boy, a stenographer other than your own, the porter who moves the desks around your office, and two of your friends' wives can understand every idea you have put into your radio copy, merely from having it read to them, probably every listener who hears it over the air will grasp what you are trying to say."[142] While such a caution was no doubt sound business, it revealed the ways advertisers distanced themselves from the masses they supposedly served and addressed in their own native tongue. The working class, women, children, blacks: all were indistinguishable. For the educated, affluent occupants of Madison Avenue, the consumer was the Other.

This distance also influenced advertisers' sociology of consumer tastes. Copywriters, in fact, thought of the vast audience as symbolized by the goods and mass entertainment they sold the public. The movies, tabloids, Model Ts, dance band jazz, and even radio itself all became convenient symbols for the ad men's vague and condescending notions of the mass audience. "The people who buy toothpaste" was one such characterization. Similarly, a Thompson man eloquently articulated this Madison Avenue vision of consumers in general: "After all, the market for most products is the people who flock to the talkies to see Greta Garbo—who travel in Fords and Chevrolets munching hot dogs en route. In infancy they are attracted by bright colors, glitter and noise. And in adulthood they retain almost a similar set of reactions." This notion applied equally to the radio audience; as Roy Durstine reminded his colleagues, "The great mass of radio listeners are no higher than the average motion picture audiences in intelligence and purchasing power."[143] Engaged in selling to the masses, advertising agents conceived of goods and entertainment, the products that they sold, as the telling symbols of consumers themselves. The result was that advertisers often could not distinguish the commodity from the customer.

This process of symbolization went on, in part, because radio seemed to blur or eliminate other signs of class divisions. Like mass consumption itself, radio seemed to promise an unprecedented social and cultural leveling. Spokesmen had long celebrated the democratizing potential of radio and its capacity to elevate the masses. While, as Roland Marchand has shown, radio spokesmen believed that possibility was destroyed by full ascent of commercial programming, many still remained convinced that the medium provided the masses access to culture, particularly drama and classical music, they had ordinarily been denied.[144] Moreover, in offering common and simultaneous experience to listeners of all classes, radio had the potential to obliterate distinctions among them. Social scientists Hadley Cantril and Gordon Allport described the democratizing pretensions of radio: "Millions of people listen to the same thing at the same time—and they themselves are aware of the fact. Distinctions between rural and urban communities, men and women, age and youth, social classes, creeds, states and nations are abolished. As if by magic the barriers of social stratification disappear and in their place comes a consciousness of equality and of a community interest. . . . In short it seems to be the nature of radio to encourage people to think and feel alike."[145] Advertisers applauded such tendencies, however exaggerated, and defended their work as servants of the consumer in precisely these terms: advertising cultivated common habits and tastes among all consumers.[146]

However, among themselves advertisers expressed exactly the opposite sentiments. While they openly celebrated the democratizing potential of mass consumption, privately advertisers held themselves aloof from it to preserve their own identities. Clinging to the idea of a cultural gulf, ad men continued to think of consumers in terms of their lowbrow habits. As one executive put it, "Social and cultural levels tend to parallel economic levels."[147] Advertisers could study consumers, measure their preferences in programming and products, evaluate their living conditions, and compile inventories of pantries, closets, and even bank accounts. Yet the closer advertisers came to the mass of consumers and the more the cultural boundaries separating them from the masses blurred, the more fiercely advertisers sought to distinguish themselves from their audiences.

By 1930 advertisers had established firm ideas about the spending publics they addressed. Clinging to their own elevated cultural plane, ad men saw consumers as childlike, irrational, ungovernable, and unpredictable. Fabricating standardized and easily sold traits for consumers was good business, but it left professionals unprepared for the variety of behaviors and desires they encountered in real consumers. Their portraits of women and audiences were abstractions and types, suitable for selling to clients; their sales messages likewise were often simplistic and unpersuasive. In turn, actual consumers often behaved very differently than advertisers hoped: indifference or resistance often greeted sales messages. Buyers evaded and defied, as well as complied with, advertising. Everyday market behaviors thus invalidated the generalities of the ad man's invented consumer. Despite many selling successes, ad men could neither contain nor control actual consumers. Their prescriptions remained just that, the exhortations of authorities that contended with other values for popular allegiance. But equally true, consumers encountered these sales messages and ideals every day, repeatedly. If consumers ignored some, advertisers followed up with new methods and messages. A campaign or commodity might fail, but advertising would go on.

Advertisers offered a vision of consumption and consumers based on a premise of personal transformation and social distinction through accumulation and spending. Locating and addressing prospective purchasers led advertisers to imagine them as simple-minded, childlike, and irrational. They attempted to teach consumers to think of themselves as symbolized by goods, but in truth only ad men themselves viewed consumers solely through their possessions and tastes. Claiming to be public servants, advertisers contended that they knew and fulfilled popular desire. Their vision of consumption and their claims to public legitimacy were based at best on highly partial, myopic understandings. In contrast to later motivational researchers or today's retail anthropologists, most advertisers cared little why people actually bought goods. Their attempts to study purchasers understandably were aimed to increase sales, not to grasp higher truths or even the complex diversity they glimpsed in society. In the final analysis, consumers remained elusive to advertisers—fearsome and contemptible one moment, gullible and easily led the next, always aggregates to be managed rather than understood. Urging constant consumption in their social portraits, dominating the structure of commercial media, advertisers preempted other perspectives. Little penetrated the magazine pages or the airwaves that did not urge consumers to buy more or to view themselves as an extension of their things. Advertisers saw modern America as a heterogeneous society with increased wealth and comforts but with little common culture. They proposed to fill that void with consumer goods. In material modernity—mass-produced abundance—they saw the foundation of an American identity secured by spending, an identity they could shape. They envisioned a nation imagined and unified through goods. To that end, they offered a profoundly political and nationalist portrait of consumption, and it is to that vision we now turn.

CHAPTER 2

THE

NATIONALIZATION

OF CONSUMERS

THE POLITICAL

LANGUAGE OF

AMERICAN

ADVERTISING,

1890–1930

Advertising seems to have been accepted by the American people, voted for and elected as the medium through which they choose to learn of new things to eat, to wear, to protect themselves, and to add to their pleasure.[1]

Every Day in Philadelphia new declarations of independence are signed. . . . Men and women are making it the birthplace of their own independence. And to each individual the Penn Mutual policy gives the same freedom to progress and achieve that the famous declaration gave to our nation.[2]

A pervasive presence in American culture, advertising recast ideas of citizenship and nationality. As advertising became a national institution after 1890, its practitioners drew on political metaphors and imagery to designate consumers, products, and consumption as important elements of a distinctly American public life. The images that filled magazines and newspapers, roadsides and streetscapes, store windows and even scrapbooks equated goods and spending with becoming and being American. At a time of vast demographic expansion and emerging national culture industries, advertisers showed American life as defined and fortified by consumption. Moreover, they cast advertising in the argot of American political traditions, patriotic emblems, and nationalist ideals. While they invented consumers from their encounters with buyers of differing social groups, advertisers remade the abstract figure of "the consumer" as a citizen naturalized by spending.

Business advocates had long argued that trade and enterprise must be kept free from both government and politics, although they often called on the state to safeguard commercial interests.[3] But Madison Avenue readily adapted political language and nationalist rhetoric to its wares. Advertisers used such language and symbols to imagine markets in the likeness of the American nation, portraying consumption as a political process of consent, where Americans exercised their most important public power: buying. In comparing spending and suffrage, advertisers imparted the aura of democracy to the distribution of goods. Yet consumption superseded political democracy, as advertisers' civic language subverted traditional associations of citizenship and politics. Even as seismic demographic shifts, social movements, and new ideas transformed American citizenship, advertisers crafted a compelling vision of consent and belonging based on consuming.[4]

This new language and figurations of citizenship as consuming could only attain a hold as traditional ideas and practices of American citizenship underwent significant changes, beginning in the late nineteenth century and cresting in the 1920s. Widespread reform campaigns gained national success over decades in extending suffrage, enhancing direct elections and referenda, and attempting to bring capitalism under democratic control.[5] Yet as these campaigns waged prolonged battles to expand the vote, grave doubts grew among social critics and expert social scientists regarding the citizen's capacity for public participation. Questions regarding the individual's fitness to exercise political power challenged long-standing ideals of widespread civic culture.

Political analyst Walter Lippmann gave such concerns prismatic focus in *Public Opinion* (1922). He attacked lingering Jeffersonian notions of the common people's fitness to shape the course of human events. The pursuit of self-determined self-interest, claimed Lippmann, did not assure good government. He noted that people were unable to perceive a "true" picture of the world beyond "the picture in their heads," and thus people remained mired in their own prejudice, unable to transcend their provincial views. The political system's rhetorical subservience to a public both poorly informed and incompetent guaranteed the eclipse of significant issues by "the more obvious failings of democracy . . . violent prejudice, apathy, preference for the curious trivial against the dull important, and the hunger for sideshows and three-legged calves." Without a responsible system of experts delivering carefully analyzed and digested information to the public for their "opinion," no democratic form of government would be possible. As it was, the idea that every citizen's native intelligence, abilities, and communal spirit would ensure a good or just government was both unfounded and dangerous. A serious and realistic assessment of political democracy led to the inevitable conclusion that its foundation—the competent citizen—could no longer be the individual.[6]

Social critics identified disturbing irrational formations within mass society—crowds and publics—that seemed patently ill-suited for deliberative, effective politics or enduring social cohesion. From the mid-nineteenth century the rise of mass society and popular revolutions in Europe had filled some observers with dread, contempt, or despair. "Crowd psychology," which developed in the wake of urbanization, further disturbed Enlightenment notions of the autonomous and self-interested individual as the foundation of political life. Such European thinkers as Gustave Le Bon and Gabriel de Tarde found the urban masses to be a threatening social phenomenon, a huge group seemingly incapable of independent mental activity, completely irrational, and ultimately susceptible to external manipulations.[7] In the United States the response to the rise of mass society was somewhat less strident. Such commentators as Robert Park and Gerald Stanley Lee hailed the ascension of masses to a prominent place in public life. Yet even these commentators cautioned that crowds needed guidance and by themselves could not articulate their desires or devise a rational plan of action.[8] The self-reliant, autonomous individual came under attack as an insupportable fiction; human beings were really products of a social environment. Most prominent in the United States, sociologist Charles Horton Cooley and philosopher George Herbert Mead claimed that human identity and character were in essence socially determined.[9] Neither autonomous nor rational, the individual as delineated in psychological and philosophical theories differed sharply from the model citizen enshrined in American political thought.

Beyond the diminished and dependent individual, urban commercial culture provoked fierce criticism. With its basis in new sensory entertainments of spectacle, display, and sexuality, urban amusements threatened traditional associations of popular leisure and moral order. Lippmann's comment about sideshows and three-legged calves reflected the consistent unease of many intellectuals with commercial culture. Fearful of irrational crowds and skeptical of the competent individual, writers concerned with democratic renewal through culture expressed repeated concern for the quality of popular entertainment. Critics as different as Randolph Bourne, H. L. Mencken, and Simon Patten all disparaged popular commercial entertainments as shoddy, lacking in substance, degrading, and dehumanizing.[10] Usually cast as aesthetic arguments, such criticisms of mass culture and popular entertainment barely disguised the social or political fears of the commentators. The low moral and spiritual nature of American people as reflected in their amusements would ultimately shape the nation's political and social destiny. The poor quality of public amusements would harm the republic itself. Those arguments and attitudes echoed in the debates between defenders of commercial culture and its critics throughout the century.[11] The ideas and practices of citizenship were changing under the centralization of politics, the fragmentation of urban masses, and the promulgation of new ideas of public life and individual competence. In this setting advertisers developed a political language of consumption to sell goods, but in the process they also created an enduring vision of citizenship based on purchasing, ownership, and display.

ADVERTISERS AND POLITICS: THE METAPHOR OF PROFESSIONS

Advertisers sought legitimacy by comparing themselves with established groups. As JoAnne Brown has argued, emerging turn-of-the-century professionals adopted metaphoric comparisons to older professions to claim exclusive control of their specialized expertise and to popularize it with lay publics.[12] Of the many vocations they summoned to explain their work, ad men found none more appealing or useful than politics. Advertisers identified their work of persuasion as public service and leadership akin to politics—the promulgation of ideas and programs for the common good, publicly affirmed through a communal, voluntary process. At the height of advertising's public prestige during the 1920s, advertiser George Frederick proudly staked advertisers' claims to leadership in the manner of politicians:

> To call one a writer and the other an advertiser; one a statesman and the other a seller of merchandise, is, after all, a very faint distinction without a fundamental difference . . . . The measure of all public men, as well as of business concerns, is the extent to which they can carry public opinion and responsive action with them for their ideas, and the extent to which these ideas increase the wealth and happiness of society. The advertiser need no more be afraid of this test than the statesman.[13]

To be sure, neither advertisers nor the corporations they spoke for were true statesmen. The public did not entrust them with governance, and they were not sworn to uphold or make laws. Yet Frederick's overheated rhetoric was not unusual: advertisers often compared themselves to politicians, pursuing similar goals with like means. "Without public opinion, nothing can be done in a world of democracies," claimed Bruce Barton. "We advertising people work with the tools by which public opinion is formed and directed."[14] More important, the corporations that advertisers spoke for wielded power in the economy and in politics. While advertisers were no politicians, their work and their views had political impact.

It should not be surprising that political metaphors became pervasive in advertising language. The two major strains of American political thought—liberalism and republicanism—had long enshrined commerce as a bedrock of society, and political thinkers throughout the West had long noted the close connections of marketplace and polis.[15] Madison Avenue used political language to reflect both its claims of public service and its aspirations to power. Addressing large aggregates of an often undifferentiated public; identifying public problems and offering specific solutions "for the public good"; seeking consent to their proposals; promising to promote progress in daily life; and finally, seeking continually to be named as trusted stewards of public interests—all were claimed equally by politicians and advertisers. As Murray Edelman has argued, politics itself is not only the system of allocating power and resources through the state, but also a symbolic communicative process by which a society's collective tensions and anxieties are raised or quieted.[16] Indeed, by continually raising fears and offering solutions to masses of consumers, advertisers did not simply employ political metaphors but in effect assumed the functions of politicians themselves. Roland Marchand and Jackson Lears have shown that one of the principal strategies of advertisers in these years was to raise anxieties about the complexities, treacheries, and dangers of everyday living in the modern world. By emphasizing that products could solve such "problems," advertisers claimed to be therapeutic advisors, easing popular fears of the unknown.[17] Advertisements became political not least as they continually invented, raised, and resolved collective problems.

Since advertisers used political language consistently, understanding specific cognitive and social aspects of metaphor will highlight the importance of that language. The essence of metaphor is to understand one thing in terms of another (for example, argument is war, good is up). More important, metaphor links all the meanings of one concept to another. George Lakoff and Mark Johnson have argued that metaphors systematically evoke not only the particular words in a given comparison but also the entire range of concepts related to such terms, spoken or unspoken. So, for example, describing or conceptualizing argument as war entails language and ideas about defense, attack, positions, strategy, and winning. Furthermore, this systemic aspect of language in metaphor in fact makes those concepts distinct. The related attributes of war, such as competition, victory, and positions, are what distinguish the very idea of argument from discussion or disagreement.[18] Yet metaphors are only partial; any comparison stresses only some connections while shading or suppressing others. Arguments may resemble war in our culture, but warfare differs strikingly from most verbal conflicts. The interests of those who employ the metaphor determine which elements are suppressed. The hidden dissimilarities usually illuminate the social uses of the metaphor.[19] For advertisers, the suppressed aspects of their metaphors shaped their persuasive power.

Like all elements of language, metaphor is born in social experience and does not evolve or survive at random. As Lakoff and Johnson observe, "The two parts of each metaphor are linked only via an experiential basis . . . . It is only by means of these experiential bases that the metaphor can serve the purpose of understanding." Metaphors could not persist if they did not serve as explanatory devices. They exist in numerous cultures precisely because they cohere with social reality. Like most fundamental aspects of culture, they explain and help structure interpretations of common events.[20] Yet metaphors are more than semantic devices: they shape and determine the meanings we make in our lives. Societies perfect and preserve metaphors in rituals, the repeated forms of behavior that societies evolve to create coherence and meaning.[21] Thus preserved in both language and ritual, such commonsense metaphors shape "reality" by constraining the meanings available to interpret varieties of experience. Such limitations, in turn, oblige us to pay special attention to metaphors concerning political and economic matters, including consumption. Since politics helps determine the allocation of power and resources, and economics normalizes our discussions of that allocation, the capacity of metaphor to structure meaning shapes the material conditions of our lives. In that sense, advertising is explicitly political. Common metaphors we use to interpret political and economic experience thus help determine the ways in which those resources are allocated. As Edelman notes, "It is language that evokes most of the political 'realities' people experience."[22]

Advertisers used the imagery and concepts of politics and suffrage to characterize their work, their wares, and consumers themselves. Using metaphors, advertising professionals established claims to possess exclusive expertise. The metaphoric process that distinguished advertisers' professional skill also established their legitimacy with the public.[23] Their particular choice of metaphors identified consumption with American nationality and citizenship. Persistent, successful use of these metaphors in advertising over time suggests this language's resilient ability to explain the world for consumers.

CONSUMERS AS CITIZENS: THE ELECTORAL METAPHOR

The political language of advertising rested on the identification of consumers as the sovereign rulers of a democratic marketplace. Equating the market with society, advertisers portrayed consumption as a political exercise in resonant accord with the rituals of American freedom. By casting consumption as the ritual of citizenship, and equating marketplace choices with political freedom, advertisers not only elevated consuming to a civic plane but also eroded distinctions between spending and politics. That blurring fully served corporate interests, but it sowed contradictions that would endure for decades. Powerful connections between buying and voting, economic choice and political sovereignty, undergirded advertising ideology. Between the 1890s and the Depression, advertising established strong associations between consuming and voting that have held sway, albeit with challenges, ever since. Although markets are not societies, this political language, itself a residue of the liberal equations of economics and politics, took hold.

The political language of consumption centered on an electoral metaphor. Advertisers repeatedly equated the consumer's dollar with the franchised citizen's vote. Consumer-citizens wielded their sovereign power through choosing among brand-name advertised goods. Much in the manner of voters at the polls, buyers chose "candidates" that would serve them best; their purchases "elected" certain products to public service and thus elevated businesses to rightful positions of national leadership. Advertisers consistently proclaimed that consumers, not corporations, exercised the true power of the great market democracy by their collective power of the purse and the leverage of their demand. This consumer sovereignty justified the electoral claims of successful businesses to public confidence and social authority. The advertising trade journal *Printers' Ink* linked consumption and voting in urging businessmen to court the consumer's favor: "Just as the ultimate success of the political chieftain depends upon the goodwill of the people who 'never resign,' so in the long run, the prosperity of the business man depends on the goodwill of the consumer . . . . He casts the deciding vote." Home economist and advertising consultant Christine Frederick claimed that consumers "vote in broad democratic fashion at great popular elections, the polls being open everyday at a million or more retail stores."[24] Through the votes of consumers, advertisers won the privilege of public service and trust, and the marketplace sustained only those businesses fit to gain the public's patronage. Since spending was easily interpreted as the voluntary exercise of choice, equating consuming with voting seldom elicited protest either from clients or consumers. Yet as they compared consumption to voting and the marketplace to representative government, advertisers continually implied that consumption was a more effective means of securing the popular will and common good than politics. Advertisers used the electoral metaphor to assert that spending was the proper activity of citizenship, a much more important civic activity than governance or debate.

Moreover, this voting was continual. In marked contrast to the political system, where elections were sporadic and communal participation was limited, consumption perpetually subjected goods to approval. Consumers "voted" every day, reaffirming the legitimacy of their chosen representatives and the system of choosing them. A 1928 ad expressed this sentiment: "On November sixth we'll all be doing something we do but once every four years. And the newspapers will refer to the result as the people's choice. . . . Every day is election day for the products of industry. The office to which they are elected is a place on the shelves of the nation's retail stores. And day after day, week after week, year after year, this priceless preference must be sought actively, intelligently, unremittingly by means of advertising—the campaign rostrum of commerce."[25] A continual election meant that manufacturers faced an unending campaign to win consumers to their goods. No successful business could ever take consumers' allegiance for granted, and no market remained fixed and unchanging. Advertisers continuously had to win consumers away from their distraction and indifference and then convince them of their product's worth. Christine Frederick crowed, "We consumers are 'turning out the rascals' among commodities . . . simply by that decimating failure to buy, or at least failure to buy a second time." The allegiance and votes of consumers had to be won constantly.[26] Advertisers argued that the dynamism of the market made it superior to politics because the marketplace was more deeply ingrained in the rhythms and concerns of daily life. In this democratic spirit advertisers did not shrink from proclaiming themselves the true and only representatives of consumer interests. They alone claimed to understand consumers' needs, tastes, and interests.[27] Interpreting the public to their client and their client's goods to the public, advertisers had to learn buyers' habits and traits. To be sure, ad men never fully believed this self-serving portrait, since clients and *not* consumers paid their livelihoods. Yet advertisers still tacked between interpreting the public and serving the client, maintaining that they could serve two masters.[28]

Foremost among the implications of the electoral metaphor was that marketplace success embodied majority rule. Edwin Balmer allied national advertising of branded goods squarely with the workings of true American democracy:

And just as politically the people's control is being reestablished by direct primaries and direct election, so commercially the consumer is regaining the right of selecting his products through the medium of advertising. And, precisely as direct nominations and direct primaries are bringing out the better men in politics, so our commercial direct choice is bringing forth some of our very best present day commodities. . . . In America we believe that the people should select. And *advertising is the direct primary of the people.* Through advertising the people need not take the selections others make for them; they can take into their own hands the choice and determination of our commodities.[29]

Consumer choice was political sovereignty. If consumers continually voted, then citizenship was expressed and protected best in the marketplace, and selling was central to "that big, all-comprehensive job of achieving an ideal social state."[30] For advertising professionals, every "vote" for a product also conveniently counted as a vote for national advertising. Bruce Barton, whose career path from agency chief to congressman perhaps best exemplified the close relationships between elite advertisers and politics, observed in 1930 that "advertising seems to have been accepted by the American people, voted for and elected as the medium through which they choose to learn of new things to eat, to wear, to protect themselves, and to add to their pleasure."[31] Because consumption represented the individual voluntary actions of millions—spending—advertisers easily interpreted consumption as a referendum. Commercial success entailed democratic legitimacy.

Many advertisements reinforced the electoral metaphor, depicting shopping as voting and showing consumers exercising their suffrage in the marketplace. The American Woolen Company described itself as " 'Of the People' . . . 'By the People' . . . 'For The People,' " while in 1908 Sapolio Cleanser pictured a political torchlight parade (fig. 2.1). "ELECTED—The People decide for Clean Government," pronounced the ad, which called Sapolio "the servant of all the people all the time." Peter's Milk Chocolate advertised its popularity "By Direct Vote of the People," while Parker pens announced the favorable results of a national survey as "a National Election of Fountain Pens."[32] National ad campaigns masqueraded as plebiscites of popular will. Many advertisements portrayed consumption as a social activism, where buyers campaigned for products, as in a 1914 ad, "Votes for Women," which featured a parade of little girls carrying boxes of Kellogg's Corn Flakes aloft as pickets. This ad played on the suffrage movement, noting that "women of this country have always voted 'aye' " for the breakfast cereal (fig. 2.2). The implication that consumption superseded politics in securing the common good was clear. While the ad's composition paid tribute to the suffrage movement, it asserted that women already had the vote in the arena that suited them best. Kellogg's metaphoric linking of consumption and voting showed

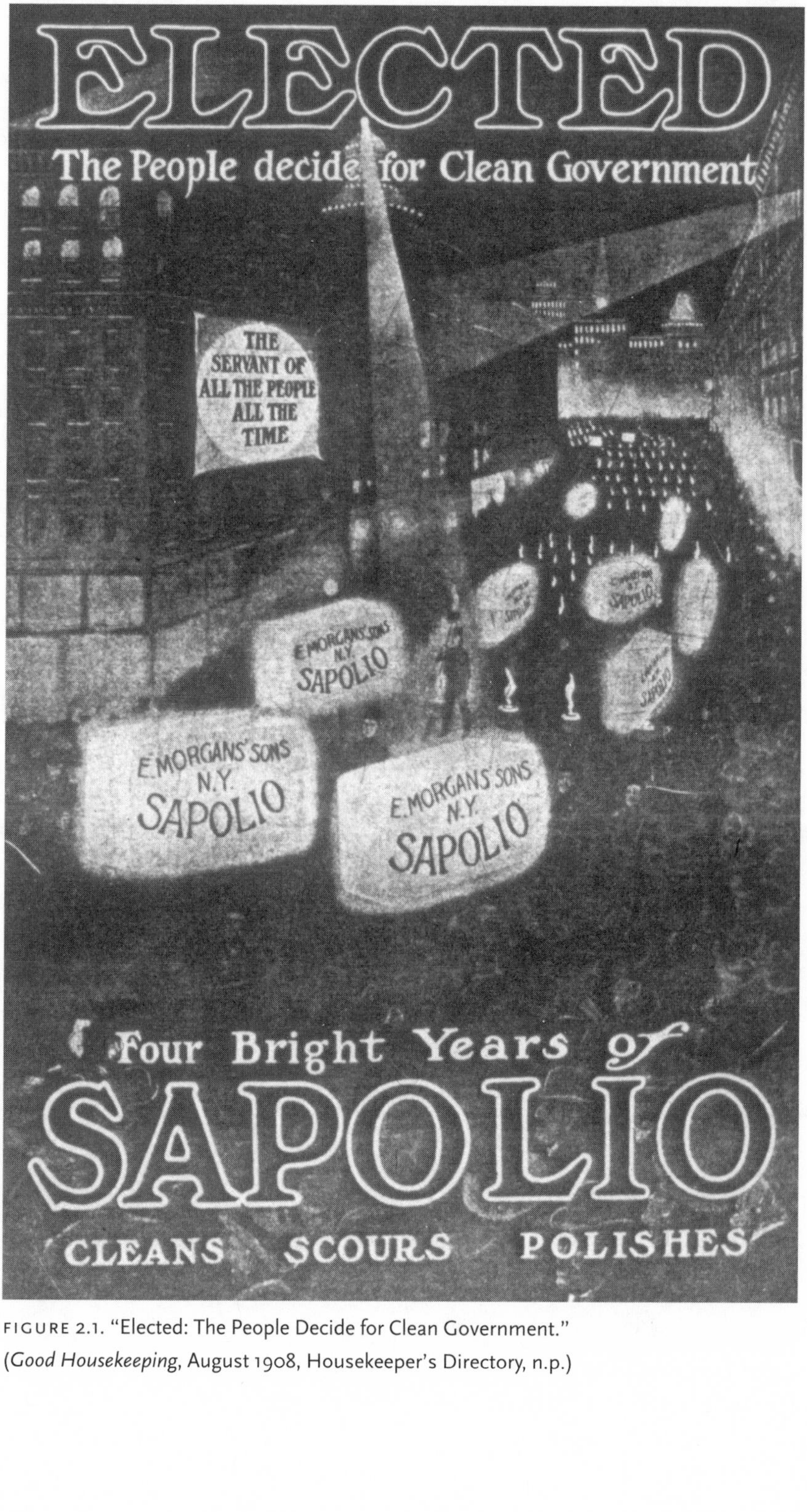

FIGURE 2.1. "Elected: The People Decide for Clean Government."
(*Good Housekeeping*, August 1908, Housekeeper's Directory, n.p.)

FIGURE 2.2. "Votes for Women." (*Woman's Home Companion*, November 1914, cover III)

that consumption took precedence, especially for those children carrying the political placards. True political action centered on the cupboard.[33]

Even as they routinely used political language, advertisers criticized politics and government by stressing the comparative virtues of consumption. Although they equated spending and voting and sought the authority and legitimacy of statecraft, advertisers also believed that politics was just another business. As early as 1896, advertisers were commenting on the similarities between the politics and marketing. A *Printers' Ink* reporter observed that "campaign work is nothing more than advertising . . . . Methods adopted in booming a Presidential candidate differ from those used in pushing a patent medicine, but the result aimed at in each case is the same: 'I am what you want. Insist on having me. Avoid all substitutes!' This in substance is the appeal to the people of both the patent medicine and politician." The reference to the disreputable and shady peddler of nostrums, a double-edged reminder of a lucrative business and notorious enterprise, made the writer's point clear. Politics was no better than the worst of all sales rackets.[34] The metaphor worked both ways: if advertising resembled an election, politics was just another sales job. Seeking legitimacy by comparing themselves to politicians, advertisers in fact devalued politics by denying the ideal of a common good that transcended parties, candidates, or commerce. By equating a politician's principles or a party platform with any other commodity for sale, ad men anticipated the development of modern political campaign techniques and, not incidentally, contributed to the commercialization of politics.[35]

Advertisers believed that politicians themselves could benefit from treating voters as consumers and that increased advertising would improve politics. In their view, a candidate had to sell himself aggressively to masses of uninterested voters. Proven sales techniques, such as aggressive sales messages and appeals to voters' self-interest, would win elections. High-minded discussion of principles or an aloof style of campaigning ultimately produced a dull and unsuccessful candidate, whatever his merits. Furthermore, politicians needed to use paid advertising to get their messages to voters, instead of relying on free placement of speeches and stories in the press, the customary method of campaigning through mass media at the time.[36] Advertisers thus prodded politicians to be more like them.

Yet when discussing the American political system, many advertisers claimed that even if the politician's vocation and their own were identical, commerce and consumption were more important and valuable to society than government. Comparing the two, they redefined politics as shopping and subordinated common concerns to individual private interests best served by consumption. The corporate populists at the *New York Daily News* drove the point home: "The candidate that Bill and every other businessman should worry about, if he wants to worry, is his Customer . . . . Most of them think a lot more about what they are going to do with next week's pay envelope—than about the next administration!"[37] In effect, advertisers argued that consumption was replacing politics as the forum through which citizens sought their common happiness.

This striking transition appears in a series of advertising premium booklets made for the Liggett & Myers Tobacco Company and distributed in national election years. *Political Information for 1896* contained national election results by state, as well as information on voting registration and immigrant naturalization, furnished "in the hope that it may prove of interest and service to all citizens, as well as to those who desire to become citizens." The advertisements avoided any attempt to sell products by linking them explicitly with the political information or the upcoming election. Typical of early corporate advertising, the ads instead addressed particulars of Liggett & Myers's productive capacities with the nearly obligatory illustration of its factory.[38] Here consumption was completely divorced from politics, despite their juxtaposition in these booklets. However, this was soon to change.

The 1912 version of the booklet offered much less information on citizenship and more space for advertising, urging the consumer/voter, "Whatever your Politics vote for your Favorite Brand: STAR." Another ad, showing two men in heated argument, suggested, "What's the use! Don't get excited; be smooth like VELVET." Taking a cue from the Progressive electoral reforms in the name of democracy, a third ad redefined political ideas as consumption: "INITIATIVE is to buy STAR, take it home and Chew it. REFERENDUM is to tell your friends and neighbors of the smoothness of 'VELVET' as a smoke, and refer them to any first-class tobacconist. RECALL: That's easy—recall all the pleasant moments of your life by smoking a 'Fatima'—the distinctly individual cigarette."[39] Nevertheless, the new meanings these political metaphors assumed indicate the extent to which advertisers now viewed consumption in terms once reserved for matters of state.

Completing this redefinition of politics as consumption, the 1916 booklet featured the homespun aphorisms of "Velvet Joe," an established and durable advertising character best described as a New England version of Finley Peter Dunne's Mr. Dooley. "Argyfyin' on religion and politics . . . thar's a heap of noise an' action but it don't get nowhar. Better discuss smokin' tobacco an' reach a verdick easy—VELVET," urged this corporate cracker-barrel sage. "When Timothy Jimson has a good crop he's a' administration man, but when crops is bad, he's agin' the gov'ment. I say principles is one thing, an' pocketbook another. Both of em's right when you smoke Velvet."[40] Velvet Joe's moral was clear enough: there was no comparison between divisive public political issues and the private pleasures of consumption. The only voting that mattered was for things. Political democracy did not exist outside freedom of choice.

THE SOVEREIGN PEOPLE: CONSUMERS AS KINGS

Advertisers showed consumers as the ruling sovereigns of business, a portrait with the specific and potent resonances of political power and social authority. Merchants and manufacturers had to please consumers in order to survive; the whole of business, in advertisers' views, depended on the constant goodwill and sufferance of the consumer. Businessmen insisted that even if they were uncrowned, consumers ruled nonetheless. "That's the glory of our great American democracy," proclaimed the N. W. Ayer agency. "The people rule the business world by their Right to Choose."[41] Reflecting the commonplace attitude that consumer demand dominated business, the Curtis publishing organization observed in 1911 that "the determination of millions of consumers to purchase, where possible, only those goods which they themselves can identify is the great 'outside selling force' with which all modern producers must reckon." Whereas previous generations of businessmen contended primarily with problems of production and capital, by the early twentieth century they faced the necessity of catering to the needs and interests of whoever might comprise their markets.[42]

Ad men adopted this characterization of sovereignty quite literally, often referring to consumers as ruling potentates and business as their royal domain. Charles Coolidge Parlin of Curtis publications unequivocally stated this view: "The consumer is king. His whim is law and his preference makes and unmakes merchants, jobbers and manufacturers." The Lord & Thomas advertising agency described the manufacturer's advertising appropriation as "giving hostages to Caesar . . . that modern 'Caesar' who is the Consuming Public.' " Advertisers consistently referred to consumers as the royalty of business, noting that their power constantly grew.[43] Sermonizing before the National Electric Light Association, Bruce Barton dubbed the consuming public a "king" whose attention and interest had to be sought and served continually, since "every day and hour the 'king' dies, and there arises a new 'king' to whom you and all your works mean absolutely nothing."[44] Consumer sovereignty meant that advertisers constantly flattered and paid homage to consumers' power, influence, and ultimate control. In different Ayer agency characterizations, the consumer could be both "the Supreme Court of business" and "the most courted and sought after man in America."[45] The consumer was an absolute monarch, whose power advertisers often felt was mysterious, unpredictable, and intangible.

However, businessmen did not accept the rise of a demand-driven economy and consumer sovereignty easily or universally. Some resisted granting consumers too much influence over production and retailing, and they harbored resentments against the power that consumers gained in competitive markets. Some businessmen fought being dependent on satisfying what they charged were the whimsical, unpredictable demands of unseen, unknown, and unnumbered masses. Accustomed to tangible production realities, corporate clients scoffed at the prospect of paying attention to a "public" that was diffuse, transient, and removed from their daily business affairs.[46] Clinging to older conceptions of selling as dependent on the authority of the shopkeeper, many executives claimed that consumers were unsure or unaware of their wants. Instead, they asserted that manufacturers, distributors, and merchants were best able to choose for consumers. "The public must be coaxed in its needs; it doesn't always know just what it wants and its requirements can often be shaped by the clever advertiser who knows the art of creating a demand for its goods," wrote one businessman in 1896. The public needed the authority of the retailer and merchant. A leading sales manager even more explicitly declared that merchants and distributors were the true sovereign powers of retail trade; consumers would take what was put before them: " 'King consumer' is largely a myth—a false treacherous god set up to wheedle the dollars from the pockets of the credulous . . . . We cannot do without the consumer, but we must place him squarely where he belongs, in the rank and file of the soldiery of trade."[47]

In the cold light of business reasoning, few advertisers assumed that consumers were fully sovereign. Yet even such skeptical opponents of consumer sovereignty shared in the pervasive imperial and political metaphors about the marketplace. They also grudgingly admitted the necessity of catering to the consumer, acknowledging that whether advertiser or retailer wielded the greatest influence, ultimately consumer choice and satisfaction determined successful sales. While manufacturers, advertisers, wholesalers, and retail merchants still fought for control over the distribution system, by 1910 few seriously denied that consumers' demands had to be met, in explaining marketing practices or market relations.[48] As one advertising agency noted, "These people who are asking for known merchandise in thousands of stores today are *buying*. They are not *being sold*. More and more each year, people are insisting upon their own preferences . . . . 'Manufacturer, wholesaler, retailer —all must observe the buying habits and listen to the demands of the consumer.'"[49] Perhaps the most explicit elaboration of consumers as the sovereign imperial power of business came in a 1925 series of advertisements featuring the fictional monologues of "Andy Consumer." The humor magazine *Life* created Andy to "advertise advertising" by telling the reading public about consumers' influence and power in commerce. Announcing as he set off to market, "I'll check up on this new advertiser and see if I want to let him live," Andy celebrated the power of life and death over businesses vested in consumers through advertising.[50] The consumer possessed the greatest power in the marketplace through an ultimate veto over commerce (fig. 2.3).

SELF-DETERMINATION: CONSUMPTION AS INDEPENDENCE

"Man, the Liberty Bell is Ringing for You, Do you have the spirit of '76? Have you declared your independence as a free-born, American pipe-smoker? . . . You haven't, listen to the ringing of the Liberty Bell. Swing your old jimmy pipe into action and load up with the real American man's tobacco, PRINCE ALBERT, 'The National Joy Smoke'"—thus the Liberty Bell rang for readers of the *Saturday Evening Post* in 1911.[51] The copywriter who created this ad for the American Tobacco Company most likely did not consider himself a political theorist. Yet such copy made clear a central tenet of advertising's political language: products ensured the individual freedom that was the basis of all self-determination. Commercial language linked consumption with the sacred American devotion to liberty. Advertisers used the language of politics to encourage self-determination through consuming things. Concerned with selling goods, advertisers crafted and peddled ideas of self-transformation.[52] The electoral metaphor invoked ideas of personal liberty and autonomy, transforming their meaning. Advertisers diverted emphasis from the freedom from state power over lives and property to freedom for self-cultivation and, ultimately, freedom of choice among already selected brands and goods. Advertisers argued that freedom was not the product of labor but the fruits of proper consumption. Consciously equating the Declaration of Independence phrase "the pursuit of happiness" with purchasing and goods, advertisers portrayed spending as the means to secure personal autonomy, an inalienable American right and blessing provided by the mass market.

Republican political traditions in the nineteenth century celebrated inde-

ADVERTISING CAN'T PUT
ANYTHING OVER ON ME

—or anybody else.

I'm pleased that advertising is an expensive sport for you big business boys. Ha! ha! ha! ha! ha! ha!

We consumers laugh.

The high cost of nation-wide advertising puts the situation entirely in our hands. Yes, we must laugh.

If you advertise, you can't afford to sell us just ONCE. You can't advertise and then run off and hide. We are poor pickin' until we repeat our purchase and pass the good word.

And what if we don't repeat our purchase and pass the good word? What then?

You may ballyhoo us into buying one package or box or can, but remember where you'll be if we don't buy two.

Fool us once if you will, Jack Dalton, but remember that after that we have you in our pow-wower.

Continuous advertisers are, therefore, birds who have passed our acid consumer test.

FIGURE 2.3. "Andy Consumer." (*Life*, July 9, 1925, cover III)

pendent artisans, laborers, and yeoman farmers as the foundation of American political democracy. White male laborers, preferably skilled, were the ideal citizens. Their productive skills ensured their independence in both marketplace and polling place while guaranteeing their unfettered pursuit of their self-interests.[53] As historians have shown, industrialization redefined the conditions and control of labor for workers and the meaning of labor for citizens. The skill and knowledge that had once made some workers independent in the market was eroded by the machine. Laborers fought the loss of their autonomy, just as they organized to secure a living wage and better working conditions. The large factory and the corporation both destroyed the basis—one, without question, that was restrictive and narrow—of labor's exclusionary claims of citizenship at the core of the republic. Yet the white working man's loss was offset by new possibilities. As James Livingston reminds us, the ascendance of the corporation reconfigured not only the relations of production but also the conditions of subjectivity—self-definition and identity.[54] By eroding the connection between production and personhood, the new economic order relocated value in the marketplace itself—and opened the door for a much greater range and number of participants. While this new order still discriminated against women, people of color, and the poor, a consumer economy offered a greater number of conditions of freedom. But only over time would Americans be in a position to determine the meanings and worth of that freedom.

Nowhere were independence and consumption joined more explicitly than in advertisers' treatment of women as sovereigns of the marketplace. Advertisers depicted consumption as the best means for women to achieve both their individual freedom and their full public power as citizens. In the very years when the suffrage movement demanded equality under law through the vote, commercial imagery privileged spending and not civics as women's sphere, the means to her independence. In this way "Mr. Advertiser" offered "Mrs. Consumer" a profoundly apolitical vision in an explicit political disguise.[55] Women's predominant role as shoppers and as the implied subject and object of national advertising specifically shaped advertisers' political language. Since advertisers believed most consumers were women, their political language prescribed proper female behavior in both the market and the home. By treating women as natural consumers, advertisers "naturalized" them as citizens—spending was women's ritual of citizenship. Advertising's naturalization of women encouraged them to channel both individual aspirations and social impulses through the market. The political language of advertising urged women to believe that consumption was their proper role and the most effective means of attaining power in their lives and of improving national life.

In their selective focus on homemakers, mothers, and the independent New Woman of the age, advertisers linked political ideas of freedom, equality, and sovereignty with women's roles. So fundamental to advertising portrayals of women and consumption were ideas of independence and freedom that they permeated all manner of sales messages. The first major episode in the process of naturalizing women as consumers was the commercial battle over brand names and substitutions. Turn-of-the-century conflicts among manufacturers, wholesalers, and retailers centered on brand loyalty.[56] Store owners and wholesalers often preferred locally made or unpublicized brands that generated higher profits than nationally advertised products. National advertisers termed merchandisers' attempts to supply the customer with unadvertised goods "the substitution evil." They mounted extensive campaigns to protect their brands and prices, which culminated in a media campaign in 1906–7. As one manager put it, consumers had a simple but profound dilemma: "Advertising does not mean much to them. They know the retail merchant or his clerk—they do not know the advertiser. The known dealer is a responsible individual to them while the unknown advertiser is not. The consumer in ninety-nine times out of a hundred will take the advice of the dealer unless she is fortified with information and is convinced before she enters his store to make a purchase."[57] Advertisers reinforced the idea that consumer sovereignty was *women's* sovereignty. They depicted brand-name choice as a means for women both to exercise their superior taste and judgment and to defend their individual rights as consumers. Advertisers privately joked of Mrs. Consumer's preadolescent mentality and conscientiously proclaimed their duty to tell her what to do. Yet to combat substitution, they adopted the language of individual equal rights. Consumer demand was literally engendered as the sphere of women's power and women's rights. The phrase "accept no substitutes," in common use from the turn of the century, bore the political meanings of liberty and self-determination. Refusing the temptations of substitution became a defense of sacred liberty. "Insist Upon Your Rights!" thundered one woman's magazine. "Tell him [the clerk] you know what you want. That you are convinced that the goods are all right or they would not be advertised."[58] The customer always had rights.

Insistence on their chosen brands asserted women's independence from male distributors and merchants. Antisubstitution advertising shifted authority for purchasing information from merchant to corporations and sowed distrust between women customers and male storekeepers. Advertisers argued that the shifty clerk who offered a "just as good" substitute did not have the consumer's best interests at heart. Such offers resembled the deceptions of the confidence man, the seductions of the rake, or the orations of the patent medicine show huckster. Scores of advertisements encouraged women to defend themselves and their sovereign choice with the eternal vigilance necessary for a female consumer. "Excuse me—I know what I want and I want what I asked for—TOASTED CORN FLAKES—Good day" was the haughty dismissal given to an unseen grocer who dared offer his female customer anything but the pride of Battle Creek (fig. 2.4). "Take it back and send me Tetley's," said an irate housewife to a sheepish delivery boy in a 1922 ad. "And tell Mr. Jones that when I order Tetley's Orange Pekoe I want Tetley's—and *not* a cheaper substitute."[59] According to this view, only advertised products were worthy of patronage; manufacturers who did not advertise had something to conceal or nothing at all to recommend their wares.[60] Even Christine Frederick, as loyal an ally as merchandisers could want, warned against alienating Mrs. Consumer with substitutes. "She does not want 'brand switching' advice at all," she admonished. "She has plenty of brand knowledge at her fingertips"[61] Women knew what they wanted, argued brand advertisers, and it was their right to buy it. Consumer sovereignty for women recast individual liberty as freedom of choice, not merely an abstract political right but one with important personal consequences. Freedom of choice ensured the unfettered expression of individual character. Advertising thus presented consumption as the means to self-determination. Gillies Coffee cautioned, "Don't let anyone tell you what to buy. . . . Get a coffee that suits *your* taste."[62] But this also implied that women depended on the product to realize their true individuality. Only in the marketplace could women be truly sovereign and truly themselves.

Such sales talk always invoked women's demand for the vote. Suffrage offered the most resonant connections of sales talk and the language of rights. Advertisers addressed women's claims to equal rights by defending consumption as the key to equality. Political rights, which derived from the social contract, became inalienable consumers' rights arising from mass production. Advertisers recast such sales features as convenience, economy, and novelty as the natural and inevitable rights to be enjoyed by all. Thus Old Dutch Cleanser claimed to be "Champion of Women's Rights," including "the right to freedom from household drudgery" and "the right to a clean home and the leisure to enjoy it." The Hoosier Kitchen Cabinet blended an appeal to labor saving with a political appeal to rights. "Save hours of time, and save your vitality . . . . A million women have realized the right to the

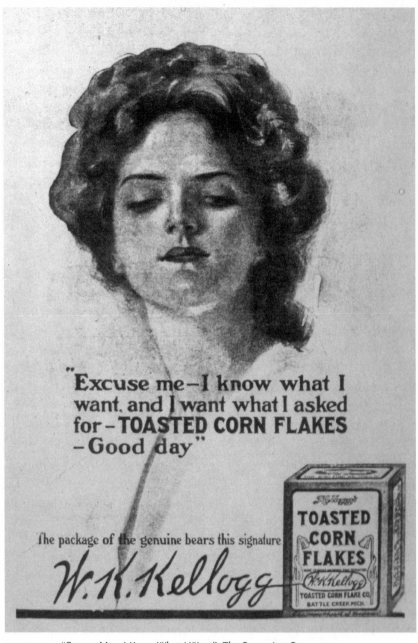

FIGURE 2.4. "Excuse Me—I Know What I Want": The Sovereign Consumer.
(*Good Housekeeping*, April 1908, Housekeeper's Directory, n.p.)

Hoosier. Are their time and health worth more consideration than yours?" one ad read.[63] Hoosier cabinets were inexpensive (an installment plan required just one dollar down); therefore, price should pose no barrier to entitlement, at least among the middle class.

Similarly, advertisements treated labor-saving devices as the "freedom" from arduous and unrelenting imprisonment in housework, as goods promised to save women labor or time. Such appeals often intertwined concepts of independence, rights, and autonomy. Serving Shredded Wheat became a woman's "Declaration of Independence" from onerous kitchen work and the constant "servant problem." A leading soap manufacturer promised "More Liberty! For Belles who save time and strength by using SAPOLIO."[64] "Lincoln Freed the Slaves," announced Juergens Bakeries, "but a lot of housewives are yet slaves of the housework." TIP-TOP factory-baked bread would set women "free from baking bondage." Lorain Stoves and the 1900 Cataract Washer both promised to liberate women from bondage in the kitchen.[65] Along these lines, General Electric, in campaigns comparing American civilization with preindustrial or "primitive" living, claimed, "Back of every great step in woman's progress *from a drudge to a free citizen* has been some labor-saving invention." Through mass production the slave was made citizen, and enlightenment triumphed in proportion to consumption of labor-saving appliances (fig. 2.5).[66] Even Remington Rand boasted that its typewriter held "the Keys that gave her FREEDOM" because it allowed women to enter business as typists: "She tap . . . tap . . . tapped her way to economic independence. . . . Throughout the world millions of women still prefer the Remington. And millions of them still find economic freedom at its keyboard." The New York Vacuum Cleaner Company took this metaphor to its logical extreme, titling a 1909 advertisement "Up from Slavery."[67]

The new electrical appliances offered advertisers untold opportunities to champion freedom through consuming. The Gainaday Electric Washer Company, whose advertising centered on its eponymous sales appeal, told women the machine gave them "new hours of FREEDOM every week" and conferred upon them "Washday Independence." The American Laundry Machinery Company claimed that "2,000,000 women have gained new Freedom" through its services, while the Simplex Electric Ironer urged women to "take the step *now* that will bring you freedom."[68] The Western Electric campaigns for its line of appliances in 1915–16 introduced a remarkable female figure, helpfully named Liberty, to demonstrate the advantages of electrical living and to offer a sisterly vision of comfort and independence to women readers. Dressed in classical robes and Phrygian cap, she invoked the enlight-

Generations of travelers in Europe have seen women washing clothes, like the woman in this illustration, on the banks of rivers.

Shall the river work— or shall you?

Back of every great step in woman's progress from a drudge to a free citizen has been some labor-saving invention. Back of most inventions in electricity's progress from a mystery to a utility has been the research of General Electric Company scientists and engineers.

Too many women, abroad, are still washing clothes like this.

They go to the river. Our American rivers are being trained to come to *us*. Water-wheels drive electric generators—thus water is supplied to your home, and electric current runs the washing machine which has banished so much toil.

GENERAL ELECTRIC

FIGURE 2.5. "Shall the River Work—or Shall You?" (*Light* 2, no. 1 [May 1924]: 47)

enment, nurture, and freedom associated with her statuesque namesake in New York harbor. As these Western Electric advertisements noted, Liberty brought women a host of new appliances symbolizing "The New Enlightenment." She conveyed to her sister consumers a "vision of a better way" (figs. 2.6 and 2.7). For women broken in health, if not spirits, by housework, Liberty defended their interests and heralded a "new freedom" in the electrical conveniences that would add years to their lives.[69]

Consuming offered women the means to achieve their collective rights as well. Advertisements presented consumption as a social and political movement, with women publicly united in purchasing to elevate the status of all their sisters. A long-running campaign illustrated consumption as a collective movement. Claude Hopkins's advertising for Van Camp's Pork and Beans, begun in 1910, transformed convenience, the most common selling point of canned foods, into a story of "How a Million Housewives have Created a Co-Operative Kitchen." Both manufacturer and consumers became the "New Crusaders" for "Shorter Hours for Women." Here women abandoned days of arduous, uncertain effort in the kitchen to join a movement where an "army of expert [and exclusively male] cooks now bake the beans for those million homes." If this were not sufficient, the new crusaders referred to Van Camp's as "the National Dish"; beans were "our racial food," the dish of all good Americans. This advertising invoked the rhetoric of the labor movement and the imagery of suffragism, with clear political, nationalist, and eugenicist implications. Consumption was central to being American, and women were responsible for proper consumption in order to make themselves and their families better Americans. Women united by consumption joined a movement to secure their rights to leisure and to freedom. Even so, while women were still sovereigns of domesticity, clearly men were more competent to do their work.[70]

What did this new freedom mean? As advertisers presented consumption, freedom entailed not only the lessening of women's onerous household tasks but also liberation for activity outside or within the home, to pursue their social or personal aspirations. While advertisers frequently linked women's extra leisure time with other family duties, especially child care (itself dependent on proper consumption), they frequently portrayed women's self-determination as consumption itself. Consuming to save labor or gain time often ironically implied that a principal goal of the new leisure was more consumption. Freedom arose from and gave birth to opportunities to spend. Advertising for Libby's canned foods, for example, offered women relief from the lengthy chores of preparing full, nutritious meals, thus promising (and

FIGURE 2.6. "The New Enlightenment." (N. W. Ayer Collection, Series 2, Box 319, Book 548, Archives Center, National Museum of American History, Smithsonian Institution, Washington, D.C.)

FIGURE 2.7. The Better Way: Western Electric Vacuum Cleaner. (N. W. Ayer Collection, Series 2, Box 319, Book 548, Archives Center, National Museum of American History, Smithsonian Institution, Washington, D.C.)

selling) them freedom; ad copy defined this new freedom for women as "Time to watch the papers for announcements of special sales. Time to be constantly on the alert for special bargains. Time to shop around and secure the utmost for their money."[71] Women's citizenship became the public activities of shopping and consuming, for themselves and their families.

As historians have noted, women's workload and time spent in housework may have actually increased in the complex ecology of "labor-saving" technologies.[72] Despite this actuality, the lure of freedom from the house and housework became a principal justification for household products and appliances. In scores of advertisements, new products freed women to leave the house with newfound time and the right to spend it in spending. The presence of watchful clocks in numerous advertising depictions of women at household chores only further emphasized important connections between consumption, time, and freedom. The producers of California Canned Asparagus warned that "the kitchen clock is the fastest clock in the house!" The American Laundry Machinery people reminded women, "Remember a day a week at *home-laundry-drudgery* means 52 days taken from *living* each year."[73] Consumption restored freedom by saving time. "What will you do with the time you've saved?" asked Gold Dust soap. "That question is something which we mere men wouldn't try to answer." Nevertheless, the implication was clear that most women would spend their outings shopping or consuming. Campbell's Soup promised women "much more freedom to make her home and herself more attractive."[74] Advertising depicted freedom for women as liberty to consume. Consumption, in turn, guaranteed women's independence.

LEADING BRANDS: ELECTING THE CORPORATION

By the turn of the century, the rise of bureaucratic corporations, and its attendant growth of trusts and monopolies, left Americans feeling at a much greater remove from crucial economic institutions than in the localized economies of the mid-nineteenth century.[75] The rise of corporations and trusts inspired both public celebration and fear. Protests against concentrated economic power fueled crucial aspects of the mass movements of the day— Populism and Progressivism. For millions, the corporation's power and isolation threatened the good of worker and voter alike. Corporations were widely viewed as a force powerful enough to erode democracy itself.[76] Even before corporations hired public relations firms to build public support for their policies and power, advertisers were defending corporation's disproportionate influence as natural and desirable.[77] They asserted that consumers "elected" not only particular goods but also those corporations that made them: consumers democratically and voluntarily empowered these institutions. In advertisers' terms, consumers elevated to national public "leadership" the major corporations that were already transforming American business, politics, and social relations. Thus, the electoral metaphor enabled corporate defenders to make the astonishing claim that "the people" caused and justified the major economic centralization and consolidations of the trust era, movements over which in fact they had little influence, and which represented no small loss of their power. This logic brought forth the dubious claim that consumers were sovereign over organizations that in fact answered to no one but boards of directors. Moreover, equating corporate with political leadership again favored business: corporate success indicated that the public acknowledged business's right to govern as well as serve. Advertisers claimed that consumers endorsed the leadership and service of those corporations whose products they purchased and argued that corporate leadership instituted the benign reign of duly elected representatives. As department store magnate and self-styled consumer champion Edward Filene declared, "The masses of America have elected Henry Ford. They have elected General Motors. They have elected the General Electric Company, and Woolworth's and all the other great industrial and business leaders of the day. . . . This election of business leadership is constant. The polls are open every day, and voters vote when they feel like voting."[78]

To defuse hostile public sentiment toward corporations and enlist public support for corporate interests on controversial issues, advertisers developed "institutional" campaigns. Such advertising aimed to counter widespread antitrust sentiment (as in the cases of American Telephone and Telegraph [AT&T] and Swift & Company, which both faced persistent allegations of monopolistic practices) and to alleviate public suspicions that such secretive organizations were neither immediately nor ultimately accountable for undemocratic or predatory behavior.[79] Such advertising generally sold no particular product but instead described in flattering terms the organizations that made or sold goods. Institutional ads portrayed such enterprises as "public" (whether publicly or privately owned) organizations devoted to service, much in the manner of representative government. AT&T's agency N. W. Ayer explained the rationale for its campaign of "editorials" designed to "humanize" the corporation: "The consumer's contact with the Bell System is personal. His judgment of the telephone organization might naturally be based upon limited knowledge and a personal reaction were it not the policy of the

Bell System to take the public into its confidence—to discuss on the printed page its aspirations, problems and accomplishments."[80] Such advertising played a significant role in business propagandizing, as the most overt campaigns to justify corporate leadership. Long-winded editorial copy compared corporations to historical heroes, lobbied for corporate interests, and offered paeans to progress. As mass-circulation magazines veered from muckraking to celebratory portraits of business in both journalism and fiction, the advertisements alongside the editorial matter often carried the same messages: the size, scope, and goals of big business served Americans better than the outmoded political and economic order of the nineteenth century. Most recently, Roland Marchand has argued that corporate imagery cast such enterprises in a human light to persuade people that corporations were moral institutions, responsible community members, and of course, the most successful businesses. Yet what remains striking is the political and civic language and imagery in this advertising. Corporations did not just give themselves "a soul," as Marchand claimed, but portrayed themselves as legitimate *public* representatives and rulers.[81] Corporate advertising thus echoed and amplified the political assumptions of product advertising. With the consumer often deprived of meaningful influence on corporations, advertising claimed that business power was the legitimate product of democracy and freedom.

Everyday product advertisements promoted a similar agenda, portraying products and their makers in the familiar contexts of home, family, and community. Corporate leadership was domesticated through the acceptance of products sold by advertising. Brand-name ads created "identities" for corporations and simulated personal relationships between producers and consumers. Trademarks, a practice that originated in ancient times, substituted a symbol for the maker's physical presence in the market to guarantee satisfaction to the buyer. The maker's mark symbolized both the producer's handiwork and his or her relationship with the customer. Advertisers quickly claimed this venerable history: brands assured consumers of quality in every purchase, they argued, since manufacturers would suffer if products failed to satisfy the consumer.[82] The corporate trademark, trade character, or brand name served as the maker's bond; consumers knew who stood responsible for the goods they bought. The people's recourse—the refusal to buy—formed the basis of corporate legitimacy. Like any elected official, manufacturers could be held accountable.

To humanize the corporation, advertisers again deployed political language. Leading agencies such as the George Batten Company, N. W. Ayer, and

J. Walter Thompson noted that consumers hungered for the impression of human contact from corporations. They stressed the importance of conveying not only quality but also the human and responsible attributes of an organization's "character." No agency better typified this approach than N. W. Ayer & Son, founded in 1869 and led for over fifty years as a limited partnership by Frederick Wayland Ayer. Emphasizing that an institution or business was the "lengthened shadow" of one man, Ayer boosted clients, its own services, and advertising itself in long-running campaigns. Dwelling on the virtues of commerce and advertising in general, Ayer copywriters often returned to this motif of personalizing the corporation: "Just so there is the shadow of a man, so is there a shadow of a business and its products—a shadow that reflects the ideals of the one and the quality of the other . . . its advertising." Another ad in this series showed that the ideal of character depended on advertising for public recognition. In a world where personal contacts were no longer possible, advertising conveyed a corporation's values and integrity: "No one can deceive time, and no one can prevent time's displaying character. . . . [Advertising] has a great opportunity and a great responsibility. On it rests the sensitive task of conveying the character of a house and its wares to all consumers. Advertising offers the vital first impression. It is the only point of contact a house may have with the great body of consumers. It is building reputation, and reputation is of greater worth than all else—save character."[83] The George Batten Company summed up a similar philosophy, asserting, "It is the business of the advertising agency to prepare advertising for the advertiser which represents faithfully his institution, his product and his ideals."[84] Corporations thus claimed to place their "character" into goods and encouraged buyers to treat the products as embodying the moral qualities of businesses. Such qualities justified corporate wealth and influence.

To show consumers just whom they had "elected," advertisers often created public personae for leading corporate executives or concocted fictional corporate representatives to lend human form to their faceless clients. This introduction of "personality" attempted to assuage fears of corporate rule by providing a comforting aura of personal accountability and face-to-face contact. Razor blade manufacturer and social prophet King Gillette and motion picture executive Carl Laemmle were just two executives who during the 1910s initiated long-running national campaigns in the form of personal editorials that emphasized both their business achievements and their personal devotion to public service and leadership.[85] Many advertisements had previously featured editorials or comments from company presidents, but agency professionals usually scorned these as ineffective and self-serving.[86] In contrast, Gillette's editorials on personal grooming for men wrapped sales messages in sermons on class and sex relations, democracy, and national progress. For Gillette, consumption, especially of his company's razor blades, signified the unfolding of social equality through democracy in action; his long-running campaigns linked sales messages and social ideals while clearly establishing him as a business celebrity who was sold to the public along with safety razors. Gillette's public persona as both manufacturer and philosopher linked his product with democracy, implying that consumers who bought Gillette were shaving their way to a more democratic and egalitarian social system.[87] Independent motion picture executive Laemmle had gained national fame in successful legal battles against the Edison-dominated Motion Picture Patent Organization cartel. His self-interested trust-busting helped democratize the film industry by opening up film distribution and exhibition to outside studios and theater owners.[88] He placed a personalized advertising "column" in the *Saturday Evening Post* at a time when advertising for movies in magazines was uncommon. He democratically urged readers, "I wish you would drop me a line—tell me what you think of this advertising—tell me about UNIVERSAL PICTURES—the kind you like and the kind you don't like." With such signed pieces, Laemmle personified the progressive manufacturer seeking direct rapport with those citizens who elected his product to public service.[89] Such campaigns revealed the lucrative potential in fabricating selective "portraits" of corporate executives.[90]

Sympathetically personalizing organizations, advertisers put forward corporate claims to leadership while countering critiques of business. Some businessmen, most notably Henry Ford and Thomas Edison, became folk heroes, beloved for their products' social benefits and admired for their inventive skills and personal fortunes. But the extensive public veneration and nearly unquestioned trust those two men enjoyed were exceptional, rooted more in their heroic status as inventors than as capitalists.[91] Comparatively modest images of dedication, service, democratic leadership, and integrity shaped the campaigns created for such manufacturers as John and Horace Dodge, A. Atwater Kent, Walter Chrysler, and King Gillette. Yet such campaigns proved important to justify business leadership. Theodore MacManus, creator of the personalizing campaign for the Dodge brothers, claimed, "Insofar as their public identity was concerned, John and Horace Dodge were unmistakably and unequivocally a creation of sales and advertising. . . . The process of conferring an identity upon them was almost as deliberate as the process pursued by a sculptor carving a figure out of marble."[92] The leadership of a corporate chief or his organization proved as much a fabricated product as the goods he sold.

Advertisers invented fictional corporate spokesmen as well to "humanize" the corporation and personify its ideals. Like Liggett & Myers's "Velvet Joe," these fictitious characters appeared in advertisements to spread the good news about their product or corporation.[93] Earlier durable trade characters, such as Sunny Jim (Force Cereal), the Campbell's Soup Kids, or Aunt Jemima, established proprietary visual identifications for products, and occasionally advertisers would create narratives for such established trademarks as Aunt Jemima.[94] But fictional corporate representatives served as specialized voices, not trademarks. Created for editorial-style copy, seldom pictured (Betty Crocker being a notable exception), they were as anonymous as the corporations they represented. Their specific social roles—doctor, engineer, nurse, salesman—strengthened both the sales message and corporate legitimacy while lending specific authority unattainable in most advertisements. For example, Mennen's "Jim Henry" provided weekly homilies on the virtues of grooming, Mennen products, and advertising. He claimed expert authority as a traveling salesman, an occupation known to be meticulously concerned with appearance and grooming.[95] Similarly, numerous corporations, notably Libby-McNeill, Washburn-Crosby, Kimberley-Clark, and Proctor & Gamble, all created fictional experts, "Mary Hale Martin," "Betty Crocker," "Ellen Buckland, Registered Nurse," and others. These characters "signed" editorial-style ads and premium booklets and pronounced the values of their companies. As members of "helping professions," they were both experts and confidantes of the women who used their products. Never did such copy indicate that these were not actual expert home economists, professionals, or interviewers. The voice of corporate interests occupied the fabricated bodies of characters assumed to be both factual and objective.[96] This form of ventriloquism especially appealed to advertisers, painfully aware of the gap between their social position and that of their readers. Here advertisers presented corporate leadership as unbiased professional expertise, a simulation at best misleading and at worst dishonest. In this form of advertising, such characters were meant to convey corporations' most attractive guise, but consumers in effect elected phantoms fronting for corporations.[97]

The electoral metaphor implied the similarity of political and corporate leadership, but the two differed radically. Advertising's use of the metaphor disguised or ignored substantial gaps between the two spheres in order to portray consumption as ultimately superior to politics. Primarily, they differed in accountability to their publics, which were the source of their power. Unlike politics, corporate enterprise was collective, anonymous, and very often hidden: there was no visible official, no single individual, responsible for the public service and leadership corporations were supposed to render. The anonymous nature of most corporate decisions, along with private control, usually ensured that no one would be publicly accountable for corporate actions. Then, as now, corporate leaders and industrial statesmen, with some prominent exceptions, remained largely unknown to the mass public, even while their brand names grew more familiar every year.[98] Similarly, the public authority of businessmen differed from the authority of politicians because it originated in fundamentally different sources. Political legitimacy derived from power expressly awarded by citizens explicitly assembled for that purpose; commerce enjoyed no such direct mandate. While politicians at all levels of government certainly employed public relations to create favorable portraits of themselves and their achievements, ultimately their claims to rule depended on their performance in office. Despite pretensions to public esteem, leading businesses attained marketplace power through their ability to control distribution channels and supplies, undercut or stifle competition, create new markets, dominate labor, and not least, use influence to gain favorable government legislation when needed. Consumers were hardly the sole factor that kept corporations "in office."[99]

CONCLUSION

Despite their similarities, consuming was not just like voting after all. But political metaphors enabled advertisers to humanize complex organizations and condense them into convenient symbols.[100] Advertising shaped perceptions of corporate leadership in distinct and specific ways. Equating corporate with political leadership ultimately favored the corporation, rendering it superior in serving "the will of the people." As national politics grew more distant from citizens, corporate leadership, embodied in goods, assumed a growing prominence in American homes. Linking leadership with products in fact located symbols of corporate power in everyday experience. If American consumers "elected" corporations to national office, they were also urged to consider these leaders as part of their own communities. This constituted a deception, as most organizations were neither present in nor responsive to individuals or communities. However, the resemblance of consumption to politics—private individuals exercising choice in matters of consequence— suggested that consumption might become a powerful force in public life were it ever to challenge politics directly for predominance in Americans' priorities. By the 1920s the two realms were certainly equated in the electoral metaphor.

In advertising's political language Madison Avenue professionals crafted a vocabulary that connected sales messages with some of the most important and cherished ideals in American life. Spending and voting were distinct activities with divergent consequences, yet their equation in the pages of magazines and newspapers hid those differences. By portraying consumption as a civic exercise, advertisers altered meanings of the political, the public, and the social. Casting consumption as an affirming ritual of American democracy planted seeds of long-term political quiescence and positioned commercial interests to claim their right to rule in a society that recognized no legal but many de facto elites. Of course, simply equating consumption with politics did not blur all boundaries between the two. The franchise and political participation were precious and treasured for many Americans; the unending fights to expand suffrage and gain equal citizenship waged throughout American history give eloquent testimony to that drive. The broad antimonopoly sentiment of these years shows that citizens fought corporate dominance. Yet by equalizing politics and consumption over time, in print, the radio ether, and public space, advertisers staked a large claim for the commercial over the communal and reduced politics to just another commodity. Although history has unmade that equation again and again, as social movements challenged business rule in politics, still it endures to the present. While many Americans question whether commerce can serve as the overriding public good, relatively few have criticized the link between purchasing and voting.[101] The electoral metaphor has persisted over time not only because it made sense to many, but also because advertisers used it as a key idea in a broader discussion about national identity. Advertisers forged an even more powerful and enduring metaphor that linked consumption with Americanism; acquiring goods became an explicitly nationalist activity.

CHAPTER 3

MAKING

CONSUMPTION

AMERICAN

ADVERTISERS,

CONSUMERS,

AND NATIONAL

IDENTITY

Who can say that advertising has not played a part in welding our people together by directing their thoughts and habits into common channels? In a country made up of many diverse races, it may well be that one of the strongest national ties is the common use and possession of the same kinds of foods, the same kinds of clothing, the same kinds of automobiles, and the same kinds of countless other things that advertising has helped make national necessities.[1]

Advertising is an American product. We are the only nation on the face on the earth that knows how to advertise.[2]

Although we Americans cannot claim to be the wisest and best of men ourselves, we can at least claim that we are helping provide the substratum on which a wiser and better civilization for someone can arise. From this point of view, education, Ford cars, motion pictures and chewing gum for everybody can be looked upon as good.[3]

The business portrayal of spending vested power in consumer-voters who wielded sovereignty in a demand-driven economy. This vision rested on advertising's openly nationalist vision of consumption. Between 1890 and 1930 national advertising consistently offered images of American life as defined by consumption. Agency copywriters depicted the United States as distinguished by a common culture dominated by getting, spending, and accumulation, its democracy characterized and sustained by consumption and goods.[4] Copywriters celebrated America as a unique land of manufactured plenty where the ritual of becoming American was purchasing and using consumer goods. Although ideals of individual liberty and independence did not always readily harmonize with egalitarian sentiments, sales messages cast democracy and equality as the fundamental aims of mass production. Advertisers ignored the decidedly inegalitarian conditions in American life in order to portray a nation in which goods were both the measure and the source of social equality. Consumption was the democratic institution of an egalitarian nation.

THE BUTLER AND THE HOUSEWIFE: CONSUMER DEMOCRACY

Advertising professionals understood that consumer goods marked clear distinctions between classes. National advertising most often addressed the most prosperous, the upper-middle and upper classes. The vast majority of workers and the poor participated, much less and more intermittently, in the national branded goods system. Still, great numbers of middle-class and working Americans were buying a living every day.[5] Advertisers regularly asserted that American people lived in an inclusive democracy, equal in their access to goods. Certainly, many contemporary observers between 1880 and 1930 praised as nothing short of revolutionary the mass market's ability to manufacture and distribute large quantities of goods to middle- and working-class consumers. As *The Delineator*'s advertising manager wrote in 1907, "The whole idea of modern manufacture is to secure the profit on the wideness of the sale—a fraction on each article but so many articles that the total will represent financial success. . . . [for] the manufacturer who has brought within the reach of all the best quality at the fairest price."[6] The consumer marketplace ensured happiness and social stability by rewarding all with the benefits of mass production. Although advertising executives generally distrusted beliefs in political or cultural equality, as a group they saw themselves as messengers of democracy, providing equal access to information about new products or desires. They claimed to promote greater equality by encouraging spending: mass distribution itself was proof of America's inherent democracy. The electoral metaphor implied (and advertisers happily assumed) that the consumption patterns accurately reflected popular tastes, desires, and self-interest. Advertisers aided democracy by instituting majority will and preserved democracy by improving social conditions through their wares. Since advertising assisted business, as N. W. Ayer claimed, by guaranteeing "the common welfare of the common people," increasing mass consumption demonstrated that "democracy is gaining ground."[7] Advertising also promoted commercial democracy by allowing firms both great and small to communicate with the public (for a 15 percent commission, of course). Paid space on the printed page, public space, or airwaves served a true commercial meritocracy. Advertising worked equally well for anyone: an enterprise of any size could advertise successfully, and any meritorious product could succeed.[8]

Yet as elites who worked for America's wealthiest corporations and executives, agency men and women were acutely fixated on class divisions. In public they would claim that the United States was a classless society, but privately they endlessly studied and remained invested in the class divisions that consumption supposedly would dissolve. Successful market analysis depended both on finely tuned observations of buyers and sensitivity to goods as symbols of social distinction. With precisely such class issues in mind, modern advertising tailored specific sales appeals to differentiated markets, the A, B, BB, C, and D order of incomes and propensities to spend. Large national advertising agencies often identified different specialized and segmented markets, and as we have seen, they perfected a sociology to support that effort. Yet the advertising business as a whole balanced two distinct portraits of American social life, one in which products produced and maintained strict if flexible social and cultural hierarchies, the other in which a classless social order rested on universal access to goods. The promise of equality in things was undercut by the fiercely guarded privileges and exclusions in American society. This dynamic of invitation and rejection, in turn, was driven by advertising's ability simultaneously to provoke desire and leave it unsatisfied.

The democratic implications of mass production were most appealing to ad crafters. Processed foods, breakfast cereals, soaps, cosmetics, cleansers, ready-made clothing and furniture—all seemed to promise better living. Resources and privileges once enjoyed only by elites were now available to all. By the 1910s, the apparent ubiquity of inexpensive products now offered widespread happiness, social equality, and long-term economic stability. Consumer goods promoted a classless society through popular access to similar experiences. In the face of varying patterns and uses of consumption by different groups, advertising's explicit connections of goods and spending with American democracy provided powerful sanctions to buy. The mass availability of consumer products proved for ad men that America was a harmonious organic society, where all were equal in needing and having many goods. Superior and inexpensive products in effect made the laborer and clerk equal to the wealthiest. Even a millionaire's money simply could not purchase better things. This central myth, which Roland Marchand has called the parable of the "Democracy of Goods," assumed special significance in light of the political language that often accompanied such depictions.[9] While Marchand emphasizes the parable's individualist implications, its message of social leveling offered an important collective insight as well. Consumption made the United States a democratic society of equals, marked by consumer goods as symbol and the source of that equality. "All ages, classes and sexes drink COCA-COLA," declared a 1907 ad; Jello advertising pointed out that "the Butler Serves and the Housewife Too," demonstrating that social status meant little in comparison with an opportunity to enjoy one of five delicious flavors. A 1910 King Gillette editorial boldly asserted, "There are no idle rich in this country today—no leisure class. It is asked of every man—what is he doing? . . . The Gillette Safety Razor is a symbol of the age— it is the most democratic thing in the world. The rich man is not shaved in

There are no idle rich in this country today—no leisure class. It is asked of every man—what is he doing? Life has a meaning. Men are up and dressed betimes—and shaved.

The Gillette Safety Razor is a symbol of the age—it is the most democratic thing in the world. The rich man is not shaved in bed by his valet as he was a generation ago. He uses a Gillette and he shaves himself—in three minutes.

Get up—get busy—get a Gillette. Don't be an effeminate dawdler and let another man shave you. There is more boost in a Gillette shave at 6.30 than there is in a cocktail at nine.

Buy a Gillette and take a brace. It costs $5.00 but it lasts a lifetime.

Write and we'll send you a pamphlet—Dept. A.

King C Gillette

GILLETTE SALES CO.
22 W. Second St., Boston

FIGURE 3.1. Gillette's Consumer Democracy. (*Saturday Evening Post*, April 16, 1910, 56)

bed by his valet as he was a generation ago. He uses a Gillette and shaves himself—in three minutes" (fig. 3.1).[10] Inexpensive abundance equalized all strata. But by reducing class status to possessions, such advertisements recast social inequality as marketplace diversity. By asserting that money could no longer separate plebian from plutocrat, whether in motor oil or mayonnaise, advertisers claimed that Americans lived on a great plain of equality measured in things. Such symbolism contained the outlines of a new nationalist culture where consumption was the foundation of citizenship, the individual's membership in a vast American society through ownership. A 1916 campaign celebrated the "Maxwell Democracy," composed of a community of satisfied consumers that was "based on characteristics soundly American . . . born of thrift, intelligence and enterprise . . . held together by a uniformly high appraisal of the Maxwell Car."[11] Such advertising implied that products made social relationships equal. Moreover, such advertising asserted that true political democracy was secondary to a democracy of things, in which all people were equal in their common possessions, without regard to the social consequences of power or class.

This form of democracy connoted universal access to luxury. Here advertisers were among the most forthright boosters for the American economic system, and they claimed that modern worker-consumers enjoyed benefits once reserved for royalty or nobility. Such thinking was enshrined in ads for products as diverse as automobiles, perfume, soap, and food. It proved especially useful in popularizing new items such as the phonograph. Although inventor Thomas Edison intended it as a business machine, the gramophone found commercial success as an entertainment medium and had made substantial inroads into the upper reaches of the middle-class market at the turn of the century. By 1910 several million homes had phonographs.[12] A widespread national appetite for classical music played a significant role in the phonograph's popularization, and its advertisers often argued that talking machines democratically offered universal access to good music and high culture, formerly the sole province of the rich. The Columbia Graphophone's advertisements declared, "Time was when this acquaintance [with good music] was a cultural advantage open only to a privileged few. . . . Today, through Columbia records, all the music of all the world is available to every child." The Victor Orthophonic Phonograph brought aristocratic pleasures to all by delivering absolutely true fidelity: "Only a fortunate few can attend the concerts. But, through the Orthophonic Victrola, you can bring the great symphony orchestras to your home, precisely as you would hear them at a public performance!" The Victrola (and Victor records) thus promised any consumer riches beyond the dreams of royalty because the Victrola brought the greatest (and most expensive) artists of the world into any home to perform.[13] But this version of cultural uplift championed by Victor, as well as by advertising experts, often fell on deaf ears. Enjoyment of classical music had never belonged exclusively to the rich. For many turn-of-the-century European immigrants, the arias and melodies offered by Caruso, Nellie Melba, Ernestine Schumann-Heink, Jascha Heifetz, and other stars of the day were popular songs of their homelands and not an exclusive commodity reserved for the aristocracy. Yet advertisers felt compelled to stress the uplift in promoting this product.[14] A common version of this idea was that new products conveyed to the masses benefits that the richest could not surpass. Ivory Soap stepped across the centuries to make the point in 1908: "It is a fact that John

Smith, Everyday American, can enjoy one luxury that Julius Caesar himself could not; and that is a real bath . . . . He steps into a tub of water, as warm or as cold as he chooses to have it . . . and feels the equal of Caesar and as much the Master of the World." Chase and Sanborn told an eager world, "Something you can share with kings and princes. . . . Good Coffee."[15]

Even communication and conversation could be reified as democratic products and practices. Striking democratic claims appeared in American Telephone and Telegraph's (AT&T) long-running institutional campaign, prepared by the N. W. Ayer agency. AT&T advertising originated in 1907, as the Bell company directors attempted to integrate their systems fully and consolidate markets. Disguising its designs on monopoly as "universal service," these ads emphasized that the telephone served everyone equally well. It was a truly democratic instrument, which provided the same opportunities to everyone. Noting that the Bell system "serves all the people all the time," AT&T advertising claimed, "Membership in the Bell democracy of the Bell System means equal opportunity for every man, no matter who he is or where he is. Each member of this Bell democracy has the same chance of communication."[16] Again, the language of democracy obscured social inequality. The Ayer copywriters presented the consistent technological performance as egalitarian innovation: "The telephone is essentially democratic; it carries the voice of the child and the grown-up with equal speed and directness." Thus Bell Telephone could claim to be "the most democratic system that could be provided for the American people." But more than simply uniting its users, Bell functioned as a great instrument of democracy itself by bringing equal privileges to all classes. "The telephone knows no favorites," its ads proclaimed. "It does the bidding of the country store and of the city bank. It is found in the ranch house kitchen and in the drawing-room of the city mansion." The Bell System claimed to be "a great telephone democracy," whose fruits were, as one advertisement's title claimed, "within the means of all."[17] Bell ads also stressed how its system served political democracy by quickly assuming a central role in the electoral process and in government.[18] And finally, AT&T advertising cited the social diversity of its stockholders to persuade consumers that the Bell System was, far from its apparent virtual monopoly of communication, in fact a commonwealth, a "Democracy '—of the people, by the people, for the people'" (fig. 3.2).[19] Here, democracy suffused the characterization of a decidedly undemocratic organization—the Bell Corporation—and in the process transformed the telephone into an essential component and symbol of the American social system: democratic, classless, and egalitarian.

Democracy

"—of the people, by the people, for the people"

People of every walk of life, in every state in the Union, are represented in the ownership of the Bell Telephone System. People from every class of telephone users, members of every trade, profession and business, as well as thousands of trust funds, are partners in this greatest investment democracy which is made up of the more than 175,000 stockholders of the American Telephone and Telegraph Company.

If this great body of people clasped hands they would form a line more than 150 miles long. Marching by your door, it would take more than 48 hours of ceaseless tramping for the line to pass.

This democracy of Bell telephone owners is greater in number than the entire population of one of our states; and more than half of its owners are women.

There is one Bell telephone shareholder for every 34 telephone subscribers. No other great industry has so democratic a distribution of its shares; no other industry is so completely owned by the people it serves. In the truest sense, the Bell System is an organization "of the people, by the people, for the people."

It is, therefore, not surprising that the Bell System gives the best and cheapest telephone service to be found anywhere in the world.

"BELL SYSTEM"

AMERICAN TELEPHONE AND TELEGRAPH COMPANY

AND ASSOCIATED COMPANIES

One Policy, One System, Universal Service, and all directed toward Better Service

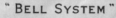

FIGURE 3.2. "Democracy." (N. W. Ayer Collection, Series 2, Box 21, File 3, Archives Center, National Museum of American History, Smithsonian Institution, Washington, D.C.)

Consumption symbolized the social equality available in American life and established only through the marketplace. By 1930, commentators would proclaim that consumption was not only the symbol but also the guarantee of democracy in America. Broad distribution of numerous goods hid systemic social inequality. Although advertising agents maintained a gulf between consumers and themselves, along with sharp differences between "class" and "mass," they nevertheless viewed consumption as a fundamentally benign and classless institution. They projected their visions of equality through the consistent use of democratic terminology. With the Depression, the fundamental inequalities of American life would challenge their views and the political language of advertising would then adapt to new conditions.

CONSUMPTION, NATIONALITY, AND AMERICANISM

The associations of suffrage, democracy, and independence all converged in advertising's reconstruction of the American nation through consumption. Between 1890 and 1930 advertisers consistently linked Americanness to goods and spending. As unprecedented immigration, new communications, and the emergence of a complex bureaucratic state all reshaped the contours and experience of nationality, advertisers presented consumption as the manifestation of American identity while trumpeting goods as the bedrock of its characteristic culture. Madison Avenue wedded nationalist icons, language, and heritage to products and purchasing. Copywriters crafted a vision of the United States as a distinct culture and people, for whom goods embodied the binding ideals of Americanness. Advertisers showed consumption as the means of naturalization, the ritual process of becoming a bona fide American. They linked goods to heritage and history, geography and language, ethnicity and folkways—all traditional symbols of a distinct nationality—to ground a distinct American nation in consumption.[20]

The contemporary emergence of the modern state and mass market in the United States ensured that consumption and nationalism would shape each other.[21] As Wilbur Zelinsky argues, "Cultural elements have been indispensable in the rise of modern nations and states."[22] In the United States advertisers reworked the powerful common language and symbols of nationality and nationalism. In so doing, they also imparted a material and market-oriented sensibility to nationalism. Of course, the elective affinities of consumption and nationalism were hardly unique to the United States. In western Europe, the Netherlands, England, France, and Germany all spawned distinct national consumption dispositions—habits, values, and goods—over the span of modern industrial capitalism.[23] Even as capitalism and commodities increasingly attained transnational influence, particular cultures, state systems, and local interests shaped national consumer economies. Despite the increasing erosions of national boundaries and challenges to the nation-state posed by mobility of capital, nationalism nevertheless continued to influence consumption. Advertisers promoted a nationalist ethos of consumption among American consumers and used powerful national language and symbols to that end.[24]

Twentieth-century Americans have debated two varieties of nationalism, according to Gary Gerstle. "Civic nationalism" emphasized the cohering force of a common creed: the commitment to political equality and economic opportunity for all was the foundation of a nation composed of diverse peoples from around the world. "Racial nationalism" rested on a much more exclusionary criteria: ties of blood and ancestry distinguished the United States as a nation and people inherently adept at self-rule.[25] I argue that advertisers' vision rested on a commercial variant, a "material nationalism," that blended the affiliating spirit of the civic strain and the essentialism of the racial. Emphasizing the pursuit of happiness, copywriters aligned with the inclusionary traditions of civic nationalists. However, their consistent erasures of minorities and people of color in their representations echoed racial nationalism. Advertising's material nationalism conferred American-ness through and in things. For Madison Avenue, the pursuit of goods offered an alternative to divisive political debates and social views; goods, in their widespread desirability, promoted comity and social harmony, not least by offering a more peaceful means of assimilation and conformity. Advertisers saw the nation as united in and defined by getting and spending. As we have seen, national advertisers did not address or consider the entire populace. Many Americans lived at a minimum subsistence level and did not participate to any extent in the consumer system, while other well-to-do folk distanced themselves critically from the excesses of material modernity. Advertisers' exclusion of those outside their marketing framework may have been business sense, but material nationalism applied to all. The true mark of an American for advertisers remained full participation in the consumer economy.[26]

Whereas civic and racial nationalists built on concepts (tradition, lineage, law, and shared sacrifice) to unify the nation, advertisers located material nationalism in the concrete reality of everyday goods. Indeed, nationalist rhetoric of all types informed cultural, as well as political, sources, including the material modernity made pervasive through the mass market—popular entertainment, music, foods, commodities.[27] Connecting sacred political and historical symbols with purchasing and products legitimated being a consumer and consumption. While many Progressive-Era authorities advocated racial and ethnic containment to combat the social and cultural fragmentation they feared from immigrants, advertisers claimed consumption would forge a united nation and a stable culture from their disparate origins. Advertisers invoked national symbols recognized by millions to invest buying with powerful cultural authority. Material nationalism made references to history, tradition, heritage, and self-sacrifice removed from abstractions and set in everyday material terms. These national metaphors and symbols, however, downplayed consumption's connection to a market system that served corporate interests and instead highlighted consumption as furthering ideals of patriotism. Glossing over this contradiction, advertisers argued that consumption transcended the narrow interests of business by claiming to serve all "the people" rather than a particular corporate sponsor.

Twentieth-century American nationalism took shape in an emerging state with new imperial responsibilities, extensive immigration, and a burgeoning mass communications system. Consumption influenced significantly the cultural aspect of nationalism. Anthropologist Benedict Anderson famously denoted the modern nation as an "imagined community," with distinct limits, but "always conceived as a deep horizontal comradeship."[28] To its people, the nation exists ideally as a mutual, organic society where all are deeply bound in ties that transcend social relations, kinship, or even self-interest. Nationality functions expressively, originating in culture and symbols among those sharing a common geography, heritage, and interests. As a nation, people believe "that they are united in the possession of a unique and cherished social and cultural personality." Built on the commitment to a unique history and character that is deliberately reinforced through cultural practices, nationalism articulates a people's devotion to both nation and nationality. Nationalism allows, and in fact demands, the articulation of that unique character. Culture becomes the site of a nation's distinct attributes, the manifestation of its particular "genius." Nationalism fabricates and then invokes the so-called natural bonds that join members of the same nation. Thus, nationalism has often produced exceptionalist narratives in different settings. This is not to argue for a special American "exceptionalism," still too frequently an unexamined assumption among American historians. But nationalism is predicated on the very idea of national distinctiveness, if not exceptionalism.[29]

Advertisers thus found nationalism attractive. In Ernest Gellner's formulation, nationalism equates the boundaries of the social (a people) with the political (a state).[30] Advertisers adapted nationalism to equate the commercial with the social. We have already seen that advertisers invented consumers as markets, conflating commercial and civic aggregates. In adapting nationalism, advertisers identified the nation as a market. They defined that market not only as the customer base for goods, but also as people characterized primarily by their appetites for goods, in what William Leach has called a culture of desire.[31] The language and symbols of nationality implied both official approval and social inclusion. As mass communication networks made it possible for Americans to attain a nationwide awareness in their daily lives, advertisers explicitly undertook the nationalist project of communicating to consumers that they shared material experiences with their fellow citizens around the country.[32] Understanding consumption as American nationality allowed advertisers to present material modernity as an extension of American heritage and folkways. Advertisers' use of nationality and nationalism legitimated consumption by casting it as the distinct, characteristic activity of Americans; they also thus domesticated consumption by linking individual daily life with history and the nation.

Advertisers promoted consumption as a means to unify American people by providing them common experiences and aspirations. The mass market made many goods available throughout the entire country. Advertisers easily adapted widespread distribution of commodities to ideas of nationality. "The United States is developing the quality of nationalism. We are coming to think of things in terms of our nationality. . . . We have established a national point of view and are thinking with a national mind"—so the Ayer agency wrote in 1916, reflecting its awareness not only of far-flung markets, but also of the opportunity to foster distinct and standardized habits among Americans.[33] Scores of advertisements identified consumption as the distinctive trait of American people, and no greater endorsement could be conferred on goods than to link them with broad acceptance. Advertisers sought to create "national" tastes, not only because potential profits were vast, but also because they were fascinated by the prospect of a national American culture characterized by consumption. As one agency pronounced, "Day after day, wherever there is human habitation, whenever there is need to buy, a nation's shopping list is made."[34]

Advertisers conflated national distribution with national significance, portraying goods as "national," that is, as approved by the whole nation. Scores of ads urged consumers to select "the Nation's Choice" or the "National Brand." Long before scholars discerned "consumption communities," advertisers made them the staple of their campaigns: everything from food products to timepieces to farm equipment bore a "national" designation that indicated a far-flung nationwide community of users. Welch's Grape Juice for years used the slogan "the National Drink," and its jam Grapelade became "the National Spread," while Van Camp's billed its pork and beans as "the National Dish." Ad men offered Hires Root Beer as "the National Beverage" and "the Nation's Drink as it Ought to Be." Buying Borden's, consumers bought "the Nation's Milk," while both Puffed Rice and Shredded Wheat claimed to be the national breakfast. Another campaign urged consumers, "Tonight, join the nation in a 'night-cap,'" Chase and Sanborn Tea, "The 'night-cap' of a nation." Campbell's Soup, one of the most prolific national advertisers, often used national imagery and language, calling its wares "the banquet of the nation from the greatest to the least."[35] Further, advertisers reminded consumers that "America" had chosen particular products, implying a national plebiscite to legitimate goods. Overland Autos breathlessly announced, "Exacting, appreciative, practical, hard-headed America has, as one unit, O.K.'d the small, light economical $615 Overland."[36] Ads for goods used in daily life, such as canned foods, as well as ads for special products of great expense, legitimated consumption by the authority of a widespread national consensus.

The electoral metaphor underpinned such "national" designations, using the idea of widespread acceptance to imply that the products had achieved prominence through popular will. Advertisers thus implied that such goods had been sanctioned by American society at large. Bearing little intrinsic relationship to products, the national designation was explicitly political, as solemn a ritual of public approval as an election itself. As a Lehigh Cement advertisement indicated, the company's "square deal policy" was "a sign of national distribution and national endorsement."[37] Misrepresenting pervasiveness as significance, advertisers interpreted the pervasiveness of the mass market as a measure of its importance in civic and communal life. A J. Walter Thompson advertisement arrayed its various clients' wares, proudly noting, "Go up and down the streets of any American city or town. In rich neighborhoods and in poor ones, you will see from the druggists' windows and counters, how much a part of the life of every community these products have become."[38]

Advertisements also employed the "national" designation to encourage consumers to select goods because they performed a national service. Appealing to nationalist sentiments, advertisers portrayed consumer goods as integral to a nationwide community, personifying them as public servants in the manner of heroes and historical figures. Thus, National Biscuit Company paraded Uneeda Biscuit as "the Soda Cracker that Makes the Nation Strong"; Pearline Soap was dedicated "for National Cleanliness"; and Hires proclaimed itself "Old Philadelphia's best contribution to the comfort of the nation." Kellogg's Bran promised to "remake the health of the nation." In 1919 Welch's boasted incredibly of its role in preserving civilization in the recently ended world war. "There are about a million men of the A.E.F. [American Expeditionary Force] who will tell you that Grapelade helped them win the war."[39] The Arch Preserver shoe claimed to be "the shoe that changed the idea of a Nation." A leading tire manufacturer claimed, "The Goodrich Record is a National Record." Even the venerable Sears catalog by 1925 had become "the Thrift-Book of a Nation."[40] Such advertising declared that consumption enhanced national well-being, since these products fostered the public good while they symbolized the nation they served. Advertisers showed products as national benefactors and implied that consumers would serve their country as well by purchasing them.

Advertisers often boldly cast their products as contributors to better social conditions. Proper consumption achieved painless social reform. By 1908 Proctor & Gamble could announce, "Every minute of the day and night, Ivory Soap is being used somewhere, some way, to keep our nation clean." Buying Campbell's Soup promoted "the United States of Good Health." Styleplus Clothes linked the endorsement of a nation of citizens with public service in a typical argument from 1914: "Styleplus Clothes $17 have become a national institution! . . . They have won a popularity as big as the nation itself. Styleplus clothes were originated and made to fill a national need—the need for all-wool clothes of a style and fit at a price which all men could afford. And the men of a whole Nation have answered 'Fine.' "[41] The Victor Phonograph announced its "great constructive service to the nation" in "Moulding the American Citizen of Tomorrow" through its use in over 25,000 American schools.[42] The Southern Pine Association, a lumber industry organization, unabashedly connected its wares to national service. Homes were "the Nation's Greatest Need," announced a 1920 ad. "National patriotism and civic spirit demand that every community concentrate greater attention on the building of more homes." Caterpillar Tractor's superior efficiency promised to uphold the public trust faithfully in building roads and other public works projects: "It is to your interest, therefore, to encourage and support your officials in the use of the most modern and most economical machinery and methods. 'Caterpillar' Tractors protect the taxes you pay."[43] According to advertisers, these products all met the exacting standards of public service, and consumers spread their benefits to the entire nation by acquiring them.

Advertisers sold some products by stressing their contributions to making American society more cohesive and harmonious. AT&T, for example, emphasized the telephone's role in promoting national unity. "The Telephone Unites the Nation," claimed the Bell System. "We are truly one people in all that our forefathers, in their most exalted moments meant by that phrase. . . . The Bell System has become the welder of the nation." The telephone, according to Bell, "has given greater force to the national motto, 'E Pluribus Unum.' " In providing the broad access to communication, the phone gave each user the length and breadth of the country to survey: "When you lift the Bell Telephone receiver from its hook, the doors of the nation open for you." More than many other products, Bell Telephone promoted not only individual convenience or service but also enhanced nationality and nationalism (fig. 3.3).[44]

Stressing national service did more than encourage consumers to buy: it consciously called on the obligation implied in nationalism for all citizens to transcend their individual self-interest for a national good. At the same time, advertising did not insist that consumers sacrifice their own interests in purchasing, but rather that the national interest and their own were harmoniously joined. A World War I ad for Campbell's Soup linked patriotism, service, and nationalism: "*Where is the American who doesn't know about Campbell's Soups?* They belong to America like the Washington Monument belongs—or the White House or the Lincoln Highway. Their name is a familiar word in practically all American homes. Why is this so? Because these wholesome soups meet a national need and fulfil *a national service*" (fig. 3.4).[45] Dedication to a greater common good certainly justified a product's existence, but such rhetoric also invoked the citizen's duty. The American who did not know Campbell's Soups ignored national heritage (the Washington Monument), national grandeur (the Lincoln Highway), and political duties (the White House). In such references, advertisers urged consumers to identify their self-interest with national welfare and their products.[46]

Perhaps the most powerful and significant connections between consumer products and American identity were forged through visual elements —icons and figures of American heritage and government. Advertisers made prolific use of political symbols and national icons. Although patriotic symbols never overshadowed other visual conventions, they remained a continual presence, used to strategic effect.[47] As easily recognized and widely accepted symbols, Uncle Sam, the Statue of Liberty, the American flag, his-

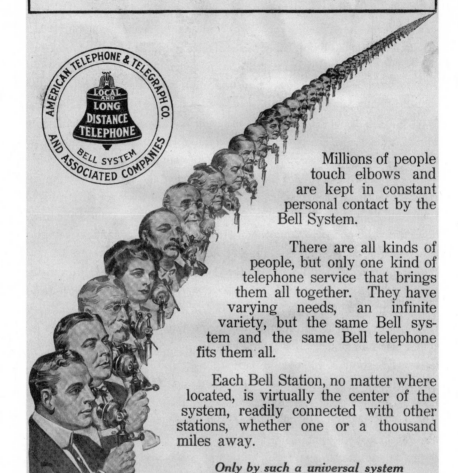

A United Nation

Millions of people touch elbows and are kept in constant personal contact by the Bell System.

There are all kinds of people, but only one kind of telephone service that brings them all together. They have varying needs, an infinite variety, but the same Bell system and the same Bell telephone fits them all.

Each Bell Station, no matter where located, is virtually the center of the system, readily connected with other stations, whether one or a thousand miles away.

Only by such a universal system can a nation be bound together.

AMERICAN TELEPHONE AND TELEGRAPH COMPANY
AND ASSOCIATED COMPANIES

FIGURE 3.3. "A United Nation." (N. W. Ayer Collection, Series 2, Box 21, File 2, Archives Center, National Museum of American History, Smithsonian Institution, Washington, D.C.)

"I belong to the U. S. A.
'Tis here I take my stand
For health and vim in work or play—
For strength in heart and hand."

A national Institution

Where is the American who doesn't know about Campbell's Soups?

They belong to America like the Washington Monument belongs—or the White House or the Lincoln Highway. Their name is a familiar word in practically all American homes. Why is this so?

Because these wholesome soups meet a national need and fulfil *a national service.* You see this, for example, in

Campbell's Vegetable Soup

Here is the choice yield of fertile farms and gardens gathered at its best, daintily cooked and prepared, hermetically sealed, distributed to millions of city home tables with all its freshness and flavor, all its nourishing quality perfectly retained.

We combine in this tempting soup more than a dozen delicious vegetables beside fragant herbs and strength-giving cereals — all blended with a rich nutritious stock made from selected beef.

No home kitchen has the facilities to produce such a perfectly balanced combination. It provides the very food elements most needed and most lacking in the average diet— elements which regulate the system and create energy and active strength.

And this invigorating soup is most convenient and economical. It involves no cooking cost for you. No labor. No waste. It is ready for your table in three minutes.

A dozen or more at a time is the practical way to order it. Then you have it always at hand.

21 kinds   12c a can

Campbell's Soups

LOOK FOR THE RED AND WHITE LABEL

FIGURE 3.4. "A National Institution." (*Cosmopolitan* 65, no. 2 [July 1918]: 101)

torical figures, and historic monuments all illustrated advertisements for virtually every conceivable product. They conferred visual endorsements on both the products of large manufacturers and small local businesses. Yet advertisers used these figures cautiously, fearing criticism that their huckstering would demean such semisacred icons of patriotism and heritage. One business writer offered the general sentiment about the flag in advertising: "It won't sell goods. It is the symbol of the republic and not of your brand of toothpicks, or plows or automobiles." Beneath the hard-nosed tough talk lay squeamishness about corrupting precious symbols of patriotism with base motivations of commerce. The potential offense to consumers from commercial usage advised against using these esteemed symbols.[48] Yet even with such qualms, scores of advertisers were willing to risk civic indignation: advertisers commonly used these icons to bequeath the aura of official endorsement to goods.

No national symbol appeared more often than Uncle Sam. According to *Printers' Ink,* using Uncle Sam as a trademark, testimonial figure, or a consumer surrogate provided "the double value of a decidedly likeable, lovable personality, plus the dignity of country-wide recognition. He is a symbol of the whole United States; he is everybody rolled into one. . . . He *is* America."[49] Uncle Sam's presence implied that the whole country used the product, and imaginative advertisers melded his image with that of the nation (fig. 3.5). However, employing Uncle Sam in connection with consumer products courted legal difficulties. While the national government allowed its suppliers to publicize the government's use of their products, federal law prohibited advertisers from implying government sponsorship or official sanction of a product or organization.[50] Uncle Sam so universally symbolized the United States government that to depict him risked falsely conveying official federal government endorsement. Yet that ambiguity was precisely the reason for Uncle Sam's appeal: advertisers hoped that the credulous consumers would assume the government approved the advertised goods. Advertisers had ample reason to suspect that many customers might mistake Uncle Sam for something more than a pleasant and well-known folk hero: "He may at once mean government sanction or merely be indicative of the country at large."[51] He always embodied public approval, and thus advertisers eagerly put him to work promoting products from typewriters to condensed milk, radios, and breakfast cereals. Whether he appeared as an emblem of the government, a representative consumer, or a symbol of nationality, he conveyed widespread national acceptance and usually a broad hint of nationalist sentiment and official approval.

FIGURE 3.5. "Uncle Sam Drinks Hires Rootbeer." (N. W. Ayer Collection, Series 2, Book 217, Archives Center, National Museum of American History, Smithsonian Institution, Washington, D.C.)

The Statue of Liberty similarly proved an attractive symbol for advertisers. Frederick Bartholdi's monument to political freedom and independence had grown in public perception from an embodiment of abstract principles to a personification of American nationality and loyalty. By 1920 the statue had become perhaps the equal of Uncle Sam in social recognition and evocative power.[52] Although she had come to be associated primarily with immigration, her presence in advertising brought ideals of individual liberty, enlightenment, wisdom, and political freedom to a variety of products. She promised "Soap Enlightenment" to Ivory users, for example (fig. 3.6). Even Campbell's adapted her figure for an ingenious ad, "Common Sense Enlightening the World," which showed how soup eaters enjoyed the blessings of liberty (fig. 3.7). Other advertisers capitalized on her symbolism to connect national grandeur and glory with specific products such as phonographs, tractors, and perhaps most tellingly, Coca-Cola (fig. 3.8).[53]

Other national and political symbols were used in advertising with like effects. Presidents, the Founders, Christopher Columbus, the Washington Monument, the Capitol, and the American eagle all hawked goods during these years.[54] Although appeals to patriotism and nationality generally enjoyed public support, advertisers usually skirted these issues, in fear of offending some readers. Nevertheless, these motifs appeared continually in national magazines over decades, marking moments when the political unconscious of American advertising in fact became explicit and overt.[55] The consistent appearances of such figures as Uncle Sam or George Washington outweighed in significance their frequency. Even if such advertisements were atypical as sales appeals, their choice of subject was telling: advertising "narrative" linked consumption with American identity.

Whatever their own patriotic sentiments, advertisers generally rejected economic nationalism as a bad business ploy that was both undemocratic and unworthy of competitive American business practices. Few advertisers supported campaigns to encourage spending based on parochial or national loyalties, even in times of economic crisis. Local manufacturers' or merchants' attempts to create enthusiasm for "Buy at Home" campaigns generated opposition from advertising agents who feared that economic localism would harm their national clients.[56] They contested the numerous campaigns organized by small-town merchants, editors, and manufacturers against mail-order, department, and chain stores; indeed, advertising agents led the battle against a 1935 California chain store tax.[57] Advertising spokesmen argued that individual self-interest in economic considerations outweighed community loyalties and that society would benefit most by allowing all to

FIGURE 3.6. "Soap Enlightenment." (*American Magazine*, March–April 1907, 120)

FIGURE 3.7. Soup Enlightenment. (*Pictorial Review*, July 1919, 29)

FIGURE 3.8. The Glass of Liberty. (*Woman's Home Companion*, June 1918, 47)

buy as they pleased. They also claimed that appeals to buy based on civic pride or duty were ineffective, if not absolutely repugnant, to consumers when less expensive or more appealing goods were available. Furthermore, advertisers maintained that those who urged buying at home as a rule had inferior products to sell.[58] These claims applied especially to campaigns that urged consumers to purchase American-made goods. As one merchandising executive sniffed, "There is no patriotism in the purse." If consumers preferred foreign-made or mail-order goods, appeals for self-sacrifice to benefit manufacturers and merchants would be impractical, wrongheaded, and unjust. Thus, advertisers most often refrained from asking consumers to buy for the greater good of the hometown or the republic, preferring instead a less divisive stance that supported consumers' pursuit of their individual self-interest.[59] Even during World War I, when advertisers thrust themselves into national prominence by creating propaganda for recruitment and bond drives for the government, they remained unenthusiastic about economic nationalism.

Moreover, advertisers fought economic nationalism on political principles. They resented merchants' attempts to prescribe consumer tastes based on anything but their individual happiness. "Buy at home" and "Made in America" campaigns proposed different criteria for consumers other than free choice. The electoral metaphor asserted that consumer choice was as sacred as freedom from coercion in political voting. "Do we like one thing better than another? We have a right to buy it, foreign-made though it may be," one advertiser insisted.[60] Always, advertisers asserted the primacy of private individual interests, even when discussing the collective good that consumption might bring to the American economy as a whole. Advertising agents fought any economic localism, whether it pitted towns or nations against one another. The politically sanctioned right to choose overruled other formulations of national interest.

CULTURAL NATIONALISM AND CONSUMPTION

Advertisers rejected economic nationalism, but they ardently embraced cultural nationalism, asserting that their products were central to a specifically American mode of living. Frequent reminders that their wares served explicitly "American" ideals and needs allowed advertisers to position consumption as the material expression of national identity. They consistently and self-consciously placed goods and spending in explicitly American settings, familiar and comfortable contexts for new goods and habits. Moreover, they presented material modernity as the distinct heritage and privilege of living in the United States. Advertisers depicted consumption as American folkways—characteristic modes of living that expressed political ideals, national cohesion, and cultural distinctiveness. They claimed that common possession of commodities unified American society; the national market itself melded a diverse and divergent populace. Building coast-to-coast markets, advertisers fostered a material nationalism based on spending. Thus, they offered goods less as the fruits of an industrial economy and more as the distinctive artifacts of twentieth-century American civilization. Consuming symbolized the uniqueness of the United States as a nation and a civilization; getting and spending affirmed one's Americanness.

For Madison Avenue, American culture and history embodied the triumph of the market. Merchandising, selling, and of course buying cemented a unified national culture and society. Ayer executive William Armistead noted that advertising "has played its part in making this country a united nation. The same food, the same tobacco, pipes, automobile tires, the same shoes, clothing, hats, the same toilet articles, and thousands of other commodities are sold under nationally known brands in every section of this country, in cities and towns and cross-roads."[61] Advertising and possession of brand-name goods provided the common references and experiences that made a harmonious, unified, and organic American culture. As agency founder Frank Presbrey noted, advertising and mass consumption were responsible for "most of the growth of a national homogeneity in our people, a uniformity of ideas which, despite the mixture of races, is found to be greater here than in European countries whose population is made up almost wholly of people of one race, and would seem to be easier to nationalize than in all respects. Constant acquisition of ideas from the same sources has caused Americans living three thousand miles apart to be alike in their living habits and thoughts, in their desires and in their methods of satisfying them."[62] Mistaking material unity for social cohesion, advertisers took credit for making a unified people out of a population beset by seismic demographic changes.

This material nationalism resonated with a broader contentious conversation in American life. Since the late nineteenth century, critics, pundits, and activists had engaged in a long-running, passionate debate over the essential characteristics and potential of American civilization. Such "Young Intellectuals" as Van Wyck Brooks, Lewis Mumford, Randolph Bourne, and Waldo Frank all came of age during the Progressive Era. Along with other critics and pundits they sought a "usable past" in a distinctive and nurturing American artistic culture. They searched for lost literary traditions and advocated new

relationships of community and creativity. Although they did not all necessarily reject business civilization, many of these critics condemned the corrosive role of marketplace logic in American life and culture. Some located
alternatives in organic and authentic cultures that predated industrialization
or that neutralized its worst effects through traditions and new forms of
creativity. In those same years Progressive-Era historians, led by Frederick
Jackson Turner, Vernon Parrington, and Charles Beard, offered interpretations of American history and literature as distinct and exceptional, rooted in
western expansion, abundant land, and the twinned pursuits of democracy
and commerce.[63] The aesthetic critics, in their search for a usable past, and
the Progressive historians, in their interpretation of American exceptionalism, viewed industrialization with ambivalence. For the Progressives modernity and industry meant the end of the frontier, a crisis of both meaning and
democratic institutions. For the Young Intellectuals, the dominance of business values was an impediment to true community, as well as to any enduring civilization. But unsurprisingly, advertisers offered a counter-celebration
of American manufacturing and enterprise as the source and not the solvent
of a distinct American culture. National advertising's depiction of self, society, and goods powerfully and pervasively located in consumption the material embodiment of American distinctiveness.

Material nationalism thus understood commodities as embodying ideal
and intangible qualities that made them truly "American." Thus, the National
Biscuit Company could assure an anxious world that "the Spirit of America is
exemplified in America's greatest food product—Uneeda Biscuit." Proctor &
Gamble's greatest product was "American soap. Ivory Soap. The two are synonymous. Ivory is the national soap because it embodies the American spirit
of cleanliness, efficiency and economy." Similarly, in urging consumers to
have their houses painted, advertisers identified "the Gospel of Paint" as "distinctly an American development." Buying a Packard meant that consumers
expressed "the American ideal of first class travel." Using concrete would
give consumers a "thoroughly American Home."[64] The Ingersoll Yankee,
one of several competing brands marketed as "the great American watch,"
claimed that "there is something truly American in spirit about this watch.
About its sturdy, faithful nature, its fairness, its price, its honest good looks."
The smiling Quaker Oats trade character urged consumers to try "the Great
American Breakfast."[65] By purchasing goods that expressed American values
and ideals, consumers asserted their own American nationality, vesting it in
the things they purchased. Connecting nationality and consumption reaf-

firmed the essential harmony of self, society, and nation, all linked through commercial products.

If economic duty to the nation fell short as a sales appeal, advertisers did invoke cultural obligations. They urged consumers to consider their spending habits and purchases as symbols of American civilization. Just as taste subjected the individual to social judgment, the international community judged the United States for the goods it made and consumed. Advertisers emphasized that American goods signified not just the quality of the firm but also of the culture that produced them. In such logic, Chiclets, Maxwell House coffee, Simmons bedding, Knox hats, and other domestically manufactured brands constituted a declaration of cultural independence, one that thus far had eluded the critics and practitioners of fine arts. So, Royal Tailors celebrated the "American ingenuity that produces the best at the least cost." Selz assured consumers that "American men are the best shod in the world," while Notaseme hosiery simply proclaimed that "American ways are best."[66] To label a product "American" or "for Americans" gave it a superior distinction from the rest of the world. Anger Spaghetti promised "American-Made Foods for American Homes" as the best guarantee of its product's quality. Elgin trumpeted its goods as "American watches for American life. Built for their time and place." The Oakland "All American Six" advertising named it "A New Car Built for American Use and Sold at an American Price." Welch's Grape Juice celebrated nationalism as exceptionalism: "One of the Joys of 'home again.' A real honest to goodness American drink that has life and healthfulness in it. . . . Welch's has been an American institution for 50 years."[67] American goods were worthy symbols of American civilization.

Not surprisingly, such celebrations of American manufacturing masked a great deal of insecurity. American manufacturers had long fought against the aura of European superiority in craftsmanship, countering such fears through assertions of cultural pride and nationalism. Even as ad men castigated "Buy American" sentiments, their "Made in America" slogans elevated products by appealing to nativism and patriotism; they might condemn a blanket principle of economic nationalism but would support the particulars of buying some American-made goods as they embodied the nation. Thus, Packard argued, "Many American buyers of foreign cars have been influenced largely by habit. But invariably their first purchase of a Packard has shown them the superior worth of the American-made car." Calling its pianos a "National Triumph," Steinway often appealed to cultural nationalism, invoking national pride as the great reward of Steinway's artisanship and quality: "Whenever an American victory is proclaimed, whether in the fields of sport or industry, every heart is filled with pride. Hence conquest of all countries and nations by the STEINWAY Piano should be regarded in the light of a national achievement."[68] American manufacturers could compete with the best the world had to offer, but only the market would validate the worth of American civilization.

The industrial economy made consumer goods the most powerful symbols of American culture. The "new American tempo" of modern life, described in an influential 1926 essay by advertiser Robert Updegraff, meant constant change. That tempo embodied modernity itself—"the public's disconcerting willingness to turn its back on established institutions, products, methods, ideas," rapid replacement and renewal, continual change and innovation.[69] Moreover, Americans' spending habits in this accelerated regime of change were key aspects of cultural distinctiveness. Christine Frederick argued that since the European approach to consumption elevated scarcity, durability, and stability over abundance, novelty, and renewal, Americans should avoid European designs and goods. She opposed American imitations of European approaches to consumption, which meant choosing, according to her, "the expensive automobile that will not wear out; the suit of clothes that will last five years . . . the contentment with very, very few things." Frederick's criterion was not value but culture: European integrity would not express Americans' ideals or serve their needs. The rapid, fluid pace of modern life required consumers to be as flexible and adaptive as the rate of changes in production. Durable values of quality and timelessness could not supply protean goods to changing consumers. Frederick recast planned obsolescence as both flexible accumulation and cultural exceptionalism. She preached that mass consumption (specifically the "American" system of rapid turnover and inexpensive wares) typified American culture. Domestic goods were superior because they fit American needs: "If the interior designers and the standardized furniture makers had been allowed their way, America in another twenty years would have been a vast pasteboard imitation of all the antiques of Europe, a bedlam of styles and periods, hopelessly mixed, entirely impractical and not expressing the personality or manners of the modern present period. But Mrs. Consumer has called a halt. Our America is to be something better than a shoddy Europe."[70] Arguing that Mrs. Consumer preferred the cheap and cheerful, Frederick asserted that buyers were best served by goods that aided them socially and psychologically. The "new American tempo" set the pace for a machine culture, symbolized by mass-produced goods.

Other advertisers reaffirmed American culture by seeking European endorsement. Led by the Social Darwinists at J. Walter Thompson, some agencies built campaigns around testimonials from European socialites and royalty, such as Romania's Queen Marie, certainly the most active advertising figure among heads of state. The European aristocracy's endorsement of popular and mass-produced American products became cultural commentary that marked the superiority of American goods. Reversing traditional perceptions of European craftsmanship and conventional beliefs about the tastes of the ruling elite, such advertising elevated common products to examples of American cultural distinction.[71] Perhaps the most telling example of Europeans' endorsing American goods came in a 1915 Royal Tailors advertisement. Featuring a stylishly attired "Uncle Sam" (with Capitol dome in view), the ad shows two German military men pointing out his new fashions: "I wish we had his Royal Tailored Look!" The text sums up American claims of cultural elevation through its consumer products: "The Royal Tailored Look is the Look of Civilization; the Look of Peace and Plenty; truly the Made-in-America Look. Royal Tailoring typifies Americanism; the kind of Americanism that secures the best in whatever it goes after." Such endorsements of American products for Americans drew on and cultivated the consumer's sense of cultural nationalism.[72] Attentive readers might have noticed the anomaly of Americanism touted by the Royal brand.

IMAGINED COMMODITIES:
CONSUMPTION AS NATURALIZATION

Why did advertisers so enthusiastically embrace a commercial and material vision of a cohesive American culture? Beyond giving themselves credit for uniting America under the banner of brand names, why did copywriters and executives eagerly paint a vivid portrait of Americans made one through common possession of things? We have already seen that advertisers feared the rise of commercial culture and zealously policed the borders between themselves and the great masses to whom they sold. With little hope for a cultivated citizenry and fearful of the ethnic and racial diversity manifest in urban life, they saw in consumption and entertainment the only means to cohesive society. Common pursuits and similar possessions would effectively substitute for a unified *Kultur* and indeed might comprise the foundation for a new American civilization over time.[73] Suspicious of immigrant and working-class culture and squeamish at the prospect of ethnic and racial democracy, advertisers viewed consumption as benign and efficient Americanization. Spending and ownership could transform any immigrant or worker, no matter how benighted, into a modern, assimilated, and unthreatening American.

Buying and using goods Americanized the immigrant and modernized the native-born. Certainly, advertising spokesmen assumed that consumption effectively accustomed masses of immigrants to American political and social values. When one executive described "Mrs. Typical Consumer" as "dancing before me in a medley of all the peasant costumes I had ever seen in Americanization parades," he underscored his colleagues' belief in consumption as the emblem of "American" living. Many remained uncertain whether foreign immigrants could successfully adopt American values and habits through products. They nevertheless viewed consuming as an essential indication of full participation in American life, a view that many immigrants and their children came to share.[74] Foreign-born consumers in fact did not simply accommodate themselves to the American national market on its own terms. Immigrant consumers compelled American businesses to adapt to preferences and traditions brought from their homelands and to develop "ethnic" products and markets even as these immigrants slowly adjusted to American-made goods. American advertisers sought to convince immigrants that becoming American meant becoming a consumer.[75]

Copywriters also used history to depict consumption as the distinctive trait of American culture. American history, in their unabashed view, was an unbroken procession of material improvement and cultural betterment. History and traditions informed sales messages by presenting goods as emblems of national progress.[76] Though concerned with contemporary times, advertising portrayed consumption, and more important, an ever-increasing demand for goods, as the result of American history: consuming was the unique behavior of Americans from past to present. This commercial version of the usable past depicted a common history that justified consumption in the present. In turn, modern advertising led Americans—now unified by that common heritage of appetite and acquisition—to new products that exemplified ideals forged in the past. Thus, as advertisers invoked history, they praised the present. Goods were the means through which the past was preserved and improved.

Advertisers believed that through the marketplace consumers reclaimed past traditions and asserted their nationality. Even more than revered historical figures such as Lincoln or Columbus, advertisers drew on vague but evocative depictions of American historical scenes and traditions to place their wares in the hallowed aura of past experience.[77] Historians Roland

Marchand and Jackson Lears have emphasized that ads on the whole maintained a distinct bias toward the modern in depicting and interpreting human experience. While advertisers often used history to link products with the American past, the necessity of selling always skewed ad men to favor the present. Validating change for its own sake, advertisers thus cast history and traditions as marginal and disposable elements of life, important only to evoke for their embodiment or transcendence in modern goods. Advertising images of the past emphasized that the marketplace offered an escape from history. Embracing the erasure of the past in consumption, selective historical imagery portrayed consumption as a means of reaffirming traditions, of maintaining continuity in a changed world, and of participating in time-honored "American" customs. Advertising created links for consumers with traditions, folkways, and mores that were increasingly being erased in the modern world.[78] At the same time, ad men promised a future unencumbered by any residue of tradition or obligation.

Modern goods thus served as appealing symbols of history and a unique cultural heritage. Corporate or institutional advertisements in particular suited such invocations of history. N. W. Ayer's campaigns in the *Saturday Evening Post* to advertise its services often named events and actors from American history as the source for the agency's ideals and the true nature of advertising.[79] For example, a cooperative campaign financed by mutual insurance firms featured a frontier circuit rider to stress that mutual insurance was "typically American in Origin and Principle." Swift and Company's 1923 campaign invoked the Pilgrim Fathers, among others, to link its modern service with revered historical ancestors.[80] One Portland Cement campaign featured historical figures, including William Penn and Lewis and Clark, to show how the company carried on their stirring examples of service and leadership. American Radiator pledged its fidelity to "the spirit of development which is the instinct of America." AT&T frequently featured episodes from American history to identify its service with the historic growth of the nation and its national heroes.[81] Advertising for everyday domestic goods deployed historical traditions as well. Chase and Sanborn advertisements in the 1920s featured its coffee's history as bound up with the history of the republic. Del Monte canned goods invoked the pioneering spirit of conquest and settlement of the nineteenth-century West to ground its products with the air of history. Advertisers touted the "true colonial spirit" and old "New England craftsmanship . . . imbued with a spirit of mastership—independent, individualistic, proud, unshaken by industrial and social upheavals."[82] These all played on and reinforced sentiments of cultural nationalism by linking consumers and goods to a sense of sacred traditions, nationality, and distinct cultural destiny.

Similarly, advertisers urged consumers to express their Americanism and cultural pride by owning those things that embodied distinctly American traits. Advertisers taught consumers to think of purchasing as public affirmation of the greatest elements of American culture. International Silver introduced a new line of products by claiming its embodiment of American ideals: "The American people are realizing that they have inherited a true American style, a style expressing the finest characteristics of their life and ambition . . . the inspirational basis of a real American decorative art."[83] In a sales campaign promoting what might be called "manicure destiny," Cutex solemnly assured *Ladies' Home Journal* readers that "well kept hands" were "a national characteristic" and that "nowadays Americans abroad are known by the grooming of their finger nails."[84] Consuming was ultimately to serve as the characteristic folkways, rituals, and communal activity of nation defined by things. Thus, a leading tobacco could contend that smoking its product was "a National Custom" and "more than a national form of enjoyment—it is an expression of American character. The millions of 'Bull' Durham smokers are the self-reliant energetic Americans who make the United States the most progressive nation in the world." King Gillette assured men that using his blade was "typical of the American spirit . . . . Its use starts habits of energy, of initiative. And men who do for themselves are men who think for themselves." Consumption embodied American ideals, through rituals where consumers reaffirmed their Americanness through their products.[85]

What were these American ideals? Advertisers used their selective history and sociology to identify as "decisively American" precisely those habits or traits most conducive to avid spending: an open mind, fierce individuality, a boundless appetite and curiosity for new things, a readiness to accept the modern, and a determination to find quality and satisfaction.[86] The representative American possessed the traits of an ideal consumer. Lest advertisers worry that such a vision was unfounded, no less a body than the 1928 Committee on Recent Economic Changes, chaired by Secretary of Commerce Herbert Hoover, echoed the same sentiments: "Underlying recent [economic] developments is an attitude of mind which seems to be characteristically American. Our nation is accustomed to rapid movement, to quick shifts in status; it is receptive to new ideas, ingenious in devices, adaptable. Our economy is in large measure the embodiment of those who have made it."[87] Advertisers projected these habits and aptitudes onto their vision of history and of a distinct culture; they not only flattered consumers' tastes but also essentialized them as the birthrights and traits of all Americans. According to the Overland Auto Company, "American" consumers were "pretty shrewd buyers. By instinct they look at everything from a commercial standpoint. . . . When they make an important purchase, their judgement makes the choice; not some warm or pretty picture." The Stevens-Duryea Motorcar praised consumers for fostering American craftsmanship through the "sense of discrimination among our countrymen which, by demanding such things, provides a stimulus and an answer to creative instinct."[88] These criteria were not simply expressions of taste and standards but what distinguished Americans from others. An early Chrysler ad referred to the "American demand for comfort without waste, for highest quality without excessive cost, for exceptional beauty without extravagance."[89] Being an active, attentive consumer was not simply the result of living in a complex modern economy but an expression of American identity through participation in this most characteristic ritual of American society. Christine Frederick flatly declared that American women were better consumers than their sisters in other nations: "I have no hesitation in saying that American housewives are in the mass more responsive to new ways, new foods, new devices than are foreign housewives."[90]

Here taste and acquisitive aggression emerged as national ideals, a precious legacy bequeathed by history and ratified in sacred national traditions and lore. That such traits imbued continuous, ceaseless demand was more than coincidence. Advertisers' rechristened demand as an "American ideal" rooted in the past: the new American tempo fulfilled national destiny. Americans were born consumers, and their aptitude for getting and spending fulfilled their destiny for more and better things. International Silver introduced a new design by claiming that it exemplified an American ethos. "What is the spirit of modern America?" asked International Silver. "It is restless, intolerant of cramping dictates. It is expressing itself in art literature, music, in sculpture and architecture . . . a freedom from narrowing precedents." Simmons mattresses took credit for creating the healthy appearance of citizens who always " 'look different' from European men and women." The free expression of individuality was held up as the fulfillment of American ideals in consumption. Royal Tailors used the Founding Fathers to advertise American ideals in ready-to-wear suits (fig. 3.9). "Your real American has always stood for self-determination: for freedom of choice and action, not only for the nation but for the individual," the ad insisted.[91] Christine Frederick argued that changing consumer appetites and the willingness to try the newest were not only habits that drove the consumer economy but in fact the most

FIGURE 3.9. "Men of Independence." (*Saturday Evening Post*, July 10, 1920, 130–31)

characteristic and valuable elements of American culture. By claiming that Americans should embrace consumption without reservation, Frederick reasoned that consumption was the highest fulfillment of American ideals.[92]

All these elements of cultural distinction, national destiny, American identity, individual freedom, and consumption were interwoven in an N. W. Ayer advertisement. "Something to Grub For" discussed consumption as national custom, a unique characteristic of American people. "Perhaps this is a nation of money grubbers as we have often been called," the ad conceded, but "Americans are the greatest spenders as well as the greatest earners in all economic history."[93] American history, economic development, and culture were all joined in consumption: "Through three hundred years of pioneering . . . of pushing back the frontiers of so vast a land . . . three traditions have become established traits of the American people. *The necessity for labor . . . the necessity for education . . . and the need for mechanical power to free workers for other pursuits*" (fig. 3.10).[94] Labor and education stimulated innovation. The dispositions that drove demand became the distinctive features of American culture and identity. These traits existed not only to serve individuals but also to realize the nation's utopian ideals. "Here is a new independence . . . a new democracy built on the permanent foundations of economic freedom."[95] The

SOMETHING TO GRUB FOR

Perhaps this is a nation of money grubbers, as we have so often been called. Certainly no other people has ever produced so much individual wealth.

Yet we do not grub for the sake of money alone . . . for Americans are the greatest spenders as well as the greatest earners in all economic history.

It would be interesting to know how we have become The Money Grubbers.

*   *   *

Look back for just a moment to those bleak shores where the founders of the nation found themselves confronted by the rugged task of feeding, sheltering and defending their families . . . with little equipment other than their bare hands.

There was neither a leisure class nor an organized serfdom. Everybody worked. Being people of intelligence, resource and courage, they soon made their brains do for them what hands had always done before. Labor-saving devices were born and manual workers were freed for the more difficult problems of education, government and defense.

Schools were established so the children of these ambitious people could reach cultural standards their parents had never known.

And through three hundred years of pioneering . . . of pushing back the frontiers of so vast a land . . . three traditions have become established traits of the American people. *The necessity for labor . . . the necessity for education . . . and the need for mechanical power to free workers for other pursuits.*

The necessity for labor has made us want labor-saving devices. The application of mechanical power to manufacturing has made them available to us. The use of the printed page in the disseminating of information has permitted the picture of their rewards and benefits to be held constantly before us. Our national ability to *read, think* and *reason* completes the cycle. We want these machines which will ease our burden and improve our living . . . and we are willing to work harder for them. Advertising has stimulated more work . . . more buying. By creating more manufacturing, it is providing work for those who would *buy* the machines they are helping to make.

Automobiles, washing machines, electric refrigerators, telephones, talking machines, tractors, harvesters, each the application of power to some simple need and a whole nation aware of and wanting them.

Here is a new independence . . . a new democracy built on the permanent foundation of economic freedom.

If we *are* money grubbers, it is because *we have something to grub for!*

N. W. AYER & SON
ADVERTISING HEADQUARTERS
PHILADELPHIA
NEW YORK   BOSTON   CHICAGO   SAN FRANCISCO

FIGURE 3.10. "Something to Grub For." (N. W. Ayer Collection, Series 14, Box 1, Archives Center, National Museum of American History, Smithsonian Institution, Washington, D.C.)

American people had fostered a new nation, conceived in liberty and dedicated to the proposition that all were created equal. They realized and expressed that proposition fully through things. Consuming was the foundation of a distinctly American way of life, a new order of the ages. By 1930, material nationalism cast the nation not as imagined communities but as an aggregate of appetites expressed in goods. Advertisers defined the nation as imagined commodities.

CONCLUSION

By 1930, American advertisers had built up over the previous four decades a clear, consistent identification of consumption with American nationality and a distinct American culture. The proliferation of goods that transformed the landscape, domestic environment, and daily life symbolized both a "modern" age and a specifically American civilization. Nationality and culture were inextricably rooted in consumption. For millions, consumption came to be identified with the goals and virtues of American life, and for many millions more it symbolized aspirations beyond reach, visible only as pretty pictures in a magazine, display window, or on a movie screen. Advertisers made such linkages because they seemed socially and commercially advantageous. Their own privilege and ambivalence about the consuming public fostered a myopic vision of America. Although many powerful and successful executives came from village, rural, or petty bourgeois backgrounds, advertisers could not imagine a society where marketplace values did not rule. Just as they did not acknowledge immigrants, the poor, and people of color as consumers, advertisers imagined a nation bound only by spending and by things.

Advertisers' ready use of political language, nationalist rhetoric, and patriotic icons had two results. The first was the sustained identification of market activity with democracy; no matter how unequal American social conditions became, the public would readily view consumption itself as democratic. Any liberal critique of material inequality would be impaired by the political rhetoric that associated consumption and popular will. Second, the ubiquitous presence of commercial images and language and insistent intrusions of marketplace imagery in public life eroded American's political and civic vocabularies. If consumption indeed were citizenship, and liberty were freedom of choice, there seemed to be few alternatives to the market as the measure of the public good and the common weal. Yet this democratic language and nationalist imagery struck deeply resonant chords. The utopian appeals of new goods, higher standards of living, and new forms of personal identity in goods were powerful and unmistakable. Even if most Americans did not have full access to material modernity, they still knew its promises. By 1930, the modern consumption regime had become thoroughly nationalized, and Americans knew that they lived in a consumer culture. The Depression that followed would destabilize that culture and imperil the nation's economic and political institutions. Americans would ultimately give allegiance to the leaders that protected them in turn as citizens, workers, and consumers.

Promoting spending as the basis of identity and the foundation of community and nation undoubtedly served commercial interests. However, advertisers did not get the final say on the subject. In those decades when advertising became the voice of corporate capital and brought forth the political language that would conflate marketplace interests with American identity, other professionals were creating a vastly different vision of consumption. The burgeoning enterprises of social science and the new profession of product testing would bring forth sharply contrasting ideas of consumption. These professionals would challenge conventional business wisdom and economic theory to offer a radically different vision of consumer citizenship.

CONSUMERISTS

CHAPTER 4

SOCIAL

SCIENCE

AND THE

PRAGMATIC

CONSUMER,

1890–1928

No matter how efficient may be our mines and farms and factories, we cannot regard our economic system as efficient if it induces consumers to spend a large part of their income for goods which yield little or no satisfaction.[1]

The modern consumer movement emerged in the late 1920s. The publication of Stuart Chase's *The Tragedy of Waste* (1925) and *Your Money's Worth* (1927), written with F. J. Schlink, sparked a popular response to their exposé of consumers' difficulties. Shortly thereafter, Chase and Schlink founded Consumers' Research, a membership organization devoted to fostering dialogue among consumers, dispersing information about products, and increasing public awareness of the interests of citizens as consumers.[2] Chase and Schlink's highly publicized work appeared in the wake of sporadic but increasing attention to consumers in the newly professionalizing social sciences. They clearly followed in a tradition with long roots.

From the mid-nineteenth century onward, social thinkers had been discussing consumers as significant elements in the polity and economy and describing the conflicts and constraints faced by consumers. They articulated ideas on the individual buyer's place in the economic order and made tentative steps toward discussing consumers as citizens, the inhabitants of the American polity.[3] While the intellectual history of consumption and social science requires a book-length treatment in itself, this chapter traces important clusters of ideas offered by three writers who shaped the consumerist program that emerged in the 1920s.

ECONOMISTS AND CONSUMERS IN THE LATE NINETEENTH CENTURY

Attention to consumption by economists evolved intermittently in the late nineteenth and early twentieth centuries. With the initial appointments of scholars trained in German research universities, some American scholars by the 1890s were engaged with European revolutions in economic theory.[4] By this time, the major social and technological changes of industrialization had begun to challenge the assumptions—shared by both classical economists and Karl Marx—that material scarcity posed the greatest constraint on the economy and that, consequently, production was the preeminent economic activity. Instead neoclassical economists of the "marginalist revolution" recast their theories around economic demand, instead of the traditional emphasis on production and labor, and thereby made consumption a focal point of economic analysis.

Marginalism located demand at the center of economic exchange, displacing the labor theory of value, which postulated that the economic worth of a commodity was determined by the time, labor, and resources necessary to produce it. The marginalist position has been neatly summed up by James Livingston: "the value of a commodity was greater or smaller according to the state of demand for it. . . . Unless effective demand validated the prior expenditures of labor-power, commodities would have no value regardless of the labor-time contained in them. In short, [marginalists] argued that if production was the necessary condition of value, demand was the sufficient condition."[5] Led by Alfred Marshall and W. Stanley Jevons in England and John B. Clark in the United States, these theorists stressed that demand for goods and satisfactions—the appetites and desires of individuals—were the heart of economic activity, the wellspring of all production and the justification of any economic system. Rather than being a consequence of production, consumption stimulated it: humans produced in order to consume. Marginalism also held that the genesis of demand lay outside the sphere of economics, in the realm of psychology, and that beyond physical needs, human desires were made socially, through imitation and emulation. As the "political economy of consumer culture," marginalism, Livingston reminds us, justified both wages paid to labor and the profits and economic power of capitalist firms.[6] Thus, its adherents tended to ignore or, more precisely, assume issues of economic value. One result of this position was a surprisingly simple model of economic motivation as the rational calculus of benefits, a concept that almost immediately met criticism.[7]

Marginalist economists had little interest in the specific characteristics or genesis of demand. They assumed that the market would ascertain "human needs" and supply them. Some marginalists argued that consumers' preferences had no explanation other than the vagaries of individual personalities, and indeed most marginalists eventually turned away from psychological explanations of particular demands.[8] Once basic questions of subsistence had been answered, marginalist theory asserted, consumer demands were virtually interchangeable, with no choices more important than others. As Livingston argues, while such mutable categories enabled economists to justify the existing distribution of wealth and wages, marginalism's overall result was to enshrine the free market not simply as the ideal arena of exchange but as a metaphor of society. Marginalism validated the outcomes of capitalist enterprise.[9] Consumer preferences could not be theorized or charted with the scientific objectivity necessary for the formulation of true economic "laws." Thus, consumers were taken for granted, even as marginalists placed them at the heart of the economy.[10]

The industrial economy's capacities seemingly promised unheard-of affluence for all, thus challenging traditionally held assumptions about the relationship of frugality and success, restraint and indulgence. Commentators debated the new possibilities offered by machine-made affluence, focusing on what Daniel Horowitz has termed "the morality of spending."[11] Longstanding beliefs had linked spending and indulgence with moral corruption and sinfulness. Thomas Malthus had theorized that competition for a fixed food supply in an ever-expanding population would lead to catastrophic famine and warfare. While Malthus's dire predictions were not always shared, his emphasis on the limits of food and the pressures of population on resources painted a grim picture of scarcity, want, and survival. Only those who worked hard and saved up could survive in the competition for food and shelter. Moreover, middle-class Puritan traditions of plain speaking and moralism hostile to ostentation and artifice lingered as powerful indictments of spending, especially by the poor and working class. Yet new technical possibilities for mass production and a recognition of the grinding poverty faced by urban workers in the late nineteenth century prompted some to pose alternatives to the morality of thrift and denial. Among them was economist Simon N. Patten, who cast consumption and, more important, a philosophy of abundance as the "new basis of civilization." Patten charged that denial, saving, and thrift were not only inhumane when applied to a working class barely subsisting on meager wages but also ineffective in raising the general level of prosperity. Patten claimed that people needed to consume to satisfy physical and spiritual wants. Rather than draining a society's economic resources, consumption would stimulate them. Moreover, fostering consumption represented a more humane ethic of treating the poor and setting policy for social responsibility.[12] Consumption was not a threat but the key to a family's economic health and security.

Even as Patten developed this challenge, social investigators were collecting information on how people actually spent their money and how they lived on the money they made. Researchers from government, private organizations, and social work agencies studied household budgets and spending patterns among the working and middle classes, hoping to ameliorate the problems of the poor and workers through close analysis and re-education on their tastes, spending, and housekeeping habits.[13] These investigations perpetuated long-standing assumptions that consumption choices exemplified the moral character of the spender. While private social workers used budgets to investigate the actual constraints under which the poor and working class lived, government investigators used them to shape policy debates and recommendations. Commentators often argued that the poor could improve their lot by restraint and wiser choices in spending. The spending habits of the middle classes, by contrast, offered a preferred model of modest thrift and restraint. While not all middling families met such standards, and in fact provided the greatest challenge to nineteenth-century ideals of thrift and restraint, middle-class habits served as benchmarks for the debates about proper levels of family spending.[14]

Between 1890 and 1924 several economists began to pay attention not only to consumers but also to their demands and the conditions under which they spent. Three in particular analyzed the cultural sources of demand, as well as the constraints in which people spent. In that way, Thorstein Veblen, Wesley C. Mitchell, and Hazel Kyrk all placed consumers, not business or markets, as the fulcrum of the economy and argued that consumers should assume center stage as citizens. The three also forged a critique of business treatment of buyers that would directly inform the consumer movement. They argued that the consumer was a potentially powerful but disfranchised "sovereign" of the economic system. Their arguments filled in a sketch of consumers that now assumed very specific class, gender, and cultural characteristics. While these three were not the only economists to write on consumers, their assessment of both consumers' powerlessness and agency, and their calls for pragmatic experimentation in the marketplace, helped prepare the emergence of a consumer voice in the 1920s.

THE THEORIST OF PECUNIARY SOCIETY

Although he completed his major works a century ago, Thorstein Veblen (1857–1929) remains one of the greatest analysts of the American economic system. Trained in philosophy, Veblen incorporated sociology and anthropology into his studies of economic institutions and processes.[15] From the 1890s through the 1920s, he produced an interwoven series of writings on the logic of business enterprise, the role of technology in industry, society, and culture, and the relationship of consumption to social status. Though eclipsed today as an economist, Veblen left a legacy of terms and concepts that still influence social analysis and criticism.[16] He influenced the writers and thinkers who mapped consumer interests and options in the years after World War I. Though the modern retail consumption system and everyday commodities never attracted his sustained attention, his critique of consumption's influence in invidious social hierarchy and his criticism of capitalist logic in culture set the stage for the consumer movement. Even as his contemporaries in economics departments struggled to chart abstract and objective economic "laws," Veblen placed economic activity squarely within the framework of culture and history, and he argued that social customs and cultural practice shaped economies. Along with the newly professionalizing anthropologists, Veblen interpreted uses of goods in social and cultural structures. He characterized consumption as both symbol and product of social relations, an emblem of inequality and an instrument for reinforcing social hierarchies. With a few notable exceptions, his was a lone voice applying such concepts to the contemporary world. It has taken the better part of a century for scholars to catch up.[17]

Veblen served a long and vexing academic apprenticeship, earning a Ph.D. in philosophy in 1884 from Yale and spending the 1890s at the new University of Chicago, where he was a colleague of philosophers John Dewey and George Herbert Mead and economist J. Lawrence Laughlin. He composed his most famous book, *The Theory of the Leisure Class* (1899) while living in the Second City, at that time the nation's innovative hub of merchandising and advertising.[18] His subsequent work, *The Theory of Business Enterprise* (1904), was the first of the series of treatises on capitalism and industry that comprise his legacy. Throughout his career he followed out implications set forth in those first two volumes.[19] Since Veblen's general analysis of capitalism was as influential on the consumer movement as his discussions of conspicuous consumption, a review of those arguments will illuminate his impact.

Insisting that economies were specific products of human history, Veblen dismantled prevailing assumptions that economic laws and institutions were timeless, universal, and natural.[20] Distinct from the dialectical unfolding of history in the work of Hegel and Marx, or the Whiggish view of history as an unbroken series of triumphs as understood by his late Victorian contemporaries, Veblen saw history as both contingent and evolutionary. The economy was a product of the past, inexorably shaped over time by a society that was remade by that economy in turn.[21] He rejected the commonplace presumption of historical progress and caustically questioned Victorian notions of inevitable moral improvement and technological advancement. Veblen thus reconnected capitalism with the history it supposedly transcended. Demonstrating the origins of production, labor, property, and exchange among the earliest recorded civilizations and those remote indigenous peoples then being "discovered" by anthropologists, Veblen upended conventional wisdom.[22] From this starting point, he raised serious questions about the ends of American capitalism and identified criteria for judging its effectiveness and social worth.[23]

Central to Veblen's economics was the systematic conflict between business and industry. By "industry," he referred to the productive activity of machine technology and human labor. For Veblen, technology and the material conditions of a civilization were among the most significant determinants of human development. Under machine technology, industry had become centralized and efficient, susceptible to specialized control and coordination, and capable of producing an abundance of materials and goods. Industrial logic entailed the rational application of scientific principles to increase efficiency (the performance of a given task with a decreasing expenditure of energy) and productivity (increased output for a given expenditure of energy or labor). Whatever did not increase functionality, efficiency, and productivity was antithetical to industry as such.[24]

However, industry was controlled by business, whose guiding principles Veblen termed "pecuniary logic," institutionalized as "the price system." Businessmen ran industry to serve their financial interests, and pecuniary logic dictated preserving profit levels by maintaining prices over efficiency. Consequently, business hampered the industrial process; as a rule, business was unproductive, industrially and socially. In business the customary reliance on credit for growth wasted resources (since the money used to finance such debt was not directly used to increase production) and ultimately harmed overall prosperity. In good times businesses borrowed to enlarge output; with prosperity came rising prices, wages, and interest rates. But increased loans led to a rising debt service, thus making it unprofitable to maintain production levels once interest rates rose or profits fell. To stave off losses, businessmen routinely cut production rather than prices, resulting in reduced wages and cycles of depression, idle plants, and unemployment. The waves of prosperity and depression, expansion and contraction, wasted machine and human resources. Since there was nothing intrinsically wasteful in the machine process, and no inherent limitation on potential productivity, such administered curtailment of production by pecuniary logic attacked industry and eroded its social benefits.[25]

With typical sarcasm Veblen termed this pattern of events the "theory of modern welfare." As he observed, "The corporation is always a business concern, not an industrial appliance. It is a means of making money, not of making goods."[26] Business logic fostered "overproduction," where supply exceeded the market's capacities but never the human need. Veblen noted that this term and "underconsumption," both frequently used by businessmen, referred only to pecuniary or business inadequacies, not to flaws in the industrial process.[27] "Overproduction" only had meaning in the context of the profit system: in restricting production, the businessman effectively acted as a saboteur through "the conscientious withdrawal of efficiency" to support profits. In Veblen's words, "the rate and volume of output must be adjusted to the needs and resources of the market, not to the working capacity of the available resources, equipment and man-power, nor to the community's need of consumable goods."[28] Since society still faced scarcities of its basic needs, restricting production in Veblen's view was not only harmful, but criminal.[29]

Veblen saw two major implications of this conflict. First, business logic stifled the "instinct of workmanship" common to all cultures and peoples. This instinct, the human propensity to make things and to act upon the material environment, was as deeply rooted in human psychology and biology as instincts of procreation and survival. Workmanship shaped the forms of human activity and brought about "serviceability for the ends of life." It was the key to social evolution as well. "The instinct of workmanship brought the life of mankind from the brute to the human plane," Veblen wrote, "and in all the later growth of culture it has never ceased to pervade the works of man." Not surprisingly, this instinct underlay industrial logic—for Veblen, the pursuit of efficient production for the common good—and opposed pecuniary interests.[30] Moreover, this clash meant that subjugating industry to business represented a continual sacrifice of the welfare of the many on the altar of private gain for the very few. This loss was made bitter by the knowledge that industrial capabilities could fulfill the common need. Businessmen or "Captains of Industry," as he dryly dubbed them, won praise in the press and public as leaders and heroes of American civilization, but for Veblen they were "barbarians" who sabotaged productive capacity. Despite the businessman's reputation as a sober, conservative decision maker, he was at best a delusional "visionary" whose quest for profits led him to disrupt the inherent order of industry regardless of consequences.[31]

Because they did not operate or understand machinery, businessmen were, in effect, "absentee owners," removed from the human and technical costs of their decisions.[32] Businesses essentially could only destroy: whatever industry produced came about in spite of business. Businessmen threatened not only productive capacity but also the very lives of those who depended on industry for a living. The fruits of business civilization were "a regime of continued and increasing hardship and dissension, unemployment and privation, waste and insecurity of person and property," which "the rule of the Vested Interests in business has already made increasingly familiar to all the civilized peoples."[33] The only remedy he saw was to liberate industry from business control and return it to the stewardship of engineers. The engineer stood outside the system of pecuniary thinking and pursued the very efficiency, productivity, and common welfare that businessmen routinely sabotaged. As Veblen wrote in *The Engineers and the Price System*, "The technicians are indispensable to the Vested Interests and their absentee owners, as a working force without which there would be no industrial output to control or divide; whereas the Vested Interests and their absentee owners are of no material consequence to the technicians and their work, except as extraneous interference and obstruction."[34] Veblen wisely doubted the engineers' willingness to take control of industry and operate it for the common good, but he still held out that possibility. When the engineer-turned-publicist Howard Scott led his short-lived Technocracy movement to prominence in the early Depression, promising to end hard times by coordinating control of production, it seemed as if Veblen's call for rule by a "Soviet of Engineers" might come true.[35] When a consumerist movement emerged in the late 1920s to expose the inefficiencies, waste, and dangers facing consumers, it would be spearheaded by an economist steeped in Veblen's ideas and an engineer who personified Veblen's analysis.

VEBLEN ON CONSUMPTION

Veblen's most famous work dealt directly with consumers and consumption. *The Theory of the Leisure Class* (1899) brought him recognition as a satirist of the American ruling class and the aspiring bourgeoisie and imparted "conspicuous consumption" permanently to the lexicon. Yet, this influential book was more than just a wicked comedy of manners disguised as sociology.

Leisure Class carefully analyzed the historical circumstances that shaped taste and attitudes toward material accumulation, uniting an economic analysis of cultural practices with a cultural analysis of economic activity.[36] Comparing the habits and behavior of contemporary elites with those of indigenous peoples then being "discovered" by anthropologists, Veblen established crucial continuities between the deep past and the more recent industrial revolution. More important, he revealed clear similarities among peoples and communities across time and around the globe, among small tribes, feudal societies, and his own contemporaries.[37]

Veblen argued that the acquisition and use of possessions were social activities, rooted in ancient history and human instincts, especially emulation: "With the exception of the instinct of self-preservation, the propensity for emulation is probably the strongest and most alert and most persistent of all economic motives proper." Emulation fueled consumption and acquisition, as people sought to imitate one another through their objects.[38] Property originated in struggles between people and among social groups; its early form, the trophy, symbolized the triumph of specific contestants. But the trophy embodied the instinct of workmanship: it was above all practical, representing the killing of food or the defeat of a hostile tribe. Social distinction and leadership, however, soon accrued to the warriors and providers with the most trophies. As a result, possession of wealth, which originally stood for workmanlike competence and craft, came instead to symbolize high social status itself. The instinct of workmanship was replaced by distinction of possession.[39] Social hierarchy was inextricably linked with property; goods served as markers of difference and inequality. Conversely, since groups tended to make their less physically powerful or subordinate members slaves and laborers, workmanlike labor lost its associations with the high status once accorded to efficiency. Thus, labor came to embody a lower status, while hunting and war signified social leadership. In Veblen's view, people never shunned labor as intrinsically distasteful. Only as society's lowest members exclusively became laborers did people avoid work in pursuit of higher status.[40] In the quest for a laborless life, attaining the visible signs of "conspicuous leisure" became the goal of emulation.

Thus, Veblen undercut the associations of wealth and possessions with social prestige. By unveiling property's origins in struggle, warfare, and theft, he questioned the claims of a ruling class to rule or possess great wealth by any "natural" or "just" criteria. Demonstrating that property emerged from efficient labor, he criticized the social relations that sanctioned accumulation as the greatest good, and he made clear that socially honorable goods embodied calculated waste. There was no status in owning purely functional goods, once workmanlike qualities lost their honored associations along with labor.[41] Status that derived purely from ownership simultaneously frustrated the instinct of workmanship and demonstrated the unproductiveness of social inequality. In Veblen's mocking logic, society thus placed the greatest value on the least worthy goods. His theory was the fun-house mirror of marginalism: economic and exchange values did not embody utility and the social good, nor did they justify the distribution of wealth and power.

What made the emulation and institutionalizing of invidious social distinctions through consumption so powerful was their perpetuation in habit, the socially ordained behavior that groups enforced and passed on to succeeding generations. Habits set standards over time; a member of any society had to uphold those "standards of decency" at all costs. Consumption was conspicuous in order to signal conformity: "Ordinarily his motive is a wish to conform to established usage, to avoid unfavorable notice and comment, to live up to the accepted canons of decency in the kind, amount and grade of goods consumed as well as in the decorous employment of his time and effort."[42] Since habit was very difficult to transgress and broken only under great duress, emulation of social betters occurred at a level "as high as the earning capacity of the class will permit—with a constant tendency to go higher" and with a tenacity approaching permanence.[43] Consumption as social emulation became apparently natural, seemingly even preordained.

The emphasis on workmanship implied that Veblen favored only efficient goods and shunned adornment, decoration, or polish, as these qualities invariably represented waste and social honor rather than workmanship.[44] Critics have noted that his insistent contrast of consumption with workmanship, the wasteful and useful, meant nothing less than a critique of the basic, human propensity to adorn and display. In Theodor Adorno's phrase, Veblen conducted an "attack on culture" itself. Veblen focused attention only on the invidious ways that consumption reinforced social inequality and neglected its role in fostering identity.[45] While he certainly discounted the ways people used possessions to make sense of their world, to fabricate an identity, or to indulge a necessary bent for play and display, Veblen did acknowledge the cultural aspects of goods. Although he was no aesthete, Veblen separated consumption as a pecuniary activity from the appreciation of goods. The relevant measure of any commodity was "whether, aside from acquired tastes and from the canons of usage and conventional decency, its result is a net gain in comfort or the fulness of life." Consumption depended on the social usages to which goods were put; those goods that exclusively fostered divisive comparisons or inequity failed his standards. That most goods were used for pecuniary distinctions did not make that brutal process inevitable.[46]

Veblen believed consumption itself should serve the aims of life. No less than industry, goods should exemplify workmanship.[47] Moreover, he even favored goods without a tangible functionality as long as they facilitated "idle curiosity," the human propensity to explore and speculate with little thought of practical ends or immediate use. That curiosity, almost a spirit of play, was essential to intellectual and scientific development. While Veblen treated idle curiosity largely in relationship to science and research, he made clear that it served everyday life as well. In this regard, the ideal consumer was a pragmatic experimenter, seeking serviceability and functionality, who indulged in idle curiosity and sought workmanlike goods.

The Theory of the Leisure Class famously drew attention to the "barbarian" status of women consumers. Veblen argued that women were central to the history of consumption, not just as participants, but in effect as the original "objects" of exchange. Once primitive groups had passed from the peaceable (pastoral) to the predatory (hunting, war) level of sustenance, Veblen argued, women were probably traded or awarded as trophies of triumphant conquest. Similarly, either as such trophies, or as a result of the fact that the honored positions in society generally went to males, women became associated with menial labor. The social aversion to labor emerged from women's inferior status within warlike tribes. In the modern era women were still associated with domesticity, the tasks accorded the least respect in pecuniary logic. This conjunction made them the central laborers of consumption. Women had become symbolically central to the economic order as well. Especially among the urban middle class, women had lost much of their productive function and were reduced to serving as emblems and arbiters of male achievement. Their lives increasingly revolved around conspicuous waste, as they ostentatiously decorated bourgeois homes and themselves. They continued to function in effect as trophies.

For Veblen, women were hurt by such objectification and by the wastefulness of consumption: they were the group most identified with social inequality and status aspiration. In his analysis women were made to embody the wastefulness of pecuniary society carried out and institutionalized by men. Yet he stopped short of critiquing the double standard under which women were judged. Veblen never noted that consumption reinforced unequal gender relations, which allotted respectable domesticity to women but accorded privilege and power only to men.[48] Veblen noted women were capable of useful labor as much as men, yet he clearly felt their limitation to consumption was unfortunate. His feminism remained implicit: if there were nothing natural or predetermined in the scheme that made accumulation a sign of prestige or superiority, equally artificial was any logic that assigned consumption to women and production to men.

Veblen probed the conditions that consumers faced in the business system. In a striking dissent from neoclassical and marginalist economics, he noted that the consumer was hardly the ultimate sovereign of economy but rather was powerless to influence pecuniary institutions. Certainly, business did not make goods for consumers' benefit or at their behest. In addition to restricting production to stabilize prices, business attempted to create demand and to limit choice. As this strategy succeeded, consumers themselves were the foremost products of business. "Judicious and continued expenditures on publicity and the like expedients of salesmanship will result in what may be fairly called a quantity production of customers for the purchase of the goods or services in question," Veblen contended.[49] From a business viewpoint, standardizing customers was a necessary corollary to standardizing goods. To maximize profits, business had to restrict consumers' demands and spending options. The buyer did not rule; he could only acquiesce in purchasing, inexorably constrained in his thinking as well as options. The result was that "the consumer (that is to say the vulgar consumer) furnishes his house, his table, and his person with supplies of standard weight and measure, and he can to an appreciable degree specify his needs and his consumption in the notation of the standard gauge. . . . Idiosyncrasies of individual consumers are required to conform to the uniform gradations imposed upon consumable goods."[50]

Industry produced goods, but business manufactured customers. By the 1920s Veblen was arguing that salesmanship—the process of manufacturing customers—was the characteristic activity of American business, "the end and animating purpose of all business that is done for a price, that is to say business as usual." Salesmanship had replaced workmanship so thoroughly that substantial competition no longer existed among businesses, but only between business and the consuming public, as enterprises fought to gain the public's attention and money by telling half-truths and playing upon its ignorance. For Veblen, selling was "little else than prevarication."[51] The most dangerous and disruptive elements of salesmanship were advertising and the popular press.

Veblen attacked advertising as wasteful for society, industry, and even business itself. Advertising harmed industry by seeking a wasteful monopoly of trade and custom in consumers' habits. Brand loyalty, a form of monopoly in trade, was for Veblen a waste, since the price system guaranteed not the lowest price for the consumer's benefit but the maximum possible profit for the manufacturer. Advertising achieved these "monopolies of custom, prestige, prejudice" by accommodating to prevailing standards of decency and social norms. Advertisers traded in accepted prejudices and half-truths and sold by using irrelevant or unclear arguments rooted in the common culture:

> A declaration of fact, made in the form and with the incidents of taste and expression to which a person is accustomed, will be accepted as authentic and will be acted upon if occasion arises, in so far as it does not conflict with opinions already accepted. . . . A reiteration of the statement is the chief factor in carrying conviction. The truth of such a formulation is a matter of secondary consequence. . . . The aim of the advertiser is to arrest attention and then present his statement in such a manner that it is easily assimilated into the thoughts and habits of the person whose conviction is to be influenced. When this is effectually done a reversal of the conviction so established is a matter of considerable difficulty.[52]

Advertising thus was a cultural institution that succeeded by confirming accepted norms. The products themselves were often wasteful, fraudulent, or destructive. Here Veblen turned to the perennially disreputable patent medicine business for pointed examples, terming them the "organized fabrication of popular conviction."[53] Advertising in fact epitomized business wastefulness in its attempts to divert the consumer's dollar from one product to another. "Each concern must advertise chiefly because the others do," he pointed out. While advertising occasionally provided information of interest to the consumer, most advertisements offered deception, distortion, or irrelevant information. For the consumer, advertising was most often, literally, useless: "It gives vendibility to the seller, but has no utility to the last buyer."[54] Advertising thus cohered with business logic in general, seeking profit rather than use.

Similarly, Veblen criticized the role of the press in the advertising system, arguing that newspapers and magazines disguised their structural connections to business interests and salesmanship. The press, he charged, did not exist to convey information about the public world; it was an instrument of selling, "a vehicle for advertisements. This is its *raison d'être*, as a business proposition, and this decides the lines of its management without material qualification."[55] Instead of serving as a voice of public concern, information, and entertainment, the press unabashedly served business interests, disingenuously proclaiming impartiality. Since publications depended heavily on advertising for revenue, they had to serve business in their news coverage and editorial stances. Although most national publications commonly segregated advertising from editorial content, Veblen argued that, in fact, both the stories and ads promoted business interests and salesmanship. Here he identified the commercial orientations of national publishers like Cyrus Curtis and Frank Munsey and editors Edward Bok and George Horace Lorimer, who built the great magazines—*Ladies' Home Journal, Saturday Evening Post, Collier's,* and others—on probusiness fiction and journalism. Veblen claimed these editors avoided anything critical of business or harmful to the claims of advertisers. "The first duty of an editor," Veblen argued, "is to gauge the sentiments of his readers, and then tell them what they like to believe. . . . His second duty is to see that nothing is said in the news items which may discountenance any claims or announcements made by his advertisers, discredit their standing or good faith, or expose any weakness or deception in any business venture that is or may become a valuable advertiser." Even periodical fiction had a fundamental pecuniary purpose: "it should conduce to a quickened interest in the various lines of services and commodities offered in the advertising pages, and should direct the attention of readers along such lines of investment and expenditure as may benefit the large advertisers particularly. At least it must in no way harm the interests of advertisers."[56]

National magazines did make limited attempts to combat certain forms of commercial excess, as in the *Ladies' Home Journal*'s stand against patent medicines during the 1890s and *Collier's* 1906 exposé of the patent medicine business by Samuel Hopkins Adams. Yet Veblen's critique struck home: he unveiled the decidedly interdependent relationship of editors and advertisers, which has been echoed by critics and scholars through the years.[57] The implication was plain: Dependence on advertising revenue fostered self-censorship. The press would not criticize business interests. Though Veblen always acknowledged that common cultural standards shaped opinion and reinforced existing norms, he feared the repercussions of the absence of a public voice critical of the business regime. The press's reliance on paid space threatened its integrity as an educational resource and imperiled its ability to foster new opinions and ideas. Pervasive salesmanship, Veblen implied, in the end could poison culture.

Until late in his life, few people outside academic circles knew of Veblen's ideas. After his death in 1929, cumulative sales of his ten books totaled

40,000, a modest accounting by any standard.[58] Although the phrase "conspicuous consumption" passed into popular use, his critiques of structural waste, of women's subordinate and symbolic roles, and of business's dominance of consumers did not. Yet his emphasis on efficiency and functionality shaped the articulation of consumer interests for a generation afterward. Consumerist critics of the business system would focus on waste and sabotage, and specifically on its role in proliferating harmful or unnecessarily obsolete goods. Veblen was hardly the first or only critic of waste; both the industrial efficiency movement and the arts and crafts movement, from vastly different perspectives, shared his dislike of business waste. But his formulation, rooted in industrial production, inspired advocates of the ultimate consumer. The consumer movement's crusades to promote greater knowledge of the qualities of goods, to ensure durable and functional products, and to curb excessive and false advertising were fully grounded in Veblen's perspective.

Veblen's ideas on consumption may today seem limited by their distinct lack of interest in forms of human symbol making. As did his targets the neoclassical economists and Karl Marx, Veblen viewed production and consumption as inextricable, with production clearly the important human activity. Along with Marx, Veblen considered production to be the activity that made people distinctively human. But despite his anthropological insights, he never considered the possibility that people used goods not only to enforce social hierarchy but also to establish identity apart from such distinctions. He never could entertain an instinct of consuming similar to that of workmanship, based on creation and use for the ends of life. Moreover, particularly as practiced by women, consuming was a form of labor, essential to the maintenance of home and family. Buying and using commodities, though they embodied the laborers' loss of control in production, still drew on the individual's laboring talents to serve the ends of life.[59]

Veblen also never turned his attention to the daily difficulties of consumption. His interest in technology and industrial systems lay in the interactions of large-scale economic institutions. Perversely, his most famous work on consumption actually paid little attention getting and spending. Yet if, as he argued, production suffered due to business sabotage and sales imperatives, consumption was just as inefficient, due to wasteful practices in business and in the home. It remained for one of Veblen's most famous students to apply his perspective to the economics of daily life and to identify specific difficulties for consumers.

Wesley Clair Mitchell (1874–1948) earned a name as one of the foremost economists and social scientists of his time. Having studied with J. Lawrence Laughlin, John Dewey, and Veblen at the University of Chicago, Mitchell pursued lifelong interests in economic processes and institutions. His explorations of business cycles, efforts in statistical collection, and advocacy of strong governmental economic administration all influenced economic thought and public policy throughout his long career.[60] He first earned national attention in 1913 with *Business Cycles*, a Veblen-influenced study that used extensive empirical evidence to evaluate fluctuations in economies.[61] A founder of "institutional" economics, Mitchell studied interwoven elements of the macroeconomy—businesses, government, currency—yet, unlike many colleagues, he never lost sight of the individual. Implied in the institutionalist outlook was a commitment to managing the economy for social betterment. Advocating strict and open-ended empiricism in investigation, Mitchell shared a deep faith in social science as a tool for improvement throughout his life.[62]

Mitchell adopted a "behavioral" viewpoint, tracking economic activity empirically and charting its organizational and personal implications. He felt strongly that psychology and social relations were integral to economics, and he chided his marginalist peers for ignoring factors that influenced human motivation. "When economic theory has been purified so far that human nature has no place in it," he claimed, "economists become interested perforce in much that lies outside their theoretical field." For Mitchell, economics was less a study of an abstract subject than "a science of human behavior" pragmatically concerned with "how men act."[63] Although his research was mostly built on massive quantities of empirical data, from the outset Mitchell believed the purpose of economics was to aid human welfare through knowledge of the actual decisions, motivations, and actions of people in economic contexts.[64]

Not surprisingly, he viewed consumption as a fundamentally necessary activity. He argued, contrary to the marginalists, that people's motivations and desires were proper subjects of study. In a brief article published the year before *Business Cycles*, Mitchell challenged the conventional economic assumption of "consumer sovereignty" by discussing the limitations on consumers' position in the marketplace. "The Backward Art of Spending Money" was one of the first inquiries into everyday consumption from a pragmatic standpoint. He declared that consumers' position in the economy was largely powerless, and he offered suggestions to address the imperfect conditions of their decision making.[65] He argued that consumption deserved the same detailed analysis regularly accorded to business.[66] Building on Veblen's ideas, Mitchell presented modern consumption as a women's issue because it was almost exclusively women's work through its primacy in households. While he was hardly original in viewing consumption as principally associated with women, he was an early scholar of women's roles within a specifically economic framework, rather than treating consumption as "domestic economy" or "family life."[67] He differed from feminist pioneers of domestic science from Catherine Beecher to Melusina Peirce and Ellen Swallow Richards, but Mitchell's work continued in their traditions.

"The Backward Art" contended that while Americans paid great attention to earning money, most were incompetent in spending it. Both women and men lacked skills in judging and selecting goods and did not even have sufficient knowledge to identify their wants. Mitchell invoked a metaphor of the home as business, a comparison already favored by advertisers. "Ignorance of qualities, uncertainty of taste, lack of accounting, carelessness about prices—faults that would ruin a merchant—prevail in our housekeeping," he wrote. Unlike businessmen, who could plan expenditures and investigate their purchases before buying, consumers spent blindly.[68]

Mitchell contrasted the conditions of spending in the home and in business. Economic theorists viewed consumers as rational profit-seekers, who used their spending to attain their precise desires by making them known through the responsive mechanisms of the market. Economists then held that consumers behaved like businessmen, seeking the best and most for their money and making decisions from a position of equal knowledge and power with others in the marketplace. But Mitchell argued this model was inaccurate: women were ill equipped for their tasks in business terms because consumption in everyday life was highly inefficient. Families did not benefit from the division of labor or economies of scale practiced in industry. Extending the arguments of Charlotte Perkins Gilman, Melusina Peirce, and other reform feminists, Mitchell noted that homemakers performed diverse tasks too numerous for practical or informed decision making: "She must buy milk and shoes, furniture and meat, magazines and fuel, hats and underwear, bedding and disinfectants, medical services and toys, rugs and candy. Surely no one can be expected to possess expert knowledge of the qualities and prices of such varied wares." Moreover, family size thwarted businesslike efficiency. The hand-to-mouth frequency and incremental nature of family consumption, especially for the poor, prohibited scientific testing of goods or the systematic use of labor-saving machinery. Volume purchasing was impractical for most families; thus they forfeited savings from possible economies of scale.[69]

The numerous undivided tasks of homemaking made it virtually impossible for women to organize their labor efficiently. Indeed, the diversity of their tasks kept women from conceiving of homemaking as a profession:

> But the woman must do most of her work at home, amidst the countless interruptions of the household, with its endless calls from children and friends. She cannot divide her duties as a human being so sharply from her duties as a worker. Consequently, her housekeeping does not assume objective independence in her thinking, as an occupation in which she must become proficient. Household management, under the conditions of family life, is not sufficiently differentiated from other parts of the housewife's life to be prosecuted with the keen technical interest which men develop in their trades.[70]

Mitchell declared that, in fact, numerous women became efficient homemakers (in proportions similar to those of men who made successful managers, he noted), but the limitation of consumption to individual families meant that superior home management was never shared communally. "What ability in spending money is developed among scattered individuals, we dam up within the walls of the single household," he pointed out. As long as basic tasks of consumption were not socialized beyond individual families, no gains in efficiency would permanently be won.[71]

Mitchell argued that improving consumption depended on providing consumers with technical knowledge of goods. Apart from recent food and drug reforms, consumers had little objective information about goods or criteria for determining how to best satisfy the family's needs.[72] Again, consumers suffered in comparison with business: a manufacturer could learn more from engineers about his materials "than the housewife could learn from all the living physiologists and psychologists about the scientific laws of bodily and mental development. . . . Hence the housewife's work presents more unsolved problems, is more a matter of guesswork, and cannot in the nature of things be done as well as the work of making and carrying goods." Mitchell called for research in nutritional chemistry and psychology to assist the housewife in making purchasing decisions.[73]

Most important, standards and goals of the family differed from those of business. Consumers had few concrete or universal norms to measure success in their purchasing. While businessmen had a universal principle, profits, through which to judge their actions and decisions, a homemaker's "gains are not reducible to dollars, as are the profits of a business enterprise, but consist in the bodily and mental well-being of her family." Mitchell questioned American society's overwhelming emphasis on pecuniary standards, noting, "Only in the crudest way can subjective experiences of different orders occurring to different individuals be set against each other."[74] Thus, the true interest of consumers lay in identifying as specifically as possible their goals. Neither technical training nor greater socialization and rationalization of consumption's tasks alone would help women identify their needs or promote their happiness. In his most Veblenian vein, Mitchell criticized the pursuit of higher status through spending, especially in extravagance. But he explicitly rejected the moral criticism of indulgence as the fault of an undisciplined working class or a decadent middle class: "Our faults as spenders are not wholly due to wantonness, but largely to broad conditions over which as individuals we have slight control."[75] Arguments over living costs and extravagance had little meaning unless consumers could understand those costs outside of pecuniary terms. Happiness and well-being did not readily translate into dollars. The market was not the measure of society.[76]

Here Mitchell questioned orthodox theories that placed individual experience beyond the realm of economics. In contrast, "The Backward Art" located the process of forming consumer values and making choices at the center of debate. Mitchell thereby rejected marginalist assumptions of rationality among consumers and equity between seller and customer.[77] The irreducible diversity of experience, along with the unsuitability of pecuniary/business standards for family life, made the homemaker's most pressing problem the development of an adequate "philosophy" of spending. "To make money becomes an end in itself; to spend money requires some end beyond the spending," Mitchell contended. The homemaker "must decide what happiness and development mean in concrete terms for her particular husband and children."[78] The rational consumer of marginalist theory was clearly inappropriate; a socially useful, pragmatic, and realistic philosophy would be needed instead.

Mitchell's own pragmatic emphasis made him skeptical of universal aesthetic or functional values for goods. He distrusted overarching prescriptions that were untested by specific studies of spending as it actually took place. Such investigations, similar to those in *Business Cycles*, he could only leave to others. Although his view of the social uses and origins of consumption were derived from Veblen's *Theory of the Leisure Class*, Mitchell did not claim that consumers should follow precepts of spartan functionality or simplicity. For

Mitchell, functionalist criticisms of consumer choices were meaningless because they ignored the contexts in which those choices took place. Critics who attacked consumers' taste, incompetence, or extravagance conveniently ignored the conditions in which these people spent money every day. Consumers needed new values: only scientific expertise, self-knowledge, and experience could develop them. He believed that specific technical problems could be addressed by scientifically trained experts. Mitchell called for the kind of specialized research into household science that the home economics movement was beginning to offer. Women's organizations and magazines could disseminate useful information more successfully, and communities could socialize efficiently many tasks currently performed by individual families, such as cooking, recreation, and hygiene. But no one but the individual could formulate values of consumption, which supported life. For Mitchell, this remained the most important task of consumers and the vital intersection of economics, science, and philosophy. The marketplace might provide goods, but consumers could best determine their own needs.

Although Mitchell never lost interest in the subject, and this article remained one of his best-known pieces, the publication of *Business Cycles* the next year changed his career. No one emerged immediately to take up the challenge of developing the philosophy and the empirical data for a better understanding of consumption. Some advertisers became familiar with the article.[79] Home economists, largely with different training, would embrace the challenge to articulate a professional scientific approach to consumption as women's work. (There would remain, however, an ambivalence toward treating consumption as only women's concern, born of the professional requirements of disinterest and objectivity and the biases against women in the social sciences.) Mitchell's call for greater technical training for consumers would indeed be achieved through doctors of domestic science. "The Backward Art of Spending Money" can be read as an important statement of the ideals of the still fledgling home economics movement. Appropriately enough, the next major analyses of the pragmatic dimensions of consumption came from a home economist, trained in economics.[80]

CONSTRUCTING A THEORY OF CONSUMPTION

One of the first to accept Mitchell's challenge to construct a philosophy of spending and to outline the practical difficulties facing consumers was economist Hazel Kyrk (1886–1957). She taught for many years at the University of Chicago; trained in economics, she developed an institutional and economic approach toward the problems of spending in the family.[81] *A Theory of Consumption* (1923) expanded Veblen's and Mitchell's insights to argue that the processes by which consumers selected and used goods were significant activities not only of the economy but also of everyday life: consumption was essentially a cultural institution. Her work had few precedents, and upon its publication she received the prestigious Hart, Schaffner, and Marx Award for business monographs. Combining economic analysis with pragmatic philosophy, home economics with psychology, *A Theory of Consumption* placed the individual consumer at the intersection of economic, political, and cultural issues. "The term [consumption]," she argued, "carries with it the thought of activities and interests which manifest themselves in wants, and choices on the market. . . . It is this which makes individuals as consumers, significant factors in industrial affairs."[82]

While commentators had linked consumption with morality and aesthetics with moral uplift, Kyrk rejected any single criterion for spending.[83] For Kyrk, consumption involved "almost all the desires and purposes which move men to action." A theory of consumption would necessarily address three major areas: economic activity, the values embedded in action, and the distribution of resources.[84] A proper theory of consumption would link economics, morality, philosophy, and politics. This ambitious agenda reached beyond the scope of her book, but Kyrk nevertheless established the connections between the individual and cultural standards of consumption, on the one hand, and between the consumer and the political and economic system, on the other.

Who were consumers? Kyrk noted that they comprised the general public and "do not constitute a group who can be differentiated and isolated from their fellows." Like a mirage, consumers vanished when observers approached. Kyrk acknowledged that the individual's interest as a consumer was obscured by other identities, and yet "the interests of consumers are definite distinct realities, which may be differentiated from the interests of individuals in their other capacities."[85] Because consumption was primarily a process of making choices, individuals acted as consumers when choosing and spending in the marketplace; their identities as consumers did not necessarily exist outside this context. Thus, for Kyrk, consumers' interests did not depend particularly on improving marketplace regulation (although she by no means advocated a laissez-faire approach to markets) but in increasing and facilitating consumers' choices.

Kyrk argued that studying both constraints on choice and the formation of values was necessary, since traditional economics thus far had failed to provide guidance for consumers or build them adequately into economic theory. She criticized both classical and neoclassical economists for ignoring consumption as an ongoing activity in daily life. Most important for Kyrk, consumers were real people and not theoretical projections:

> These early writers and their latter-day followers recognized consumption as the raison d'être of production, but once having recognized this obvious fact, having assumed wants over against which can be set the niggardliness of nature, economic inquiry ceased. Formally, the consumers' existence was recognized; they were always there, a sort of bottomless pit into which a continuous and ever-increasing stream of commodities must be kept flowing. But the chosen field for investigation was not the consumer's activities, but the organization of effort they necessitated.[86]

She agreed with Mitchell's prior criticisms of marginalists and noted their interpretation of value was ahistorical and abstract, universal for all consumers in all circumstances, and "seemingly divorced from all realities of life."[87] Not only did marginalist theory ignore critical questions of how consumers established values for goods, but it also, in truth, was merely a theory of price, addressing the conditions under which prices proved to be either a barrier or incentive to purchase. Marginalism sought to justify what the traffic bore. Thus, it could not guide consumer choosing.

Choice entailed selecting goods, allocating resources, and most important, testing values. Consumption was a moral activity. Kyrk believed that values should neither be prescribed collectively, as in a socialist economy, nor simply assumed under the guise of individual freedom, as in many liberal nation-states. Both socially and individually, people determined consumer values. Implicit in Kyrk's treatise were beliefs that an important role of citizens was to purchase and use goods, that consumers exercised crucial influence over the direction of society and culture, and that greater understanding of consumer identity would improve the welfare of society as a whole.

Freedom of choice—the ability to meet material needs through the market —was the issue most critical to consumers. But "freedom of choice" entailed more than fifty-seven varieties or a plethora of brands. Under capitalism the consumer enjoyed a formal freedom, since the government exercised little coercion or constraint on purchasing or production. Kyrk acknowledged, "Only in a price-organized society does the consumer have the power of choice and is the process of production even nominally under his control." Since business success depended on creating and meeting demand, consumers generally benefited from capitalistic competition.[88] But Kyrk's study was not a brief for capitalism; consumers hardly enjoyed a perfect choice in that system, despite the economists who anointed them as its theoretical sovereigns. Most important, consumers encountered vast disparities between "formal" and "real" freedom of choice, between the absence of formal or physical constraint and the opportunity and means to choose and spend.[89] "It is possession of purchasing power which gives a positive content to freedom of choice, and which gives the consumer the power to 'live out his individuality,'" Kyrk wrote. "This one economic limitation upon the expression of choices and preferences is so obvious and so keenly felt, that individual freedom in any real sense seems quite formal and negative. Property controls; it is only owners who have real freedom of demand."[90] Like Veblen, Kyrk charged that business was oblivious to the needs of society. Her swipe at marginalism argued that economic inequality affected more than disposable income; those with less could neither influence the market nor make something of themselves with goods. What one could become depended on what one could spend or possess.

The pecuniary system determined conditions of consumption. Like Veblen, Kyrk argued that business attempts to control demand limited the character and content of goods available. Aggressive sales messages surrounded consumers and sought to break down their resistance to purchasing. By contrast, consumers had little control over what they could buy: freedom of choice often meant a decision whether or not to choose:

> Certainly the individual consumer under such a system feels that his freedom of action is only exercised upon terms laid down by the producer, and that the latter controls the situation. In many cases the consumer cannot wait nor can he boycott the goods offered. He cannot expect to have his individual tastes consulted in details of workmanship or minor matters of quality. Further, even if he should make up his mind to enforce his own will there may not be adequate machinery for giving voice to his protest. The producer may be unknown, remote, or difficult to access, and the consumer's infrequent and weak protest could only reach him as transmitted through a long chain of middlemen.[91]

Kyrk admitted that buyers' resistance could effectively nullify business manipulation. Consumers' habits were uncertain and unpredictable, their desires irrational, their attention fragmentary; the complexity and scope of strategies to control and sway consumers testified to the difficulty of compelling them to spend. But generally, she maintained, consumers held but few cards.

The profit system itself further disadvantaged consumers. Producers

foisted shoddy and inferior materials, frauds, and adulterated goods on unsus-
pecting buyers. Taking a leaf from Veblen and Progressive-Era muckrakers,
Kyrk charged that the profit system encouraged substandard wares, whose
cheapness made them exceptionally profitable. The boundaries blurred easily
between outright deception, adulteration, substitution, and selling dubious
goods through irrelevant claims, such as patent medicines.[92] Kyrk argued that
the producer's ignorance was far more dangerous than the buyer's: "Producers are not necessarily moral, aesthetic or hygienic experts; they have no
special qualifications to pass upon the qualities of commodities; they cannot
speak with authority as to what is good and what is bad." Nevertheless, she
charged, the legal system allowed businesses to make extravagant claims for
their products despite that ignorance.[93] Kyrk echoed "The Backward Art of
Spending Money" in describing consumers' own disadvantages in the marketplace: ignorance, lack of criteria, overwhelming varieties of goods. To compensate, buyers often resorted to price as the index of quality. In turn, producers often felt compelled to maintain high prices to keep customers who
valued quality. Thus, prices were often artificially elevated. Buying by price
was perhaps worse than complete ignorance. Since consumers' ideals of
health, convenience, preference, and pleasure were so vague, regulation at
best could only supplement consumer protection. The rest depended on
consumers themselves.[94]

Consumers' satisfaction depended foremost on having specific criteria for
goods and firm determination to see those criteria met. This self-awareness,
Kyrk argued, depended in turn on the values that shaped consumers' behavior and choices.[95] She rejected the traditional utilitarian or hedonistic
calculus of both classical and neoclassical economics, asserting that consumers chose by far more complex criteria than strict rationality or the simple
pursuit of pleasure. Borrowing from John Dewey, Kyrk stressed that all values
were instrumental, affirming that particular objects or concepts were good
for specific things. They were never abstract but were "qualities of our world
as real as the sense qualities," grounded in social experience and habit. Consumers, then, were of necessity pragmatic, continually experimenting, expressing, and seeking values in their choosing.[96]

People did not choose randomly but by criteria, similar to Veblen's standards of decency, that emerged from a historical process in which social
groups asserted control over the individual. Economists, she thought, incorrectly focused on consumers as isolated individuals and ignored the social
process that produced culture, which nurtured standards of value. Consumer
"standards" varied, "not at haphazard among individuals, but by classes, by

countries and by periods of time."[97] As prescriptions for behavior, they projected neither an ideal state nor a bare minimum level of subsistence but the "norm" of every group, the expectation that every member felt compelled to meet. Penalties for failure—ostracism, shame, isolation—were too great to risk.[98] Standards however, were dynamic, changing over time as groups experimented with luxuries and eventually adopted them as necessities.[99] Changes in living standards occurred much more frequently in the modern era; the erosion of traditional ways, the growth of communication, the rise of science, and capitalism's expansion of the realm of choice all encouraged consumers to experiment more than in times past. Thus, the modern consumer was perforce a pragmatic investigator, whose purchases were directed at solving problems.[100]

Kyrk's theory ended with an outline of a high standard of living, an attempt to theorize a philosophy of ideal consumption. Arguing that a high standard would promote "individual and social well-being" and require greater resources and an increased number of essential goods, Kyrk concluded that the consumer's real freedom of choice would depend on improving the quality and range of goods.[101] She called for extending such freedom and linked choice in consumption to political freedom, arguing that no attempt to dictate or legislate better consumer standards could be successful in the American political system. A higher standard of living, realized in increased choice, would improve individual tastes and self-expression. Freedom of choice for consumers enabled individual self-determination; ultimately, the true purpose of consumption was freedom.[102]

Kyrk's emphasis on freedom of choice for consumers was the distinctive element of her theory, but it was abstract, with no particular form. She insisted that most consumers required greater discretionary income and purchasing power, but she did not discuss how they could achieve those ends, or even what consumers might accomplish with them. Perhaps most troubling, she claimed that consumers needed practical guidance in the actual selection of goods, but she could offer few new standards. She left the question of freedom of choice undeveloped, much as the marginalist economists whom she criticized.

Ironically, the economists most interested in choice as the basis of economic activity founded a libertarian strain of economics that advocated less, and not more, regulation of the economy for the benefit of consumers or anyone else. Led by Kyrk's colleague Frank Knight, such economists viewed politicians and the political process as the worst possible guardians of individual economic interests. Knight and his students developed a theory of economics that advocated maximizing the free choice of "responsible individuals" and ultimately explained decision making in political and public life by analogies to market decisions.[103] In the process they rehabilitated the laissez-faire market-driven economics that Kyrk criticized.

A Theory of Consumption advocated a philosophy of consumption that relied on a carefully worked out set of values aimed to maximize freedom of choice. But although Kyrk knew that people would determine such values through experimentation and error, and that consumers needed protection beyond the wisdom gained thorough experience, A Theory of Consumption falls short of any political analysis or even context. Barely acknowledging the liberal assumptions of her theory, Kyrk could not criticize or transcend them. Beyond noting that the American political climate fostered freedom of choice, Kyrk's essay did not evaluate the social, political, or even bureaucratic framework in which consumption took place. Her later work, emphasizing consumers and family life, would begin that inquiry. Solutions to dilemmas of purchasing power, the need to educate purchasers to their interests as consumers, and the enforcement of measures protecting consumers against fraud and deception all required a political articulation and the recognition that the political sphere was the place for consumer interests to be framed and realized. That political analysis, fragmentary and partial in the 1920s New Era, would wait until the Depression.

CONCLUSION

By the late 1920s, Veblen, Mitchell, and Kyrk were joined by other social scientists who were interested in the consumer's place in the social order as well as economics.[104] With Veblen's example, a few institutionalist economists made consumer "interests" a focus of their economic analysis.[105] Others, most notably sociologists Helen and Robert Lynd and the economist Elizabeth Ellis Hoyt, adopted an anthropologically inspired approach to consumption. For the Lynds and Hoyt, consumption was a focal point of contemporary American culture—the folkways of a diverse society recently wrenched into modernity by rapid urbanization and industrialization.[106] For yet others, such as economist Paul Douglas and the social activists Wilbur Phillips and James P. Warbasse, consumption not only characterized the modern economy but also held the key to greater social justice.[107] Their advocacy of planning, socializing resources, and most important, consumer cooperatives—all approaches rooted in European social democracy—sought to adapt modern economic systems for maximum benefit to the mass of citizens. Despite the hopes of public influence entertained by these writers, most discussions of consumption generally remained within academic discourse. These writings all revealed their debts to Veblen, notably his cultural perspective on consumption in society and his advocacy of efficiency and utility.

A sketchy but discernible portrait of consumption had thus emerged in American social thought by the 1920s. From Veblen came the idea that consumption served as the principal means of social emulation and status, the symbolic substitutes for war and conquest. He asserted that consumers were victims of a destructively wasteful business system that produced shoddy and unnecessary goods while turning consumers themselves into products. Finally, Veblen offered a caustic and symbolic account of women as the ultimate consumers. Once the object of early economic exchange, women were now the principal agents and arbiters of wasteful consumption of useless goods, the symbols as well as the forces behind consumption. Wesley Mitchell asserted that consumers could not be competent, independent judges of goods without drastic changes in their knowledge and practices. American women's lack of preparation and training as consumers threatened the health and well-being of their families. He argued that consumers required reliable, scientifically sound information about the contents and qualities in goods, along with a strong sense of the important purposes of consumption, a philosophy of purchasing. Hazel Kyrk stressed that consumption was ultimately an expression of human values in economic choices. People acted as consumers primarily in their choosing. They developed preferences and habits as much according to cultural expectations as economic constraints.

These thinkers firmly grounded consumption in the particulars of time, place, and culture and shunned the idea of timeless economic "laws" as abstract, inaccurate, and insufficient to explain actual social behavior. All emphasized that consumers were engaged in an ongoing pragmatic and instrumental determination of values and preferences. They stressed that consumption was an evolutionary refinement of knowledge and skills, based on individual needs. They implied that consumption was a key ingredient of individual self-expression. They all argued that pecuniary values were insufficient, if not antithetical, to a useful approach to consumption. The marketplace could not be a universal measure of the good.

Finally, all stated explicitly that consumption was made in the United States as women's work, although none fully explored the implications of spending in an economy run by men. While Mitchell and Kyrk argued for its significance, consumption in fact did not receive the same sustained analysis or respect as other economic issues.[108] In addition, those who did analyze

consumption often minimized its crucial distinctiveness due to their professional dedication to scientific objectivity and the attempt to legitimize the
subject by molding it along scientific lines. While Mitchell, Kyrk, and Veblen
all argued that consumption was not fully comparable to business, they offered no other point of comparison, and analysts of the field would adopt
business metaphors, until they were challenged by new comparisons in the
Depression that made clear consumption's connection to citizenship. These
analysts lacked a political perspective to explain or redress consumer vulnerability. While noting that consumers were the public, they did not elaborate on the connection, and they did not establish a firm link between the
American political system and the interests of consumers. The modern consumer movement arose in the late 1920s because it successfully amplified
Veblen's line of analysis with practical useful information and a political
perspective, persuasively argued in plain language. To this emergent movement we now turn.

CHAPTER 5

THE SCIENCE OF PURCHASING

Marketing is an attempt to mold the consumer's valuations, to influence the importance which he attaches to things—in other words, to do the very thing that religion and education endeavor to do. . . . Well may we ask whether it is wise to permit our valuations, our philosophy, our desires to be molded by men who are guided by no higher aim than to make a profit for themselves or for their employers.[1]

When you contemplate the eastern sky ablaze with chewing gum, the northern with tooth-brushes and underwear, the western with whiskey, and the southern with petticoats, the whole heavens brilliant with monstrously flirtatious women, when you glance at magazines in which a rivulet of text trickles through meadows of automobiles, baking powders, corsets and kodaks, you begin to accumulate a sense of the disastrous incompetence of the ultimate consumer.[2]

Yet no matter how much money a consumer may have, he cannot buy knowledge with it. . . . Pecuniary civilization is making morons of consumers as 2 billions of advertising a year testify only too eloquently.[3]

Who wants a tub of boric acid?[4]

Thorstein Veblen, Wesley Mitchell, and Hazel Kyrk offered important insights on the limits consumers faced under corporate capitalism while arguing that spending and acquisition reflected American cultural mores. However, their hopes for a science of consumption would not bear fruit until the late 1920s. The first comprehensive approach to consumers' problems from a specifically Veblenian standpoint came from Stuart Chase, an accountant turned economist, and by Frederick J. Schlink, a physicist and engineer. Together they wrote the best-selling *Your Money's Worth* (1927), termed by Robert S. Lynd "the *Uncle Tom's Cabin* of the abuses of the consumer," and they created the first independent product-testing organization to operate solely on the consumer's behalf. The consumer movement emerged in their book's wake. Though consumers had organized since the nineteenth century, particularly in the Progressive Era, to achieve specific political and economic goals, *Your Money's Worth* marked a founding moment and manifesto for a loosely organized but powerful movement, which imbued consumption with both the rights and the aura of citizenship.[5]

Although buyers have sought protection and regulation in markets throughout history, the Progressive Era witnessed the first sustained efforts to protect consumers in the United States. Most significant was the 1906 Pure Food and Drug Act, which provided minimal regulations and enforcement in the production and marketing of some foods and medicine.[6] At the same time, as part of a broad uprising against concentrated economic power, popular movements using consumer pressure—most prominently the National Consumers' League under Florence Kelley—used buyers' pressure to compel manufacturers and merchants to remedy exploitative labor conditions.[7] These important interventions laid the groundwork for both government protection and activism in behalf of consumers. Consumers deserved goods that were safe and whose production did not immiserate others. But what were desirable characteristics of goods in themselves?

Answers to that question emerged from an unlikely source. During World War I, the federal government assumed control of the national economy on an unprecedented scale. The War Industries Board centralized production in key sectors to speed output and increase efficiency. The federal government now oversaw industrial production and purchasing, regulated intermediate and retail pricing in industries essential to the war effort, and took control of wages, hours, and working conditions. The streamlined output from American factories ultimately proved crucial to the Allied victory, yet efforts to coordinate production met frustrating obstacles. It was often difficult to interchange parts, measurements, or procedures between firms; interfirm production foundered on an array of dissimilar or incompatible processes.[8] Thoughtful observers saw a clear need for planning and cooperation if industry were ever to outstrip current levels of production or adequately function in the event of another war.

One such observer was Herbert Hoover, the head of the wartime Food Administration.[9] In 1920, as president of the Federated American Engineering Societies, he chaired a pan-industrial committee to investigate waste in production. The resulting report helped to generate the standardization movement within American manufacturing. Advocating cooperation and interchange among industries, proponents of standardization sought higher productivity and efficiency through the adoption of common terms, units, and techniques.[10] Spearheading the movement was the American Engineering Standards Committee (AESC), which resided in the National Bureau of Standards.[11] The bureau had been established in 1901 as the government authority over weights, measures, and physical constants, but it had gradually expanded its activities to assist American industries in solving production problems, especially regarding testing materials and ingredients. According to its official historian, "little that was measurable in the home, in the market, in commerce, industry, science, or Government but had at one time or another become a subject of investigation at the Bureau, and as often as not a sustained investigation."[12] The AESC served as an information clearinghouse and helped industries prepare voluntary standards for its members. By the late 1920s some 365 organizations had affiliated with the committee, including 140 trade associations, to generate and promote universal standards.[13] By 1929 the organization had over 10,000 approved and adopted specifications on file, a stunning reorientation of American industry.[14]

Additionally, the bureau made modest efforts to involve retail consumers in the movement in a series of guides to standardization within the home. These pamphlets illustrated uniform measurement and scientific efficiency for technically untrained consumers.[15] *Measurements for the Household* (1915) comprehensively surveyed the role of standards and measurements throughout the home, from gas and electric meters to kitchen tools. The circular explained scientific techniques in lay terms and dispensed practical advice, such as ordering in specific quantities rather than by "a can" or "a box." The bureau argued that insisting on buying by quantity offered a stable indicator of value. Familiarity with measurements would protect consumers from misleading prices and deceptive packaging and offer protection from faulty home equipment and wasted energy in heating, lighting, and plumbing.[16] The bureau, in essence, urged consumers to adopt scientific practices and follow the rational methods of industry. Endorsed by Edward Bok of the *Ladies' Home Journal*, it was far and away the most successful pamphlet circulated by the bureau. Homemakers sent in over a half million requests for a handy card with a table of common household measures and weights.[17] The success of this first venture led to additional pamphlets on safety and proper materials in the home. None offered any specific brand-name recommendations, although they did prescribe desirable designs and types. This policy of silence protected manufacturers and merchants, but it proved a burden to individuals untrained in technical issues. Consumers could acquire most retail products only by brand, and consequently the bureau's commercially neutral policies severely limited its effectiveness. Clearly, if consumers were going to profit fully from scientific testing and specifications, someone would have to name names, identify products by brand, and otherwise connect the science of the testing laboratory to the pragmatic decisions of the grocery, department store, and pharmacy. One bureau physicist who worked on these circulars was prepared to do just that. His name was Frederick John Schlink (1891–1995).

Schlink grew up in Peoria, Illinois, the son of a German immigrant merchant.[18] At the University of Illinois he earned a master's degree in engineering in 1917, with a thesis on high-tonnage precision scales. His entire scientific career centered on measurement, testing, and the properties of devices and materials under stress. He worked for a number of firms, including Western Electric (he helped develop the rotary telephone dial) and Firestone, where he supervised measuring and testing instruments. Most significant, he spent six years at the National Bureau of Standards from 1913 to 1919, where he served as technical assistant to director Samuel Stratton and contributed to "Measurements for the Household." There Schlink learned the complex web of industries, corporations, trade associations, and government agencies involved in standardization. From Stratton he also learned rapidly to sift and distill great quantities of technical data and to route and answer a heavy volume of correspondence from the military, government, and businesses. When bureau physicist Paul Agnew became executive director of the AESC in 1921, he hired Schlink as his assistant. For the next ten years, Agnew and Schlink helped direct the standardization movement during its greatest growth and influence.[19]

As assistant secretary of the AESC, Schlink devoted himself to publicizing the benefits of standards and the advantages of cooperation among competitors. He edited the AESC bulletin and circulated data among AESC members, including estimates of savings in money, safety, and time generated by standardization.[20] As a liaison between government and business, the AESC promoted "simplified practice" in manufacturing, which Schlink defined as the "elimination of unnecessary variety of types, forms, sizes, ranges, capacities, qualities, etc. of materials or manufactured products." The AESC's other principal task involved helping draft specifications for products and processes. These constituted precise qualitative descriptions of ingredients, components, and characteristics to be used as the formula for their fabrication, performance, and purchasing.[21]

The little discussion that the standardization movement afforded consumers cast them only as passive beneficiaries of savings and efficiency.[22] However, Schlink's interest in measurements and materials ideally suited him to thinking about the home. He began applying to his own interest in consumers the knowledge and data he had accumulated in daily contacts with manufacturers, engineers, and businessmen. With Agnew's assistance, he pressed the case within the AESC for standards for consumer goods and publicized the benefits of standards for consumers.[23] Agnew used his own position as secretary to prod AESC members to pay more attention to these issues. Agnew and Schlink established collaborations with other groups, notably the American Home Economics Association and the government's Bureau of Home Economics, to develop consumer goods standards. Early projects concerned refrigerators and bed sheets.[24] Without Agnew's support, it is unlikely that Schlink would have been able to promote even basic consumer interests in the standardization movement.[25]

Schlink took up Wesley Mitchell's challenge to modernize consumption with professional expertise and socialized resources. He spoke and wrote urging consumers to adopt scientific business practices. Standards promoted increased quality of production, interchangeable parts, and lower prices, all of which made "the best available to the many."[26] At this early stage Schlink believed that the interests of consumers were aligned fully with those of producers. The marketplace under capitalism was the consumer's best source of protection from shoddy and harmful merchandise. But within a short time, he abandoned his beliefs that consumers were well served by the existing business practices. He had been with the AESC a little more than two years when he made an acquaintance that would change his life and his views. His decade-long collaboration with Stuart Chase would propel questions of consumer interest fully into public discourse.

Son of an established Boston accountant, Chase (1888–1985) grew up in and outside of Boston, and throughout his life Chase remained attached to small-town values of community. He received his degree from Harvard in 1910 and spent the next decade working as an accountant before embarking on a long career writing on political and economic subjects for popular magazines.[27] As a young man, he sympathized with the romantic aspects of socialism; his wife, Margaret, and he spent their honeymoon living among unemployed workers seeking jobs. It was an early foray into the anthropology of the underclass.[28] The war's restrictions on wages shifted Chase's attention to the problems of middle-class buyers, such as the cost of living and household budgeting.[29] Like Schlink, his technical training informed his interest in the daily problems of getting and spending. By the war's end, Chase was working for the Federal Trade Commission, investigating scandalous charges of monopoly and profiteering by major meatpacking firms that supplied American forces in Europe. When Chase uncovered damaging information about the packing trust, he was fired.[30] Working as an economist in New York, he began his journalistic career in earnest. He made the acquaintance of Veblen,

Dewey, and other intellectuals who would greatly influence his thinking; both Veblen and Wesley Mitchell were important influences on Chase's approach to economic questions. In New York he also befriended Paul Agnew, who most likely introduced him to Fred Schlink.[31]

The pair met sometime in 1924 when Chase was at work on his first major book, a survey of wastes in production, manpower, natural resources, and consumption in industrial society. Taken with the subject, Schlink offered his friend data, evidence, and anecdotes on wasteful practices from the AESC's own voluminous files.[32] The two were compatible collaborators. Schlink, who was somewhat shy and retiring, found the perfect foil for his interests in the more outgoing and well connected Chase; indeed, Schlink preferred to write with partners throughout his career. Chase, in turn, had his eyes opened wide by a torrent of information, insights, and business connections. They both excelled at relating complex technical issues accessibly in lay terms, and they both could enliven economic abstractions with everyday examples. Their shared pragmatic outlook made them ideal proponents of new approaches to consumption.

Chase's book *The Tragedy of Waste* (1925) took a Veblenian tour of production in America, using the Hoover committee's report as a road map. Chase highlighted tremendous wastes in industry due to manpower shortages, unemployment, strikes, and technical inefficiency. He charged that industry and agriculture wasted up to 50 percent of the labor invested in production and squandered nearly as great an amount of natural resources simply through poor planning, technical ineptitude, and the excesses of competition.[33] Chase laid the blame straight at the door of capitalism's unrestrained pursuit of short-term profits. Along with the familiar Veblenian contrast of engineering and business, Chase borrowed R. H. Tawney's condemnation of the "acquisitive society," where rights of property superseded all basic human needs and justified a grossly unequal distribution of wealth. Chase found it appalling that industrial practice sanctioned restrictions on production, underemployment, and life below a minimum standard of decency for half the population. He leveled these indictments from Veblen's perspective but added anecdotal detail and illustrative figures to ground an abstract analysis in vivid everyday terms. While *The Tragedy of Waste* lacked Veblen's theoretical verve and corrosive tongue, Chase more than compensated with lively prose and telling examples that showed what waste meant in everyday human terms.[34]

Not surprisingly, he found consumer goods to be a chief source of waste. He argued that 8 million workers wasted their labor on manufacturing and selling harmful, specious, and unnecessary products. He termed such waste "illth," borrowing from John Ruskin. The antithesis of wealth, "illth" contributed nothing to either physical or psychological well-being. Narcotics, patent medicines, crime, commercial vice, quackery, and adulteration all represented illth's most harmful presence in the economy.[35] Chase's argument rested on a moral judgment of what was truly "necessary" to meet human needs and wants, yet he took pains to avoid simple utilitarian concerns. He included as primary needs not just the bare essentials of food, shelter, and clothing, but also love, recreation, communication, worship, government, expressive forms of culture, health, and sexuality. Waste only emanated in those classes of goods tainted by adulteration or shrouded in aggressive salesmanship.[36] As long as he claimed an "objective" treatment of illth, Chase inevitably passed judgment on activity which society had decided was a matter of the individual's choice. Nevertheless, he insisted on describing illth because such issues were seldom raised, particularly in the 1920s New Era economy.[37] Illth embodied the inequality and misery caused and aggravated by the competitive system. If competitive society had brought true equality or happiness to most people, no analysis of illth would have been necessary or plausible:

> If all consumers were reasonably well educated, if all had roughly equal purchasing power in the market, if the goods and services offered for sale were free from adulteration and defect, it might be impertinent to make inquiry at all into human wants. One might accept what the consumer demanded as the real criterion. But the consumers are not educated for their own protection against deleterious goods, they have not equal purchasing strength in the market, and are thus led to buy cheap imitations of the goods held by their economic superiors; adulteration and quackery are rampant, the modern advertiser has developed a technique of artificial stimulation which would make Cleopatra blush; and finally the very number and complexity of goods for sale today, make it impossible for the consumer to test and value what he buys. He must, in most instances, take somebody's word for it—and three times out of four it is the advertiser's word. In these circumstances perhaps our inquiry loses something of its impertinence.[38]

Thus Chase challenged the rational economic man enshrined in Adam Smith and rejuvenated in marginalism. Economic value might emanate from consumers, but since manufacturers did not produce uniformly acceptable goods, consumer choices were neither equal nor free.

Chase shared Veblen's view that society could overcome waste only through technocratic planning and collective control of productive resources. His analysis was too general and moderate to call for, let alone inspire, a Veblenian uprising of engineers. Even so, it pointed him in a new direction, laying the groundwork for a full analysis of consumption and consumers. In the aftermath of *The Tragedy of Waste*, Chase and his new collaborator Fred Schlink turned their full attention to spending in everyday life.

YOUR MONEY'S WORTH

The Tragedy of Waste brought Chase moderate notice. Emboldened by its success, he worked on a new study with Schlink examining the difficulties, frustrations, and powerlessness of modern consumers. Their jointly authored *Your Money's Worth* (1927) was a full-scale exposé of consumer exploitation through inefficient production and distribution, defective and dangerous products, and fraudulent advertising.[39] Its blunt protest against the practices and conditions of the consumer marketplace made it a best seller. With grim wit and striking anecdotes *Your Money's Worth* highlighted the many ways in which consumers were duped and denied the satisfaction promised by advertisers and assumed by economists and New Era boosters. *Your Money's Worth* portrayed consumption as an important everyday task that many people increasingly found difficult to perform. The authors underscored that as prosperity increased, ironically, individuals found more, and not fewer, obstacles to satisfaction in getting and spending.[40]

Pundits and politicians of the 1920s praised industry for the boom economy that seemed to increase material abundance for the masses. Chase and Schlink turned the narrative of progress on its head.[41] Modernity, in their view, was the source and not the solution of everyday difficulty in purchasing; modern consumers were alienated from direct knowledge of things. The transition from rural villages to a modern urban industrial society altered the fabric of social relationships and permanently changed the conditions under which people made, understood, and used goods. Mass production and bureaucratic organizations brought about a new consumer affluence but also made it virtually impossible for people to know what they were buying; people lacked firsthand experience making or using simple goods. In the local economies of the nineteenth century, relatively few goods were available that were not manufactured nearby; both economic value and satisfaction depended on the personal relations and community standards among makers, merchants, and customers. Moreover, nineteenth-century consumers purchased relatively few goods, and the household production required of women taught them to know and judge accurately the finished goods they did purchase. By contrast, the modern consumer encountered industrially produced goods shipped over great distances from uncertain origins. With the erosion of the communal, face-to-face basis of commerce, consumers were at a disadvantage. Whether in the kitchen or parlor, consumers did not necessarily know who made their goods or what was in them.[42] With an increasing number of products for sale, consumers were handicapped in judging composition, performance, or value save through the bitter experience of trial and error. They knew less and less about more and more.[43]

At the heart of *Your Money's Worth* stood a compelling image borrowed from Lewis Carroll: "We are all Alices in a Wonderland of conflicting claims, bright promises, fancy packages, soaring words, and almost impenetrable ignorance."[44] The commercial marketplace was not simply unreliable or incoherent but also positively surreal. Consumers were unwitting if not unwilling guests in a mysterious and illogical realm. The consumer market seemed an alluring arena promising universal pleasure but delivering confusion, contradiction, and frustration.[45] Like Alice, consumers possessed imminent common sense but little knowledge or real power. Strikingly, the Alice of *Your Money's Worth* resembled the childlike Mrs. Consumer enshrined in advertising lore—incessantly curious and ultimately dependent. But if advertisers trusted themselves to guide the consumer, Chase and Schlink told Alice she was on her own. Ultimately, the consumer's interest depended on making her independent of the March Hares on Madison Avenue and the Mad Hatters of magazines and shops.

If material modernity had made consumers ignorant, business practices kept them in thrall. Intense competition among firms directly affected consumers, who faced an onslaught of salesmanship. "The consumer is under mounting pressure, directed by ever increasing astuteness, to buy, buy, buy—while very few sources are offered him whereby he may use intelligent selection in his buying," Chase and Schlink wrote. These business pressures begat a host of modern plagues: pesky door-to-door canvassers, garish billboards that ruined the natural landscape, promotions and offers everywhere, and a deafening roar of sales talk that threatened to drown out all other conversation and disturb citizens at home and out of doors. Most troubling, individuals were virtually powerless against organized industries intent on capturing their dollars:

> In the face of the new competition, utterly disorganized, with no defense except a waning quality of common sense, the ultimate consumer makes his blundering way; a moth about a candle. To talk of his bargaining power

is to talk about a non-alcoholic America. There is no such thing. He can break a business, but only when a rival stimulates him into breaking it. . . . He is sunk in an indiscriminate sea of door-knockers and other things; he grabs as the strings are pulled, but too often grabs only to find sand and ashes in his hand.[46]

Not surprisingly, Madison Avenue was the chief culprit. Advertisers kept consumers ignorant and inundated them with misleading information. "The ultimate consumer is buried under tons of advertising matter," Chase and Schlink claimed, "and shot this way and that as the sluice gates of distributive pressure open and close."[47] Advertisers ran a "Mad Tea Party" of claims, counterclaims, and attention-getting devices, instead of using their powerful tools of publicity to impart factual information about products' ingredients and performance. *Your Money's Worth* documented the principal crimes of advertising: false labeling and misleading and deceptive claims of performance. Chase and Schlink noted that such practices were endemic not only to the disreputable arena of patent medicine but also to soaps, solvents, baking powder, radio speakers, insecticides, textiles, pharmaceuticals, and other prosaic items and respectable industries. More than merely misinforming people, such claims often endangered consumers' health from harmful or adulterated ingredients.[48]

Equally dangerous was advertising's pandering to modern Americans' fragile sense of self. Chase and Schlink charged that ad men used envy, shame, and fear to keep consumers in a perpetual state of agitated anxiety. Advertising thus dwelled upon personal and psychic needs that few products could address, let alone fulfill. Advertising too often played shamelessly on emotions, a province that by rights stood outside commerce altogether.[49] "Advertising being the able technique that it is today," the authors wrote, "it is possible to take simple goods, such as soap or cereals, and surround them with a halo of characteristics which are non-existent, or of no consequence, but which sound like galleons from Cathay." By avoiding factual discussions of empirical data, advertisers conveniently ignored how competing goods were often more alike than different. Thus advertising offered little meaningful aid.[50]

Such sales messages bred unreal expectations. By training individuals to expect a happier social life from their purchases, advertising made claims that no product could meet. *Your Money's Worth* underscored this point in critiquing the campaigns for Listerine mouthwash. Consumers might be swayed by claims that Listerine cured the fictional disease of "halitosis" and would improve their social lives, but at best they received only a poor disinfectant, marked up 15,000 percent.[51] Advertising misled as well by vague language and irrelevant reasoning such as embodied in testimonials. Babe Ruth's selling cigarettes or Queen Marie of Romania's endorsing a clock undermined common sense and conveyed that scientific experts on clocks and cigarettes had little to say about these products. Agencies, such as Famous Names, Inc., existed to provide celebrities who were willing to endorse products for a fee, which thus completely destroyed the presumption of voluntary endorsement at the heart of testimonials.[52]

The authors indicted the branded goods system for perpetrating waste, as ad men sought to overthrow "that keen price competition which usually accompanies the sale of simple, known materials, and to build up a monopoly based on unknown quantities, governed by ghostly and magical laws." They quoted an agency advertisement that claimed, "The object of advertising is to TAKE IT OUT OF COMPETITION, that it will no longer be compared but will be accepted by the buyer."[53] If business traditionally defended brand-name advertising as giving the consumer convenience and reliability, Chase and Schlink directly charged just the opposite—that brands *undermined* consumer choice. Brand-name products were not necessarily uniform and reliable, they claimed; proprietary formulas changed constantly, and testing revealed enough variance in products to question their overall uniformity. Chase and Schlink argued that most brands of a given type were essentially the same. Proliferation of similar items that did not compete on a price or performance basis actually made consumer choice more difficult. Ignorant of ingredients, production, or performance, consumers relied on price to judge goods, and advertising undermined consumers' ability to judge differently. Yet *Your Money's Worth* demonstrated no intrinsic links between cost and quality and argued that consumers often paid much more for articles marginally better, and frequently worse, than much cheaper alternatives. Fancy packaging and deliberate markups deceived buyers who were unable to tell the shoddy from the superior.[54] Gaudy styles and deceptive packaging further made it difficult to test prices and quantity and diverted attention from performance, composition, and price.[55] Advertising thus ensured that consumers could not trust their senses.

The authors of *Your Money's Worth* took pains to explain that the marketplace as a whole provided many guarantees of quality and safety in products. They blamed advertising's failings on the need to divert competition from the issue of price. That need drove the promotion of spurious distinctions and the shrouding of quality in meaningless claims:

Probably the greater part of branded merchandise now sold is untouched by quackery so far as the physical product goes. But in the confusion of sales pressure, quackery tends constantly to come into the picture by reason of inflated and technically unwarranted claims. Meanwhile the temptation is great to adulterate, cheapen, weaken or change the quality of the basic product. The consumer is too bewildered to ever be the wiser. He has long since been de-educated to the point where he has ceased to know things by their real names.[56]

As symbols of social status, and as influences on self-image and self-worth, products could and did serve an important place in people's lives. Chase and Schlink professed no quarrel with the psychological aspects of consumer goods, a point that their numerous critics ignored. "Man does not live by bread alone," they conceded. "Mystery and wonder are implicit in his psychological make-up. But do we want it in soup, plaster, wall board, soap, fertilizers and bug killers?"[57] Consumers did not have to invest themselves in *all* of their possessions, as advertisers urged. *Your Money's Worth* implied that each individual had to determine his or her own hierarchy of values. Psychological satisfaction would likely emanate from goods that were most invested with personal significance. By assuring consumers that some commodities were totems and others just tools, Chase and Schlink urged their readers to claim independence from the market. Consumers needed to make meanings for themselves. To do so, they needed accurate scientific information in order to spend successfully.

Where could consumers find accurate and unbiased information? A model did exist for satisfactory shopping and spending, derived from the very businesses that defrauded consumers on a daily basis. Business and governments fulfilled their needs by purchasing on the basis of standards and specifications. They defined their needs exactly and stated them in impartial, universally understood terms. Manufacturers competed to meet their demands as cheaply as possible, without reliance on subjective advertising appeals. Schlink had estimated that the government saved $100 million using standards.[58] What worked for large organizations could also benefit consumers. Competition would be limited to the level of price and would eliminate fraud and poor quality.[59] Standards would perform true public service by equalizing relationships among consumers, manufacturers, and retailers. Consumers would need no longer depend on another party with a financial stake in their ignorance.

Yet standards and specifications were only available to large-scale purchasers, and individuals could scarcely afford testing and experimentation on a full range of everyday goods. *Your Money's Worth* revealed that the government already gathered important consumer information in the Department of Agriculture's Bureau of Home Economics, state agricultural extension stations, and most important, the Bureau of Standards. Public dissemination of test results that were already in the bureau's files could increase consumers' knowledge of thousands of goods. As policy, the government kept the results anonymous and restricted access to those organizations that requested the tests, but Chase and Schlink argued forcefully that consumers had the same rights under law to those taxpayer-funded results as corporate citizens of the republic.[60] The consumer was the public.

The authors concluded with a call for consumer skepticism and activism. Consumers could safeguard their own interests only through vigilance and investigation. Chase and Schlink called for consumers to question their merchants, to complain to local and congressional officials, to encourage colleges and high schools to test goods, to cultivate severe skepticism and antagonism toward sales claims and advertising, to manufacture simple products for themselves when necessary, and to organize community groups to test products and share information. Most of all, they argued that consumers had to take matters into their own hands and not rely on manufacturers, merchants, or advertisers on their behalf. Only by such activism could consumers secure what they wanted because only then would businesses find it necessary to provide it.[61] While such a program of activism would demand time and effort, the authors contended that it was the only way for people to get true satisfaction from the marketplace.

Only with collective resources could consumers stand up to business. They needed experts to cull the considerable information already available and an organization to voice their interests. That enterprise would require professional scientists and engineers, as they alone had the requisite skills to test products and impartially sift data. In addition, such an outfit could only operate independent of commercial publications, trade associations, or even the government:

A multi-millionaire of an inquiring turn of mind could probably perpetuate his name to eternity by endowing a laboratory and information bureau on a scale sufficiently large to make a real impression upon the buyer's consciousness. "The Consumer's Foundation," he might call it. Under a group of public-spirited and disinterested trustees, chosen mainly from the professions, its experts could afford to tell the truth and nothing but the truth, and they could furthermore put their efforts into fields where the protection now afforded is particularly inadequate. . . . It would be based squarely on the assumption that facts duly published would bring their own reward. If the institution were large enough, and the staff authoritative enough to command wide respect, one suspects that the effect of its facts would ultimately be very great, even upon the advertising agencies.[62]

In this hopeful passage, the authors described the outlines of what would eventually emerge as Consumers' Research, a sort of Bureau of Standards for consumers.

Far beyond a call to rise up against cheats and frauds, at its heart *Your Money's Worth* was an anguished cry against material modernity and the market's growing influence in daily life. "We are deluged with things which we do not wear, which we lose, which go out of style, which make unwelcome presents for our friends, which disappear anyhow—fountain pens, cigar lighters, cheap jewelry, patent pencils, mouth washes, key rings, mah jong sets, automobile accessories—endless jiggers and doodads and contrivances," its authors lamented.[63] The two observed but did not fully endorse contemporary theories of "overproduction," which claimed that business made more than it could distribute without substantial increases in consumers' purchasing power.[64] Purchasing power depended not only on how much but on what quality of goods Americans could buy. While Chase and Schlink had no quarrel with modern technology of production and communication, they bitterly condemned business's aggressive pursuit of customers. They recoiled from the therapeutic emphases of salesmanship, the incessant appeals to consumers' feelings of insecurity and incompetence. Chase and Schlink granted that goods played a powerful cultural role in American life and that advertising was critical in shaping the self by promulgating ideas about goods. But by arguing that some goods were only functional—only tools created to perform specific tasks—they encouraged consumers to erect and patrol a barrier between their private lives and the marketplace. As much as they acknowledged the importance of consumption in everyday life, Chase and Schlink claimed that people retained an essential self that transcended material goods, a self that should not be subject to the dictates of the market. *Your Money's Worth* saw that border as fragile and vulnerable to invasion by advertising, and the authors protested the market's disrespect for individual peace and privacy.

Moreover, as much as they advocated standardization, Chase and Schlink were alarmed at the homogenizing tendencies of mass-produced goods and culture. Along with other critics on the left and right, they feared the debasing influence of mass-produced goods: mass-produced experience, an assembly-line life in which everyone became the same in response to identical, standardized stimuli. They wrote:

> But standardization of design and pattern of clothing, houses, furnishings, from the standpoint of submerging individual tastes and differences in a vast pattern of uniformity, is an intolerable thing. Syndicated editorials and "boiler-plate," standardized revues and movie plots, standardized gum chewing, permanent waves, automobile talk . . . booster clubs, comic strips, sleek hair, popular songs, cemetery sculpture—all such tend to reduce us to one dead level. In which no influence is more powerful than advertising and canned publicity. "Repetition is Reputation."[65]

Clearly, Chase and Schlink attributed great power to the corrosive force of things. Standardized goods and experience, they inferred, would turn everyone into essentially similar people. Assigning such power to goods hinted that they shared that fragile sense of self they decried in others. They saw a distinction between standardized things, which they applauded, and a standardized experience, which they feared.[66]

Independence from the market depended on both scientific information and psychological insulation from the totemic powers assigned to goods by Madison Avenue. In an essay written just after *Your Money's Worth*, Chase complained that high-pressure salesmanship was eroding traditional ethics, honesty, and "honor." He protested the commodification of human relationships, wherein commerce was one of the few things that brought people together. " 'Sell thyself' rather than 'Know thyself' is the categorical imperative of the age," he pronounced. "And the end of that selling is always and forever to be reckoned in thirty pieces of silver or its multiples. . . . The problem is to break down consumer resistance to the product. The common citizen must be made to want it, demand it, wake up at night and cry for it. In the struggle, all the sometime considerations of human decency and humanity are thrown to the winds."[67] Salesmanship thus eroded society.

Both Schlink and Chase grew up connected to small communities of moderate means that honored republican traditions and a Jeffersonian suspicion of commercial institutions; indeed, other contemporaries who became interested in consumers, such as the economists Colston Warne and Wesley Mitchell, came from similar backgrounds.[68] *Your Money's Worth* was an antimodern critique of a world given over to commerce, the world of chain stores, radio, and national advertising. But unlike Robert and Helen Lynd, the *Middletown* sociologists who shared the same analysis of the corrosive effects of modernity on local knowledge and everyday life, Schlink and Chase did not condemn material change. Consumers might be confused and cheated by business, but neither the authors nor their readers desired to turn back the clock. Nevertheless, their nostalgia for an era of greater individual competence and communal resources was palpable. A deep desire to retain the social relations of the earlier era while remaining firmly rooted in the material conditions of the present shaped *Your Money's Worth*'s demanding regime for activist consumers. Its program for consumers required the same commitment of time as nineteenth-century home production, except that consumers would now research and not make goods. Paradoxically, the authors advocated a consumption ethos far more, not less, rigorous than that envisioned by advertising. To have the best of the past in the present, consumers had to devote time to investigating goods.

Despite its harsh criticisms of New Era business, *Your Money's Worth* revealed no fervor to overthrow capitalism. Both authors admittedly had clear sympathies with central economic and technological planning, along with socialism. Chase was one of a small group of social scientists, including John Dewey, Rexford Tugwell, and Paul Douglas, to visit Russia in 1927. Schlink supported socialist candidate Norman Thomas in the 1928 presidential election rather than the engineer-reformer Herbert Hoover.[69] But the two, especially Schlink, were more interested in planning to better capitalism for consumers than in bringing about a revolution to ensure collectivism. Although they drew heavily from Veblen ("I want to emphasize that the shadow of Veblen was over this thing," Chase recalled later), they did not yet share Veblen's conviction that capitalism, ultimately, was incapable of economic justice for all.[70] Such questions did not specifically arise in *Your Money's Worth*. They would, however, recur as central issues in both men's later careers, as well as in the future consumer movement. By remaining focused on waste in the consumer economy, and by advocating that individuals should enjoy the same information and protection as businesses and government, Schlink and Chase eluded for the moment the deeper political implications of their work. Those implications would soon become clear once the economy collapsed and consumption itself became a political problem.

BUSINESS BITES BACK

The response to *Your Money's Worth* was swift and telling. A selection of the new Book-of-the-Month Club (along with Mary and Charles Beard's *The Rise of American Civilization*), it garnered attention from the middlebrow audience the club targeted.[71] It became a best seller, with two dozen print-ings. Home economists found it evenhanded and stimulating; its advocacy of scientific purchasing fitted the goals of the home economics movement, and Chase acknowledged a debt to Henry Harap, the home economist and educa-tor whose work predated his own.[72] Other social scientists found little in the book to surprise them. Writer Max Lerner and Columbia economist Rexford Tugwell, among others, argued that the book made no great contribution to economics, but it served an important popular niche by lucidly explaining the issues first articulated by Veblen.[73]

Among advertisers, the book became almost required reading, attracting the attention and responses of some of the profession's most prominent figures and a generating a good deal of publicity.[74] One incensed manufac-turer devoted an entire book to a fevered point-by-point response.[75] Their defensive and dismissive responses revealed vulnerability to criticism on both economic and cultural issues. While acknowledging the just critiques of advertising's less savory aspects, ad men complained that *Your Money's Worth* harbored an unreasonable bias against Madison Avenue. Kenneth M. Goode complained, "No hired copy writer could more skillfully have played up our weak points. Or more studiously avoided facts in our favor." Even worse, advertisers charged that Chase and Schlink unfairly grouped the honest and reputable advertisers in with some "sensational and isolated episodes."[76] This protest ironically confirmed one of *Your Money's Worth*'s points. The authors had claimed that the mass of unreliable and irrelevant advertising damaged reputable copy as well, by making it impossible for consumers to trust any advertising. To complain that the book lumped the bad with the good only proved the authors' point.[77]

Beyond questioning its "objectivity," advertisers attacked *Your Money's Worth*'s advocacy of standards and specifications and its criticism of name brands. They protested that consumers would not heed "dull" technical speci-fications; businessman Charles Carpenter asked pointedly, "Can anyone imagine a more monotonous, brain-decaying process of living than to have the housewife go into the corner grocer, pull out a Bureau of Standards specification catalogue and say, 'I'll have a can of B-64 please?' "[78] Ad men argued that purchasing by brand itself provided all the necessary assurances of quality and satisfaction; brands *were* specifications.[79]

Worst of all, critics argued, Chase and Schlink condescended to consum-ers: promoting specifications assumed that people did not know their own desires or how to satisfy them. In copywriter Harford Powell's words, stan-dards helped only those "who have no confidence in their abilities to tell good wares from bad." Christine Frederick, who spent part of her famed *Selling Mrs. Consumer* sternly reminding businessmen of the twelve-year-old mentality of women buyers, criticized Chase and Schlink for presuming that women needed outside help. The consumer "does not believe in the capacity of any one organization to make sound judgements as to what brand of any or all types of goods is 'the best' . . . . Few women are willing to subordinate their shopping judgment in this wholesale manner." Advertisers had privately called consumers incompetent for years. When *Your Money's Worth* offered a similar argument, Madison Avenue was shocked. More threatening was Chase and Schlink's proposal that other authorities assume advertisers' function in determining the meanings of goods. Advertisers promised the buyers would resist: "Man wants to do his buying unhampered by forms, rules or standardized specifications . . . and he does not want to be criticized for his choice by some self-constituted authority in the name of science."[80] As *Printers' Ink* editorialized, "Continued advertising automatically establishes a quality grade. Advertising is a grading bureau that offers real rewards for improved quality and better value."[81]

The authors' idea that consumers could produce floor wax, disinfectants, or ink for themselves met with even more ridicule. Agency executive Roy S. Durstine sneered, "Where is the housekeeper today who wants to follow their suggestion of obtaining a good cereal breakfast food by grinding her own wheat in an ordinary coffee mill? It is busy time that Mr. Chase and Mr. Schlink have designed for the American woman—running out to the store to buy 4 cents worth of this and 3 cents worth of that and mixing it with 7 cents worth of something else." Frederick more bluntly called Chase and Schlink's enthusiasm for home production "hopeless."[82] Consumers were more interested in saving time than saving money.[83] Some critics even implied that home producers attempted to worm out of the civil contract, by usurping others' jobs and trying "to get something for nothing."[84] These critics ignored Chase and Schlink's point that home production was acceptable only when commercial goods did not meet specification quality; as soon as such products were available, there was no sense in manufacturing them at home.[85] But the finer points of the argument were lost in the barrage of enraged replies from business. J. Walter Thompson star copywriter Mildred Holmes got the last word. Defending the subjective and imagination ("bunk" was her term) in advertising and goods, she argued that without imagination, buyers must reduce everything to unadorned facts: "You must quarrel with the cost of a prepared eyewash because its chief ingredient is boric acid and 'a nickel should buy a tub of boric acid.' Who wants a tub of boric acid?"[86] The doorbell ringers in Thompson's research department apparently had never posed that question, but the best-selling authors were determined to find out.

The book's criticism of overcompetition and the arrogance of marketplace values drew fierce, throat-clearing counterattacks. Creators of demand are the builders of civilization, thundered Charles Carpenter. To create demand was to stimulate discontent and desire for better things, argued Theodore Mac-Manus: "The most contented individual is an untutored savage with a full stomach. . . . To cry out against the prodding of the age is to admit the possession of a lazy mind and the total lack of any appreciation for the comforts and refinements of civilization."[87] New York University marketing professor George Burton Hotchkiss even denied that advertising could create demands; they already existed as unarticulated desires within everyone. Desires, like energy, could be neither created nor destroyed, and advertising merely spurred consumers to satisfy them. Advertising was thus central to current civilization.[88] Schlink and Chase were thus criticizing American life itself.

To defend salesmanship ad men invoked American individualism. No one, whether a dissenting accountant or the entire National Bureau of Standards, had the right to determine what those values should be for individuals. Christine Frederick restated the marginalist claim: "Authentic economic value is made in the consumer's mind, we must remember: not, as the old economists believed, in the cost of labor and materials." Any attempt to determine or prescribe value across the board was doomed to founder between the rock of incoherence and the hard place of elitism. Similarly, there was no way to justify categorizing some goods as necessities and others as luxuries since "everything and anything which may aid in obtaining happiness is a necessity."[89] Only the consumer could judge. Advertisers and businessmen advocated a consumption ethic that owed more to Simon Patten than Adam Smith, claiming that consumption offered a richer, fuller life and that thrift and denial were no longer necessary.[90] By contrast, they argued, *Your Money's Worth* preached a backward nineteenth-century economics, which expected the consumer to behave according to a rational economic model, calculating costs, allocating satisfactions, and following "outdated" practices of thrift.[91] Advertisers drew on twenty-five years of advertising psychology to claim that consumers did not behave rationally; they chose goods by all manner of criteria, of which cost was decidedly secondary.[92] Consumers sought value in styling, convenience, and social prestige. Though seemingly illogical and capricious to an outsider, consumers' choices made sense.[93] As to thrift, advertisers not surprisingly argued that people should consume more, and not less; *Your Money's Worth*, they said, encouraged precisely the wrong behavior for social and economic health. Kenneth Goode, author of *How to Turn People into Gold*, proclaimed, "Until the great mass of solid citizens loses its fear of poverty and learns to play—cheerfully—comfortably—confidently—while the machinery does the drudgery, we shall still have to lure them with over-colored advertisements and trap them with intensive selling." Goode completely ignored the authors' claims that they did not advocate a return to thrift. More important, "the great mass of solid citizens" were unable to participate in the consumer economy and thus conceivably needed to make every cent of their purchases count.[94] For Goode, the social role, if not duty, of people was to consume and not to save money.[95] The nation and American civilization depended on the consumer.

Despite their bluster, business readers took Chase and Schlink's charges to heart. The authors had evidence to back their claims, quoting advertisers conversing among themselves in trade journals and industry reports. They understood ledgers, technical data, and inside jargon; their charges were not easily dismissed. Very quickly advertisers recognized that these new advocates of scientific purchasing asserted a professional authority in competition with their own. Schlink and Chase challenged advertisers' exclusive claim to speak for and to consumers. Advocating skepticism and sales resistance, Chase and Schlink competed not for buyers' dollars but for their beliefs and their habits. If consumers lost their faith in advertising, there would be little point in selling. And so among advertisers the pair became marked men. Columbia economist Rexford Tugwell speculated on possible effects of the book: "A slaves' revolt this, rather than a civil war! But for all that it may come to something." The subsequent months would reveal how correct he was.[96]

THE FOUNDING OF CONSUMERS' RESEARCH

Your Money's Worth touched a raw nerve on Main Street as well as Madison Avenue. The book proved to be a popular success, sought after in libraries and bookstores; it sold over 100,000 copies in the decade after its publication. Readers wrote the authors in droves, and the pair spent their free time in evenings and on weekends answering as best they could.[97] While most letters sought information on specific brands, many letters revealed a general dissatisfaction with high-pressure salesmanship or criticized the growing dominance of American life by commercial interests.[98] *Your Money's Worth* tapped a well of antimarket resentment beyond frustration with shoddy merchandise. There was reason to believe that consumers might welcome alternatives to advertising's influence and embrace a different role than passive choosers.

The book's success prompted a search for possible sequels and related enterprises. The pair sought to build an organization to serve their goals of providing consumers with scientific data on goods, free from assumptions and pressures of the marketplace. Their publisher, Macmillan, proposed an encyclopedia of consumption, a companion to *Your Money's Worth*, that would contain specific product recommendations. Schlink's estimate of $70,000 needed to generate and compile the necessary information quickly killed the idea.[99] The authors were often approached to endorse products, but they categorically refused. They fiercely guarded their independence, and they studiously avoided all commercial ideas.[100] As Chase wrote, they were committed to "the establishment of an impartial, disinterested clearing house and laboratory set up for the purpose of furthering a genuine science of consumption, and incidentally debunking the more extravagant claims of the high pressure salesmen and advertisers."[101]

Even before the book's publication, Schlink had begun airing his ideas for helping consumers. From a church in White Plains, New York, he began a Consumers' Club, which for a nominal membership fee provided and exchanged product information. The club offered tales of unsatisfactory goods, recipes for the home manufacture of simple household staples, and sources of further data on products. From the first, the club pursued the same goals and suggestions offered in *Your Money's Worth*: buying by specifications, avoiding advertising claims, undertaking home production when necessary, and most of all, encouraging members to test for themselves. Moreover, the club made clear its critical but not implacably opposed attitude toward nationally advertised goods. As the club's newsletter insisted, "The high unit prices charged for package goods are in part the penalty paid by the consumer for not knowing the names, ingredients or properties of the things he uses. In other cases, particularly with staples such as food, condiments, etc., they represent a desirable protection from dust and dirt, extra convenience in handling, and often though not always, a reliable uniformity of characteristics or benefits. *It is for each consumer member to decide whether for him these benefits are worth what they cost.*"[102] Rather than rejecting marginalism, as ad men claimed, Schlink urged others to utilize it in their decisions. Despite recommendations and information from experts, and reliance on scientifically developed standards, in the end the consumer's judgment was the most important criterion in purchasing. In practice, the sometimes melodramatic assertions of *Your Money's Worth* were now limited by Schlink's commitment to at least one tenet of marginalist economic theory: value was ultimately the province of the individual. Technocratic expertise could generate information but never determine a person's experience.

From the beginning, Schlink envisioned the club as a community. Consumers would only be sharing information and experience. As Wesley Mitchell had argued, buying had to be socialized for people to benefit. The club explicitly invited corrections, emendations, and revisions of its recommendations. From the outset, Schlink claimed that, while the club's commodity ratings and descriptions were based as often as possible on empirical tests conducted by experts, they were nevertheless private suggestions and opinions, subject to modification pending new data. The work of testing for consumers, and the consumers' own evaluations of such tests, had to be experimental, pragmatic, and evolutionary.[103] The club membership of 565 continued to grow, which encouraged Schlink and Chase to expand. Edith Copeland, an instructor at New York University, volunteered to run the club's office, working at first out of a borrowed apartment. Throughout 1928, interest in both the book and club grew, and a second " 'Your Money's Worth' Club" formed in Scotia, New York.[104]

Encouraged, Chase and Schlink put together a proposal for a Consumers' Foundation, which reflected the arguments of *Your Money's Worth*, Schlink's AESC experience, and Chase's broad social sympathies. The authors sought to found "a strictly impartial scientific, non–profit making, goods-investigating body" to run a clearinghouse of information on products gathered from government and private tests and to establish a laboratory to test goods.[105] The information would be supplied "so interpreted and simplified as to be directly usable in a main street store."[106] Ultimately, the foundation would promote new product standards and specifications, "which the consumer would be educated to call for, and which honest manufacturers would be only too glad to meet." These standards would change the market by "substituting science for magic and persuasion" and by supplanting name-brand products with "goods of known, tested and dependable character."[107] Chase and Schlink sought $75,000 to establish both the clearinghouse and laboratory for a year. The Elmhirst Foundation of philanthropist Dorothy Straight, backer of the *New Republic* (which itself previewed *The Tragedy of Waste* and *Your Money's Worth*), provided $10,000. In December 1929, as the nation tumbled into depression, Consumers' Research, Inc. was incorporated as a nonprofit organization in New York, with Chase as president and Schlink as technical director.[108] Neither officer gave up his day job.

Consumers' Research continued the Consumers' Club practice of compiling information in the form of specific recommendations, recipes, and test results, issuing a series of bulletins, as well as a cumulative annual volume, *Scientific Buying* (later the *Handbook of Buying*), which rated products by their brand names as "recommended" or "not recommended." Later on, an "intermediate" category was added. This system became the basis for the rankings of products based on test results and prices similar to those that are still used in many consumer publications today.[109] From the outset, the approaches of Consumers' Research to gathering information and testing goods were unconventional and controversial. If advertisers had been disturbed at the portents of a "slave's revolt" in *Your Money's Worth*, they would find the new organization a much greater threat.

If all consumers should wake up literate tomorrow morning, the commercial fabric would be torn to pieces. It has been patiently reared on the assumption that we are natural born damn fools.[1]

This quality of being a consumer is so common and so inescapable that like the air about us, we mostly take it for granted.[2]

In short we believe that consumers were born with the same rights as manufacturers, although that belief is contrary to the current folkways of America.[3]

From the beginning, Consumers' Research (CR) was engaged in a struggle to redefine the meanings and practices of consumption with and for its members. Stuart Chase and Fred Schlink drew on familiar traditional ideas of thrift, along with Veblen's analysis of business, to promote better consuming. Introduced at the height of the 1920s prosperity, their ideas seemed fresh.[4] For both critics and members, CR was radical.[5] The organization proposed a vision of consumption that fundamentally challenged the claims of national advertisers to represent, portray, and address consumers.[6] Its efforts to provide scientific information on goods, along with its determined opposition to sales pressures, comprised a meaningful alternative to the consumer ethos set forth in advertising. During the nation's descent into the Depression and the first New Deal, CR forged an economic, social, and cultural program that articulated and campaigned for a distinct consumer's interest. Seeking to build consumer communities and reach an engaged national audience, CR pursued a path that ultimately led to political engagement and activism. While its program for a consumer's interest in the end reached far fewer people than the competing agendas of business, mass media, or even other civic groups, CR's challenges to American capitalism greatly influenced public debates throughout the 1930s.

Schlink and Chase hardly dared entertain or utter such aims when they founded the organization in 1929. Due to Schlink's experience and temperament, CR began as an imitation Bureau of Standards for consumers. The organization gathered and disseminated scientific and economic data while assisting other consumer-minded groups.[7] CR as a rule at first eschewed political issues and social theorizing for empirical study and reliable testing, as its initial prospectus made clear: "Consumers' Research holds no brief for any particular kind of economic conduct or social or political order. It is founded only on the belief that consumers have as much right to increase their purchasing power of their dollars as have business enterprises, and that many consumers, given an income above the subsistence level, will as a practical matter achieve better results by learning how to get more for their money than by continually striving to get more income, as the sole defense of their economic rights." Collecting information about goods remained CR's principal activity and the chief service that attracted most of its members.[8] Yet by positioning itself as an alternative to the sales messages and merchants' interests, Consumers' Research offered members not only facts about goods but also a philosophy consciously opposed to the commercial system's unbounded promotion of material modernity. While grounded in liberal assumptions about the marketplace, CR embraced a political stance that challenged the tenets of liberalism. Pursuing the path to better consumption inexorably led the fledgling organization toward a critique of American capitalism. Just as advertisers identified themselves with America itself, their opponents would find themselves ultimately criticizing the foundations of American business enterprise. CR's work would inevitably be politicized. Perhaps the best way to understand the contours of this different consumerist vision is to examine its primary work of testing, evaluating, and making prescriptions for goods and behavior in the marketplace.

MAKING MEANINGS FOR THINGS: CONSUMERS AND GOODS

Consumers' Research began as a modest operation in borrowed quarters. The original personnel consisted solely of Schlink, who worked in off-hours from AESC, and Edith Copeland, a home economist who produced the voluminous correspondence that was the backbone of CR's work. Stuart Chase, the group's president, stole time for CR from his work as an economist at the Labor Bureau. Schlink ran the organization's daily operations from its inception; he designed tests, gathered information, and generated correspondence. As president, Chase set broad policy issues, appeared as the organization's principal spokesperson in numerous speeches, and served as treasurer. Within a few years his involvement in CR's daily affairs ended due to extensive outside commitments. Chase admitted later that as the Depression and the crisis of capitalism worsened, he lost interest in the consumer cause to concentrate instead on economic planning, technology, and the relationship of government and the economy.[9]

During its first half-decade, Consumers' Research continually emphasized the need for consumers themselves to become knowledgeable about goods and merchandising, more self-conscious of their own requirements, and more effective as a force within the marketplace. While its avowed goals were providing better information on goods and more choices for consumers, CR also tried to redefine what it meant to be a consumer by rethinking the relationships of people, goods, marketing, and consumption. Fundamentally, CR argued that to get more satisfaction from purchasing, people would have to become much more actively involved in all aspects of the process. CR could never substitute for knowledgeable consumers active in their own localities.[10]

Consumers first had to determine the goods they wanted, the performance they desired, and the prices they were willing to pay. The more fluently people could articulate such values, the more likely were they to find satisfaction. Next, buyers needed information on what in fact the marketplace offered them. CR not only evaluated the properties of goods but also informed its readers what was feasible for manufacturers to supply, along with an estimate of how much it ought to cost, relative to comparable items. Consumers needed to become informed about the conditions in which goods were sold, including irregularities in packaging, weights, measures, and ingredients.[11] Moreover, consumers required an awareness of their legal rights, as well as of the various techniques used to make sales on the unwary. CR urged members to read labels carefully, question merchants, become versed in sales strategies, and recognize the often vague and questionable language in advertisements.[12] Above all, Schlink and CR urged consumers to remember always that neither manufacturers nor retailers operated for the public's benefit.

Despite their own strong labor sympathies, neither Schlink nor Chase felt it appropriate for CR to investigate or report on labor conditions. Other organizations, such as the National Consumers' League, had done that work for years, and the pair believed that any effective articulation of a consumer's interest rested on a distinct consumer position independent of other social questions: what affected all consumers was their disadvantage in the marketplace, what Robert Lynd called their "illiteracy." While many, if not most, consumers were workers, Schlink and Chase determined to report strictly on the composition, performance, and economics of goods, leaving issues of both production and distribution to be addressed by unions, civic groups, and private organizations. Though this commitment remained a pillar of CR policy, the Depression's worsening pressures on consumers would compel the group to broaden its scope to include labor, even as other organizations explicitly linked working conditions and wages to consumer issues.

Perhaps most important for consumers to learn was sales resistance, a steely refusal of all invitations to buy.[13] CR's bulletins attempted to inoculate consumers against all sales strategies and advised them never to participate in a sales situation that they did not fully control. This meant never purchasing except on their own initiative, never accepting anything from door-to-door salesmen, and never allowing vendors to assume any unwarranted familiarities with them.[14] Instead, CR urged that all purchases be deliberately planned and executed only when the consumer felt fully ready. In addition, CR advised members to become aggressive in the marketplace, repeating their demands frequently and uncompromisingly and using their patronage to ensure that merchants and manufacturers responded to them. As one CR report insisted, "Too much weight cannot be put on the part which the consumer could play in remedying these conditions if he would only assume a determined and forceful attitude. . . . It is only by acquiring a knowledge of conditions and then effecting something very akin to a boycott, that the consumer can express himself."[15] CR's leaders believed that business would only respond accurately and promptly to consumers' needs if it were clear that the public would accept nothing less.

Lacking funds or facilities for testing, CR concentrated on gathering and publicizing existing information from government and private sources, compiling recommendations for an ever-growing product list for its buyer's guide, recruiting new members to the organization, and answering subscribers' questions. One of the greatest difficulties facing the organization was the decentralization of scientific information, and Schlink constantly sought new consultants to conduct specific tests on goods, answer reference questions, and think through technical and economic questions in connection with specific goods.[16] The staff grew slowly, but the work attracted highly educated personnel, and Schlink soon had a reliable circle of outside scientists, bureaucrats, and professors eager to aid in the effort. In these early years CR attempted to build bridges to as many like-minded individuals and organizations as possible. The organization had good working relationships with scientists at the National Bureau of Standards, Electrical Testing Labs, universities, state extension bureaus, and even a few manufacturers. Through his contacts with home economists, Schlink recruited a number to the organization, including Mathilde Hader, a home economist at Washington Square College, economist Eleanor S. Loeb, and consultants Pauline Beery Mack of Pennsylvania State University and Evelyn Roberts of the University of Washington.[17] The American Home Economics Association welcomed a new ally in consumer education, and Schlink addressed home economists numerous times over the first few years of the organization's existence.[18] CR's early bulletins were filled with information generated by these contacts, helped by

Schlink's own persuasive powers. This largely voluntary effort suggests that Consumers' Research struck a chord with professionals in different fields who desired to turn their technical expertise to public, populist ends.

The organization aimed to provide consumers with accurate information to aid in their spending. Agreeing with Hazel Kyrk that the consumer's principal problem was choosing, CR presented their recommendations in the most practical form possible, with specific references to brands and trademarks. The group's efforts would be merely academic without "naming names."[19] The organization gathered evaluations from expert engineers and scientists and also secured results from hundreds of studies already conducted by government and private laboratories.[20] As a rule, CR's presented its findings in comparative checklists that could easily be used in a store. Although CR harbored no illusions about the finality of its work, Schlink nevertheless aimed at producing reliable data.[21] CR's specific recommendations were meant to help consumers avoid learning solely through the process of trial and error.[22] The group hoped that by educating consumers on the state of those wares available to them, people would demand better, cheaper, and safer goods and force the market to respond accordingly.

Consumers' Research produced for its members bimonthly bulletins, which contained recommendations on goods, and an annual cumulative *Handbook of Buying* that covered a wide array of products. Membership cost a dollar per year. CR product tests appeared in its confidential bulletin circulated privately to member-subscribers. To avoid the possibilities of libel and lawsuits, CR created and enforced a confidential pledge from subscribers to not share the material with anyone outside of immediate family. Within a few years CR started a second, public *General Bulletin* that was circulated through public libraries and other venues; it contained no specific product tests but featured practical information on a wide variety of consumer issues and product types.

Yet CR's potential task was daunting, if not impossible. Hundreds of thousands of trademarked articles were sold in the United States; there were over one hundred different varieties of toothpaste sold in Milwaukee, Wisconsin, alone! The group reported on a wide array of products, including household cleaners, building materials, processed and canned foods, electric appliances, autos and auto accessories, over-the-counter drugs and patent medicines, cosmetic items, and apparel. In its first full year CR rated over one hundred different types of products, and by 1933 it would cover well over one thousand brand-name goods. CR could never hope to test the full range of branded goods, yet no other citizen organization gathered such information on as many different brands.[23]

CR's product criteria reveal both the meanings they sought for goods, as well as the habits and tastes they encouraged in buyers. Responding to wide-ranging requests from its members, CR developed a broad basis for testing, evaluating, and reporting. While certain tests were applicable only to par-ticular classes of products, CR's basic concern for quality influenced virtu-ally every form of product evaluation. Such ideals were anticipated in *Your Money's Worth* and the standardization movement, but they became fully defined and more powerful as CR applied them to hundreds of items over time. The group emphasized the utilitarian, assuming the most important products addressed the physical needs for food, shelter, clothing, rest, and transportation; most goods CR reviewed fell into these categories. Function-ality was perhaps the single most important quality under consideration: CR tested specific and general claims made by manufacturers, advertisers, and retailers.[24] CR argued that many products did not necessarily perform consis-tently well and seldom met their advertised claims.[25] Yet these tests did more than institute the obvious: in order to evaluate functions, CR had to define them, thereby creating prescriptions for goods. Thus, for example, CR ex-pected vacuum cleaners to remove dirt as completely as possible from a variety of surfaces, and refrigerators to emit a desired low temperature at a constant rate under varying atmospheric conditions. CR also evaluated effi-ciency, the performance of a given task with the least expenditure of energy in the design or by the operator. Long before the middle-class market under-stood energy efficiency, Consumers' Research tested it regularly. Where ap-plicable, technicians monitored the amount of power required to run a given product to determine the optimum energy for a job.[26]

The group devoted its most painstaking attention to safety. CR's most sensational revelations concerned the hazards in everyday products other-wise considered harmless. Consumer health and safety influenced all its tests, from food and drugs to appliances and even clothing. Did the product pose any potential hazard to consumers or to their environment?[27] Addi-tionally, since such products as cleansers and paints were used in contact with other goods, technicians also investigated their potential harm to posses-sions.[28] Such concerns underscored a growing conviction in the group that consumers often depended on goods at their peril.[29]

The organization also tested durability, the propensity for things to retain their qualities and usefulness over time.[30] Schlink and his consultants devoted special attention to devising tests that simulated the normal use and misuse of goods in everyday household or work conditions. For example, when Electrical Testing Labs surveyed washing machines, Schlink insisted on running them under a variety of abusive conditions and overloads to reflect likely conditions in consumers' homes.[31] CR tested rugs by subjecting them to a constant stream of foot traffic and tested automobile finishes by exposing them to extreme weather conditions. In a long series of tests on shoes, orthopedic specialist Dr. M. B. Howarth played the role of an "ignorant" consumer. The tests covered the whole process of obtaining shoes: shopping, including whatever information the clerk might pass on in transacting the sale, through trial wearing and actual use after purchase. Thus, CR tests covered consumers' practical experience in purchasing, as well as using, goods.[32]

CR paid attention to expense, the cost of purchasing *and* using goods. CR argued that price generally shaped most consumers' decisions, directly contradicting advertisers' contention that people preferred higher prices to gain higher quality.[33] As far as possible, CR reported comparative retail prices in its reports. Schlink felt that this was one of CR's most useful services.[34] As a *Consumers' Research Bulletin* editorial noted, "In so far as advertising has any justification, it is that it tells the consumer things he needs to know, and advertising that does not state the price in a specific and fully informing way does not do that, but leaves the field open to further waste of time and investigation and to badgering and follow-ups and telephone prospecting by run-of-office salesmen and even that special breed of pest known as the expert closer."[35] CR recommendations often give the nod to the cheapest products.[36] By analyzing costs of ingredients and production, CR argued that many commonplace goods featured shockingly high markups over manufacturing costs.[37] For example, its report on breakfast cereals compared the retail prices of such best-selling branded cereals as Corn Flakes (20 cents per pound) and Puffed Wheat (68 cents per pound) with the wholesale prices of their main ingredients. With corn at $1\frac{1}{4}$ cents and wheat $2\frac{1}{2}$ cents per pound, CR implied that consumers paid far too much for their breakfast food.[38] Such information enabled consumers to make their own judgments of an item's value, without relying on the word of manufacturers or retailers.[39]

Packaging and design attracted CR's enduring scrutiny. The group contended that packaging techniques deceived the consumer and wasted resources.[40] CR reported numerous cases of inaccurate quantities and slack filling that left containers partially empty.[41] Often, CR displayed its own Veblenian bias: short of sanitary or safety concerns, the design of any container mattered little, as long as it adequately housed and plainly revealed the contents. Consumers always paid for extraneous, beautified packaging, thereby wasting money in unjust markups.[42] CR viewed Madison Avenue's and marketers' strong emphasis on design and artwork as a diversion to avoid cutting prices or making improvements in utility and efficiency.[43] For example, CR engineers critically assessed "streamline" design in autos, complaining that it "consists mainly in rounding corners, removing visors, and placing a sheet of stamped steel over the gas tank. All these changes improve the appearance of the car far more than they lower wind resistance."[44] Although attractive designs were often important to consumers, CR contended that emphasis on appearance was not only frivolous but also harmful.

Behind all these criteria lay a more fundamental question: what benefit to the individual or society did products offer, and under what conditions? CR warned consumers against clearly useless or harmful products and also challenged the necessity for new types of goods. If advertising made the creation of desire its principal task, CR encouraged members always to question such new "needs."[45] For example, CR bulletins criticized electric food mixers as unnecessary, wasteful, and burdensome: "It is our opinion that an electric food mixer is not a desirable addition to the kitchen of a small household, and there are undoubtedly many small families who, after having purchased one and used it a few times, have relegated it to the back of the closet, never to be used again, simply because of the nuisance involved in setting it up, changing the attachments, cleansing after use, and keeping it in satisfactory running order."[46] In this manner, CR urged consumers to examine the role of various products in their lives, along with the amount of time and energy they devoted to them.

These interlocking criteria—functionality, efficiency, safety, durability, cost, and utility—reveal CR's thorough Veblenism. Committed to functionality, CR labored to devise test procedures that would yield quantifiable, practical data on consumer goods' abilities to perform their tasks. Yet while CR did make considerable room for a second class of aesthetic or luxury goods, consumers typically sought many products for what CR felt were subjective values, and the organization adopted a vastly different attitude toward these types of goods. By default, luxuries had no specific physical function; consumers used them rather to evoke a particular feeling or emotion. Luxuries did not promote physical survival, and whatever labor they performed was secondary to their subjective attributes. Because CR staff members perceived a greater social need for information about functional goods, they paid little attention to things they defined as luxuries. Schlink argued that consumers who could afford items that were strictly in the category of luxuries could well afford the ill-informed buying through trial and error that CR sought to relieve.[47] The most important aspects of luxuries, the psychological benefits, could not be quantified and thus yield practical information. Often, CR reports on such items as cosmetics or furs made clear that these types of products were morally suspect. M. C. Phillips's analysis of cosmetic hand lotions was indicative. Calling the advertising of cosmetics "hokum, dear ladies, mere hokum," she argued that hand lotions' ingredients made them ill equipped to perform their function, the "relieving of chapped hands," which was "more successfully performed by other means."[48] At best, such lotions were expensive and relatively harmless. They were irrelevant goods and, as Phillips made clear, unworthy of consumers' concern.

Despite this disposition, CR received many requests to report on items that the staff either defined as "luxury" goods or deemed too expensive for most American families. CR's middle-class, educated readership clearly had ideas of its own that differed from those of the editors. For example, in response to some subscribers' interest, CR devoted an entire special bulletin to the purchase and care of fur coats.[49] CR's audience had varying tastes, and their relatively affluent members sought to apply CR's techniques to high-priced goods. When analyzing luxuries, however, CR still scrutinized their functional aspects. Even the most expensive cars still provided transportation and the highest-quality German cameras offered a means for taking pictures.[50] Without denying consumers' needs to make their own meanings for goods, CR focused almost exclusively on functionality, insisting that such criteria trumped any subjective qualities that consumers might seek. Moreover, CR strongly implied that most people should not be concerned with luxuries, as they were antithetical to consumers' more important interests in reliable and safe staples for everyday living. Economically, luxury features were a smoke screen for advertising deception and irrelevance. Advertisers often claimed that psychological appeals distinguished one product from similar competitors.[51] CR charged instead that advertising used psychological appeals to avoid competition by the measurable, empirical standards that should be applied to all goods.

This fundamental difference between product testers and advertisers underscored their ongoing struggle over the meanings of goods. CR urged that the meaning of goods be limited to their ingredients, price, and function; for ad men, goods shaped and informed the consumer's sense of self.[52] CR believed advertising taught people to treat commodities as reflections of themselves and to measure social distinctions through possessions, which thus created artificial divisions in society. The group instead urged its members to treat goods not as symbols but as tools: they were mere things. The organization's disciplined and narrow interpretation of goods opposed advertising totemism and the use of goods as social markers.[53] In CR's ideal society, goods were largely the inanimate extensions of human physical capacity. Ultimately, CR envisioned a society in which possessions held little significance: as humans, consumers were socially and morally independent of things, no matter how much they physically relied on them. Put differently, CR espoused a pragmatic approach to truth about commodities but rejected pragmatism's equation of thought and thing. Despite this, these consumerists recognized that even basic commodities contained a host of subjective meanings whose diversity was inevitable in a heterogeneous nation. CR never attempted to deny or repudiate this psychological behavior. But it emphasized that with most goods, the physical trumped the subjective. On this issue CR stood in sharp conflict with advertisers: common social interests lay in the physical, shared qualities of products, their functionality. Since advertising depended on the distinct, individual aspects of goods, Madison Avenue and CR fundamentally clashed on the meaning of things.

CR seldom presumed to dictate the desires of its members. "It is only in rare cases—and then on competent authority—that we would endeavor to correct the general direction of consumer purchases," Schlink wrote. "It would undoubtedly be cheaper were all women to wear cotton stockings instead of silk, and healthier were men's summer clothing reformed on the direction of the lighter weight, but it is not in our place to crusade for such causes."[54] Even in evaluating certain features of goods, CR claimed to chart a neutral course: "We are not making decisions for people as to whether a convenience is worth this or that money to them; we are telling them what the costs are and allowing them to evaluate their convenience in terms of those costs for themselves."[55] Individuals' own criteria for choosing were private matters; Schlink felt that his organization's duties began and ended with supplying information. Yet the CR bulletins and correspondence demonstrated certain tastes that it clearly encouraged consumers to cultivate. The inclinations of CR's own staff tended toward the utilitarian and the antimodern: Schlink admitted that CR sympathized with those who preferred the straight-edge razor to safety razors and those who favored older home remedies and simple goods.[56] They believed that consumers who sought functionality, durability, safety, utility, and economy in goods, rather than psychological benefit, would gain greater satisfaction. Rational and utilitarian tastes could be met predictably and realistically.

This belief was borne out even in the ways in which CR shaped its testing procedures and selections. For instance, when setting up an elaborate investigation of footwear in 1934, technician Dewey Palmer instructed the orthopedic consultant to seek shoes for comfort rather than style and restricted the tests to areas of orthopedic design, satisfactory fit, and durability.[57] In ongoing discussions to evolve a philosophy of consumption, the staff distinguished between "durable" and "ephemeral" goods and sought to encourage durability in production and use, even at the expense of style or price. These preferences were clear even in the first CR buying guidebooks, which provided prescriptions on what goods should contain when the organization was unable to name specific brands. The recommendations invariably emphasized long wear, mechanical integrity, safety, and economy. The CR handbooks never concentrated on style or external design and frequently offered alternatives to brand-name goods.[58]

Useful standards for goods would amount to little unless consumers countered advertising misinformation. CR's second challenge to advertising was in questioning and disproving ad copy. Schlink sought a common language for goods and expectations truer to actual consumer experience than the grand fantasies promoted by Madison Avenue and the "high-pressure boys." CR tests often revealed that ingredients of proprietary trademarked goods were commonplace and inexpensive, no different than their generic or unadvertised counterparts. Brand names defrauded consumers by capitalizing on their ignorance.[59] Contrary to advertisers' assertions, Schlink argued that the brands themselves imparted no economic or material value. "Secret" or proprietary ingredients he scathingly referred to as "bear oil," a term that reeked of advertising's illicit origins in patent medicine days.[60] CR reminded its members that advertising misled buyers and, more important, was useless in helping consumers make informed decisions:

> The methods that are of any use for differentiation of such products are the only ones that have not been applied. Such methods will not be employed because in developing a critical and discriminating audience, through cost and quality comparisons, an advertiser rouses the ire and invites the attack and business pressure of competitors whose product will not stand discriminating examination, and, in the great majority of cases . . . will tend to ruin the market for other of his own goods on which the consumer might be led to use the same sort of critical approach. . . . Thus it is that practically all advertising of competitive products is either a). false or misleading, or b). useless from the standpoint of the consumer's being enabled to make a sober unbiased judgment in light of all the essential facts.[61]

Far from offering useful information about goods, advertisers were engaged in a conspiracy of silence.[62]

Member-subscribers often announced their own suspicions that advertising inflated retail costs, a popular prejudice that CR encouraged. A substantial portion of the retail price represented selling and not production costs. As CR argued, "Everyone who has had experience or contact with manufacturing of any kind realizes that cost of production and selling price in many cases bear no direct relationship on one another."[63] CR also encouraged the use of generic goods and pointed out that many unadvertised, private-retailer-label, and nationally advertised goods in fact were all the same products, manufactured in the same place at the same time.[64]

CR tests also refuted the scientific claims put forth in ad copy, often concluding that many proprietary goods could not exceed the performance of inexpensive and simple alternatives. For example, CR argued that toothpastes and dentifrices were inherently flawed, unable to cleanse, protect, or abrade teeth any better than a simple combination of baking soda and chalk.[65] Similarly, CR's evaluation of certain cosmetics and lotions revealed that expensive brands could provide no safer or more effective protection and cleansing than those that were long known to virtually every pharmacist.[66] For CR, the answer to "what's in a name?" was "nothing."

By insisting on the importance of physical properties and performance and by denying that most goods could truly affect the consumer's self-image and status, CR fought advertisers' creation of meanings for products. Although consumerists could not counter the therapeutic attractions of spending and goods, their persistent opposition cast them as implacable enemies not only of Madison Avenue but also of the commercial basis of American culture.

Despite the merit of CR's position as virtually the sole alternative to advertising discourse, its anticommercialism flew in the face of consumption's widespread popular appeal. By marginalizing the human propensity to give meanings to goods, Consumers' Research, like Veblen, underestimated the cultural importance of consumption. Although *Your Money's Worth* echoed Veblen's emphasis on the historical roots of the social and cultural construction of consumption, consumerists tended to ignore them. At best, culture lay beyond CR's ken. By simply asserting that the subjective meanings of goods were the province of individuals, CR lost sight of the powerful social role of consumption and mass-produced goods and, as a result, dismissed the importance of personal attachment to things. Lacking that understanding, the organization could never fully address the ways in which mass consumption was reshaping American life nor even effectively offer information for consumers on important nontechnical issues. By denying the human and animating aspects of consumption, CR severely undercut its potential for providing a useful alternative to the corporate definitions of goods.

ANTIMARKET AND ANTICOMMERCIAL SENTIMENT

Your Money's Worth had offered hope of harmony between consumers and business, but Consumers' Research quickly abandoned those beliefs. Implicit in the CR consumerist program was the firm conviction that the interests of consumers and those of business and commerce were fundamentally, irreducibly opposed. The small organization argued that no group or institution with commercial, profit-oriented interests could be relied upon to act in the consumer's behalf. CR declared that business exploited consumers so thoroughly that no commercial organization could protect their welfare. Buyers needed new institutions and new strategies; a consumer's interest would have to be articulated and pursued separately from other movements. From the outset, Consumers' Research kept a distance from other reform and commercial organizations. Although the organization did work with other groups (which was usually followed by acrimonious quarreling), CR maintained its strict independence and policed the borders of its autonomy obsessively. The hostile reception given *Your Money's Worth* made Schlink and Chase determined not to provide their critics with any evidence that CR adopted the same questionable practices that they had themselves criticized. Schlink told consumer educator Henry Harap, "Naturally our friends in the advertising profession have not been slow to suggest that Mr. Chase and I are in this business for what we can get out of it and we are open to approach by manufacturers whose goods are recommended in the lists."[67] The organization took seriously its independent nonprofit status; virtually all monies to support CR came from subscribers, and any surplus funds were turned back into the organization.[68]

From the beginning, the anticommercial values at CR restricted its engagement with consumers, allies, and of course, enemies. To distance its work from commercial interests, the CR board instituted stringent policies that employees terminate all financial connections to any firm likely to fall within CR's critical sights.[69] Potential staff members were rigorously screened for technical competence, ideological sympathy, and—most important from Schlink's point of view—personal honesty and integrity. Moreover, new employees also signed a confidentiality pledge to safeguard the sensitive materials under investigation. Staff had to refrain from accepting any outside employment, research positions, or consulting, without prior permission.[70] So rigorous was CR's drive for integrity that the organization dictated the private lives of its employees, keeping them as isolated as possible from the snares of commerce. What began as a healthy suspicion of competing agendas and interests ultimately grew into an overzealous aversion to the complexities of contemporary life. Fred Schlink and others in the group drew on and eagerly sought contacts with other like-minded professionals in government, industry, and the academy, but they hid and hoarded those contacts. Isolating the ideals, interests, and actions of the consumer from all other possibly corrosive or conflicting concerns, CR ultimately distanced itself from the consumer's friends as well as foes.

The group sought a wide-ranging membership but barred almost as many as it admitted. Businesses (corporate, retail, or manufacturing) were ineligible for membership in CR, and the staff monitored its subscription lists for names of known corporate executives whose products came under its review. "We do not knowingly accept contributions . . . from persons connected (as presidents or vice-presidents of corporations, owners of businesses, etc.) in a major executive capacity with firms whose products have been listed or discussed in the Handbook or bulletins," CR policy stated. Consumers would not be found among producers; one could not have two competing interests. Schlink bluntly asserted that CR's findings and activities could not aid business enterprise. The group's tests and bulletins would offer little help to those who were still convinced of the harmony between capitalism and consumers. CR thus eliminated from potential membership:

> Those who believe, and wish to believe that advertising generally tells the truth, that all or most nationally advertised products are dependably maintained at a high level of quality, that all large corporations carefully guard the interests of their customers, that a trade-marked article is in some mysterious way better, and therefore rightly more costly, than the same commodity under its real name, that all customs imposed by aggressive merchandising and shrewd appeals to pseudo-science are right because the millions who have already bought an article can't be wrong.[71]

CR further emphasized its suspicions of commercial firms by insisting on conducting all contacts with business (and subscribers) exclusively in writing in order to keep a documented record of the discussions and deter "any effort on the part of manufacturers and others to conduct backstairs arrangements of any sort."[72]

CR's policies and platforms not only criticized commerce but also fought its influence throughout society. Many members of CR, as well as its leaders and staff, disliked the modern commercial order as an artificial and unwelcome intrusion into private life. This critique, offered on moral grounds, assumed central importance for CR's program. Ultimately, consumers' common welfare depended on changing the relationships of people, goods, and the commercial system that brought them together. Even before it began seriously attacking capitalism during the New Deal, CR sought make consumers more independent of the market. Advertisers' goal of "awakening desires" was anathema to CR. As one editorial stated:

> In refusing to purchase things which they do not need and do not want, consumers will be providing the best foundation for the lasting prosperity of the greatest number. The fact that so many consumers have become sick of being continually sold new gadgets and have painfully acquired a wish to conduct their affairs without a continual stream of calls from super-salesmen or a daily orgy of aimless and needless shopping, is the price which business enterprise has paid for applying an ever increasing and ever more unscrupulous pressure on the masses of our population—to spend without any regard for their needs or resources.[73]

Desire should originate with the consumer: the more people controlled and determined their desires, the greater their chances of satisfaction. The marketplace crassly intruded in daily life, commodifying all sorts of private experiences that properly stood beyond the realms of commerce. Advertising, especially, was the culprit here, as its search for new subjective values to impart to goods encroached increasingly on emotions and experiences previously deemed private, intimate, or even sacred. If advertisers claimed to address and solve for the first time many of the intimate personal problems of modern life, Consumers' Research replied that their efforts were unwelcome and unnecessary.[74]

Commercial interests, in Schlink's view, by nature corrupted and undermined independent critical thought. CR fought back through its criticism of media, the schools, and other public institutions and argued that as long as businesses supported publications and communication through advertising, useful critical information about business would not reach the public.[75] As professionals whose work depended on disseminating information, CR paid great attention to the ethics and operations of the press, periodicals, and broadcast radio.[76] CR bulletins and stories constantly cited the media's total dependence on advertising revenue as de facto evidence that the press could not produce an unbiased record of events.[77] Journalists were torn between two incompatible masters, business and the consuming public.

CR reserved particular scorn for the numerous household "institutes" of magazines and newspapers, which ostensibly tested and reported on goods but, CR contended, had a different purpose: "We cannot ascribe motives to the commercial services but we think it is safe to say that while the magazines may often refuse large advertising accounts from firms manufacturing substandard goods, the net effect of their service is to encourage more and more buying of expensive advertised articles, to create wants as well as to indicate how they may be filled."[78] The *Good Housekeeping, Delineator, Modern Priscilla*, and *New York Herald* consumer laboratories were thus severely compromised by advertising patronage. CR had some justification for its suspicions. Not only did these institutes adopt widely varying procedures to evaluate products, but their reports and features seldom employed critical language or technical references. Their testing methods often did not adhere to scientific procedures customarily used in university and industrial research labs, the Bureau of Standards, or CR. While such bureaus clearly held great sway with some readers, CR argued there was a clear distinction between their operations and consumerist science. The determining difference was profit; no magazine would condemn goods freely if advertising revenue were at stake.[79]

CR bulletins vehemently charged that commercial journalism censored information critical of business, products, or the consumer economy in general. CR encountered this censorship firsthand. When the group attempted to advertise its own service, CR met fierce resistance from national magazines. After running small notices successfully in *The New Republic* and *The Nation*, the organization embarked on a more ambitious publicity campaign in 1932. CR attempted to place ads in *Harper's* and *Time* magazine, and both refused to accept the paid space.[80] *Time* evaded the issue for months, contending that " 'further investigation of the claims of the organization and observation of its operation is desired,' " before finally refusing to accept any CR advertisement. *Harper's* relented by September 1932, as inexplicably as it had refused.[81] After a number of CR subscribers wrote angrily to *Time*, the magazine's ultimate explanation was, "It is obvious that in many cases it [CR] has not established laboratory and staff necessary to conduct adequate analyses and tests in articles it chooses to recommend or ban. These private opinions and individual judgments often prove wrong. . . . The point is *Time* is not convinced." The magazine also contended that CR had not followed accepted advertising procedures of submitting a definite order for space through a bona fide advertising agency.[82] CR reported the refusal in its bulletins and in 1934 duly tried again, hiring an advertising agent to submit proofs to the magazine. With no explanation, *Time* flatly rejected the advertisement, which was headlined "The Attack on the Consumer's Dollar," with no explanation.[83] After some months, Mildred Edie of *Tide* magazine, an advertising journal sympathetic to CR, secured an explanation. Apparently, *Time*'s first refusal sparked a flood of protesting mail from CR member-subscribers. After that the Luce flagship wanted nothing to do with the consumer group.[84] By contrast, the fledgling *Newsweek* was more candid, telling CR's representative that it rejected the organization's business on the advice of other ad agencies.[85]

When attempting to publish staff writer M. C. Phillips's book *Skin Deep*, a 1934 exposé of dangers and fraud in women's cosmetics, Consumers' Research encountered similar censorship. Richard Walsh, an editorialist for *Woman's Home Companion*, as well as president of John Day Publishers, canceled his company's contract to publish the book by ordering Phillips to remove sections that criticized advertising and magazines. Such behavior only seemed to confirm CR's worst suspicions, leaving the staff to conclude that its critical stance toward commercial journalism threatened both advertisers and publishers. Such hardheaded resistance from a press that published many liberal works only reinforced CR's suspicions of commercial media.[86]

Consumerists fought commercial inroads into schools. CR argued that schools and institutions of higher learning generally failed to equip students with a critical attitude toward business and its products. Concerned with the quality of education, CR directed a great deal of attention to teachers, who made up a substantial core of its membership. CR staff devised consumer courses for college and high school use and created a special school membership plan. Working with instructors, the staff devised simple classroom tests and answered questions from students and teachers.[87] In what CR saw as an even more troubling development, businesses corrupted education by placing commercial propaganda in the schools. By directly intervening in curricula and by donating textbooks, supplies, or commercially sympathetic "educational materials," businesses kept schools from educating children to be truly critical.[88] As CR warned, "A school system which does not dare even to supply its pupils with inoculations against misleading advertising and salesmanship, we may be sure will turn out consumers more distinguished for their gullibility and intellectual ricketiness than for discrimination and judicial temper."[89] CR would ultimately break with its earliest ally, the home economics movement, over the issue of commercial influence on education. CR charged that the American Home Economics Association depended too much on advertisers and business for revenue and equipment to teach students critical objective methods, or to investigate its subjects impartially. "We . . . have found that it's just as well to have the consumer sold out by those who dislike him and exploit him as it is by home economists and professors of marketing and the like who pretend to be his friend and often indeed think they are his friend," Schlink wrote.[90]

Consumers' Research reserved its most passionate critiques for commerce's attack on individual identity, however. By assessing everyone's worth through possessions, advertising and the market obscured the individual's true self behind a veil of mass-produced commodities. Heirs of a Puritan belief in plain speaking and social relations, consumerists at CR held to a nineteenth-century psychology that viewed the self as anchored in "character," an internal moral compass unaffected by social relations.[91] The modern plethora of goods created pernicious social distinctions, marking individuals by external images unmoored from character. Paradoxically, CR recognized that material modernity had radically altered the conditions of individuality producing a modern social self, and yet they clung to a belief that the self existed outside the material realm. They felt that the commercial marketplace imparted a phony conformity on society by making things the democratic measure of people. Lacking any interest in social well-being beyond selling goods and keeping the consumer economy running, business could only measure values in its own terms—the commercial values of manufactured possessions.[92] The result, for CR, was that American society emphasized getting and spending at the expense of self-knowledge and independence. Advertising encouraged people to measure themselves only through things, and CR's antidote was to encourage consumers to resist intrusions of the market into their lives. While advertisers claimed that consumption was the means to achieving both self-transformation and personal freedom, CR held that true liberty lay in freedom *from* consuming. Numerous similar items did not constitute meaningful choice. The less people had to do with the market, the better: it engaged precious time primarily for the benefit of manufacturers and merchants. Acknowledging that consumption required labor on the consumer's part, CR still contended that consumers would welcome reduced time in spending.

Despite its technical expertise, commitments to mass production, and eventual emergence into public life, CR's advocates ultimately embraced an antimodern sensibility. They shared little with other antimodernists who sought refuge from contemporary life through immersion in crafts, medievalism, or similar cultural movements. The group held that consumers had to live and choose in the present; moreover, as public professionals and as individuals, CR staff believed themselves to be very much part of the twentieth century. Unlike followers of John Ruskin or William Morris, CR's leaders did not celebrate crafts for their own sake or despise mass-production technology.[93] Far from this, the group argued that only in mass production could consumers reap the benefits of new scientific knowledge. Yet CR leaders and members often showed signs of profound distrust of their own time and milieu. CR contrasted material modernity with an American past with radically different relationships of people and goods, a bygone age where individuals firmly controlled their own desires and spending. The only antidote for the discontents of contemporary life, manifest in consumer exploitation, was a materially grounded individualism. Despite the knowledge that the United States had been utterly transformed by the industrial revolution, and despite a growing commitment to the collective management of the economy and government, CR remained paradoxically wedded to a nineteenth-century individualism that would leave people free from outside suggestion or influence. That commitment would receive a fuller exposition in the group's consumer-oriented republicanism.

CONSUMER REPUBLICANISM

In its first several years, Consumers' Research seldom offered extended social or political critiques; the group's views on society appeared occasionally in its bulletins and, more revealingly, in the voluminous correspondence carried on with subscribers, activists, businessmen, academics, and technicians.[94] Even so, a vivid picture emerged of the group's own ideal of a consumer-oriented society. Despite the commitment to modern science and technical expertise that underlay its entire program for consumers, CR's vision of a healthy society for consumers was grounded in a nostalgic vision of the mid-nineteenth-century American republic. CR strove to preserve its sense of the relationships of people and goods from that era within the twentieth-century state. The mid-nineteenth-century American village exemplified an ideal society, where consumers' interests were paramount, because there consumers possessed in their daily lives the knowledge necessary for good spending. The figure who embodied the ideals closest to CR was the homemaker of the preindustrial village, in "your grandmother's time." According to Schlink, grandmother had exemplary consumer skills. As the homemaker responsible for producing food and clothing for her family, "Grandma" had firsthand experience with the qualities of many goods. Consumers' Research was not alone in this estimate: it was a fundamental assumption of post-Veblen writers on consumption that the homemakers of the mid-nineteenth-century American village were more knowledgeable and skilled consumers than their grandchildren.[95] Grandmother's skills rested on her complete social knowledge of the production and manufacture of goods. She knew the circumstances and the people responsible for them. On that local scale, fraud and adulteration were difficult to perpetrate. Moreover, grandmother herself had extensive knowledge of things through personal experience in home production.[96] The homemaker-consumer was well acquainted with the comparative properties of fabrics, of her tools and foods. She was a shrewd and keen shopper; since values were fairly stable and fixed, she knew the relative worth of goods and was not easily out-bargained or deceived. Such was CR's romanticized portrait of the ideal consumer.

Consumers were far more ignorant in the twentieth century because mass production had made available a dizzying array of goods, a range too wide for consumers to attain encyclopedic knowledge.[97] With fewer goods, nineteenth-century consumers had far fewer desires. Moreover, Schlink hinted, in a life where labor and consumption blended inextricably, people had much greater self-knowledge. With far fewer things to want, and with a different morality that suggested that possessions were not the key to happiness, consumers had a much healthier relationship to goods. Because labor occupied so much time and home production was critical to a family's survival, grandmother understood the real costs of goods. In an era before money had dissolved differences in value between things, consumers understood the relative worth of goods much more clearly than did their descendants. In the twentieth century mass production rendered social relationships opaque, and the qualities of goods were only "known" through advertising.[98] But if science could not restore the face-to-face relationships of the previous century, it could revive the technical knowledge of things. Grandmother's world was gone, but her expertise could be preserved, through science, education, and consumer activism.[99] To restore the competence of grandmother's world became CR's mission.

Other aspects of that village life and culture offered a far preferable vision of consumer happiness. Schlink shared the same background with many at CR and other sympathizers and consumer activists. They hailed from small towns in and near farming communities.[100] The city might have spawned the reform sentiments among the middle class and intelligentsia that first nurtured CR, but the city also fostered institutions and practices that alienated consumers.[101] CR protested the diminishing of prime sensory aspects of life in the twentieth century: packaged and preserved foods were inferior to fresh, urban air was dirtier than rural. Moreover, new technologies and media meant that people relied less on the senses of smell, touch, and taste to interpret the world. These could only be restored through new attitudes, not by deliberately running back to the land but by a conscious effort to restore that experience, in diet and exercise and through periodic escape from the cluttered, overcivilized modern world.[102] CR solved this difficulty—along with the need for adequate space to house its own laboratory—by moving from New York City to rural Washington, New Jersey, in 1933.

Perhaps the most questionable aspect of CR's nostalgia for the antebellum republic was its lionization of the nineteenth-century diet. Schlink and others at CR crusaded against dietetic reforms and habits of the twentieth century, including the emphasis on dairy products, vegetables, citrus juices, and fruits.[103] Schlink argued that a much more "primitive" diet emphasizing rare meat was far healthier, and he urged people to cook like their ancestors. Claiming that many modern nutritional "discoveries" were in fact sales campaigns of the food industries, Schlink held that Americans' ancestors were much healthier and ate better and that modern diets were often poison.[104]

CR's advocates contended that preindustrial American life was more cohesive, as well as healthy. The classic gemeinschaft of early sociology was in fact grandmother's village, untainted by an excess of machine technology, with family and kinship structures intact. There, the community of producers and consumers, sellers and buyers, lived together. This consumer's Eden was explicitly American, associated with both the small town and the agrarian past. Without directly invoking nationalism, CR portrayed an ideal manner of consumption, expressive of a characteristically American form of living, threatened by modernity, but that could ultimately be preserved through CR's program.

Schlink did not simply invoke the nostalgic aura of the bygone republic. Running throughout his entire consumerist critique of modern advertising and commerce was a political discourse that might best be called "consumer republicanism." Like advertisers, the founders of product testing borrowed specifically political concepts and terms to describe consumption, the aspirations of consumers, and the relationship of people and goods. CR's purpose was to provide people with the knowledge that would allow them to evaluate independently the claims and pressures brought to bear on them by sales messages. Advertisements preyed on consumers' ignorance, vulnerability, and fears. Consumers were given a choice of accepting or rejecting the word of powerful institutions with interests distinctly different from their own, or relying on their own inadequate resources. For CR, providing people with information to evaluate sales claims would restore their independence in the marketplace.[105] This represented a vision of the consumer as a latter-day descendant of the Jeffersonian yeoman, the individual who exercised the franchise in the marketplace confidently, independent of powerful larger interests, economically secure.

Like advertisers, CR understood consuming essentially as an exercise of the franchise. Schlink seldom referenced traditional political ideas, yet his prescription for wise consumption clearly echoed republican ideas of citizenship, suffrage, suspicion of commerce, and the role of the virtuous commoner as citizen. Better buying was possible only by liberating the individual from powerful commercial interests and making him their equal in the marketplace. Moreover, the call to consumer protest and activism invoked republican ideals as well. Standing up to manufacturers, merchants, and Madison Avenue with boycotts, complaints, and skepticism echoed the republican opposition to commercial corruptions of society that accompanied an expanding marketplace.[106]

CR's nostalgic portrait of the nineteenth-century village linked the social relations and individual psychology of republicanism to the local market relations necessary for ideal consumption. Whether fighting the corruptions of large landowning interests in the eighteenth century or the false messages of corporate advertisers in the twentieth century, republicanism's emphasis lay in strengthening individualism and independent thought. The modern consumer had to interact with the market but live beyond it, not by productive self-sufficiency, but through self-reliance in consuming.

CR's republican-derived critique was limited and open to serious question. Full, self-sufficient independence in the twentieth century was impossible, as CR often admitted; technical specialization involved in evaluating goods, along with the numbers of available products, made it impossible for consumers to be experts themselves, and thus truly free. CR's own expertise protected consumers, but ironically, this entailed replacing one dependence with another.[107] Beyond this, CR underestimated the extent to which consumers made decisions outside advertising's sway; spending was a much more complex process than either advertisers or consumerists claimed. Constrained by shifting needs and desires, limited by access to goods and money, consumers ultimately spent money with a wide-ranging and diverse set of criteria. CR's refusal to acknowledge other aspects of consumers' lives beyond spending—to understand consumers as workers or women, for example— seemed almost perverse. By reducing buying to a rational exercise using skills that lay outside people's daily ken, CR made consumer reform unnecessarily narrow. Just as much as the advertisers they opposed, consumerists insisted on managing and controlling consumers. Consumers may have been citizens, but CR's Jeffersonian model only barely acknowledged the complexity of their needs, or the many forms in which their rights took shape.

Consumerists did seek to reconcile the republic to the new organizational state. For CR, science replaced cheap, available land and an agrarian life in the republican vision as the guarantee of stability and equality. Science was the great egalitarian force stabilizing the relationships between consumer and corporation, the individual, and capital.[108] Just as businesses portrayed science as progress embodied in new products, consumerists claimed that science would close, not widen, the gap between the individual and the corporation. Through the impartial evaluation and testing of advertising claims, science offered the consumer a means to reduce the corporation to human scale. Translating technical data into plain language made it possible for all consumers to protect themselves. Science was potentially the truly democratic language: ideally objective, transparent, incapable of misinterpretation.

Finally, CR advocated a serious, aggressive consumer sovereignty. Capitalists and consumerists alike contended that consumers were the sovereigns of the market, but CR asserted that the public had to lead business and not simply follow in paths laid out by commerce. This activist sovereignty directly contradicted advertisers' notions of the public's power; for Madison Avenue, consumers were king, but a constitutional monarch and "court" assumed the job of determining their needs and desires. For consumer sovereignty to be meaningful, argued CR, consumers would have to take active control of determining what came to the shelf, or they would continue to get inferior goods. Consumers had to assert and reclaim their power in the marketplace. CR saw the consumer as playing a new social role, as significant in the economy as the producer, worker, or capitalist. Consumers' interests were more legitimate than all others, since virtually everyone bought goods.[109] The Depression and the New Deal would compel CR to develop a political perspective advocating for consumption and consumers' rights within government and against capitalists, a full articulation of consumption as American citizenship.

CONSUMER SOCIOLOGY

Consumers' Research was a membership organization, and its relationship with its subscribers shaped its entire approach to the sociology of consumption. CR's specific prescriptions inevitably reflected the notion that proper spending should proceed along broadly defined middle-class lines. But while claiming to speak to and for a broad constituency drawn from many segments of society, CR remade consumers in its own specific image, that is, of the bureaucratic, white-collar, professional sector of the middle class. CR's construction of a universal consumer's interest that transcended class and gender inevitably inscribed the perspectives of its own staff and members. There was almost never any mention of specific ethnic or racial groups in CR writings, and little attempt to address specific problems that different groups faced in the marketplace.[110] Concerned primarily with class divisions, Consumers' Research envisioned mass consumption as a force for overcoming social barriers instead of reinforcing them.

As with ad men, CR's relationships with member-subscribers left the CR staff distinctly ambivalent about people's abilities to guide their own affairs and about spending habits as a reflection of American civilization. CR fought for a democratic approach to consumption and envisioned consumption as a key to greater democracy, yet from a distance, these consumer activists inevitably developed some elitist ideas about consuming and goods. As reformers, the staff of Consumers' Research strove to encourage democracy and participation. In private, they wondered whether consumers were competent to handle their own affairs, even with scientific information in hand. Their professional training left them ill equipped to treat their members as full equals, even working in the public's behalf.

Ironically, CR's perpetual conflict with advertisers masked their similar beliefs and attitudes toward the buying public. Ad men and product testers disagreed with each other about consumers' needs, desires, and welfare, but they both viewed the broad mass of consumers through their own professional, sophisticated self-image. Although CR indignantly and effectively pointed out Madison Avenue's contemptuous attitudes about Mr. and Mrs. Consumer, in private CR staff and members often shared those same beliefs.[111] Fiercely committed to consumer equality and democratic market participation, many at CR nevertheless privately believed in a hierarchy of taste, of consumers, and of goods. In that hiatus between their commitment to the consumer cause and their often patronizing attitudes toward actual people lay the key to CR's limitations as a social force and a media enterprise. In turn, those limitations determined its fate in public affairs and national politics. CR won the allegiance of an extraordinarily loyal and avid group of members. Its own snobbish opinions of mass consumption, of middle- and working-class people, and of American culture in the end undercut its overall effectiveness as a reform group and as a publicist for consumer issues.

Like their advertising opponents, CR saw consumers as benighted, child-like, and unintelligent, although they seldom were as explicit as the Madison Avenue stereotype of the "12-year-old mentality."[112] Also like advertisers, CR members and staff took pains to distinguish consumers' "limited" attitudes and abilities from their own, and at times they went out of their way to criticize the low taste of the majority. But CR differed fundamentally and crucially from its adversaries in holding that even if consumers' appetites were degraded or juvenile, consumers nevertheless deserved accurate information about those products. Whereas advertisers pointedly refused to try to elevate consumers to their own plane, CR made such education the center-piece of its efforts. CR claimed that taste did not play a significant role in the economy and ecology of goods and that the organization merely responded to the interests of its members when choosing the subjects for tests or articles. Yet inevitably the group's utilitarian values shaped their investigations, as much as relationships with subscribers and their tastes. Schlink had built the first Consumers' Club as a community, but CR substituted uncompromised expertise for majority rule among its members.

While CR held a dim view of most consumers' intelligence, its bulletins, buying guides, and correspondence never "talked down" to consumers.[113] The staff expended great efforts on conveying technical materials in accessible language, but the end results were still erudite. The CR editors and contributors wrote as if their readers were literate, adult, and capable of evaluating several different kinds of criteria. While product grading came down to "recommended," "not recommended," or "intermediate," CR staff covered complex issues and assumed subscribers would devote their energy to them. Schlink never compromised his vision that the most important things CR could offer its members were accurate distillations of carefully gathered data and the awareness that being a successful consumer required more effort than picking from brand names in stores or through the mail. This vision meant an absolute fidelity to test results and technical questions: CR succeeded if it reached an intelligent and avid audience on this basis.

CR's principal criticism of consumers themselves was their unwillingness to "think critically." Buyers possessed plenty of intelligence, CR argued, but their critical faculties were dulled by years of advertising's false promises that made them unwilling to apply their skills.[114] Seductive advertising promising what no product could deliver confused consumers and diverted them from realistic, and thus proper, expectations of goods. Even the relatively high levels of education among CR's members did not prevent them from being duped. As Schlink told a subscriber, "we are continually being startled by inquiries from intelligent and sophisticated people—readers of *Harper's*, the *Mercury*, and *The New Yorker*—whether they should use Mrs. So-and-So's depilatory or Mr. Blank's poisonous hair dye. A person's desire to be beautiful or successful constantly outruns his mental capacity to examine a situation."[115] The organization came to believe that if consumers were unable to resist advertising, it was partly because they were already too accustomed to its false promises; for CR, "the average consumer cannot be so easily influenced by honest factual information as by the glamorous extravagances of advertising. One cannot undo years of conditioning by misinformation over night."[116] While generally content to warn consumers about exploitative advertising schemes, occasionally the staff revealed their beliefs that consumers were, in the words of writer M. C. Phillips, "pretty dumb as a whole."[117]

Ambivalence about members' intelligence was partially offset by faith in the democratic potential of science and the pragmatic experience gained in daily interactions with goods. Science determined the impartial values in goods, while advertising could only create subjective and socially divisive traits. CR believed that a certain amount of consumers' own experience of trial and error, when not harmful, might prove as valuable in the long run as any information conveyed in its bulletins. "We believe that consumers ought to flounder a bit themselves and experiment in order to acquire a certain self-reliance and ability to stand on their own feet," Phillips wrote.[118] In Schlink's vision, people had to experiment with their goods and appetites. Only through persistent trial and error in evaluating goods, testing claims, and tenaciously pursuing their own satisfaction would consumers prevail in the marketplace. This meant that being a consumer was an ongoing obligation, and not a passive exercise in choosing brands. By adopting an experimental attitude, consumers would ultimately train themselves to demand more from industry and to learn more easily when they were satisfied. But only individuals' personal experiences and their willingness to change in light of them would provide a lasting independence and power within the marketplace.[119]

CR argued that the consumer's interest was the general public interest, yet the organization's actual membership was concentrated in certain groups. Examining CR's relationship with these groups who made up its members reveals the limits of its claim to legitimacy with a mass public and will illuminate the strengths and weaknesses of its overall program. From the earliest days of the Consumers' Club, avid CR members came from the educated middle class; schooling, even more than income, defined its subscribers. The organization defined its mission as serving the general reader, a member of

the consuming public who was neither so affluent as to be exclusively interested in luxuries, nor so poor as to live at a subsistence level of income and
thus unable to use and profit by CR's recommendations. Within those broad
and admittedly vague categories CR attracted people from several specific
groups. A substantial proportion were professionals working in white-collar
jobs, often with highly specialized training. CR counted not only many doctors, lawyers, engineers, scholars, and the clergy among its members but also
a substantial number of highly educated, if not especially affluent, public and
private educators, students, clerks, and government and office workers.[120]
Numerous businessmen and advertisers were regular subscribers, despite
the group's Orwellian efforts to purge them from the ranks.[121] Schlink's
copious professional contacts made Consumers' Research known to professional organizations. High school and college instructors as a core group
of CR supporters spurred the organization to develop some programs for
schools, students, and teachers.[122] What united most of these subscribers was
an interest in the recommendations and information about goods and a
lesser but still noticeable interest in the consumer's place and rights in the
American society and economy.

The type of goods chosen for analysis reflected readers' interests. CR's
methods of selection and testing revealed its ideas of the typical goods
in which educated, middle-class consumers were, or should be, interested.
Schlink and his staff paid great attention to such technically complex items as
cameras, radios, and electric appliances, as well as the constellation of automobile products, goods that otherwise were seen as luxuries. Such items, of
course, were generally more expensive than the basic household products
covered in CR bulletins. Did the organization serve a predominantly upper-
middle-class taste? CR justified its coverage in these areas on the basis of
readers' inquiries and interest. CR argued that many of these products had
such wide appeal that they transcended rigid class lines and that goods were
not simple indicators of social status or income. Certainly, goods often traveled beyond the class boundaries seemingly drawn by marketers, retailers, or
even by price tags. But the group paid little attention to testing secondhand,
used, remaindered, or otherwise budget-line goods that might have been
welcomed by poorer or working-class consumers. Like the advertisers, CR
presumed to address the broad middle class, yet in practice they spoke to a
much smaller public.

Many member-subscribers were activist as well as educated. A number
came to CR through references in *The Nation* and *The New Republic*, which
both ran articles by Schlink and Chase and frequently discussed the organiza-

tion.[123] Despite the potential appeal of saving money and getting better goods to people both on the left and right, at first political liberals and progressives supported CR's consumer advocacy. Schlink admitted in later years that its initial base of subscribers, its first endorsements, and critical public support came almost wholly from leftists.[124] Eventually, even some conservative journals discovered CR and consumers, including *American Mercury*, which by the mid-1930s had become a voice of both political and cultural reaction. Yet despite the broad appeal to the pocketbook, CR's critical attitude toward the marketplace and corporations found its greatest support among those sympathetic to progressive political and social reform and New Deal policies. It would remain that way until CR broke with liberalism and social reform in 1935.

However, CR's unbending adherence to its ideals made it insular and limited its impact. The bulletins were cumbersome and difficult to use, especially compared with mass-circulation magazines or newspapers. With minuscule print and almost no illustrations (to save subscribers money), the CR confidential *Bulletin* and the *Handbook of Buying* resembled government reports or legal briefs more than magazines. More troubling, the group's impact was severely constrained by its membership rules, which made it more of a secret society than an organization sharing information in the public interest.[125] Fearing legal action (which largely never materialized), CR instituted a pledge of confidentiality among members to avoid libel suits. Offering the *Bulletin* as a private service and not public speech protected CR's crucial policy of naming names in rating goods. However, in the end the secrecy isolated the group and the consumer cause from a broader public suspicious of signing a "pledge." This policy also kept CR's specific information, arguably its most useful, out of public libraries. Even with a second "general" bulletin covering broad consumer issues, CR did not succeed in drawing in the widest possible net of subscribers.[126] More than once, Schlink turned down publishing offers from major firms to compile CR product information that would have garnered much greater recognition for the group.[127] Most subscribers willing to take the magazine on its own terms came from the educated professional and managerial class. This was perhaps the most curious irony of all: CR staff campaigned for public access to government information and worked tirelessly to spread its consumerist message, and yet the organization's very form ensured most Americans would never encounter it. On some level Schlink clearly enjoyed being the uncontested ruler of a small domain.[128]

Beyond its relationships with other professionals, CR did attempt to reach out to certain other groups of consumers. The most important group was women. Certainly, CR shared the conventional views of advertisers, social scientists, and home economists—that women did the spending in most American households and made the purchasing decisions for virtually every product.[129] CR regularly covered and tested goods deemed to be within women's province as homemakers. Some of CR's earliest employees were home economists, whose interests lay in adapting the group's program of technical expertise and specifications for women. Its first regular touring speaker after Chase, Katherine Engel, addressed dozens of women's groups exclusively on women and consumption. Like the advertising agencies it battled, CR employed many women, especially in the clerical and bookkeeping departments, which were the heart of CR's operations.

CR's first home economist, Mathilde Hader, devoted her efforts to reaching women by teaching them specific home testing techniques and developing projects specifically targeted to women. One unfinished project when she left the organization was a CR cookbook that combined the organization's ideology with older nineteenth-century recipes, in keeping with CR's antimodernism.[130] CR's first book devoted to a specific type of product was directed at women and came the closest to voicing CR's version of a feminist consumerism. Written by M. C. Phillips, a Wellesley graduate who was one of the highest-ranking women in the organization and by then Schlink's wife in private life, *Skin Deep* revealed a vision of women's interests as consumers that combined feminism with scientific testing and CR's customary suspicions of the marketplace. Women were especially taken advantage of as consumers, Phillips argued, because manufacturers not only capitalized on the prevailing pressure on women to be beautiful, but also took advantage of women's comparative lack of technical training, to cheat them and peddle phony wares.[131]

In assuming that women were as capable as men of understanding its findings, CR revealed its commitment to equal rights for all consumers. Advocating scientific testing for household equipment, canned foods, and beauty preparations, the organization placed women's needs on a par with men's. Yet CR's relationship with women was marked by ambivalence. The many articles and features directed to women emphasized homemaking but ignored women's status in society. The magazines and bulletins seldom addressed consumers as women, even when covering goods specifically of interest to them. Most CR writings seemed directed at a male reader: even when addressing a convention of home economists, Schlink referred to the consumer as "he."[132] While CR writers often remarked that women had even less technical training than their male readers, the bulletins made few efforts to address this issue. More revealing was the fact that CR often discussed consumer incompetence in feminine terms, with frequent cautionary tales of inept shopping and weak sales resistance.[133] In CR's vision, women consumers and women's products were associated with the most troubling consumer behavior. The two models of good consumers that CR adopted—the rational, technically astute purchasing agent of the present and the mid-nineteenth-century grandmother—were far beyond the realm of the contemporary homemaker. In each case the contrast was clear. Consumer incompetence was feminine. Once again, CR embraced the same ideas as the advertisers they opposed.

CR also cultivated but ultimately drew away from working-class consumers. The group originally aspired to reach workers as those most vulnerable to economic exploitation, with the least education and the least discretionary income. In its first few years, CR struggled to determine the relationship of labor and the labor movement to the consumer's interest. Many staffers were active in unionizing and labor issues. The group assumed a harmony of interests between laborers and consumers, and virtually all CR's progressive supporters felt the same way. It seemed like an ideal fusion of two important social interests.

This was a misperception. CR never fully gained the sympathy of the labor movement because it explicitly ruled out discussions of wages, hours, and social conditions. Concerned with the end product of labor—goods themselves —the organization left to others issues of labor's greater concern.[134] The level of education and narrow focus assumed in the bulletins and the lack of funds for outreach made it difficult for CR to speak to or for masses of working people. Moreover, CR proved unwilling to change the specifics of its presentation to reach a working-class audience. While its leaders assumed that the working class stood to benefit most from its service, CR never tailored its reports or interests to working-class concerns. When some dissident CR employees founded a rival organization some years later, it immediately found a niche by forging a close relationship with the labor movement.[135] CR never understood that working-class buyers might have different interests, assumptions, needs, or tastes from those of the educated professional class who effectively shaped CR's policy.

While CR sought ways for the consumer to save money by spending wisely regardless of social class, in the economic upheaval of the Depression, its message of frugality, rationality, and product testing did not appeal as strongly as concerns of economic security, wages, and working conditions. CR advertising got its worst results from labor papers; apparently, despite its pro-labor sympathies, CR was not a service most workers wanted or could afford. The organization concluded that labor groups were more concerned with producer-oriented issues and that the union movement's commitments were too archaic to embrace a consumer-based viewpoint.[136] By 1934 CR had begun to consider that the labor movement opposed consumers' best interests—labor's commitment to wage and price increases acted against the consumers' goal of the best goods at the lowest prices possible.[137] While many members argued with the organization's leaders that being a worker and a consumer were virtually inseparable, the consumer organization refused to blend the interests of producers and consumers. In turn, consumerists always acknowledged that workers had legitimate grievances under capitalism, and CR developed a strong pro-union hiring policy, often giving preferences to those with union backgrounds or sympathies.[138] Yet in the end Schlink and staff refused to compromise their vision of the consumer's interest, even if it meant losing the good wishes and concern of many workers and labor groups.

In hindsight, it seems inevitable that CR would be out of touch with working-class tastes, needs, and expectations. CR's technically informed language and uninviting format contrasted sharply with the tabloid media that had found favor with working people in the era. CR's layout put off all but the dedicated reader armed with a good light source and a magnifying glass. Moreover, CR's utilitarian bias meant that the *Bulletin* discounted aspects of goods that could and did appeal to workers. As Roy Rosenzweig, Kathy Peiss, and others have shown, working-class and ethnic groups' distinct fascination with and influence on mass consumption and culture came precisely in the symbolic aspects of goods that CR excluded from its purview.[139] Although we know little about the relative tastes, it is quite possible that the appetite for the symbolic in goods was far more pronounced among working people than among the educated middle class of CR's primary audience. Beyond this, it is likely that CR's emphasis on frugality did not appeal to workers, inasmuch as organized labor's emphasis heavily favored increasing wages. Here CR's frustrations were not alone. Certainly, settlement house efforts to create a consumer consciousness and educate consumers encountered similar difficulties; only when attached to specific communities and commodities did efforts succeed in educating poorer consumers.[140] Moreover, labor's interest in increased wages meant, under capitalism, that costs were invariably passed on to the consumer. Higher wages meant higher prices, and CR insistently noted this tendency when other consumer advocates and labor groups alike evaded it.

Further complicating the relationship was CR's resistance to rapid growth or expansion from its mandate of testing and informational activities. To become involved heavily in labor activity would mean a disservice to other consumer-members who were not working class, and Schlink was adamant about responsible use of subscriber funds according to readership interests. Although for several years CR explored labor's relationship to consumption, and in the end the organization characteristically stuck to a narrow, technocratic vision of consumer interests, Schlink and his compatriots made a national impact through their initial program of scientific information about goods and knowledge about sales pressures and frauds. Yet its limited ideas about consumers' interests, habits, and needs ultimately vitiated CR's potential. The onset of the Depression and New Deal would forcefully bring consumption to a public political urgency, and then the battle between consumer advocates and commercial interests would erupt into politics and the press. Then, the two competing visions of consumption would clash publicly, and the established commitments of both groups, along with the government response to the Depression, would make clear the connections between consumption and citizenship.

III

CITIZENS
AND
CULTURE

CHAPTER 7

CONSUMER

PROFESSIONALS

IN THE

DEPRESSION

The consumer, disinterred from his grave, reappears in the political arena as the "common man," the "plain people," the "strap-hanger," the "man on the street," "the taxpayer," the "ultimate consumer."[1]

Perhaps this progressive and more liberal administration will come to realize that after all it is the consumer who is "the Forgotten Man."[2]

The deep-rooted Puritan tradition of abstinence is being undercut by the new citizenship, which makes it a civic duty to spend to make the wheels of industry turn.[3]

As things are now, it is a terrible responsibility to be a consumer. It is like being a doctor—you feel you ought to be on call every minute, lest the patient weaken. Sometimes I wake in the middle of the night, thinking about the country's emaciation, and throwing on my shirt and trousers and coat I trudge out to the corner drugstore to make a small purchase from patriotic motives. Some aspirin tablets or a Tootsie Roll. I would much prefer having society ordered so that, if I chose not to purchase a thing for six years, I would not be jeopardizing my fellow countrymen.[4]

The Depression was a crisis of capitalism that permeated American life. Horrified observers witnessed long breadlines in city streets, the collapse of meager social services under the weight of unemployment, poverty, and homelessness, the withering of industrial and agricultural production, and the frightening specter of want amid plenty. A sickening cycle of losses, unemployment, and curtailed production accelerated the economic crisis as it revealed the centrality of consumer spending to the overall economy. As a consequence, the interests and prospects of everyday buyers assumed new urgency in polity and culture. Over the span of the New Deal, federal economic priorities shifted from reviving industry and agriculture, through production control and price stabilization, to a combination of fiscal policies, regulatory reforms, and welfare programs.[5] By the mid-1930s, reforming everyday purchasing power had become a persistent minor theme of public discourse.[6] Before the New Deal era ended, Americans had become at least vaguely familiar with the figure of "the consumer," the everyday citizen who would play a critical role in any revived economy. At the same time there emerged a widespread, loose, and distinct movement to fight for a variety of consumer aims—better goods, market regulation, and buyer protection—that has persisted into the present.[7] The cultural reorientation initiated by depression and war made clear that consumption was a fundamental practice in everyday life and a pillar of American national culture.

Central to this transformation were the conflicts among professional consumer experts. The New Deal provoked an often bitter public debate between advertisers and consumerists that lasted through World War II. Their views on the economy, society, and culture clashed, even as the New Deal and the war effort engaged both camps. Consumers' Research (CR) and the product-testing movement entered into open battle with corporate enterprise and, later, the federal government. Civic and consumer groups allied themselves with and against the government, with and against labor. Advertisers, media, and corporations wrangled with consumer advocates, product testers, and the government. They all fought to define the relationships of consumers with the state and with goods, and they struggled over the scope of the market in daily life. Although advertising's service to corporate capital granted its professionals true hegemonic influence, the oppositional consumer republicanism of Consumers' Research, along with other grassroots groups, earned public allegiance as well.[8] As the Herbert Hoover administration ineffectively grappled with the prolonged economic crisis, and then as Franklin D. Roosevelt's first New Deal experimented with state-sanctioned cartels and central economic planning, consumer professionals were pitted against one another. While both advertisers and consumerists privately thought most buyers unintelligent and ill educated, they agreed that consumption held the key to the economy and future prospects of American culture. If consuming were to become a new form of citizenship, what form would that citizenship take? Economic recovery was not the only prize in this confrontation: at stake were the meanings of belonging, nationality, and citizenship.

Questions of consumption's significance played out in many sites—politics, popular entertainment, intellectual forums, business, the home, and the workplace. As many scholars have shown, consumer questions most often were articulated in connection with other broad national concerns, such as the rights of labor, the questions of racial equality, social democracy, and antimonopoly that were raised by the center-left Popular Front, or discussions on the definition and direction of American life.[9] Yet in order to understand the ways Americans understood consumption as citizenship, we must first examine the conflicts of advertisers and consumerists during the Depression and early New Deal.

The divergent views held by these experts meant that no common ground would be reached easily. From 1930 through the end of World War II, advertisers played a leading role in business's nonstop wars against the New Deal and labor. Ad men fought for the broader interest of business in unregulated capitalism. They waged an unending campaign to wrest influence and attention from governmental programs and grassroots movements that challenged businessmen's market-dominated vision of society and their claims to lead. In this struggle advertisers further refined their own relationships with consumers and built countermovements to contain and defeat consumer reform. In turn, CR and other groups of consumer professionals found their perspectives fundamentally challenged in the Depression. Even as the New Deal brought consumer interests into the government, Consumers' Research pursued a radicalized vision of consumer interests, articulated as citizenship and embraced as a fundamental right. These two programs and the broader movements they represented would reach a partial truce during World War II. But even before the war, advertisers and consumerists circled each other repeatedly, as the Depression's economic crisis propelled consumer issues to public scrutiny.

SLAUGHTER ON MADISON AVENUE:
PROFESSIONAL SURVIVAL IN THE DEPRESSION

The Depression hit advertisers hard.[10] Beset with business paralysis and challenged by the loss of popular confidence, advertising professionals saw their economic prospects and cultural authority dramatically decline.[11] Only a few years had passed since President Calvin Coolidge had publicly proclaimed the profession as indispensable to the national economy; now, in 1932, Madison Avenue had to justify its work all over again to financially strapped and skeptical clients.[12] Customary expectations of painless economic growth, so central to the profession's social vision since the 1910s, gave way to grim evocations of a Social Darwinist struggle for survival. The long New Era party ended in a harsh reveille for tough times. For many advertisers, the utopia of growth and prosperity had now become the third circle of hell.

More explicitly, the Depression set off a price-cutting war among advertising agencies, which competed ever more aggressively for a shrinking pool of client dollars. Between 1929 and 1933, clients slashed spending, demanded extra free "service" (usually ancillary marketing and promotional assistance or materials), and changed agencies frequently.[13] Nearly one-quarter of the 150 leading advertising clients switched their agencies between 1929 and 1931, nearly double the rate of the mid-1920s.[14] Profits sunk so low that

Printers' Ink reported that the average operating costs of nearly a hundred leading advertising agencies exceeded 99 percent of their gross receipts.[15] Such ruthless cost-cutting affected the very structure of advertising economics. The American Association of Advertising Agencies squared off in a prolonged battle with the Association of National Advertisers (the trade group of corporate clients) to reduce or eliminate the entire agency commission system (customarily 15–17 percent of gross billings went to agencies).[16] Magazine and newspaper publishers also faced intense pressure to cut space rates; Curtis Publishing's price reduction for a full page of its bellwether *Ladies' Home Journal* sent a shock wave through the industry in 1932. Advertisers were hard-pressed to justify the very bread they earned.[17]

"Now is the time for advertising to sell!" cried the Ruthrauff and Ryan agency. "Now if ever, is the moment to view advertising for what it really is . . . and to realize that advertising men, after all, are a species of salesmen." Moralizing on "fundamental principles," "sound values," "confidence," and the "honor" of business leaders, ad men sought to keep clients within the fold. Only advertising could help businesses hold or build their markets in tough times. Agents bellowed that aggressive selling would give the individualist, risk-taking businessman an advantage.[18] Praising the "stimulus of adversity," Madison Avenue's denizens claimed that businesses could only prosper by accentuating their individuality, improving their products, and promoting them extensively.[19] "Fundamental principles" apparently entailed making no substantial changes in marketing, design, or selling. Agents and clients alike believed the Depression would end if manufacturers produced, retailers stocked their shelves, advertisers sold, and consumers bought. Executives told themselves that despite rising unemployment, people still had money to spend.[20] Some advertisers argued that the Depression only *enhanced* consumer desire. As N. W. Ayer argued, "Conditions may limit spending for a time but they cannot stop for very long the eternal pushing forward that is characteristic of the American nation." Another writer noted, "Buying capacity has shrunk . . . . But the desire for new clothes, new furniture and a thousand and one other commodities has not shrunk . . . . The resultant opportunity for advertising to produce at a profit, especially in the field of merchandise that comprises the necessaries of life, must be self-evident."[21] Ad men cheered themselves by remembering that people would have to buy.

To win back business, advertisers adopted aggressive, once taboo, sales tactics. Screaming headlines, sensationalist designs, and lurid "scare copy" focusing on a plethora of horrific physical ailments and social stigmas now swept through the magazine pages. One copywriter complained that "the back pages of our better magazines are rapidly becoming" a "chamber of horrors." Fierce competition and aggressive selling surfaced in what another observer described as "the frantic battle of today to animate or force the attraction power of advertising with extra big type, trick photography, professional testimonials, and quotations of imaginary, exaggerated, impossible conversations."[22] Hard-sell tactics, now renamed "back to basics," dominated the business as leaders gave the call: sell the consumer *by any means*. Agency executive William Day claimed that advertising's fundamental purpose—increasing sales and profits—depended on "tough copy—that direct truthful competitive stuff telling how a scientific advance in an industry has conferred a benefit on the ultimate consumer."[23]

The clearest sign of advertisers' crisis of nerve came in their rehabilitation of P. T. Barnum as a heroic ancestor. Before the Depression, Barnum was the yardstick of morality for ad men: respected for his business acumen, dangerous for his deceptions. Professionals commonly acknowledged his pioneering importance as a publicist but distanced themselves from his characteristic "humbug"—the fakery, deception, and exaggeration that marked his great triumphs. Barnum belonged to the patent medicine and snake oil days of advertising's preprofessional past.[24] Yet in the early Depression, professionals claimed him as the "father of advertising," whose ingenious entertainments fascinated the masses and made him the world's greatest salesman. Barnum's true legacy was showmanship, the ability to attract and entertain.[25] If sober truthfulness could not stimulate sales, ballyhoo and genial fakery would. The pious Batten, Barton, Durstine and Osborne (BBDO) agency now declared, "We believe in showmanship. It is the essence of selling—and of advertising. . . . It isn't reasonable or logical. It has nothing to do with studied technique. It need not be relevant to the product. Very likely it has no sales appeal. But an advertisement which has it will be read and will do a good job of selling, and one which lacks salesmanship will accomplish little."[26] J. Walter Thompson, long concerned with "the mass mind," now intensified its studies of the entertainment business to explain consumer behavior. The comics, radio, movies, vaudeville, mass magazines, popular music, and pulp literature all received obsessive scrutiny by ad men looking anxious to tap the irrational, instinctive impulses of the masses.[27] Through entertainment, advertisers would learn the secret of backward, unsophisticated hordes.[28] The rehabilitation of showmanship and "Barnumizing" highlighted advertisers' difficulties. Their praise for Barnum's flamboyant ease with popular tastes and low culture barely masked their own discomfort with mass culture and the masses themselves. Even as they continuously sold their sober profession-

alism to hard-nosed clients, they resorted to extreme methods of sensationalism and defended humbug and hyperbole.

In such an environment of fear, crisis, and competition, the Depression
quickly became a test of masculinity on Madison Avenue. Executives exhorted colleagues to put on overalls, adopt a "shirt-sleeve" or "flannel-shirt"
approach, and assert control of their fate.[29] Advertisers suffered a crisis of
besieged manhood. They cast themselves as virtuous and virile laborers acting to reclaim their livelihoods and reassert their masculine prerogatives.
They now scorned the "feminization" of products, especially the modern
artwork and designs of the 1920s boom, which they viewed as decadent and
corrupt. "Hail the Male!" one advertising writer noted of ad men's revolt
against the feminine dominance of copy and imagery. "Here's to a new day of
vim, vigor and vitality. We've been a nation of softies too long."[30] Some
ad men even railed against the rising popularity of radio, where advertisers
had "to accept the role of 'sugar daddy' to the gold-digging public who must
be entertained."[31] Now, ad men sought to control and compel fickle and
hoarding females, whose reluctance to spend, they believed, prolonged the
Depression.

Taking control meant taking no chances. Advertisers launched campaigns
to sell the profession to business and the public. N. W. Ayer, for example, began a decade-long campaign, blanketing hundreds of local newspapers along
with several dozen magazines, whose purpose was to "advertise advertising"
to consumers. The Ayer ads appeared nationwide, once more taking up an
old line: advertising in itself clearly guaranteed product quality and subtly
pressing people to spend more.[32] Several major household magazines began
similar campaigns boosting advertising and brands. *Woman's Home Companion, Better Homes and Gardens*, and *Good Housekeeping* all urged women to
manifest their faith in advertising by purchasing only nationally publicized
brands.[33] *Woman's Home Companion* even recruited Mrs. Consumer to be a
junior copywriter in a contest where readers would submit "talkies"—little
dialogues—on the advantages of buying "*Companion*-advertised products—or
the service which *Companion* advertisements have rendered you in your buying." All the winning stories, not surprisingly, concerned the advantages of
brand names for women shoppers. With their own revenues down, the publications circled the wagons and hectored readers to buy.[34]

In addition, agencies took control by reviving the political language that
had served them so well in the past. Now advertisers adopted a hard-line tone
of patriotism: new campaigns promoted advertising as embodying fundamental political principles. The leading agency, J. Walter Thompson, had

always eschewed such idealistic copy, preferring to win clients and sales with rational business language. Their no-nonsense sales pitches emphasized thorough study of consumer markets, distribution channels, and Spencerian theories of mass society.[35] Yet in 1934 the agency began a long-running series that portrayed its campaigns as exemplifying the great ideas of American history. These ads discussed the right to self-government, equality, freedom from entangling foreign alliances, westward expansion, and woman suffrage, among others, as the great motivating ideas of American history and as the stuff of Thompson's own work.[36] Comparing the Gettysburg Address to advertising, Thompson stated their case bluntly: "One basic idea is enough to overturn a government, to make a war or win it, to carry an inconspicuous product to world leadership. Nothing else approaches the force of a basic idea because nothing else communicates itself to the minds of so many people. And in politics, war or plain selling, it is the minds of the plain people which must be reached."[37] Advertising carried important ideas of American history to the masses, leading and serving them at the same time.

Similarly, several major corporations began radio campaigns centering on patriotism, nationalism, and a business version of American history. Coaxed and courted by agency chief Bruce Barton and NBC head Merlin Aylesworth, a reluctant Alfred Sloan authorized General Motors to begin a long-running and influential broadcast in 1931, in the teeth of the Depression. "The Parade of the States," intended as General Motors's first large-scale foray into radio, revived a patriotic "Story of the States" campaign first done by Ayer in 1915. But whereas Ayer's campaign sold advertising to business, Barton's addressed General Motors customers. The program fused nationalism, patriotic pride, and American history to sell automobile travel. The weekly program presented portraits of the different states, explored their histories, commerce, and distinct cultural traditions, and ended with an appeal to visit, preferably by automobile.[38] Moreover, NBC and General Motors offered "The Parade of the States" tributes (penned by Barton) to listeners as premiums; they were eventually published in book form. The radio program thus emphasized national unity and civic pride while selling transportation and travel. The state "tributes" often set transportation at the core of American history, associating that history with the sponsor's automotive products: "Along the trails of Michigan the stagecoach followed the oxcart. Then came the automobile . . . Michigan's gift to the world [which] has made these states a United States . . . this nation a neighborhood."[39] Each week General Motors products became integral elements of American history and nationality, legitimized by their part in sustaining the republic.[40]

The program's success elated sponsor, network, and agency. A pleased Sloan wrote, "The United States has grown and become unified, as means of travel have been enlarged. . . . If this volume [of tributes] makes us know each our neighbors better and increases the desire to visit them more often, it will have contributed something to the more perfect uniting of our United States."[41] But of course, the program served more than good will: General Motors promoted "Parade" extensively with its dealers and manufacturing plants. The corporation also sent copies of the programs, along with letters from Sloan, to state governors and legislators, as well as "presidents of banks, newspaper editors, chambers of commerce, fraternal organizations, advertising and automobile clubs, women's clubs, superintendents of schools and libraries, in fact anyone of any consequence." Listeners responded in kind; within the first ten weeks, over 48,000 separate requests came in for the tributes, including many from "school children, patriots, historians, professors or Senators."[42] A later BBDO history summed up the program this way: "The merchandising of the program to each state's official, fraternal, business, club women, [and] educational organizations was a snow job. A handsomely printed framed copy of Bruce Barton's tribute was sent to each State's Historical Society."[43] In a similar vein, NBC developed an audience participation program, "The Buick Hall of Fame," in which listeners, along with a panel of prominent business and political leaders, would honor current civic heroes and organizations for their acts of public service and patriotism.[44]

Advertisers' determination to coax the coin from resisting buyers also surfaced in the brief vogue of "consumer engineering." Its chief advocates, Roy Sheldon and Egmont Arens, claimed that consumer engineering was a new approach to selling, which embodied "the science of finding customers" and, more important, "the making of customers when the findings are slim."[45] Manufacturers had largely solved production, but most consumers lacked sufficient means to buy. However, consumer engineering was more than a plea for progressive obsolescence, market research, or centralized planning. It was a totalized approach that advocated psychological and behavioral study to learn consumer preferences and the retooling of businesses to meet them. Led by both advertising agents and industrial designers, the movement's frankly acknowledged concern was to manufacture customers, not goods.[46] Through market research, package redesign, industrial styling, and business psychology, consumption engineers proposed to match products to people.[47] As agency chief Earnest Elmo Calkins asserted, "Producing customers is one of the legitimate objects of mass production. . . . The consumer engineer is one of the big jobs of the future. He will outrank the sales manager and give orders to the production manager. It is not his job to sell what the factory makes but to teach the factory to make what the customer will buy."[48] Consumer engineers now openly campaigned for business what Thorstein Veblen had criticized three decades before: the mass production of standardized tastes and aspirations among the buying public, exactly matched to the products rolling off the assembly lines. Yet consumer engineering never really generated a movement, as businesses proved unwilling to invest in the research necessary to develop the methods.[49] The only aspect of the program to survive was its least original: progressive obsolescence. Throughout the Depression, manufacturers' emphasis on obsolescence battled with long-lived popular practices of thrift and reuse. While consumer engineers castigated older advertising ideas of "forced selling" on the customer, their project of manufacturing consumers was in reality a similar agenda.[50]

FLEEPS, MORONS, ANTS, AND MASSES: THE NEW SOCIOLOGY OF ADVERTISING AND SELLING

Beyond taking such steps to control sales conditions, markets, client expectations, and their own professional image, advertisers renegotiated their relationships with consumers. In the punishing economic climate, copywriters and artists now drew harsh, manipulative portraits of consumers. Marketing strategies lost the New Era veneer of genteel sophistication. Advertisers revised their views of consumers downward and assumed a churlish, punitive attitude. However, working so intimately with the instruments of mass culture and mass marketing threatened to dissolve the barriers separating ad men from consumers. As long as the cultural status of consumption and the future of capitalism remained in flux, advertisers strove to keep their distance from "the people." The more advertisers became shrill entertainers, the more fiercely they guarded the boundaries between themselves and their audiences. Peddling showmanship and sensation, advertisers felt the barriers blur.[51]

Back-to-basics selling bred a Machiavellian approach to the mass mind. "We are talking to *Daily News* Readers, not to university students," admonished one copywriter. William Esty summed up the attitude toward the masses: "Captain John Smith, in one of his papers referring to the Indians of Virginia called them, 'Poor and miserable souls, wrapped up unto death in almost invincible ignorance.' I sometimes wonder if that isn't a pretty good characterization of the population today."[52] Advertisers now customarily referred to the consuming public not as large aggregates or markets but instead as a mass—an irrational, impulsive, instinctive herd, called by one cynic "the vast army of half-wits who have learned to put Bolt 37 into part 48."[53] "Markets are PEOPLE," N. W. Ayer reassured anxious clients, telling them that consumers really all were alike under the skin. Yet representations of large crowds often told the opposite story, presenting not folks but a faceless anonymous crowd: mass society was alien, impersonal, and threatening (fig. 7.1).[54] As advertisers faced ever-worsening conditions, they conflated their own private anxieties with the social realities they depicted in their ads. In a sensibility that we might best term "corporate naturalism," Madison Avenue recast consumers as incompetent, fearful, irrational, and dangerous. The people, in fact, were the horde.

Some experts even embraced theories of animal behavior and authoritarian control to explain consumers. Thompson executive William Day urged his colleagues to consider consumer behavior as if they were entomologists: "Study of the ants and bees shows that in their simple scheme of things one lever is sufficient to provide control. Appetite, response to taste or smell, this is the lever . . . . For centuries human beings have been ruled by similar means. A nation is only a human mass united by belief in the validity of a political theory." Human behavior was determined by laws governing emotions and instincts; attempts at persuasion through other channels would fail because the great mass of people did not "think" as those on Madison Avenue understood the term. Day told a class of junior salesmen, "If I go to an ant hill and blow a horn the ants pay no attention. They have no ears. They don't hear. To them hearing is absolutely unknown. I can blow a horn all day. But if I put a drop of sugar down, ants come right away. . . . Large quantities of people you have to sell to cannot reason; you have to handle them through the lowest forms of reason—or through their emotional reactions."[55] The staid *Better Homes and Gardens* trumpeted its "typical" readers, "Mr. and Mrs. John Homer," as having "The Buy-ological Urge." Thompson, the agency perhaps most taken with the sociobiological approach, phrased it best: "Advertising . . . is perhaps the Greatest Agency of Natural Selection in the Business World."[56]

But in the early 1930s the Buy-ological Urge seemed less frequent than cicadas. As the economy worsened in 1931–32, executives took to blaming the victim. Advertisers told themselves that consumers were not financially strapped but were on a "buyer's strike" that prolonged the Depression and crippled business.[57] Advertisers, merchants, and business leaders all countered with "Buy Now" campaigns, home improvement drives, "Buy American" campaigns, "National Bargain Days," all of which were couched in the rhetoric of public interest and patriotism.[58] "Buy Something from Somebody

Where do
they get their
Ideas?

At first glance you see a crowd, a weaving mass of people. Look again. They are individual bodies governed by individual minds.

And every mind is swarming with ideas just as this open space is swarming with people. Ideas about what vegetables to cook for dinner tonight, what clothes to wear to the theatre, what roofing to put on the new house, what cigarettes to smoke . . .

Where do they get their ideas? From conversations with other people? And from observations of other people?

Suppose we assume that they do. Then where do those other people get the ideas? From the newspapers . . . morning, evening and Sunday?

From the magazines? From the radio? From the talking pictures? From the car cards and posters that surround them? From other forces less tangible?

How can you profit most from the utilization of these tangible forces? And how can you set intangible forces in motion to influence their ideas in behalf of your product?

From seven cities in the United States and from the center of every large population area in every land, except Russia, Japan and China, where offices will be opened as soon as conditions warrant, the J. Walter Thompson Company is co-operating with a group of distinguished clients in seeking out the fundamentals

that lie behind human motives in the purchase of things and services from day to day.

Through its consistent policy in searching for basic facts in the actual field of the given enterprise, this company is today a leader with those products which lie in the highly competitive trades and industries.

New York · Chicago · St. Louis · Boston · Cincinnati · San Francisco · Los Angeles · · Montreal · Toronto · · London · Paris · Madrid · Berlin · Stockholm · Copenhagen · Antwerp · Warsaw · · Alexandria · Port Elizabeth · · Buenos Aires · Sao Paulo · · Bombay · · Melbourne · Sydney · · Batavia · · · Wellington

J. Walter Thompson Company

FIGURE 7.1. "Where Do They Get Their Ideas?" (J. Walter Thompson Archives, John W. Hartman Center for Sales, Advertising, and Marketing History, Duke University, Durham, N.C.)

—We All Prosper Together!" clamored the Standard Home Utilities Company of Ohio. Chevrolet sent to all its customers a booklet, *71 Days of Work*, that explained how much labor was contained in a single new car and urged consumers to spend immediately.[59] Dana Frank reminds us that the national "Buy American" movement, which "rose in exact correlation with the economy's degeneration," indeed overshadowed the "Buy Now" sentiments of advertisers and merchants. Yet at the heart of both ideas a simple belief thrived: the economy's difficulties originated in a distinct scapegoat: alien manufacturers or unpatriotic buyers. The "Buy Now" editorials that filled both trade literature and mass publications appropriated nationalist and political language. Consumption and patriotism were united in urging Mrs. Consumer to spend. "Let's stop being Mickey Misers," cajoled one automobile executive. "Everything we buy at retail, from pins to pianos, means an order on the jobber, on the factory. Multiply you and me by millions and we are really On Our Way."[60] The editors of *Printers' Ink* invoked revolutionary traditions to describe consumer behavior: "Come what will, the Missus is going to call in a paper hanger. Also she's going to call in a painter and a plumber. She's been put off long enough. Now she's going to re-paper that front bedroom, refinish the floors throughout the house, and modernize that bathroom. . . . The citizens of America, and in particular, *those of the upper levels of intelligence and culture and taste and aspirations*, are taking up arms against dinginess."[61] A Wanamaker department store editorial made the connection between spending and nationhood explicit. "America is not a cheap nation," it asserted. "Our people are not shoddy people. The American Standard of living is known the world over as better—better homes, better things to wear and live with, better and cleaner foods, better education and amusements, better working conditions . . . . Cheapness in itself is destructive—it tears down. It cheapens the mind of the worker, his job in making a good product, his ambition. It cheapens the morale of business, of industry, of the people."[62] Demand and quality directly reflected the intrinsic traits of the nation and in turn shaped national destiny. While merchants and retailers had long encouraged consumers to use goods as mirrors for themselves, the Depression made explicit the connections between citizenship, national identity, and consumption.

A most telling instance of the "Buy Now" sentiment appeared in a *Ladies' Home Journal* campaign, organized by public relations guru Edward L. Bernays. Once the costliest national advertising medium in the 1920s, the *Journal* by 1931 had fallen on hard times. It cut its famous cover-page rates and had seen its advertising matter dwindle from over two hundred pages per

FIGURE 7.2. Mrs. Consumer Foils the Depression. (*Ladies' Home Journal*, April 1932, 9)

issue to less than forty. Late that year, editor Loring Schuler initiated a campaign to rescue the economy through Mrs. Consumer, the *Journal* reader. "It's Up to the Women!" the *Journal* announced. American women would have to get out and spend money to buy the nation back to health. The *Journal* urged its readers to understand any purchase, no matter how inconsequential —a new hat, a repainted house, new upholstery—as investments in the community as a whole. Schuler appealed to *Journal* readers to spend their money: buy or improve a home, start a family and not postpone one, buy an auto or trade up to a newer model, invest money in new things rather than save in banks, and generally maintain or increase spending levels. New goods or services meant increased prosperity for the community. The very products advertised in the magazine's pages were not only the means to meet an individual woman's needs, but the symbols and manifestations of new jobs and opportunities for other families (fig. 7.2). Here, material modernity not only mirrored individual personality and desire but also enhanced the civic realm.[63] Consuming threw a lifeline to businesses and workers. The emblem of this campaign was a determined and stylish young shopper, packages clutched in one hand, dragging a reluctant Uncle Sam with his wallet off to market (fig. 7.3). Far from being merely individual property, goods were the fundamental glue in economic and social relations.[64] "Based on recommendations from the American Economists' Committee for Women's Activities," the *Journal* rallied its readers to "pocketbook patriotism," urging them to spend in the present. The republic's future lay in the hands that fished through the purse; inflation and economic collapse would result if American women continued to hoard.[65] The "It's Up to the Women!" campaign enlisted women's civic organizations from the League of Women Voters through the

FIGURE 7.3. "It's Up to the Women!" (*Ladies' Home Journal*, February 1932, cover)

American Home Economics Association and secured statements from such figures as Carrie Chapman Catt, Eleanor Roosevelt, and even Elizabeth Arden.[66] The endorsement of this veiled appeal to spend money by such prominent social or political leaders emphasized the connections between a woman's civic duties and her private familial interests as Mrs. Consumer. However, without the price-cutting commitments from industries and retail to encourage spending, the "movement" was less a social force than a well-organized publicity campaign. It offered little meaningful reassurance to families fearful of further economic disruptions. But the campaign iconography emphasized clearly the connection between citizenship and consumption.[67] Mrs. Consumer stood at the heart of the great economic order.

In their new shirtsleeve sensibility, however, advertisers now rebelled at their dependence on women. Frustrated at Mrs. Consumer's unwillingness to spend Uncle Sam out of depression, advertisers began to challenge and openly discredit women's abilities as consumers.[68] Some stressed that women were in the thrall of forces beyond their control—namely, the imperious desires of other family members. "The Shadow of a Man Stands Behind Every Woman Who Buys," intoned a long-running trade journal campaign for *Redbook* magazine. Large expressionist shadows loomed behind Mrs. Consumer, "unseen by the salesclerk, yet ready to help or hinder the sale of your goods." This Mrs. Consumer was easily manipulated (fig. 7.4). Giving the female consumers in these advertisements such humorous names as "Fleep," "Nerp," and "Whuff" also reflected the advertising backlash.[69] Similarly, a campaign for "Magnetic *McCall's*" celebrated women as consumers: "Who Says It's a Man's World?" Yet the illustrations of a lone male consumer, outnumbered and outmaneuvered by avid female shoppers, did not celebrate women's status as the great American consumers but depicted them as a herd sweeping over the hapless middle-class man. The image of stampeding women enthralled by the irresistible magazine depicted psychological suggestion out of control: these women shoppers were an irrational force of nature far removed from the competent Mrs. Consumer whom ad men had praised only a few years before.[70] "What did you do with that $11,000,000 we gave you last week?" asked an endless row of husbands of their wives, symbolizing *The American Home's* readership. Celebrating Mrs. Consumer's buying power also offered opportunities to criticize women for their irresponsibilities in handling it.[71]

Madison Avenue infantilized women consumers. Visually, illustrations gradually reduced portrayals of women to childlike imagery over the 1930s. The modernist and abstract stylings of the 1920s gave way to cartoonish,

"MORE ICE CUBES" WHISPERED THE SHADOW

REGARD the tableau above. The salesman is unleashing a flood of oratory in praise of Chillblain Refrigerators.

His customer is Mrs. Chesterton Whuff. For some reason Mrs. Whuff is in a mood of abstraction. In spite of the salesman's skill, she seems hardly to hear his voice.

She *does* hear it. But she hears another voice, too. The voice of the shadow. The remembered voice of Chesterton Whuff, complaining about the paucity of ice cubes in their present refrigerator. In this respect, she notes that the otherwise excellent Chillblain is scant improvement.

Presently, counseled by the shadow of her husband, Mrs. Whuff will excuse herself with the remark, "I'll have to think it over."

Really she means to *talk* it over—in family conference with Mr. Whuff. Tonight the whole subject of refrigerators will be aired. If Mr. Whuff has seen and heeded the advertising of the Chillblain Refrigerator, he will know the miracle of speed with which it makes ice cubes. And he and Mrs. Whuff may agree to buy a Chillblain.

But if the only refrigerator he knows and approves is some other kind—the Frostbyte, for example — there will have to be a compromise somewhere. Until husband and wife think alike, the money stays in the pocket.

This necessity of selling two people in order to dominate the Family Conference is not limited to refrigerators. It takes two votes to approve an automobile, or a vacuum cleaner, or almost anything on which family money is spent. The daily food is a compromise between his tastes and hers. Even the clothes Mrs. Whuff buys for herself are bought with an eye to inspiring his admiration.

Would you have the husband champion your product in the Family Conference? Tell him about it, as well as the wife. Is it cheaper? More stylish? Easier to use? Tell him, too, and rest assured that he will remind her.

You sell both sexes when you tell your story in Redbook Magazine. Redbook is deliberately edited to appeal to both wife *and* husband. Every thousand copies are read by 1480 women and 1420 men. Moreover, in Redbook you pay 30% *less* to reach wives *plus* husbands than you pay to reach one sex alone through other magazines. Even if you shut your eyes to its masculine circulation, it would still cost you less to reach women alone in Redbook.

Sell the family and you sell all. Use Redbook and save 30%. Redbook Magazine, 230 Park Avenue, New York City.

REDBOOK
MAGAZINE

THE SHADOW OF A MAN STANDS BEHIND EVERY WOMAN WHO BUYS

FIGURE 7.4. The "Shadow of a Man" Campaign. (*Advertising and Selling*, May 25, 1944, 7)

juvenile depictions. Women (and men) became more youthful, even adolescent, in appearance. Spurred on only in part by comic strip advertising, illustrators now presented adult women who seemed barely out of school.[72] More significantly, advertisers attributed women's prominence as purchasers to their "natural instincts" for bargains or quality; no longer did advertisers frequently praise women's skills or talents as anything but inborn nature. As one observer put it, "She will buy an automobile for its radiator ornament or refuse to buy it because she doesn't like the salesman. And the surprising thing (to a mere man) is that she is so often, so mysteriously right!"[73] In the Depression women were celebrated for their instincts, not their abilities as shoppers.[74]

The harshest judgment of women consumers came from popular self-help author and radio commentator Walter Pitkin, who called woman "the economic imbecile." His massive 1932 tome, The Consumer, was an ill-conceived hash of Wesley Mitchell and H. L. Mencken. Pitkin asserted that women bought under the influence of their passions, encouraged by the deferential or flirtatious suggestions of salesmen and sensory judgments irrelevant to quality or cost. Pitkin's bilious critique turned Robert Lynd's consumer illiteracy into depravity. For Pitkin, female consumers were incapable of reason, abstraction, or calculation. They were by nature consumers, "closer to our primordial animality" than men, the producers.[75] However, women lacked the skills for ascertaining value. As spenders, women were enemies of civilization: they wasted industry's resources by insatiable demands for meaningless style changes and cheap shoddy goods for variety. Pitkin charged that their devotion to ephemeral goods and their extravagance caused and prolonged the Depression. Women were unable to buy wisely for themselves and their families; their irrational demands curtailed the production of necessary commodities. When the 1920s boom burst, women had not set aside enough money for themselves or their families.[76] For Pitkin, women caused the Depression and could not cure it. The feminine character of consumption symbolized and produced the sickness of the American economy. As economics, Pitkin's work was substandard in its own time; he quoted raw figures without context and based his analyses on dubious assertions of human behavior. Moreover, his reasoning seems peculiarly myopic, focused intently on women consumers but paying little attention to any structural causes of the Depression. His analysis evoked "The Backward Art" of his Columbia colleague Wesley Mitchell, yet Pitkin's work was notably inferior as both economics and social observation. As cultural commentary, however, his abrasive attacks spoke volumes for businessmen who were frustrated and angered by the Depression. In that regard, Pitkin foretold the 1940s misogyny of Philip Wylie's best-selling *Generation of Vipers* (1945) more effectively than he continued the traditions of Veblen and Mitchell. Pitkin's formulation of Mrs. Consumer revealed an extreme backlash against women, along with business's fears of the purchasing public.

Pitkin-style copy also appeared in national magazine advertising. "The Little Woman, GPA" (see fig. 1.4) now gave way to an invasion of incompetent mothers, shrewish wives, and unskilled newlywed brides, all unable to perform basic chores. "Manage these or they'll manage you!" snarled the Cleanliness Institute to a homemaker cowering before her tools (fig. 7.5). "She complained to the plumber . . . but the plumber blamed her" for using the wrong cleanser and ruining her bathroom. Too many difficulties in the home overwhelmed the incompetent Mrs. Consumer, who could only admit her helplessness and rely on the "magic" of Mr. Advertiser's products.[77] Being a good consumer or homemaker truly stood outside her control. The honeymoon of Mr. Advertiser and Mrs. Consumer ended, thus setting the stage for women's grassroots criticism of advertising that would propel them into the emerging consumer movement.

Decades-old ideas of the "twelve-year-old mentality" now hardened into a more cynical view of all consumers as children. The telltale episode occurred in the rise of comic strip advertising. In a 1931 survey of newspaper reading habits, researcher George Gallup learned that the comic pages far outstripped all other features in popularity. Virtually everyone who picked up a paper read the funnies. Gallup's finding both shocked and galvanized Madison Avenue (one pundit called it a "startling commentary on our national tastes and mentality") and initiated a vogue for comic strip–style advertising, which told dramatic stories featuring products in cartoons with ballooned captions. Comic strips were "the swiftest and most compelling way to tell a story in print . . . [through] an underlining and a diagraming of ideas that can make them clear to any intelligence."[78] Advertisers plainly viewed these forms of entertainment as debased and low; they clearly felt superior to those people who embraced them. One senior copywriter dismissed comic strip ads this way: "[Since] much of the copy sounds like the mouthings of a moron, maybe a good name would be baloonatic advertising."[79] Nevertheless, advertisers used them.

The new attitudes also emerged in portrayals of children. If ad men had once seen women as ideal consumers, now they bestowed that honor on juveniles. What made women ideal consumers were their childlike qualities, and as ad men never tired of reminding each other, all consumers were really

FIGURE 7.5. "Manage These or They'll Manage You!" (*Woman's Home Companion*, July 1930, 79)

children at heart.[80] But the metaphor of consumers as children could be reversed; increasingly, ad men pointed out if consumers were like children, likewise children were ideal consumers. One hard-boiled agency pronounced, "After all, men and women in the mass are apt to have incredibly shallow brain pans. In infancy they are attracted by bright colors, glitter and noise. And in adulthood they retain a strikingly similar set of reactions."[81] Advertisers and merchants alike had long been fascinated with the possibility of selling directly to children and selling parents through children. Historian Lisa Jacobson has shown that in the 1920s advertisers portrayed a new children's consumerism that countered standard visions of women. They showed boys as connoisseurs, progressive and modernist consumers who educated their whole families in taste and brand preferences. This child (really adolescent) consumer embodied both technological sophistication and limitless appetites—an avid buyer who did not need education.[82]

For ad men, then, children became the perfect consumers, possessed of short attention spans, limitless desires, and hearty appetites and ignorant of logic or sales resistance. As a Thompson man reminded his colleagues, "One nice thing about children is that they have a sense of values." One agency advertisement explicitly discussed adults as consumers in these terms: "He can't be forced to buy any more than a baby can be forced to walk. His attention, like that of a baby, is drawn to a thousand different things. Man and baby, each sees something he wants, starts for it, is interrupted, turns to something else. Out of these distractions comes something that finally commands attention. The baby takes his first step. The grown-up buys."[83] Children also were the best barometers of advertising, the best people on whom to test sales ideas because they responded openly and spontaneously, trusting the advertiser. "Have you a six-year-old?" asked one advertiser. "Or maybe your neighbors have. If so take time to show him or her the pictures and advertisements in the magazines, or go for a walk and look at the poster boards and in store windows. Notice how quickly complicated illustrations, fancy hand-lettering or freak spelling draw comment and question. Then remember that thousands stumble over the same things."[84]

Although advertisers and merchants had long been accustomed to using children to untie parents' purse strings, during the 1930s they increasingly sought out children on their own. Advertisers saw children as collectors with a great desire to accumulate.[85] As such, ad men argued, they constituted a ripe market for the premiums and giveaways offered with a wide range of goods.[86] Radio presented the ideal portal to children; it offered direct, unguarded access to children's pliant minds and avid desires without the mediation of adults. Such access was risky, however. By the 1930s broadcasters and agencies faced a mounting chorus of criticism over both the content of children's radio programming and advertising appeals directed to young listeners. Parental and progressive critics claimed that advertising eroded adult authority within the family by stirring children's desires without invitation.[87] Still worse, they charged that children's programs such as *Little Orphan Annie* were lurid and sensational, resulting in harmful effects on children's nerves and behavior.[88] At issue was the right of advertisers to enter homes and address as equals those who were not full citizens; if children needed guidance in the marketplace, parents alone wanted to supply it. The irony is that in many ways advertisers viewed parents as no different from their offspring.

With the resentment against women as consumers and a new focus on children as ideal buying influences, advertisers turned anew to the gathered nuclear family as the source of consumption. Ad men now claimed that the whole family made purchasing decisions on everything from breakfast cereals to automobiles. According to many advertisers, within the family no one person dominated, despite mother's responsibilities and father's breadwinning status. In defiance of the facts that many families were patriarchal in nature, that many extended families still lived under one roof, and that there were limits to any outside authority, advertisers redoubled their efforts during the Depression to influence the family as a group, each composed of childlike, irrational, and highly impulsive members.

Thus, in the Depression advertisers recalibrated their relationships with consumers. Although they had long been used to raising and resolving difficulties through products and helping consumers to address problems of everyday life, in the early 1930s ad men depicted consumers in much harsher ways than before. As they were well aware, they risked a negative response from readers and listeners, and they got it. Those consumers who were frustrated and angered by aggressive salesmanship and insulting portrayals found kindred critical spirits in Consumers' Research and the loose federation of organizations and agendas that would come to be known as the consumer movement.

GUINEA PIG NATION: RESENTMENT AND REFORM

The cultural upheaval of the Depression brought forth intense examination of business civilization. Once the restricted province of intellectuals, these considerations now found a wider and more receptive audience. Much of the journalistic reportage, cultural analysis, and proletarian social fiction of the early 1930s bitterly castigated business values and laid the blame for the economic crisis squarely at the boardroom doors of corporate enterprise.[89] With less fanfare, signs appeared of anticommercial sentiment that rudely questioned corporate capital's presumption to rule. Some critics even belittled the business contention that America would meaningfully benefit from restored industrial growth, urban expansion, and economic recovery.[90] A persistent strain revived in the cultural crisis of capitalism was a critique of advertising, selling, and the excesses of consumption.

Some of the most cutting criticisms of the commercial system came not from its proletarian victims but from cynics close enough to know its operations. The satirical magazine *Ballyhoo* appeared in 1931, taking as its special targets commercial enterprise and entertainment. Its very name evoked disreputable publicity stunts and insignificant, sensational ephemera.[91] A frequent recipient of its barbs was advertising: *Ballyhoo* cartoons and collages viewed the Barnumesque aspects of commerce as the focal point of selling. *Ballyhoo* featured fictional parody advertisements that announced that the gleaming products on display were shoddy or unnecessary and that advertisers thought consumers were morons. The magazine's mascot character, "Elmer Zilch," appeared alternately as the hapless victim of aggressive sales pitches and the cynical consumer wise to advertising fakery.[92] His very name yoked the common citizen with the cipher. In *Ballyhoo*'s cynical vision, the common folk who bought advertised goods were victims of a shell game. Commercial culture was intrusive, deceitful, and irrelevant. "Ballyhoo's Radio Log," a parody guide to programs, irreverently made the point: "WABC—Threats about losing your teeth. . . . WEAF—History as filtered through the Standard Oil Co. . . . WEAF—Voice of Firestone—including 12 mins. (Gawd help you) of the 'eldest son of the founder.' . . . WABC—Pebeco wheedles and threatens. . . . WEAF—Beware of other Aspirins."[93] The humor worked: within a year the magazine had a circulation of 1.5 million.[94] Even as ad men more aggressively promoted a new rapprochement with popular entertainment as a means of getting closer to the commoner, *Ballyhoo* used entertainment to warn readers away from advertising. The magazine's jovial but caustic portrayal of modern life perhaps limited its appeal, and the venture faded after a few years—but not before it resonated with other equally biting critiques.[95]

Radio provoked strong criticism as well. Commercial broadcasting had become established by 1930 as radio's prevailing economic structure, although educators, activists, and businesses would fight over its form and governance until the Communications Act of 1934 ratified the business enclosure of the airwave commons.[96] Advertisers assumed a pivotal role in the new radio order, but in the early 1930s procedures and practices were still inchoate. Industry policy that favored so-called indirect advertising would end in 1931–32's worsening economy. By then, radio announcers regularly delivered full-fledged, unabashed sales talks.[97] At this development many listeners who had long opposed radio advertising rebelled, complaining to advertisers about the length and content of many commercials. Some spokesmen warned advertisers that listeners just barely tolerated commercials. As a typical critic put it, "The public doesn't want them. We don't give a damn about your toothpaste or your hats. We want entertainment. . . . We're not listening to find out how to get rid of Athlete's Foot and B.O."[98] Opponents of commercial broadcasting mounted drives to limit on-air advertising and to shape radio according to a public interest, educational agenda.[99] Such groups as the National Committee on Education by Radio and the Women's National Radio Committee, along with educators and audience groups such as the American Listeners Society, pushed for strict controls and limitations on commercial messages. They argued forcefully that the air belonged to *all* Americans and that government should not permit commercial enterprises to charge a toll to gain access to it. Viewing radio as a tremendous force for social betterment through education, these groups fought its dominance by commercial sponsors, whose true interests, they charged, centered on increasing sales.[100] Moreover, they feared that exposure to advertising "propaganda" and "jazz" would further debase an already uneducated populace. These critics shared a great deal with the elitist worldviews of ad men and broadcasters who ran radio. Yet like consumerists, advocates of radio uplift sought to rein in the influence of the market in daily life. As such, they posed a threat to advertisers; many in the trade felt that their powerful, simmering resentments against commercialization could be the industry's undoing.

Radio figured prominently in the work of one dissenter whose inside knowledge of advertising made his critique especially galling. James Rorty, a former copywriter at some large New York agencies, offered a stinging indictment of his old business and its deleterious effect on American culture. *Our Master's Voice: Advertising* (1934) was a leftist critique of business and consumer culture that minced few words.[101] Building on the work of Veblen and Stuart Chase, Rorty attacked advertising as a morally bankrupt enterprise beyond repair. Advertisers purveyed cheap goods and inane sentiment to a public they held in contempt. Advertisers were, in his words, "profit-motivated producers of customers," who believed it "right and beautiful to make a customer out of a woman, even though this involves making her into a fool, a slave and a greedy neurotic."[102] Further, advertising embodied everything wrong with capitalism: it created false expectations, exploited people's misery, and hypnotized them into a pursuit of worthless things. Copywriters played fast and loose with public beliefs, serving up a "body of doctrine" that molded "the economic, social, moral and ethical patterns of the community into serviceable conformity with the profit-making interests of advertisers and of the advertising business." The interweaving of advertising with the structure of communication and publishing resulted in "reader-exploitation, cultural malnutrition and stultification."[103]

Rorty dedicated the book to his friend Thorstein Veblen, whose influence would appear to discerning readers on every page. But Rorty provided a political prescription that the skeptical Veblen had avoided and the circumspect Chase downplayed. To counter the exploitation and self-deceit of business society, Americans needed to adopt a collectivist economy, where goods would all be "functional" and advertising would be either based purely on facts and standards or scarcely exist at all. Rorty asserted confidently that advertising and capitalism were ultimately obsolete, for "there is nothing the matter with the machine, with industry, except that its productive forces cannot be released, nor its dehumanizing effects controlled, under a profit economy." For Rorty, the critical issue was whether Americans "have enough residual mind and character to achieve the necessitated transition to a collectivized economy and a classless society."[104] Only collectivism could save the worthy aspects of American culture.

Rorty's work had little immediate impact beyond the intelligentsia and his former haunts on Madison Avenue. As with *Your Money's Worth*, advertising's noteworthies rushed to downplay the book's significance. Yet their nervous air of dismissal and patronizing tolerance—Rorty's former boss Roy Durstine sniffed, "Honestly Jim, you can write more lucidly than that"—revealed how deeply the critique hit home. "Comrade Rorty" was derided as a malcontent, a failed ad man, an "artiste" who fancied himself too good for the profession, an outside agitator. What advertisers could not dismiss was that he had been one of them; his revulsion at what he had helped to build provided a cautionary tale for professionals already stung by severe setbacks and undergoing an identity crisis.[105]

To advertisers, however, one lapsed copywriter's plodding Veblenisms paled in comparison to the monthly barbs from Consumers' Research. Comrade Rorty himself was one of a growing number of subscribers to CR's confidential bulletin.[106] The product-testing agency flourished throughout the early Depression, reaching 58,000 members by 1935.[107] By 1934, the consumer organization was advertisers' most hated enemy, second only to the New Deal itself. The Depression awakened the organization politically, and CR journeyed from a volunteerist faith in consumer and commercial cooperation to an ardent advocacy of thorough government regulation. In the months after Franklin Roosevelt's election, CR traveled a tortuous path toward grassroots activism. Faced with bitter business opposition, garnering slowly growing public support, and weathering fractious relationships with other reform groups, CR steadily politicized. The organization moved away from promoting scientific standards for goods, rational purchasing, and functional tastes in products. Instead, CR now concluded that consumers could only be protected in the market if they became politically aware and active themselves. Only by compelling the political system to protect their rights as citizens would consumers ever extract satisfaction from the marketplace.

Just as a popular book gave CR its start, a second best seller placed it in the national spotlight. Written by Arthur Kallet and F. J. Schlink, *100,000,000 Guinea Pigs* marked the first flowering of the group's new political awareness. Like Schlink, Kallet had worked at the American Standards Association; the two shared similar backgrounds, although Kallet, an electrical engineer by training, was more at ease in public forums and with publicity.[108] Published early in 1933, *100,000,000 Guinea Pigs* struck a popular chord of resentment and fear among its readers. Kallet and Schlink argued that corporate greed and scientific ignorance turned consumers into unwitting victims, no better than lab animals, of products that were all too often harmful or toxic. An ineffective and inadequate Food and Drug Administration (FDA), a probusiness Federal Trade Commission, and business's own determination to quash adverse criticism left consumers endangered and betrayed by the very organizations set up to safeguard them. Even worse, corporations knowingly exposed consumers to dangers, confident that lax regulation would spare them from punishment or restraint. Advertising furthered this exploitation by spreading misinformation about products in its columns; publishers who fed off advertising revenues quietly suppressed critiques and damaging information on commercial products or consumption itself.[109] The only protection for guinea pig consumers was protest and organization, to demand government action to safeguard their rights. The book argued above all that, as Americans, consumers had explicit rights to protection from fraud and harm caused by dangerous products.[110]

The book's powerful central image demonstrated how far CR's critique had evolved in the six years since *Your Money's Worth*. Where confused and infantilized buyers had once inhabited the surreal Wonderland of the market, now buyers were helpless animals caught in a maze of health hazards at every blind turn. The epithet "guinea pig" struck a raw nerve, conjuring up a creature with neither consciousness nor strength to fight those who would experiment on it. Summoning both powerlessness and ignorance, the name entered Depression-era slang as a highly charged term used by advertisers and critics alike to describe consumers. The portrait of the helpless individual whose fate lay in the hands of an indifferent government and a malevolent business system resonated deeply in a society with millions out of work and millions more seeking new ideas about the relationships of the government, the economy, and themselves. Kallet and Schlink's work revealed the dark side of capitalism's consumer utopia. If advertising visions of consumer goods offered self-transformation and boundless possibility to buyers, *100,000,000 Guinea Pigs* played on fears of the unknown and stoked popular suspicions of large corporations that made and sold goods.

The book was an impressive popular favorite; throughout the 1930s, *100,000,000 Guinea Pigs* remained in great demand on municipal library shelves, reaching a wide working- and middle-class audience; it was an even bigger success than *Your Money's Worth*. Publisher the Vanguard Press ran eighteen printings in as many months; both the RKO Radio and Fox film studios even pursued the idea of a movie version.[111] A lasting impact was seen in the second generation of muckraking literature that appeared in its wake; these were universally known as "guinea pig books."[112] Kallet and Schlink's book brought more interested readers and a national recognition to CR.

Kallet and Schlink presciently raised concerns about poisons and pesticides such as DDT and highlighted the dangers of lead in gasoline. Yet the book also recycled old warnings about poisoning from toothpaste and patent medicine horror stories dating back several decades. By pointing out the FDA's utter failure to identify hazardous products, *100,000,000 Guinea Pigs* conveyed that consumers above all were helpless, abandoned by those obligated to protect them. The hyperbole provoked passionate responses from reviewers, political commentators, and business spokesmen. Kallet and Schlink's radical sensibilities surfaced in the uncompromising language and the stark conflict of parasitic businessmen and hapless citizens. That sensationalism impressed reviewers far more than the volume's technical information. Popular press reviews mixed admiration and criticism, lauding its indictment of the profit system while reproaching it for exaggerations, vagueness, and circular logic. Those sympathetic to business, as might be expected, found the book dangerous and unreliable. In *The Nation*, whose editorial stance was usually sympathetic to CR, biologist and Mencken crony Raymond

Pearl savaged the book more for its political tone than its science, his area of expertise. Accusing the authors of demagoguery and propaganda, he argued that *100,000,000 Guinea Pigs* exaggerated the relatively few instances of food adulteration while downplaying the existing norm of healthful goods. He charged that Kallet and Schlink were "singularly oblivious to the profound waves of resentment which has gone over this country against the prohibitionist and all his ways." The book savaged the FDA as wholly inadequate to the task of protecting Americans, yet Department of Agriculture publicist T. Swann Harding was given space in the *Saturday Review of Literature* to review the book. Accusing Kallet and Schlink of being poor scientists, he charged that they "lack the objective knowledge upon which alone intelligent reform can be predicated. . . . They remain passionately prejudiced reformers when faced with facts which do not happen to please them in their priestly functioning as Keepers of Dogma."[113] Even other sympathetic business critics found that the book too often strained the limits of credulity. One of Schlink's admiring correspondents, sociologist Robert S. Lynd, deplored the book's "snarling, plunging attack" and sensational overstatements. Jim Rorty, also a friend of CR, found "a lot of honest, well-made Grade AA Swiss cheese in the argument of this book; it is full of holes."[114] Kallet and Schlink's extreme positions on the safety, reliability, and integrity of consumer goods struck many readers as unjustified; nevertheless, the pair had served notice that CR would tread an independent path in its relationships with other critics and with commerce. While usually reserved and scrupulous in analyzing test results and cautious in making recommendations, Schlink kicked over the traces in *Guinea Pigs*. In the dark times of the Depression, Kallet and Schlink wrote from a belief that temperate language would only hurt consumers.

Business spokesmen and advertisers declared war on the book and on CR. *Printers' Ink* and *Advertising and Selling* declined to publicize the book with formal reviews, yet both continually referred to the book and its authors and regularly disparaged the consumer movement's critical attitude. The conservative *Printers' Ink* repeatedly criticized the unreviewed tome, as well as Schlink personally. C. B. Larrabee portrayed Schlink as the uncharismatic leader of an enthralled cult of middle-class consumers. The "Guinea Pig engineers" kept ignorant consumers trapped and needlessly fearful; if consumer products were so bad, more people would have died.[115] Only *Tide*, the Madison Avenue journal most open to business criticism, praised *100,000,000 Guinea Pigs* while offering only mild correctives. For *Tide*, the book's indictments, even if more extreme than expected, were justified: "It could not have been written if the food and drug industries and the public presentations of their products were not considerably more vulnerable than they ought to be."[116]

Significantly, the book also catalyzed a movement for reform in the Food and Drug Act of 1906, long regarded by informed observers within and outside the Food and Drug Administration as inadequate. Even before Franklin Roosevelt assumed the presidency in March 1933, he authorized his future assistant secretary of agriculture Rexford Tugwell to overhaul the legislation. Tugwell sought Schlink's advice, and the organization played a central role in shaping Tugwell's version of the legislation. FDA staff combed CR files, and Schlink lavished the brain truster with a flood of information, clippings, and opinions. Tugwell also contacted Stuart Chase, but Chase's interests had moved into macroeconomic matters, and he begged off.[117] Tugwell produced a bill that sought sweeping regulatory and police powers over a wide variety of products. His bill would have given the FDA far-reaching powers over the content, as well as the operations, of advertising, which was then only loosely monitored by the Federal Trade Commission. The proposal touched off a pitched battle in Congress that lasted five years, spawned more than a dozen competing bills, and produced the 1938 Food, Drug, and Cosmetic Act.[118] From the outset of FDA reform efforts, advertisers, manufacturers, and media executives made war on the administration for trying to interfere with brand-name goods, advertising claims, and what business deemed "the consumer's right to choose."[119]

The nation's economic collapse revealed the importance of consumption to the economy, and the New Deal fitfully but unmistakably addressed consumption as part of its overall programs. The administration's National Industrial Recovery Act (1933), for example, created a specific role for consumers in industrial reform. Along with business and labor groups, consumers were to participate—through a Consumers' Advisory Board (CAB)—in drafting operating codes that would regulate practices, pricing, labor standards, and distribution. The CAB seemed a portent that government would finally acknowledge all citizens in their roles as consumers by recognizing their economic rights.[120] Thus, the Roosevelt administration's first hundred days found CR staff and members cautiously optimistic that the government would finally begin to step in to protect consumers in a manner and scale commensurate with their problems.[121] In turn, federal interest in consumers spurred CR to participate in specific political aid. The advent of the New Deal propelled Consumers' Research into the forefront of the nascent consumer movement both within and outside government. As the only organization that had studied industrial, governmental, and individual perspectives on ultimate consumer questions, and certainly the only organization with its substantial breadth of technical and social information on goods and consumption, it seemed clear that CR would figure prominently in government reform efforts. With allies and acquaintances in the government and among reform groups, Consumers' Research had the opportunity to lead a new consumer movement.

Yet CR squandered its chance. Despite its interest in political reform and the growth of numerous groups claiming to represent consumer views and interests, CR proved at best ambivalent about acting through government mechanisms. While calling for federal help for consumers, CR proved unwilling to assist admittedly inadequate federal efforts. Eager to see Tugwell bring Madison Avenue to heel, CR nonetheless perversely set limits on assisting the food and drug reform or the CAB. Perhaps mindful of his own frustrations at the Bureau of Standards, Schlink balked at throwing CR's activity fully behind any federal consumer program. Although CR allowed government workers to use its extensive files, the organization peevishly refused full-time staff support for government projects. Schlink complained that to do the work for consumers properly, the government would need to assign several people to comb the CR files and shape that information into usable forms. He bitterly complained that none of the federal programs allocated resources for necessary technical research. CR did promote broad policy recommendations and provided technical assistance to their contacts in the government, especially in the areas of product standards, education initiatives, and food and drug adulteration. In the end, however, Schlink backed down from immersing CR in the most significant effort yet seen to bring together technical, economic, and policy information in behalf of a consumer interest.[122]

However obstinate, Schlink's hesitance was sound. As historians have noted, the National Recovery Administration (NRA) generally ignored consumer interests, and the minimally staffed Consumers' Advisory Board could not adequately represent consumer needs in the code-making process. The NRA essentially sanctioned industrial cartels: in many cases the code-making benefited the largest business enterprises by favoring wage and production cuts. Moreover, code-making ignored the interests of labor.[123] The CAB, too, was often excluded from code meetings; Schlink heard complaints from CAB members Robert Lynd and economist Robert Brady of their frustrations in trying to maintain a voice for consumers in the code process. Yet Schlink and CR took a strong, unforgiving position on CAB activities. Even as advertisers denounced the CAB as hostile to all advertising and competition, Schlink was criticizing the board both privately and in print. He cited its lack of technical expertise and its leadership by economists instead of scientists; its lack of cogent economic theory; its timidity in the face of hostility from NRA leadership, especially NRA chief General Hugh Johnson; and above all its woefully inadequate responses to the concentration of business power against the consumer.[124] Writing to Brady, Schlink charged that the CAB's personnel lacked technical training, and he bitterly objected to CAB members' seeking help from CR and other groups in code making and consumer protection. "It just is not possible for us to drop what we are doing and suddenly supply you with information on all sorts of standards, nor is there any reason why we should," Schlink insisted. "It is a government function which the government should work up, for God knows it pays for little enough on the consumers' side." In effect, Schlink was still arguing against the Bureau of Standards's style of business orientation. Unable to generate or gather sufficient technical data for sound and useful codes and unable to mount effective opposition to corporate dominance of the NRA, the CAB was worse than inadequate. Rather, Schlink charged the board was "selected by NRA officials as a screen for their price-fixing codes, and competition-preventing code authorities." With no prospect of reform, "the most honest and candid course on the part of the Consumers Advisory Board is to announce that fact to consumers so that they may not mistakenly be led to rely even in a small way on the operations of the Consumers Advisory Board as though it were in their protection."[125] Brady answered, reasonably enough, "At this time we are so short of facilities ourselves that we area able to do very little of a research character. Besides, what reason is there for us not 'soaking up' anything we possibly may from any source whatsoever? Certainly you would not advise us to duplicate work already done."[126] Yet Schlink's own hardening viewpoint left little sympathy for others in the consumer cause. A partial effort in the consumers' behalf was worse than none.

Moreover, as early as autumn of 1933, Schlink grew suspicious of the New Deal. Political reform struggled through entrenched methods of bartering, lobbying, and compromise. The slow pace of reform, along with the marginalization of scientific expertise, dampened CR's belief that the government could provide strong, meaningful consumer protection. The Tugwell version of the Food and Drug Bill, already under heavy lobbying from canners, proprietary and pharmaceutical firms, advertisers, and publishers, was watered down and stalled in committee. Senate stewardship of the bill was claimed by Royal S. Copeland of New York, a homeopathic advocate who broadcast for Fleishmann's Yeast.[127] That company's advertising was handled by J. Walter

Thompson, which regularly used massive testimonial campaigns that featured foreign doctors without American Medical Association accreditation and offered flagrantly false claims.[128] A Consumers' Research–endorsed alternate version of the Food and Drug Bill did not even make it to consideration. Arthur Kallet's testimony at the congressional hearings on the bill met a rude reception, the committee treating him as a hostile witness and barely concealing their contempt. "But after I finished testifying," he remembered years later, "there was a stir in the room and in the back of the room the door opened and a very elderly woman came in, in the arms of a couple of men. . . . [Chairman Bennett Champ Clark] came down and helped escort this woman to the stand. She was to testify. She was the daughter of Lydia Pinkham. In other words the representatives of the patent medicine makers were receiving a very cordial reception; representatives of consumers were not."[129]

In late 1933, alarmed at the slow pace or blocking of consumer reform in the NRA and other programs, an ad hoc Emergency Conference of Consumers' Organizations, representing a number of different organizations from Consumers' Research to the leftist League of Women Shoppers, journeyed to Washington at the invitation of the CAB's head Mary Rumsey. In attendance were a number of activists including Caroline Ware, progressive engineer F. R. Hoisington, economists Leon Henderson and Colston Warne, and Schlink. When finally cornered in early morning hours by a delegation from the group, the bellicose Hugh Johnson made it plain that consumers' interests or demands played no significant role in the NRA's agenda. "Who is a consumer? Show me a consumer?" he shouted. From that confrontation came an informal invitation for Henderson and Schlink to come to Washington and work with him. Henderson soon got an official appointment, but Schlink never did.[130] Schlink's presence certainly would have been anathema to the business powers within the NRA, and undoubtedly Schlink would have refused such a position. Yet privately the engineer was piqued, for he planned to use the opportunity to demand publicly that the government initiate substantial testing and advocacy on behalf of consumers. By spring of 1934, CR had lost its waning faith in the NRA and soon turned to critiquing the administration for betraying consumer interests by inflating prices, restricting production, and writing production codes that preserved profits by authorizing low-quality goods.[131] CR became convinced that little short of a radical revolution in government itself would ever ensure meaningful protection of consumer interests. Even as government was experimenting with the economy in unprecedented ways, CR moved much further to the left.

Ultimately, Consumers' Research did not exercise significant direct influence on government reforms. Despite its claims that consumers needed pragmatic present-day guidance, CR was unwilling to surrender its gadfly independence to become even a consultant to another consumer agenda. The real conflict here was technocratic. Schlink refused to subject professional and scientific standards to the political process and economic concerns, especially if the politics only enhanced what he came to see as the inadequate liberalism of the New Deal. While the members of CR proved foresighted in assessing the tendencies and weaknesses of New Deal regulation, they also displayed a naive suspicion of compromises made with supposed political devils. Schlink always used the pressing daily needs of CR's confidential bulletin and product testing to avoid commitments to programs other than his own. Faced with the prospect of sharing power and control, Schlink balked. His critics argued that Schlink treated CR as a personal domain, and his guidance of the organization easily bore this out to many observers. CR did not achieve its fullest potential because the organization refused to grow beyond prescribed limits. Despite democratic ideals, those at Consumers' Research could not yet put the fate of the consumer in the hands of the political process.

Despite its criticism of the New Deal, CR still pinned its hopes for the consumer on government intervention. Concluding that all consumer efforts should be centralized, the group carried on a campaign for a federal Department of the Consumer. CR counsel Oscar Cox drafted a bill for the purpose and designed an informed administrative structure for the department; Schlink exhorted subscribers to urge the president to recognize consumer concerns as a distinct interest with a formal cabinet post. Schlink entertained no designs for CR's staff or himself for personal influence in such a department (although office manager M. C. Phillips noted, "we are going to stay outside and tell the boys how to run it, which is more fun"). Indeed, by the end of 1933, CR's personnel policy prohibited employees from joint service to the federal government or any outside employment. The board also extended that policy to include staff membership in outside activities, a stipulation that would later haunt the board.[132]

Although CR still looked to federal power for consumers, the group criticized as insufficient the regulatory liberalism of the New Deal. Most damning in Schlink's view was the manner in which New Deal liberals "betrayed" the public by underestimating the implacable opposition of powerful commercial interests against consumers. When it became clear that business would prevent and politicians would not support any thorough structural reform of the FDA, or that General Johnson would shut consumers out of a meaningfully equal voice in the NRA, consumer-minded liberals should have demanded satisfaction. A few, like the first Consumers' Advisory Board chairman, William F. Ogburn, quickly resigned. But as most stayed on, CR argued that liberals' participation in programs that could not significantly serve consumers only worsened the buyer's plight. Liberals thus obscured the conflict between business and consumers by making it appear that something was being done. Their persistence in the government, Schlink claimed, revealed that they valued their own power more than consumers' welfare.[133] Liberals failed to recognize how businessmen, politicians, and even the labor movement were all willing to sacrifice the consumer for their own interests.[134] According to Schlink, the worst aspect of liberals was that they did not recognize that their commitment to "objectivity" and "fairness" was completely trampled by the business dominance of politics. Following such compliance with a business regency, Schlink darkly hinted, fascism would not be far behind. Producers of all kinds—manufacturers, labor, and businessmen— had declared war on the consumer, and liberals pretended it was simply the legislative process. Better for the true friend of the consumer to resign and expose the conflict.[135]

CR's break with liberals represented a tough-minded critique of the relationship of intellectuals and power. Disillusioned, CR moved steadily leftward, seeking radical alternatives both to American politics and the specter of a business-run fascism.[136] The organization articulated an uncompromising vision of consumer interests, unaffected by practical politics, organizing concerns, or business's needs. By 1934, CR was beginning to examine the need for a broader social basis for a consumer movement and had started exploring tentatively avenues of popular education and political organization on its own terms. The First New Deal taught them that consumers would have to organize politically; the only difficulty they faced was how. Not even Schlink could have predicted where attempts to organize would lead.

GETTING OFFENSIVE: ADVERTISERS AGAINST THE CONSUMER MOVEMENT

Organized business met both New Deal–centered and private movements for consumer protection with vigorous counterattacks waged in Congress, the trade press, and popular media. Government, corporate, and consumer advocates all debated central issues: who would take the lead in speaking for and to consumers? Who would define and control the attributes of goods for the consuming public? Who would determine the best ways to promote consumption, and what instruments would they use to achieve those ends? If, as Meg Jacobs suggests, the New Deal institutionalized a distinct emerging consumer's interest, represented (however falteringly) in government itself, how would government establish that vision, and what would determine its limits?[137] Businessmen, home economists, product testers, social workers, and federal policymakers all acknowledged that consumption justified production; they all positioned themselves as rightful stewards of the consumer's best interests. In the decades before 1930, product-testing advocates, advertisers, and social scientists drew on different strains of political and nationalist language and imagery to reach divergent conclusions about safeguarding those interests. When the mass-consumption economy broke down, those differing positions came into highly charged conflict. These professionals claimed to be consumer representatives, using democratic concepts to describe their relationships with consumers and to justify their own agendas. Against a fervent antibusiness sentiment voiced by many consumers, business began a counteroffensive, first with specific campaigns against New Deal regulation and ultimately with a long-lasting cultural and political initiative to recast business as consumers' natural ally and to neutralize, if not destroy, the nascent consumer movement. Corporate enterprise entered the New Deal fighting to survive; by 1940 business was waging a full-scale war to restore its rule over politics and culture.

When Franklin Roosevelt took office in March 1933, many businessmen and their advertising spokesmen viewed lagging consumer spending as the critical stumbling block to recovery. Whether due to insufficient purchasing power—an explanation embracing the underconsumption theories of William Foster and Waddill Catchings that were broached in the 1920s—or to fear and hoarding, many businessmen believed that consumers prolonged the Depression.[138] The shrewdest among them detected a troubling public skepticism and displeasure with the aggressive sales practices that had mushroomed since the crash. Some advertisers indeed found much to reform: scare-mongering and "chamber of horrors" copy, doubtful testimonial advertising, fictitious diseases and "complexes," intrusion into the most intimate details of hygiene, and copy that consumers found condescending and presumptuous. Agency chief William D'Arcy sounded the alarm: "You all know what I mean: Advertising that reeks with vulgarity for the sheer sake of being; advertising that is suggestive merely for the shock it will cause; offensive advertising that succeeds only in offending." He warned that such advertising revealed a contemptuous attitude toward consumers as "a nation of morons, morbid in tastes, perverted in desires and unclean in lives and persons."

D'Arcy concluded, "How much lower do we think it can go before the American consumer quite properly kicks all advertising out the door."[139] Such critics questioned advertisers' aggression in selling, from door-to-door canvassing to intrusive and disrespectful sales messages. Trade journals brimmed with tales of consumer anger and skepticism.[140] With good reason advertisers feared a dwindling public faith in their words as well as their wares.

Consumerist critics of business among homemakers, professionals, and pundits identified three interrelated means to improve goods: standards, grades, and labeling. Advocates claimed that each would make new forms of information available to consumers to aid purchasing. All three would offer other authorities besides business the right to determine the qualities and meanings of goods. The proposed Food and Drug Administration reform in its several guises (especially the sweeping initial "Tugwell" version), along with the NRA and Agricultural Adjustment Act (AAA) consumer programs, all sought stricter minimum standards for consumer goods than business had previously granted or tolerated.[141] The 1933 Tugwell bill called for technical specifications to define the content of goods, along with the attributes that consumers would be trained to demand. Grade labeling—of a simple A, B, C, D hierarchy—would provide accessible universal nomenclature, especially for canned goods and textiles. To meet the requirements, manufacturers would provide labels stating compliance with technical standards, rather than customary, so-called descriptive labels, which seldom indicated adherence to standards. The bill also called for strict prohibitions against false advertising, either on labeling or in other forms.[142] Labeling, standards, grading, and truth claims all in turn affected brand names, trademarks, and proprietary formulas. Both the proposed Tugwell bill and Consumers' Advisory Board recommendations required that brand-name goods have government grading and standards on the labels, to identify minimum standards of quality and content.[143] Thus, the particular brand would be less important than its conformity to universal standards.

Such attempts to institute legislation in a consumer's interest emphatically distinct from that of business prompted immediate and vehement responses from corporations, advertisers, and media.[144] Even as businesses first accommodated and then eventually broke with the New Deal, corporate spokesmen fought against government, community, and private groups claiming to speak for and with consumers. As in their battles with the labor movement, business spokesmen declared that producers and consumers shared essential interests, as did management and workers. Those relationships, business argued, required neither regulation nor outside interference.

Government intervention in consumption—whether through the NRA, AAA, or Food and Drug Administration—would not only ruin the mutual understanding and trust of business and buyer, it would cripple business's ability to deliver the goods to consumers at desired qualities and prices.[145]

Federal and private reform efforts for consumers threatened marketing and sales practices, and businesses mounted extensive efforts to turn them back. Their attempts first centered on convincing the consuming public that the business vision of consumption was preferable; that meant rebutting and discrediting critics in consumer groups and the government. Consumers' Research was a natural target for many business commentators, some of whom held the small organization directly responsible for the negative criticism they received from consumers. They wondered with a mixture of bitterness and bemusement about CR's disproportionate influence.[146] Business opponents attacked consumer advocates on political grounds in several ways. They charged that CR's and other consumer groups' activities were presumptuous and illegitimate: consumers were perfectly capable of determining and safeguarding their own best interests. Business spokesmen relied on the metaphor of representation; no one had "elected" consumer advocates to speak for the public, whereas General Electric, General Motors, and hundreds of national and local businesses had won literally millions of "votes" in American homes.[147] Second, businessmen argued that consumerist critics not only had un-American methods but an un-American goal as well: socialism. They alleged that consumer activists entertained aspirations for greater power and sought to usurp both business's and consumers' sacred American rights of self-determination. If advertising reforms, strict grade labeling, or product standards were adopted, a cabal of "pink-cheeked professors" and government bureaucrats would be the ones who determined the content and qualities of goods. If Fred Schlink and his allies worried that the New Deal was breeding fascism, his business enemies warned that grade labeling and specifications were first steps toward Russian-styled collectivism. Some thoughtful observers disagreed; C. B. Larrabee, no friend of CR or regulation, sternly warned business not to "conduct a propaganda on the basis that consumer movement is entirely subversive, that it is inspired by Stalin and therefore must be met by stupid, flag-waving gestures." Even so, it was easy for beleaguered businessmen to conclude that government consumer protection meant measures were nothing short of communism.[148] Such corporate spokesmen saw (quite incorrectly) an unholy alliance of consumer advocates and government bureaucrats that sought to place manufacturing in thrall to federal control. Claiming to protect the common citizen, businessmen argued that consumerists waged war on American freedom—the freedom of choice.

Finally, business defenders accused the consumer movement, and CR especially, of having little knowledge or understanding of consumption. The twin goals of buying through specifications and simplification showed the movement's profound ignorance of consumers; women hardly desired to return to nineteenth-century home production, to buy in great bulk for small savings, or to utilize obscure technical standards for goods.[149] Commercial home economist Christine Frederick (who by this time was styling herself arrogantly as "Mrs. Consumer") and women's magazine editor Anna Steese Richardson attacked CR's methods, as well as its mandate. They argued standards and grade labeling were lost on the female consumer (without explaining how the proposed "A, B, C, D" order would confuse women more than such descriptive terms as "Fancy," "Fine," "Grade A" or "Best").[150] According to Richardson and Frederick, manufacturers, media, and merchants best understood the daily problems of Mrs. Consumer. These three groups alone met women's needs of labor saving, ease, and imagination. Whether by government or private reformers, rationalizing consumption would fail. Mrs. Consumer wished to choose easily and confidently; she desired commodities that appealed to her emotions, her aspirations, and her self-image, not her underdeveloped logical faculties. Mr. Advertiser knew what she needed most.[151]

The brand-name system had become the most prominent target of consumerists in and out of government. Both the food and drug legislation and the Consumers' Advisory Board activities made brand regulation and reform a distinct possibility. Arguments against brands were familiar. Clair Wilcox stated the case bluntly: "Brands are convenient. They often carry a guarantee of quality. But these advantages are purchased by the consumer at the cost of increased prices, lowered living standards, and industrial instability. Buying by brand is no substitute for buying on the basis of comparative prices and standard specifications. Its costs, in general, are far in excess of its worth." The prospect of reform gave this Veblenian critique a new political charge.[152] While most reformers had no desire to eliminate brands, widespread standardization, grade labeling, and regulation of copy would undoubtedly alter brands' influence and advertising practices. With both their revenue stream and business methods at stake, Madison Avenue and publishers led the counterattack against consumer protection. First, brand names themselves served as the best standards and grade labels, argued business representatives. The integrity of the maker was inscribed with each brand, representing millions of dollars of equity that no rational businessman would risk by selling inferior goods. Manufacturers simply could not get away with foisting poor quality on the public.[153] Second, grade labeling and standardization would kill brands by destroying years of effort and expenditure in building up good will and public recognition for advertised goods. Furthermore, advertisers charged that the proposed government reforms could not assure quality in its grade labeling; the proposed standards would be too cumbersome and complex to be useful or too broad to offer any substantial protection for consumers. Brand names represented higher achievements in quality than any government could mandate. Finally, and most important, consumers were democratically represented in the brand system. Business knew best how to produce goods; its ultimate proof was that consumers bought them. Market tests, polls, and constant feedback ensured that products would always serve the buying public. Businessmen again spoke of representation: consumers designated manufacturers to fulfill their needs through brand-name goods and changed their delegates when those needs were no longer met. Continued brand loyalty demonstrated that consumers approved their existing relationships with manufacturers, despite the radical claims of the self-appointed friends of consumers.[154]

The end of the brand-name system would mean the end of advertising itself. Along with publishers and broadcasters, advertising executives circled their wagons against the prospect of federal interference, stricter accountability, or limits on the ways they could describe or sell goods. Even as they agonized among themselves over the rise of hard-sell tactics and sensational scare copy, they invoked freedom of speech to claim that advertising was a distinctly American tradition.[155] They also defended their work as protecting American freedom. Indeed, they boasted that advertising, not the Constitution, guaranteed a free press by liberating editors from patrons, government support, or other sources that might censor materials. The elimination of advertising would mean government-run media, censorship, and the specter of collectivism.[156]

Advertisers viewed consumers' criticism and reform ideas as nothing less than attacks on capitalism and Americanism. In a mixture of pique and pathos, Roy Durstine asked, "How can anything be justified if this creative force of education, desire and consumption has no reason to exist? What are we living for—to learn as little as possible, to want as little as possible, to have as little as possible? Isn't it clear that Americans like advertising?"[157] Their defense first hinged on advertising's truth. More than anything else, consumers questioned advertising's factual reliability and relevance. If skeptical and frustrated consumers permanently lost faith in advertising, false and misleading claims would be to blame. The "truth in advertising" campaigns of the Progressive Era, which had largely been symbolic efforts, were reactivated during the 1930s; ad men claimed to reform from within, even as they fiercely accused consumer advocates as wrongheaded and un-American.[158] Professionals debated the minute shadings of truth, filling their conferences and journals with hot debate and agonized discussions of ethics and public skepticism of their honesty. Yet they turned a defiant face to potential regulators and consumer groups, claiming that the substance of advertising was usually and dependably truthful. More troubling, they claimed for themselves the right to "puffery," best described as fanciful and evocative description that endowed a product with its sales points and "personality." Puffery was the essence of advertising; as long as it did not become outright deceit and falsehood, such language was perfectly permissible. It was what distinguished one product from its competitor.[159] Consumer-minded skeptics, however, pointed out that in fact puffery made advertising wasteful: bestowing specious and extrinsic traits on similar products masked the important characteristics of goods.

Most important, advertisers and publishers fought back with goods. They argued that advertising made possible the world's highest standard of living. Amos Bradbury spoke for many on Madison Avenue when he expressed his resentment of consumer advocates such as CR and women's clubs:

> When I told that particular women's club that the only reason they were able to meet to take a crack at advertising, about which they knew nothing, was because of the added leisure advertising had produced for them, it was the truth. Ladies don't always care for it. They all took too much for granted, I told them. Things like garbage pails that open when you push your foot on a lever, sinks of the right height, dishwashers, oil furnaces, canned soup, electric refrigerators, fly-killing sprays, all made possible and made known by advertising.

Ad men were growing angry with consumers for not being properly grateful; if they were the consumers' true representatives, advertisers nonetheless resented those they served. An editorial attempt at humor barely masked the seething anger at the new turn of events: "It's all the fault of the advertisers—the skunks! . . . They've inveigled him into putting down his hard-earned dollars for electrical conveniences, radios, bathtubs, comfortable homes and all the other conveniences that have made poor John Q. Public an object of derision the world over."[160] Even as consumers had the impertinence to demand a greater voice in how they were sold, advertisers cast about for effective ways to respond. Much would depend on suppressing their own anger at buyers' ingratitude for the uplift that business provided them.

CONCLUSION

Throughout the New Deal debates over consumer interests, controversy centered on who would create and police the attributes of goods. Business claimed that right as part of private property and competition, while consumer advocates asserted their place in representing and shaping popular uses and ideas of products and, increasingly, commerce itself. Each group ultimately claimed to be the consumers' true, democratically sanctioned representatives. In this war over representation, business did more than argue with its critics. By the mid-1930s, as public opinion hardened against business, corporate leaders adopted new strategies to blunt growing sentiments for consumer protection and for restraints on harmful advertising and media. Business would begin anti–consumer movement campaigns in earnest while also courting public favor for corporate prerogatives and a business vision of the American economic future. Its success would be achieved not in economic but in cultural terms. Ultimately, advertisers recast the corporate version of consumption as the folkways, political ideals, and national heritage of American citizens.

CHAPTER 8

THE AMERICAN

WAY OF LIFE

FOLKLORES OF

CAPITALISM,

1935–1939

My consumers have listened to the extravagant promises of politicians, labor leaders, social reformers, and entertainment producers, until when I present my products in simple, truthful language, I am laughed at. . . . I am tired of every politician riding into office upon his abuse of an economy that makes his office and salary possible. . . . I am tired of being blamed for unemployment and maldistribution, by these same politicians, who have wrecked business and brought on a depression by political handicaps, both Federal and State; who have thrown my employees out of work and destroyed the purchasing power of my customers; who have attempted to repeal the laws of supply and demand; who favor organized voting groups; and who now prevent my doing anything constructive to undo their wrong. . . . Finally, I am tired of supporting the whole mess by taxes.[1]

Every day more than 28,000,000 "General Motors people" are casting a vote for or against us in a sort of informal nation-wide poll with their friends. These 28,000,000 "General Motors voters" represent our own huge organization—employees, stockholders, dealers, suppliers, product owners, together with their families. . . . Our size now makes us vulnerable, but "bigness is as bigness does," and our "bigness," instead of a sin with the American people, will become our greatest virtue.[2]

The organized discontent of some consumers with the things they buy and the way they are sold has become a major marketing problem.[3]

There is one thing that every manufacturer in this country can paste in his hat and that is that this consumer movement cannot be met by evasion or by shrill cries of "Bolshevik."[4]

The Depression debates of consumerists and advertisers largely took place in political and economic precincts: congressional hearings, the business press, political and reform journals, occasional radio programming on public affairs, club and union meetings, lectures. Yet inevitably these debates entered popular culture. The government addressed consumer programs and interests, but broad questions of who would define the parameters of consumption, control the meanings of goods, or gain the allegiance of consumers would not be resolved by federal programs or executive fiat alone. Nor, for that matter, would they be resolved strictly in political action or spending choices. As warring consumer professionals struggled to represent consumers and define goods, they increasingly turned to the familiar plane of everyday life—the quotidian experience of things and varieties of commercial entertainment and leisure. Here, both advertisers and consumer advocates defined the national dimensions of consumption.

In the mid-1930s public opinion seemed to harden against corporate enterprise even as the labor movement and allied groups propelled class politics to the fore. Franklin Roosevelt's 1936 reelection was a surprising and crushing defeat for the New Deal's opponents. Corporate leaders adopted new strategies to blunt growing sentiments for consumer protection and government regulation of private enterprise. Business would, of course, continue its anti–consumer movement campaigns by contesting new legislation and regulatory reforms: Roosevelt's second term saw Madison Avenue lobbying against food and drug legislation, for example. Yet it also brought growing federal interest in specifications and standards and, perhaps most threatening, the 1938 Temporary National Economic Committee's inquiry into monopolistic business practices. Even before the election, however, business leaders were taking their fight beyond political debate to the more intimate realms of everyday life.[5] These campaigns turned away from economics and politics to culture. Ultimately, advertisers recast the corporate stake in free enterprise as the folkways, political traditions, and nationalist myths of American citizens. They portrayed consumption as the American Way of Life.

THE AMERICAN WAY OF LIFE:
PRIVATE RENEWAL AND PUBLIC RELATIONS

By the end of 1935, most influential leaders of corporate enterprise had broken their tenuous ties with the Roosevelt administration. Recovery efforts and prospects had halted, and the future of regulation seemed uncertain.[6] The National Recovery Administration (NRA) and Agricultural Adjustment Act (AAA)—which had offered regulation and reorganization generally favorable to large enterprise—had been declared unconstitutional, and attempts at food and drug, advertising, and retailing reforms had all been diminished or stalled. Yet the prolonged depression found big business growing further out of favor among Americans.[7] While Roosevelt's most conservative opponents had taken comfort in the demise of flagship New Deal economic programs, business estrangement from the New Deal only grew. Although business leaders had fought off or diluted regulation they perceived as inimical, they still fretted that public sentiment opposed them.

Facing a popular leader and a restive populace, some businessmen sought a new path to approach working-class and especially middle-class Americans. Most articulate among this group was Bruce Barton, head of a major Madison Avenue agency and popular writer. Widely known for his best-selling treatment of Jesus Christ as a modern salesman, Barton was a confidant of the powerful.[8] He had been instrumental in Calvin Coolidge's ascent to the presidency and had made over Coolidge's public image from taciturn loner to stoic statesman. Barton also befriended preeminent corporate leaders, including Alfred Sloan of General Motors and General Electric's Gerard Swope. Few in advertising were more steadfast opponents of the New Deal, and fewer still understood the connections of selling and politics better.[9] In a major speech before the conservative National Association of Manufacturers in 1935, Barton summed up his own disillusionment with his chosen field, his doubts about the Depression, and his concerns for the future:

> Industry and politics, at the moment, are competitors for the confidence and favor of the same patron, the public. Politics knows it; industry, for three years has acted as if it did not. Industry has stuck out its tongue at its political competitor. It has pouted and scolded and sulked. But it has not rolled up its sleeves and sold. We in industry say that Business keeps its promises better than [politics]. We say that Business does not find the people poor and leave them poor. . . . The politician says to the people: "Give us your money in taxes and we will redistribute them." Industry says: "Give us your money in exchange for goods, and we will use it to produce more and better and lower-priced goods." On this issue the competition is joined. . . . We have a story to tell but we do not tell it. We have great benefits to confer upon the people if they will give us the opportunity, but we must persuade them that we are more reliable than the politicians; that we will work for them more cheaply and with more satisfaction. . . . The politician makes people believe that he is thinking in terms of their welfare and happiness of their children. Industry, in the long run, can and will do more for the people and their children than politics can ever do. But it must first beat politics with its own weapon; it must speak not to the mind only but to the heart.[10]

Barton's solution was, not surprisingly, more advertising. He urged promoting not products but the "human" aspects of business in daily life. Businessmen had to publicize their part in creating jobs, as well as the products that increased the public's happiness and satisfaction. Business needed to advance its central role not only in the political economy but also in culture. "No major industry has any moral right to allow itself to be unexplained, misunderstood or publicly distrusted, for by its unpopularity it poisons the pond in which we all must fish," Barton argued.[11] The super-salesman urged his audience to become involved in politics itself, not through checkbook support of national candidates, but through personal participation in local communities.

Barton urged businesses to redefine the relationships of corporations and consumers—the working and voting public. In so doing, business would recreate the civic importance of consuming. He presciently observed that the competition of business and politics would not be played out in the realm of abstract ideas but in the everyday lives of plain people. Daily life and private interests were the focus of the public's most important concerns. He pounded home that the true realm of politics, in effect, was consumption, and the products of American industry were the most powerful ideological weapons that private enterprise could employ to make a case for its unfettered operations.[12] If businessmen failed to convince Americans that private enterprise would provide a better life than the New Deal, business would lose its standing with the public.

After years of extravagant use of political language to sell apolitical goods, agents and clients now confronted the need to learn political communication to sell themselves and to sell capitalism. The J. Walter Thompson agency observed, "Successful political leaders understand the principles of advertising better than many of those engaged in advertising as a business. Political leaders know the force of an idea—a single simple idea that makes contact with human need and emotion. They know that it is only through their emotions that great masses of people can be influenced quickly." This Thompson ad featured William Graham Sumner, whose phrase "The Forgotten Man," the agency grudgingly noted, was picked up by the Roosevelt administration to sell "an unfamiliar product, 'The New Deal.'" The ad thus suggested that what politics could do, advertising should do as well.[13] Kenneth Goode put these sentiments slightly differently: "On March 4, 1933, Mr. Franklin D. Roosevelt inaugurated modern advertising."[14] If politicians were at heart advertisers, ad men had to become politicians. Although few took this directive as seriously as Barton (who served as a Republican congressman from New York City in 1938–40), the die was cast.[15] The advertising industry joined battle against government and consumer reformers by presenting its political vision in the material terms of consumption.

Barton's oration became a rallying point, not only for his agency's tony clientele—DuPont, General Electric, General Motors, and U.S. Steel—but also for big business as a whole over the next decade, for public relations.[16] His call set the tone for an aggressive campaign against the New Deal and reform that would surface in many guises and locations over several decades. An extended, multifaceted campaign to sell American business through public and corporate relations sprouted in several venues of American culture: radio and film; pageantry, fairs, and exhibitions; billboards and posters; magazines and the press; the sales floor and the shop floor.[17] Almost always, such efforts had the twin goals of creating favorable public impressions of individual firms and of business overall.[18] Public relations campaigns were themselves a contested terrain within the world of advertising and marketing. Such giants in the field as Edward Bernays and Ivy Lee commanded grudging respect (if only for their fees and clientele), yet public relations seemed to embody the ephemeral, vaporous aspects of advertising that hard-nosed professionals deplored. Nevertheless, public relations promised to present goodwill messages to the public in a form radically different from the conventional sales talk or, for that matter, the typical political speech.

These initiatives shared a common objective of displacing government in popular esteem by retraining consumers to internalize business perspectives and prerogatives. Over the years historians have debated the effectiveness of this business public relations movement. Richard Tedlow has asserted that the campaigns had little to do with big business's eventual rehabilitation after World War II. William Bird and Roland Marchand each conclude that the campaigns were not cohesive but still decisively influenced the resurrection of corporate approval between the Depression and postwar years. Most recently, Inger Stole has argued that these campaigns were highly coordinated, effective instruments that muted opposition to business and placed advertising beyond public criticism. Although she downplays how such campaigns often worked at cross-purposes and met a variety of responses, her argument, like Bird's and Marchand's, remains persuasive.[19] In the late 1930s corporations spent substantial sums on such image making; advertisers and executives continually emphasized its importance. On the lecture circuit, in conventions, and throughout the trade press, business spokesmen recurrently called for more and better public relations. These campaigns arose from the crisis of American confidence in big business and the loss of its moral authority. The campaigns shifted focus when capitalism faced far fewer challenges to its legitimacy in the postwar decades.

These campaigns built a material nationalism, an interpretation of an American nation distinguished by spending and goods. The new public relations campaigns centered on everyday life, consumer products, and American identity. By linking consumption and Americanism through corporations, advertisers drew on their own traditions of political language and national imagery. For many years they had conflated their own interests with those of the consuming public. Now, they fought to preserve private enterprise by equating their concerns with American national heritage. Business leaders concluded "that they must do something more than talk to the public at large; in short, that they must deal *politically* with the various 'publics' on which depend the day-to-day conduct of business-as-usual, at the same time reorganizing, or creating new organizations, adapted to the purpose."[20] To that end, advertisers promoted business by portraying consumption as the badge of American nationality, a citizenship symbolized in goods and realized in marketplace democracy. They asserted that the people not only expressed but indeed attained and preserved their American heritage—nationality, culture, and rights—in consumption. This ideology rested on material possessions, family living, and a vague but powerful nationalism—the American Way of Life.

Specifically, these campaigns illuminated abstract political ideas by situating them in local, historical, and nationalist events, scenes, and characters. As with previous generations of advertisers, the campaigns placed "progress" at the center of American history.[21] Advertisers had long characterized the past primarily by its lack of modern goods: present-day goods were solutions to the "problems" that made up the "past." The "American Way" vision of progress that surfaced in the mid-1930s contained a nationalist twist. It emerged in a 1936 General Motors (GM) campaign, "Who Serves Progress Serves America," begun in time for the presidential election. Each month, in lavish double-page spreads, scenes depicting mythical elements from American history (western pioneers, young Abraham Lincoln reading by the fireplace) and rendered in a romanticized visual style, linked the course of American history with GM's innovations for the common people. The series rested on a simple premise: the promise of American national history was realized in consumer products, and corporate free enterprise was the engine of that progress.

This series marked a turning point; while corporations had often pointed to "progress" as a driving force in American history, the source of great fortunes, companies, communications, and transportation, the GM advertising self-consciously tied American history and empires to symbols—the goods and services made possible through corporate capital. Even so, the ads could not conceal the gulf between American history and modernity, between the old producer's republic they nostalgically invoked and the modern state they battled. On closer examination, these ads emphasized the gap between the autonomous individual and corporate bureaucracy; they made clear that the individualism they celebrated was archaic if not impossible. Heroes like Abraham Lincoln or Benjamin Franklin stood in stark contrast to the anonymous GM researchers and scientists featured in every advertisement's inset. Even spreads that celebrated communal efforts, such as western pioneers or the gold rush, stumbled on the paradox. GM highlighted their rugged individualism but depicted anonymous communities. The GM series could not praise large corporate enterprise without evoking the associations of collectivism it was trying to discredit.

The themes converged in an October 1936 advertisement, "Lifting the American Standard," which linked research, free enterprise, abundance, and American exceptionalism (fig. 8.1). Framing the text was a picture of a nineteenth-century election scene. The inset, entitled "The People's Choice," showed men from GM's "Customer Research" Department, "the 'ballot box' of a great business," reviewing consumer questionnaires and tabulating "the tastes and desires of the public." With the introduction of its Customer Research Department in 1933, GM had portrayed the mechanics of market research as the mysteries of a national plebiscite. GM boasted that Customer Research was its "proving ground of public opinion," engaged in fulfilling the solemn responsibility of providing what the public wanted.[22] In the name of business, General Motors assumed responsibility for safeguarding democracy and spurring Americans on to greater achievements.[23] These ads embodied Barton's prescription for the counterattack by business against the New Deal; beneath the hagiographic portraits of past leaders and innovators, small-print sermons delivered a tough anti-Roosevelt message to go with the warm imagery. One pronounced, "The place America holds in the world is the fruit of the diligence of its people. . . . Ask yourself: is it the part of diligence, or of the American character, to heed defeatist counsels now? Shall we divide our wealth—or multiply it? Shall we 'stabilize' under restriction and regimentation—or go forward?" Or, as another ad insisted, "In the United States one hour's wages will buy more food—and fewer hours of work will buy an automobile, a radio, a package of cigarettes or an electrical refrigerator —than any country in the world. . . . It comes by working steadily for greater output at lower prices, with wages maintained at high levels by the efficient use of machines. The comforts and luxuries the average American enjoys today are convincing evidence that this is the course of progress."[24] Once more advertisers measured America as a nation and culture by the proliferation of things.

WHO SERVES PROGR

Lifting the American Standard!
The American standard of living is the envy and marvel of the world. Its maintenance and advancement depend directly upon the amount of wealth we are able in future to create. Now ask yourself this: How shall we best create that needed wealth? By dividing what we have? By "stabilization" under restriction or regimentation? By imposing limitations upon agriculture and industry, the sole creators of wealth, so that both produce fewer things at higher prices for fewer people? *Not one of such proposals squares with American experience or with the process which brought the*

YOUR MONEY GOES FARTHER

FIGURE 8.1. "Who Serves Progress Serves America."
(*Saturday Evening Post*, October 28, 1936, 48–49)

SS SERVES AMERICA !

The *"ballot box"* of a great business: Members of the General Motors Customer Research Staff tabulating replies to more than a million inquiries sent to car owners.

THE PEOPLE'S CHOICE

Before its new cars are introduced, General Motors checks engineering developments, style trends, improvements in convenience and advancements in design with the tastes and desires of the public by sending out more than a million letters to car owners. Thus, on a scale which early industry could not undertake, it safeguards its employes, its stockholders and the buyers of its cars against the errors or penalties of guesswork.

merican standard of living to its present matchless place! On the con-try, we outstripped the nations of the world because the energy d enterprise of our people were free to *multiply* wealth, to *go for-rd* instead of "stabilize," to succeed in the productive task of aking *more* things at *lower* prices for *more* people. Have condi-

tions changed? They have to this extent: today in America more people want and need more and better things than ever before! In the satisfying of these wants is America's opportunity to serve progress in a measure never heretofore known, and to attain for our people a standard of living beyond anything we have dreamed!

N A GENERAL MOTORS CAR

Beginning in the mid-1930s, advertising sociology turned to a folksy realism in copy, visuals, and trade literature. Advertisers had long equated the national market with political democracy: these dual democracies were the foundation of Americans' daily lives. But with the emergence of the American Way ideology, ad men now portrayed economic democracy as superior, more important to Americans and more critical to their future as a free, independent, and prosperous people than politics. This argument, in turn, spurred new representations of consumers and new configurations of markets. Ad men had long been accustomed to remapping the country according to commercial considerations and to objectifying communities as markets. But the new American Way easily recast the alien nation of 100 million guinea pigs and fleeps as a small, intimate community. As they materialized the American Way, advertisers abandoned their cynical, self-protective distance from consumers. In market surveys, advertisements, and even editorial matter, advertisers and media now emphasized typical American communities to replace abstract or smug summaries. Commonplace but never nondescript, these communities all boasted prosperous middle classes, industrious laborers, and a common ideology of consumption. From the lofty heights of Manhattan's Graybar Building and Philadelphia's Independence Square, ad men began to think of and address consumers as *neighbors*.[25] Markets were people again.

Boardroom sociology of class and mass gave way to a rosier vision of the public. Chastening criticism of the corporate naturalist style with its insulting portrayals of juvenile, incompetent shoppers compelled Madison Avenue to modify its images and ideas considerably. To win purchasers from politicians, advertisers addressed their audiences in intimate tones and respectful terms. Whereas only a few years before advertisers had snarled at consumers, they now purred. Where they once scornfully dismissed consumers as morons behind the scenes, they now sought an understanding with "the plain folks." Indeed, advertising now brought to the fore a new consumer, celebrated not for modernity, sophistication, or instinctive gifts, but for the very opposite of such distinctions: the common and typical. In Madison Avenue's detour down Main Street, copywriters and artists highlighted "typical" American families and communities. While they still balked personally at identifying too closely with the habits and tastes of common people, in their counterattack on the New Deal advertisers acknowledged their own participation with the masses in a common culture marked by consumer goods.[26] As corporations developed ever more rationalized marketing schemes that reflected growing professional and instrumental distance from actual consumers, the folksier and more populist their language and imagery became.

This revised advertising sociology took its cue, in part, from the new community studies in government and academia. These studies offered some of the first widely disseminated empirical information on everyday habits, beliefs, and material resources throughout the broad spectrum of American social structure. With the new techniques of public opinion and market research, these studies also propelled to prominence the figure of the "average" or "typical American."[27] Warren Susman first pointed out the relevance of the average American for understanding Depression culture, and recently Olivier Zunz and Sarah Igo have offered instructive perspectives. They both argue that constructing and accepting the average American proved critical in the coming of mass society. In the United States, Zunz notes, the invention of the statistical and demographic "average" cast an aura of democratic consent and individualism over a strikingly managed and fabricated phenomenon. Further, he argues, social scientists used "responses to questionnaires as a proxy for what people thought" and thus reconfigured momentary opinion as consensus. Advertisers developed an appealing twist on the construction of the average: long adept at uniting democracy and markets, they now proffered the figure of the average American as the symbol uniting mass taste and political sovereignty, not in the abstractions of consumer as king or queen, but as the common person. Selling the average also offered advertisers the most direct means to gauge both consumer taste and voting preference. Bruce Barton underscored the link between the average consumer-citizen and his American Way goals in a 1936 speech:

> These millions have been made literate and have been given the ballot. They have been taught in the very schools that were given them that they have natural rights. They now believe in those rights and are fully conscious of their power. . . . Who are these buyers? *They are not anybody; they are everybody.* They are folk whose ancestors battled for the mere necessities, but they themselves accept it as a matter of course that every luxury shall be theirs. . . . My plea is that we should be as diligent, as ingenious, and as resourceful in our approach to them as voters as we have proved in our approach to them as buyers."

Thus, advertisers created a new means to construct and manage markets while appearing simply to serve them.[28]

No studies influenced advertising sociology more than Robert and Helen

Lynd's *Middletown* (1929) and *Middletown in Transition* (1937). After the first volume appeared, inhabitants of Muncie, Indiana, the Lynds' subject town, endured frequent polls by marketers, business organizations, and pundits. Experts viewed the town as a divining rod of dominant popular sentiment. Robert Lynd originally planned a quick return to Muncie simply to gather material for an appendix to *Middletown*. His new project quickly attracted public attention, and he labored under expectations that its findings would constitute a definitive barometer of national attitudes and adjustments to the Depression.[29] Lynd's own increasing frustration with consumers' power-lessness—stemming from his hopeful but disappointing time on the NRA's Consumers' Advisory Board—permeated the second study. *Middletown in Transition* became a much more somber account of the effects of commercial culture and a harsh portrait of Muncie's ruling Ball family and business class. Noting bitter resentment among labor and a disregard among the city's bour-geoisie for the extent or degree of poverty, want, and inequality, Lynd was quite pessimistic about Muncie's response to the Depression:

> Middletown is overwhelmingly living by the values by which it lived in 1925; and the chief additions are defensive, negative elaborations of al-ready existing values, such as, among the business class, intense sus-picions of the centralizing tendencies in government, of the interference of social legislation with business, of labor troubles, and of radicalism. . . . Such changes as are going forward in Middletown are disguised by the thick blubber of custom that envelops the city's life. The city is uneasily conscious of many twinges down underneath the surface, but it resembles the person who insists on denying and disregarding unpleasant physical symptoms on the theory that everything *must* be all right, and that if anything really is wrong it may cure itself without leading to a major operation.[30]

Yet what the sociologist saw as conflict, indecision, and stultifying re-sistance, the account executive delightedly viewed as pliant optimism. No sooner had the ink dried on *Middletown in Transition* than market researchers from *Life*, *Look*, and *McCall's* magazines invaded Muncie to turn Middletown into a mirror for the middle class.[31] Business commentators interpreted the book very differently, in accordance with their new outlook. What made Middletown significant was its allegiance to a business-friendly American Way. The Lynds' careful and complex explication was reduced by executives to business-friendly, anti–New Deal shorthand: "Two parties, one religion, one country. Move slowly, avoid extremes. 'American Ways.' Bigger and better. Business can run its own affairs. Competition. The home town is best. 'The Constitution should not be fundamentally changed.' 'Taxes should be kept down.' Out with the Communists, whoever they are!"[32] Lest its readers miss the point connecting the Lynds' work to the business of selling, the *Wall Street Journal* review of *Middletown in Transition* was titled "Guinea Pig Revisited."[33] In actuality, the city's homogeneity—its apparent typicality—was deceptive. The Lynds had chosen the city to investigate the dynamics of tradition, modernization, and change precisely because Muncie lacked the strong divisions of race and ethnicity prevalent in larger cities. The city proved so appealing as a "typical" American community for business spokesmen because the nation as a whole was much more complex. The portrait of Muncie fulfilled business leaders' fantasies of an America without class conflict or consciousness. A quiescent working class in Muncie did not typify labor as a whole, of course. Advertisers recommending *Middletown in Transition* ignored its disavowal of the alleged business-labor consensus. They utterly disregarded the political implications of Roosevelt's strong win over Republican Alfred Landon in Muncie, despite the unrelenting opposition of all the city's major institutions. Nor did business reviewers mention such telling details of local color as the joke widely told at Muncie factories about the worker who broke his leg tripping on a pile of "Landon" buttons discarded outside the plant gate.[34]

In the Middletown spirit, advertisers sought to depict, as well as understand, the masses sympathetically to gain their trust. *Printers' Ink Monthly* urged ad men to see themselves in the people of Muncie, "so much like all of us," to determine if their selling messages would touch the plain people's desires. J. L. Sowers urged his colleagues, just as advertisers had done for years, to get out among common folk. But all trace of alienation or superiority that customarily informed that advice before the Depression now evaporated: "Immerse yourself in humanity—where thousands never know the luxury of a bathtub after a day of grime, or the comfort of an indoor toilet on a stormy night! . . . Listen to the palaver at filling stations, repair shops, bus stations and trailer camps . . . . Ponder the mental processes of the rank and file of men off duty and after hours." Sowers reminded his readers, "Be decent— attentive—you'll find friendliness and learn a lot." Once an involuntary observer in the field, the advertiser now served as devout documentarian. The photographs accompanying Sowers's prescriptions only amplified this point —street scenes, railroad terminals, filling stations, and Ladies' Aid meetings, all earnest and slightly mannered images of humble everyday life.[35] Such scenes, usually recorded only by federal documentary projects or leftist photo leagues, proved necessary now for advertisers to reconnect with the public.[36]

As Sowers indicated, advertisers perfected a commercial version of the same documentary impulse that swept through Depression culture. They depicted small localities and communities as telling representatives of self-consciously "American" culture and markets. Thus, they borrowed expressly and implicitly from folklorists, folk artists, preservationists, and others who chronicled American daily life. Ad men aped the techniques and vocabulary of the federal investigators and leftist documentarians who uncovered vast disparities in American life but then ignored those findings. Copywriters and advertising researchers did not seek so-called average Americans but pro-duced fictional models of that average, fulfilling the now mandatory commit-ment to defend business against the New Deal.

The modern city, the symbol of material modernity in pre-Depression layouts—receded into the deep background as copywriters instead turned their attention to Middletown-style villages and small communities. They abandoned the urban centers now associated with the laboring classes of the emergent New Deal coalition, rushing to the more hospitable precincts of neighborhoods, small towns, and suburbs. There, advertisers hunted the behaviors, tastes, and Republican-tinged political ideals that characterized their favored American Way of Life, now conceived as "typical" of America. This search generated both feature series and advertisements, presented side by side in mass-circulation magazines. "*Liberty* went to White Plains—and Discovered America!" crowed one campaign. The magazine boasted that those communities where it reached high circulations and influence among readers symbolized "worthwhile America," the cream of the U.S. middle-class markets. What made these people "American" was being ardent, active consumers and members of the "business classes"—small merchants and white-collar employees whose devotion to free enterprise and individual ini-tiative comprised the American Way of Life.[37] These campaigns neither por-trayed nor addressed the bulwarks of the New Deal coalition, the workers and lower white-collar folk who made up 40 percent of potential markets. Despite the sizable markets for consumer goods among working-class urban dwell-ers, the small town now emerged as Madison Avenue's *heimat*. Additional marketing studies led to an industry consensus that such communities were bellwethers of American markets; as late as 1943, one executive still referred to them as "simon-pure American," neither "union-ridden nor plagued with class dissensions, racial hatreds."[38] Not surprisingly, such studies rewrote the social and cultural aspects of communities strictly from a commercial viewpoint. Despite their resolve to get closer to great numbers of people, address them in their own language, and portray them without bias, advertisers still showed them only in light of their consuming habits and tastes.

Once more advertisers turned again to a favorite device, praising "typical American families" as the great consuming unit. In both trade ads that emphasized families as the ideal types of an avid market and in different feature stories, magazines took up the American Way banner by holding a mirror to their readers. Such portraits took on a new nationalistic and political turn. "Mom and Pop and Sis and Bud" had long been familiar stock figures to ad men, but the American Way depictions now added that such families were not only typical consumers but also "typically American."[39] Most emblematic was a series from the leading women's publication, the *Ladies' Home Journal*. In February 1940 the magazine embarked on an elaborate, yearlong series, "How America Lives." These articles (and the corresponding campaign to promote the series) offered up a mixture of intimate interview and Farm Security Administration project. The *Journal* described the families as "your neighbors," bathing them in rosy patriotic hues—"as real, warm and American as pumpkin pie straight out of the oven." How America lived translated to an index of spending habits. "These neighbors of yours own more cars, read more magazines, hear more radios than the rest of the world put together," the *Journal* asserted. "How they live is the point—what they eat, drink, wear, and talk about, what gives them a kick, where the shoe pinches most and least, what they dream about and believe in."[40] What most typified American families were their tastes and spending habits. For *Journal* advertisers, "How America Lives" afforded an opening into lucrative markets (fig. 8.2).

The *Ladies' Home Journal* series opened to readers the logic of the market research that had been carried on by advertisers and media for years; the families were graded along standard scales similar to those used in marketing studies and by the Bureau of Home Economics and Bureau of Labor Statistics in their massive investigations into consumer purchasing. There was nothing random about the featured families. Although editors Bruce and Beatrice Gould advertised the families as typical, the *Journal* in fact handpicked the subjects. The magazine presented its initial family, the Griffins of Cedar Rapids, Iowa, as "*Elected* to represent six million families." In truth, the Griffins were chosen not by popular poll but by purposeful research, first in the Department of Commerce statistics to arrive at demographic prescriptions (community, income, occupation, number of children), and then through careful culling from community authorities. Ultimately, the *Journal* staff pinpointed their families by door-to-door canvassing, like a J. Walter Thompson

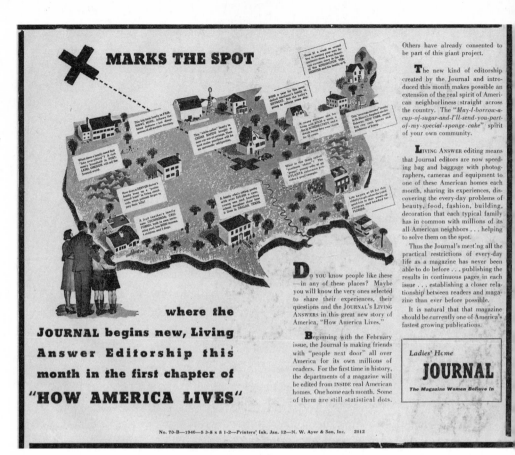

FIGURE 8.2. Advertising "How America Lives." (N. W. Ayer Collection, Series 3, Box 311, File 2, Archives Center, National Museum of American History, Smithsonian Institution, Washington, D.C.)

field representative or vacuum cleaner salesman.[41] Billed as an investigation into the economics of family life, "How America Lives" was a collective portrait of families like the *Journal*'s own business-class subscribers. "The degree to which their problems were common to many of our readers, problems with which our readers could identify themselves, determined which of the families in the same income brackets would be surveyed for the *Journal*," the magazine explained. In the end, it was the magazine staff's own eye for intangibles—taste, spending habits, appetites, child-rearing ideas—that shaped the choice of subjects, in order "to cover ways of life representing income brackets all the way up and down the line."[42]

Yet "How America Lives" was neither survey nor census. From the outset,

series writer J. C. Furnas made clear that nationalism loomed large in this study of how America consumed:

> If democracy exists and works, if it is worth the conscious effort we are all making to preserve it, if it is not just a mask of words wearing thin over the same violence, poverty, and spiritually bankrupt hatreds that are wrecking Europe, then America is the place to see the difference proving something. Everybody knows his own neighborhood pretty well, his own state and re-gion better than people from other states and regions. That is not enough. Some of us are more, some less prosperous. . . . Each of us ought to know all his 130,000,000 neighbors in our American democracy.

Editor Mary Carson Cookman recalled that this text and these sentiments, which she presented to every family under consideration for the series, were the most powerful arguments in persuading families to participate. Consumers themselves wished to see their own material habits as the stuff of political democracy, the foundation of citizenship. "How America Lives" neatly joined neighbors, material possessions, spending habits, political democracy, and American exceptionalism.[43]

The series focused on family possessions and spending choices; this engaged the magazine's decorating, food, fashion, and home departments, whose staff descended on the homes to transform them. Beyond their possessions, the Griffins' democratic approach to consumption itself became a feature of the first article. Both parents and children constituted a "board of directors" who debated and ratified each purchase by majority: "When Mrs. Griffin was thinking of running for the Woman's Club Presidency, when the old Ford and the aging Studebaker were traded in with $300 cash for the secondhand 1937 Dodge; when the buying of supplies was transferred from one store to another, the board of directors passed on the scheme each time." The Griffins had little specific interest in formal politics or world affairs, although the *Journal* quickly noted that they were "Republican as a rule."[44] The contrast between their avid democratic politics of consumption at home and their slight participation in public issues was striking. The American Way of Life showed that the true politics took place in the living room and the grocery store, not in the ballot box or on the shop floor. The families featured in these articles always chose consumption over politics. When it came to showing social harmony and homogeneity, the local community was the focus. In purchasing power and spending decisions, the family was the locale. In both arenas consumption superseded politics as the best way to ensure the good life for all, and it was pointedly assumed that everyone desired the same things. Freedom was redefined as freedom of choice—of color, of size, and style— freedom seldom defined beyond the realm of the marketplace. Emphasizing the nonideological and individualized aspects of consumption, this series showed families as neither political nor class-conscious but instead as interested only in the better things in life—newer and more products.

The series editors chose their subjects carefully, in calculated exclusion of much of American society. The series transformed the idea of a living standard into cultural cohesion and posited that association could only work in small, homogeneous communities. The magazine did take pains to show indigent families, including a black tenant family in Warren County, Mississippi, a New York City family on relief, and a Works Progress Administration family of eight. Of poverty and struggle, series writer Furnas was candid but brief; these portraits eschewed any consideration of the social or structural causes of the families' situations. Only one factory worker made the *Journal*'s vision of America—Dearborn resident Stanley Case, a Cadillac machinist who was not of the rank and file. Yet nothing was said of the United Auto Workers save that the General Motors strikes of 1937 had torn the community up. "How America Lives" thus served the same ends as Bruce Barton's speeches or General Motors's public relations. Neither labor concerns nor politics surfaced much, if at all. When underemployed West Virginia mine worker Charles Gillespie reported "kind words" for President Roosevelt, Furnas dutifully noted that they were *despite* Gillespie's normally Republican affinities. Portraying the nation as "neighbors" was the American Way antidote to recognizing a class system.[45]

As advertisers abandoned the masses, and the focus on neighbors brought forth portraits of "typical" individuals, some "others" now found inclusion as average Americans. Despite advertisers' private knowledge that the "average American" was a statistical construct at best, this fabrication appeared frequently throughout the late 1930s, as an endorsement of consumption as the characteristic form of American behavior. Whereas earlier testimonial campaigns of the late 1920s and early Depression had highlighted celebrities, civic leaders, and foreign scientists, testimonials in the mid-1930s often featured everyday people, distinguished only by their commonness. Ad men took great pains to show their subjects as average, in order to combat populist claims that they were out of touch with their customers. Even "Tell it to Sweeney," a venerable campaign of the tabloid *New York Daily News*, reflected this change. Created in the early 1920s, "Sweeney" was writer Leo Mc-Givena's composite of the lower-middle-class and working-class readers who made up the *News*'s audience. More often than not, Sweeney represented an abstract personification of the working-class common man and woman. But in the mid-1930s the *News* presented Sweeney as the "average" New Yorker, with character sketches of consumers, such as "Bella," a young single office worker, and "Joe Smith," once poor, now a respectable businessman. What made the Sweeneys important was not only their great numbers, but also that as consumers "they make your business tick, any business tick. They're great wanters, great getters, great customers."[46] The Sweeneys were now recognizable more as people than props, yet they were still chiefly distinguished by the buy-ological urge.

"Average" Americans appeared in numerous guises. Some portraits featured regional differences, local color, or even class attributes, but advertisers softened those distinguishing characteristics to emphasize that these quaint folks were in fact all united beneath the skin as modern eager consumers. "To sell the small town sell 'Carrie Staunton' first," proclaimed one trade journal. Carrie was the "leading club woman" of her small community, neither the richest nor smartest, but the woman to whom others looked for guidance. "She is the town's champion salesman," the trade journal explained. "In everything that smacks of progress or reform, she is the central figure." Although possessed of unyielding moral principles and abundant opinions, "Carrie" also proved open to new ideas, especially if they were presented as educational and factual. Once convinced of a new idea, she would be relentless in spreading it to a wider audience. She represented the informed consumer, the earnest reformer whom advertisers had alternately resented and spoofed since the emergence of Consumers' Research and the consumer movement in the early 1930s.[47] Advertisers were coming to the conclusion that the only means of outwitting consumers was by recruiting them.

Moreover, farmers and their families now were modernized as just as up-to-date and eager to spend as their urban cousins. Despite the fact that less than 25 percent of family farms had electricity in the mid-1930s, the Madison Avenue image of rural folks down home changed to reflect the growth of their own national aspirations.[48] Whereas before the Depression ad men had spent years claiming that rural consumers were different and that only appeals to them in their own language would sell, by the late 1930s the trade now argued, "Don't Talk Down to the Farmer." Rural Americans' aspirations, tastes, and habits were the same as suburbanites'. In spite of continual evidence of cultural difference, ad men began to tell themselves that country and city people were the same.[49] This was a truly imagined community in which difference and diversity were fantasized away.

Average Americans proved most crucial in both surveys and representations as clairvoyants of mass buying preferences. The average Americans' demands and tastes guaranteed mass sales, advertisers told themselves. Their outlooks and perspectives were the most valuable asset any national advertising agent or client could have. Accordingly, different agencies and media offered fictional portraits of average Americans to illustrate their skills in reaching and fascinating the Average American. The BBDO agency presented an early typical consumer in Grace Ellis, the fictional host of their *G-E Circle* NBC radio program:

One day the President of the G-E Company said: "Mrs. Ellis, how would you like to be a sort of hostess or directoress of our radio program?" I just sat and stared at him. "Me? on the radio?" I asked. "Why, I'm not important enough a person to direct a huge nation-wide program like yours," I said. "I'm just a wife and mother." "That's why I think you're just the person for us," Mr. Swope answered. . . . So here I am! There isn't much to tell about myself. I think I've been through all the experiences that most of you have had. I grew up in a middle-sized house in a middle-sized town. I went to school and church socials and picnics on the river. Later I worked, and finally held a pretty good job, and then I fell in love and got married. I've worried about croup and mortgages and what to have for dinner. I've had two children and not too much money. I've known joy and sorrow, birth and death, plenty of hard work and lots of fun—and so I guess I'm typical of women the world over.

What seems particularly interesting about this portrait is that the fiction was not only carried out over the air but also in the BBDO agency's in-house publication, whose readers all knew that "Grace Ellis" was a composite of a male copywriter's wife, two female writers' words, and a radio actress.[50]

Not to be outdone by NBC, CBS offered its clients a portrait of "Jake," a fictional common man who acted as consultant to major corporations. His tastes matched those of the mass, and his reasoning saved his corporate bosses from their own boardroom insularity. Jake was a marketers' fantasy come to life, a fortune-teller for products. A member of the working class, he had been "a farmhand, a mechanic, a taxi-driver, a rubber in a Turkish bath. . . . His ideas, his likes and dislikes, his enthusiasms and prejudices, seemed consistently to cross-section those of the company's 25,000,000 customers. As Jake thought, so the nation would think."[51] In addition to his barometric appetites, Jake was the most pliant of common men, willing to work for corporate bosses. Despite his proletarian background, he was an antisocialist's dream. He utterly lacked class consciousness, holding no animosity toward the wealthy and professing no particular solidarity with workers. He spoke of society—in CBS's terms, the radio audience and consumers—as "most folks," with no reference to any differences among the people he met. For Jake and the corporate sociology he voiced, the world consisted of two groups—neighbors and strangers. For advertisers to succeed, all they had to do was become the consumer's "friend." It is also worth noting that as the typical American consumer, Jake was decidedly a man, with masculine

FIGURE 8.3. "What Does Jake Think?"
(Library of American Broadcasting, University of Maryland, College Park, Md.)

appetites and reactions; advertisers might be selling mostly to women like Carrie Staunton or Grace Ellis, but they still had a rocky relationship with the actual Mrs. Consumer. It was easier to put their thoughts into a male voice. Most telling in this respect was the CBS brochure's cartoon illustration of "Jake." Rather than present him as some fantastic combination of Popeye the Sailor and Dagwood Bumstead, the brochure artists rendered him as another typical American: a guinea pig (fig. 8.3).

Such portraits celebrating typical and average Americans blurred the relationship between corporate and civic interests. The very notion of typical, connoting both democracy and the absence of privilege, clouded the fact that advertisers varied their criteria of the average to suit their clients' interests. The search for the typical culminated in 1939 when the National Retail Dry Goods Association chose Mrs. J. Richard Powell, a thirty-one-year-old homemaker and mother from Flushing, New York, as "Mrs. Typical Consumer." With an annual income of $2,700, "intelligent, observant and discriminating," Mrs. Powell fell statistically well within the income range of desirable dry goods and department store shoppers, according to the trade association. A spokesman said of Mrs. Powell, "she is one of the many millions of up-and-coming young American women who look to the future of their families with eagerness and a desire for better things. . . . Mrs. Powell, we think, typifies well that vast group of women who are the backbone of the nation and the store's best customers of tomorrow. What she and the women like her think of stores and the things they buy there is of much more basic importance to us than anything which may be gleaned from a chart or a table of statistics." Powell addressed the association, on behalf of women consumers, about the quality of goods and service she regularly received. In her talk she criticized high prices, annoying advertising, the glamour appeal in goods, and condescending clerks. It is worth noting that as an ex-librarian, with her children immersed in arts lessons and her husband taking postgraduate classes at Columbia, Powell's circumstances, if not unusual, were hardly typical. Even as her selection revealed the association's earnest desire to understand consumers as people as well as customers, more powerful currents of commercialism eroded their efforts.[52] As the trade journal *Tide* reported, Mrs. Powell was turned from "an omniscient oracular symbol of all the lady shoppers that ever were" into yet another guinea pig, "the prey of every promotion-minded retailer, manufacturer, testimonial grabber and crank in the country."[53] Once crowned, she met a barrage of offers for endorsements and requests to test scores of products. For a brief time, she became a minor public relations sensation, with manufacturers, retailers, and others seeking to link themselves and their wares to her, and in the process perhaps to learn more about consumer attitudes toward goods and business. Here, corporate public relations, Barnumesque publicity stunts, and aggressive marketing overshadowed the association's attempts to reach consumers. Advertisers could not resist their own impulses to commercialize every issue, even if wisdom plainly dictated restraint.

It is important to point out whom ad men regularly excluded from all these portraits, real and fictional: African Americans, the visibly poor "one-third of a nation" who fell below the poverty line, working small farmers, white and black southerners, and immigrants who proudly clung to their ethnicity. Warren Susman has observed that even as American Way proponents claimed that the nation had solved its problems and settled on its core values, they ignored numerous signs of cracks and rifts beneath the supposedly uniform veneer of American life.[54] Defining community and country only by shared participation in the marketplace, advertisers still excluded those whose opportunities to buy were most constrained by economics, cultural bias, geographic and racial segregation, or taste. To be sure, advertisers paid more attention than previously to some in these groups as potential customers, but the boundaries of representation in national media or in most marketing studies scarcely stretched to include them. Although advertisers subtly changed their attitudes toward consumers, they were still unwilling to confront American society in its stubborn diversity and insolent resistance to corporate overtures.

NEITHER MASS NOR CLASS:
CAPITALISM AND THE FULLER LIFE

To accompany the new sociology, business pundits reinvigorated their political economy. Business mounted concerted "educational" campaigns about capitalism as an institution to combat populist sentiment about corporate size and profits and to counter specific leftist criticisms of capitalism. These campaigns assumed many forms and penetrated the country. From the mid-1930s through the late 1950s, when the relationship of business and the labor movement had again realigned, corporate enterprise preached the gospel of the wonders, benefits, and essential superiority of capitalism for the good of the American people. An indispensable part of Barton's call to fight New Deal politics, this education in capitalism was multifaceted and ultimately involved conflicting views within and beyond business.[55] Advertisers were heavily involved in the fray; moreover, such corporate leaders as Colby Chester of General Foods and the National Association of Manufacturers, and Lee Bristol of pharmaceutical firm Bristol-Myers and the Association of National Advertisers, had long advocated educational public relations. Leading agencies such as Ayer, Thompson, and BBDO produced pamphlets and educational materials to spread the corporate gospel of free enterprise.[56] Agencies, corporations, and trade organizations all got into a second business—producing short didactic pamphlets, films, posters, and other materials expounding "the free enterprise system" for workers, clients, and customers. These pamphlets were part of a multidimensional outreach campaign that took place in factories, schools, civic gatherings, clubs, and churches. Educational films, plays, and school materials all brought this message of free enterprise, classless harmony, management's benevolence, and consumer sovereignty to millions.[57]

The political economy that poured forth from business spokesmen was, first, a defiant restatement of free enterprise prerogatives typical of the 1920s. Both the prolonged Depression and the 1937 recession seemingly emboldened big business to reject all responsibility for the economy and combat Roosevelt's policies on every level. For corporate apologists, defending capitalism now meant linking it explicitly to the political basis of the American

Way of Life: political liberty and economic freedom of choice were insepar-able. The unfettered pursuit of private interests secured the public good, and business liberty ensured consumer abundance. One representative example of this propaganda came in J. Walter Thompson's *A Primer of Capitalism* (1937). A graphic example of what some Thompson people still thought of consumers, the tract was illustrated with childlike line illustrations. Thomp-son contrasted state-run economies with private capitalism, arguing that pri-vate enterprise made the consumer the "boss" of the economy. In capitalism, the consumer was king. The visual contrast between private and state capital was obvious: the "Politician" of state capital sat on a throne too large for his pint-sized frame, looking confident but ridiculous; the "Consumer," a larger middle-aged woman, squarely occupied her throne, modestly but uneasily (fig. 8.4). The primer's graphic style, ironically, paid tribute to Otto Soglow's satirical comic *The Little King*, whose eponymous figure possessed a con-sumer sensibility beneath his royal robes. The cartoon's humor came from the contrast of the king's plebeian tastes with his royal station, his lowbrow appetites in highbrow garb (fig. 8.5). The consumer might be king, but this king was just another consumer.[58] Thompson's *Primer*, appropriating Adam Smith, asserted that all business was performed for the benefit of the con-sumer, and that private enterprise had replaced professional politics as the guardian of public welfare and the precious American heritage. The con-sumer's place was explained through the electoral metaphor: "The consumer is the voter, the juror, the judge and the executioner. And he doesn't even have to wait for election day to vote. . . . The consumer 'votes' each time he buys one article and rejects another—every day in every ward and precinct in the land. . . . In all history there has been nothing remotely like modern Ameri-can business as a sensitive index to popular likes and dislikes. It is democracy plus."[59] Capitalism was not perfect, the pamphlet conceded, but it was the greatest engine of growth in world history, and it was responsible for the fact that the United States had most of the world's wealth and luxuries. The American Way of Life was measurable by its fruits, its consumer goods.[60]

Second, like other corporate counterattacks against the New Deal and labor, proponents of the new political economy like the *Primer* trumpeted an organic theory of society. There were no meaningful divisions in American life: consumers and workers were both capitalists, along with managers and owners. The idea that producers and consumers were irreconcilably opposed by their economic concerns, it contended, was patently absurd; big business still refused to acknowledge consumers as having a distinct interest. At the very least, the pamphlet hinted, most consumers were also producers, and

What is the difference between state capitalism and private capitalism?

In state capitalism the *politician* is the boss. He may call himself a king, a general, a dictator, a fuehrer or a super mass-man. But whatever he calls himself, he is a politician.

He commands factories to open or close. He tells consumers what they can buy.

No workers can quit a job unless the politician says so. Everyone works where he is told to work, and everyone is told how much he may earn.

If the *consumer* doesn't like what he gets, or if the *worker* doesn't like his job, there is nothing they can do about it. In a nation under a dictator, or a nation waging war, or one populated by people who simply can't manage their own affairs, a high degree of state capitalism may be the only answer.

FIGURE 8.4. *A Primer of Capitalism* (1937). (J. Walter Thompson Archives, John W. Hartman Center for Sales, Advertising, and Marketing History, Duke University, Durham, N.C.)

Under private capitalism, the *Consumer*, the *Citizen*, is boss

The consumer is the voter, the juror, the judge and the executioner.

And he doesn't have to wait for election day to vote. He needn't wait for Court to convene before he hands down his verdict. The consumer "votes" each time he buys one article and rejects another—every day in every ward and precinct in the land. He dooms the business which, because of bad management, greedy stockholders or inefficient, unwilling workers, fails to *satisfy* him. For the consumer with his own private money—no matter how little he has—can spend it when and where he wishes.

In all history there has been nothing remotely like modern American business as a sensitive index to popular likes and dislikes. It is democracy plus.

FIGURE 8.5. *The Little King* (1933).

few were implacably opposed to all products they used, as defenders of capitalism hastened to point out.[61] Everyone who owned a home, some stock, or even an automobile was a capitalist. If most Americans were capitalists, pursuing their private interests in the honorable American way, and if most consumers were also producers, then the people could not honestly be against themselves. To equate consuming goods with business investment as a form of capitalism tortured the definition of capitalist as most Americans understood it in their daily lives. Owning several shares in Metropolitan Life or AT&T did not necessarily make one a capitalist, any more than owning a Chevrolet made one kin to Alfred Sloan. Still, business commentator Walter Pitkin estimated that over 60 million Americans were capitalists. "They try to give and get value received for goods and services. They strive to make profits, earn interests on investments, compete fairly with rivals, use individual initiative in starting and carrying on enterprises and careers. Here we find most of the middle-class, millions of skilled and semi-skilled workers and some of the rich."[62] Similarly, AT&T—the most entrenched, though state-regulated, monopoly in American business—ran a campaign arguing that the vast majority of its stockholders were common folk, especially women and widows: "Their average holding is 28 shares. No individual or organization owns as much as one per cent of the stock. There are no secret reserves or hidden assets. This structure . . . has been fundamental in making the Bell System a distinctive American business."[63] Such ads in fact ignored the concentration of stocks and power within AT&T, in favor of a corporate populism that emphasized distribution over influence. The corporation was really the community, and any attempt to attack, dismantle, or regulate the business was to interfere needlessly and harmfully in the business of 130,00,000 neighbors.

The third aspect of this new political economy addressed industrial workers and the labor movement. Convulsed by the union uprisings of the late 1930s, manufacturers were fighting not only the unions but also growing sympathy for workers among the general public. Business spokesmen steadfastly held that the United States had no class system and that to consider class solidarity before individual interest betrayed the American heritage. The staunchly conservative *Nation's Business* weighed in on this issue: "The most precious thing in America is the spirit of enterprise which management supplies . . . which has given this country the highest standard of living in the world. Isn't it time to quit talking about this land of ours as if it were split into hard and fast 'classes,' and to think of it for what it really is, the greatest spot on the globe, if not the only one, where classes do not really exist . . . ?"[64] In effect, this argument claimed that it was un-American to choose collective solutions to common problems. The surest evidence that Americans did not divide along class lines was not political democracy but the democracy of luxuries, the vast proliferation of consumer goods. "Now MILLIONS of People Are Wealthy" announced General Electric, celebrating mass ownership of autos and appliances.[65] Accordingly, an *American Magazine* profile of American Communist Party leader Earl Browder emphasized that even his family enjoyed typical American consumer comforts (although his un-American sentiments were best symbolized by his never owning a car).[66]

Advertisements portrayed corporations and businesses at work in communities, and many adopted a pseudodocumentary approach to depict typical American workers and their families, content in the workplace and grateful for both the benefits of the American Way of Life and their kind employers. "I'm glad my old man came to America," pronounced the friendly filling station owner. "The average fellow gets a whack at more of the good things in life and I see proof of it everyday right here in my gas station. Take most of my steady customers. Not one in a hundred makes a whopping big salary. Do you think they could even afford to run cars in most other countries, let alone buy them? Not on your life!"[67] The American standard of living, as embodied by mass-produced goods, was invoked repeatedly to demonstrate the capabilities of management and labor, "working together," to spread this level of accumulation throughout America.[68] For business spokesmen, those goods symbolized America's heritage of freedom and liberty, its exceptional national destiny, and the blessings of material plenty.

Corporations produced or commissioned hours of so-called sponsored film to make these points. These industrial films uniformly presented corporate interests in pictures made to resemble Hollywood fiction or newsreels. In 1937, just after the traumatic sit-down strikes in Flint, Michigan, General Motors employed the Jam Handy Company, pioneers in industrial and sales films, to make a documentary about the auto industry.[69] *From Dawn to Sunset*, like most Handy films, reached thousands of salespeople, customers, and civic and business groups. The film depicts the might of American industry in GM plants across the country. But whereas earlier films portrayed the work process or craftsmanship, *From Dawn to Sunset* offers a vision of labor that is presented almost entirely in consumerist and material terms. Opening with shots of workers arriving at factories in eleven different cities, the film clearly establishes these men as individuals in their communities and families yet speaks of them also as "a mighty army of builders . . . of a new prosperity in a land where that prosperity brings a fuller life to everyone who labors and who serves. And as each builder marches forth to shape his own destiny, tens of thousands go with him marching side by side." Such tortuous narration reveals the split in the film's political unconscious. Intent on countering labor's solidarity, the film insists on individualism but must immediately and repeatedly acknowledge the masses of workers that fill the plants. As if reflecting on this contradiction, the didactic narrator thereafter falls silent for most of the film. The problem of insisting on individualism within a mighty army remains unresolved as the film turns away from work to consumption (fig. 8.6). In fact, most of the film follows workers' families spending money. The camera lingers longingly on men in pay lines and on checks pressed into satisfied hands; on fresh cuts of meat, cheese, and other foods; on women picking out clothing and furniture; on men buying tools, musical instruments, or toys for their children; and on at least one entire family selecting a new auto. "The fuller life in the Great American Way," invoked by the narrator, clearly refers to the spending and goods that cement families and communities.[70] Here the cinematic eclipse of the producers' republic is complete. Citizenship and belonging are defined in and through goods, not labor itself.

This vision was not only presented didactically but also entertainingly. For many years, Ford Motors sponsored a Sunday night radio program of light classical music, whose centerpiece was a series of popular "talks" by W. J. Cameron, Ford's publicist. These invariably argued for corporate prerogatives, praised small town values, and castigated the New Deal. Cameron's talks were very well received among the Ford audience (the company gave away some 2 million copies within two years). Yet in 1938 the nonprofit, nonpartisan Institute for Propaganda Analysis charged that Cameron engaged in unabashed (and more important, unanswered and unidentified) political speech making, mixing Liberty League sentiments with Vienna waltz accompaniment. The content of the *Ford Hour* speeches was highly political, without the network's customary and required attention to balance normally given to political party representatives at the microphone.[71] Other sponsored programs similarly filtered free enterprise ideology into the network lineup throughout the late 1930s. The National Association of Manufacturers presented a continuing drama series, *The American Family Robinson*, whose plotlines continually presented the superiority of the free enterprise system. More famously, the DuPont *Cavalcade of America* similarly presented episodes from history to highlight the greatness of individualism and the human spirit, or in business terms, private enterprise. These programs were conceived of and executed as direct challenges to the New Deal philosophy of shared responsibilities for common welfare; garbed in the guise of entertainment, such attacks often attracted little fanfare.[72]

FIGURE 8.6. Scenes from the film *From Dawn to Sunset* (1937). (Rick Prelinger and the Prelinger Archives)

Industry readily claimed responsibility for abundance and democratized wealth through the union of individual initiative and social benefit through mass production and technology. Yet in the American Way campaigns, corporate spokesmen cast this as a nationalist question. As war darkened over Europe, business apologists repeatedly criticized foreign collectivism and dictatorship in contrast to American freedom. The Warner and Swasey Company told its workers, "The tools you operate are both the weapons and the badge of democracy and freedom."[73] The Erwin, Wasey agency produced an editorial ad, "The Old Man," portraying a paternal capitalist in his factory. He was of the generation of managers and captains of industry who rose through merit—the "Old Man" even lived in a log cabin as a boy—and whose success was both democratic and virtuous. That system of achievement, however, was endangered by foreign ideas, as the "swarthy" soapbox orator outside the gates reminded the big boss:

> He is worried more about what is happening in America today and about the eager bright-eyed son of Charlie Pedersen. He is worried lest the sickness that has seized the rest of the world spread its infection in America; worried lest all the isms and the insidious doctrines of alien places destroy our greatest heritage. . . . It would be too bad if America should become like other countries, so regimented and politician-ruled that it would no longer be possible for a man to toil and climb and pluck the prime fruits of reward. For then this country would cease to be—America sweet land of liberty.[74]

Labor conflict, populist hostility to entrenched wealth, and government activism threatened not just business prerogatives but national foundations as well. Any criticism or attempt to alter existing economic arrangements, under any guise, was simply un-American. Indeed, such campaigns held that the most important values and behaviors of American life depended on the maintenance of unregulated enterprise. The corporate American Way testified that the distinct traits and folkways of Americans lay less in the vernacular speech, crafts, humor, or racial and ethnic backgrounds than in the fruits of the economic and political system. The distinctive attributes of American nationality, corporate spokesmen emphasized, were the material benefits accorded to every American regardless of origin through free enterprise. All Americans, then, shared a mythic history that reinforced the interconnections of individual economic freedom, nationality, and consumer abundance. The corporate American Way agenda was succinctly distilled in a Scripps Howard advertisement: "Business, Not Politics, Developed America. . . . In

America, the term 'business' doesn't merely define a commercial technique —it defines the life force of the nation. The business of every American is, directly or indirectly, business. Business—which is to say, the American way of life, has created for the American people the highest standard of living of any great people in history."[75] This editorial made crystal clear that the American Way of Life was *only* business; a market, not society, formed the central core of the nation, and its citizens were really passive consumers.

This union of consumer progress and American distinctiveness culminated fittingly at the 1939–40 World's Fair, held in New York. The concurrent Golden Gate Fair in San Francisco also partook of this vision. Billed as "the greatest merchandising opportunity of the decade," the New York fair featured dozens of displays that celebrated mass production, classless interdependence, and corporate leadership. As the New York fair opened, one advertising journal summed up the fair's importance: "The World of Tomorrow is selling a concept. . . . [It was] time for business to show that it wasn't just the New Deal that was thinking in terms of a planned more abundant future."[76] Over four thousand different firms, selling typewriters to toothpaste, signed licensing agreements for "collateral advertising" with the fair. While the product advertising took place in the fairground pavilions and amusement areas, corporations also heavily promoted their participation in the fairs.[77] Westinghouse trumpeted its New York exhibit with a massive public relations program whose centerpiece was the film *The Middleton Family at the New York World's Fair* (fig. 8.7). In this film the evocatively named Indiana family learns in Flushing Meadows the superiority of the American Way of Life, courtesy of Westinghouse.[78] Led by patriarch Tom Middleton, an optimistic small businessman, the Middletons are hosted by a hometown friend and Westinghouse employee Jim Treadway, who touts the virtues of corporate research and free enterprise. Treadway's foil is a communist-inspired radical, Makaroff, whose collectivist sentiments pointedly echo Consumers' Research critiques. The two belief systems compete on the battleground of products; the Middletons' allegiance would be determined by the quality and performance of consumer goods and technologies. The film resolves with the triumph of free enterprise on the fairground and with the fair sex. The Middleton daughter, Babs—next generation's Mrs. Consumer—renounces the Russian for the hometown engineering student Jim, who will help deliver the World of Tomorrow to consumers like her.[79]

The fair's much-studied and celebrated futuristic utopias played up these same ideas. New technologies offered the promise of new products; the revolutions heralded in the various pavilions in essence came down to better

FIGURE 8.7. "The Middleton Family at the New York World's Fair."
(*Saturday Evening Post*, April 15, 1939, 60–61)

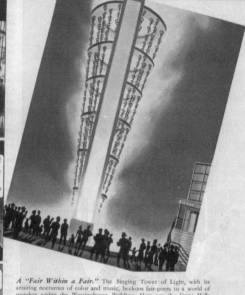

FIGURE 8.8. "Ford Cycle of Production." (Edward Orth World's Fair Collection, Archives Center, National Museum of American History, Smithsonian Institution, Washington, D.C.)

products to help future families live happier middle-class lives.[80] The fair's pavilions also hosted displays embodying explications of management views, trumpeting the classless harmony of worker, capital, and consumer administered by the beneficent wisdom of management. Tellingly, this often was manifested as the erasure or caricature of workers and consumers themselves. For example, the Ford exhibition, created by celebrated designer Walter Dorwin Teague, featured workers designed to look, as well as move, like puppets or automatons; the net effect was to dehumanize workers even as it celebrated a production cycle (fig. 8.8). The vaunted Futurama exhibit of General Motors, created by theatrical and industrial designer Norman Bel Geddes, displayed vehicles in a metropolitan landscape with neither workers nor consumers. This consumer "autopia"—the most popular exhibition of the fair—lacked any semblance of society at its center. Futurama, as built, contained a half million scale models of buildings and fifty thousand cars, yet no passengers or pedestrians except at the very last moment.[81] In this futuristic tomorrowland of automobiles, citizens disappeared (fig. 8.9). Buying the cars that filled the future, consumers performed their economic roles even as they abandoned their civic duties.[82]

The erasure of consumers took place even within the fair's administration. Managers had planned a consumers pavilion dedicated to portraying consumers' interests. Yet a scant few weeks before the fair opened, twenty-one

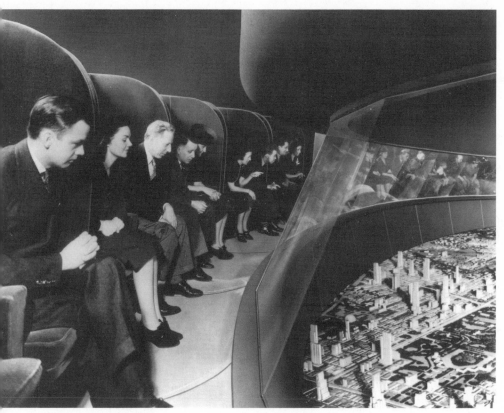

FIGURE 8.9. General Motors' Futurama. (Edward Orth World's Fair Collection, Archives Center, National Museum of American History, Smithsonian Institution, Washington, D.C.)

prominent consumer advisers to the pavilion committee resigned en masse. Among them were familiar and long-time officials and activists from government agencies, the American Home Economics Association, the American Standards Association, Consumers Union, and the academy. Their letter charged that fair managers had never taken consumers' interests seriously and had denied them any meaningful role in shaping the content of the pavilion. The letter further charged that the committee had scuttled the two most important purposes of the consumer exhibition, a conference on consumer interests and a public survey of visitors. The dissidents concluded that the exhibition could not display consumers' interests but only those of business and retail. Paul Willis of the Associated Grocery Manufacturers ran the consumers' committee for the fair, which lent some substance to the charges of bias in favor of retailers and business. Eventually the Hall of Fashion, sponsored by a number of large department stores, took up residence in the

Consumers' Building, along with an exhibition that stressed distribution issues but not consumer problems. Consumers Union was permitted to lease space but not to make available its literature that rated goods by brand.[83] The organization took advantage of this limited autonomy to display samples of testing methods and consumer education materials. It also offered a chance to meet the Consumers Union mascot—Sylvia the guinea pig.[84] The World of Tomorrow and the business American Way promised a consumer's paradise, yet this utopia depended on consumers disappearing from public view and public life.

CONCLUSION

The American Way of Life celebrated by business retaliated against the New Deal by using nationalist images and historical exceptionalism to counter democratically made political choices. This American Way told consumers that material modernity—an endless future of more and better goods—distinguished their nation from others. Being an avid, loyal consumer was everyone's civic responsibility; neither politics nor social movements would ensure that future of new and improved. True Americanism depended on spending, and only with unlimited prerogatives for business could citizens both achieve happiness and preserve their freedoms. The business American Way thus placed consumer choice at the center of American liberty. When Americans confronted prospects of communist subversion and the real threats of war, consumption, freedom, and citizenship would be joined. Freedom would become freedom of choice.

CHAPTER 9

FIGHTING FOR THE

AMERICAN WAY

CONSUMPTION

AND AMERICANISM,

1935–1945

The most precious possession we have in this country is freedom of choice.[1]

Advertising is predicated on the validity of the pursuit of happiness. . . . Democracy is meaningless if the pursuit of happiness is invalid.[2]

Brands, trademarks, labels, displays, even the merchant's proud sign over his own door, are therefore vivid if humdrum symbols of your freedom. And especially so is advertising. . . . Long words like dictatorship, totalitarianism, corporate statehood, stand for the bleak burned-over wastelands of old worn nations. Other long words are democracy, liberalism, individualism, and these stand for the rich foliage, the wide branches, the high trunk, of our fresh and living culture. But the taproot, strong and straight and deep, is simple freedom—freedom to speak, read, think, worship, work, make, sell, and buy—freedom of choice.[3]

This war is the test of the selling way. It is a war of those who believe in compulsion against those who believe in persuasion. Our enemies in this struggle are warring upon our selling way of life as surely as they are upon democracy itself. Compulsion and persuasion can no more exist side by side than can tyranny and democracy.[4]

An economy which serves us, which produces and distributes to us all the things which make the good life for us and our children, and in which we participate as responsible citizens, will give the lie to the enemies of our way of life both without and within. We are not fighting this war for the Captains of industry, for the movie stars, for the big-league baseball players, or for the great cotton planters. We are fighting the war for John Q. Citizen and his wife and children.[5]

The battles over the American Way of Life among business, government, and consumerists were conflicts of ideas and images that spilled over from political arenas to cultural sites and back. Business's counterattack to the New Deal and the consumer movement escalated such skirmishes to specific confrontations that cast consumption as Americanism. Even as they revealed the porous boundaries of culture and economy, such struggles specifically linked consumers' interests with American identity. Prospects of war, fears of communist subversion, and disagreements over the terms of buying and selling all imbued consuming with conflicts over the meanings of nation, patriotism, and citizenship. The coming of war brought the clash of consumerists and corporations onto the national stage, every day. During World War II, consumption shaped daily home-front experience and the conscious articulation of wartime ideology. In the imagery and practices of nationalism and wartime patriotism, Americans came to see consumption as an integral part of American culture and to experience it as citizenship. But even before Pearl Harbor, consumer interests became linked not just to consuming but also to Americanism itself.

CONSUMPTION AND AMERICANISM, I: THE BATTLE FOR CONSUMERS' RESEARCH

After its disillusionment with the New Deal and political liberalism, Consumers' Research (CR) radicalized. Sympathetic to collectivism but critical of government, by 1935 CR staff members began investigating possibilities for direct political activity. As the staff became convinced that consumer protection could not be gained without direct political power, they contemplated organizing consumers and building a consumer's party at the grass roots. This was not necessarily an unprecedented departure. CR had often reached out to labor groups and held town meetings frequently with subscriber-members. Despite its disappointment with Franklin Roosevelt and the New Deal, CR nonetheless stepped up its campaign for a federal Department of the Consumer, to establish a permanent presence for the consumer in the cabinet.[6] Also in that year, with managing editor J. B. Matthews taking a leading role, the organization itself became more explicitly political. In mid-August CR hosted a conference on organizing consumers, and Matthews took exploratory soundings for a New Jersey State Assembly campaign. A former missionary, socialist, and member of numerous leftist organizations, Matthews possessed a certain hard-boiled organizational experience matched by few others on the staff. A veteran of infighting at numerous religious and political groups, he was a seasoned pamphleteer when he joined the consumer cause. One of CR's most radical believers, he was a firebrand found at the center of controversy throughout his career.[7]

Yet Matthews saw his plans for elected office fade as CR became engulfed in serious labor difficulties. Staffers otherwise loyal to F. J. Schlink had grown restless under an unyielding workload, low pay, job instability, and his stringent criticisms. Their loyalties did not extend to other members of the CR board of directors, including office manager M. C. Phillips (Mrs. Schlink) and Matthews, who ran the editorial department.[8] In the late spring of 1935, employees formed a union, which by August had become Local 20055 of the American Federation of Labor's (AFL) Technical, Editorial, and Office Assistants Union. Schlink and CR management explicitly encouraged the organization. Yet on September 4, forty-one clerical and technical workers—much of CR's core staff—walked out over working conditions and the dismissal of three temporary employees who were union members (fig. 9.1). The strikers demanded reinstatement of the fired union members, the elimination of a policy that employees could not engage in outside organizations and activities without the CR board's consent, a $15 a week minimum wage, and a greater voice in determining policy.[9] Schlink, Phillips, and Matthews comprised the majority of that board, and they summarily dismissed from their ranks Dewey Palmer, CR's chief technician, who sympathized with the strikers and criticized CR labor policy. Arthur Kallet was subsequently dismissed from his post as CR board secretary as well. Management rapidly circled its wagons, in the process cutting ties to anyone who might have opposed or debated them.[10] Matthews took the lead in combating the strike and dealing with the union; once the walkout began, CR steadfastly refused all offers of arbitration and fought virtually any attempt to settle the strike. More comfortable conducting his confrontations in writing than in person, Schlink retreated to editorialize against the strikers from behind the scenes.

Some form of labor unrest had been probable at CR ever since 1933, when the organization relocated from New York City to expansive new quarters in rural Washington, New Jersey.[11] Under self-imposed pressure of heavy workloads, and a characteristic inability to brook disagreements, Schlink over time had alienated numerous CR board members, such as former treasurer Bernard Reis, Schlink's executive assistant Eleanor S. Loeb, and E. J. Lever, a former CR employee who ran Cooperative Distributors, a firm that sold recommended products through a cooperative. Many of the most active and passionate staff members had resigned or left the organization, frustrated with Schlink's unwillingness to compromise his own specific vision or share

FIGURE 9.1. Consumers' Research Strike, 1935. (Special Collections, Alexander Library, Rutgers University, New Brunswick, N.J.)

authority. Schlink in turn shed CR's board of directors of anyone outside the organization's daily affairs, effectively merging internal and external management and gutting the function of a board. Leaving New York had provided needed room for testing labs, but it increased CR's isolation. At a moment when the organization was poised to augment its national influence, Consumers' Research was fighting with and criticizing its potential allies among consumer and government groups. That prickly isolation harmed the rank and file as much as management. As longtime observers of the organization noted, cosmopolitan workers interested in the consumer's cause in bohemian New York were likely to become restive in the narrower confines of rural New Jersey.[12] As local residents now joined and replaced the transplanted staff, the sense of a small and finite community only intensified.

Negotiations begun in earnest in late August quickly broke down; Matthews's abrasive style killed off most hope of compromise.[13] The escalation of demands and tensions leading up to the strike gave CR management ample opportunity to depict strike leaders as untrustworthy and therefore unfit for employment at CR. Management claimed that the union misrepresented events and issues in the press and other public forums. Confrontations and violence on both sides of the picket lines only provided the excuse for CR to label strikers (and their supporters, for that matter) as being fundamentally dishonest and unreliable. Participation in the strike by definition disqualified workers from returning to CR.[14]

Within weeks after the strike began, CR management was charging that the walkout was engineered by communists bent on taking over the organization. Some union activists—most notably Susan Jenkins, a CR proofreader who led the strike; John Heasty, the local president; and Kallet—had ties to the Communist Party along with other progressive organizations. This was not surprising given the overall interests of labor-oriented activists in questions of consumption. Decades later, a number of former CR strikers remembered being helped by "reds."[15] There is no direct evidence of Communist Party planning or leadership of the strike, however, even after sixty years of charges and countercharges. Clearly, some radical activists were interested in CR as a means of helping working people and the labor movement; a consumer movement led by others less independent than the mavericks at CR would likely appeal to a broader spectrum of leftists and radicals with party and organizational connections. Schlink's handling of power at CR revealed a fundamental unwillingness to share authority or join coalitions. In October 1935, in the heat of the strike activities, Matthews filed a sworn statement concerning a secret meeting he had attended in July, along with Arthur Kallet and Dewey Palmer. There, he learned a number of communists and progressives "were determined to control, or failing this, to wreck Consumers Research and any movement of a political or economic character which it might be influential in launching." Matthews claimed he made clear his disagreement with this goal at the time, although he may have been wishing to preserve his own options: he apparently did not think to inform Schlink about this meeting until close to the strike. In addition, Charles Wyand, an economist friendly with both Kallet and Schlink, also reported attending two meetings shortly before the strike, where a number of staff members and allies, including Heasty, Palmer, Jenkins, and Kallet, discussed an impending strike at CR to "take over" the consumer movement from Schlink.[16] While it seems clear that communist or radical presence in the strike was not the initial cause of management's opposition to the union's demands, by the third week of the strike, management was claiming in the press and in its letters to subscribers that CR faced "no strike at all in the ordinary sense of the term but rather an attempt to stage a revolutionary capture movement or *putsch*."[17] Thus, already having determined to never take the strikers back under any circumstances, CR management then added charges of communist subversion to the struggle. This modest strike of clerks, stenographers, typists, and technicians escalated from grievances over commonplace labor issues to one of Americanism: CR management now claimed that the consumer movement itself was at stake.

Oh Mr. Matthews! Oh, Mr. Matthews,
You are looking very worried nowadays.
You have turned from Red to pink
And your frowns are black as ink
Is it a headache, Mr. Matthews?
No it's a REDACHE, Mr. Schlink.[18]

This lighthearted tune sung by the picketers belied the seriousness of their situation. The CR strike opened a deep and unhealed schism in the ranks of the consumer activists and sympathizers.

The convulsive strike lasted several months. Fledgling and inexperienced union members, many of them young local women from the clerical staff, were aided (and often outnumbered) on the picket lines by tough veterans from the local mills, particularly Local 20 of the AFL Hosiery Union. As a CR worker recalled decades later, "We were playing at being union members . . . . we really didn't know what we were supposed to do."[19] CR, for its part, employed a few local residents as strikebreakers. CR also hired a strikebreaking detective agency, Foster and Roberts, as a private armed security force to defend the premises and combat the strikers if necessary, and the newly trimmed board engaged a law firm to secure injunctions and file suits against the union.[20]

The CR strike case made national press, as liberal journals rushed to defend the strikers and condemn Schlink and the board's dictatorial control of the organization. Coverage highlighted both workers' grievances and CR's denial of influence in policies to both workers and subscribers.[21] Despite the board's steadfast refusal to arbitrate, theologian Reinhold Niebuhr and Roger Baldwin of the American Civil Liberties Union set up a special investigation team to attempt a settlement. Their report, based on testimony from both strikers and CR management, further supported the public impression that CR was run as the board's personal fiefdom and that consumers were ill served by a nonprofit organization run in such fashion. A dissident group of members, the Association of Consumers' Research Subscribers, also organized to encourage compromise. Continually rebuffed, the group subsequently organized other subscribers in order to make their displeasure known to CR.[22] On October 25 strike supporters staged a mock trial in New York City, to air grievances and to bring the charges against CR into open discussion. No one from management attended. The business press had a good laugh at CR, erstwhile sanctimonious defenders of the people, now having an old-fashioned capitalist dustup. As CR's old enemies at *Printers' Ink* were quick to wonder, if the strikers had regularly misrepresented facts, as Schlink claimed, why should readers trust any of magazine's criticisms of advertising and goods?[23]

The same stubborn and righteous persistence that had made Schlink an enemy of business now alienated him from the labor movement and many liberals. Strikers and critics both claimed that Schlink's autocratic manner and inability to work with others made him a menace rather than a friend to the consumer. To outside observers, the firing of union activists so close to the formal presentation of union demands was at best ill timed; at worst it was dictatorial and heavy-handed. Schlink's long-winded, technical, legalistic defense of management's conduct translated poorly as well. To outsiders it seemed as if CR dodged the moral issues of justice to workers. The trumped-up dismissal of Dewey Palmer just after the strike began indicated to union supporters that Schlink was determined to prevent any influence other than his own in the organization. Just as CR had some basis in alleging that the strike was a veiled attempt to disrupt and damage CR permanently, strikers and their allies hit the mark in charging that management ran CR as if it belonged to them instead of members.[24] Schlink limited subscribers' communal participation in CR: members either accepted or ignored the magazine's recommendations and observations, participating through feedback and suggestions but never in a democratic process. Subscribers had no veto or direct influence on policy. The new National Labor Relations Board took up the strike, ultimately concluding that CR had unfairly and unlawfully dismissed the three union employees. Yet the walkout was never resolved. By November Schlink was referring to them as "ex-employees" and not strikers, reiterating his total unwillingness to take them back under any circumstances.[25] For its part, the union announced the end of the strike on January 13, 1936.[26]

Whether or not a takeover of CR had been planned, as Schlink charged, Arthur Kallet emerged as a spokesman for the rebels. As a well-known author and public figure, a man of radical sympathies and passions, his criticism of and rapid dismissal from the CR board made him a natural leader of the dissidents. In February 1936 the strikers chartered a new organization, Consumers Union (CU). Headquartered in New York's Union Square, a center of the labor movement, Consumers Union advocated similar methods and techniques—testing, standards, grade labeling, home experimentation—as its predecessor, along with union membership for all employees. The group published test results, identified inferior and superior products, and reported news of interest to purchasers.[27] Yet the new organization pursued a much broader constellation of goals than had CR. CU from the outset aimed for a high degree of member participation and governance and made concerted efforts to reach low-income workers. Unlike CR, Consumers Union systematically cultivated its ties to the labor movement and other progressive organizations. The group developed a low-price, limited-focus edition especially for working-class readers who could not afford the standard $3 yearly subscription for *Consumers Union Reports*. This edition, frustratingly, never gained much success: like its predecessor, CU would struggle to reach low-income readers.[28]

The organization made the labor conditions under which products were manufactured a critical focus of its work. CU thus reinvigorated concerns of older movements such as the National Consumers' League and contemporary leftist groups such as the League of Women Shoppers.[29] *Consumers Union Reports* separated the labor information from its product ratings but consistently reminded reader-members of the mutual significance of both issues:

> "Decent living standards for ultimate consumers" will never be maintained simply by reporting on the quality and the price of products. All the technical information in the world will not give enough food or enough clothes to the textile worker's family living on $11 a week. They, like the college professor or the skilled mechanic, are ultimate consumers; but the only way in which any organization can aid them materially as consumers is by helping them, in their struggle as workers, to get an honest wage. . . . Despite the fact that a small minority of consumers are not workers and that others do not recognize themselves as such, by and large the consumer and the worker are the same person, a person who must carefully guard his interest both as wage earner and as consumer.[30]

Like CR, the new group claimed that most consumers were workers, but CU from the outset insisted that workers' interests could not be addressed by product ratings alone. CU also cooperated more closely with other groups that were working on consumer issues, including cooperatives and civic and women's clubs. Most tellingly, Consumers Union repeatedly addressed its reader-members as a community, seeking input and opinion; the CU editors addressed members as equals and not customers, in distinct contrast to CR's emphasis on its own distanced professional expertise. Committed to the consumer's welfare at the core of a host of reforms, CU became a very different voice on consumer concerns, even as its principal focus remained better purchasing. As a popular front organization, linked in constituencies and affiliations to other progressive groups, CU's membership soared. Within three years, the new organization boasted more subscriber-members (71,000) than rival CR.[31] Like its competitor, Consumers Union garnered business criticism and opposition from the beginning.[32]

Hardened by the strike and ostracized by former allies, CR now broke entirely with liberals, statist politics, and social reform, careening down an ideological path that would have been unthinkable even a few months before the strike. From Schlink's vantage point, the strike revealed the labor and consumer causes as fundamentally opposed; the investigation of CR by the new National Labor Relations Board further convinced him that a meddling, incompetent government was the consumer's enemy, as well liberals and labor. This truculent stance saddened and alienated many prominent support-ers and hundreds of subscribers. Early allies and sponsors gave up on Schlink, and some turned to the new organization. Besides Kallet, activist social scien-tists like Stuart Chase, Robert Lynd, Robert Brady, and Colston Warne, home economists such as Louise Edwards and Hazel Kyrk, and pundits such as George Soule and Bruce Bliven all broke or let slip their ties to CR. With old friends and colleagues unable to comprehend his actions, Schlink in turn repudiated former beliefs. Before the strike Schlink had spoken openly of redistributing wealth, and he warmly promoted "genuine, i.e. class-conscious consumer interest." Schlink had characterized capitalism as "the indefeasible opposition of economic interest of the factory-owning class to the factory-product-making-buying- and -using class of workers, farmers and other con-sumers." Before the strike Schlink clearly viewed the consumer's interests and labor's as mutual; according to some coworkers, Schlink and CR had supported the labor cause explicitly and vocally.[33] But by the end of the decade, Schlink had become a full-fledged apologist for unregulated capitalism. He soon embraced the ideas of libertarian theorists Ludwig von Mises and Frie-drich Hayek. The onetime propagandist for an activist, consumer-friendly state now preached the gospel of free markets as fervently as Bruce Barton or the National Association of Manufacturers. The turnaround was both striking and sad.

Embittered against his old colleagues and allies throughout the consumer field, Schlink quickly became a rabid anticommunist. To his new way of thinking, anyone that sympathized with Consumers Union or worked with that organization was suspect, if not communist, as well. The fierce energy he once spent compiling data on testing and products he now turned to assembling endless lists of alleged leftist consumer activists. In the manner of Elizabeth Dilling, author of the guilt-by-association tome *Red Network*, Schlink kept a ballooning "Red Rope" file of consumer activists and groups with purported ties to communists. Well into the 1960s he dogged his progressive ex-associates and critics. CR fed information to the government and the press about the purported communist activities of progressive consumer activists Mildred Edie and Dexter Masters, along with old colleagues Robert Brady, Dewey Palmer, and Arthur Kallet.[34] Collaborating with him in this new obsession was J. B. Matthews, who left CR, fittingly enough, for a position as research director of the House Committee on Un-American Activities (HUAC) in 1938. Working for the anticommunist watchdog group chaired by Texas representative Martin Dies, Matthews soon made a national name for himself. His indiscriminate reasoning and take-no-prisoners rhetoric found a welcome home with the publicity-conscious Dies, and Matthews would influence many in the anticommunist era to come. If consumption were American citizenship, both Matthews and Schlink were each in their own way determined to control definitions of Americanism, just as CR had once aimed to influence the properties of motor oil and washing machines.

Thus, by choice Consumers' Research relegated itself to a marginal, oppositional place in consumer reform. No longer able to lead the consumer movement, Schlink refused to follow. CR struck its own path, still suspicious of advertising, but now more opposed to government intervention on behalf of consumers than to business predation on buyers. After the strike, CR lost few opportunities to assert that free competition was the consumer's most effective protection. In CR's eyes, not only labor-oriented organizations but also federal regulation of markets inescapably meant communism. By 1938 Schlink and Matthews were arguing, "This nation cannot long endure with an economy which is half collectivism and half free-enterprise. . . . Increasing misery for the many is the fundamental condition for 'progress' in the communist sense of the word. Naturally they welcome as an ally an Administration which is . . . moving toward the collapse of free and private enterprise."[35] Such rhetoric bears the stamp of Matthews's intemperate pen and undisciplined logic, but undoubtedly Schlink endorsed and echoed such thinking. While the movement it fostered grew closer in the late 1930s to extracting meaningful consumer protection from the government, Consumers' Research turned away from nearly every reform it once championed, other than better products for consumers. In a final irony, Schlink found his lasting ideological home among his former enemies in business.

This evolution poses questions about the long history and prospects for consumers in the market. Do CR's positions before and after the strike reveal a fundamental change in views? Were the interests of the consumer fundamentally opposed to labor? What insights can we draw about consumption and citizenship from the strike and its repercussions? Lawrence Glickman's excellent interpretive essay on the CR strike and the politics of consumer interests contends that CR's activism was always largely asocial. Price and pocketbook defined consumer interests as interpreted by the testing organization. Glickman also maintains that Schlink clung to interest-group liberalism both before and after the strike, placing more trust in the overall mechanisms of the market to aid the consumer than other sources, whether government or social organizing. CR had advocated a consumer interest that stood alone, independent of labor or other social interests, from the first.[36] Certainly before *and* after the strike, CR argued that consumers were members of the social body and the body politic who deserved representation and protection at least equal to that of labor or business. Yet to argue that CR's consumerism never varied from the interest-group and pocketbook perspective of liberalism ignores both the utopian possibilities glimpsed by some movement leaders and also the extent of CR's critique of capitalism. Such a view also shortchanges the drastic shifts in its expressed views both in public and private, shifts that reflected both the volatility of political thought in the Depression and the search within CR for a viable and consistent economic philosophy to best serve the consumer. Between its founding and the strike, CR did move steadily leftward, eventually espousing strong government action and the possibility of collectivism on behalf of consumers. At the same time, its criticism of both government and industry mounted; by mid-1934 the organization contended that these institutions in their present form could not give consumers full value or protection. CR held that business under a profit system was overall unwilling, and perhaps incapable, of delivering high-quality, reliable goods at a fair price to consumers.[37] Government, even with a history of consumer neglect and betrayal, was the only institution that offered some meaningful protection to consumers as a class, to fortify them against "sellers['] greed or overreaching."[38]

Although CR still publicly preached a version of interest-group liberalism to argue for consumers' representation in government, Schlink angrily denounced other political liberals and repeatedly pointed out the inadequacies of a liberalism so heavily dominated by business and markets. The New Deal experience under the National Recovery Administration (NRA) led Schlink to characterize liberals in government as unprepared politically and technically to fight for substantive protection for consumers. During the early New Deal, CR's faith in the market and science gave way briefly to faith in the government. The NRA experience led CR to believe that consumers ultimately would have to attain their own direct political power to force much more drastic change. Consumers simply could not rely on a business-dominated government or the market to protect them; they would have to enter politics themselves. In the heady days of 1934 and 1935, CR could not be characterized as a typical interest-group liberal organization.

Moreover, CR was not simply interested in an exclusive pocketbook basis for consumption. The group supported the union movement up until its own strike, viewing labor and consumption as complementary issues. In part because both groups suffered at the hands of big business, CR continually referred to the worker's interests as distinctly connected to the consumer's. Schlink lectured for the League for Industrial Democracy, attended organizing workshops at Brookwood Labor College, and supported union causes, not least of which was the formation of an employee union at CR. Schlink might have criticized what he considered labor's overemphasis on wages and hours instead of broader consumer concerns, but he still enthusiastically supported the union movement. While Consumers' Research bulletins and editorial matter seldom discussed specific labor causes, the organization did address workers' disadvantages under American business and made clear that only a solution that provided justice for workers, as well as consumers, could have a lasting impact.[39] Yet CR contended that consumption could possibly unite even more people in common cause than labor: more people consumed than produced. In the fragmentary context of Depression-era reform, the appeal of consumption to unite large disparate groups of citizens proved tempting for consumer activists as well as advertising apologists for capitalism.[40]

At the peak of its insurgent interests, then, CR was hardly a typical "liberal" organization. Schlink, Kallet, and the staff would have been appalled at that designation; between 1933 and the end of 1935 CR positioned itself as radical. Careful to serve its middle-class constituents through product information and not political theory, CR nonetheless embraced social views that would have shocked many members. Writing to political scientist E. Pendleton Herring, Schlink emphatically stated, "My plea is not, as you assume for a redress of the present balance or unbalance [of interest groups] but for a fundamental change. Certainly the economic underpinnings and the political structure must be brought into line with the purposes of a consumer-oriented society if we are to have one. . . . [The lower middle class's] interests as consumers constitute such an economic ground for alignment on the basis of self-interest with the dissidents that plan for fundamental change."[41] While CR had initially accepted the reality of interest-group pressure and had gained a thorough education in interest-group politics during the New Deal, by 1934 the group placed much less faith than other consumer activists in interest-group liberalism. Its campaign for a federal Department of the Consumer and for adequate federal resources put to grade labeling and regulation pushed its radical sympathies in the early 1930s toward central government control, but not without misgivings. Schlink had broken with liberals before the strike; their almost universal condemnations during the strike ensured he would never consider himself one of them ever again. Writing to a member in Flint, Michigan, Schlink declared, "If your judgement that 'the Consumers' Union of the United States [composed of a staff whom we have had to exclude from our organization because of a demonstrated lack of integrity] represents a more liberal attitude' truly reflects present day 'liberal opinion,' then our break with 'liberalism' will have to be complete and permanent."[42] CR's eventual settling to embrace corporate-friendly free enterprise and a severely restricted government role in protecting consumers should not obscure the significance of its intervening journey. CR's odyssey revealed the limits of liberal reform for consumers: a business-dominated government would not adequately protect consumers from the market, and the market itself could not be trusted to deliver the best, safest, or most efficient goods. While Schlink ultimately embraced a laissez-faire version of marginalism, his own work showed with undeniable clarity how the marketplace was neither the best nor the sole protection for consumers. Consumers might only gain protection in alliance with other groups, which inevitably meant a melding of purposes and goals. Standing between New Deal liberalism and untried collectivism, fearful of fascism and wary of socialism, CR sought a politics that placed consumers not as another interest group but as the first among equals, superior to both business and government. Schlink's unwillingness to compromise or share power doomed CR to the sidelines, but consumers themselves would not be so easily marginalized. By the time of CR's crisis, dozens of organizations were taking up the consumer cause from a variety of political and social positions. Their activities demonstrated conclusively that even diffuse groups of citizens would organize to challenge business prerogatives and ill treatment of consumers. The many local organizations of buyers proved that consumers were becoming a political force.

CONSUMPTION AND AMERICANISM, II:
CORPORATIONS, MEDIA, AND THE CONSUMER MOVEMENT

Public confidence in business remained low in the wake of the 1937 recession, and some businesses and publications aggressively accelerated their defense of business against consumer groups and regulation. They created a shadow business consumer movement to win the buying public from the likes of Consumers Union or Consumers' Research. Just as corporations in the 1920s had set up company unions, funded worker publications, and touted a paternalistic version of welfare capitalism, now some firms established consumer "institutes."[43] Leading the business consumer "fronts" was the staunch opponent of "Guinea Pig theorists," Collier-Crowell publishing executive Anna Steese Richardson. A longtime vocal enemy of consumer groups, she launched an intense campaign against CR and similar organizations, promoting advertising, media, and branded goods. Between 1934 and 1939 she traveled 145,000 miles and by her estimate addressed as many people.[44] Incensed at the "increasing evidence of an unjustified suspicion towards all advertised brands, fostered by sources inimical to advertising," she founded the Crowell Institute on Consumer Relations in 1937 to coordinate the firm's considerable resistance to consumer groups.[45] The institute published educational materials and pamphlets with such titles as "A Primer on Rayon" and "The Canned Food Label and What It Represents," which argued positions friendly to industry on standards, grade labeling, the economics and veracity of advertising, class relations in the United States, and shopping. All addressed civic groups interested in consumer questions. Richardson sought to neutralize guinea pig "propaganda" by "telling the truth" about American business. Her institute had a regular forum before over 2 million monthly readers of the *Woman's Home Companion*, and she toured the country using her extensive contacts in civic and women's clubs to present the business message to consumers. No evidence points to the institute ever having tested one product itself or authorizing independent tests conducted outside manufacturing facilities. Instead, Richardson's institute encouraged clubwomen and community organizations to learn "the problems of the manufacturer" as the first step in understanding the consumer's role and benefits under free enterprise. In other words, the consumer's job in a market economy was to think like and act in consideration of the manufacturer. Those benefits, Richardson implied, conferred responsibilities; Mrs. Consumer was to work with and not criticize business to seek satisfaction. She was not to organize.[46] As a businesswoman, Richardson firmly asserted that women needed to learn the business perspective on consumer issues; homemakers would not adhere to their protests if they learned business's needs and understood how business served them. In turn, she urged businessmen and advertisers to address groups of homemakers and women's clubs and persuasively inform them that their demands for lower distribution costs, grade labeling, and regulation were either unnecessary or unfair. The institute helped procure speakers and secure materials from local chambers of commerce for a grassroots campaign for the hearts and minds, as well as the pocketbooks, of consumers.

Other organizations followed suit. The *New York Herald Tribune*, which had its own product-testing institute, brought together clubwomen and business leaders for a series of consumer forums in 1937. *McCall's* founded an "institute" explicitly designed to counter the critical viewpoints of Consumers' Research and Consumers Union. Sears, Roebuck initiated consumer outreach lectures and information services as a way to boost telephone sales. Even the advertising agency N. W. Ayer set up an Institute on Consumer Relations.[47] Macy's set up its own Bureau of Standards and then pushed consumer expertise into entertainment, debuting a "Consumer Quiz Club" game show on New York's WOR radio in February 1938.[48] More important, the American Association of Advertising Agencies instituted a Consumer Advertiser Council, and the National Retail Dry Goods Association (NRDGA) established working committees with consumers. In cooperation with a coalition of different groups (from which both CR and CU pointedly were excluded), the NRDGA met with and heard the concerns of consumer representatives from women's clubs and university groups. The NRDGA deemed this public relations program very successful, establishing long-standing connections between department and chain stores and consumer groups.[49] Similarly, William T. Foster, theorist of underconsumption and purchasing power, emerged in 1937 touting a proposed Consumers Foundation. This organization, which would act as a clearinghouse of information and programs for consumers, had the financial backing of the Institute of Distribution, a trade group for chain stores. The chains were facing strong legal and political challenges in courts and Congress and apparently intended the foundation to generate social support for the chains. However, its first official bulletin falsely advertised prominent consumerists as its sponsors and was quickly discredited. Yet Foster's prominence and the deep pockets of the chains and like sponsors gave consumer advocates pause. The business consumer movement could easily overpower grassroots or nonpartisan consumer organizations.[50] Such business-run shadow consumer groups were built around publicity campaigns (the *McCall's* "institute" seems to have been nothing but a public relations office) and enjoyed access to millions of consumers through magazines and other outlets. They were designed to combat the consumer product-testing groups by showing that, in effect, business already went through all the steps that CR and CU advocated for testing products. The consumer move-ment was unnecessary since businesses and women's magazines already took care of the consumer's needs.

Such business-run fronts naturally drew sharp criticism from consumer advocates. Most prescient, Robert S. Lynd warned that "the whole movement can be aborted if the present plans of manufacturing and retailing trade associations to set up 'kept' consumer pressure groups [are] allowed to go forward unchecked." Likening such groups to company unions, Lynd and others worried that they would only pursue business-friendly issues and their existence would either obviate or discredit other consumer organizations with less funding and different programs.[51]

"Who's a Guinea Pig?" demanded one advertisement in Hearst's *Cosmopolitan*. "The woman who buys *unadvertised* goods" was the answer. This business counterattack, orchestrated by the Hearst publications, turned the guinea pig comparison back on consumer advocacy (fig. 9.2). Consumers were guinea pigs only as they followed the advice of harebrained government theoreticians and private consumer "experts" instead of national advertising from established manufacturers. Unadvertised products did not face the revealing glare of national publicity, and they did not endure the trial of popular use and opinion. Without the backing of national advertising and marketing, any product could be dangerous; far from being a sign of public deception, advertising was the surest sign of reliability.[52] Hearst's campaign ran for over a year, underscoring the conflict between consumer advocates and private enterprise at the close of the decade.[53] It was a conflict over who would keep consumers' trust and retain the right to speak for and to them. Similarly, Crowell initiated a magazine campaign that modeled its own Institute on Consumer Relations. Lavish ads showed earnest clubwomen interviewing uncomfortable-looking executives to learn that advertising was Mrs. Con-sumer's best tool in homemaking. Establishing such intimate ties, in the manner of the best product selling, would restore consumers' faith in adver-tising. Yet awkward poses and obvious staging revealed that even in their attempts to mingle, businessmen still viewed Mrs. Consumer as more foe than friend (fig. 9.3).[54]

The Hearst company soon encountered a more troublesome pest than rapidly multiplying guinea pigs. In 1939 the Federal Trade Commission (FTC) capped a four-year investigation by launching hearings into the business practices of Hearst's *Good Housekeeping*. The commission charged that the magazine published highly exaggerated and fraudulent advertising claims. CR and CU had long insisted that magazine institutes' inadequate science

WHO'S a guinea pig?

● "After all, I'm perfectly sure about the quality of the products I buy. Because I buy only products which are backed by a well-known reputation. I KNOW I never take a chance this way!

"Despite sensational, destructive propaganda, I know for example, that when I buy nationally known drug products I don't have to wonder about their quality, purity, and ability to give me my money's worth in satisfaction.

"The real guinea pigs are the people who experiment . . . take chances . . . with products which are NOT backed by a well-known house.

"I know that exact methods and precise tests maintain the high quality of drugs and cosmetics which bear a nationally known name, and that therefore I can buy with complete confidence.

"And I know that, all in all, I don't pay more for this extra assurance. In fact, my dollars go farther because I don't risk them on un-

known and untried merchandise.

"I know that the manufacturer who makes his product nationally known through advertising wins success because of the proved merits

of his goods. He sets a standard of quality and service and maintains it because he cannot afford to risk disappointing me and thousands of others who use his products. He has his good name to uphold.

"I know that the widely advertised product shows by its widespread use that it must be satisfactory.

"And I know that responsible publishers protect me further by refusing to accept the advertising of products which fail to pass tests for quality and performance.

"Thus no matter how tempting the bargains in unknown, unbranded merchandise, I know — and tell all my friends — that it is still the better part of buying wisdom to prefer the products you see regularly advertised — and to refuse all substitutes for them."

LOOK FOR THESE PRODUCTS ON DISPLAY THIS MONTH IN YOUR FAVORITE DRUG STORE

ABSORBINE, Jr.*	GILLETTE *Brushless Shaving Cream*	PEPSODENT *Tooth Paste*
ALKA-SELTZER*	GILLETTE *Safety Razors and Blades*	PRO-PHY-LAC-TIC
APRIL SHOWERS TALC*	HEINZ *57 Varieties**	*Tooth Brushes*
ASTRING-O-SOL*	INGERSOLL *Watches and Clocks*	PYREX *Nursing Bottles*
BAYER ASPIRIN	IPANA *Tooth Paste**	RAY-O-VAC *Flashlights and*
B-D *Fever Thermometers*	JERGENS *Lotion*	*Batteries*
BLUEJAY *Corn Plasters*	JOHNSON & JOHNSON	SARAKA *Laxative*
BOND *Flashlights and Batteries*	*Band Aid*	SCHICK *Injector Razor*
BROMO-SELTZER	*Drybak Corn Plasters*	SCOTT'S *Emulsion*
CALOX *Tooth Powder*	*Red Cross Cotton*	SEIBERLING
CHAMBERLAIN'S *Lotion**	KOTEX *Sanitary Napkins*	*Drywear Latex Baby Pants*
COLGATE *Dental Cream*	LISTERINE *Antiseptic**	SERGEANT'S *Dog Medicines*
DAVOL *"Anti-Colic" Nipples*	LUXOR *Face Powder*	SILEX *Glass Coffee Makers*
DR. SCHOLL'S *Foot Remedies*	MENNEN *Antiseptic Oil*	SIROIL *Aids Psoriasis*
FEEN-A-MINT *Laxative*	MENNEN *Lather and Brushless*	TAYLOR *Binoc Fever Ther-*
FITCH'S	*Shaving Cream*	*mometers*
Dandruff Remover Shampoo	MILLER *Water Bottles*	TEK *Tooth Brushes*
FLETCHER'S CASTORIA	MODESS *Sanitary Napkins*	WHEATAMIN EXTRACT
Laxative	MUM *Deodorant**	*Vitamin Products*
GEM MICROMATIC	NEW HAVEN *Watches and*	*Please refer to advertisement
Singledge Razor Blades	*Clocks*	in this issue of Cosmopolitan.

FIGURE 9.2. "Who's a Guinea Pig?" (*Hearst's International Cosmopolitan* 105, no. 5 [November 1938]: 103)

FIGURE 9.3. Countering the Consumer Movement:
Mrs. Consumer Seeks Out Mr. Advertiser. (*Woman's Home Companion*, June 1939, 96)

and commercial dependence neither informed nor protected consumers reliably.[55] The commission alleged that the magazine's vaunted product "Seal of Approval" misled readers, who assumed it applied to all goods advertised in the magazine, when in fact it concerned only the very few products actually tested by the Good Housekeeping Institute. The FTC contended that, through the use of a similar "Guaranteed as Advertised" seal, *Good Housekeeping* implied that *all* products contained in its pages were guaranteed. Thus, as an advertising trademark, the seal was false and misleading, said the FTC. *Good Housekeeping*'s seal implied that all goods had met a series of rigorous scientific tests of composition and performance, tests that the magazine simply did not perform.[56]

Hearst executive vice president Richard E. Berlin vowed to fight this action, arguing that the FTC charges were trumped up to destroy the American free press by weakening advertising. "Certain radical and communistic groups in and out of the government service," charged Berlin, were bent on destroying capitalism by undermining the confidence of consumers in its wares.[57] Berlin's own rebuttal was sent to two thousand businessmen and a thousand publishing executives, who in turn offered hundreds of supportive responses. In early 1939 the Good Housekeeping Institute began an advertising series that specifically responded to the FTC charges. "Merit is the sole basis upon which the Seal of Approval is awarded. We do not charge manufacturers to test their products. Nor do we require manufacturers to advertise in *Good Housekeeping*. Any product within our testing scope which is sponsored by a responsible manufacturer and has reasonably wide distribution is eligible for our testing services," editorials proclaimed.[58] In other words, only products that were nationally advertised (and thus more likely to purchase space in the magazine) were eligible for testing. Much was at stake, both for Hearst and for the middle-class general publication. Although one trade journal described the institute's $500,000 per year expense as a "constant drain," the *Good Housekeeping* Seal of Approval served for thirty years as a symbol of product quality and the trustworthiness of consumer goods in general.[59] The FTC case could have struck a major blow to consumer beliefs in their goods. The seal signified the public's faith in the magazine, and an adverse FTC judgment would prove that Hearst betrayed consumers for advertisers' interests. Startlingly, Hearst admitted as much as a 40 percent rate of error in its tests, certainly an alarming number for anyone who relied on the seal. Such a high rate of error, of course, was unacceptable in independent consumer bureaus such as Consumers' Research or Consumers Union.[60] The government's attack reinforced a building public skepticism in advertising and American business. If the *Good Housekeeping* seal was a racket, was there much hope left for consumers?[61]

Berlin's charges of communism might have fallen on deaf ears had they not aired simultaneously with a special report of the House Committee on Un-American Activities. The first phase of the FTC-Hearst hearings finished on December 7, 1939. On December 10 HUAC chairman Martin Dies called a special session of a subcommittee, attended by him alone, to receive a "report" from HUAC researcher and ex-CR board member J. B. Matthews. The Matthews document charged several prominent consumer organizations (notably CU but not CR) with communist intentions and activities. According to Matthews, consumer organizations sought to "discredit advertising of reputable American firms and products through propaganda issued by the consumer organizations which is designed to make the American public dissatisfied with the profit system." Thus, he charged, they served as "transmission belts" for Communist propaganda.[62] Furthermore, the report singled out the *Good Housekeeping* investigation as an example of the influence of communism in the consumer movement and government.[63] This highly irregular set of unsubstantiated charges soon after appeared on Hearst mimeos and in the business press.[64] It seems likely that Matthews, and possibly Dies, planned this with Berlin to derail the FTC case and discredit free enterprise critics in and out of government, and not incidentally win HUAC some needed attention and renewed funding.

That certainly was the interpretation of some consumer groups and business pundits. Donald Montgomery of the Consumers National Federation bluntly charged that the committee report was "pulling Mr. Hearst's chestnuts out of the fire." Undeterred, Berlin shot back: " 'Unless the publishers and business[es] of the country act promptly to check these Communistic influences there will be no free press in the United States of America.' "[65] In rebutting Matthews, Consumers Union alleged that this HUAC attack on the consumer movement originated in a direct meeting of Schlink and Matthews with several corporate leaders at the home of conservative columnist George E. Sokolsky.[66] Other HUAC members, most notably California congressman Jerry Voorhis, immediately howled in protest at both Dies's flagrant procedural violation and the content of the report. Indeed, HUAC member Joseph Casey charged that both the Matthews and Hearst versions of the report originated on the same typewriter. Consumer groups immediately denied the accusations, vilifying Matthews and seeking hearings to air the issues laid out in the Matthews document.[67] Within two days, both President Roosevelt and First Lady Eleanor Roosevelt publicly condemned Dies's actions in presenting the Matthews report.[68] The Matthews screed never became part of the official record; however, the damage was done: thereafter, insinuations of communism dogged consumer movement advocates, including Arthur Kallet, well into the McCarthy era.[69]

Although many advertisers quickly conceded that the consumer movement generally wasn't "red," as a practical matter they supported Hearst in its battle with the FTC.[70] By the spring of 1940, the American Newspaper Publishers Association petitioned unsuccessfully to intervene in the case, claiming that the outcome would affect the fundamental operations of a free press.[71] Corporate spokesmen continued to denounce the far-reaching critiques by the consumer movement as inaccurate, dangerous, and communist-inspired. After a prolonged set of hearings that featured witnesses who defended *Good Housekeeping*'s institute, disgruntled manufacturers who had failed its tests, and homemakers who disputed the seal's reliability, the FTC ultimately rendered a decision against Hearst. Having been found guilty of deceptive advertising and misrepresentation, *Good Housekeeping* consented to change the wording in its "guarantee" to consumers. The magazine also altered institute procedures to ensure stricter standards of testing and accountability.[72] Matthews, for his part, remained a fixture at HUAC and in Washington anticommunist circles over the next fourteen years.

The final attack on consumer groups was made to order for publishers and emerged from the same stew of business opposition to an increasingly militant consumer movement. George Sokolsky, a conservative columnist, had gained national fame denigrating the labor movement and New Deal as a broadcaster for the National Association of Manufacturers. Macfadden Publications, publishers of *True Story* and other magazines aimed at working-class Americans, also owned a slightly more upscale news weekly, *Liberty*. At the behest of its editor Fulton Oursler, Sokolsky penned a series of articles denouncing the consumer movement and fulsomely praising advertising. Oursler ordered the series to rebut the Consumers' Research material used in his daughter's school. Collected and published as *The American Way of Life* (1939), Sokolsky's propagandistic pieces served as a breathless ode to manufacturing. "By the mysterious alchemy of political freedom and private enterprise," he wrote, "we have managed to produce on this continent the most satisfactory procedures of living. . . . That is the essence of the American ideal." An anti–guinea pig tome, *The American Way of Life* recycled by then familiar arguments about the low cost of advertising, the wonders of consumer goods, and the innate independence of consumers. Updating advertising's decades-old tropes of progress and barbarism, Sokolsky invoked China and Russia, communism and fascism, noting that "the mass of people suffer not only from the government suppression of the spiritual qualities of man from the abolition of every human right . . . but they have so stabilized consumption that human beings live on a physical basis which we do not recognize in this country as fitting for human beings." At times overbearing, the book nonetheless neatly tied together nationalism, American culture, free enterprise, and consumer abundance.[73] *The American Way of Life* served as well as the basis for a sponsored film, *I'll Tell the World!*, which played daily at the Macfadden exhibit at the New York World's Fair, decamping afterward to a theatrical run and long rounds in the customary venues of corporate-sponsored films—churches, factories, Republican clubs, and the Young Men's Christian Association.[74] The corporate interpretation of the American Way of Life rested on and was realized in free enterprise, advertising, and the fruits of mass production.

At the decade's end business groups could tally at best a mixed result in their ongoing campaign to halt regulation and defuse anticorporate sentiment. The Advertising Federation of America had spent ten years in a campaign to defend and promote advertising; in 1939 it used over two thousand periodicals and over three hundred radio stations nationally to that end.[75] Despite the slowing of the New Deal, business still faced stiff challenges from government and consumers. Economic and regulatory reforms had placed notable checks on certain aspects of selling and marketing. Though no sweeping reform of advertising, the Wheeler-Lea Act of 1938 empowered the Federal Trade Commission to regulate truth in advertising claims beyond the scope of patent medicines. The commission was proving itself willing to take on and curb abuses of prominent advertisers such as Fleischmann's Yeast and *Good Housekeeping*.[76] More important, the congressional Temporary National Economic Committee (TNEC) of 1938–39 initiated a wide-ranging investigation into the effects of economic concentration and monopolies. The TNEC's many inquiries often uncovered advertising's tendency to promote monopoly in various anticompetitive and anticonsumer practices. Led by Assistant Attorney General Thurman Arnold, Justice Department investigators worked with and testified before the TNEC. Arnold's widely reported comments that advertising fostered wasteful competition and inessential information thus incorporated Thorstein Veblen's insights into the official record, nearly four decades late.[77] Under fire, Arnold subsequently went to great lengths to profess that advertising per se was not the TNEC's target, even as Madison Avenue—and indeed TNEC's chair, Wyoming senator Joseph O'Mahoney—defended the right to puffery.[78]

Although business spokesmen had been urging outreach to consumer groups, it remained unclear whether an effective understanding between buyers and sellers would result.[79] A 1939 *Business Week* intelligence report on the movement displayed a thin veneer of curious tolerance that barely concealed fear and dismissive contempt of organized consumers: "The malcontents have fomented a movement that has vitally affected the business of marketing goods. Today, the consumer movement is something that must be considered as unemotional reality. Whether its program is good or bad, sound or unsound, sane or insane, is pretty much beside the point. . . . In that confused but consecrated army there are perhaps at present only two common denominators: (1) a vague resentment against advertising 'because it gyps the buyer' and (2) a desire for lower prices and more facts about merchandise."[80] The *Business Week* report urged readers to manage the consumer movement while appearing to take its demands seriously. It suggested a course of action similar to the response to the 1934 food and drug reforms: "compromise on a platform of minimum reform" to gain consumer confidence "helpful in withstanding the demands of some of the more zealous and militant consumer leaders." More thoughtful was a study commissioned by the Advertising Retail Federation, which warned that consumers resented business attempts to organize or speak for consumers.[81] While many advertisers advised their colleagues to acknowledge that consumers had valid complaints, others stubbornly ignored that counsel. Instead, they followed the *Business Week* strategy. Executives had to manage the "malcontents" by defusing their militant anger and offering symbolic concessions. The trick for business was to maintain the appearance of exchange and compromise while giving little or no ground.

The consumer movement at decade's end embodied a broad interest that had neither been fully plumbed nor tested in national politics. While organized consumers comprised a coalition that stood equal in theory with labor and business, they had neither an overarching political presence nor a single dominant issue to focus their influence. Effectively promoting specific reforms or a public education agenda might prove difficult for such a broad alliance. The movement's dispersion, it must be said, frustrated its foes as well as friends, as it made difficult a uniform response to consumer demands, even as it hampered the articulation of their common interests. Still, through community groups, clubs, and national organizations, consumers had become visible and vocal.[82] That new prominence spurred some in business to seek cooperative and constructive relationships with consumer organizations. With a million dollar grant from the Sloan Foundation, the Institute for Consumer Education at Stephens College in Missouri held a series of high-profile conferences that brought together consumer activists and some sympathetic businessmen to chart paths to consumer empowerment in government and the marketplace. Some business commentators not only predicted but even welcomed prospects for a long-desired consumer cabinet post.[83] Yet on the whole business groups remained frightened and determined to control or neutralize the movement, especially its most critical members, and consumers in turn remained skeptical and at times defiant of business. Although the Committee on Consumer Relations in Advertising, the National Retail Dry Goods Association, the Crowell Institute on Consumer Relations and a few other trade groups—candidly dubbed the "right-wing consumer movement" by one business writer—had made numerous contacts among community groups, advertisers and businessmen in general still feared the greater consumer movement's emphasis on labeling, standards, grading, regulation, and transparency.[84] In 1940 business stepped up the criticisms offered by Hearst, Matthews, and Sokolsky. The consumer movement, they charged, contained radical communists bent on the destruction of the American free press. If communists crippled advertising, they warned, the American Way of Life would perish as well.[85] Despite assurances of such critics as Thurman Arnold and Donald Montgomery that they did not oppose advertising, business spokesmen now pilloried advertising's critics as un-American enemies of free enterprise. Even Roosevelt's proclamation that advertising was a necessary and vital force in the economy and in any war effort could not dissuade advertisers in their quarrels with government and consumers.[86]

What did *Business Week* fear? With considerable militance and strong feelings, consumers themselves were organizing. More than 20 million consumers were represented in over eighty different organizations, according to one 1940 survey.[87] Many shared key goals and criticisms that challenged business's dominance of the consumer marketplace: the desire for accurate and useful labeling, standards, and product reliability, along with strong opposition to deceptive manufacturing claims and aggressive salesmanship. Consumer activists critiqued advertising as a needless expense transferred to the buyer, and they passionately argued that consumers alone, *apart from business*, should determine their own needs. These common goals cut across the fissures that otherwise divided such groups.

Underneath the push for labeling and standards, consumer groups most significantly wished to reorder their relationships with manufacturers, retailers, and advertisers. Just as the labor movement was remaking the compact of workers, owners, and the state, consumer activists desired a similar renewal. The broad consumer movement sought to transcend the market-place logic of high volume and low price and rejected the price-cash nexus as the sole point of contact between Mrs. Consumer and Mr. Advertiser. In their public complaints, in appearances at congressional hearings and public meetings, in forums with business representatives, and in the numerous publications emanating from outposts around the country, consumers made clear they needed a different moral compact with business. Consumers desired to change how businesses addressed them and to exert active and meaningful influence over the values and attributes of goods. Some progressive groups indeed wished to alter the social relations in spending itself. Thus, consumers not only reached for more influence on the conditions and constraints of trade, but they also articulated a basis of consumption that moved beyond marginal utility to broader conceptions of social good. For some consumer groups that meant support for the labor movement, while others worked toward greater freedom from the expanding influence of the market.

The move to seal a new social compact between businesses and consumers cut across programmatic differences and political alliances. Such thinking was fundamental to such progressive proconsumer groups as the Consumers National Federation and Consumers Union.[88] Yet the same basic impulse, with decidedly different applications, underlay business-run initiatives like Anna Steese Richardson's institute at Crowell Publishing and the National Consumer-Retailer Council. Moderate civic groups such as the General Federation of Women's Clubs, whose large membership swelled the ranks of organized consumers, shared these impulses as well. These groups, particularly those representing women's groups and consumerists, sought new relationships of buyer and seller, new expectations of one another, and new understandings of consumption. Seeking greater satisfaction in spending, many consumer activists wished to heal what they viewed as the alienated social relations of the marketplace.[89]

Nevertheless, serious conflicts would remain. Business operations would yield to demands for change and shared authority only under extreme pressure. Richardson claimed that business's welfare and Mrs. Consumer's were identical. Most consumerists knew different. Could producers and consumers reassign and share control over the meanings of goods and the conditions of selling? What did consumers and producers owe one another beyond the exchange of money and merchandise? What were their relationships with labor to be? Clearly, corporate enterprise would only allow a narrow range of consumer influences over the quality, kind, and labeling of goods. The food, canning, and textile industries, publishers, and advertisers had all bitterly fought grade labeling since 1933 with no signs of relenting to women's demands for clear and consistent standards. Businesses had fiercely contested both consumers' and government's demands to regulate advertising messages or manufacturing content. Many business consumer initiatives were unabashed attempts to neutralize public discontent by overwhelming grassroots buyers with business-friendly information and contacts.[90] Large-scale enterprise would tolerate different relationships with consumers only on its own terms.

Yet diffuse as it was, the consumer movement sent a wake-up call to business. More ominously, businesses understood that skepticism and frustration would destroy loyalties and erode demand. "The organized discontent of some consumers with the things they buy and the way they are sold has become a major marketing problem," noted *Business Week* frankly.[91] The president of the General Federation of Women's Clubs put the matter bluntly to the National Consumer-Retailer Council: "Today advertising is up against an emotional resentment [from consumers]. You advertising men are experts on emotion. Is it wise to let this resentment grow? Discontent is the path which leads to the ideologies which we see in Europe. Are you going to meet this condition or are you going to tell the gals to stick to their knitting?"[92] In its continued nervous hand-wringing and surveillance of consumer groups for signs of rebellion and pink-cheeked propaganda, by 1940 business had arrived at an important moment. Consumers were insisting on more influence over advertising and over relations with manufacturers and merchants. The costs of business's failure to meet and defuse consumer dissatisfaction would be long lasting and serious: damage to consumers' allegiance to business and erosion in the public's commitment to the system of private enterprise. Agency chief Raymond Rubicam asserted, "American freedom is, or should be, based on the willingness of the individual to accept such limitations on his personal freedom as will serve the rights and interests of all. There is no question that business and its instrument advertising must serve the great consuming public to its satisfaction or that the public will find ways of compelling that satisfaction."[93] But who would determine the nature of that satisfaction? Who would define and control areas of concern between buyer and seller, corporation and citizen? Would government support for consumer-friendly regulation further erode business autonomy? Would consumers define freedom as more than freedom of choice? Would government or business win the allegiance of consumers, or would they share it? The answers would emerge in World War II.

"AN ECONOMY WHICH SERVES US":
CONSUMERISTS AND CITIZENS AT WAR

Advertisers, consumer advocates, and government officials all struggled to win allegiance for their competing visions of consumer citizenship. Although advertisers had the greatest resources to defend their interests, advocates of consumer organization and government administration competed with some success against business to shape long-term associations of consumption and Americanism. World War II's role in remaking consumption deserves a book-length treatment in itself, but even the necessarily brief account that follows will reveal that consumption became a principal vehicle for the articulation of citizenship during the war. The ideological battles between advertisers and consumerists, as well as the domestic wartime programs, cemented an understanding of consumption as an exceptional unique American identity and a material embodiment of freedom that has underpinned citizenship and culture ever since.

Robert Westbrook has argued that Americans understood the nation's war aims, and indeed their individual participation in the war, through appeals to private, not communal or social, interests. Drawing on political theorist Michael Walzer, Westbrook suggests that the contractual basis of liberal society—the obligation and consent of citizens—made it difficult for Americans to conceive of their war effort in communal terms. Citizens would be hard-pressed to defend a government whose principal function of offering protection had manifestly failed with the outbreak of war. Instead, he notes, both the wartime discourse of obligation (seen in government propaganda) and the "lived theory" of everyday citizens (embodied in their own expressions of obligations and in popular culture) translated the war's aims into a defense of private interests. World War II became a fight to protect the family and the domestic realm.[94] The greatest challenge to the nation and the global community was interpreted officially and unofficially in individualist terms. Westbrook perhaps underestimates the importance of the attack on Pearl Harbor for motivating and sustaining the war effort, but his argument remains compelling because he has located an important source for the war's specific popular support that also influenced the eventual eclipse of political reform and social obligation during those years. Just as Americans understood the war effort through the "subnational" affiliations of domesticity, over the 1940s they gradually abandoned the state-sanctioned politics of welfare and obligation instituted in the New Deal.[95] Associations of consumption with self and home united liberal political institutions, nationalism, and war with home, family, and material abundance. Consumer plenty and private domesticity together undergirded obligation for servicemen and civilian alike.

World War II unveiled new implications of material nationalism. In their everyday experience of wartime—apprehension regarding loved ones overseas, material and economic constraints at home, pressure for communal and national unity in both thought and action—Americans recast the nationalist meanings of consumption. If the Depression had marked a crisis of economy and culture, the war indisputably revealed the union of spending and civics: how people consumed would affect the outcome. In addition, the war made it necessary to define a unified national purpose and a distinct American culture to defend against the Axis. Americans used consumption to answer them. In outlining the stakes of the conflict, consumerists, advertisers, government officials, and shoppers all acknowledged spending's importance to the war effort. Yet the war occasioned a complex resolution of consumption's different meanings. Both the corporate American Way that justified free enterprise as the material foundation of a distinct American culture and the consumer republicanism that opposed unchecked business power and marketplace dominance flourished during these years. Business without doubt emerged from World War II a stronger, far more formidable element in American life than before; however, consumer republicanism and activism still survived as an ideological and popular force.

To win the war at home, the federal government created a massive, cumbersome, but necessity-driven system of economic control and regulation. The successful mass mobilization of American participants in the war effort has been inscribed in history and in memory as a signature element of World War II.[96] Unprecedented levels of civilian voluntarism characterized the war effort in industry, in financing, and in the domestic economy. Even a cursory glance would acknowledge the deep connections of consuming and citizenship that emerged on what Marquis Childs called "the household front."[97] American consumers spent the war years as rational and rationed consumers. Shortages, preservation, planning, rationing, and home production all constrained Americans' choices and directed their labor as consumers. Even before December 7, 1941, key materials and goods were scarce and some rationed. Everyday consumption fell under the purview of the government, which restricted access to materials (rubber, metals, steel, fabric) and commodities (sugar, meat, coffee, automobiles, and appliances) to aid war production and provision the armed services. The Office of Price Administration

(OPA), particularly its Consumer Division, oversaw consumer markets—prices, supply, rationing—while other agencies, including the Office of War Information (OWI), the War Production Board, the Office of Defense Health and Welfare Services, and the Cabinet Secretariats of Agriculture, Commerce, and Labor, all assumed responsibilities for production, distribution, and civilian information.[98] The federal government trumpeted that, as citizens, every consumer played a critical role in the war effort. Under the auspices of civilian defense and the War Production Board, young people conducted scrap and salvage drives to reclaim needed materials.[99] The culture industries, celebrated for the well-remembered programs, films, comics, and music that entertained the troops, produced much more than diversion. Broadcasting, movie studios, advertising, and the commercial press churned out a continual stream of consumer-directed, didactic stories for the home front, along with prescriptive messages on the necessity for rationing, sharing, conservation, and buying war bonds.[100] From many quarters, the war called on Americans as citizens to be better consumers.

The war effort thus associated consuming not only with civics but also with democracy and the distinctiveness of American life. The atmosphere of necessity vindicated two long-held consumerist beliefs, namely, that consuming and citizenship were the same and that equitable consumption would bolster American democracy. In 1943 economist Leland Gordon wrote, "The concept of democracy includes our economic as well as our political life. . . . Although you may never have thought of it, the concept of representative government in our economic life includes your freedom as a consumer to choose whatever you wish in the way of economic goods or services to satisfy your wants. To such fundamental freedoms as freedom of worship, freedom of speech, freedom of assembly, should be added the economic freedom of choice exercised by consumers in our normal peacetime economy."[101]

A successful war effort would require all citizens, most importantly "average Americans," to change their customary consumer behavior. No longer could people simply purchase and use items without considering the greater overall need. No longer could the individual pursuit of private interests guarantee either national safety or economic growth. Consumer activist Caroline Ware made this clear: "As individuals, we must give up our accustomed ease, perhaps walk long and wearying distances, face actual hardships, empty larders, cold houses. In fact to exist, we must learn to be good consumers. At the same time, by being good consumers we make our contribution to the war effort." Buyers were no longer atomized choosers at the ultimate end of the distribution chain; citizens in wartime now made purchasing and use decisions with overall national resources and needs in mind. Only by putting the collective interests of the nation ahead of family and self would Americans win the war. Most eloquently, Ware made clear the civic significance of consumers to national war aims and war making. She wrote, "A strong consumer front thus means that we must release all possible resources to work for our fighting men, and that we must make the best possible use of the limited supplies which our armies can spare for civilian living. It means an all-out attack on inflation, with war bonds, taxes and effective price control. It means wise buying by consumers and careful conservation of all our possessions. . . . This is a battle which each of us fights individually, in each detail of his life." These consumer efforts did not simply support the armed forces. Rather, battlefield effort resounded on the domestic front: "Democracy lives or dies in our home towns."[102] Ware, who had explicitly made connections between consumption and citizenship since the New Deal, argued strongly that Americans had to do much more than follow directives and imbibe government information. Instead, the consumer front actively served the government's whole war program. Consumers' efforts were central, not ancillary, to the struggle against the Axis. "In this war for freedom and democracy, fought by a free and democratic people, one of the major weapons on our side is our own initiative, responsibility and resourcefulness. Our Government must, and does, rely on *us*."[103] By participating in community consumer programs and civilian defense activities, Americans strengthened democracy itself. Indeed, the wartime consumer system itself could only succeed through voluntarism, that measure of true freedom. Complying with rationing and spending guidelines, consumers made choices that bolstered democracy by ensuring the continuance of American-style freedoms.

Perhaps most significantly, Ware offered a cultural argument that linked consumption, citizenship, and American life. Americans must now "keep down with the Joneses," limiting spending and prolonging the life of goods. Here, citizens could defend and reinvigorate their characteristic civilization, particularly the "American standard of living." This standard originated in the ideals of plain living (derived, she claimed, from the Puritans and the Founders), familiar folkways that had resurfaced in the republicanism of the 1930s. The American standard entailed decency for all, in food, housing, labor, and leisure. While citizens treated this standard as a birthright, millions had not yet reached it. Ware saw this standard as a deep-rooted ideal, shaped by economics and technology, but ultimately preserved and refined in common culture.[104] And this distinctly American standard of living was the focal point of the war effort.

For Ware and other consumerists, Americans' chief aim in the war was the preservation of democracy, expressed in and ensured by a shared access to plenty, determined by and for everyone. Her eloquent peroration summed up the consumerist-republican version of the American way of life:

> For we, the people—our standards, the welfare of our families, the right and responsibility to take a part in controlling our own lives are what this war is all about. An economy which serves us, which produces and distributes to us all the things which make the good life for us and our children, and in which we participate as responsible citizens, will give the lie to the enemies of our way of life both without and within. We are not fighting this war for the captains of industry, for the movie stars, for the big-league baseball players, or for the great cotton planters. We are fighting the war for John Q. Citizen and his wife and children.[105]

The consumer's war would guarantee not just a world free of the Axis but a more equal, democratic world as well. "Perhaps the greatest adjustment, one with which we are all faced is the realization that this is not a war of classes or groups," Marquis Childs reminded. "This war is being fought in behalf of the democratic ideal, and the fight must be democratically conducted."[106] The war would win freedom and abundance for all.

As historians Meg Jacobs and Lizabeth Cohen both contend, the vast entry of wartime government into consumers' everyday lives empowered consumers even as its directives constrained them. In the face of scarcity and substitutions, government efforts to train citizens in patriotic spending and use placed a great deal of economic and social initiative in everyday Americans' hands.[107] Thousands of consumers volunteered for OPA community activities, working in the Office of Civilian Defense Volunteer Organization with local merchants, neighbors, and government officials. Eventually, OPA volunteers reported on rents, retail prices, and supplies, investigated complaints of hoarding and price gouging, and explained the intricacies of the ration system to neighbors and community members. OPA workers and volunteers created and staffed local consumer information centers to educate and work with homemakers, shoppers, and groups interested in everyday buying problems and questions.[108] Echoing some wartime observers, historians have asserted that while Americans participated in the home-front effort enthusiastically, shortages and government-authorized planning and discipline nonetheless bred resistance and hostility. Alan Brinkley contends that popular experience of the planned economy, especially the OPA, undermined grassroots support for the New Deal, even as an alliance of anti-Roosevelt forces in Congress and business overturned state economic planning and other established liberal programs. "The OPA became, in short, a target for all the frustrations and disappointments of people unaccustomed to regimentation and control," he concludes. "It was, in effect, a jarring reversal of the New Deal of the 1930s: government acting now not to distribute largesse but to restrict access to goods and services."[109] Jacobs, on the other hand, argues that the OPA did enjoy widespread support throughout the duration of the war from active consumers who were willing to put up with shortages and rationing in exchange for stable prices, a sense of socially shared sacrifice, and an implicit promise of managed abundance for all. While Americans chafed at the restrictions, and the OPA became undoubtedly one of the most unpopular government offices, its work still elicited strong support from segments of the consuming public. Cohen and Jacobs both show that consumers across the country organized at the local level to influence retailers, to protest price hikes and shortages, and ultimately to lobby for the extension of the OPA itself, which they contended would ensure fair prices and equitable distribution.[110] Either way, scarcity, substitution, and compulsory rationing of wartime were inextricably associated with government. Savvy citizens could distinguish between wartime necessities and permanent conditions, but overall far fewer apparently would support long-term policies that threatened to substitute a collective good for private interests.

Consumerists aided in the home-front activities in a variety of programs. While prominent advocates such as Persia Campbell, John Cassells, and Caroline Ware worked in local and federal organizations to formulate consumer policies, larger consumer organizations from the Consumers National Federation to the General Federation of Women's Clubs found their efforts focused by the war. With its support of labor organizations and willingness to work with consumer and popular front groups, Consumers Union had by 1941 outstripped erstwhile rival Consumers' Research in membership. The advent of war found CU making a firm commitment to the government's war effort and vowing to work to align consumers' interests with the government war aims. "For American consumers—along with Americans as producers—personal interests must be subordinated to the needs of the whole people at war," CU pronounced. "And for consumers there is now an absolute obligation to spend their family earnings in such a way as to maintain health and efficiency at a peak while putting the minimum strain on vital materials and services."[111] Specifically, CU brought to the war effort two important agendas. First, the organization continued its testing and information service, gearing its reports to encourage preservation and upkeep of existing goods, appliances, and other commodities. Second, the group dedicated itself to informing consumers on the plethora of new and often confusing and conflicted directives emerging from Washington bureaus. The group began a weekly newsletter, *Bread and Butter*, to keep up with the flow of information from the capital. CU thus served as both critical advocate for, and often loyal opposition to, government consumer programs. It encouraged its members to follow OPA directives, particularly OPA's famous "General Maximum Price Regulation." More important, CU encouraged members to become activists, to join in consumers' councils and local neighborhood committees, to aid in conservation, to share information and work with retailers. But as much as CU made clear the vital importance of individual and organized consumers to the war effort, it also inveighed against what it deemed were the inadequacies and inequities of government consumer programs. CU campaigned against rising prices and inflation, urging the government to adopt stronger anti-inflationary measures. It also railed against retailers who overcharged and flouted the schedules set by "General Max."

Even as CU thus spent the war advocating for stricter OPA enforcement, fairer pricing regulations, and higher purchasing power, its rivals at CR charted a much different course. Consumers' Research approached consumption issues almost as if they were divorced from the war. It criticized the OPA for lax and incompetent enforcement but directed its most powerful barbs against the Roosevelt administration for needlessly rationing materials and for using federal power to curtail rather than increase production. Schlink claimed that government's intervention in the economy would predictably produce want, not plenty. Wartime collectivism led to unnecessary scarcity. The consumer was paying for the war not only in bonds and reduced purchasing power but also in a needlessly curtailed standard of living at a moment when Americans required abundance to do their patriotic duty. Reliably critical of government's ineptitude in organizing and coordinating the production effort, CR could offer no alternative to the needs of production, other than a firm conviction that neither the government nor reformers could serve consumers in their capacities as citizens. While CU saw the war as a battle between the forces of democracy and fascism, CR viewed it as much as a battle against state collectivism at home and abroad. It was an outlook shared by CR's former enemies on Madison Avenue.

"THE WAR THAT BUSINESS HELPED TO WIN":
ADVERTISING'S TWO FRONTS

During the war Americans behaved like faithful members of Consumers' Research while entertaining advertising's visions of the dream world to come. Citizens learned to ration even as they were promised a future without rationing. In its official tasks of creating thousands of messages for wartime programs, the advertising business teamed up with the government to fight the Axis on the communications front. Ad men undertook the daunting task of coordinating and deploying information to educate a diverse, at times demoralized, people about a war that involved all Americans. But advertisers did more than convey official propaganda, sell bonds, or provide vital public information. As Frank Fox, Roland Marchand, and others have argued, in these years advertisers also conducted a private campaign against Franklin Roosevelt and the government, against business regulation, the consumer movement, and labor. Under cover of their war efforts, advertisers fought against economic planning and the social claim to regulate business. Madison Avenue used its privileged position in circulating messages to sell the war effort not as the joint effort of government and the people but as the struggle being won by American enterprise and individuals for the benefits of freedom, defined in familiar terms of commodities and private life.[112] The United States entered and won the war as a nation, but advertisers largely interpreted and presented the war as the experience of individuals. While perfectly harmonious with advertisers' beliefs in free enterprise as the paramount American value, these wartime ideological messages stood in sharp conflict to the collective goals of federal officials, consumerists, and their allies in numberless communities throughout the United States.

The escalation to this private war was underway long before Pearl Harbor. By 1940, the advertising business had come to acknowledge the need for an all-out commitment to fight the consumer movement and government economic regulation. After years of public relations counterthrusts to the New Deal, advertisers still confronted a restive populace hostile to business's visible public power. Veteran researcher L. D. H. Weld proposed a $5 million industrywide campaign to sell the public on the idea that advertising lowered the price of goods.[113] Advertising writer E. B. Weiss put the case even more bluntly: "Propaganda and advertising have the same goal—molding the minds of millions of people. We have had a vast experience with advertising. Our propaganda efforts have been feeble. But our weakness in that respect is not inherent; it is constitutional. Our enormous advertising abilities can easily be sluiced into propaganda channels. Will we do it ?"[114] Like many agency veterans, advertiser James Webb Young thought his profession was at a cross-roads in the lengthening days of 1941. The war in Europe, an American economy still not recovered from the 1937 recession, sluggish advertising, and a restive consumer movement all threatened business and advertising with years more of uncertainty and struggle. When the American Association of Advertising Agencies and the Association of National Advertisers met in November 1941, participants gloomily discussed the charges hurled by government and organized consumers: that advertisers promoted unjust monopoly, wasted money and resources, and offered misleading, irrelevant descriptions instead of useful facts. By now a well-known senior executive, Young had won respect for his prodigious success selling everything from rifles to pancake mix, as well as his leadership saving the agency commission system during the Depression.[115] He gave a fiery speech designed to settle forever the issues of advertising's place in the economy and consumers' impudent skepticism of its benefits:

> Here is the crux of our problem: To bring about in this country a new faith in the possibilities of the dynamic economy: to make that faith so strong that business will be ready to back it with the necessary capital investments —in spite of political deterrents to such investments. . . . What will it profit us to win the battle of advertising and lose the war of business? . . . Let us ask ourselves whether we, as an industry, do not have a great contribution to make in this effort to regain for business the leadership of our economy. We have within our hands the greatest aggregate means of mass education and persuasion the world has ever seen—namely, the channels of advertising communication. . . . Use it to give the whole of business a new faith in our destiny—a faith that will start flowing again all the little waters of enterprise.[116]

Young contended that business was in a death-fight with government over control of the American economy. Advertisers had acquiesced in the public's hostility to business. Only a thorough counteroffensive demonstrating business's centrality both to daily life and prosperity ("not frothy speeches about the American Way of Life") could wrest public confidence and support away from their enemies in the Roosevelt administration. Young's rhetoric inspired his listeners, capping years of frustration with new plans to defeat government and consumer opposition.[117]

The nation's entry into war after Pearl Harbor focused those plans that simmered after his address. A group of executives from large ad agencies, media outlets, and corporations soon came together as the Wartime Advertising Council. Offering their services to the government, this group took the lead in volunteer coordination of wartime advertising and information production. The council created thousands of ads for military recruitment, bonds, morale, and home-front programs. In addition, the council worked closely with the government's Office of War Information, under the direction of former newspaper editor Elmer Davis. The owi's writers, many of them progressive, sought to portray the war as a battle against international fascism, viewing the United States as a central element in an international conflict. Expert in crafting campaigns, the Wartime Advertising Council also worked to ensure that business perspectives appeared everywhere government messages penetrated.[118] In April 1943, scarcely a year after the owi opened, a host of its writers and intellectuals resigned to protest the commercialization of its war messages at the hands of radio and agency veterans in the office.[119] As advertising veterans then took near-total control of the diminished owi, the Wartime Advertising Council—and its selling allies—were positioned to dominate the government's messages for the duration. The shift in owi from a broad-based effort to portray the war as an internationalist effort against fascism to a fight against the Axis for an American Way of Life echoed the shift away from the regulatory strength of the New Deal in wartime government. The election of a conservative anti-Roosevelt Congress in late 1942, along with resignation of the consumer-minded Leon Henderson from opa (ultimately replaced by advertising executives Lou Maxon and Chester Bowles), signaled similar turns in the tide.[120] Throughout the war business executives would staff or influence key posts in opa and other war agencies, formulating messages and policies that favored the interests of business and producers, even as consumers fought for their own.

Selling the war to Americans, advertisers sold the American Way. In turn, they also promoted themselves as its guardians and advocates. In this atmosphere, advertisers fully implemented the vision of Barton, Young, and numerous others to portray business, instead of government, as the source of Americans' happiness and security. During the war advertisers redefined the interests of capital—unregulated enterprise, a quiescent government, and public good as defined by market dictates—as the critical means to win the war as well as the aims for which it was fought. Business represented its interests as the common good of all Americans in the war. Frank Fox has called this the "private war" of American advertising—its conflation of America's enemies with its own assailants. Advertisers saw the war as both crisis and opportunity: the crisis threatened the American economy and freedom, but they glimpsed in the war a chance to vanquish America's foreign foes and in the process reposition themselves as the unquestioned leaders of a society firmly devoted to the prerogatives of free enterprise. Lord & Thomas's copy director Walter Weir summed up the situation: "For, don't forget, this is a war on the psychological front as well as the physical front, and the prime mover of public psychology in this country is advertising. And if ever advertising had an opportunity to prove its worth, if ever advertising had a chance to silence its critics, this is it. And if advertising muffs this chance, it will never get another one."[121] But the psychological battles Weir foretold would accompany a battle of perceptions. As advertiser Edward H. Gardiner put it, "At this most critical time in American history . . . the nation is engaged not only in its greatest war, but in a civil war of the intellect. The object of this second conflict is to determine whether the business man and his ways are serviceable to society, or whether he must be held in subjection allowed to perform allotted tasks, subordinate to an aristocracy which is considered capable of judging the true interests of all our people. The civil war of the intellect is not a politicians' war. It is an economists' war."[122] Walter Fuller, president of Curtis Publishing, went even further: "We are proving to the world today that advertising is more than the power to move goods. It is the force that makes great and strong nations."[123] Advertisers would assist the government in winning the war, but they would also ensure that business got credit for the victory.

Following Pearl Harbor, then, advertisers volunteered their services, casting the war as a defense of free enterprise that also safeguarded the nation.[124] The ubiquitous Bruce Barton once again gave the rallying cry as president of the Advertising Federation of America in June 1942: "The President has asked for a name for the war. So far as we in industry are concerned, the name that we hold in our minds, whether we speak it out loud or not, should be the War that Business Helped to Win. . . . If American business rises to its full opportunity in this crisis, makes the right kind of record and unfolds that record, in simple language, to the common man, we need have no fear of the verdict. That common man and his wife, and their boy home from the wars, will register that verdict at the ballot box."[125] In this war that dared not speak its name, advertisers had to sell victory to the American people in the packaging of free enterprise and consumer plenty. With a sufficiently vigorous campaign to a public weary of wartime sacrifice, business would reap the spoils. Over the next few years advertisers regularly drafted plans for large-scale efforts to promote the free enterprise system over government programs; most never appeared, yet the ideas behind such proposals were incorporated into the advertising business's regular war work.[126]

The first shot fired in that shadow war to justify business and sell advertising was a report commissioned by the Advertising Research Foundation and authored by Neil H. Borden of Harvard Business School. *The Economic Effects of Advertising*, an exhaustive and exhausting compendium, argued that advertising was an engine of economic growth, which created demand that far outstripped its expense to consumers or business. Advertising propagandists seized on the Borden tome as a definitive rebuke to consumerists like Colston Warne and bureaucrats like Thurman Arnold and Donald Montgomery, who sought to regulate the industry because it reinforced monopoly and inefficiency.[127] The Borden volume never took its place with *Liberty* or *Ladies' Home Journal* as household reading, yet advertisers celebrated this work as an unimpeachable academic defense against the pink professoriat. With Harvard on their side, advertisers took confidence.[128]

Wartime advertising did not sell simple victory or patriotism, and seldom the abstractions of freedom or sacrifice. Nor did copywriters undertake war messages lightly. On the eve of the war, executive Kenneth Groesbeck warned against flippant and irrelevant copy and urged ad men to put on "work shirt and flannel pants" in their messages. Throughout the early days of the war, copywriters agonized over the best ways of inspiring the public for the war effort while exaggerating neither extreme of confidence or gloom. Moreover, many advertisers wrestled with their portrayals of servicemen and war conditions; fearful of producing copy that insulted those who were making the ultimate sacrifice overseas, advertisers held themselves continually to standards of serious and sober salesmanship. By promoting the business vision of the American Way, advertisers cast corporations as the war heroes, assisted ably and cheerfully by the citizen-consumer.[129]

Selling the war meant highlighting the difference between the United States and the Axis powers. A materially oriented vision of American exceptionalism was the result; the difference between a free America and an enslaved Axis was the superabundance of goods enjoyed by Uncle Sam's families. A *Printers' Ink* editorial captured these commonplace associations of American exceptionalism, abundance, and nationalism: "The United States is the greatest, happiest, wealthiest and most powerful nation on the face of the earth. Our standard of living is something that the Germans and the inhabitants of the other Axis nations have never enjoyed—simply because they could never create such a system. Their plans of Government, their economic setups, were of the wrong kind. And so madly jealous, they are trying to steal from us what they could not possibly build by themselves."[130] Curtis Publishing chief Walter Fuller offered a stark nationalist contrast between a people raised in the "selling way" of life and citizens of the Axis. "We have far more to defend than a crumb of bread or a bowl of rice," Fuller wrote. "And we will defend more fiercely and more intelligently than those who, lacking initiative and understanding, do only what they are ordered."[131] To embody such sentiments advertisers revived the nationalist imagery that had so often served them in the past. "How *American* it is . . . to want something better!" observed Ballantine's Ale. The campaign celebrated innovation as American cultural patrimony—new appliances, postwar housing, and television all depicted as the American birthright and defining characteristics (fig. 9.4). The Metropolitan Life Insurance Corporation assured the readers of the *Saturday Evening Post*, "Life Insurance Is as American as Free Speech and Apple Pie." (If this headline were not sufficiently convincing, the accompanying photo showed a mother placing the pie in the oven, watched over by her young son, who was presumably reciting Webster's reply to Hayne.)[132] "A good table is an American tradition!" crowed Heinz. "In your grandfather's time and now—whether it be in the little cottage on Main Street or the Mansion on the Hill, there is no greater contrast between this and other nations for there the superiority of the American standard is most clearly found." Material nationalism thus served as the basis of a patriotic American exceptionalism that came to dominate depictions of the war effort. The United States was not only different but also superior because of its abundance of consumer goods. "How does this bathroom illustrate America?" asked the American Rolling Mill Company. The answer was that the United States had three-quarters of the world's bathtubs. "The Modern American bathroom is an example of the highest standard of living ever known . . . A Standard of Living Worth Fighting For," the advertisement concluded.[133] Consumer goods expressed ineffably American traits.

The war made preservation of goods and rituals of consumption—and the businesses that made them possible—all the more critical because they symbolized the nation and its institutions. A Coca-Cola ad set in a typical soda fountain made the connections with political institutions unmistakable: "As American as Independence Day—the soda fountain is the very expression of the democracy that is America." The airlines of the United States celebrated "America's Sense of Time" by editorializing, "We have often been frowned upon by our elders for being so much in a hurry. But it gets the results we want. That is why air transportation fits us so exactly. It is the perfect

How <u>American</u> it is... to want something better!

MAYBE MOTHER'S NEW MIXER will be one of the few remaining or maybe she'll have to wait for it till after the war. But whenever it comes, you can bet she'll exclaim "Now this *is* something better!"

And how American to want "something better"—in kitchen equipment or airplanes or threshing machines or what-have-you.

Why, we're even fighting a war on the promise of a better tomorrow!

THIS FINE AMERICAN TRAIT goes right through our lives—helps us decide what we will wear or eat or drink. There is an ale—one with a 3-ring trade mark like the dewy rings your glass leaves on the table. "Purity," "Body," "Flavor," say the words in the rings. "Something better," say millions of Americans when they try this moderate beverage. And so *many* say it that this has become...America's largest selling ale.

 America's largest selling Ale

 To speed the day when we can have more "better things" buy war bonds and stamps

P. Ballantine & Sons, Newark, N. J.

FIGURE 9.4. "How *American* It Is." (*Life*, February 1, 1943, 70)

instrumentation of the value we put on getting things done quickly . . . for work or leisure, whichever we choose."[134] Thus offering a wide variety of goods as typically American, advertisers not only adapted their products to patriotic feeling but continually informed their audiences that consuming, even in the reduced circumstances of wartime, confirmed their citizenship and nationality. What made the American Way worth fighting for was what made America unique. The ritual affirmation of spending assumed a heightened importance as the "object" of the American war effort.

Advertisers vowed to contribute to the war effort not only by supporting the war aims enthusiastically but also by selling their wares patriotically. When Congress declared war, *Printers' Ink* urged its readers to adopt a platform of service to the effort: its planks emphasized ethics, research, marketing, competition, brand maintenance, and government service to finance and staff the war effort and to maintain morale.[135] As the trade journal put it, "But the new objective of advertising is not only to increase sales and profits; it is also to teach the most people, in the fastest time, at the least cost, how to make the best use of all the products and services necessary to keep the people on the home front in fighting trim—without interrupting the production and flow of supplies to the armed forces."[136] Advertisers adapted selling to wartime themes and featured goods themselves as the centerpiece of American values. In wartime advertising, goods took on totemic status as emblems of the war effort and aims. In asking "What Are We Fighting For?" the United States Rubber Corporation asserted, "Words like freedom or liberty draw close to us only when we break them down into the fragments of daily life."[137] Those homey fragments—the familiar goods, entertainments, and rituals of consumer society—stood in for and ultimately supplanted abstractions of freedom, equality, and democracy used by the owı early in the war. For those on Madison Avenue, goods, the "selling way of life," and Americanism were all inseparable. Although copywriters feared that they would trivialize the sacrifices of servicemen and civilians alike if they linked selling too closely to war, advertisements inevitably connected the commodified fragments of daily life to the sacred mission at hand. For example, the ad "Elm Street Miracle" epitomized the connection of war and the everyday. A father peers in his serviceman son's room. "There, in the half light, were the things that clutter up the closets of all happy, carefree boys of eighteen . . . a broken hockey stick . . . cracked phonograph records . . . a mudstreaked football helmet. . . . Suddenly I knew the true meaning of a service star. And I saw a million fathers standing before a million closets all over the land. Feeling this war for the first time. Feeling it like a white hot iron in their souls."[138] As Americans experienced the war as the defense of home and family, advertisers symbolized that effort in goods. Indeed, the home itself, according to one advertiser, was "the real and enduring American Headquarters," where "the course of the nation is plotted, its destiny directed."[139]

For some advertisers, the fragments of daily life were best symbolized in the brand-name system they sought so fervently to protect in a time of pressure for standards and grade labeling. In addressing the Association of National Advertisers, Henry Link of the Psychological Corporation not only summed up the findings of the association's surveys but also sounded the fondest hopes that Madison Avenue entertained for business expansion in the postwar world. He noted that the consumer's "faith in brand and brand makers is a phenomenon which the social sciences, fifty years from today, will most likely describe as one of the greatest contributions of all time to social harmony and social progress." He went on:

> Literally people in the United States have more confidence in Campbell Soups and the makers of Campbell Soups than in any dozen of the highest government officials we might name. More people elect Campbell Soups every month than elect the President every four years. People throughout the world have more faith in Coca-Cola than in the system of international law which is supposed to govern nations. According to Mr. Willkie it is one world because the airplane has made it small. It is more likely to be one world because Coca-Cola has come to stand for something which all its inhabitants trust. . . . Its use represents an act of faith in which all men, regardless of nationality, are friends.

Brands here were not just reliable indices of trade but instead became the preservers of civilization. If the Allies won the war, Link implied, the world would be safer for brands, which themselves would guarantee social harmony and peace, as well as economic progress. The eclipse of governance by private enterprise was complete.[140]

While consumer advocates like Caroline Ware and Colston Warne strongly emphasized the role of democracy in promoting the everyday buyer's wartime efforts, advertisers almost always promoted individual freedom as the paramount ideal in the war efforts. Material goods instantiated freedom in ad copy, uniting war, enterprise, and everyday citizens. Consuming became the act of free peoples. The Fidelity-Phenix [sic] Company assured readers, "Right of Choice is Yours! That is one of the American ways of life we're fighting to preserve. It is your privilege and duty to express that right at the polls on election day. You express that same freedom in your everyday life."[141] Numerous campaigns played on President Roosevelt's 1941 articulation of the Four Freedoms to connect consumption and the war effort. Metropolitan Life encouraged, "To these four freedoms . . . add another," the "Freedom to Plan One's Own Future." Enna Jettick shoes assured its customers of "FREEDOM in every step you take. You're taking plenty of steps these days—and Enna Jetticks will support you in every cause, on every occasion." Gold Cross shoes promised "Freedom from Doubt."[142]

Some advertising extended the critical connection of consumer freedom to the freedom at stake in the war. Alcoa solemnly announced that "Freedom of the Air is the beginning of All Freedoms. . . . Along its broad highways course the hope of democracy. Here then is a high purpose that gives democracy its meaning. Here is something bigger, more final than our old earthborn belief in the Freedom of the Seas. For we have found the controlling freedom without which all others wither and die. America's very hope of existence as a good place to live depends on Freedom of the Air."[143] A picnicking family exemplified "freedom—American Style," according to Quaker State. The ad's copywriters offered this definition of that essential freedom: "It's asking you to try Quaker State—in order to care for your car for your country in the best way possible. And of course, it's your right to disregard this friendly advice if you feel so inclined. That's freedom—American Style!" Advertising thus styled itself in no uncertain terms as the essence of American liberty, the reason to fight the war.[144]

"Pearl Harbor Changed His Buying Habits!" reported the Exide Battery Corporation. "Before that Sunday in December he was just the average American citizen—patriotic but easy-going. Farthest from his mind was the notion that his buying habits could help win—or lose—a war."[145] Advertisers downplayed the war's collective effort and gave little notice to the social compact of consumers, merchants, and producers instituted by the government war agencies and community organizations. Instead, advertisers most often portrayed the war as necessitating private sacrifices by consumer-citizens to support the armed forces and businesses fighting for the American Way. In official war information, as well as in product advertising, copywriters depicted home folks as worthy partners and aides to troops overseas. The requirements of rationing, armament, and war financing transformed representations of consumers' choices and capabilities in ads. The new emphasis on consumers' frugality and patriotism emerged directly from wartime imperatives. Nevertheless, the zeal of advertising's embrace of the wartime constraints on consumption suggests a deeper strategy. By celebrating thrift and honoring "typical American consumers," advertising held onto an audience that might presumably have other concerns. Substituting an attractive ethos of abstinence for one of abundance, advertisers continually hailed the consumer-citizen even when they had nothing to sell.

In wartime advertisers once more made peace with Mrs. Consumer, praising her patriotism, born of generations of frugal American living. After years of behind-the-scenes observations that consumers had lost the knowledge of their ancestors, advertisers now claimed again that American women were good consumers by birthright. After all, noted Budweiser, "rationing came over on the Mayflower." Pillsbury compared the hardships suffered by western pioneer women and their present-day "resourceful daughters and granddaughters." Pequot sheets celebrated "our favorite Heroine . . . the GREAT AMERICAN HOUSEWIFE," noting that she bought as cannily as her grandmother—"No wonder you've made the American Standard of Living the highest the world has ever known.!"[146] *Ladies' Home Journal* similarly paid tribute to the newly thrifty Mrs. Consumer: "Washington Goes to Mrs. Smith . . . Because Mrs. Smith Goes to Market. . . . the Government itself must come to Mrs. Smith. For the duration, Mrs. Smith is *taking over the job of minding America.*" A *Woman's Home Companion* layout pictured a defiant Mrs. Consumer, legs akimbo, groceries on one hip and pocketbook on the other, in the manner of a western gunslinger. "She's the One SURE MARKET in a Topsy Turvy World!" the ad proclaimed. Women thus once more took their place as the bedrock of home provisioning, celebrated for their thrift, praised for their determination. As one market researcher observed, "The same basic ingenuity that inspires our wizards to invent the things we need to win the war inspires our women to seek what they can get, when all that the news columns tell them is what they cannot get. How typically American!"[147] Consumers were accustomed to the world's highest standard of living, yet advertisers portrayed them as adjusting easily to scarcity and constraint. Even thoughtful consumerist critics such as Marquis Childs accepted this view. "American habits of luxurious waste are deeply ingrained," he wrote. "Fortunately there is still a bedrock of American thrift on which to build. While it has been overlaid with a plating of chromium and embroidered with rhinestones, down beneath it is still there, a solid inheritance out of the past."[148]

Extending their prewar documentary focus, advertisers frequently offered portraits of war workers. Once, depictions of manual laborers seldom appeared in national advertising, but the acceleration of wartime production saw factory laborers now working their way onto magazine pages. However, the layouts showed these workers as individuals, not members of crews, groups, or "labor." As individuals, these typical Americans would aid business in winning the war: "Mike Anders . . . that's me. Married. You bet . . . four kids. Age . . . forty-three. And a first-class mechanic . . . airplane assembly. And tired out. AND how! . . . after another overtime shift on the 'line.' But still thinking. Thinking about how to do more work. This country's been good to me. I can't let this country down." (fig. 9.5).[149] In this advertisement and dozens more, the patriotic laborer of indistinct ethnicity became a commonplace figure, in much the same way as each unit in World War II combat films had its resident Pole, Italian, Jew, and Iowa farm boy. Oldsmobile, Studebaker, and Heinz, for example, all ran campaigns featuring typical employees engaged in defense occupations. Here, labor's devotion to business as well as the war—exemplified in overtime work, long years of service, and company loyalty—outshone any specific social identity.[150]

The war offered advertisers daily opportunities to emphasize the organic nature of American society and to argue forcefully that the United States had no class system. During the war years, capital and labor may have been at odds on the shop floor and in the boardroom, but in the fantasy world of advertising, there was only the neighborly harmony of an organic society. In this period, labor unrest actually rose with the chafing demands of accelerating production quotas and speed-ups. At the same time, government-mandated wage ceilings eroded labor's newfound gains, and inflation inexorably spiraled prices upward.[151] Yet this unrest was belied by, if not suppressed in, advertisements celebrating a classless society where all citizens got along regardless of social station. As one ad put it, "Americans find kinship in a glass of mellow beer or ale. No one needs to worry about democracy, as long as the man in the dress shirt and the man in the flannel shirt can swap opinions over their beer, smile and like each other. That kind of American spirit baffles, and will defeat any tyrant in the world." The *Ladies' Home Journal* described its own subscribers in similar terms, as a "cross-section of America." Compressing the social coverage of its 1940 "How America Lives" series, wartime *Journal* ads featured random groupings of subscribers gathered in war-related activities—buying bonds, participating in civil defense, voting. The "cross-section of America" both embodied democracy and represented the new consumer markets that war had created. Similarly, the Wartime Advertising Council portrayed the typical American family, invoking their role in the war in language that might have come from Caroline Ware: "We're just little people. We're not brass hats. We're not big shots. We're just plain folks . . . but we're the ones who made this country! And we're the ones who will save it!" Consumerist emphasis on classes was all but absent in such product advertising.[152]

ME

Mike Anders . . . that's me.

Married. You bet . . . four kids.

Age . . . forty-three.

And a first class mechanic . . . airplane assembly.

And tired out. AND how! . . . after another overtime shift on the "line." But still thinking.

*   *   *

Thinking about how to do more work.

This country's been good to me. I can't let this country down.

*   *   *

Today the big boss said we men could produce more work if we relaxed properly when we went home. He said that's been proved by people who study those things.

*   *   *

So . . . tonight I relax. I'm going to forget all about the plant and the machines. But I'm going to take it easy, too.

I'm going to sit on the porch and watch the kids play ball. I'm going to have a glass of nice, cool beer. Will that taste good! And it sort of eases the strain, too. Beer always helps me relax.

*   *   *

Later, after supper, I'll get together with a couple of friends. For a quiet, sensible evening. Lots of good talk . . . and maybe another glass of good beer or ale. We'll take it easy.

And then I go to bed and get some sleep.

*   *   *

Tomorrow I'll show them how to do some *real* work . . . for Uncle Sam.

By providing wholesome relaxation in these days of stress and strain, Beer contributes to national morale. To protect beer . . . the beverage of moderation . . . the brewing industry is providing active industry cooperation in the maintenance of wholesome conditions wherever beer is sold. An interesting, free booklet tells about this important "Clean-Up or Close-Up Program."

Write: Brewing Industry Foundation, Dept. A 16, 21 East 40th Street, New York, N. Y.

FIGURE 9.5. "Me . . . Mike Anders." (*Life*, May 11, 1942, 10)

Numerous ads depicted Americans of all stations pitching in to make the tools necessary to win the war. Routinely, advertisers domesticated the war, literally by depicting weapons and materiel as familiar goods transformed or everyday habits newly reborn as patriotic sacrifice. So advertisers showed homemakers how to "cook" a tank, depicted a group of Americans from all walks of life building weaponry, and revealed that common everyday items were indeed the stuff of war (fig. 9.6). So the familiar neighborhoods of the American Way campaigns now became "fighting streets" (fig. 9.7).[153] Freedom, abundance and neighborliness were all united under the banner of enterprise. But if wartime advertising showed average Americans fighting the home-front war, Madison Avenue left no doubt that it was corporate capitalism, not the government or even the nation's vast resources, that provided the means for victory. In advertisers' visions, the American Way brought forth the weapons to win the war, as well as the incentive to fight it. Many years of consistently stressing the centrality of the American Way allowed advertisers to entwine patriotism with business interests, Americanism with capitalism. At a moment of national vulnerability, with leaders and civilians calling for national unity and purpose, the most powerful segment of the American communications complex contended that the national interest was laissez-faire enterprise. "The American Way of Life" thus claimed the prerogatives of private capital after years of government intervention in the economy.

"Capitalist . . . American Style," one of a remarkable series of Republic Steel advertisements, pictured a latter-day reincarnation of the Horatio Alger hero, the newsboy: "He's in business for himself, this kid. He invests his own money in his newspapers because he has confidence in his own ability to sell them at a profit. He has learned by experience that business grows through hard work, salesmanship and thrift . . . . He is capitalist, laborer and consumer combined. He is typically American. . . . Each of us is free to take his own future in his hands—and pull himself up by his own bootstraps. That is the grand American privilege. . . . There are no restrictions on ability in America . . . and there must be none." Republic, whose fierce opposition to the New Deal and the labor movement led to the Memorial Day massacre of strikers by police in 1937, developed the series to argue for a pre–New Deal restoration of business freedoms. Another in its series shows two workmen at a lunch counter discussing the need to abandon all wartime controls as soon as the fighting stops. "When you add it all up, workers and management are *partners* in business, the business of being Americans and keeping this country American. Our problems and the boss's problems are really very

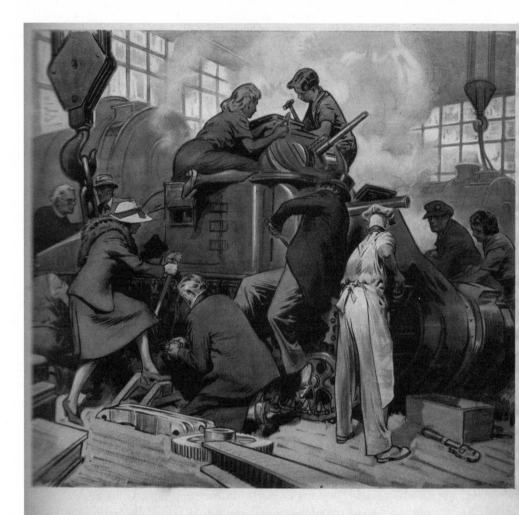

Here Are You!

PERHAPS you haven't really got a wrench in your hand...perhaps you're not actually swinging a hammer.

But it's you who are building the tanks, gun carriages, rifle springs, turret parts, bombs, steam and Diesel locomotives coming out of our plants...

and hundreds of other factories in this country.

It's *you*, the American people, with the money you put into war stamps, bonds, taxes, who are turning out the weapons coming off America's production lines...a volume of mobile power that will help to assure a decent world.

AMERICAN LOCOMOTIVE
A NATIONAL ARSENAL OF MOBILE POWER

TANKS · GUN CARRIAGES · ARMY AND NAVY ORDNANCE · STEAM-LINERS AND DIESEL-LINERS

FIGURE 9.6. "Here Are You!" (*Life*, November 2, 1942, 85)

FIGURE 9.7. "Corner Main and Pine." (*Saturday Evening Post*, August 5, 1944, 62)

much the same. Whatever hurts business hurts us too," the workers conclude (fig. 9.8).[154] On the surface, business acquiesced to regulation in its advertising, depicting willing sacrifice while at the same time promising a return to growth. Behind the scenes, advertisers in fact strenuously fought production limits and price ceilings, many of them arguing that the economy could support both war production and expanded domestic production unrelated to defense.[155] They were much less responsive, in contrast, to labor demands to lift the ceiling on wages or to shore up purchasing power.

The centrality of free enterprise to American life emerged as well in campaigns produced by the Sheldon-Claire Company, the Wartime Advertising Council, and General Motors. However, the Nash-Kelvinator Company in particular struck a powerfully resonant theme: GI Joe knew that he was fighting for free enterprise. In the final seconds before his bombing run, a fighter pilot admonished Americans to keep the country just as it was before the war, a place "where *every* man can be free to be somebody . . . where every man is free to grow as great as he's a mind to be . . . where every man has an unlimited opportunity to be useful to himself and to his fellow men." He continued, "And tell them no matter what they say . . . no matter what they do . . . to stay *free* . . . to keep America a land of *individual freedom!*" for "That's the America we want when we come home."[156] One Stromberg-Carlson layout presented a soldier who spoke to the same urging: "Promise to have a good America when I return. This time I'll want a job instead of your dimes. . . . I'll want freedom and bread . . . justice and plumbing . . . equality and a stout pair of shoes."[157] Free enterprise as defined by corporations served as the real object of the war; that was America's irreducible core.

But what would the country be like after the war? What would consumers have? Here arose advertising's second great wartime campaign: selling the future when the present was out of stock. With so many goods either unavailable or scarce for the duration, many advertisers felt that they should not promote unavailable goods. Indeed, they faced internal, as well as consumerist, pressure not to advertise at all. Consumers Union president Colston Warne had proposed a moratorium on wartime product advertising as a waste of paper and other restricted resources and as an economic waste, promoting goods that could not be produced. Yet corporations generally viewed the war as a both an advertising necessity and a selling opportunity. With firms granted a tax deduction on advertising expenses, promotion was virtually free, and they fought Warne's proposals aggressively. "Sell Tomorrow Today!" advertisers clamored, to entice consumers, maintain brand and corporate names before the public, and to fill a reservoir of interest to be tapped when

"... before it goes any farther"

"Tom, it sure worries me when I hear all this talk about *keeping wartime restrictions on business after the war*. I actually get scared."

"But Jim, why should fellows like you and me worry about that. We don't own stock or clip coupons. How business is regulated—and to what extent—those are problems for the big shots. They don't affect us at all—do they?"

"You're so close to your job, Tom, I'm afraid you don't see the whole picture. Why, when I worry about business, I'm worrying about you and me and our families. Any way you look at it, it affects us—and how!

"This old fashioned idea of drawing a line between the men in the office and the men in the plant is a lot of bunk. When you add it all up, workers and management are *partners* in business, the business of being Americans and keeping this country American. Our problems and the boss's problems are really very much the same. Whatever hurts business hurts us too.

"When you come right down to it, we all work. We all furnish capital in one way or another to some kind of business enterprise. And we're all customers of somebody.

"The heads of our business depend on us to produce goods. We depend on them to supply the plant, the equipment, the materials, the engineering, the management—and to develop sales and markets for the goods we produce—so that we can produce *more* of them.

"As production goes up, costs per product go down. We can make more money and buy more of the things we want. The company can plow more money back into more jobs, better plants, and improved equipment—and the customers get lower prices.

"It's a cinch that business has got to have freedom from a lot of this unnecessary outside meddling if it's going to get anywhere—*and if you and I are going to get anywhere.*

"All of us, from the boss on down, are ready and willing to do most anything to finish this country's number one job—*winning the war*—and will put up with almost anything to do it.

"But when our boys come back from the war, they've got to have jobs and opportunity. And business can't give it to them if we don't give business the green light.

"Take it from me Tom, peacetime regimentation is dangerous—no matter who it applies to. And the trouble is, that once something like that gets started, it grows—and grows. As I see it —it's up to us, and millions more like us, to stop it *before it goes any farther.*"

REPUBLIC STEEL

GENERAL OFFICES: REPUBLIC BUILDING, CLEVELAND 1, OHIO
Export Department: Chrysler Building, New York 17, New York

ALLOY, CARBON, STAINLESS STEELS · COLD FINISHED STEELS · PLATES · BARS · SHAPES · STRIP · SHEETS · PIPE · TUBING
TIN PLATE · NUTS · BOLTS · RIVETS · NAILS · PIG IRON · FARM FENCE · WIRE · FABRICATED STEEL PRODUCTS

FIGURE 9.8. Talking over the Postwar World. (*Saturday Evening Post*, August 12, 1944, 73)

domestic production resumed.[158] Advertising pundits urged their peers to sink more, not less, money into the maintenance and even the increase of demand during scarcity.[159]

While preaching patience and restraint, Madison Avenue also promised Americans lavish abundance; urging rational consuming in the meantime, advertisers foretold a material modernity beyond measure. Arguing that war production and new research would usher in a world of undreamt conveniences and scientific marvels, corporations asserted that the postwar era of safety and security would also provide wealth and happiness to redeem the suffering and uncertainty of the war. Americans would each receive a private payoff for their collective sacrifices.[160]

Advertisers trumpeted that Americans' unique beliefs and institutions served as the hallmark of their freedom and wealth. That exceptionalism dominated the vision of a postwar world of abundance. Madison Avenue bridged a postwar utopia of goods with the wartime defense of distinct national culture. General Electric typified this trend. Merging the American Way with the frontier myth, the corporation announced that through electronics it had discovered a "furrow that has no end," one that would generate an endless stream of benefits through research and new technology.[161] The postwar world would be brought to Americans by corporate largesse, typified by American values of freedom and enterprise, and ratified by the American equation of market and democracy. Thus, the goods of tomorrow, awaited during wartime sacrifice, embodied the true aims of the war (fig. 9.9). Nash-Kelvinator claimed that only in the transition from war to peace production would victory "be made real for those who are fighting for it." The tank of today was really the toaster of tomorrow (fig. 9.10). Unlike in ancient agrarian civilizations, returning servicemen would not beat their swords into plowshares but instead would find carbines made into freezers.[162] Westinghouse displayed a tantalizing gallery of goods, "a promise of what's to come," for a young couple dreaming of their future (fig. 9.11). General Electric, Hotpoint, Norge, and other manufacturers offered ads that showed consumers dreaming of postwar bounty. As Revere copper somewhat ominously foretold, "After total war . . . total living" (fig. 9.12).[163] Makers of appliances, building materials, and household furnishings, along with the architectural and construction industries especially, developed sales copy and merchandising plans to sell goods that could only arrive in an indefinite future.[164] All was made possible by corporate wisdom and managerial freedom, and a war fought to preserve home and democracy easily became a war fought by business for consumer plenty. As one executive put it, "Today we need production to save America. But tomorrow we are going to need super-selling to save both production and America."[165]

As so often in the past, advertisers turned once more to political language. A 1944 General Electric ad, for example, underscored the connections of consumption, war, and the deepest American political ideals. Yet this campaign addressed the emerging postwar world in a new blend of political ideology, corporate interest, and private appeal. Against an image of a young GI, an unseen homemaker detailed the "things my Bill has a right to after it's over." The rights of Bill included a job, General Electric appliances that made possible his favorite creature comforts, and a house, "ALL-ELECTRIC from the ground up" (fig. 9.13).[166] The war would guarantee a new American *right* to consumer abundance. Not merely the freedom from want promised by President Roosevelt, General Electric gave veterans and their families the *right* to consume, a guarantee of an ever-increasing number and kind of goods, along with a single family home in which to enjoy them. While the ad intoned, "These things after the war cannot be for the few. They must be for ALL AMERICANS," the illustration belied the democratic promise. The ad pictured one individual along with a well-appointed suburban home. GI Bill himself did not represent all Americans, and the new abundance for which he fought would not be distributed or enjoyed equally. The actual GI Bill of Rights adopted by Congress during the war bestowed upon returning soldiers entitlements to work, education, and access to housing. Yet those promises were inconsistently and unfairly realized, as many returning veterans would learn.[167] General Electric indeed promised consumer rights to all, but the fulfillment of tomorrow in reality did not resemble its promise in the magazines. Even so, the equation was clear: the war would guarantee new and better things for Americans, earned by the soldier and delivered by the corporation.

EVERYTHING AND NOTHING:
THE HAPPY-GO-SPENDING WORLD OF TOMORROW

Anyone who has seen the 1946 Frank Capra film *It's a Wonderful Life* remembers its harrowing final sequence. Facing ruin on false charges of embezzlement, George Bailey wishes he never had been born, and his guardian angel, Clarence Oddbody, grants this request. Bailey plunges into a nightmare in which he nearly loses all sense of himself. At every turn his familiar and stifling hometown of Bedford Falls is now a ghastly doppelganger, Pottersville. Under the rule of greedy banker Mr. Potter, the town is a cheerless, noirish hell of unchecked commerce and degradation. Gambling,

FIGURE 9.9. "Producing for War, Preparing for Peace": Firestone's Two Fronts.
(*Life*, July 10, 1944, 40–41)

stone

PREPARING FOR PEACE

VICTORY must come first, of course. But victory will be hollow indeed unless those on the home front plan now to help build that wonderful world of tomorrow for which millions of Americans are fighting. So Firestone is also preparing for peace. And after victory, when Firestone is again concentrating on peace-time products, its advantages in "know-how" will help provide work for its men and women now in service and enable Firestone to make and sell a wide variety of products which will set new standards of quality, durability, comfort and economy. So it is only natural that Firestone, while producing for war, is also preparing for peace.

HOME, PORTABLE AND AUTOMOBILE RADIOS

WASHING MACHINES

FOAMEX FOR MATTRESSES, FURNITURE, UPHOLSTERY AND SEATING

VELON FOR CLOTHING, HATS, SHOES, HOSIERY AND HUNDREDS OF OTHER USES

REFRIGERATORS

GAS AND ELECTRIC RANGES

TIRES AND TUBES FOR ALL TYPES OF VEHICLES AND AIRCRAFT

CONTRO FOR FOUNDATION GARMENTS, SWIMMING SUITS AND MANY OTHER USES

ON THE HOME FRONT

FIGURE 9.10. "A Refrigerator and an Automobile Go to War."
(*Saturday Evening Post*, October 24, 1942, cover II)

THE ART OF BETTER LIVING

Yesterday . . . Today . . . Tomorrow . . .
it's Electrical Living by Westinghouse

Let's hope it's not too far away . . . that bright new day when you'll again know the lift of living electrically. And when it does come, Westinghouse will be a name to remember. It stands for the know-how and experience acquired in making 30 million pre-war electrical home appliances.

More than that . . . it stands for years of tried and tested background in making not just one or two appliances, but *twenty-two* different types of electrical servants for your home.

At the moment, we're head over heels building essential war material. And we'll stick to that job until it is done. But when the go ahead signal flashes, you can count on Westinghouse to turn out all the fine new appliances you need to banish

that "never done" feeling about housework. In war or peace, we take your homemaking problems to heart. The pre-war masterpieces shown above are just a promise of what's to come.

WESTINGHOUSE ELECTRIC & MANUFACTURING CO., MANSFIELD, O.
PLANTS IN 25 CITIES . . . OFFICES EVERYWHERE

30 MILLION PRE-WAR

Westinghouse

ELECTRIC HOME APPLIANCES

YOUR PROMISE OF STILL FINER ONES TO COME

TUNE IN JOHN CHARLES THOMAS • SUNDAY 2.30 EWT., N.B.C. • HEAR TED MALONE • MON. WED. FRI. 10:15 EWT., BLUE NETWORK

FIGURE 9.11. "The Art of Better Living." (*Life*, September 25, 1944, 57)

"After total war...total living"

You could read, relax, hold First Aid and other courses, in this comfortable meeting room.

You and your neighbors could produce plays and concerts in this little theatre of your own.

You could have a hobby shop with work benches, power tools, potter's wheels and looms.

A neighborhood fun center for children in the daytime—a gymnasium for grownups at night.

Floor plan of the complete community building, showing how the rooms would be arranged, with the swimming pool outdoors.

...at a single family can...possibly afford, a group ...milies can easily pos-...After the war, we will ...e the discovery of what ...can mean for happy ...g. Neighbors can have ...mming pool, a gym-...um, a little theatre, ...bby shop with power ..., in a community building within walking ...nce of tomorrow's home.

By working together to win the war, groups ...s are learning to be teammates and friends. ...cting together afterwards, we can create a ...community spirit through which we can ...e buildings to house the recreations and ...ies we have in common, to make them more ...fying and more fun.

...n such a building, rust-proof metals and ...plastics will make possible the admission of ...ight wherever wanted, while beams of artifi-...light and heat may be focused where they ...needed—not scattered wastefully in the hope ...eaching the right spot by accident. Already I ...helping to plan several such neighborhood ...ers, and I know how well we are mastering ...techniques and economies that can bring ...kind of total living to communities every-...re."

LAWRENCE B. PERKINS
Perkins, Wheeler and Will, Architects
Chicago, Illinois

Almost daily, out of the tremendous effort we are making to win this war, come new reasons why our sacrifices are worth while. New inventions, new ideas that can be used for peace as well as war, new production techniques and materials— all of these can bring us new homes and better living in days to come.

In this rebirth of living, copper will play an even more important part than it does today. Not only will it protect tomorrow's homes and build-ings against weather and termites, insure rust-free water, help reduce heating costs, but it will also help to make possible the new comforts and con-veniences which American inventive genius is al-ready planning for us all.

Today the copper industry is working all-out for Uncle Sam. There is no copper available for any purpose except winning the war. But in Revere's laboratories, research is steadily pressing forward in preparation for the better homes and better living that victory can bring.

* * *

Naturally, in this limited space, Mr. Perkins could only begin to tell you about his con-ception of a community house. So Revere has prepared an illustrated booklet giving more information. This, and former book-lets describing the low-cost homes conceived by other leading architects, will gladly be sent to you free. Write us.

* * *

REVERE
COPPER AND BRASS INCORPORATED
Executive Offices: 230 Park Avenue, New York

FIGURE 9.12. "After Total War . . . Total Living." (*Life*, October 19, 1944, 109)

THINGS MY BILL HAS A RIGHT TO

AFTER IT'S OVER

A JOB — the War Bonds you are buying will hasten the victory and will provide money to spend for the new post-war conveniences that will make jobs for the men who do our fighting and the men who're now making their weapons.

ALL THE CUPS OF COFFEE HE WANTS How he wants it. When he wants it. With a new G-E flavor-guard Coffee Maker that will brew perfect coffee and then keep it just the right flavor and temperature automatically for hours.

A SET OF SPARKLING ICE-CUBES in his glass for every sip of tepid, brackish water he is drinking now. (And a new G-E "zoned" Refrigerator to keep all his foods at the most tempting temperature.)

NO MORE K. P. And no guilty feeling for not helping me with dishes and emptying garbage when our new G-E Electric Sink will let us forget that kitchen drudgery forever.... Small things? Not if you know Bill. But if they seem to you too picayune to build a post-war world, I'll add the *big* ones: OUR HOUSE — less expensive than we'd dreamed — but ALL-ELECTRIC from the ground up. ME, free as a pre-war millionairess. . . . OUR CHILDREN, growing up in what their father fought to make it — *a good world with opportunity for all.*

These things after the war cannot be for the few. They must be for ALL AMERICANS. That is why General Electric from the midst of total war production is devoting this series of messages to you to say, most seriously: "In Time of War, Prepare for Peace." * * * Whatever your income, YOUR WAR BOND SAVINGS can buy you everything mentioned on this page—things finer than ever before because of our war skills. So begin to save and plan for the things your savings will buy. Each after victory purchase you make will help create more jobs. General Electric Consumers Institute, Bridgeport, Connecticut.

Hear the General Electric radio programs: The G-E "All Girl Orchestra" Sunday 10 p.m. EWT, NBC. "The World Today" news every weekday 6:45 p.m. EWT, CBS.

EVERYTHING ELECTRICAL FOR AFTER VICTORY HOMES

GENERAL ⊛ ELECTRIC

FIGURE 9.13. General Electric's Postwar Rights. (N. W. Ayer Collection, Series 3, Box 245, Drawer 303, Folder 1943–47, Archives Center, National Museum of American History, Smithsonian Institution, Washington, D.C.)

prostitution, violence, alienation, and death reign. Bailey's friends and family are miserable wrecks: stumbling drunks, outcasts, bitter cranks. In place of community George finds feckless mobs bent on brutal sensation and numbing pleasure. He confronts a world whose inhabitants have lost their souls and their ability to love. All they have is a relentless grind of getting and spending: misery-making work in a suffocating prison of cheap stores, billboards, saloons, and dance halls, all awash in a ghastly neon glare. Bedford Falls without George Bailey is enslaved to unbridled commerce, a market in place of society, commerce without purpose or limits.

Pottersville is the dark shadow of the world George helped create. In his Bedford Falls, economic institutions, including those of consumption, operate for communal and spiritual benefits, to help make everyone better citizens and better people. When George finally escapes his nightmare, he finds redemption in the community, and Capra's political economy becomes clear. The town's working-class, ethnic, and racial minorities all come to George's aid in solidarity and loyalty. In his nightmare, amusements embodied the destructive power of unbounded commerce, but here they aid the community. "I busta the juke box!" cries Mr. Martini, bringing a load of nickels from his café. Industry rallies to George's aid, as manufacturer Sam Wainwright wires a line of credit ("Hee Haw and Merry Christmas!"). The state itself sanctions the communal values of Bedford Falls: the bank examiner and sheriff happily add their contributions to George's basket. Decorated hero Harry Bailey, back from personally downing Japanese planes and saving hundreds of American troops, toasts his brother, "the richest guy I know." The community returns to George what he has dispensed so liberally throughout his life—faith and trust in the form of money, a personal bond symbolized in a paper obligation. George Bailey's Bedford Falls was a consumer society where commercial and communal values endured in delicate balance, safeguarded by his own wonderful life.

Capra's film has, of course, been a Christmas favorite for many years with audiences who cherish its sentimental holiday message of love conquering necessity, of redemption and grace. To be sure, the film is regularly satirized by those impatient with the story's easy resolutions. But as a version of midcentury American history and political economy, a coda to the "Why We Fight" propaganda films Capra made during the war, the film merits a short discussion. World War II did come to Bedford Falls. George served as an OPA volunteer, rationing tires and encouraging civic restraint on the home front, just as he had once kept the Building and Loan from closure in the Depression. The return of war hero Harry Bailey—destined for a postwar life of success in industry—brought the purpose of the war home. Capra implied that the war was fought to preserve and uphold the values, institutions, and relationships of such small communities, not for material abundance. As consumers, workers, and citizens, the people of Bedford Falls were a community cemented by homes and family. As a banker, George defended their right to a home, a decent living, and freedom from care and worry, all elements of the Four Freedoms outlined by Franklin Roosevelt. That vision, not the shiny future of better things for better living outlined in magazines, inspired the people of Bedford Falls. Only George has witnessed a future where private interests eclipse community and commerce rules untamed by either morality or politics. George will never forget his nightmare, but he will work to the end of his days to keep those competing interests in harmony. Capra echoed the consumerist civic vision of Caroline Ware: the United States fought the war for John Q. Citizen and family. Consumers ensured the triumph of democracy at home only as they supported it by both wise consumption and in knowing the difference between more goods and a greater good.

A life measured by more, newer, and better things implicitly promised to heal the wounds of war and the traumas of the Depression. Yet goods in themselves could neither address the damage and dislocations of war nor provide compensation for the fighting men in the trenches or their anxious families at home. In their struggle to establish a corporate-dominated, privatized consumer world of the future, advertisers were not the only contestants, and they did not have the only say. Wartime copywriters' feared that sales talk and patriotic imagery could potentially trivialize servicemen's experience; in some instances, their worries were justified. Near the war's final days, the armed forces newspaper *Yank* printed a letter that questioned ad men's claims to speak for the postwar serviceman or civilian. In doing so, the letter questioned the whole commercial interpretation of freedom, Americanism, and war:

> A fair examination will reveal that, next to his rifle, GI Joe's best friend is the typewriter tycoon of the advertising agency. For the advertising profession not only knows what we are fighting for; it knows exactly, down to the last uplift bra, what we want when we come home. And it also knows precisely how we live on the various fighting fronts. It is the copywriters of advertising who nurse the carefully guarded secret that this war is, in reality, a luxury cruise. They know we aren't alone in our foxholes. Everything from Aunt Elinor's radio to Uncle Eben's toothbrush has "gone to war" with us. If you don't believe this, look at the ads. On page after page

you will see a picture of a hungry civilian asking for a rib roast, a new convertible, a crushproof necktie, or some nylons for his honey. And, on page after page, you will see the advertising man brush him off rudely for his lack of patriotism with the stirring slogan: "Meat has gone to war! Superdupermobile has gone to war! Kravatko has gone to war! Honey has gone to war!" It's nice to know that our more abundant life in ODs [olive drabs] is at last getting some recognition.

Some servicemen criticized both the presumptions of advertising to speak to the horrors of war. More important, this letter answers back to the home front and the proponents of American Way ideology that goods in themselves could not sustain war aims or compensate war service. This serviceman at least was not battling for freedom against dictators abroad only to return to them at home. The letter continues:

The world we come home to will be laid out in advance by these same thoughtful moguls. It's none too soon for us to get down on our knees and start thanking them. We haven't had to make a single peep as to our preferences. Advertising has figured them all out in advance. Our girls, guided by scintillant copy, will have become such paragons of charm that Hedy Lamarr will look like a barracks bag besides them. . . . The homes that wait for us will be a tidy combination of Hans Christian Andersen and Jules Verne. . . . Television receivers, thinly disguised as tiger-skin rugs, will disgorge fried chicken from a hidden glove compartment. It will be a world like you've never seen this side of a Section VIII ward. It will be homey, and new, and shiny and soft, and robust and restful, and cheap and expensive, and thick and thin, and sharp and dull. It will be everything and nothing.[168]

The sarcastic GI chastised advertisers for their sunny representations of both war reality and postwar fantasy. Servicemen resented the tidy ease of war depicted in the ads, and they scorned Madison Avenue's awkward fusion of corporate patriarchy and popular freedom. If American democracy and liberty were to be realized in the homey fragments of everyday life, this letter served notice that many viewed those fragments as more than promises of new and better in the World of Tomorrow. For such GIs, advertisers' neat linkage of goods, war, and freedom could not remotely address their experience. "Total living" would be more than a bounty of better things. Freedom could not adequately or plausibly be defined as choice, nor democracy as commodified plenitude. For these GIs and their families at home, what was worth fighting, and perhaps dying, for was no thing. Far from the rosy pictures in magazines or battles between Mrs. Consumer and Mr. Advertiser, the most profound lessons of the war pointed soldier and civilian both to a truth that the good—freedom, democracy, security, or happiness—could not simply or always be reduced to goods.

Even so, the war marked a decisive victory for the material nationalist vision of consumption. As Americans fought to uphold freedom, democracy, and a distinct culture, they defended a way of life centered on getting and spending. In the new Cold War that dawned so soon after V-J Day, American freedom would symbolize affluence, material abundance, and the promise of leisure. For millions at home and abroad, American free enterprise stood superior to collectivist economies that simply could not deliver the goods.[169] That assumption underlay such different visions of the postwar world as Henry Luce's interventionist "American Century," Henry Wallace's popular front "Century of the Common Man," and Wendell Willkie's multilateral "One World."[170] The material symbols of that postwar prosperity—autos, appliances, synthetics, plastics, television—conveyed to a world split in three the utopian potential of modern production, sophisticated design, and boundless appetites. If the returning GIs and their families had rights, they would be expressed and fulfilled in goods. The new consumer paradise would take root most visibly away from both cities and small towns and flourish in the new suburban communities that would mushroom in the twenty years after World War II. There, families would continually reaffirm Americans' unique and superior heritage; as consumers destined to enjoy the best and most modern goods, delivered seemingly without any effort or cost other than price. It would be, as a 1957 sales film intoned, a "happy go spending world."[171]

Both the corporate vision of the American Way and activist consumer republicanism emerged from the war strong; consumerists' moral economy and the advertisers' market vision of society enjoyed a prolonged engagement in the postwar era. Consumerists left a permanent imprint on American life. Product testing and information became a staple of middle-class consumer culture in the postwar era. The activist strains of the consumer movement, so visible in the grassroots participation in the OPA and the social progressivism of the New Deal era, met important but not fatal setbacks. As Meg Jacobs has shown, pressures from businesses (including a meat producers' boycott) on a conservative Congress and a frustrated public doomed the OPA. Even with firm, albeit divided, public support for its extension, Congress eliminated the agency soon after the war's end. Organized shoppers subsequently staged boycotts, often in conjunction with a resurgent labor activism that reached historic heights in 1946.[172] More important, allegations that linked consumer activism with communism had a chilling effect on outspoken reformers and propelled consumer activities squarely toward pragmatic product testing in the postwar era. In an ironic twist, Arthur Kallet was ousted from Consumers Union in 1957 over his reluctance to push the organization back to social action.

Activist consumers continued to organize around specific commodity-centered approaches to social, economic, and environmental questions that arose throughout the postwar decades. A new consumer movement would flourish in the 1960s and beyond. Consumers Union's widespread and durable success, punctuated by several crises, perpetuated the successful format of product testing and ratings pioneered by Consumers' Research; that basic approach now appears in hundreds of consumer-oriented publications around the world. In the postwar era, scandalous safety and health revelations about numerous products generated new interest in test results and independently generated information, particularly about automobiles, medicines, foods, and tobacco, leading to organized campaigns for individual consumers' rights, in what Lizabeth Cohen terms "third-wave consumerism."[173] Although Americans on a nationwide scale have not since practiced such a form of civic-oriented consumption, the legacy of that wartime activism remains both in memory and in latter-day movements that organize consumers to boycott and to campaign for reform. But in the years after World War II, involvement in the moral economies of retailing and conservation inexorably declined, with neither firm programs nor a sense of prolonged crisis to sustain them. Making do gave way to making more.

The same years saw striking and perhaps more important victories in business's campaigns to displace New Deal liberalism. Business may not have won Americans' hearts and minds as Bruce Barton had sought, but citizens acquiesced in business's resurgent authority and influence. Large corporations enjoyed a new popularity in postwar years. Criticism of free enterprise dissipated in the postwar aura of prosperity, anticommunism, and hostility to ideology and mass movements. With anticommunism and the Cold War sustaining free enterprise (and keeping the consumer movement at a low profile), and a rejuvenated economy pouring out goods for both middle- and working-class consumers, postwar America indeed became a consumers' republic, as Lizabeth Cohen has asserted. Lacking serious international competition and benefiting from a surging population, wage growth, and high demand, the American economy enjoyed sustained twenty-five-year expansion beyond all expectation.[174] Corporations exercised growing dominion over culture and everyday life, as well as the economy and public policy.

Americans in this era would tack from boisterous embrace to querulous defense of their unprecedented wealth in things.[175] Skepticism and opposition to advertising could easily coexist with a general acceptance of corporate power and influence. Encouraged by consumerists and cultural critics, many Americans leavened the embrace of plenty with wary disbelief, derision, or from some quarters, outright hostility to the claims and the influence of the consumer marketplace and the influence of a commodity-centered way of life. Culturally, such dissent surfaced in everything from beat literature to *Mad* magazine in the 1950s. During the 1960s, critics of the affluent-society consumption emerged from left, centrist, and self-consciously fringe positions. Cultural forms such as underground comix, "sick" humor, and rock music featured critiques of conformist consumption and material plenty, echoing the widely read critiques of Herbert Marcuse, Betty Friedan, Michael Harrington, Ralph Nader, and Thomas Merton that entered the mainstream. Yet commentators have noted the irony of such critiques, finding their characteristic shape and audiences as commodities themselves. What power can these critiques have if they cannot transcend the very form they attack?[176]

Committed to an expanding economy, valuing "newer" and "more" as the material measure of modernity, Americans have sporadically confronted limits to the corporate ideal of growth without consequence. When they did, they encountered a paradox. The associations of consumption with nationalism and citizenship limited their options in thinking through the consequences and meanings of consumer plenty. As pollution and environmental challenges, shortages and health concerns, underscored the costs of postwar consumption, Americans confronted the limits of the nationalism and exceptionalism that sustained their faith in economic expansion. Such strong belief in a distinct culture defined by consumption and in identities moderated through the market meant that Americans could not easily entertain alternatives to a nationalism grounded so strongly in things. In the 1970s complex and intractable environmental issues, shortages, and economic stagnation revealed that the postwar boom could not last indefinitely. In an increasingly interdependent, international economy, Americans could not easily sustain the fiction of a unique nation distinct and isolated from the world. If consumption defined what it meant to be an American, citizens, in turn, would discover that as Americans they had to choose how well, and not just how much, to consume.

We began with one Christmas story; we end with another. The 1947 film and novel *The Miracle on 34th Street* arrived scarcely a year after *It's a Wonderful Life*, but in tenor and tone it ushered in a different world. The story cheerfully maps a postwar United States in which consumption eclipses community under the pretense of defining it. An elderly gentleman named Kris Kringle finds work as Santa Claus in Macy's department store. His boss, Doris Walker, a no-nonsense, cynical divorcée, shuns intimacy of any kind while raising her daughter Susan to avoid childhood make-believe and innocence. Doris has a grim attitude toward Christmas itself, anxiously tracking her own job security through the toy department's sales. Kris is befriended by Fred Gailey, an attorney who has unsuccessfully wooed Doris. Kringle claims to be Santa Claus and confounds store management with his peculiar brand of customer service. He does not steer shoppers to items that must be moved but helps them search for the perfect choice and refers them to competitors if necessary. Delighted and impressed, customers loyally flock to Macy's, whose business booms. Within days the entire American retail establishment adopts the same competitive altruism. After failing a routine intelligence test from the store's staff psychologist, Kris undergoes a widely reported sanity hearing in state court. Aware of the trial, sharp-witted postal workers deliver Christmas letters for Santa to Kringle at the courthouse. When thousands of letters arrive, Kringle is legally declared the true Santa Claus.[1]

This whimsical story indeed pointed to a new society far from Bedford Falls. The political economy of this tale does not serve community but institutions. All the principals live alone in a lonely, if stylish, New York City, lacking friends and loved ones. Workplaces, such as Macy's and Gailey's law firm, are inhumane, indifferent bureaucracies. Gailey must give up his pro bono work on behalf of Kris or be fired. While Macy's intelligence tester is an ideal comic villain—humorless, suspicious, and bullying—he personifies the logic of large-scale enterprise. Minimizing risk and rationalizing operations according to standard templates, he streamlines workers to fit the Macy's machine, just as Macy's itself produces customers. Even Kris's gerontologist sees him, albeit affectionately, as one of many delusional cases in his practice.

The film turns on the intersection of Christmas and consuming with politics and the state. Kris's trial reveals the holiday's critical role in the economy. Savvy political ward heeler Charlie Halloran challenges trial judge Henry Harper with a blunt explanation of the Christmas political economy:

All right. You go back and tell 'em that the New York State Supreme Court rules there's no Santa Claus. It's all over the papers. The kids read it and they don't hang up their stockings. Now what happens to all the toys that are supposed to be in those stockings? Nobody buys 'em. The toy manufacturers are gonna like that. So they have to lay off a lot of their employees—*union* employees. Now you got the CIO and the A F of L against you, and they're gonna *adore* you for it. And they're gonna say it with votes. Oh, and the department stores are gonna love you too, and the Christmas card makers, and the candy companies. . . . You go back on in there and tell 'em that you rule there's no Santa Claus . . . and you can count on getting just two votes, your own and that district attorney's out there!

Harper's own job directly depends on keeping Santa Claus alive, as do the economy and the polity. While Valentine Davies's New York possesses none of the alienated despair of Frank Capra's Pottersville, the two communities are united in thrall to business dominance. Selling trumps everything. The only person to stand up to the cold-blooded rationalism of commerce is Kris, and he is, of course, thought by all to be daft.

Spending undergirds human relationships in *Miracle on 34th Street*. From a conversation with a displaced Dutch orphan to the new medical machine he procures for his old-age home, Kris's good works center on consuming. His kindness encourages others to spend, thus ensuring both happiness and a prosperous economy. But the community he builds—satisfied customers, retailing executives, coworkers—seems to be evanescent. The adults in the film get involved with Kris largely from self-interest, in direct opposition to Kris's message of love and giving. Even those whom he transforms remain wedded to the bottom line. Mr. Macy perjures himself on the witness stand, rather than admit he does not believe in his own Santa Claus. Even as workers save the day, they do so to get rid of the overflowing sacks of mail cluttering up their loading docks. Fred Gailey befriends Kris to help his love life. Kris believed the world had lost the true meaning of Christmas, but his success in encouraging consumption makes clear that the world very well understands the holiday's overarching importance.

The film's romantic resolution depends on the wounded Doris rediscovering love and on rational, precocious Susan acknowledging her deepest girlhood desire for domesticity. On Christmas Day Kris directs Doris and Fred to Susan's present from Santa—a suburban house complete with a backyard swing set, for sale in a smart bedroom community. The two confess their love for one another and unite to give Susan what she has always really wanted, a house and a family. Here, consumption initiates the flight to the suburbs and constitutes the family. The Cape Cod procured by Kris for his friends will no doubt contain love and happiness, redemption and grace, as did the Bailey's drafty old house in Bedford Falls. Yet that world where consumption served the community is in the past. As Gailey's last, ambiguous line in the film has it: "Maybe I didn't do such a wonderful thing after all."

The postwar world ushered in unprecedented abundance that buoyed a family-centered consumer boom, accompanied by political retrenchment. The postwar political climate solidified the associations of nationality and consumption, traced in this study, into everyday common sense. One of the triumphs of postwar political conservatism has been its successful promotion of the market as a model for society itself. That persistent equivalence took root in no small way in the widespread use of the electoral metaphor. Advertisers and consumerists linked marketplace choice with democracy, spending with voting, possession with participation, and consumption with civics; continual trumpeting of these associations set the stage for metastasis into their present forms as truisms. As much as they fought one another, advertisers and consumerists alike built up common associations of consumption and citizenship between the late nineteenth century and World War II.

The competing visions of consumers and consumption explored in this study each found avid support in the decades beyond 1945 and still shape spending practices today. Americans have internalized the professionalism of consumerists. From public radio's Car Talk to consumer reporters broadcasting on local affiliates, from the "Fab Five" of Queer Eye for the Straight Guy to financial maven Louis Rukeyser, Americans rely on expert authority for their spending decisions. People habitually comparison shop with expert technical information for everything from watches to sport-utility vehicles. That practice owes its origins in no small way to Consumers' Research. Cameras to colleges are all rated, ranked, and evaluated, with results published in celebrated lists and compendia. Many old-line consumerists would have reservations about the scientific integrity or unbiased reliability of this information, but there is little doubt that their advocacy of expert information has borne fruit.

Consumers' Research, and later Consumers Union, pioneered an engaged buyer activism to secure better products, more accurate information, and greater satisfaction. That activism, often expanded into alliances with the environmental movement, antiglobal campaigns, and social reform causes, thrives today. Scientific and moralistic advocates of product testing raised issues that today form a basis for an environmentally conscious and ethical consumption, pursued in numerous contemporary movements.[2] Contemporary critiques and satires of consuming excess appear regularly in such publications as *Ad-Busters* and *The Baffler*. Cartoonists ranging from Charles M. Schulz and Cathy Guisewite to Robert Crumb and Bill Griffith regularly treat consumption as a source of alienation and disaffection. More polemically, authors Kalle Lasn, Naomi Klein, Juliet Schor, John De Graaf, and Thomas Frank, among others, contend that accelerated consumption threatens our ethics and saps our social institutions. For these writers, rampant spending and uncontrolled commerce erode family and community bonds. As they see it, we already live in Pottersville.[3]

Consumerists' longtime opponents among advertisers and commercial spokesmen have of course attained even greater success. After 1945, spectacular economic growth, along with a conservative political realignment, reestablished the social authority of private enterprise. The consumer's republic saw a decisive redirection of state policy from social welfare concerns to private consumption, a shift enabled largely through fiscal mechanisms that minimized taxation, subsidized white suburban home ownership, and promoted automobility. Associations of patriotism, spending, and exceptionalism have risen and fallen with the fortunes of American commercial and military empires. Madison Avenue has continually found success in associating consumer abundance and a unique American heritage. The sacred ideal of the pursuit of happiness has assumed the form of consumer goods. Many Americans turned away from government as the guarantor of a standard of living and a source of happiness; anti–New Deal sentiments grew stronger as citizens came to view private enterprise as the sole institution delivering on World War II's promise of more new and better things for everyday Americans. A younger generation with no personal connection to the New Deal legacy sees no viable alternative to the market. For their part, advertisers have generally surrendered their pretense of transcendent public leadership. While the Advertising Council and other groups have steadily offered public service announcements that call on civic participation or even commercial sacrifice, such messages overall are few; moreover, these campaigns generally seek to alter behavior, not rearrange the civic fabric.[4] Save for such public service campaigns, national advertisers claim to represent only the interests of their clients, and seldom any larger public good. Yet in moments of national triumph or crisis, consumers can still find products from cars to cereals bathed in an iconic wash of Americanism. Observers unconvinced that consuming is central to mass-mediated images of the American Way of Life might reflect on the continual post–September 11 stream of patriotic imagery and language in commercial messages.

The civic camouflage of commerce has concealed its cost. Associations of consumption, citizenship, and nation, especially when grafted to the pervasive idealization of a distinct material American culture, have proved durable. Americans have no doubt enjoyed and benefited from a vast universe of goods and choice. Yet the continued equation of political suffrage with spending has narrowed our expectations of political and social democracy. American icons, nationalist imagery, and political language all evoke institutions that embody self-sacrifice and communal obligation, not self-interest and atomized gratification. The imagery of civic virtue to promote spending on its face denies the self-serving logic of the market but embodies it in substance. More troubling, such language eclipses other models and examples of citizenship, of civics, and of a common culture. The material nationalist claim that nationhood and freedom are symbolized in a preponderance of products has diminished the bonds of society and left citizens groping for alternatives to its market system. Freedom of choice, as Daniel Rodgers has shrewdly observed, "bound in a phrase the consumer benefits of postwar society with the political fact of choice in open reasonably contested elections. It did so, however, at the expense of what everyone knew, once the words moved closer to the grain of experience: that private choice of economic opportunities and public choices of policy were not really the same thing at all."[5] Although consumption has offered up a new form of citizenship, at best it has changed and at worst undermined civil society. Consuming may promote a sense of belonging, but it is in practice as exclusionary as the ascriptive definitions that have determined political citizenship since the Revolution.[6] Moreover, a political economy devoted to maximizing privatized spending for a white middle class has ill served those beneath the privileged stratum and has accelerated widening disparities in income between haves and have nots over the past three decades.

In the end, perhaps spending and owning goods have not been the same in practice as personal interaction and community participation. Advertisers' dreams of forging a stable culture, based solely on common commercial experiences, might ultimately be neither possible nor desirable. Certainly, previous iterations of vast unified "mainstreams"—commercial or political— have proven easily undone by a marketplace logic that finds greater profit

now in addressing niches, not masses, and in capitalizing on imagined difference at the expense of meaningful commonality.

Contemporary consumption mixes strains of frugality and individual desire. As each new generation redefines for itself the boundaries of public and
private interest, meanings of good consuming inevitably shift. Those fluctuations keep demographers, marketers, pollsters, and pundits ceaselessly
busy, tracking and measuring consumer citizenship in action. Current critics
of the American consumer system do not merely echo older antimarket
critiques. Contemporary opponents to consumer excess array themselves
against more than material accumulation. They criticize the global impact of
American and Western material demands on a fragile, interdependent system of economies and ecologies. They point us to questions of equity—how to
share fairly the resources of the planet—and of purpose. What are economies
for? What are goods for? The new culture jammers, ad-busters, and critics of
"affluenza" offer a far-reaching analysis that outstrips the charges of Veblen,
Chase, and Schlink and builds on the work of postwar social critics like Vance
Packard, Michael Harrington, and Betty Friedan. Today's dissenters define
consumption through its excessiveness, and they see the pervasive marketplace as numbing, harmful, addictive. People use and take in unhealthy
goods, sickened by both the tenacity of unfulfilled consumer desire as well as
its hollow fruits. Contemporary consumption, accelerated and aggressive,
harms Americans and promotes privation and suffering around the world.

Such critics offer us a good deal to consider. First, politically established
associations of American nationalism, freedom, markets, and exceptionalism
cannot be easily sustained in an interdependent world. Such related ideals
have been historically linked to an imperialism that has undermined treasured claims of democracy and self-governance as the highest American
principles.[7] Second, in an interdependent world economy American consuming has consequences far from home. Whether or not one believes in
environmental stewardship, the United States consumes a vastly disproportionate amount of global resources. Critics abroad and at home note that
American material abundance depends on the misery of others. From Wal-
Mart to Nike, American access to low prices, deep discounts, endless varia-
tion, and technological advancement—now viewed almost as entitlements—
depends on a worldwide economy responsible for exploitation and ecological
spoilage. In turn, American life is shaped by conditions around the globe. As
I write these words, current economic news notes that fully 80 percent of
American income goes to consumption; Americans produce much less than
they consume, and they have built up a massive trade deficit to subsidize that

spending. Economies from China to Canada in turn depend on that continued American consumer debt; American spending has worldwide impact.[8] Changes in labor prices and policies elsewhere influence prices and availability within the United States. No longer can American consumers easily ignore the global conditions in which they spend.

And yet, those who question American consumption might note that one observer's economic exploitation is another person's job that supports a family spread perhaps over several continents. In its unending pursuit of resources and lower costs, transnational capitalism has accelerated both growth and privation. The experiences of a diasporic global workforce complicate existing notions of fairness and exploitation. While Americans may be aware in many cases of the consequences and costs of their consumer system, they do not have a uniform response to that knowledge. The past generation's neoliberal market policies and ideology may have aggravated social inequality and eroded governmental capacity to address common problems, but they have not as yet generated an opposition large or compelling enough to win over the majority of Americans. Consumer abundance remains attractive, useful, and liberating for many in the United States. Not surprisingly, consumerism generates strong allegiance among Americans. Its costs remain largely hidden and are literally displaced onto other countries and another time.

Whether celebrated or castigated, goods themselves comprise a fertile and undervalued resource. Critics of materialism miss the point, as both Jackson Lears and Barry Shank remind us. People have long used goods to make themselves, even as the modern world has spread alienation. Shank makes us consider how commodities have become our daily vernacular, the very grammar and vocabulary of feeling, not solely an instrument of alienation but also a voice of an authentic self.[9] Anthropologist Daniel Miller makes the case thus: goods symbolize our alienation from one another and nature, but as they are used in social relations, they can help us overcome that condition.[10] Mary Douglas and Baron Isherwood observe that "commodities are good for thinking . . . a non-verbal medium for the human creative faculty." As that is true, goods not only symbolize status or ideas but also offer connection. They are prosthetics that reunite us to the natural and social world.[11] As we further think with and through goods, we can use them purposefully in human relationships. This alone can never heal the wounds of exploitation and disfranchisement—goods maintain their capacity to symbolize and perpetuate alienation—but goods can bind us as makers and users of things to the world and to one another.

The United States hosts a consumer abundance that surpasses that of the rest of the world, yet the sway of commodities in daily life remains contested and ever changing. While consumer spending has continually expanded over the long run, everyday Americans have seen and in many cases have embraced shifts in the ways they spend, in response to different critiques and concerns. Environmental issues now impinge on everyday consumer decisions ("paper or plastic?"). Health concerns have sparked fierce popular resistance to such industry-led modernizations as irradiated food or new vaccines. Wal-Mart, America's largest retailer, faces mounting criticisms of its labor policies, of its impact on local communities, and not least of the effect of its pricing and supply policies on a global economy.[12] Culturally, the popular success of the auction/yard sale Internet site eBay and the *Antiques Roadshow* television program reveal more than the search for bargains or unexpected windfalls. They also trace a popular desire to integrate and reuse items from the past in everyday life. Recycling thus preserves not only the earth but also our sense of self. If a marketplace calculus of monetary costs and benefits remains a primary arbiter of public values, we have daily reminders that Americans hold other values important, even sacred, as well. Olivier Zunz assures us, "For no matter how hard we try, marketplace and society cannot be made congruent." Access to goods is not political democracy, and the market is not the only standard of value.[13]

Consumption has become both badge and practice of citizenship in modern America. It symbolizes belonging to the nation even as it divides those within the nation. Consumer plenty materializes Americans' understandings of their distinct national heritage in the world. However, just as nationalism voices the claims of a unique heritage for citizens of *any* nation, exceptionalist claims based in material nationalism may prove illusory. Capital does not respect borders, and Americans may discover that their material way of life is neither unique to the United States nor tellingly distinct. If McDonald's, Nike, Apple, and Major League Baseball all seem *typically* American, can it be said that they are *uniquely* American?

As citizenship is redefined by multinational diasporas, economic and technological developments that move capital and jobs across borders with dizzying speed, and changing claims of the nation-state itself, consumption also will undoubtedly influence new meanings and practices of citizenship.[14] Multinational identities are a reality in late modernity; communities are made from affinity and interest, as well as descent and obligation, across once solid barriers of space, language, and custom. Both the contemporary economy and the antiglobalization movement are, well, global. Whether a new citizenship centered on complex identities as consumers and workers and as transnational subjects can itself lay a foundation for a just economic and political order remains to be seen. Even if capital undermines national boundaries, reports of the death of the nation-state are premature. Without doubt, consumers will shape any process of renewal. As they remake the relationships of identities, nations, and markets, they will be an indispensable part of that new order to come.

NOTES

ABBREVIATIONS

AC   N. W. Ayer Collection, Archives Center, National Museum of American History, Smithsonian Institution, Washington, D.C.

BBDO   BBDO Archives, BBDO Inc., New York, N.Y.

CBS   Columbia Broadcasting System

CR   *Consumers' Research* (publication)

CR   Consumers' Research (organization)

CRB   *Consumers' Research Bulletin*

CRGB   *Consumers' Research General Bulletin*

CRP   Consumers' Research Papers, Special Collections, Alexander Library, Rutgers University, New Brunswick, N.J.

CSCM   Center for the Study of the Consumer Movement, Consumers Union, Inc., Yonkers, N.Y.

CUA   Consumers Union Archives, Center for the Study of the Consumer Movement, Consumers Union, Inc., Yonkers, N.Y.

FJS   Frederick J. Schlink

GH   *Good Housekeeping*

JHE   *Journal of Home Economics*

JWT   J. Walter Thompson

JWTA   J. Walter Thompson Archives, John W. Hartman Center for Sales, Advertising, and Marketing History, Duke University, Durham, N.C.

LAB   Library of American Broadcasting, University of Maryland, College Park, Md.

LHJ   *Ladies' Home Journal*

NBC   National Broadcasting Company

PI   *Printers' Ink*

RG   Record Group

SC   Stuart Chase

SEP   *Saturday Evening Post*

SHSW   State Historical Society of Wisconsin, Madison, Wisc.

WCBA   Warshaw Collection of Business Americana, Archives Center, National Museum of American History, Smithsonian Institution, Washington, D.C.

INTRODUCTION

1. Quoted in Lynd and Lynd, *Middletown*, 88.

2. Chase and Schlink, *Your Money's Worth*, 2.

3. See Capra's own autobiography, *Name above the Title*; Carney, *American Vision*; Basinger, with the Trustees of the Frank Capra Archives, *"It's a Wonderful Life" Book*; Ray, *Certain Tendency of the Hollywood Cinema*, 179–215; and Smoodin, *Regarding Frank Capra*, 182–202.

4. See Jameson, *Postmodernism*; Hardt and Negri, *Empire*; Wood, *Empire of Capital*;

Desai, *Marx's Revenge*; Hertz, *Silent Takeover*; and Kuttner, *Everything for Sale*. More sanguine is Westbrook, *City of Gold*.

5. President Bush and others in the cabinet called for Americans to go back to work and to go shopping to resume economic behavior. For two relevant speeches, see Mike Allen and Greg Schneider, "National Guard to Be Used at Airports; Bush Calls for Public Confidence in Flying, Details Security Plan," *Washington Post*, September 28, 2001, A1; and Richard W. Stevenson and Joseph Kahn, "A Nation Challenged: The Economy; Bush Tries to Steady Economy Jolted by Attack," *New York Times*, September 23, 2001, A1. Such urgings were bipartisan: see Jose Martinez, "War on Terrorism: Mayor, Kerry Say Spending Can Revive Hub Economy," *Boston Herald*, September 23, 2001, 6; Robert Reich, "How Did Spending Become Our Patriotic Duty?" *Washington Post*, September 23, 2001, B1; Frank Rich, "War Is Heck," *New York Times*, November 10, 2001, A23; David Leonhardt and Louis Uchitelle, "A Body Blow to the Economy," *New York Times*, September 16, 2001, 3-1; Liz Kowalczyk, "Patriotic Purchasing: Americans Are Being Urged to Spend, but Analysts Doubt the Strategy Will Have an Impact in the Long Run," *Boston Globe*, September 28, 2001, C1; Glenn Kessler, "Riding to the Economy's Rescue: In Days after Attacks, Bush Team Bent Rules to Stabilize System," *Washington Post*, September 25, 2001, E1; and Maureen O'Donnell, "What, Me Worry?" *Chicago Sun-Times*, September 24, 2001, 9.

6. Jennifer Davies, "Marketing Sensibility; Companies Must Return to Selling Products While Avoiding Perception of Cashing in on Terrorist Attacks," *San Diego Union Tribune*, September 23, 2001, H1; Chris Reidy, "Public Mood Challenges Advertisers," *Boston Globe*, September 28, 2001, C1; Crayton Harrison and John Kirkpatrick, "In Dallas, Shoppers Head Back to Malls," *Dallas Morning News*, September 17, 2001. For two viewpoints critical of the emphasis on consumption, see Tom Feran, "Ask What You Can Buy for Your Country," *Cleveland Plain Dealer*, October 28, 2001, L1; and Derrick Z. Jackson, "Bush's Plea: Onward Capitalist Soldiers," *Boston Globe*, October 3, 2001, A19.

7. The following are a short sampling of studies published across the twentieth century that concern these basic categories of inquiry. For social differences see Veblen, *Theory of the Leisure Class*; Lynes, *Tastemakers*; Galbraith, *Affluent Society*; and Brooks, *Bobos in Paradise*. For national civilization see Siegfried, *America Comes of Age*; Borsodi, *This Ugly Civilization*; Mumford, *Technics and Civilization*; Packard, *Waste Makers*; and Potter, *People of Plenty*. For cultural diversity see Gunther, *Inside U.S.A.*; Kouwenhoven, *Beer Can by the Highway*; Venturi, Brown, and Izenour, *Learning from Las Vegas*; and Lippard, *Lure of the Local*.

8. See Cullen, *American Dream*; Baritz, *Good Life*; Baxandall and Ewen, *Picture Windows*; Martinson, *American Dreamscape*; Frank, *Luxury Fever*; Samuelson, *Good Life and Its Discontents*; and most defensively, Lebergott, *Pursuing Happiness*. Two much more critical accounts are Schor, *Overspent American*; and De Graaf, Wann, and Naylor, *Affluenza*.

9. Leuchtenburg, *Perils of Prosperity*, is still a useful account of the American economy and society. See also Olney, *Buy Now, Pay Later*; and Hawley, *Great War and the Search for a Modern Order*.

10. Phelps, *Our Biggest Customer*; Galbraith, *New Industrial State*; Chase, *Economy of Abundance*.

11. On New Deal economic policy see, most helpfully, Hawley, *New Deal and the Problem of Monopoly*; Brinkley, *End of Reform*; Jacobs, *Pocketbook Politics*; Barber, *Designs within*

Disorder; Bernstein, *Great Depression*; May, *From New Deal to New Economics*; Reagan, *Designing a New America*; and Leff, *Limits of Symbolic Reform*.

12. See Ward, *Produce and Conserve, Share and Play Square*; Westbrook, *Why We Fought*; and Tuttle, *Daddy's Gone to War*.

13. Lipsitz, "Consumer Spending as State Project"; Cohen, *Consumers' Republic*.

14. On Cold War consumerism see Haddow, *Pavilions of Plenty*; Rydell, *World of Fairs*; Horowitz, *Anxieties of Affluence*; Wagenleitner, *Coca-Colonization and the Cold War*; Pells, *Not Like Us*; De Grazia, *Irresistible Empire*; Belmonte, *Selling America*; and Belmonte, "Selling Capitalism."

15. See Fox, *Discovery of Abundance*; and Horowitz, *Morality of Spending* for two convincing interpretations of the intellectual shift toward consumption and the considerable ambivalence with which many intellectuals encountered the notion that abundance, not scarcity, was the key fact of American economic life, and consumption rather than saving was thus more important for the economy. Donohue, *Freedom from Want*, traces these ideas into the 1940s. Birken, *Consuming Desire*, offers provocative links between the changes wrought in economic thought by a concept of abundance and ideas about sexuality, procreation, and social groups.

16. See Weber, "On Bureaucracy"; Abbott, *System of Professions*; Larson, *Rise of Professionalism*; Haskell, *Emergence of Professional Social Science*; Mills, *White Collar*; Krause, *Death of the Guilds*; Haber, *Quest for Authority and Honor*; Ross, *Origins of American Social Science*; Starr, *Social Transformation of American Medicine*; and Bernstein, *Perilous Progress*.

17. Home economists, academic social scientists, the originators of "public opinion" polling, and journalists were also among those instrumental to this coming of a mass consumer society. See Samson, "Emergence of a Consumer Interest"; Hollitz, "Challenge of Abundance"; Wolfe, "Women, Consumerism, and the National Consumers' League"; Sklar, *Florence Kelley and the Nation's Work*; Goldstein, "Mediating Consumption"; and Stage and Vicenti, *Rethinking Home Economics*.

18. Meikle, *Twentieth Century Limited*; Wilson, Pilgrim, and Tashjian, *Machine Age in America*; Nickles, "Object Lessons"; Robinson, *Measure of Democracy*; Bartels, *History of Marketing Thought*; Strasser, *Satisfaction Guaranteed*; Tedlow, *New and Improved*.

19. McGerr, *Decline of Popular Politics*.

20. Higham, *Strangers in the Land*; O'Leary, *To Die For*; Gerstle, *American Crucible*; Jacobson, *Whiteness of a Different Color*; Jacobson, *Barbarian Virtues*; Guterl, *Color of Race in America*; Michaels, *Our America*; Black, *War against the Weak*; Ngai, *Impossible Subjects*; Daniels, *Guarding the Golden Door*.

21. Purcell, *Crisis of Democratic Theory*; Smith, "Personalities in the Crowd." For two, still influential, defining statements in this debate, see Lippmann, *Public Opinion*; and Dewey, *Public and Its Problems*.

22. Nasaw, *Going Out*; Boyer, *Urban Masses and Moral Order*; Brantlinger, *Bread and Circuses*; Levine, *Highbrow/Lowbrow*; Blake, *Beloved Community*; Gorman, *Left Intellectuals and Popular Culture*; Kammen, *American Culture, American Tastes*; Rabinovitz, *For the Love of Pleasure*; Register, *Kid of Coney Island*. See also Schwartz, *Spectacular Realities*; and Starr, *Creation of the Media*.

23. Marchand, *Advertising the American Dream*; Lears, *Fables of Abundance*; Fox, *Mirror Makers*; Pope, *Making of Modern Advertising*.

24. Mayer, *Consumer Movement*; Pertschuk, *Revolt against Regulation*; Silber, *Test and Protest*; Creighton, *Pretenders to the Throne*.

25. The literature on these ideologies is multifaceted and vast. Key republican interpretations include Pocock, *Machiavellian Moment*; Bailyn, *Ideological Origins of the American Revolution*; McCoy, *Elusive Republic*; Nelson, *Liberty and Property*; Wilentz, *Chants Democratic*; Foner, *Free Soil, Free Labor, Free Men*; and Ross, "Liberal Tradition Revisited and the Republican Tradition Addressed." Emphasizing the liberal individualism of American society is Appleby, *Capitalism and a New Social Order*; Hartz, *Liberal Tradition in America*; Wood, *Creation of the American Republic*; Watts, *Republic Reborn*; Diggins, *Lost Soul of American Politics*; Kloppenberg, *Virtues of Liberalism*; and Ross, "Socialism and American Liberalism."

26. This in effect represents a version of Marx's concepts of alienation and fetishism. See Tucker, *Marx-Engels Reader*, 56–86, 104–6, 215–25; Ollman, *Alienation*; and Elster, *Introduction to Karl Marx*, 41–59.

27. On money see Simmel, *Philosophy of Money*, 147, 297–303, and more generally, 429–512. For some of the relevant literature on the social origins of value, see Zelizer, *Social Meaning of Money*; Douglas and Isherwood, *World of Goods*; Graeber, *Toward an Anthropological Theory of Value*; and Dant, *Material Culture in the Social World*.

28. Frank, *Buy American!*

29. Lowe, *Immigrant Acts*, 2.

30. Shklar, *American Citizenship*; T. H. Marshall's classic account in *Citizenship and Social Class and Other Essays*; and Smith, *Civic Ideals* all influenced my understanding of citizenship. On the idea of a cultural citizenship, see Stevenson, *Cultural Citizenship*; Isin and Turner, *Handbook of Citizenship Studies*; and Stevenson, *Culture and Citizenship*. On economic citizenship see Kessler-Harris, *In Pursuit of Equity*; and Glenn, *Unequal Freedom*.

31. Cahan, *Rise of David Levinsky*, 101.

32. Heinze, *Adapting to Abundance*; Ewen, *Immigrant Women in the Land of Dollars*; Connolly-Smith, *Translating America*; Cheng, *Melancholy of Race*.

33. Anderson, *Imagined Communities*; Hobsbawm, *Nations and Nationalism Since 1780*; Gellner, *Nations and Nationalism*. For studies that usefully adapt Anderson's ideas to the American context of consumer culture, see Shaffer, *See America First*; Hilmes, *Radio Voices*; and Douglas, *Listening In*.

34. Zelinsky, *Nation into State*, 13; Lloyd and Thomas, *Culture and the State*; Bodnar, *Remaking America*.

35. Susman, *Culture as History*, is now the standard, if contested, interpretation of "the culture of abundance." Although there is no adequate account of all the changes that occurred in this period, Susman's essays have provided a starting point to understand the cultural effects wrought by the emergence of a mass-production and consumption economy. I have attempted a short and necessarily incomplete history of these changes in McGovern, "Consumption."

36. Since Marx, philosophers, advertisers, marketers, and critics have noted the possibilities of vast omnicommodification. While philosophers, most notably the Frankfurt School, have been perhaps most interested in this process, others have fitfully but not yet fully explored the implications of commodification in various aspects of the American past. See Haug, *Critique of Commodity Aesthetics*; and Horkheimer and Adorno, *Dialectic of*

Enlightenment. For commodification in social relations see Hochschild, *Managed Heart*; Zelizer, *Pricing the Priceless Child*; Horwitz, *Transformation of American Law*; and Strasser, *Commodifying Everything.*

37. Beard and Beard, *Rise of American Civilization*; Polanyi, *Great Transformation*; and Schumpeter, *Capitalism, Socialism and Democracy* are foundational works of this history for western Europe. The historiography based on modernization theory is voluminous, and scholars are now beginning to explore the social history of the theory itself. See Gilman, *Mandarins of the Future*; and Latham, *Modernization as Ideology.*

38. The historiography on the United States's change to a consumer society has proceeded in fits and starts, but its origins are in such contemporary portraits as Allen's *Only Yesterday, Since Yesterday,* and *Big Change.* Two other contemporary observations worth considering in this context are Merz, *Great American Band Wagon*; and Lynd and Lynd, *Middletown.* See also [Mitchell], *Recent Social Trends in the United States.* None of these works are explicitly concerned with establishing consumer society at a specific historical moment, but all chronicle the emergence of the socioeconomic institutions, media, demographics, and cultural changes that drove this transformation. See also Livingston, *Pragmatism, Feminism, and Democracy,* esp. 1–14; and Livingston, *Pragmatism and the Political Economy*; both propose periodization and historiographical arguments for consumer culture. For additional historiography on consumption in the United States see, foremost, Agnew, "Coming Up for Air"; Glickman, *Consumer Society in American History,* 399–413; and McGovern, "Consumption." Slater, *Consumer Culture and Modernity,* is an extended analysis that doubles as a long bibliographic essay. More specialized bibliographic guides appear in Miller, *Acknowledging Consumption*; and De Grazia and Furlough, *Sex of Things,* 389–409.

39. See McKendrick, Brewer, and Plumb, *Birth of a Consumer Society*; Walsh, "Urban Amenities and Rural Sufficiency"; Carson, Hoffman, and Albert, *Of Consuming Interests*; Brewer and Porter, *Consumption and the World of Goods*; Campbell, *Romantic Ethic and the Spirit of Modern Consumerism*; and Bermingham and Brewer, *Consumption of Culture.*

40. Breen, *Marketplace of Revolution.* See also Carson, Hoffman, and Albert, *Of Consuming Interests*; Baumgarten, *What Clothes Reveal.*

41. Livingston, *Pragmatism and the Political Economy,* 62–77.

42. Fox and Lears's anthology *Culture of Consumption* limned several of the dominant concerns of this scholarship that would emerge in subsequent years. Their follow-up volume, Fox and Lears, *Power of Culture,* further refined the concerns of the initial volume but with an expanded chronological focus and greater attention to a breadth of disciplinary perspectives. Several other volumes of essays further engaged with and ultimately challenged the terms of this debate. See Strasser, McGovern, and Judt, *Getting and Spending*; Glickman, *Consumer Society in American History*; De Grazia and Furlough, *Sex of Things*; Strasser, *Commodifying Everything*; and Scanlon, *Gender and Consumer Culture Reader.*

43. Lears, *Fables of Abundance,* 18–19, 12 (quotations); see also Cross, *All-Consuming Century.*

44. See Nelson, *Market Sentiments,* and Merish, *Sentimental Materialism.*

45. Leach, *Land of Desire,* 3–12, 147–50, 385–90. See also Leach, "Transformations in a Culture of Consumption."

46. Livingston, *Pragmatism and the Political Economy*; Livingston, *Pragmatism, Feminism, and Democracy.*

47. Donohue, *Freedom from Want*, appeared too late for me to incorporate the insights from her own inquiry into the intellectual history of consumption, but see her first chapter for the early negative ideas of consumption; and Horowitz, *Morality of Spending*.

48. Glickman, *Living Wage*; Meyer, *Five Dollar Day*.

49. Frank, *Purchasing Power*; Orleck, *Common Sense and a Little Fire*, 215–50; Storrs, *Civilizing Capitalism*.

50. Peiss, *Cheap Amusements*; Rosenzweig, *Eight Hours for What We Will*; Couvares, *Remaking of Pittsburgh*; Enstad, *Ladies of Labor, Girls of Adventure*.

51. Schmidt, *Consumer Rites*; Kasson, *Amusing the Million*; Nasaw, *Going Out*; Register, *Kid of Coney Island*; Rabinovitz, *For the Love of Pleasure*.

52. Cohen, *Making a New Deal*. See also Cross, *Time and Money*.

53. Young, *Pure Food*; Thelen, *Paths of Resistance*; Frank, *Purchasing Power*; Johnston, *Radical Middle Class*; Pope, "American Economists and the High Cost of Living."

54. Hawley, *New Deal and the Problem of Monopoly*; Leuchtenburg, *Franklin D. Roosevelt and the New Deal*; Gordon, *New Deals*; Dubofsky, *State and Labor*, 107–232.

55. Brinkley, *End of Reform*, 65–85; Brinkley, "New Deal and the Idea of the State"; Meg Jacobs, "The Politics of Plenty: Consumerism in the Twentieth-Century United States," in *Politics of Consumption*, ed. Daunton and Hilton, 223–40; May, *From New Deal to New Economics*; Collins, *More*. Jacobs, *Pocketbook Politics*, offers a definitive account of the central role of purchasing power and consumer interests in American politics and state-building over the first half of the twentieth century.

56. Lipsitz, "Consumer Spending as State Project"; Lipsitz, "In the Sweet Buy and Buy." The latter is a rewritten version of the former essay, which emphasizes connections between state policy and increasing disparities in income and resource distribution in the United States. For the decline of public amenities see Nasaw, *Going Out*; and Avila, *Popular Culture in an Age of White Flight*. For the impact of these policies on housing, including the transfer of subsidies from public to private housing, see Sugrue, *Origins of the Urban Crisis*; and Parson, *Making a Better World*.

57. Cohen, *Consumers' Republic*; Cohen, "From Town Center to Shopping Center." See also Weems, *Desegregating the Dollar*; Hurley, *Diners, Bowling Alleys, and Trailer Parks*; Hardwick, *Mall Maker*.

58. Kroes, *If You've Seen One, You've Seen the Mall*; Pells, *Not Like Us*; Kuisel, *Seducing the French*; Wagenleitner, *Coca-Colonization and the Cold War*; Barber, *Jihad vs. McWorld*.

59. Livingston, *Pragmatism and the Political Economy*, argues that philosophical pragmatism is the key intellectual innovation that made possible the reconceptualization of self in and through the regime of corporate capitalism, namely, consumption rather than labor. Mitchell and Kyrk barely but discernibly anticipate that argument, claiming that consumption was necessary for people to realize their human potential and that a pragmatic approach was necessary for consumption. While Livingston refers to pragmatism's role in redefining the broadest parameters of subjectivity—the realization and apprehension of self in the material world—I suggest that pragmatism primarily appealed to the social and physical scientists who studied consumers as an attractive description of the process of consumption in the everyday life.

60. Horowitz, *Anxieties of Affluence*.

61. See Lindblom, *Market System*; Walzer, *Spheres of Justice*; Sandel, *Democracy's Discon-*

tent; and Greider, *Soul of Capitalism*. Two works that explore the difficulties posed to individuals by the consumer system are Schwartz, *Costs of Living*; and Schwartz, *Paradox of Choice*.

62. Westbrook, *Why We Fought*, speaks of the social history of moral ideas; *Sold American* is in this aspect, I trust, a small contribution to that enterprise.

63. McChesney, *Telecommunications, Mass Media, and Democracy*; Gudis, *Buyways*; Starr, *Creation of the Media*; Ohmann, *Selling Culture*.

64. Lindblom, *Market System*; Hirschman, *Exit, Voice, and Loyalty*; Kuttner, *Everything for Sale*.

65. Habermas, *Structural Transformation of the Public Sphere*; Calhoun, *Habermas and the Public Sphere*; Robbins, *Phantom Public Sphere*.

66. Robinson, *Measure of Democracy*; Zunz, *Why the American Century?*; Wells, "Remapping America"; Gordon, *Comic Strips and Consumer Culture*; Ward, "Tracking the Culture of Consumption."

67. Turow, *Breaking Up America*; Weiss, *Clustered World*; Erik Larson, *Naked Consumer*; Frank, *Conquest of Cool*.

68. Robert Westbrook, "Politics as Consumption: Managing the Modern American Election," in *Culture of Consumption*, ed. Fox and Lears, 143–73; Allen, *Eisenhower and the Mass Media*; Jamieson, *Packaging the Presidency*.

69. Lasn, *Culture Jam*; Klein, *No Logo*; Greider, *One World, Ready or Not*; Princen, Maniates, and Conca, *Confronting Consumption*; Brown, *Plan B*.

CHAPTER ONE

1. Leverett S. Lyon, "Advertising," in *Encyclopaedia of the Social Sciences*, 1:470.

2. "The Universality of Advertising," in N. W. Ayer & Son, *Ayer Idea in Advertising*, 21.

3. Chester M. Wright, "How Much Can the Home Market Absorb?" *PI* 141, no. 13 (December 29, 1927): 4.

4. Bates, *Good Advertising*, 256.

5. Key works in tracing the emergence of industrial-managerial capitalism, modernity, and the consumer system include Perrow, *Organizing America*; Roy, *Socializing Capital*; Chandler, *Visible Hand*; Scranton, *Endless Novelty*; and Sklar, *Corporate Reconstruction of American Capitalism*. An overall celebratory but insightful history of the corporation is Micklethwait and Wooldridge, *The Company*. For everyday life and pivotal cultural changes see Trachtenberg, *Incorporation of America*; Schlereth, *Victorian America*; Schivelbusch, *Railway Journey*; Schivelbusch, *Disenchanted Night*; Thompson, *Soundscape of Modernity*; and Kern, *Culture of Time and Space*.

6. Leiss, Kline, and Jhally, *Social Communication in Advertising*; Lears, *Fables of Abundance*; Marchand, *Advertising the American Dream*; Schudson, *Advertising, the Uneasy Persuasion*; Fox, *Mirror Makers*; Kilbourne, *Can't Buy My Love*; Cronin, *Advertising Myths*.

7. Leiss, Kline, and Jhally, *Social Communication in Advertising*, 47.

8. For two genealogies of the term "consumer," see Williams, *Keywords*, 78–79; and Ulrich Wyrwa, "Consumption and Consumer Society: A Contribution to the History of Ideas," in *Getting and Spending*, ed. Strasser, McGovern, and Judt, 420–47. See also Strasser, *Satisfaction Guaranteed*, 25–26.

9. Jameson, "Reification and Utopia in Mass Culture," remains the classic statement of the utopian possibilities in mass entertainment. Some influential studies, shortened from a

long list, of communities using consumption and entertainment to construct their own political and social claims are Gutman, *Work, Culture, and Society*; Small, *Music of the Common Tongue*; Cohen, *Making a New Deal*; Kelley, *Race Rebels*; Denning, *Cultural Front*; and Enstad, *Ladies of Labor, Girls of Adventure*.

10. "The Highest Paid Ad-Man Talks to the Sphinx Club," *PI* 66, no. 3 (January 20, 1909): 117; see also Claude C. Hopkins, "Chicago as an Advertising Center," *Judicious Advertising and Advertising Experience* 7, no. 3 (January 1909): 20–24. Testimonies to Hopkins's importance through the years from advertising men (some of whom were his peers and some of whom got their training at Lord & Thomas) include Lasker, *Lasker Story*; Mark O'Dea, "To Know Advertising, You Must Know Claude Hopkins," *PI* 161, no. 1 (October 6, 1932): 65–68; Ogilvy, *Confessions of an Advertising Man*; Cone, *With All Its Faults*; O'Toole, *Trouble with Advertising*; and Fox, *Mirror Makers*, 52–56, 192, 261.

11. Pope, *Making of Modern Advertising*, 108–9; Strasser, *Satisfaction Guaranteed*, 3–29, 93–123; Tedlow, *New and Improved*.

12. C. E. Raymond, "Memoirs," part I, section 2 (typescript, 1932), 30, Raymond File, JWTA; Pope, *Making of Modern Advertising*, 112–83. The fullest study we have of advertising professionalism in these years, focusing principally on the creation of professional organizations and journals and the organization of knowledge within the profession through science and reform efforts, is Schultze, "Advertising, Science, and Professionalism."

13. This professional code was often self-serving: at times advertisers glossed over painful industrywide conflicts of interest on such issues as reliable circulation figures, secret rebates on commissions, restraint of trade, and truth in advertising. See Pope, *Making of Modern Advertising*; Rowell, *Forty Years an Advertising Agent*; Hower, *History of an Advertising Agency*, 62–88, 236–54, 402–88; Young, *Advertising Agency Compensation*; Kenner, *Fight for Truth in Advertising*; and Pease, *Responsibilities of American Advertising*.

14. I have thus far used "advertiser" in the customary sense of the time, to refer to the party with the goods or service to sell, that is, the client who paid for the advertising. "Advertising man" usually meant anyone concerned with the buying, selling, or preparing of advertising space, and professionals easily moved among jobs in agencies, media, and corporations; occasionally, that name referred to the client as well. In discussing the professionalization of the advertising business, I will use "advertisers" to refer primarily to advertising specialists, those responsible for creating and promulgating advertising in agencies and, to a lesser extent, within corporations, and "client" to refer to any business interest for whom advertising professionals worked, especially if their interests were in conflict. See Calkins and Holden, *Modern Advertising*; and Calkins, *Business of Advertising*, 16–18.

15. These changes were first presented in Rowell, *Forty Years*; Presbrey, *History and Development of Advertising*, 261–309; and Hower, *History of an Advertising Agency*. The best analytical accounts are Pope, *Making of Modern Advertising*, 112–83; Bogart, *Artists, Advertising, and the Borders of Art*, 15–124; and Laird, *Advertising Progress*.

16. To be sure, advertising agencies did not have any sophisticated approach to marketing at the turn of the twentieth century, but agencies as far back as 1879 had conducted market surveys. Indeed, preliminary attempts at market surveys were first conducted by agencies (notably, N. W. Ayer & Son and Lord & Thomas) and by C. C. Parlin of the Curtis Publishing Company, which published the two most important and influential general

magazines, the *Ladies' Home Journal* and the *Saturday Evening Post*. See Hower, *History of an Advertising Agency*, 88–94; Parlin, *Merchandising of Automobiles*; and Parlin, *Merchandising of Textiles*. See also Hopkins, *My Life in Advertising*; Walsh, *Selling Forces*; and Christopher P. Wilson, "The Rhetoric of Consumption: Mass-Market Magazines and the Demise of the Genteel Reader, 1880–1920," in *Culture of Consumption*, ed. Fox and Lears, 44. The best history of early attempts at research to develop markets for goods is Strasser, *Satisfaction Guaranteed*, 124–203.

17. Strasser, *Satisfaction Guaranteed*; Pope, *Making of Modern Advertising*, 94; Laird, *Advertising Progress*, 196–200. For candid contemporary statements of conflicts over advertising and distribution, see Cherington, *Advertising as a Business Force*, esp. 3–67, 119–56, 206–56. Cherington, one of the pioneers in marketing thought, later went to work for J. Walter Thompson, the largest American advertising agency, where he specialized in statistical analysis and problems of distribution; Harford Powel, "Gallery," *Advertising and Selling* 32, no. 5 (May 1939): 52, 70, 74. See also Tedlow, *New and Improved*; and Chandler, *Visible Hand*, 377–414.

18. Cherington, *Advertising as a Business Force*; Mahin, *Advertising*. A forthright discussion of different aspects of agency economics and conflict of interest questions can be found in the transcription of Albert Lasker's testimony at a Federal Trade Commission hearing in 1927. "A. D. Lasker Traces Advertising Agency's Development," *PI* 141, no. 2 (October 13, 1927): 140–46.

19. Bartels, *History of Marketing Thought*. For a present-day view of this same phenomenon, see Turow, *Breaking Up America*; Weiss, *Clustered World*. For accounts of this tendency in the early twentieth century, see Wells, "Remapping America"; Kreshel, "Toward a Cultural History of Advertising Research"; and Silva, "Development of American Marketing Thought and Practice."

20. Pope, *Making of Modern Advertising*, 142–43. Hower, *History of an Advertising Agency*, 88–125, 254–306, chronicles the development of client services at N. W. Ayer. The names "Uneeda Biscuit" and "Karo Syrup" were created by H. N. McKinney of N. W. Ayer, "Yuban Coffee" and "Kelvinator" by Stanley Resor of J. Walter Thompson. See Hower, *History of an Advertising Agency*, 329. On Yuban see Strasser, *Satisfaction Guaranteed*, 139; on Kelvinator see *J. Walter Thompson News Letter*, July 18, 1916, 2, JWTA. For preempting a competitor, see William H. Armistead, "Mr. Armistead's Memo," 22–24, n.d., Series 19, Box 7, File 1, AC. For package design see Calkins, *Business of Advertising*, 166–71; and Franken and Larrabee, *Packages That Sell*. On the agencies' turn to corporate advertising and public relations, see Herbert N. Casson, "Big Business Has No Choice—It Must Advertise," *PI* 77, no. 8 (November 11, 1911): 17–20; Herbert N. Casson, "Advertising as the Olive Branch of Corporations," *PI* 77, no. 11 (December 14, 1911): 24–27; "Future of Corporation Advertising," *PI* 86, no. 4 (January 22, 1914): 186; Walsh, *Selling Forces*, 202–4; "SWIFT—A Food Service," *J. Walter Thompson News Letter*, August 27, 1925, 3, JWTA; Hower, *History of an Advertising Agency*, 322, 326; Marchand, "Fitful Career of Advocacy Advertising"; and Marchand, *Creating the Corporate Soul*.

21. John Lee Mahin, "Who Pays for the Advertising?" in Mahin, *Lectures on Advertising*, 7; Thomas P. Balmer, "The Evolution of Good Advertising," *PI* 71, no. 5 (May 4, 1910): 40.

22. See Leiss, Kline, and Jhally, *Social Communication in Advertising*; Marchand, *Advertising the American Dream*; Lears, *Fables of Abundance*, esp. 40–234; Lears, "Some Versions of

Fantasy"; and T. J. Jackson Lears, "From Salvation to Self-Realization: Advertising and the Therapeutic Roots of Consumer Culture, 1880–1930," in *Culture of Consumption*, ed. Fox and Lears, 1–38.

23. Laird, *Advertising Progress*; Lears, *Fables of Abundance*. See also Lears, "Packaging the Folk," 115–16; and Marchand, *Advertising the American Dream*, 1–16.

24. Joseph French Johnson, "Making People Want More—The Basis of Civilization," *PI* 111, no. 11 (June 10, 1920): 19. See also N. W. Ayer & Son, *Ayer Idea in Advertising*, 10–11; Calkins, *Business the Civilizer*, 18; French, *Art and Science of Advertising*, 87–88.

25. "Advertising as a Measure of Civilization," *PI* 1, no. 14 (February 1, 1889): 362; Balmer, *Science of Advertising*, 28. See also French, *Advertising*, 33–34.

26. Switzer, *Who Pays the Advertising Bills?*, n.p.

27. Johnson, "Making People Want More," 19. See also [N. W. Ayer & Son], *The American Scene* (Philadelphia, 1926), 3–5, N. W. Ayer Archives, New York, N.Y.; Bruce Barton, "Human Appeals in Advertising Copy," in *Masters of Advertising Copy*, ed. French, 66–67; and Calkins and Holden, *Modern Advertising*, 7.

28. George Sherman, "The Effect of Advertising upon Our Internal Economy," *PI* 57, no. 5 (October 31, 1906): 12.

29. For a definitive account of American-style consumer capital's advent in Europe, see De Grazia, *Irresistible Empire*.

30. "The Advertiser's Right to Be Heard," *PI* 74, no. 8 (February 23, 1911): 64; Eldridge, *Making Advertising Pay*, 12; "Advertising as a Mirror of National Progress," *PI* 134, no. 9 (March 4, 1926): 199; Bruce Barton, "Four Main Accomplishments of Modern Advertising," *PI* 149, no. 1 (October 3, 1929): 3–6, 179. See also "Back Home," *Wedge* 32, no. 4 (1932): 9, BBDO; and "They Beat the Motor Car with Sticks," N. W. Ayer House Ad, House Ad Files, Ayer Archives.

31. Advertisers were hardly anthropologists in our accepted sense of the term, but they drew on popular, anthropologically informed concepts, extending at least to the Enlightenment, for their views on "primitive" peoples and the evolution of civilization. For an intellectual history of how similar views were themselves challenged within anthropology, see Stocking, *Race, Culture, and Evolution*, 73–74, 88, 110–32; Stocking, *Romantic Motives*; and Baker, *From Savage to Negro*. For the increased awareness of "civilization" in the realm of the educated middle class, see "Culture and Civilization," in Susman, *Culture as History*, 105–21; Bederman, *Manliness and Civilization*; and Hegeman, *Patterns for America*.

32. O'Sullivan ad, *Munsey's Magazine*, April 1908, Advertising Section, n.p.

33. Will B. Wilder, "A World without Advertising," *Fame* 16, no. 3 (March 1907): 51.

34. Barton, "Advertising as an Incentive to Human Progress," 77. For a similar sentiment see Johnson, "Making People Want More," 19.

35. Barton is further discussed in "Culture Heroes: Ford, Barton, Ruth," in Susman, *Culture as History*, 122–49; Lears, "From Salvation to Self-Realization," 30–37; and Ribuffo, "Jesus Christ as Business Statesman." Anthropologists' use of history to demarcate contemporary peoples as "primitive" is discussed in Fabian, *Time and the Other*; and Marcus and Fischer, *Anthropology as Cultural Critique*, 77–110.

36. For a discussion of Barton in this context, see Marchand, *Creating the Corporate Soul*, 130–63; and Susman, *Culture as History*, 122–31.

37. Marchand, *Advertising the American Dream*, emphasizes how advertisers, along with

other professionals, came to view their work as a benign, if at times deceptive, leadership; that is, for the consumer's welfare, advertisers oversimplified arguments or indulged in hyperbole or generalizations to convince consumers.

38. *The J. Walter Thompson Book* (New York, 1909), quoted in Lears, "Packaging the Folk," 116; James Webb Young, Lectures, no. 1 (1934), 3, JWTA; William Burgess Nesbitt, "Advertising the Energizer," *Fame* 19, no. 10 (October 1910): 219; Lichtenberg and Barton, *Advertising Campaigns*, 325.

39. Allen, *Advertising as a Vocation*, 2–3. See also "A Big Idea," *PI* 76, no. 1 (July 6, 1911): 67; and Edward Mott Wooley, "How Advertising Can Overcome Prejudice," *PI* 110, no. 2 (April 8, 1920): 3.

40. "The Development of Consumer-Individuality," *PI* 74, no. 4 (January 26, 1911): 60; "Change Is Upon Us," in *12 More Advertisements* (Philadelphia, 1921), n.p., Ayer Archives; Will B. Wilder, "The Great Modern Educator," *Fame* 20, no. 7 (July 1911): 155; "A Big Idea," 67. See also Higham, *Scientific Distribution*, 53; *PI* 70, no. 6 (February 9, 1910): 47; and *J. Walter Thompson News Letter*, June 27, 1916, 1, JWTA.

41. Felix Orman, "What Are the Principles Underlying Your Copy Appeal?" *PI* 88, no. 4 (July 23, 1914): 47–56. See also "Education," in N. W. Ayer & Son, *12 Advertisements* (Philadelphia, 1919), n.p., Ayer Archives.

42. "Universality of Advertising," in N. W. Ayer & Son, *Ayer Idea in Advertising*, 21.

43. J. George Frederick, "Introduction: The Story of Advertising Writing," in *Masters of Advertising Copy*, ed. Frederick, 31.

44. JWT staff meeting minutes, October 30, 1931, 2–3, RG 2, Box 4, JWTA; see also Robert T. Colwell, "The Program as an Advertisement," in O'Neill, *Advertising Agency Looks at Radio*, 24.

45. French, *Advertising*, 102.

46. See Strasser, *Satisfaction Guaranteed*, 138–61. The most detailed histories of advertising's role in the origins of marketing are Wells, "Remapping America"; Kreshel, "Toward a Cultural History of Advertising Research"; and Ward, "Tracking the Culture of Consumption." For business-centered, canonical accounts of marketing, which narrate this history of selling with the production of customers, see Tedlow, *New and Improved*; Riggs, *Encyclopedia of Major Marketing Campaigns*; and Hotchkiss, *Milestones of Marketing*. On the ever-changing composition of markets, see Roger W. Babson, "Roger Babson Looks at Advertising," *PI* 147, no. 12 (June 20, 1929): 17–20; and Bruce Barton, "Which Knew Not Joseph," *Wedge*, 1954, BBDO.

47. French, *Advertising*, 102–4; Calkins, *Business of Advertising*, 335; Phelps, *Our Biggest Customer*.

48. Scott, *Theory of Advertising*, 204.

49. This particular example is drawn from Starch, *Buying Power of the American Market*, 5, but the basics of income classification remained constant from the World War I era, when the first attempts were made to delineate family incomes as a basis for determining potential markets, through World War II.

50. See John C. Graham, "Simplicity of Language," *PI* 14, no. 11 (March 11, 1896): 8; "Face to Face with Humanity," *Judicious Advertising* 1, no. 4 (February 1903); Mahin, *Advertising*; Hopkins, *My Life in Advertising*; "Selling from the Top Down," Book 115 [Hills Bros.], AC; MacManus, *Sword Arm of Business*; Cherington, *Consumer Looks at Advertising*; JWT

Representatives' Meeting, October 22, 1927, 2–3, RG 2, JWTA; "Memo from Ben Duffy to A. D. Chiquoine," July 31, 1931, Ethyl Gasoline, Client Data Book, Vol. 2, pp. 4–6, BBDO; James Webb Young, Lectures, no. 1 (1934), 3, JWTA.

51. Oscar Hertzberg, "Human Nature as a Factor in Advertising," *PI* 13, no. 14 (October 2, 1895): 3; Saunders Norvell, " 'Us Morons' as Seen Through an Advertiser's Eyes," *PI* 125, no. 13 (September 27, 1923): 53.

52. Marchand, *Advertising the American Dream*, 25–87.

53. "Losing the Grasp of One's Audience," *PI* 89, no. 6 (November 5, 1914): 73.

54. Wallace Boren, "Good Taste in Advertising Copy," *JWT Forum*, January 7, 1936, 6, RG 2, Box 7, File 1, JWTA; "What Groucho Says," *PI* 153, no. 3 (October 16, 1930): 81. See also Lears, *Fables of Abundance*, 154, 61, 229–33.

55. Yerkes, *Psychological Examining in the United States Army*; Yerkes, "Report of the Psychology Committee of the National Research Council"; Yerkes, Bridges, and Hardwick, *Point Scale for Measuring Mental Ability*; and Yoakum and Yerkes, *Army Mental Tests*. Terman, *Measurement of Intelligence*, is an apology for intelligence testing by the leader of the American movement. McDougall, *Is America Safe for Democracy?*, is a prominent psychologist's statement connecting the test results, immigration, and the dangers of democracy; see also Purcell, *Crisis of Democratic Theory*, 97–101. "The Lippmann-Terman Debate," in *IQ Controversy*, ed. Block and Dworkin, 4–44, contains the prominent public controversy between political columnist Walter Lippmann and testing advocate Lewis Terman over the sociological, racial, and political implications of the test results. See also James Reed, "Robert M. Yerkes and the Mental Testing Movement," in *Psychological Testing and American Society*, ed. Sokal, 75–94; Henry L. Minton, "Lewis M. Terman and Mental Testing: In Search of the Democratic Ideal," in *Psychological Testing and American Society*, ed. Sokal, 95–112; Minton, *Lewis M. Terman*; and Chapman, *Schools as Sorters*.

56. Howard Henderson, "Behind the Doorbell," *J. Walter Thompson News Bulletin* 101 (August 1923): 5–9, is a brief expository justification for door-to-door surveys.

57. Charles Daniel Frey Company, "In the Hollow of Her Hand," *Fortune*, February 1930, 139.

58. James H. Collins, "The Eternal Feminine," *PI* 35, no. 13 (June 26, 1901): 3.

59. This figure was consistently quoted by the industry from the late nineteenth century through World War II, at times ranging from 70 percent to as much as 90 percent. See, for example, E. James Gibson, "Position," *PI* 20, no. 2 (July 14, 1897): 3; Nellie Ballard, "Advertising as a Woman Sees It," *Judicious Advertising* 4, no. 6 (April 1906): 51; "Advertising to Women," *Fame* 16, no. 7 (June 1907): 134; G. Albert Strauss, "Women's Magazines and their Growing Power," *PI* 67, no. 10 (June 9, 1909): 40; S. Roland Hall, "Reaching the Hearts and Purses of Women," *PI* 78, no. 6 (February 8, 1912): 62–65; W. W. Garison, "When Women's Influence Closes the Sale," *PI* 81, no. 8 (November 21, 1912): 40–41; Butterick Publishing Company, *Mrs. John Doe*; Matlack and Matlack, "Feminine Appeal in Advertising"; E. B. Weiss, "Who Buys Your Merchandise?" *Printers' Ink Monthly* 7, no. 7 (August 1923): 38–40; Kyrk, *Consumption of Wealth*; Purcell, "Why Otherwise Good Copy Fails in the Eyes of Women—the Eighty-Five Percent Buyers," 162–64; " 'I Spend Half My Life in the Kitchen,' " *J. Walter Thompson News Bulletin* 111 (January 1925): 9–14; Naether, *Advertising to Women*; "Why Women Read Advertisements," in Durstine, *This Advertising Business*, 25–42; Frederick, *Selling Mrs. Consumer*; "Southern Cooking," in N. W. Ayer &

Son, *12 Advertisements, 1929* (Philadelphia, 1929), n.p., Series 14, Box 20, File 5, AC; "To Her Ladyship!" *SEP*, February 22, 1933, 59; and Arthur Hirose, "To the Ladies!" *Advertising and Selling*, August 13, 1936, 33, 74. The idea that women were the primary or sole purchasers was tested in specific campaigns and was often modified to reflect the more likely circumstances of many middle-class homes, where men were often involved in purchase decisions even if women were delegated the actual labor of buying. See "Johns-Manville Tests Out an Appeal to Women," *PI* 124, no. 12 (September 20, 1923): 57.

60. Marchand, *Advertising the American Dream*, 66.

61. For the influence of advertising on the rise of a commercial culture typified by gender prescriptions, see Garvey, *Adman in the Parlor*; Peiss, *Hope in a Jar*; Scanlon, *Inarticulate Longings*; Ohmann, *Selling Culture*; Kitch, *Girl on the Magazine Cover*; Loeb, *Consuming Angels*; and De Grazia and Furlough, *Sex of Things*. For the mid-twentieth century see Walker, *Shaping Our Mothers' World*.

62. See Calkins, *Business of Advertising*, 335, for one of few open admissions that, as men, advertisers were at a disadvantage in writing to women.

63. Earnest Elmo Calkins, "The New Consumption Engineer and the Artist," in *Philosophy of Production*, ed. Frederick, 110.

64. Scott, *Theory of Advertising*. Scott originally published his ideas in 1902 and 1903 in *Mahin's Magazine*, a Chicago advertising journal. Scott's career is discussed in Friedman, *Birth of a Salesman*, 172–89; Jacobson, *Scott of Northwestern*; and Lynch, "Walter Dill Scott."

65. Scott, *Psychology of Advertising*, 82–83. See also Kuna, "Psychology of Advertising," 158–69, 202–11; and Kuna, "Concept of Suggestion."

66. Daniel Day Walton Jr., "Advertising to Men," *Mahin's Magazine* 1, no. 12 (March 1903): 23.

67. Oscar Herzberg, "Why Women Read Advertisements," *Mahin's Magazine* 2, no. 1 (April 1903): 20–21; Hall, "Reaching the Hearts and Purses of Women," 64; "The Relations of the Public to a Large Store," *Judicious Advertising* 6, no. 11 (September 1908): 24; Garvey, *Adman in the Parlor*, 135–83.

68. Scott, *Theory of Advertising*, 67; Balmer, *Science of Advertising*, 8–9; MacManus, *Sword Arm of Business*, 138–39; Lears, "Some Versions of Fantasy," 375–82.

69. [Kennedy], *Book of Advertising Tests* (Chicago, 1911), 44–45; Lasker, *Lasker Story*, 23–44, 81–86; Hopkins, *Scientific Advertising*; Hopkins, *My Life in Advertising*. See also Fox, *Mirror Makers*, 40–63.

70. Nellie A. Ballard, "Advertising as a Woman Sees It," *Judicious Advertising* 4, no. 6 (April 1906): 52; D. Herbert Moore, "The Ad That Leads Woman to Buy," *Judicious Advertising* 3, no. 7 (May 1905): 30.

71. Frederick, *Selling Mrs. Consumer*, 21. Frederick had been a student of Walter Dill Scott's at Northwestern University.

72. "A Woman's Idea of Advertisements," *Judicious Advertising* 6, no. 12 (October 1908): 44. See also W. W. Hudson, "The Skillful 'Class' Appeal to Influence Women," *PI* 80, no. 4 (July 25, 1912): 64.

73. Woodward, *Through Many Windows*, 205–6.

74. See Naether, *Advertising to Women*; and Frederick, *Selling Mrs. Consumer*, 43–53.

75. "What Women Want in Ads," *PI* 78, no. 3 (January 18, 1912): 120; Charles R. Wiers, "Handling of Inquiries from Women," *PI* 77, no. 10 (December 7, 1911): 57; W. Livingston

Larned, "Why Some Copy Strikes Women as a Joke," *PI* 86, no. 10 (March 5, 1914): 68–70; Frances Maule, "The 'Woman Appeal,'" *J. Walter Thompson News Bulletin* 105 (January 1924): 1–8; Sara Hamilton Birchall, "The Strong-Armed Princess," *Advertising and Selling Fortnightly* 2, no. 5 (January 2, 1924): 19–21; Woodward, *Through Many Windows*, 230–31.

76. William Thompson, "The Human Nature Element in Advertising," *PI* 69, no. 12 (December 22, 1909): 11; John S. Grey, "The Store and the Lady: A Suggestion," *PI* 22, no. 7 (February 16, 1898): 34; Calkins, *Business of Advertising*, 335; Sara Hamilton Birchall, "Ladies—Or 'Cuties?'" *Advertising and Selling Fortnightly* 7, no. 1 (May 5, 1926): 32, 90, 92.

77. As early as 1903 Kate Griswold devoted an issue to profiling women in all phases of the business and not simply in writing for so-called women's products: *Profitable Advertising* 12, no. 9 (February 1903): 711–65. See also Clair and Dignam, *Advertising Careers for Women*. For some personal reminiscences see Fitz-Gibbon, *Macy's, Gimbel's and Me*; and Woodward, *Through Many Windows*. There is no adequate history of women in advertising, but see, for a beginning, Fox, *Mirror Makers*, 79–94; and Marchand, *Advertising the American Dream*, 33–35.

78. For the Thompson women's department, see Jennifer Scanlon, "Advertising Women: The J. Walter Thompson Women's Editorial Department," in *Gender and Consumer Culture Reader*, ed. Scanlon, 201–25. Indeed, Thompson's fortunes were staked on clients' selling a variety of low unit price, name-brand articles—household goods, toiletries, and cosmetics—often identified with women. The agency was able to remain the leading agency in the 1930s largely because its clients weathered the Depression better than those producing durable goods and more expensive consumer items. For advertising women in radio, see Fox, *Mirror Makers*, 158–62; and Hilmes, *Radio Voices*, 144–46.

79. *LHJ* 37, no. 3 (March 1920): 38 (quotation); "Why Not Help Him 'Shop'?" *LHJ* 37, no. 2 (February 1920): 48; Cannon Towels, "That sixth sense which tells you 'these are finer towels,'" Cannon Client File (1928), Ayer Archives.

80. For some examples see "But Why Tetley's? All Teas Are Practically the—," Book 654 (1921), AC; *LHJ* 44, no. 4 (April 1927): 130 [Paige Automobiles]; Ruth Leigh, "Over-Feminizing the Feminine Appeal," *PI* 129, no. 11 (December 11, 1924): 99–102; and "'Mrs. Jones, Mrs. Jones, Paging Mrs. Jones,'" Cannon Towel Ads, Ayer Archives.

81. Marian Hertha Clarke, "A Little Light on That Dark Subject—Woman," *PI* 137, no. 7 (November 18, 1926): 97–101; James H. Collins, "All About Women—for Advertisers Only," *PI* 134, no. 7 (February 18, 1926): 3–6.

82. Advertisers' use of themes of women's political rights to legitimize and depict consumption is discussed in chapter 2.

83. Mildred Holmes, "Housewives Write the Copy," *J. Walter Thompson News Bulletin* 98 (May 1923): 9; Hopkins, *My Life in Advertising*, 116.

84. Louise Taylor Davis, "What a Housewife Wants in Copy," *Printers' Ink Monthly* 13, no. 2 (February 1924): 56; Lois Ardery, "She Wants It But She Doesn't Know It—Yet!" *J. Walter Thompson News Bulletin* 110 (December 1924): 18–21; Dorothy Dwight Townsend, "Mrs. Wilkes Reads the Ladies' Home Journal," *J. Walter Thompson News Bulletin* 99 (June 1923): 1–5. See also Hotchkiss and Franken, *Leadership of Advertised Brands*.

85. Frederick, *New Housekeeping*; Frederick, *Household Engineering*; Bruére and Bruére, *Increasing Home Efficiency*; Gilbreth, *Homemaker and Her Job*. See also Horowitz, *Morality of Spending*, 85–108; Strasser, *Never Done*, 212–20; and Weigley, "It Might Have Been Eu-

thenics." For evaluations of efficiency and mass production on different aspects of American culture, see Tichi, *Shifting Gears*, 75–96; Hounshell, *From the American System to Mass Production*, 303–30; Banta, *Taylored Lives*; and Brown, *Corporate Eye*.

86. *SEP*, February 2, 1923, 116 [Florence]; *LHJ* 38, no. 10 (October 1921): 69 [Nepanee]; see also Western Electric, "Why Have Two Standards of Efficiency?" Book 548 (1916), AC.

87. *SEP*, February 17, 1912, 59; *SEP*, September 7, 1912, 64; *SEP*, October 24, 1914; *SEP*, March 23, 1918, 78–79; *LHJ* 33, no. 5 (May 1916): 74.

88. *SEP*, November 30, 1918, 72 [Hoosier]; *American Magazine*, September 1925, 84 [Hoover]; *SEP*, September 21, 1912, 33 [Campbell's].

89. *SEP*, August 28, 1920, 44; *PI* 80, no. 4 (July 25, 1912): 19; "A Trade Journal for Women," *PI* 79, no. 4 (April 25, 1912): 98; "The First Factory," *PI* 80, no. 4 (July 25, 1912): 19; Walsh, *Selling Forces*, 230.

90. Garrett K. Brown, "An Adventure in Housekeeping," *PI* 111, no. 12 (June 17, 1920): 150, 153; Amos Bradbury, "The Home as a Copy Laboratory," *PI* 138, no. 1 (January 6, 1927): 93–104.

91. "Lorelei," in Ruthrauff and Ryan, *18 Shorts on Advertising*, 25; C. Foster Browning, "America's Alarm Clock of Ambition," *PI* 127, no. 10 (June 5, 1924): 105–6.

92. *SEP*, March 24, 1928, 53; Marchand, *Advertising the American Dream*, 169–71. Other examples of the general purchasing agent idea include *Literary Digest*, December 27, 1930, 33 [Ipana]; *American Magazine*, November 1927, 90 [Globe-Wernicke]; *American Magazine*, May 1932, 97 [Williams]; "Mrs. Evanston . . . 'G. M.,'" *PI* 134, no. 10 (June 3, 1926): 82–83 [Cincinnati Enquirer]; and Mary E. Matlack and William H. Matlack, "The Feminine Appeal in Advertising," *American Gas Journal*, October 16, 1922, 316–17. The industrial purchasing agent also provided the model for the intelligent consumer in the emerging consumer movement at the time; see chapter 5.

93. Frederick, *Selling Mrs. Consumer*, 336 (quotation); Christine M. Frederick, "American Woman: Gauge of Consumer Preference," *Advertising and Selling* 13, no. 10 (September 4, 1929): 36; Strasser, *Never Done*, 242–62.

94. On Piggly Wiggly see Strasser, *Satisfaction Guaranteed*, 248–49; Freeman, "Clarence Saunders"; Jones, *Piggly Wiggly Store Management*; and Lestico, *Building the Story of Piggly Wiggly*. See also Bowlby, *Carried Away*; Longstreth, *The Drive-In, the Supermarket, and the Transformation of Commercial Space*; Seth and Randall, *Grocers*, which has an international perspective on the growth of supermarkets and self-service; and Tedlow, *New and Improved*, 182–258.

95. *SEP*, March 10, 1928, 87; *SEP*, April 7, 1928, 111; *GH* 136, no. 5 (May 1928): 194; *GH* 136, no. 2 (February 1928): 164.

96. Saunders, *Piggly Wiggly*; Saunders, *National Standard for Piggly Wiggly Store Conduct and Maintenance*; Jones, *Piggly Wiggly Store Management*; Lestico, *Building the Story of Piggly Wiggly*.

97. Leach, "Transformations in a Culture of Consumption."

98. Carroll, *None of Your Business*, ix.

99. Douglas, *Listening In*, 16. For the struggle over commercialization, see McChesney, *Telecommunications, Mass Media, and Democracy*; and Newman, *Radio Active*.

100. James True, "What the Public Thinks About Advertising over the Radio," *PI* 131, no. 1 (April 2, 1925): 114–15, 120; Smulyan, *Selling Radio*, 125–53. See also "Radio Fans Vote

on Broadcast Advertising," *PI* 134, no. 1 (January 7, 1926): 52; "Radio Listeners Still Protest against Broadcast Advertising," *PI* 135, no. 6 (May 6, 1926): 137–44; "Freedom for Radio Listeners," *PI* 133, no. 10 (December 3, 1925): 178; and "A Leader or a Nurse?" *PI* 131, no. 1 (April 2, 1925): 176.

101. "Public Resistance Is Reducing Direct Advertising by Radio," *PI* 140, no. 3 (July 21, 1927): 42.

102. True, "What the Public Thinks About Advertising over the Radio," 120; Harris, *Microphone Memoirs*, 39.

103. On publicity see "Broadcasting Doesn't Belong in Advertising Account," *PI* 132, no. 6 (August 6, 1925): 125–28; "Radio as an Advertising Medium," *PI* 134, no. 12 (March 25, 1926): 152; and E. C. Barroll, "As the Radio Fan Sees It," *PI* 136, no. 2 (July 8, 1926): 144. On the issue of gaining an accurate accounting of radio circulation, see "The Little Schoolmaster's Classroom," *PI* 130, no. 10 (March 5, 1925): 188. The general business caution and skepticism regarding radio advertising are reflected in Harry P. Bridge Jr., "If You Are Thinking of Broadcasting," *PI* 135, no. 1 (April 1, 1926): 133–40; and most emphatically in Harry Merrill Hitchcock, "How to Sell Advertising over the Radio—in One Hard Lesson," *PI* 139, no. 4 (April 28, 1927): 17–20. See also Smulyan, *Selling Radio*, 2–3, 68.

104. Brown, "Broadcast Advertising"; Roy S. Durstine, "Why Advertising Agencies Should Tackle Radio Broadcasting," *PI* 147, no. 10 (June 6, 1929): 113–21; Roy S. Durstine, "Audible Advertising," in *Radio and Its Future*, ed. Codel, 52–53. See also Dunlap, *Advertising by Radio*; Arnold, *Broadcast Advertising*, 110–27; O'Neill, *Advertising Agency Looks at Radio*; Smulyan, *Selling Radio*, 52–64; also Ely, *Adventures of Amos 'n' Andy*, 47–96.

105. By July 1928, these major agencies had established radio bureaus: N. W. Ayer; Lord & Thomas and Logan; J. Walter Thompson; Lennen & Mitchell; Young and Rubicam; Barton, Durstine and Osborne; George Batten Company; Erwin-Wasey; Calkins and Holden; Frank Seaman; and Aitken-Kennett; H. K. McCann; Campbell-Ewald; Blackman; Erickson; and Ruthrauff and Ryan agencies were to follow within the next three years. See minutes of JWT Representatives' Meeting, July 11, 1928, 3, RG 2, Box 1, JWTA. These agencies stood among the top twenty agencies in business volume in 1927. Marchand, *Advertising the American Dream*, 32–33. By 1934 fifty different agencies had radio departments in New York and Chicago, with nearly forty others scattered elsewhere throughout the country; agencies at that time had just begun to produce a significant portion of programming in Hollywood. West, *So-o-o-o You're Going on the Air!* 205–9; Young and Rubicam, "Young and Rubicam and Broadcast Advertising: Growing Up Together" (1987), 12–15, typescript, in author's possession.

106. Not surprisingly, these products were everyday, low-price staples as opposed to durable goods or luxury items. Lord & Thomas and Logan, "Proving the Advertising Value of Broadcasting," *PI* 147, no. 8 (May 23, 1929): 82–83; JWT Representatives' Meeting, April 3, 1929, 4, RG 2, Box 1, JWTA; Arnold, *Broadcast Advertising*, 114–19. Advertiser William Benton recalled Pepsodent's success with *Amos 'n' Andy* in Terkel, *Hard Times*, 80. On Ipana see NBC, *Improving the Smiles of a Nation!* in NBC Pamphlet File, LAB; and Barnouw, *Tower in Babel*, 237–39. An early and extensive study of radio as merchandising aid is Elder, *Does Radio Sell Goods?*

107. JWT Representatives' Meeting, April 16, 1930, 3, RG 2, Box 2, JWTA. See also N. W.

Ayer & Son, "What about Radio?" (1931), manuscript, Baker Library, Harvard Business School, Boston, Mass.

108. JWT Representatives' Meeting, February 16, 1928, 8, RG 2, Box 1, JWTA. In a survey for NBC, one researcher estimated that some 9.6 million families owned 11,032,855 radios by 1929 (Starch, *Study of Radio Broadcasting*). See also JWT Representatives' Meeting, April 10, 1929, 1, RG 2, Box 1, JWTA; and "Forty Per Cent of Country's Homes Now Have Radios," *Broadcast Advertising* 2, no. 4 (January 1930): 9.

109. E. P. H. James, "Radio as an Advertising Medium," May 1, 1940, *NBC Discussion Group Talks*, Vol. 2, p. 4, typescript, NBC Pamphlet File, LAB.

110. Buchler and Maloney, *You Sell with Your Voice*, 5, 7, discusses the element of personal contact with consumers as crucial to sales.

111. For explorations of the development of emotional appeals in ad copy, see Lears, "Some Versions of Fantasy"; and Marchand, *Advertising the American Dream*, 13–16, 22–25.

112. Ralph McKinley, "The Radio Boys Know a Thing or Two about Copy," *Advertising and Selling* 15, no. 5 (July 9, 1930): 24. While radio restored a semblance of personal relationship to the sales message, it is important to emphasize that it could not restore actual face-to-face relations. Advertisers remained distant and isolated from their audiences.

113. Frank Libbey Blanchard, "Build Prestige with Broadcasting," *Broadcast Advertising* 2, no. 5 (February 1930): 20; Don E. Gilman, "Radio Broadcasting as an Aid to Distribution," *Broadcast Advertising* 2, no. 1 (October 1929): 25; Hettinger, *Decade of Radio Advertising*, 36. See also Mark O'Dea, "Kisses from Venus," *PI* 175, no. 5 (April 30, 1936): 54.

114. JWT Representatives' Meeting, July 8, 1930, 2, RG 2, Box 2, JWTA.

115. See JWT Creative Staff Meeting, December 21, 1932, 2, RG 2, Box 5, JWTA. Dixon, *Radio Writing*, 6, discusses the ephemeral and inferior quality of radio writing.

116. J. T. W. Martin, "Copy for the Ear," in O'Neill, *Advertising Agency Looks at Radio*, 74.

117. Stanton, *Memory for Advertising Copy*; Lumley, *Measurement in Radio*.

118. Cantril and Allport, *Psychology of Radio*, 17–18; Hettinger, *Decade of Radio Advertising*, 31–32. See also H. C. Goodwin, "Random Thoughts on Radio," *Broadcast Advertising* 3, no. 10 (January 1931): 40; Dunlap, *Radio in Advertising*, 27–55; and Lazarsfeld, *Radio and the Printed Page*.

119. [Kesten], *You Do What You're Told!* 6–7.

120. Loviglio, *Radio's Intimate Public*.

121. Razlogova, "Voice of the Listener," offers and important, sophisticated account of the relationship of broadcasters and the radio audience.

122. John Eugene Hasty, "The Emotional Kick—Radio's Priceless Ingredient," *PI* 157, no. 8 (November 19, 1931): 27; Hubbell Robinson, "What the Radio Audience Wants," in O'Neill, *Advertising Agency Looks at Radio*, 44–45. On Block see Passman, *Deejays*, 13, 47–48; [Gordon], *WNEW*. Merton, *Mass Persuasion*, is a famous study of the phenomenon of personalization. See also Douglas, *Listening In*, 22–39; and Razlogova, "Voice of the Listener."

123. Olive Sharman, "Is There Really Too Much Advertising on the Air?" *Broadcast Advertising* 5, no. 1 (April 1932), 10–11; see also Dunlap, *Advertising by Radio*, 106–7; Vallee, *Vagabond Dreams*, 117–18; Dunlap, *Radio in Advertising*, 100; Harris, *Microphone Memoirs*; Cullinan, *Pardon My Accent*; [Field], *Story of Cheerio*; and Cantril and Allport, *Psychology of Radio*, 18.

124. See Goode, *What about Radio?* 22; Dunlap, *Radio in Advertising*, 166–67; Howard Angus, "A Discussion of Radio Talent," *Broadcast Advertising* 4, no. 3 (June 1931): 36; and Jarvis Wren, "The Musical Program vs. Dramatic Radio Program," *Advertising and Selling* 15, no. 7 (August 6, 1930): 27, 46. Harrison Holloway described actual listening in "typical" homes: "In one home a group is playing bridge. In another, the family, quite oblivious to radio, is engrossed in reading. In still another a few friends are engaged in social talk that is hardly conducive to radio attentiveness." Holloway, "You Can't Make All of the People Listen All of the Time, But You Can Try," *Broadcast Advertising* 3, no. 2 (May 1930): 9.

125. Goode, *What about Radio?*, 79; Hasty, "Emotional Kick," 26; NBC, *Let's Look at Radio Together*, 6; James, "Radio as an Advertising Medium," 6. See also William S. Paley, "Radio and Entertainment," in *Radio and Its Future*, ed. Codel, 63; E. W. Donaldson, "How to Dramatize Radio Commercial," *Printers' Ink Monthly* 30, no. 5 (May 1935): 36.

126. Frank A. Arnold, "High Spots in Radio Broadcasting Techniques," *Broadcast Advertising* 1, no. 2 (May 1929): 7. Other examples of this trope include Betty Parker, "Women in Radio Advertising," in Clair and Dignam, *Advertising Careers for Women*, 224–25; H. Calvin Kuhl, "The Grim Reber," (1971), 1, typescript, "H. Calvin Kuhl—Speeches and Writings" File, RG 3, JWTA; Dixon, *Radio Writing*, ix; Herschell Hart, "The Commercial Announcement," *Broadcast Advertising* 5, no. 6 (September 1932): 10; Martin A. North, "Don't Use All of Your Showmanship in Your Program," *Broadcast Advertising* 4, no. 12 (March 1932): 13.

127. NBC, *Let's Look at Radio Together*, 2.

128. Martin, "Copy for the Ear," 72.

129. Dunlap, *Advertising by Radio*, 17 (quotation); New York News, *Tell It to Sweeney!*; CBS, *4 Hours and 28 Minutes by the Kitchen Clock*, CBS Pamphlet File, LAB; Dunlap, *Radio in Advertising*, 75; Sharman, "Is There Really Too Much Advertising," 11, 29.

130. Goode, *What about Radio?* 22.

131. Robert H. Rankin, "Broadcasting in America," *Broadcast Advertising* 1, no. 6 (September 1929): 22; NBC, *35 Hours a Day!* NBC Pamphlet File, LAB; JWT Group Meeting, July 8, 1930, 3, RG 2, Box 2, JWTA; Stanton, "Critique of Present Methods," 20. Stanton's research led him into the broadcasting business, where he rose to become president of CBS.

132. JWT Representatives' Meeting, February 16, 1928, RG 2, Box 1, JWTA; JWT Group Meeting, April 16, 1930, 4–5, RG 2, Box 2, JWTA (emphasis added). See also Dunlap, *Radio in Advertising*, 92–104; Vallee, *Vagabond Dreams*, 115, 117–19; and [CBS], *Two Letters That Took Ten Years to Write*, CBS Pamphlet File, LAB.

133. Harlow P. Roberts, "The Radio Audience," *Broadcast Advertising* 5, no. 1 (April 1932): 36.

134. Showalter Lynch, "The Cinderella of Broadcasting, Continuity, Is Paging the Fairy Prince," *Broadcast Advertising* 3, no. 10 (January 1931): 30.

135. Carroll, *None of Your Business*, 33; JWT Representatives' Meeting, April 3, 1929, 5, RG 2, Box 1, JWTA; Bertha Brainard, "The Commercial Program Division," November 22, 1939, *NBC Discussion Group Talks, 1939–1940*, Vol. 1, p. 17, typescript, NBC Pamphlet File, LAB; Hettinger and Neff, *Practical Radio Advertising*, 111.

136. JWT Creative Staff Meeting, December 21, 1932, 7, RG 2, Box 5, JWTA; Carroll, *None of Your Business*, 33. For conflict between classical music and jazz advocates, see "Jazz

Music Is Preferred by Listeners, Stations Report," *Broadcast Advertising* 4, no. 1 (April 1931): 7; Harris, *Microphone Memoirs*, 66, 92–93, 95–98; and Smulyan, *Selling Radio*, 96–97. For the class dimensions of the tensions of lowbrow and highbrow, see Levine, *Highbrow/Lowbrow*. Some clients maintained considerable control over programming decisions, even at the expense of ratings or popularity: see Carroll, *None of Your Business*, ix. American Tobacco president George Washington Hill, a client with lowbrow tastes, was perhaps the most celebrated for his autocratic control of his broadcast *Lucky Strike Hit Parade*. For a thinly fictionalized account, see Wakeman, *Hucksters*.

137. Goode, *What about Radio?* 18.

138. Marchand, *Advertising the American Dream*, 66–87.

139. William L. Day, "Copy," JWT Staff Meeting, February 17, 1931, 3, RG 2, Box 3, JWTA.

140. Hettinger and Neff, *Practical Radio Advertising*, 113.

141. Roy S. Durstine, "Radio Advertising's Future in the United States," *PI* 170, no. 4 (January 24, 1935): 42. See also Dorothy Barstow, "How to Present Your Commercial Announcement," in O'Neill, *Advertising Agency Looks at Radio*, 82; and Hasty, "Emotional Kick," 28.

142. Martin, "Copy for the Ear," 71; see also Sharman, "Is There Really Too Much Advertising," 11, 29.

143. JWT Staff Meeting, June 16, 1931, 8, RG 2, Box 4, JWTA; Durstine, "Radio Advertising's Future," 42.

144. Marchand, *Advertising the American Dream*, 88–116.

145. Cantril and Allport, *Psychology of Radio*. 20. For a dissenting, if lonely, opinion see Goode, *What about Radio?* 23–24.

146. See, for example, Margaret Cuthbert, "Women and Radio," in NBC, *Colonel's Lady an' Judy O'Grady*, 1.

147. [CBS], *Ears and Incomes*, 4.

CHAPTER TWO

1. Bruce Barton, "I Believe," *Wedge* 30, no. 13 (1930): n.p., BBDO.

2. Book 508 (1926), AC.

3. Frank, *Buy American!*

4. I have outlined the advertisers' vision of citizenship in "Consumption and Citizenship."

5. Chambers, *Tyranny of Change*, is a standard account of the Progressive Era that emphasizes the expansion of democracy along these lines.

6. Lippmann, *Public Opinion*, 230, 195–97; Steel, *Walter Lippmann and the American Century*, 171–85. See Purcell, *Crisis of Democratic Theory*, esp. 104–7, for a definitive intellectual history of the challenges to Jeffersonian ideals; my overall account follows Purcell's. John Dewey assailed this description of the incompetent citizen most formally in *The Public and Its Problems*. Their debate is discussed by Carey, *Communication as Culture*, 74–88; and Westbrook, *John Dewey and American Democracy*, 293–318.

7. de Tarde, *Underground Man*; de Tarde, *Social Laws*; Le Bon, *The Crowd*.

8. Park, *The Crowd and the Public*; Lee, *Crowds*; Leach, "Mastering the Crowd."

9. Cooley, *Social Organization*; Cooley, *Human Nature and the Social Order*; Mead, *Mind, Self, and Society*, 135–226; Mead, *On Social Psychology*, 19–42. See also Fleming, "Attitude"; and Bellomy, "Social Darwinism Reconsidered."

10. See Bourne, "Trans-National America"; "The Sahara of the Bozart" and "The Cerebral Mime" in Mencken, *Prejudices*, 69–83; and Patten, *Product and Climax*.

11. See Brantlinger, *Bread and Circuses*, esp. 154–277; Gorman, *Left Intellectuals and Popular Culture*; Blake, *Beloved Community*, 268–77; Levine, *Highbrow/Lowbrow*; and Kammen, *American Culture, American Tastes*.

12. Brown, "Professional Language," 38; Brown, *Definition of a Profession*.

13. "Introduction: The Story of Advertising Writing," in Frederick, *Masters of Advertising Copy*, 29.

14. Bruce Barton, "I Believe," *Wedge* 30, no. 13 (1930): n.p., BBDO.

15. Agnew, *Worlds Apart*; Hirschman, *Passions and the Interests*. Bourdieu, *Language and Symbolic Power*, not only notes the connection but then also systematically analyzes political decision making and language in marketplace metaphors.

16. Edelman, *Symbolic Uses of Politics*, 1–43; Edelman, *Politics as Symbolic Action*; Edelman, *Political Language*.

17. Lears, *Fables of Abundance*; Marchand, *Advertising the American Dream*. See also Laird, *Advertising Progress*.

18. Lakoff and Johnson, *Metaphors We Live By*, 5, 7–9, 58–59; Black, *Models and Metaphors*; J. Christopher Crocker, "The Social Functions of Rhetorical Forms," in *Social Use of Metaphor*, ed. Sapir and Crocker, 34. My whole discussion of metaphor is influenced by Lakoff and Johnson.

19. Lakoff and Johnson, *Metaphors We Live By*, 10–13, 41–45, 77–81.

20. Ibid., 20, 22, 117; Geertz, *Interpretation of Cultures*; Fernandez, *Persuasions and Performances*, 1–57; Sapir and Crocker, *Social Use of Metaphor*.

21. Lakoff and Johnson, *Metaphors We Live By*, 233–35.

22. Edelman, *Political Language*, 3. See also Lakoff and Johnson, *Metaphors We Live By*, 236; Edelman, *Politics as Symbolic Action*, 68, 70–71; Edelman, *Symbolic Uses of Politics*, 121; and Crocker, "Social Functions of Rhetorical Forms," 35. Pierre Bourdieu makes a similar point on the relationship of language and politics in *Language and Symbolic Power*, 4–41, 166–70. See also Burke, *Language as Symbolic Action*.

23. Brown, "Professional Language," 41; Larson, *Rise of Professionalism*; Haber, *Quest for Authority and Honor*; Ortony, *Metaphor and Thought*; Robbins, *Secular Vocations*.

24. "Overlooking the Consumer," *PI* 92, no. 9 (September 2, 1915): 86; Frederick, *Selling Mrs. Consumer*, 322–23.

25. Book 177a (1928), Series 2, Box 52, AC.

26. Frederick, *Selling Mrs. Consumer*, 323.

27. Cherington, *Advertising as a Business Force*; H. M. Horr, "Is There a Cure for Substitution?" *PI* 74, no. 7 (February 16, 1911): 22–23; John G. Keplinger, "Would Specifications in Advertising Cure Substitution?" *PI* 76, no. 2 (July 13, 1911): 32–36.

28. Carl D. Spencer, "Putting Yourself in the Consumer's Place," *PI* 85, no. 13 (June 29, 1911): 6–8; Richard A. Foley, "As Viewed from the Buyer's Standpoint," *PI* 78, no. 4 (January 25, 1912): 76–77.

29. Balmer, *Science of Advertising*, 61, 64 (emphasis in original). Balmer was the son of

Thomas Balmer, a pioneer in magazine advertising, and he later went on to write the science fiction classic *When Worlds Collide* (New York, 1933).

30. Presbrey, *History and Development of Advertising*, 618.

31. Barton, "I Believe," n.p. Barton was not the first prominent advertiser to become intimately involved with the government. Albert Lasker of Lord & Thomas served in the Republican political campaign of 1920, as well as on the Government Shipping Board during World War I. Lasker, *Lasker Story*, 55–63; Gunther, *Taken at the Flood*; Morello, *Selling the President*. F. W. Ayer of Ayer and Stanley Resor of Thompson both built powerful ties to political parties and figures; see, for example, William H. Taft, "An Address," in N. W. Ayer & Son, *Book of the Golden Celebration*.

32. *SEP*, March 25, 1911, 42 [American Woolen]; *GH* 47, no. 2 (August 1908): n.p. ["The Housekeepers' Directory"] [Sapolio]; Advertising Section, *Century* 76, no. 4 (August 1908): 66 [Peter's]; *SEP*, April 6, 1929, cover II [Parker].

33. *Woman's Home Companion* 41, no. 11 (November 1914): cover III. Some political advertisements typically appeared at predictable moments in the calendar, such as near election day. But many did not, and, more important, these occasions allowed advertisers to restate their faith in consumption as a political and civic process. See also *Cosmopolitan*, September 1918, 138.

34. Chas. L. Benjamin, "Advertising a Presidential Candidate," *PI* 17, no. 4 (October 28, 1896): 3.

35. The process by which political elections were transformed into marketing campaigns has been explored in Jamieson, *Packaging the Presidency*; Robert B. Westbrook, "Politics as Consumption: Managing the Modern Election," in *Culture of Consumption*, ed. Fox and Lears, 143–73; and with specific respect to advertising executives in Bird, "Order, Efficiency, and Control"; and Allen, *Eisenhower and the Mass Media*.

36. Charles Austin Bates, "Department of Criticism," *PI* 16, no. 9 (August 26, 1896): 47; *PI* 16, no. 4 (July 22, 1896): 52; Roy Dickinson, "Selling the Silent Voter," *PI* 117, no. 11 (September 14, 1921): 110; McGerr, *Decline of Popular Politics*, 138–83.

37. "Tell It to Sweeney . . . Perpetual Candidate," *PI* 177, no. 4 (October 22, 1936): 22–23.

38. Liggett & Myers Tobacco Company, *Political Information for 1896* (St. Louis, 1896), 2, 7–8, 12–13, 16–17, Tobacco, Box 1, WCBA; Marchand, *Creating the Corporate Soul*, 26–41; Laird, *Advertising Progress*, 120–27.

39. Liggett & Myers Tobacco Company, *Official Political and Other Valuable Information, 1912* (St. Louis, 1912), 4, 16, 19–20 [unpaginated], Tobacco, Box 1, WCBA.

40. Liggett & Myers Tobacco Company, *Official Political and Other Valuable Information, 1916* (St. Louis, 1916), 3, 18 [unpaginated], Tobacco, Box 1, WCBA. For an interpretation of the advertising use of rural types like Velvet Joe in this period, see Lears, "Packaging the Folk."

41. N. W. Ayer & Son, *Better Business*, 12.

42. Curtis Publishing Company, *National Advertising*, 2; Felix Orman, "What Are the Principles Underlying Your Copy Appeal?" *PI* 88, no. 4 (July 23, 1914): 47; "Overlooking the Consumer," 86; Cherington, *Consumer Looks at Advertising*, 22–23. Advertising literature from 1900 onward reiterated the necessity of developing sympathy with the consumer's viewpoint as the key to effective advertising. Some pertinent examples include *Ad-Art* 5, no. 7 (January 31, 1903): 4; J. George Frederick, "First Principles of Good Advertis-

ing," *Judicious Advertising* 5, no. 2 (December 1906): 30; Carl D. Spencer, "Putting Yourself in the Consumer's Place," *PI* 75, no. 11 (June 29, 1911): 6–8; Richard A. Foley, "As Viewed from the Buyer's Standpoint," *PI* 78, no. 4 (January 25, 1912): 76–77; and An Ex-Copy Chief, "Get the Reader into the Picture," *PI* 117, no. 1 (October 6, 1921): 57–58.

43. Parlin quoted in Boorstin, *The Americans: The Democratic Experience*, 153; Lord & Thomas, " 'Giving Hostages to Caesar,' " *SEP*, April 22, 1911, 51. See also "Selling the Queen," *PI* 141, no. 4 (October 27, 1927): 156.

44. Bruce Barton, "Which Knew Not Joseph," *Wedge*, 1954, BBDO. Barton delivered the speech on June 15, 1923, in New York City.

45. "The Supreme Court of Business" and "The Most Popular Man in America," both in House Advertising File, N. W. Ayer Archives, New York, N.Y. See also the Campbell's Soup ad, "The Supreme Court," *SEP*, March 2, 1918, 23, which applies the comparison in selling a specific product.

46. Cherington, *Advertising as a Business Force*, 29–66, 206–289; Lears, "Some Versions of Fantasy," 362.

47. *PI* 16, no. 2 (July 8, 1896): 24; N. W. Aubuchon, "Salesmanship Plus Advertising," *Judicious Advertising* 3, no. 7 (May 1905): 40. See also Addison Archer, "Dixey on Dixey," *PI* 22, no. 10 (September 4, 1895): 6; "The Purchaser's State of Mind an Essential of Value," in Mahin, *Lectures on Advertising*, 6; Lois Ardery, "She Wants It But She Doesn't Know It—Yet!" *J. Walter Thompson News Bulletin* 110 (December 1924): 18–21; and Strasser, *Satisfaction Guaranteed*, 89–161.

48. Most vexing and persistent was the question of wholesalers "forcing" privately produced or nonadvertised brands into the stores; these were generally brands that could be sold at a much greater profit than famous advertised brands such as Royal Baking Powder, Kellogg's Corn Flakes, and Campbell's Soup. Despite evidence of consumer preference and despite high volumes of national advertising, many distributors and retailers fought against branded goods well into the 1920s. See Cherington, *Advertising as a Business Force*; and Strasser, *Satisfaction Guaranteed*.

49. "Out of the Background," in N. W. Ayer & Son, *In Behalf of Advertising*, 39, 106 (emphasis in original); Cherington, *Consumer Looks at Advertising*, 22–23.

50. *Life*, July 9, 1925, cover III; *Life*, February 12, 1925, cover II; *Life*, March 19, 1925, 1. See also *Advertising and Selling Fortnightly* 6, no. 1 (May 5, 1925): 9; and *Advertising and Selling Fortnightly* 6, no. 3 (June 2, 1925): 9.

51. *SEP*, April 1, 1911, 71.

52. Berger and Luckmann, *Social Construction of Reality*; Goffman, *Presentation of Self*; Rochberg-Halton, *Meaning and Modernity*.

53. For analysis of republican economic ideals, see McCoy, *Elusive Republic*. Republican traditions for labor are treated in Laurie, *Working People of Philadelphia*; and Wilentz, *Chants Democratic*. For the republican ideology's persistence and its role in the second half of the nineteenth century, see Foner, *Free Soil, Free Labor, Free Men*; and Rodgers, *Work Ethic*. For its persistence in the countryside see Hahn, *Roots of Southern Populism*. For its manifestations in later reform movements see Ross, "Liberal Tradition Revisited"; Ross, "Socialism and American Liberalism"; Thomas, *Alternative America*; and Cohen, *Reconstruction of American Liberalism*.

54. Livingston, *Pragmatism and the Political Economy*, 57–131; Livingston, *Pragmatism, Feminism, and Democracy*, 17–85.

55. Finnegan, *Selling Suffrage*.

56. Pope, *Making of Modern Advertising*, 87–90; Roy W. Johnson, "Where Is the Real Market," *PI* 80, no. 8 (August 22, 1912): 22; *PI* 98, no. 5 (February 1, 1917): 21; Strasser, *Satisfaction Guaranteed*.

57. *Judicious Advertising and Advertising Experience* 5, no. 6 (April 1907): 28–29; John G. Keplinger, "Would Specifications in Advertising Cure Substitution?" *PI* 76, no. 2 (July 13, 1911): 32.

58. "The Housekeepers' Directory," *GH* 44, no. 3 (March 1907): n.p.

59. "The Housekeeper' Directory," *GH* 46, no. 4 (April 1908): n.p.; Book 654 (1922), Series 2, Box 396, File 2, AC. Kellogg's was one of the most vigorous opponents of substitution, labeling its campaign of strict (and illegal) resale price maintenance (compelling all merchants to buy and sell at universal prices determined by Kellogg) the "Square Deal." See *PI* 93, no. 1 (October 7, 1915): 38. For another interpretation of substitution, see Garvey, *Adman in the Parlor*, 159–60.

60. "Our Own Page," *Woman's Home Companion* 39, no. 9 (September 1912): 3; Walter S. Hine, "The Advertising of Foods," *GH* 48, no. 3 (March 1909): 383–85; B. W. Parker, "The Commerce of Clothes," *GH* 48, no. 4 (April 1909): 526; "You Get Only What You Pay For," *Woman's Home Companion* 57, no. 10 (October 1930): 4. See also Strasser, *Satisfaction Guaranteed*, 83–88.

61. Frederick, *Selling Mrs. Consumer*, 294–95.

62. Series 2, Box 29, Book 133, File 2 (1906), AC (emphasis in original).

63. "The Home Directory," *GH* 51, no. 1 (July 1910): n.p.; *LHJ* 33, no. 5 (May 1916): 74.

64. *GH* 49, no. 1 (July 1909): cover II [Shredded Wheat]; "The Housekeepers' Directory," *GH* 49, no. 1 (July 1909): n.p. [Sapolio].

65. Series 2, Box 302, Book 526, File 1 (n.d.) [Juergens], AC; Series 2, Box 114, Book 528 [Wards TIP-TOP Bread] (1909), AC; *LHJ* 38, no. 1 (January 1921): 99; *SEP*, July 17, 1920, 115. See also *LHJ* 37, no. 4 (April 1920): 46.

66. *SEP*, January 3, 1923, 73; "Shall the River Work—or Shall You?" *Light* 2, no. 1 (May 1924): 47 (emphasis added).

67. *Fortune* 2, no. 1 (July 1930): 101 [Remington Rand]; "The Housekeepers' Directory," *GH* 49, no. 6 (December 1909): n.p. Remington not only advertised that women were given freedom through its products. This ad was one of a long-running campaign that designated Remington Rand products "The Great Emancipators" of the modern businessman.

68. Series 2, Box 380, Book 632 (1929), AC; *GH* 68, no. 5 (May 1919): 199; *SEP*, January 6, 1923, 103; Series 2, Box 380, Book 632 (1924), AC.

69. See Western Electric, "A Vision of a Better Way" (1915) and "The New Enlightenment" (1916), Series 2, Box 319, Book 548, AC. For this figure's connections to the Statue of Liberty, see Trachtenberg, *Statue of Liberty*; and Aguilhon, *Marianne into Battle*. My thanks to Tamara Whited for teaching me so much about the statue's history.

70. *LHJ* 27, no. 14 (November 1, 1910): 4; *LHJ* 27, no. 11 (September 15, 1910): 4; *SEP*, November 4, 1911, 2; *SEP*, January 13, 1912, 2; *Woman's Home Companion* 37, no. 10 (October 1910): 61. That Hopkins, master of the forceful hard sell, would create a such a

campaign indicates that political language and concepts had deeply penetrated the vocabulary of advertising. He would never permit overt appeals to patriotism or nationalism to interfere with an advertisement, refusing to cheapen their sacred political meanings and deter a sales message from the essential appeals of convenience, self-improvement, or utility. Hopkins, *Scientific Advertising*, 6–9, 21–31.

71. *LHJ* 37, no. 3 (March 1920): 57. See also "Take a Half Holiday Next Washday," Series 2, Box 216, Book 400 (1900), AC; and *SEP*, February 17, 1912, 28.

72. Cowan, *More Work for Mother*.

73. *Woman's Home Companion* 57, no. 10 (October 1930): 104; *SEP*, April 20, 1929, 212.

74. *GH* 64, no. 6 (June 1917): 161; *SEP*, February 17, 1912, 28. For other advertising campaigns that linked consumption, freedom, and time, see advertising for Walker's Soap, Series 2, Box 216, Book 400 (1900), AC.

75. Chandler, *Visible Hand*; Lamoreaux, *Great Merger Movement*; Wiebe, *Search for Order*; Haskell, *Emergence of Professional Social Science*.

76. Goodwyn, *Populist Moment*; Rodgers, "In Search of Progressivism"; Pollack, *Just Polity*.

77. Ewen, *PR!*; Jackall and Hirota, *Image Makers*; Miller, *Voice of Business*; Tye, *Edward L. Bernays*; Cutlip, *Unseen Power*.

78. Filene, with Wood, *Successful Living*, 98–99, 101–20.

79. Marchand, *Creating the Corporate Soul*, 1–47; Marchand, "Fitful Career of Advocacy Advertising"; Galambos, *Public Image of Big Business*; Tedlow, *Keeping the Corporate Image*; Raucher, *Rise of Public Relations*. See also the treatment of John D. Rockefeller in Ponce de Leon, *Self-Exposure*, 141–71.

80. *PI* 127, no. 6 (May 8, 1924): 1.

81. Marchand, *Creating the Corporate Soul*, 7–97. For investigations into that very issue of corporate power and responsibility, see Samuels and Miller, *Corporations and Society*.

82. Black, *Family Income*, 15–20; Lord & Thomas, " 'Giving Hostages to Caesar' "; MacManus, *Sword Arm of Business*; "Protect Our Good Name," *LHJ* 33, no. 1 (January 1916): 8–9; N. W. Ayer & Son, *In Behalf of Advertising*, 59–62, 129–32; Frederick, *Selling Mrs. Consumer*, 340.

83. "By Their Shadows You Shall Know Them," House Ads, Ayer Archives; "Character," *SEP*, July 10, 1920, 132. See also F. W. Ayer's remarks to his staff on character and personal integrity in business in "Report of a Conference held at the Down Town Club," December 12, 1915, Philadelphia, Pa., 4–6, Ayer Archives.

84. *A Graphic Presentation of the Story of the George Batten Company* (New York, 1918), 35, BBDO.

85. A third example of signed editorials was a long-running campaign for Armour and Company, consisting of frequent editorials "signed" by Armour president F. Edson White. These advertisements were nothing more than corporate editorials explaining Armour's position on pricing, distribution, and most important, its service to a public utterly dependent on the corporation for its meat supplies. See Series 2, Box 280, Book 494 (1927), AC.

86. Marchand, *Creating the Corporate Soul*, 28–32.

87. On Gillette see Adams, *King C. Gillette*; Gilbert, *Designing the Industrial State*, 159–79; Segal, *Technological Utopianism*, 48–55; and Strasser, *Satisfaction Guaranteed*, 97–102.

88. Laemmle was one of many who fought the motion picture trust. Bowser, *Transformation of Cinema*, 28, 217–20.

89. *SEP*, January 6, 1923, 88. Laemmle's career is discussed in detail in Drinkwater, *Life and Adventures of Carl Laemmle*; anecdotally in Ramsaye, *One Million and One Nights*, 523–24, 580–81, 588–93; more analytically in Gomery, *Hollywood Studio System*; and in Sklar, *Movie-Made America*, 34–41. Laemmle was one of the executives who was instrumental in establishing the star system, whereby studios featured movies with favored actors well known to audiences. Fostering a demand for known performers by name, Laemmle attacked the established system, whereby film distributors had almost sole control of new product. The conflict-ridden genesis of the Hollywood "star system" is strikingly similar to contemporaneous struggles over distribution and brand goods in industry. See De Cordova, *Picture Personalities*; Bowser, *Transformation of Cinema*, 103–19; Singer, *Melodrama and Modernity*.

90. Henry Ford, the most famous and well-loved automaker in this period, also had a well-defined public personality, but he did not get it chiefly through advertising, of which he remained skeptical until introducing the Model A with N. W. Ayer in 1928: Marchand, *Advertising the American Dream*, 7. For a thorough understanding of the process of creating these public personas for businessmen, motion picture stars, civic leaders, sports figures, and others, see Ponce de Leon, *Self-Exposure*.

91. Douglas, *Inventing American Broadcasting*, discusses the popular status of the "inventor-hero," who enjoyed a long history of veneration and respect in American culture. This hero's zenith in American life was from 1880 through 1930, when a confluence of newspapers and magazines, dime novels, and the rash of technological innovations in communication and transportation created a plethora of new examples of the myth and a mass audience eager for their stories. See also Douglas, "Amateur Operators." Nye, *Image Worlds*, 1–9, discusses publicity's agenda of humanizing and personalizing a major corporation. On Ford, see Watts, *People's Tycoon*; Brinkley, *Wheels for the World*; Lewis, *Public Image of Henry Ford*; and Susman, *Culture as History*, 122–49. On Edison see Wachhorst, *Thomas Alva Edison*; and Nye, *Invented Self*.

92. MacManus, *Sword Arm of Business*, 55. Many of the most successful advertisers criticized this approach as simply a sop to the vanity of corporate clients. See Hopkins, *My Life in Advertising*, 127, for a criticism of "MacManus-style" institutional copy; and Truman A. De Geese, "Puncturing Some Advertising Airships," *PI* 70, no. 7 (February 16, 1910): 35, criticizing Gillette.

93. See, for example, the "chemical engineer" for DuPont, *SEP*, May 26, 1923, 122; the "mechanic" for Gilder Fan Belts, *SEP*, March 5, 1921, 127; and Roland Cole, "The Old Model Says Meet My Successor," *PI* 143, no. 10 (June 7, 1928): 143–46. See also Thompson, *Things to Know about Trade-Marks*.

94. There is no good cultural history of trade characters, but see Mendenhall, *Character Trademarks*. Gordon, *Comic Strips and Consumer Culture*, 37–51, offers important insights into the connection between trade characters and the emerging comic strip form; see also Henry P. Werner, "The Mistakes of 'Sunny Jim' Seen in the Light of Modern Advertising," *PI* 129, no. 4 (October 23, 1924): 3–6. For the genesis of Aunt Jemima, see Young, *Full Corn in the Ear*; C. E. Raymond, "Memoirs," part I, section II, 10–11 (typescript, 1932), Raymond

File, JWTA; *GH* 86, no. 4 (April 1928): 130; Manring, *Slave in a Box*; Kern-Foxworth, *Aunt Jemima, Uncle Ben, and Rastus*. On Cream of Wheat see "John Lee Mahin—One of Advertising's Old Guard," *PI* 153, no. 7 (November 13, 1930): 33. On Campbell's see Chen, *Campbell Kids*; and Arthur Kemble, "A Lesson from the Campbell Kids" *PI* 162, no. 4 (January 26, 1933): 49–52.

95. On Jim Henry see, for example, *SEP*, March 5, 1921, 35; *SEP*, March 21, 1921, 38; and *SEP*, January 7, 1922, 32. On the traveling salesman see Spears, *100 Years on the Road*; and Friedman, *Birth of a Salesman*, 56–87.

96. On Mary Hale Martin see Young, *Full Corn in the Ear*. On Kotex and Ellen Buckland see Spurgeon, "Marketing the Unmentionable," 30. Strasser, *Satisfaction Guaranteed*, 129–33, discusses recipe and cooking booklets as premiums; Neil, *Story of Crisco*, is an example. Fictional Proctor & Gamble spokeswomen included "Ann Cummings" (White Naphtha Soap), "Ruth Turner" and "Mildred Holmes" (Chipso), "Winifred S. Carter" (Crisco), and "Helen Chase" (Camay). These ads were often very popular and successful, offering specific information on product use, as well as the testimonials of fictionalized "professionals." For discussions of advertising "experts," see Marchand, *Advertising the American Dream*, 352–56; and Lears, "Packaging the Folk," 129–31. For testimony from an actual home economist on the appeal of such advertising, see Ida Bailey Allen, "Helpfulness—the Big Idea in Advertising to Women," *PI* 123, no. 11 (June 14, 1923): 138–40. For a revealing analysis of the relationships between actual health professionals and consumers, see Tomes, "Merchants of Health."

97. The idea of ventriloquism is suggested by Denning, *Mechanic Accents*, 82–83. Denning in turn is influenced by Mikhail Bakhtin; see Voloshinov [Bakhtin], *Marxism and the Philosophy of Language*. Although Bakhtin does not address advertising specifically, the idea that the writer as ventriloquist masks his ideology in the "voice" of a fictional figure supposedly of a different class, and speaks as a true representative of that class, seems especially pertinent to advertising.

98. Hotchkiss and Franken, *Leadership of Advertised Brands*.

99. Braverman, *Labor and Monopoly Capital*; Chandler, *Visible Hand*; McCraw, *Prophets of Regulation*; Pope, *Making of Modern Advertising*; Livingston, *Origins of the Federal Reserve System*; Tomlins, *State and the Unions*; Montgomery, *Fall of the House of Labor*.

100. Marchand, *Advertising the American Dream*, 335–63.

101. These criticisms have emerged in the present to challenge "neoliberal" regimes and globalization, which base their legitimacy on these explicit equations of suffrage and spending. See, most helpfully, Barber, *Jihad vs. McWorld*; Frank, *One Market under God*; and Chua, *World on Fire*.

CHAPTER THREE

1. Butler, "What the Advertiser Owes the Public," 27.

2. Albert D. Lasker, "What Advertising Means to America," *PI* 119, no. 5 (May 4, 1922): 105.

3. Hoyt, *Consumption of Wealth*, 321.

4. These themes were developed as a cornerstone of American historiography during the Cold War era, most prominently by Potter, *People of Plenty*, and Daniel J. Boorstin's trilogy, *The Americans*.

5. Leven, Moulton, and Warburton, *America's Capacity to Consume*; Lynd, with Hanson, "People as Consumers"; Morris Copeland, "The National Income and Its Distribution," in Hunt, *Recent Economic Changes in the United States*, 757–840. See also Susan Porter Benson, "Gender, Generation, and Consumption: Working-Class Families in the Interwar Period," in *Getting and Spending*, ed. Strasser, McGovern, and Judt, 23–40.

6. Black, *Family Income*, 6–7 (quotation); Balmer, *Science of Advertising*, 32–35; [True Story Magazine], *American Economic Evolution*, 7; Hawley and Zabin, *Understanding Advertising*, 4; Filene, with Wood, *Successful Living*, 25–38; Eldridge, *Making Advertising Pay*, 31; Calkins, *Business, the Civilizer*.

7. N. W. Ayer & Son, *Better Business*, 9.

8. Ralph Crothers, "The Democracy of Advertising," *PI* 127, no. 11 (June 12, 1924): 146.

9. Marchand, *Advertising the American Dream*, 217–22.

10. Beverages, Box 1, WCBA (originally appearing in *The Delineator* [June 1907]); *Pictorial Review* 20, no. 3 (December 1918): 66; *SEP*, April 16, 1910, 56.

11. *GH* 64, no. 6 (December 1916): 91.

12. Gelatt, *Fabulous Phonograph*, 148–49, 191–93, stresses that a substantial portion of phonographs produced were expensive. Millard, *America on Record*, 17–36, describes the context in which the Edison company developed the phonograph from a series of other inventions and discoveries; for the business machine reference, 32. See also Kenney, *Recorded Music*.

13. Series 2, Book 465 (1924), Book 511 (1927), Book 519 (1927), AC. The long-running Victor slogan, "The Music You Want When You Want It," was itself a pointed appeal to consumer autonomy.

14. Levine, *Highbrow/Lowbrow*, 219–42; Symes, *Setting the Record Straight*. Phonograph manufacturers in fact exhibited the tensions of advertising the democratic prospects of a new product. While many appeals stressed the access to formerly aristocratic privilege, still others emphasized the elevation to aristocratic status that good phonograph music provided. Kenney, *Recorded Music*, 44–87, discusses the "social reconstruction" of the phonograph as a genteel and elite entertainment medium, even as the manufacturing companies also pursued markets among ethnic, foreign-born Americans. While his emphasis differs from mine, Kenney makes a similar point—that European art music had substantial audiences among the working and foreign population in the United States, even as the music was being sold as uplift and the badge of refinement. See also Suisman, "Sound of Money"; and Miller, "Segregating Sound."

15. Advertising Section, *Century* 77, no. 3 (December 1908): 120 [Ivory Soap]; Series 2, Book 93 (1926), AC [Chase and Sanborn]. See also *SEP*, January 20, 1923, 88 [Quaker Oats].

16. "In the Public Service," Series 2, Box 21, Book 109, File 1 (1909), AC; "In the Bell Democracy," Series 2, Box 21, Book 109, File 1 (1911), AC. For a different interpretation of this campaign, see Marchand, *Creating the Corporate Soul*, 48–87. See also Fischer, *America Calling*.

17. "The Kingdom of the Subscriber," Series 2, Box 21, Book 109, File 2 (1916), AC; "The People's Telephone," Series 2, Box 21, Book 109, File 3 (1924), AC; "Telephone Etiquette," Series 2, Box 21, Book 109, File 1 (1911), AC; "Within the Means of All," Series 2, Box 21, Book 109, File 3 (1925), AC. Also see "In the Service of All the People," Series 2, Box 21, Book 109, File 3 (1929), AC.

18. "In the Public Service"; "The Telephone Commonwealth," Series 2, Box 21, Book 109, File 1 (1909), AC.

19. "Democracy" (1921), and "A Community of Owners Nation-wide" (1923), both Series 2, Box 21, Book 109, File 3, AC.

20. Smith, *Nationalism*.

21. For analysis of the emergence of the modern American state in the late nineteenth century, see Skowronek, *Building a New American State*; Bensel, *Yankee Leviathan*; Carpenter, *Forging of Bureaucratic Autonomy*; and Keller, *Affairs of State*. Still very useful is Wiebe, *Search for Order*.

22. Zelinsky, *Nation into State*, 13.

23. For the Netherlands see Schama, *Embarrassment of Riches*. For England see McKendrick, Brewer, and Plumb, *Birth of a Consumer Society*; and Rappaport, *Shopping for Pleasure*. For France see Williams, *Dream Worlds*; Auslander, *Taste and Power*; Roche, *History of Everyday Things*; and Tiersten, *Marianne in the Market*. For Germany see Buddenseig et al., *Industrielkultur*; and Leora Auslander, "Citizenship Law, State Form, and Everyday Aesthetics in Modern France and Germany, 1920–1940," in *Politics of Consumption*, ed. Daunton and Hilton, 109–28. For a pan-European perspective, see Smith, *Consumption and the Making of Respectability*; Daunton and Hilton, *Politics of Consumption*, 1–32; and most recently, De Grazia, *Irresistible Empire*. For Russia see Hessler, *Social History of Soviet Trade*. See also McCracken, *Culture and Consumption*; Campbell, *Romantic Ethic and the Spirit of Modern Consumerism*; Strasser, McGovern, and Judt, *Getting and Spending*; and Cross, *All-Consuming Century*.

24. By positing a "nationalist ethos," I do not mean a statist economy run along strict mercantile lines but instead the relationships of consumption and nationality, the influence of particular nationalist beliefs and values on consumption practices and forms in a given culture.

25. Gerstle, *American Crucible*, 1–13. Gerstle identifies racial nationalists to include Theodore Roosevelt, Anglo-partisan Progressives, eugenicists, and blue bloods and the civic partisans as including Franklin Roosevelt, New Deal leftists, affirming immigrants, and early civil rights activists. Gerstle's categories run close to those tropes identified by Sollers, *Beyond Ethnicity*.

26. Although national advertisers throughout this period seemed reluctant to admit that the majority of the populace was not the ideal middle-class consumer, some observers admitted from the outset that as much as 60 percent of the population would be unable to buy their wares. [Butterick Publishing Company], *Mrs. John Doe*, 3–15; Marchand, *Advertising the American Dream*, 63–66; Free Lance, "The Rich or the Poor?" *PI* 15, no. 9 (May 27, 1896): 8; "The Consumer's Attitude in Buying Goods," *Judicious Advertising* 5, no. 5 (March 1907): 59; "The Biggest Thing in Business," *PI* 135, no. 2 (April 8, 1926): 176–79; "Who Buys the Private Brands?" *PI* 139, no. 1 (April 7, 1927): 82–83.

27. Gerstle, *American Crucible*, 47–50, 171–80, identifies examples of such nationalist "texts" like Israel Zangwill's 1908 Broadway play, *The Melting Pot*, the movies of Frank Capra, the *Superman* comics of Jerry Siegal and Joe Schuster, and others. Other civic nationalist "texts" include early two-reel comedies of Charlie Chaplin such as *The Immigrant* and *Easy Street*; the music of Tin Pan Alley composers such as Irving Berlin and

George Gershwin; the Warner Brothers film *The Jazz Singer* (1927); Progressive-Era professional baseball, which was recast as the great American sport at the same moment as its ranks were flooded by immigrant, working-class players; and amusements parks such as Coney Island. See Maland, *Chaplin and American Culture*; Hamm, *Irving Berlin*; Melnick, *Right to Sing the Blues*; Rogin, *Blackface, White Noise*; White, *Creating the National Pastime*; Reiss, *Touching Base*; and Kasson, *Amusing the Million*. Racial nationalist texts and narratives would include D. W. Griffith's *Birth of a Nation*, the popular racial novels of Thomas Dixon, juvenile fiction featuring sports hero Frank Merriwell and inventor Tom Swift, Edgar Rice Burroughs's "Tarzan," professional football, the Buffalo Bill Wild West Shows, and the touring circus. See Lang, *Birth of a Nation*; Slide, *American Racist*; John Kasson, *Houdini, Tarzan, and the Perfect Man*; Joy Kasson, *Buffalo Bill's Wild West*; Reddin, *Wild West Shows*; Davis, *Circus Age*; and Oriard, *Reading Football*. The most useful history of the idea of "American identity" is Gleason, "American Identity and Americanization"; see also Sollers, *Beyond Ethnicity*.

28. Anderson, *Imagined Communities*, 15–16. See also Hobsbawm, *Nations and Nationalism*. For the United States see O'Leary, *To Die For*; and Bodnar, *Remaking America*. Hansen, *Lost Promise of American Patriotism*, traces connections and divergences between patriotism and nationalism at the turn of the twentieth century.

29. Zelinsky, *Nation into State*, 5. Zelinsky astutely observes that "historical circumstances have differed so greatly among the 150-odd actual and would be nation-states of the late twentieth century that the chronicle of state and national development may not be closely duplicated in any of them." Yet nationalism flourishes precisely due to perceptions of those differences. As I have indicated earlier, distinctive national consumption traditions were nurtured at particular historical junctures in different nations. The American "moment" covered the period roughly from 1900 through 1950. While consumption in the United States outstripped that of other nations in sheer volume per capita of goods, by no means did American patterns of consumption make American culture exceptional. If consumption influenced American nationalism, it did so by giving new form to old beliefs in American exceptionalism that were typical, not of American history, but of American nationalism. Zelinsky, *Nation into State*, 221. Helpful considerations of American exceptionalism as both a historiographical problem and a historical question are "The End of American Exceptionalism," in Bell, *Winding Passage*, 245–71; Veysey, "Autonomy of American History Reconsidered"; Kaplan and Pease, *Cultures of United States Imperialism*; Lipset, *American Exceptionalism*; Madsen, *American Exceptionalism*; Noble, *End of American History*; Noble, *Death of a Nation*; and Kaplan, *Anarchy of Empire*.

30. Gellner, *Nations and Nationalism*, 1–7.

31. Leach, *Land of Desire*.

32. Kern, *Culture of Time and Space*, 314–18. Boorstin, *The Americans: The Democratic Experience*, 89–165, 307–410, emphasizes the simultaneous experience possible through mass communication and consumption, while Hilmes, *Radio Voices*, 11–23, discusses radio as an instrument of nationalism through its enabling imagined communities.

33. N. W. Ayer & Son, *Story of the States*, v.

34. "A Nation's Shopping List," in N. W. Ayer & Son, *In Behalf of Advertising*, 23.

35. Series 2, Book 686, Book 694 (1919), AC [Welch's]; "The Housekeepers' Directory,"

GH 47, no. 3 (September 1908): n.p., and *LHJ* 27, no. 11 (September 15, 1910): 41 [Van Camp's]; Series 2, Book 217 (1902) and Book 218 (1909), AC [Hires]; *SEP*, February 11, 1922, cover III, and *SEP*, January 13, 1923, 125 [Borden's]; *SEP*, February 11, 1922, 42 [Puffed Rice]; *SEP*, June 1, 1935, 97 [Shredded Wheat]; Series 2, Book 93 (1924), AC [Chase and Sanborn]; *SEP*, February 16, 1918, 23 [Campbell's]. It is worth noting that such "national" endorsements included many nondomestic goods. Big Ben clocks served as "the National School Bell"; Lehigh claimed the position of "the National Cement"; Vermont Marble called itself "the nation's memory stone"; and Caterpillar Tractors claimed to be "the Nation's Road-Maker." *SEP*, January 24, 1914, 1 [Big Ben]; *SEP*, May 5, 1923, 57 [Lehigh]; *American Magazine* 111, no. 1 (January 1931): 107 [Vermont Marble]; *SEP*, January 13, 1923, 56 [Caterpillar].

36. *LHJ* 33, no. 7 (July 1916): 46–47.

37. *SEP*, May 5, 1923, 57.

38. "Selling through Drug Stores," *PI* 124, no. 9 (August 30, 1923): 8–9.

39. *LHJ* 27, no. 1 (December 1909): 79, and Series 2, Book 391 (1902), AC [Uneeda]; "Harper's Magazine Advertiser," *Harper's New Monthly Magazine* 96, no. 572 (January 1898): 26 [Pearline]; Series 2, Book 218 (1909), AC [Hires]; Series 2, Book 180a (1923), AC [Kellogg's]; Series 2, Book 694 (1919), AC [Welch's].

40. *GH* 81, no. 1 (July 1925): 133 [Arch Preserver]; Advertising Section, *Century* 77, no. 3 (July 1908): 51 [Goodrich]; *American Magazine* 99, no. 2 (February 1925): 129 [Sears].

41. *SEP*, November 9, 1912, 2; *LHJ* 39, no. 3 (March 1922): 29; *SEP*, October 24, 1914, 40.

42. *SEP*, March 23, 1918, 63–64. This advertisement's text largely celebrated not Americanization but cosmopolitan exposure to the great works of such European classical artists as Caruso, Heifetz, and Paderewski, a familiar juxtaposition of uplift and containment.

43. *Collier's* 66, no. 4 (July 24, 1920): 4; *SEP*, January 13, 1923, 56.

44. "The Telephone Unites the Nation"(1915), "The Agency of a United People"(1915), "The Telephone Doors of the Nation" (1913), all Series 2, Box 21, Book 109, File 2, AC. See also "A United Nation," *Woman's Home Companion* 37, no. 10 (October 1910): 82.

45. *Cosmopolitan* 65, no. 2 (July 1918): 101 (emphasis in original).

46. Similarly, advertisers and manufacturers designated products "American," drawing on nationalism to encourage consumption and brand loyalty to such goods as the Griswold "American" Waffle Iron and the American Beauty Electric Iron. Advertising Section, *GH* 40, no. 2 (August 1909): n.p.; *SEP*, May 5, 1923, 81; *SEP*, August 7, 1920, 106.

47. To be sure, use of nationalist imagery and iconography was not the sole significant visual strategy of advertising throughout this period. Other visual clichés, such as the radiant aura surrounding products or the business executive surveying his glorified industrial domain from a perch high up in the factory, enjoyed as prominent a presence in national advertising. Nevertheless, the national icons under discussion here all appeared frequently, for a wide variety of products and commissioned by a wide variety of advertising organizations. See Marchand, *Advertising the American Dream*, 206–84; and Cobb, "Patriotic Themes in Advertising."

48. Hollis Collins, "Two Sides of the Flag Question," *PI* 31, no. 8 (May 23, 1900): 8; "State Laws Forbid Flag Use in Ads," *PI* 71, 11 (June 16, 1916), 63; A. L. Townsend, "When 'Uncle Sam' Is the Hero of the Advertisement," *PI* 125, no. 4 (November 1, 1923): 134.

49. J. F. Richter Jr., "Uncle Sam's Endorsement in Advertising Copy," *PI* 123, no. 5 (May 3, 1923): 8–12; "Uncle Sam Buys Vast Variety of Goods," *PI* 87, no. 5 (April 30, 1914): 31–32; Townsend, "When 'Uncle Sam' Is the Hero," 140 (emphasis in original).

50. "Uncle Sam Is Touchy about the Use of His Picture by Advertisers," *PI* 144, no. 10 (September 6, 1928): 134–36.

51. Townsend, "When 'Uncle Sam' Is the Hero," 133–34.

52. Bartholdi, *Statue of Liberty Enlightening the World*; Trachtenberg, *Statue of Liberty*; Higham, *Send These to Me*, 71–80; Kammen, *Spheres of Liberty*.

53. Advertising Section, *American Magazine*, March–April 1907, 120 [Ivory]; *Pictorial Review* 20, no. 10 (July 1919): 29 [Campbell's]; *SEP*, August 14, 1920, 39 [Pathe Phonographs]; *SEP*, July 24, 1920, 71 [Twin City Tractor]; *Woman's Home Companion* 45, no. 6 (June 1918): 47 [Coca-Cola]. See also "The Bartholdi Statue," Singer Sewing Machine trade card, Sewing Machines, Box 3, File 3/14 , WCBA; and *SEP*, March 17, 1923, 85. One of the earliest cartoon images of Liberty, drawn by Frederick Opper, satirized her as a ready target for advertising exploitation; see Banta, *Imaging American Women*, 604. The cartoon originally appeared in *Puck*, April 1, 1885.

54. On George Washington see "Campaign on Quantity as Foil to High Cost of Living," *PI* 78, no. 7 (February 15, 1912): 59–60 [Washington Crisps]; and N. W. Ayer & Son, *In Behalf of Advertising*, 219–20. For Abraham Lincoln see *American Magazine* 100, no. 5 (November 1925): 94 [Waterman]; *McClure's Magazine* 22, no. 6 (April 1904): 169 [Van Camp's]; *GH* 58, no. 2 (February 1914): cover II [Welch's]; Leroy Fairman, "The Griddle," *PI* 66, no. 7 (February 17, 1909): 14–15; and *American Magazine* 100, no. 5 (November 1925): 122 [Prudential Insurance]. On the Founders see *SEP*, July 10, 1920, 130–31 [Royal]; *GH* 64, no. 3 (March 1917): 96 [Hartford]; and *SEP*, April 27, 1929, 61 [Packard]. See also *American Magazine* 99, no. 4 (April 1925): 169. For ads using Christopher Columbus see Standard Sewing Machine Company, "The Standard of Conquest" booklet (n.d. but ca. 1890), Sewing Machines, Box 4, File 4/2, WCBA; Atkinson's Cocoa, Book 163 (1896), AC; and *SEP*, February 9, 1918, 53 [Libby's olives]. On the Washington Monument see Magazine Advertiser, *Harper's New Monthly Magazine* 96 (February 1898): 69; "Housekeepers' Directory," *GH* 47, no. 1 (July 1908): n.p. [Sapolio]; and "Integrity," Ayer House Ads, N. W. Ayer Archives, New York, N.Y.

55. I borrow the concept and phrase from Jameson, *Political Unconscious*.

56. Frank, *Buy American!* On the antichain and local commerce campaigns of the 1920s and 1930s, see Lebhar, *Chain Stores*, 142–75; and Harper, " 'New Battle on Evolution.' "

57. Lebhar, *Chain Stores*, 223–36.

58. N. W. Ayer & Son, *Story of the States*, vii–viii; "The Weakest Selling Appeal," *PI* 135, no. 3 (April 15, 1926): 184–85; "The Little Schoolmaster's Classroom," *PI* 135, no. 11 (June 10, 1926): 204–6; "When the Customer Strikes Back," *PI* 142, no. 11 (March 15, 1928): 195; Wib Chaffee, "Setting 'Buy at Home' to New Music," *PI* 139, no. 11 (June 16, 1927): 33–36.

59. Isaac F. Marcosson, "Base 'Made in America' Campaign on Quality," *PI* 89, no. 3 (October 15, 1914): 44–47. See also "No Room for It Here," *PI* 77, no. 5 (November 2, 1911): 67; "Shall We Label Our Goods 'Made in the U.S. of A.'?" *PI* 87, no. 13 (September 24, 1914): 17–20; "The 'Made in the U.S.A.' Slogan," *PI* 89, no. 6 (November 5, 1914): 72–73; " 'Made in U.S.A.' Not a Boycott," *PI* 89, no. 11 (December 17, 1914): 88–89; "Can Advertising Banish the Spell of the Foreign Label?" *PI* 131, no. 9 (May 28, 1925): 10–12; "A 'Made in

the U.S.A.' Campaign?" *PI* 132, no. 3 (July 16, 1925): 154. See also the symposium on "Made in America" campaigns, *PI* 90, no. 3 (January 21, 1915): 3–38.

60. "No Room for It Here," 67.

61. William M. Armistead, "Address," in N. W. Ayer & Son, *Book of the Golden Celebration*, 42.

62. Presbrey, *History and Development of Advertising*, 613.

63. The attempt of these critics to locate distinct American cultural traditions and the historians' efforts to locate the essence of a distinct American history were entirely contemporary with commercial spokesmen's more prosaic identification of American cultural distinctiveness with the marketplace. For the key texts, see Brooks, *Van Wyck Brooks*; Mumford, *Golden Day*; Bourne, *Radical Will*; Frank, *Our America*; and Rourke, *American Humor*. The secondary literature on cultural nationalism is enormous. See Lasch, *New Radicalism in America*; Alexander, *Here the Country Lies*; Rubin, *Constance Rourke*; Pells, *Radical Visions and American Dreams*; and most important, Blake, *Beloved Community*; and Hegeman, *Patterns for America*. The literature on Progressive-Era history is as copious. Critical texts include Turner, *Frontier in American History*; Beard and Beard, *Rise of American Civilization*; and Parrington, *Main Currents in American Thought*. See Hofstadter, *Progressive Historians*; and Benson, *Turner and Beard*. Most explicit in connecting these twin traditions to consumer abundance was Potter, *People of Plenty*.

64. Series 2, Book 391 (1902), AC [Uneeda]; *SEP*, August 29, 1914, 2 [Ivory]; "Advertising Section," *Century* 77, no. 5 (March 1909): 60; Newton A. Fuesste, "What Copy-Writers Can Learn from Story Writers," *PI* 92, no. 7 (August 12, 1915): 35 [Packard]; *LHJ* 27, no. 1 (December 1909): 44 [concrete].

65. *SEP*, January 13, 1923, 55; *SEP*, April 7, 1923, 121 [Ingersoll]; *GH* 85, no. 6 (December 1927), 121 [Quaker]. Other brands marketed as the "great American Watch" included the Illinois Watch (*SEP*, April 8, 1928, 87); Waltham ("Harper's Magazine Advertiser," *Harper's* 96, no. 572 [January 1898]: 29); and Keystone (*American Magazine* 100, no. 4 [October 1925]: 165).

66. *SEP*, July 10, 1920, 131 [Royal]; *SEP*, April 28, 1928, 85 [Selz]; *SEP*, February 23, 1918, 78 [Notaseme].

67. Series 2, Book 149b (1915), AC [Anger]; *SEP*, April 20, 1929, 95 [Elgin]; *American Magazine* 104, no. 3 (September 1927): 11 [Oakland]; Series 2, Book 694 (1919), AC [Welch's]. See also *LHJ* 37, no. 2 (February 1920): 128 [Durham-Duplex Hosiery].

68. *Everybody's Magazine* 21, no. 5 (November 1914): cover II; *LHJ* 29, no. 4 (April 1912): 62. See other ads for Steinway, such as "International Fame," Series 2, Book 356 (1912), AC; and others throughout Series 2, Book 356 (1912–15), AC.

69. Robert R. Updegraff, "The New American Tempo," *Advertising and Selling*, May 5, 1926, 20. See also Updegraff, "Tomorrow's Business and the Stream of Life," *Advertising and Selling*, April 20, 1927, 19–20, 44–52; "Some American Traits that Affect Advertising," *PI* 20, no. 6 (August 11, 1897): 8; Albert Leffingwell, "They Don't Want to Read It," *J. Walter Thompson News Bulletin* 92 (November 1922): 1; Wallace R. Boren, "Mental Lunch Counters for Consumers," *J. Walter Thompson News Bulletin* 13, no. 2 (May 1930): 24–28; and Kendall, *New American Tempo*.

70. Frederick, *Selling Mrs. Consumer*, 251, 248–49.

71. An inverted variant of this cultural nationalism emerged in a long-running Thomp-

son series for Fleischmann's yeast. These advertisements featured European "scientists" (many with stereotypical heavy beards) testifying to the benefits of "yeast for health" to capitalize on notions of European superiority to underscore American cultural achievement. This was in part coincidental: the major reason Europeans were the spokesmen was that by the 1920s, American doctors were prohibited by the American Medical Association (AMA) from making paid endorsements, especially for dubious claims such as Fleischmann's. Yet the use of the less-regulated Europeans was not simply an alternative strategy: the foreigners possessed the stamp of superior training and expertise, along with the learned visage of "scientists." See JWT Representatives' Meeting, July 18, 1928, 2–5, RG 2, JWTA. On the lengths Thompson went to conceal the AMA's edict against U.S. physician endorsements and to counterattack AMA criticism of the Fleischmann campaigns, see letter to Thomas Greer, New York Office, July 12, 1933, "Fleischmann Controversy—Inactive Accounts File," JWTA. For some sample ads of the long-running campaign, see *Literary Digest* 112, no. 12 (March 19, 1932): 27; and *Literary Digest* 114, no. 4 (October 1, 1932): 29.

72. *SEP*, February 13, 1915, 1. See also Marchand, *Advertising the American Dream*, 16–18, 195–96.

73. Susman, *Culture as History*, 105–21.

74. P. K. Marsh, "Mr. and Mrs. Typical," *PI* 121, no. 3 (October 19, 1922): 4. See also "Profit in Advertising to Germans," *PI* 66, no. 3 (March 31, 1909): 8–10; *PI* 77, no. 4 (October 26, 1911): 62; Charles W. Hurd, "Oft Overlooked Markets in the Tenements," *PI* 81, no. 4 (October 24, 1912): 60–62; "Advertising Gives Immigrants Lessons in English," *PI* 134, no. 9 (March 4, 1926): 115–16; "Teaching the Immigrant Not to Fetch and Carry," *PI* 148, no. 7 (August 15, 1929): 116–17.

75. See Ewen, *Immigrant Women in the Land of Dollars*; Heinze, *Adapting to Abundance*; Cohen, "Encountering Mass Culture at the Grassroots."

76. Laird, *Advertising Progress*.

77. W. Livingston Larned, "Dipping into History for Advertising Appeal," *PI* 109, no. 6 (November 6, 1919): 85–88; "The Vogue of Historical Copy," *PI* 111 (April 15, 1920): 230; "Making an Ally Out of History," *PI* 123, no. 11 (April 25, 1923): 142–44; P. K. March "When Dame History Fills the Inkwell," *PI* 119, no. 1 (April 6, 1922): 57–58.

78. Marchand, *Advertising the American Dream*, 1–24; Lears, "Packaging the Folk"; Lears, *Fables of Abundance*. See McCracken, *Culture and Consumption*, for a discussion of the personal past and history in the ecology of consumption and goods; and Rochberg-Halton and Csikszentmihalyi, *Meaning of Things*.

79. See, for example, "The Pioneer and the Vision," in N. W. Ayer & Son, *12 Advertisements, 1919* (Philadelphia, 1920), n.p., Series 16, Box 19, File 1, AC; "Keeper of the Keys," in N. W. Ayer & Son, *12 Advertisements, 1929* (Philadelphia, 1930), n.p., Series 16, Box 20, File 5, AC; "Enter the Law" and "The Diggers," both in House Advertising File, Ayer Archives. See also "The Plow under the Wagon," in N. W. Ayer & Son, *In Behalf of Advertising*, 208–11.

80. *Fortune* 1, no. 1 (February 1930): 176; *SEP*, March 17, 1923, 39.

81. Larned, "Dipping into History," 85–86 [Portland Cement]; *American Magazine* 102, no. 3 (March 1927): 133 [American Radiator]. For typical AT&T ads see "The Pony Express," Book 109, File 1 (1912); "'Lafayette, Here We Are,'" Book 109, File 2 (1918); "Our Many Tongued Ancestors," Book 109, File 3 (1920); "The Spirit of Pioneering," Book 109, File 3 (1924); "The Meeting Place," Book 109, File 3 (1927); all in Series 2, Box 21, AC.

82. Series 2, Book 93 (1920–24), AC [Chase and Sanborn]; *Pictorial Review* 20, no. 6 (March 1919): 76 [Del Monte]; *American Home,* June 1930, 294; *SEP,* August 28, 1920, 51. For a newspaper campaign based on the spirit of the "Old West," see ads for Hills Brothers Coffee, Series 2, Book 115 (1925), AC.

83. *GH* 82, no. 5 (May 1926): 128. See also advertising for Martex towels, *American Magazine* 105, no. 4 (April 1928): 269.

84. *LHJ* 37, no. 4 (April 1921): 29.

85. *SEP,* June 20, 1914, 60 [Bull Durham]; *SEP,* July 9, 1910, 46 [Gillette]. See also *SEP,* September 3, 1910, 48.

86. Curiously but not coincidentally, Daniel Boorstin, the foremost American historian to emphasize consumption before the present surge of interest, lionized the American political ethos in very similar terms, that is, as a nonideological, practical, flexible approach to collective decisions and public philosophy. See Boorstin, *Genius of American Politics;* Lears, *Fables of Abundance,* 180–81.

87. Hunt, *Recent Economic Changes in the United States,* xxii.

88. *SEP,* June 17, 1911, 44 [Overland]; *SEP,* July 31, 1920, 41 [Stevens-Duryea]. See also *LHJ* 37, no. 3 (March 1920): 38; and "The Development of Consumer-Individuality," *PI* 74, no. 4 (January 26, 1911): 60.

89. *Life,* October 8, 1925, 1.

90. Frederick, *Selling Mrs. Consumer,* 335.

91. *GH* 86, no. 4 (April 1928): 104–5 [International Silver]; *GH* 80, no. 2 (August 1925): 180 [Simmons]; *SEP,* July 10, 1920, 130–31 [Royal].

92. Frederick, *Selling Mrs. Consumer,* 248–52.

93. "Something to Grub For," in N. W. Ayer & Son, *In Behalf of Advertising,* 226.

94. Ibid., 228 (ellipses and emphasis in original).

95. Ibid., 229–30.

CHAPTER FOUR

1. Slichter, *Modern Economic Society,* 540.

2. Silber, *Test and Protest,* 17–23; Schainwald, "Genesis and Growth of the First Consumer Testing Organization"; Campbell, *Consumer Representation in the New Deal;* Sorenson, *Consumer Movement in the United States.*

3. For an analysis of major schools of American economics, see Hodgson, *Evolution of Institutional Economics;* and Mátyás, *History of Modern Non-Marxian Economics.*

4. Dorfman, *Economic Mind in American Civilization,* vol. 3, discusses the advent of this generation of economists. See also Veysey, *Emergence of the American University,* 124–33.

5. Livingston, *Pragmatism and the Political Economy,* 49–57 (quotation on 50).

6. Ibid., 59–60.

7. See Howey, *Rise of the Marginal Utility School;* Lekachman, *History of Economic Ideas;* and Hutchison, *Review of Economic Doctrines.* For specific emphasis on the American marginalists, see Ross, *Origins of American Social Science,* 172–218; and Dorfman, *Economic Mind,* 3:190–93, 237–52.

8. Ross, *Origins of American Social Science,* 181.

9. Livingston, *Pragmatism and the Political Economy,* 50–53; Ross, *Origins of American Social Science,* 180, 182.

10. Ross, *Origins of American Social Science*, 172–95; Livingston, "Social Analysis of Economic History and Theory," 87–94. Both describe marginalism as a goodwilled effort by economists to address the social question of labor but one that ultimately wound up defending business interests and the (mal)distribution of wealth. See also Birken, *Consuming Desire*, 22–39. For a short interpretation of the marginalist shift to emphasis on consumption, as well as an example of analysis that organizes the economy around consumption, see Galbraith, *Affluent Society*, 27–34, 111–20. For a popular statement of the neoclassical consumption paradigm, see Chase, *A New Deal*, 21–25. For marginalism's role in the emergence of corporate managerial capitalism, see Sklar, *Corporate Reconstruction of American Capitalism*, 57–72.

11. Horowitz, *Morality of Spending*.

12. Patten, *New Basis of Civilization*; Fox, *Discovery of Abundance*. Dorothy Ross points out that the idea of abundance was hardly original with Patten and in fact had been emphasized by American economists since the early nineteenth century. Patten's originality was making it the centerpiece of his economics and social programs. It is due in no small part to his abstruse and tendentious language that the scope of his insight has seldom been appreciated. Ross, *Origins of American Social Science*, 196 n. 52. A helpful outline of the transformation in attitudes regarding poverty, thrift, and abundance is Donald Fleming, "Social Darwinism," in *Paths of American Thought*, ed. Schlesinger and White, 123–46. See also Horowitz, *Morality of Spending* , 30–37; and Shi, *Simple Life*.

13. Horowitz, *Morality of Spending*, is a thorough account of budgetary studies of households, occupational groups, and communities undertaken by social workers, government agencies, private foundations, and individual scholars. See also Berolzheimer, "Nation of Consumers"; Zunz, *Why the American Century?* 25–92; Pope, "American Economists and the High Cost of Living"; Samson, "Emergence of a Consumer Interest"; and Fitzpatrick, *Endless Crusade*.

14. Horowitz, *Morality of Spending*, 50–108. Lynd and Lynd, *Middletown*, became the most famous study of middle-class spending habits as indicators of change and the ideal of society; see Richard W. Fox, "Epitaph for Middletown: Robert S. Lynd and the Analysis of Consumer Culture," *Culture of Consumption*, ed. Fox and Lears, 101–41. For an analysis of one community in which middle-class consumer habits were explicitly taken to serve as a model for the good of society at large, see Gilkeson, *Middle-Class Providence*.

15. The literature on Veblen is voluminous, although much of it is quite specialized. Most helpful for the interpretations herein are Dorfman, *Thorstein Veblen and His America*, which has been supplanted but never fully exceeded by the many works cited below and elsewhere; Mitchell, *What Veblen Taught*; Lerner, *Portable Veblen*, 1–49; and Daniel Bell, "Introduction," in Veblen, *Engineers and the Price System*. A comprehensive anthology of Veblen's works and critical responses to them, which appeared too late for inclusion in this study, is Tilman, *Legacy of Thorstein Veblen*. Other important works include Horowitz, *Veblen's Century*; Edgell, *Veblen in Perspective*; Meštrović, *Thorstein Veblen on Culture and Society*; Spindler, *Veblen and Modern America*; Samuels, *Founding of Institutional Economics*, 123–320; Shannon, *Conspicuous Criticism*; Diggins, *Bard of Savagery*; Dowd, "Thorstein Veblen"; and Ross, *Origins of American Social Science*, 204–16.

16. Veblen's specific economic analyses have largely been eclipsed, first by his own disciples, who adopted his premises without his skepticism, then by the Keynesian revolution,

with which he shared some assumptions and perspectives, and ultimately by new tools of economic analysis, notably econometrics. Yet his basic outlook, focusing on the social costs and inefficiencies of corporate domination and logic in the productive system, remains influential, especially among political liberals. Most prominent among post–World War II economists who adopted a Veblenian perspective (although borrowing more from his sociological analysis than his economic discussions) was John Kenneth Galbraith. See Galbraith, *New Industrial State*. The most sustained attempt to fit Veblen into contemporary and subsequent traditions of social thought is Diggins, *Bard of Savagery*.

17. In that sense, the great expansion of scholarly interest in consumption within modern industrial societies (of which this study is a part) is derived in part from Veblen's insights in his adaptation of anthropologists such as Lewis Henry Morgan and his resonance with others such as Franz Boas. The work of Pierre Bourdieu carries on aspects of Veblen's analysis: see Bourdieu, *Distinction*; Bourdieu, *Field of Cultural Production*; and Shank, "Pierre Bourdieu and the Field of Cultural History." See also Ewen, *Captains of Consciousness*, which grafts Veblen's institutional analysis to a Marxian perspective. For the recent historical interest in consumption, see Agnew, "Coming Up for Air"; Lawrence B. Glickman, "Born to Shop? Consumer History and American History," in *Consumer Society in American History*, ed. Glickman, 1–17; and "Introduction," in *Getting and Spending*, ed. Strasser, McGovern, and Judt, 1–9.

18. Schultze, "Advertising, Science, and Professionalism," makes the case that Chicago in the 1890s was the center of American advertising, not New York. Leach, *Land of Desire*, pays a great deal of attention to such Chicago merchants as Marshall Field and Carson Pirie Scott, making a case for that city's stores' influence and innovation matching that of New York and Philadelphia.

19. During the 1890s Veblen published a series of essays that prefigured themes of his first volumes, as well as others that he developed later. While his work underwent some evolution, and thus might be analyzed chronologically, he altered his style and emphases more than his basic conceptions. For present purposes, his work can be profitably and fairly discussed synchronically and thematically. For a chronological account, see Dorfman, *Thorstein Veblen and His America*.

20. Thorstein Veblen, "Why Is Economics Not an Evolutionary Science?" [1898], in Veblen, *Place of Science*, 1–32; see also "The Limitations of Marginal Utility" [1909], in ibid., 232–33; and Dorfman, *Economic Mind*, 3:434–47. Veblen's role in a general rebellion against the notion of abstract, timeless, and universal "laws" throughout the social sciences is discussed in White, *Social Thought in America*, esp. 76–93. In the 1870s Gustave Schmoller pioneered the study of economics through economic history, but the German school of historical economics had only limited influence on Veblen. See Hutchison, *Review of Economic Doctrines*, 130–32, 180–96.

21. Thus, as Dorothy Ross argues, Veblen appears to be an exception among social scientists. In remaking social science along scientific lines, they downplayed the significance and evidence of history in order to perpetuate the timeless ideal of America's millennial purpose in the world. Veblen's skepticism of such ideals and his insistent historicism made him an exception to contemporary economic and social thought. Ross, *Origins of American Social Science*, 210–11. See also Bannister, *Sociology and Scientism*; Novick, *That Noble Dream*; and Noble, *End of American History*.

22. Here he anticipated inquiries followed by Yale scholar William Graham Sumner in *Folkways*.

23. Veblen, "Why Is Economics Not an Evolutionary Science?" 1–32.

24. Veblen, *Engineers and the Price System*; Veblen, *Theory of Business Enterprise*. Taylor, *Principles of Scientific Management*, is the famous contemporary statement that applied some of these insights to industrial practice with personnel.

25. Veblen, *Theory of Business Enterprise*, 186–89. Veblen's ideas proved a primary influence in the theory of business cycles, which his Chicago student Wesley Mitchell made famous. See Mitchell, *Business Cycles*, 14–15, 475–588, 597; and "Thorstein Veblen," in *What Veblen Taught*, ed. Mitchell, xliii–xliv; see also Dorfman, *Economic Mind*, 3:455–73.

26. Veblen, *Theory of Business Enterprise*, 185–267; Veblen, *Absentee Ownership*, 85.

27. Veblen, *Theory of Business Enterprise*, 215–16; see also " 'The Overproduction Fallacy' " [1892], in Veblen, *Essays in Our Changing Order*, 104–13. For the most popular treatment of the overproduction paradox of scarcity amid plenty before the Great Depression, see Foster and Catchings, *Profits*; and Foster and Catchings, *Business without a Buyer*. These authors created a series of popular books on overproduction, urging the increase of purchasing power as the best remedy.

28. Veblen, *Engineers and the Price System*, chap. 1; Lerner, *Portable Veblen*, 436–37; Veblen, *Theory of Business Enterprise*, 29, 39; Veblen, *Absentee Ownership*, 220–21 n. 11.

29. For contemporary business statements of problems of overproduction and distribution, see Shaw, "Some Problems of Market Distribution"; and Borsodi, *Distribution Age*.

30. Veblen, *Instinct of Workmanship*, 31, 37.

31. Veblen, *Theory of Business Enterprise*, 27–29; Veblen, *Absentee Ownership*, 420–25.

32. Indeed, Veblen, in *Theory of Business Enterprise*, 146, and throughout *Absentee Ownership*, explored the issue of the separation of ownership and management long before its classic statement in Berle and Means, *Modern Corporation and Private Property*.

33. Veblen, *Engineers and the Price System*, chap. 5; Veblen, *Absentee Ownership*, 215–17, 418–19; Veblen, *Vested Interests and the Common Man*, 90–92.

34. Veblen, *Engineers and the Price System*, 115–51 (quotation on 129).

35. Veblen had little acknowledged influence on Technocracy, despite slight contact with some of its founders and his own abortive attempt in the 1920s to organize engineers. See Layton, "Veblen and the Engineers," 64–72. Layton, *Revolt of the Engineers*; and Noble, *America by Design*, trace engineering's role in the rise of corporate capitalism, providing the history of the phenomena Veblen observed. On Technocracy see Akin, *Technocracy and the American Dream*; and Segal, *Technological Utopianism in American Culture*.

36. This is not to argue that it is the best of Veblen's writings. Veblen here simply cast a symmetry between culture and economics that assumed much different forms and emphases in his subsequent books.

37. Veblen, *Theory of the Leisure Class*, 21–33.

38. Ibid., 85.

39. Ibid., 35–38, 75–76.

40. Ibid., 40–45. See also "The Instinct of Workmanship and the Irksomeness of Labor" [1898], in Veblen, *Essays in Our Changing Order*, 78–96.

41. Veblen, *Theory of the Leisure Class*, 77–80.

42. Ibid., 87–88.

43. Ibid., 86.

44. Ibid., 87–118. Veblen was often at pains to point out that his ironic use of terms such as "waste" and "honor" was not meant to denigrate, although it clearly was intended to prove a point about the associations of such terms with the powerful in society. See ibid., 78–79.

45. Adorno, "Veblen's Attack on Culture"; Douglas and Isherwood, *World of Goods*, 4–5; Lears, "Beyond Veblen," 75.

46. Veblen, *Theory of the Leisure Class*, 79, 80.

47. Veblen had rather starkly functional approaches to dress and housekeeping in his personal life: rope for a belt, coarse heavy shoes, crates as bookshelves. Moreover, throughout his life he tinkered with numerous improvements for farm equipment and household tools in quest of labor-saving and functional devices. See Dorfman, *Thorstein Veblen and His America*, 272, 305–6, 486, 497–98.

48. Veblen's account resonated with others: Gilman, *Women and Economics*; Addams, *Twenty Years at Hull House*. For a novel that has this dilemma at its core, see Fuller, *With the Procession*. See also Cowan, *More Work for Mother*.

49. Veblen, *Absentee Ownership*, 305. This was an insight only shared by some businessmen and, much later, by Veblen's critics in the Frankfurt School. See Mahin, *Advertising*; and Horkheimer and Adorno, *Dialectic of Enlightenment*.

50. Veblen, *Theory of Business Enterprise*, 11.

51. Veblen, *Absentee Ownership*, 98, 99, 78, 85.

52. Veblen, *Theory of Business Enterprise*, 55–57 (quotation on 56 n. 2). Veblen here echoes—with a very different interpretation—Scott, *Theory of Advertising*, the first full-length explication of psychological principles of advertising's appeal. Scott was a contemporary of Veblen's in Chicago. For the distinctive and influential advertising practices in Chicago in these years, see Gunther, *Taken at the Flood*; and Schultze, "Advertising, Science, and Professionalism," 1–42.

53. Veblen, *Theory of Business Enterprise*, 56; Veblen, *Absentee Ownership*, 301–2, 309–11.

54. Veblen, *Theory of Business Enterprise*, 56, 57. Veblen did not dismiss the argument that advertising was a legitimate business expense, but he cast doubt on advertising's usefulness in reducing the cost to consumers, noting that advertising helped keep prices at the high levels necessary for profits. Ibid., 59–61. See also Slichter, *Modern Economic Society*, 556–60.

55. Veblen, *Theory of Business Enterprise*, 385.

56. Ibid., 385–91. Veblen's critique was remarkable in that he made it in 1904, even as the publishing revolution that made advertising central was still underway. His was a lonely voice then pointing out the press's fundamental dependence on advertising, a notable exception being Ellis Parker Butler's humorous tales of a sharp agent; see Butler, *Perkins of Portland*. Veblen's description of editors' goals uncannily echoes the agenda of George Horace Lorimer, the former businessman hired by Cyrus Curtis to edit the *Saturday Evening Post* in 1899. Lorimer's commitment to "business fiction," serialized novels and stories telling of the romance and favorable aspects of business, helped propel the *Post* quickly to the biggest-selling weekly magazine, as well as the most lucrative American advertising medium. See Curtis Publishing Company, *Short History of "The Saturday Eve-*

ning Post", 14–17; Walsh, *Selling Forces*, 249–50; Ohmann, *Selling Culture*, 118–74; Christopher P. Wilson, "The Rhetoric of Consumption: Mass-Market Magazines and the Demise of the Gentle Reader, 1880–1920," in *Culture of Consumption*, ed. Fox and Lears, 53; and Cohn, *Creating America*.

57. Bok, *Americanization of Edward Bok*, 341–43; Samuel Hopkins Adams, "The Great American Fraud," *Collier's* 36 (October 7, 1905): 12–14; Young, *Toadstool Millionaires*, 205–22; Cramp, *Nostrums and Quackery*. See also Wilson, "Rhetoric of Consumption," 59–61.

58. Dorfman, *Thorstein Veblen and His America*, 506.

59. Veblen's critics today chide him for ignoring the symbolic dimensions of consumption and their necessary roles in the creation of a self. See McCracken, *Culture and Consumption*, 3–31, 71–103; Miller, *Material Culture and Mass Consumption*, 156; and n. 45, above.

60. Burns, *Wesley Clair Mitchell*, contains assessments by colleagues and scholars of his influence; see also Lucy Sprague Mitchell, *Two Lives*. Homan, *Contemporary Economic Thought*, 375–436, contains a perceptive early appreciation; see also Joseph Dorfman, *Economic Mind*, 3:455–73. Mitchell was a founder of both the New School for Social Research and the National Bureau of Economic Research. For his commitment to public policy see "The Social Sciences and National Planning," and "Intelligence and the Guidance of Economic Evolution," in Mitchell, *Backward Art of Spending Money and Other Essays*, 82–136; see also Alchon, *Invisible Hand of Planning*; and Karl, "Presidential Planning and Social Science Research."

61. Mitchell, *Business Cycles*; see also Mitchell, *Business Cycles: The Problem and Its Setting*; Dorfman, *Economic Mind*, 3:455–73; and Ross, *Origins of American Social Science*, 378–83.

62. Other economists, notably Rexford Tugwell at Columbia University and the Washington Square College institutionalists, would follow Mitchell's lead in emphasizing human activity as the departure point for all economic analysis, including institutional approaches. See Tugwell, Munro, and Stryker, *American Economic Life and the Means of Its Improvement*; Atkins et al., *Economics of Modern Life*; and Atkins et al., *Economic Behavior*. See also Hamilton, "Institutional Approach to Economic Theory"; and Dorfman, *Economic Mind*, 4:360–77. Ross, *Origins of American Social Science*, 378–86, 410–20, tellingly reappraises Mitchell and the institutionalist "movement." For a perceptive treatment of Mitchell that places the tension between empiricism and activism at the center of Mitchell's work, see Smith, *Social Science in the Crucible*; and more generally, see Bannister, *Sociology and Scientism*; and Bernstein, *Perilous Progress*, 44–48.

63. Mitchell, "Human Behavior and Economics," 2, 47. See also Frederick C. Mills, "A Professional Sketch," 109–10, and Lucy Sprague Mitchell, "A Personal Sketch," 69, in *Wesley Clair Mitchell*, ed. Burns.

64. Mitchell, *Backward Art of Spending Money and Other Essays*; Ross, *Origins of American Social Science*, 384–85.

65. Mitchell, "Backward Art of Spending Money"; the essay is reprinted in Mitchell, *Backward Art of Spending Money and Other Essays*, 3–19. The article originated as part of an uncompleted project, "The Money Economy," begun in 1905. In this Mitchell proposed to examine the workings of the pecuniary system and the role money played in the function-

ing of the economy. Here his intellectual debt to Veblen was clearest, and from this project came much of *Business Cycles* and several influential essays. See Joseph Dorfman, "A Professional Sketch," in *Wesley Clair Mitchell*, ed. Burns, 129–31.

66. The piece influenced the direction of numerous analysts of consumers for the next generation, including Stuart Chase, Hazel Kyrk, Henry Harap, and Robert S. Lynd; it even became required reading at the J. Walter Thompson advertising agency. On Lynd see Fox, "Epitaph for Middletown, 128. On Thompson, see "The Backward Art of Spending," *PI* 112, no. 12 (December 23, 1920): 8–9.

67. Matthews, *"Just a Housewife"*, traces the long association of women with consumption as a domestic responsibility. See also Gilman, *Women and Economics*; and Strasser, *Never Done*.

68. Mitchell, "Backward Art of Spending Money," 269.

69. Ibid., 271–72 (quotation on 271). On Peirce and applying industrial principles to housework, see Hayden, *Grand Domestic Revolution*, 63–88; and Strasser, *Never Done*, 195–201.

70. Mitchell, "Backward Art of Spending Money," 273. The issues of professionalism and scientific efficiency became primary concerns of an important wing of the home economics movement. See, for contemporary statements, Frederick, *New Housekeeping*; and Bruére and Bruére, *Increasing Home Efficiency*.

71. Mitchell, "Backward Art of Spending Money," 273–74 (quotation on 274). The argument for the socialization of housework had been advanced since the 1880s in experimental and cooperative kitchens, which Mitchell saw as one of the most promising solutions to the dilemma he outlined; ibid., 280.

72. Young, *Pure Food*; Okun, *Fair Play in the Marketplace*.

73. Mitchell, "Backward Art of Spending Money," 276.

74. Ibid., 276, 277.

75. Ibid., 269.

76. Ibid., 279–81. Horowitz, *Morality of Spending*, 67–108, examines the context of public concern over inflation and "the rising cost of living," which emerged in the Progressive Era to fuel debates among journalists, economists, and social commentators over extravagance, frugality, and proper spending behavior. See also Samson, "Emergence of a Consumer Interest," chap. 5.

77. "Bentham's Felicific Calculus," in Mitchell, *Backward Art of Spending Money and Other Essays*, 177–202; Mitchell, "Human Behavior and Economics," 3–11.

78. Mitchell, "Backward Art of Spending Money," 277.

79. "The Press and Its Relation to Public Opinion and Government," 12–13, address at Yale, December 8, 1930, Stanley Resor—Speeches and Writings File, JWTA.

80. Goldstein, "Mediating Consumption"; Stage and Vicenti, *Rethinking Home Economics*, 235–96.

81. Perhaps Kyrk's most influential work was *Economic Problems of the Family*.

82. Kyrk, *Theory of Consumption*, 5.

83. On commentators on consumption, see Horowitz, *Morality of Spending*. On domesticity see Sklar, *Catherine Beecher*; and Matthews, *"Just a Housewife"*. On the home and the relationship of morality, character, family, and possessions, see Karen Halttunen, "From Parlor to Living Room: Domestic Space, Interior Decoration, and the Culture of Personal-

ity," in *Consuming Visions*, ed. Bronner, 157–89; Clark, *American Family Home*; and Mc-Dannell, *Christian Home in Victorian America*. On industry, aesthetics, and consumption see Ruskin, *"Unto This Last"*; Stein, *John Ruskin and Aesthetic Thought*; and Boris, *Art and Labor*.

84. Kyrk, *Theory of Consumption*, 6, 7, 131–32.

85. Ibid., 2, 119.

86. Ibid., 13.

87. Ibid., 19.

88. Ibid., 27–28, 41, 91–92.

89. Ibid, 41–42.

90. Ibid., 43–44.

91. Ibid., 101.

92. Ibid., 113–15.

93. Ibid., 116–17. This is essentially the argument that Arthur Kallet and F. J. Schlink would make to indict both private enterprise and government regulation in *100,000,000 Guinea Pigs*; see chapter 7. See also Hamilton, "Ancient Maxim Caveat Emptor"; Harap, *Education of the Consumer*.

94. Kyrk, *Theory of Consumption*, 121–24.

95. Ibid., 286–89.

96. Ibid., 153–55.

97. Ibid., 172.

98. Echoing Veblen again, Kyrk noted that the instinct of workmanship, the instinct to collect and to own, the play instinct, and the "desire for distinction" all influenced patterns of consumption. Ibid., 198–203.

99. Ibid., 238.

100. Ibid., 246–52.

101. Ibid., 280–84.

102. Ibid., 289–93.

103. For important texts of a vast literature, see Knight, *Risk, Uncertainty, and Profit*; Knight, *Freedom and Reform*; Becker, *Economic Approach to Human Behavior*; and Friedman, *Free to Choose*.

104. One telling example was an increasing coverage of consumer issues in the *Annals of the American Academy of Political and Social Science*, beginning in the 1920s.

105. Tugwell, Munro, and Stryker, *American Economic Life and the Means of Its Improvement*; Atkins et al., *Economic Behavior*, 1:263–305; Slichter, *Modern Economic Society*. Though not strictly an "institutionalist," Slichter was perhaps the most outspoken in outlining the disadvantages consumers faced in the economy and in calling for action to correct those handicaps.

106. Lynd and Lynd, *Middletown*; Smith, "Robert Lynd and Consumerism in the 1930s"; Fox, "Epitaph for Middletown"; Hoyt, *Consumption of Wealth*. See also Ogburn, *Social Change*, for the understanding of cultural evolution adopted by both the Lynds and Hoyt.

107. Douglas, *Wages and the Family*; Douglas, *Real Wages in the United States*; Phillips, *Social Unit*; Warbasse, *Cooperative Democracy*.

108. See Andrews, *Economics of the Household*, for an exception, along with the works cited in n. 105.

CHAPTER FIVE

1. Slichter, *Modern Economic Society*, 564.

2. Lippmann, *Drift and Mastery*, 53.

3. Chase, *Poor Old Competition*, 33.

4. Mildred Holmes, "Bunk," *J Walter Thompson News Bulletin* 139 (August 1929): 3.

5. Chase and Schlink, *Your Money's Worth*; Lynd, "Democracy's Third Estate," 497.

6. Young, *Pure Food*.

7. See Sklar, *Florence Kelley and the Nation's Work*; Katherine Kish Sklar, "The Consumers' White Label Campaign of the National Consumers' League, 1898–1918," in *Getting and Spending*, ed. Strasser, McGovern, and Judt, 17–35; Storrs, *Civilizing Capitalism*; Dirks, "Righteous Goods"; and Wiedenhoft, "Politics of Consumption." Stressing the mixed results of consumption as a tool for labor is Frank, *Purchasing Power*.

8. Cuff, *War Industries Board*; Baruch, *American Industry in the War*; Chase, *Tragedy of Waste*, 3–11. See also Hounshell, *From the American System to Mass Production*. On collectivization and the wartime economy see Kennedy, *Over Here*; Graham, *Encore for Reform*; and Hawley, *Great War and the Search for a Modern Order*.

9. Nash, *Life of Herbert Hoover*, treats Hoover's career through the war, which prepared him for his later position as industry leader, secretary of commerce, and ultimately president.

10. Committee on the Elimination of Waste in Industry, *Waste in Industry*; [Brady], *Industrial Standardization*, 10–11. Hawley, "Herbert Hoover, the Commerce Secretariat, and the Vision of an Associative State," discusses Hoover's broad vision of the economy and the context of the standardization movement's emphasis on voluntary cooperation among industries with government and industrial self-regulation.

11. The American Engineering Standards Committee (AESC) changed its name in 1928 to the American Standards Association (ASA).

12. Cochrane, *Measures for Progress*, 231. For this history of the bureau's expansion up to the 1920s see ibid., 38–229.

13. [National Bureau of Standards], *Standards Yearbook, 1927*, 32–33; [Brady], *Industrial Standardization*, 22–30; Schlink, "Classification of Engineering and Industrial Standards." See also Agnew, "Work of the American Engineering Standards Committee." The major efforts in standardization included nomenclature, units (of length, mass, time, and temperature), dimensions, ratings for operational use (such as horsepower), quality (material of composition, workmanship, and performance), and practice (for operation and safety in use).

14. F. J. Schlink, "How Specifications Bring Savings," address before the National Association of Purchasing Agents, Buffalo, N.Y., June 5, 1929, n.p., FJS—Papers and Talks File, Box 732, CRP.

15. "Measurements for the Household," *Circular of the Bureau of Standards* 55 (1915); "Materials for the Household," *Circular of the Bureau of Standards* 70 (1917); "Safety in the Household," *Circular of the Bureau of Standards* 75 (1918).

16. "Measurements for the Household," 30–31, 38–107.

17. The bureau sent out 33,000 circulars. Despite the volume of requests for the card, the bureau's budget permitted a print run of less than 50,000. Cochrane, *Measures for Progress*, 133–38.

18. As a boy, Schlink read voraciously on many subjects, and he pursued a fascination with mechanical devices such as waterwheels and clocks. He gave great credit to the librarians in his town for encouraging his curiosity. FJS interview with author, August 1984.

19. Cochrane, *Measures for Progress*, 170, 255–56; FJS interview with author, August 1984; "Frederick John Schlink," Box 514, File 31.1, CRP; P. G. Agnew, "F. J. Schlink, Assistant Secretary, Resigns to Direct Consumers' Organization," *ASA Bulletin* 59 (March 1931): 9.

20. Agnew, "F. J. Schlink, Assistant Secretary, Resigns," 9.

21. Hudson, "Organized Effort in Simplification," 1; Department of Commerce, *Simplified Practice*, 1–27; [National Bureau of Standards], *Standards Yearbook, 1927*, 272–74; [Brady], *Industrial Standardization*, 122–65; and Schlink, "Classification of Engineering and Industrial Standards," 122. Generally, the Division of Simplified Practice in the Department of Commerce took responsibility for simplified practice of a nontechnical nature, that is, the reduction of number of types, while the AESC oversaw standardization and reduction where technical issues remained unresolved.

22. Department of Commerce, *Simplified Practice*, 24–27; [Brady], *Industrial Standardization*, 240–55. The definitive account of consumers and standards did not come until the Depression: see Coles, *Standardization of Consumers' Goods*.

23. Agnew, "F. J. Schlink, Assistant Secretary, Resigns," 9; Agnew, "Standardization—A Woman's Problem."

24. Schlink and Brady, "Standards and Specifications," 235; see also Brady, "How Government Standards Affect the Ultimate Consumer." This entire May 1928 *Annals of the Academy of Political and Social Science* was devoted to standards. See also Schlink, "Tests and Specifications"; Schlink, "The Technique of Buying under Specifications," *JHE* 19 (October 1927): 589–90. For evidence of the interest of home economists in standards, see Cook, "Standardization, or Taking the Guesswork Out of Buying"; Cook, "Problems of Household Buying," 94; Williams, "Purchasing Problems of the Household Buyer," 727–29; Agnew, "Technical Standards for Consumer Goods"; see also [National Bureau of Standards], *Standards Yearbook, 1927* and issues of the *ASA Bulletin*, 1927–30. Both the American Home Economics Association and the Bureau of Home Economics in the Department of Agriculture were members of the AESC and later the American Standards Association.

25. It should be noted, too, that the home economics movement worked closely with the ASA to formulate standards for some consumer goods, initiating research projects and trying to work with often recalcitrant industries to establish minimum standards for bed linen, canned fruit, and other goods. See P. G. Agnew, "Technical Standards for Consumer Goods—A 'Five-Year Plan'?" *ASA Bulletin* 63 (July 1931): 15–18; and Agnew, "Standardization—A Woman's Problem."

26. Schlink, "Advantages of Standardization."

27. His Harvard classmates included a number who would make their names as writers —Walter Lippmann, Heywood Broun, T. S. Eliot, and John Reed.

28. Chase and Chase, *Honeymoon Experiment*. The basic approach of the Chases' account resonates today in current studies such as Ehrenreich, *Nickel and Dimed*.

29. There is no adequate biography of Stuart Chase, whose career as writer and interpreter of economic and political trends might make him a suggestive and illuminating example of the twentieth-century public intellectual. James Lanier is preparing one at the

present. See Westbrook, "Tribune of the Technostructure," 391–408; and Horowitz, *Morality of Spending*, 110–13, 152–53, for some suggestive treatments of the scope of his work.

30. Westbrook, "Tribune of the Technostructure," recounts this episode, which is discussed more thoroughly from an accounting standpoint in Bradley and Merino, "Stuart Chase." Chase spoke of it briefly in an oral history interview with Norman Silber, September 29, 1977, 10, Oral Histories, CUA. See also Chase, "Luxury of Integrity."

31. SC interview with Colston Warne, October 7, 1969, 1–2, Oral History Collection, CSCM. Chase and Schlink met through mutual friends, either Agnew or some of the economists associated with the Washington Square College economics department; see FJS interview with author, August 1984.

32. Schainwald, "Genesis and Growth," 34, indicates that the two met in 1926, after *The Tragedy of Waste*, but Chase singled Schlink out especially for thanks in that book's preface. In fact, Chase and Schlink were already collaborating in print by the end of 1925. Chase remembered meeting Schlink after the book was published, but Schlink was vague on the exact timing of their meeting. See SC interview with Colston E. Warne, October 7, 1969, 2–3, Oral History Collection, CSCM; and FJS interview with author, August 1984.

33. Chase, *Tragedy of Waste*, 270; Committee on the Elimination of Waste in Industry, *Waste in Industry*.

34. Chase, *Tragedy of Waste*, 23–25, 29–30, 265–68; Tawney, *Acquisitive Society*.

35. Chase, *Tragedy of Waste*, 53–107.

36. Ibid., 43–52.

37. The exception to this was Harvey W. Wiley, the first head of the Food and Drug Administration, whose career during the mid-1920s was in relative eclipse. See Wiley, *History of a Crime against the Food Law*; and Anderson, *Health of a Nation*.

38. Chase, *Tragedy of Waste*, 42.

39. Chase and Schlink, *Your Money's Worth*. It was acknowledged at the time, although not by the book's publishers, that Chase wrote nearly all the book and Schlink supplied virtually all the data. *Your Money's Worth* certainly resembles Chase's other writings enough for it to be attributed solely to him, as was often the case when the book was published. But both authors viewed it as a collaboration, even many decades later, and it will be referred to herein as a product of joint authorship. See SC interview with Norman Silber, September 29, 1977, 14, Oral History Collection, CSCM; and FJS interview with author, August 1984.

40. For descriptions of the New Era's consumer economy, see Barber, *From New Era to New Deal*; and Olney, *Buy Now, Pay Later*. In 1927 advertising expenditures peaked at a number of the most significant and lucrative magazines: see Curtis Publishing Company, *National Magazine Advertising*.

41. Such celebrations of mass production and modern industrial life were ubiquitous throughout the post–World War I era, but see especially Mazur, *American Prosperity*; Chase, *Men and Machines*; and Filene, *Way Out*. See also Prothro, *Dollar Decade*; Soule, *Prosperity Decade*; Leuchtenburg, *Perils of Prosperity*, 178–203; and Hawley, *Great War and the Search for a Modern Order*.

42. It is important to note that Chase and Schlink's explanation of the principal difference between mid-nineteenth and twentieth-century conditions of consumption was the conventional business wisdom at the time, as well as the analysis of Mitchell, Chase, and

the Lynds. See, for example, N. W. Ayer & Son, *In Behalf of Advertising*; and Calkins, *Business, the Civilizer*, 13–14.

43. Chase and Schlink, *Your Money's Worth*, 27–28, 256; Chase, *Tragedy of Waste*, chaps. 3–7. The conviction that consumers' estrangement from the material conditions of daily life originated in modern urbanization was shared by the most prominent scholars of consumption at the time. See Harap, *Education of the Consumer*; Lynd and Lynd, *Middletown*; Lynd with Hanson, "People as Consumers," 881.

44. Chase and Schlink, *Your Money's Worth*, 2.

45. Ibid., 1–26. The metaphor of the consumer marketplace as Wonderland has ironically been echoed by historians and commentators such as T. J. Jackson Lears, who has noted the surrealism of advertising's constant and promiscuous intermixing of symbols, out of context of their original clouded meanings. See Lears, "Some Versions of Fantasy"; and Lears, *Fables of Abundance*.

46. Chase and Schlink, *Your Money's Worth*, 9, 41.

47. Ibid., 25.

48. Ibid., 94–167, 246. Here, *Your Money's Worth* admittedly echoed long-standing arguments against harmful proprietary medicines; the analysis followed in the tradition of Samuel Hopkins Adams's muckraking exposé of patent medicines, "The Great American Fraud," in *Collier's* in 1905–6; see Young, *Medical Messiahs*, 30–32, 152–57.

49. Marchand, *Advertising the American Dream*, esp. 1–24, 335–63; T. J. Jackson Lears, "From Salvation to Self-Realization: Advertising and the Therapeutic Roots of the Consumer Culture, 1880–1920," in *Culture of Consumption*, ed. Fox and Lears, 17–29; Lears, "Some Versions of Fantasy."

50. Chase and Schlink, *Your Money's Worth*, 165.

51. Ibid., 19. For the significance of Listerine, see Marchand, *Advertising the American Dream*, 18–20; and Fox, *Mirror Makers*, 97–98.

52. Chase and Schlink, *Your Money's Worth*, 24–25, 141. See also Johnston, "Testimonials, C.O.D." The ethical questions generated by the revelation of widespread use of paid testimonials rocked the advertising industry in the late 1920s through the Depression, as the Federal Trade Commission investigated the practice. For a defense of such advertising by its leading exponent, see Stanley Resor, "Personalities and the Public: Some Aspects of Testimonial Advertising," *J. Walter Thompson News Bulletin* 138 (April 1929): 1–7; *Ethical Problems of Modern Advertising*; Marchand, *Advertising the American Dream*, 96–98.

53. Chase and Schlink, *Your Money's Worth*, 166.

54. Ibid., 47–48, 76–93. See also FJS, "Some Limitations of Branded Merchandise," *Journal of Marketing* 2 (January 1927): 3–7, clipped in Macy Report File, Box 737, CRP.

55. Chase and Schlink, *Your Money's Worth*, 17, 111–17, 166. For a statement of the conventional business wisdom on the side of modern packaging, see Franken and Larrabee, *Packages That Sell*. These techniques of changing packaging to disguise a reduction in unit weight or volume are commonly practiced. The "one-pound" can of coffee now weighs eleven ounces, for example. See Hine, *Total Package*.

56. Chase and Schlink, *Your Money's Worth*, 166–67.

57. Ibid., 164.

58. Chase and Schlink, *Your Money's Worth*, 61–75; FJS, "A Writer and Economist Looks

into the Store from the Outside: The Department Store and the Ultimate Consumer," 1, address before the Sales Promotion Division, National Retail Dry Goods Association, February 8, 1928, FJS—Papers and Talks File, Box 731, CRP. See also Macy File, Box 737, CRP.

59. Chase and Schlink, *Your Money's Worth*, 61–68. See also Schlink, "Improving Purchasing Methods through Specifications"; and FJS, "How Specifications Bring Savings," paper read before the National Association of Purchasing Agents, Buffalo, N.Y., June 5, 1929, Box 732, FJS—Papers and Talks File, CRP.

60. Chase and Schlink, *Your Money's Worth*, 204, 263.

61. Ibid., 264–67.

62. Ibid., 245.

63. Ibid., 12.

64. See Foster and Catchings, *Business without a Buyer*. Chase, especially, agreed that business produced too much for Americans easily to consume; however, this problem paled before a greater one, namely, that Americans were surfeited with a glut of things they neither wanted nor needed.

65. Chase and Schlink, *Your Money's Worth*, 261–62. There were numerous critics of such "standardized" aspects of American life, although mostly from elitist perspectives. See, perhaps most prominently, Lewis, *Babbitt*; Stearns, *Civilization in the United States*; and Borsodi, *This Ugly Civilization*. Janice Radway discusses the elite fears of standardization in American literary forms in *A Feeling for Books*, 205–10. See also Shi, *Simple Life*, 215–30; and Susman, *Culture as History*, 105–21. For a broad and inclusive anthology on standardization and standards of living, see Eliot, *American Standards and Planes of Living*.

66. For a differing interpretation of the same phenomenon, see Frederick, "New Wealth, New Standards of Living, and Changed Family Budgets."

67. Chase, "Six Cylinder Ethics," 26, 28.

68. Warne, the first president of Consumers Union, grew up in and around Ithaca, New York, and studied with Veblen and his student H. J. Davenport at Cornell: see Katz, "Consumers Union," 100–101. For Mitchell, see Lucy Sprague Mitchell, *Two Lives*.

69. For the impact of visiting Russia, see Chase, *Prosperity*; Chase, *Poor Old Competition*; Chase, *New Deal*; Westbrook, "Tribune of the Technostructure"; and Lawson, *Failure of Independent Liberalism*, 75–84. On Schlink's socialist sympathies, see FJS to Bruce Bliven, September 19, 1928, Box 1044, Personal Items File MC-3, CRP. Schlink asked that Bliven keep his political views anonymous since "socialism and anarchy are all of a piece with some of the conservative members of the organization I work for [the AESC]."

70. SC interview with Colston Warne, October 7, 1969, 3, Oral History Collection, CSCM. Schlink also read Veblen but never mentioned him specifically in his writings and claimed not to have any contact with him in New York, when Chase had become a part of Veblen's circle there. See FJS interview with author, August 1984. Westbrook, "Tribune of the Technostructure," 399–403, stresses Chase's commitment to rule by a technocratic elite, but that commitment grew much stronger in the Depression and New Deal than it was during the 1920s, the years under discussion here.

71. The book sold well with the Book-of-the-Month Club endorsement, and it probably sold somewhere around 100,000 copies over the next decade. See FJS to Don Wharton, August 13, 1937, Box 727, File 62.262, CRP. On the Book-of-the-Month Club see Rubin, *Making of Middlebrow Culture*, chap. 4; and Radway, *A Feeling for Books*.

72. See Day Monroe, review of *Your Money's Worth*, *JHE* 19 (October 1927): 605–6.

73. Lerner, "Book Notes," 306–7; Tugwell, "Contemporary Buncombe," 958–59.

74. See "Iconoclasm: More Buying, Less Selling," *Tide* 1, no. 3 (July 1927): 1–2.

75. Carpenter, *Dollars and Sense*.

76. Kenneth M. Goode, "Mr. Chase Broadcasts the Beans," *Advertising and Selling* 9, no. 7 (July 27, 1927): 28; Roy S. Durstine, "Twelve Cylinder Critics," *Forum* 79, no. 1 (January 1928): 37. The latter piece was reprinted in slightly amended form in Durstine, *This Advertising Business*, 57–79. See also Cherington, *Consumer Looks at Advertising*, 3–6; Tom Masson, "Beware the Jabberwock of Advertising," *PI* 140, no. 7 (August 11, 1927): 57; Edgar Quackenbush, "Economists in Wonderland," *Advertising and Selling* 9, no. 12 (August 6, 1927): 27; "The Little Schoolmaster's Classroom," *PI* 140, no. 9 (September 1, 1927): 184; and Earnest Elmo Calkins, in *Advertising and Selling* 9, no. 11 (September 21, 1927): 20.

77. Chase and Schlink, *Your Money's Worth*, 26, 43, 77. See also Kenner, *Fight for Truth in Advertising*, a self-congratulatory account of the self-policing reform efforts within the advertising profession from 1911 through 1936; and Pease, *Responsibilities of American Advertising*, 44–86.

78. Carpenter, *Dollars and Sense*, 43–44. Commercial home economist Christine Frederick claimed, "The woman consumer doesn't care to waste time on the great mass of purely technical data about household goods; she'd become a walking encyclopedia if she tried to master it all." Frederick, "Can a Consumer Club Movement Succeed?" *Advertising and Selling* 11, no. 3 (December 12, 1928): 40; see also Frederick, *Selling Mrs. Consumer*, 328–30.

79. Carpenter, *Dollars and Sense*, 6; Frederick, *Selling Mrs. Consumer*, 321, 327–30; Cherington, *Consumer Looks at Advertising*, 71–75; Hotchkiss and Franken, *Leadership of Advertised Brands*.

80. Harford Powell Jr., review of *Your Money's Worth* by Chase and Schlink, *Atlantic Monthly* 142, no. 3 (September 1927): 28; Frederick, *Selling Mrs. Consumer*, 321–22; Carpenter, *Dollars and Sense*, 240–41.

81. "Why Grading Bureaus?" *PI* 144, no. 8 (August 23, 1928): 163; Frederick, *Selling Mrs. Consumer*, 330–31.

82. Durstine, "Advertising Man's View," 305; Frederick, "Can a Consumers Club Movement Succeed?" 40. See also Powell, review of *Your Money's Worth*, 26; Carpenter, *Dollars and Sense*, 220–21; Quackenbush, "Economists in Wonderland," 27, 64; "Will Buyers Support Attacks on Advertising?" *PI* 140, no. 13 (September 29, 1927): 187–88.

83. Quackenbush, "Economists in Wonderland," 66–67.

84. Carpenter, *Dollars and Sense*, 110; see also Powell, review of *Your Money's Worth*, 28.

85. In this sense Chase and Schlink differed from Ralph Borsodi, who weighed in with his own criticism of advertising, *Advertising vs. National Prosperity*, which argued essentially that advertising was an economic waste since it added substantially to distribution costs without reducing costs to the consumer. Moreover, Borsodi echoed the criticism that modern culture was too commercialized, and in the mid-1920s he and his family began an experiment in subsistence living, producing at home as much as possible for their own use. See Borsodi, *Flight from the City*.

86. Holmes, "Bunk," 3.

87. Carpenter, *Dollars and Sense*, 22–24; Theodore F. MacManus, "Only Lazy People Are Contented," *Nation's Business* 18 (May 1930): 160. For the advertising industry anthem

on modernity and new desires, see Robert R. Updegraff, "The New American Tempo," *Advertising and Selling* 7, no. 1 (May 5, 1926): 19–20, 48–54; Updegraff, "Tomorrow's Business and the Stream of Life," *Advertising and Selling* 8, no. 26 (April 20, 1927): 19–20, 44–52; and the essays in Kendall, *New American Tempo.*

88. Hotchkiss, "Economic Defence of Advertising," 15–16. Hotchkiss's remarks were given in a debate that raised most of the same criticisms as Chase and Schlink, *Your Money's Worth.*

89. Frederick, "Can a Consumers Club Succeed?"; Carpenter, *Dollars and Sense*, 8.

90. See Mark Wiseman, "What Is Money For?" *PI* 145, no. 5 (November 1, 1928): 85.

91. See Goode, "Mr. Chase Broadcasts," 40, 65; Durstine, "Advertising Man's View," 305; Carpenter, *Dollars and Sense.*

92. For the most important studies of advertising psychology, see Scott, *Theory of Advertising*; Hollingworth, *Advertising and Selling*; Adams, *Advertising and Its Mental Laws*; and Poffenberger, *Psychology of Advertising.*

93. Christine M. Frederick, "Why Women Will Not Buy by Specification," *PI* 166, no. 8 (February 22, 1934): 91–93; Durstine, "An Advertising Man's View," 305; Goode, "Mr. Chase Broadcasts," 40, 65; Wiseman, "What Is Money For?" 86–87.

94. Goode, "Mr. Chase Broadcasts," 65.

95. Sheldon and Arens, *Consumer Engineering*, made this point explicit in the trough of the Depression: greater planned obsolescence, frequent turnover, and extended prosperity were all linked. Christine Frederick had been an advocate for increased obsolescence for some years: see *Selling Mrs. Consumer*, 245–55. The consumer's duty was to spend. See Foster and Catchings, *Profits* and *Business without a Buyer*, for the related argument that to facilitate more consumption, business had to increase purchasing power in workers' salaries.

96. Tugwell, "Contemporary Buncombe," 958.

97. Both authors later remembered devoting free time at night and on weekends to answering mail generated from *Your Money's Worth*, but Schlink likely spent more time on this chore; he had access to the technical information at the American Standards Association, and Chase spent part of 1927 on a trip to Russia with Tugwell, John Dewey, and Paul Douglas. Schlink later claimed that he alone answered the *Your Money's Worth* inquiries. While Schlink at times later tried to deny that Chase had a role in establishing the Consumers' Club and Consumers' Research, Chase was prominently named in early organizational literature, serving as treasurer and first president. See FJS interview with author, August 1984, Tape 1; SC interview with Colston Warne, October 7, 1969, 5, CSCM; SC, "*Your Money's Worth* Twenty-Five Years Later," *CR* 19, no. 2 (February 1954), clipping in Stuart Chase Papers, Library of Congress, Washington, D.C.; "Introduction to Consumers' Research," *CRB* 2, no. 6 (May 1932): 2; and Schainwald, "Genesis and Growth," 46, 52.

98. I found very little immediate consumer response to *Your Money's Worth* either in the Chase Papers or in the Consumers' Research Papers to which I had access. Yet Schlink in conversation remembered that some correspondents were more concerned with the excesses and dominance of salesmanship and advertising in American life than with information on specific goods.

99. FJS to SC, May 17, 1932, Box 502, File 13, CRP; see also FJS to Peter Hatter, February 27, 1935, Box 531, File 89, CRP.

100. FJS to Mrs. Frances Basin Parish, December 12, 1927, Foundations File, CRP.

101. SC to Professor Joseph Jastrow, November 12, 1928, Box 514, File 31.63, CRP; see also FJS to Henry Harap, January 28, 1930, Box 514, File 31.63, CRP.

102. "Foreword," *Consumers' Club Commodity List*, First Issue, October 1927, Box 11, CRP (emphasis added). See also "Introduction to Consumers' Research," 5–7.

103. *Consumers' Club Commodity List*, October 27, 1927, Box 11, CRP.

104. See "Your Money's Worth Club" (1928), mimeograph, Box 11, CRP.

105. "A Proposed Consumers' Foundation," 1, [ca. 1929], Foundation File, CRP; SC, "Memorandum for the Establishment of the Consumers' Foundation," 1–2, 1928, Stuart Chase Papers, Library of Congress, Washington, D.C. The two documents are similar, and the former appears to be a revision of the latter.

106. "Proposed Consumers' Foundation," 3.

107. SC, "Memorandum for the Establishment of the Consumers' Foundation," 5; "Proposed Consumers' Foundation," 4.

108. Schainwald, "Genesis and Growth," 52, 54–55.

109. See FJS interview with author, August 1984; Katz, "Consumers Union"; and Silber, *Test and Protest*, chap. 1.

CHAPTER SIX

1. Chase, *A New Deal*, 235.

2. Schlink, "Safeguarding the Consumer's Interest," 113.

3. "To All Those Interested in Consumers' Research," *CRB* 2.06 (May 1932): 21.

4. On New Era capitalism see Barber, *From New Era to New Deal*. On the consumer goods revolution and the expansion of national advertising see Marchand, *Advertising the American Dream*; Olney, *Buy Now, Pay Later*; *National Advertising Records*, 1929–34; and Borden, *Economic Effects of Advertising*, 47–71.

5. For a sampling of hostile and friendly opinion, see Carpenter, *Dollars and Sense*; Frederick, *Selling Mrs. Consumer*, 319–31; and Wyand, *Economics of Consumption*, 392–95.

6. I use the word "represent" to mean both "to speak for," as in the notion of political representation, and "to depict." Both of these issues were at stake in the professional tensions and battles that would erupt in the 1930s over consumers in public life.

7. See extract from *Charter of Consumers' Research, Inc.*, December 13, 1929, quoted in Schainwald, "Genesis and Growth," 54.

8. "CR's Purpose Not Propaganda," *Introduction to Consumers' Research*, CR 2.06 (May 1932): 1; FJS to Professor Robert T. Fitzhugh, October 26, 1932, Box 529, File 85, CRP; FJS to Oscar Cox, May 18, 1934, Box 501, File 12.2, CRP.

9. See Schainwald, "Genesis and Growth," 52; "Consumers' Research," Bulletin 102.b (1929); SC interview with Norman I. Silber, 21–22, September 29, 1977, Oral History Collection, CSCM.

10. *Introduction to Consumers' Research*, 6–7; FJS to A. J. McKnight, January 13, 1933, Box 530, File 88.11, CRP; FJS to Mrs. Shelton Bissell, February 19, 1932, Box 501, File 12, CRP.

11. "Weights and Measures," *CR* 0.15 (May 1930): 3–4; Pauline Beery Mack, "Improvement in Silk Weighting Depends on Consumer," *CRGB* 2, no. 1 (October 1932): 13–17; "A Study in 'Slack' Filling of Packages," *CRGB* 3, no. 3 (April 1934): 18.

12. Dallas McKown and Charles Throop, "How Not to Buy," *CRGB* 2, no. 2 (January 1933): 12–16.

13. Ibid.

14. Ibid.

15. "Three Studies of Canned Foods," *CR* 2, no. 75 (October 1932): 4.

16. "Report of Consumers' Research Fiscal Year Ending October 1, 1931," October 28, 1931, Appendix I, Box 11, CRP; FJS and Reginald Joyce interview with author, August 1985.

17. See "Report of Consumers' Research, Fiscal Year Ending October 1, 1931," Appendix C; "Report of Consumers' Research, Inc. Fiscal Year Ending September 30, 1932," October 17, 1932, Appendix I and J, Box 11, CRP.

18. See, for example, "Education for Consumption: The Home Economist's Responsibility for Education in Intelligent Buying," Box 732, CRP; and FJS, "Can One Buy Intelligently in the Modern Market?" in *Problems of the Household Buyer: Proceedings of a Conference Organized by the Department of Home Economics at the University of Chicago*, 5–7, 57–59, Box 733, CRP. The conference marked the meeting of Schlink and Hazel Kyrk.

19. See FJS to Elizabeth Ellis Hoyt, October 7, 1932, Box 871, File 13.912, CRP; and "Facts Require Interpretation," *Introduction to Consumers' Research*, 6.

20. "The 'Low-Down' on Our Recommendations," *Consumers' Club Bulletin* 102 (April 1929): 2, Box 11, CRP; "Sources of Information," *Introduction to Consumers' Research*, 8; FJS and Reginald Joyce interview with author.

21. See FJS to SC, July 3, 1931, 2, Box 512, File 023.3, CRP.

22. "General Notes," *CR* 1.20 (May 1931): 3.

23. On the number of brand names reported, see "Cumulative Subject and Brand Name Index of 'Handbooks of Buying' and 'General Bulletins' Issued During 1933," January 1934, 4–8, Box 21, CRP. On the difficulty of adequate comprehensive coverage of all brand names see Reginald Joyce to D. H. Marsh, July 6, 1936, Box 504, File 13.411, CRP; and "Testing Everything Not Possible," *Introduction to Consumers' Research*, 7. On CR's achievement in the field of specific recommendations, see "A Basis for Judging CR," *Introduction to Consumers' Research*, 6.

24. For example, CR's "A" recommendation of the 1931 Ford was given in part as it was "less likely to disappoint the user in comparison with the claims made for it in advertising." See "Automobiles," *CR* 1, no. 20 (May 1931): 1.

25. "Discussion of Test Methods and Results," *CR* 1, no. 28 (July 1931): 2.

26. "A Report on Juice Extractors," *CRGB* 3, no. 2 (January 1934): 4–5; "Mechanical Refrigerators—Some Are Pretty Good," *CRB* 1, no. 6 (April 1935): 20–22; "Automobiles of 1935," *CRB* 1, no. 7 (May 1935): 6.

27. See, for example, "Electrical Toasters," *CR* 1, no. 6 (January 1931): 1–2; "Electric Kitchen Appliances," *CR* 1, no. 12 (April 1931): 5; "A Study of Vacuum Cleaners," *CR* 1, no. 28 (July 1931): 4; "The Importance of Shock Hazard When It Involves Not Merely a Consumer's Loss," *CRGB* 1, no. 1 (September 1931): 7; D. H. Palmer, "Automobile Safety before Beauty," *CRGB* 2, no. 4 (July 1933): 10–11; "Electric Heating Pads," *CRB* 1, no. 1 (November 1934): 23–24; "Automobiles of 1935," *CRB* 1, no. 7 (May 1935): 11, 17–18; and "A Further Warning against the Use of a Power Wringer," *CRB* 1, no. 7 (May 1935): 24. Perhaps the most prominent among such reports were CR's investigations into the health hazards of everyday goods due to poisonous chemical ingredients. See "Hair Removal Presents New

Hazard," *CR* 1, no. 12 (April 1931): 6–7; "Ever-Present Dangers from Lead and Arsenic," *CRGB* 1, no. 3 (September 1932): 8–11; Cora Sanders, "Hocus-Pocus in the New Cosmetics," *CRGB* 3, no. 2 (January 1934): 3; "Arsenic Poisoning: A Reality," *CRGB* 3, no. 2 (January 1934): 6–7; and "Leaded Gas a Serious Menace to Health," *CRGB* 3, no. 2 (January 1934): 9–10.

28. "Household Lubricating Oils," *CRGB* 3, no. 1 (October 1933): 15–16; "Shoe Polishes and Dressings, and Shoe Dyes," *CRB* 1, no. 1 (November 1934): 4–5; "New Test of Electric Washing Machines," *CRB* 1, no. 1 (November 1934): 13.

29. See, for example, FJS to H. L. Nichols Jr., April 21, 1937, Box 531, File 88.3111, CRP; Reginald Joyce and FJS interview with author; "Dear Subscribers," *CR* 0.25 (December 1930): 1 [on aluminum cookware]; "Color on the Boulevard," *CR* 0.15 (May 1930): 8; "Attention Diverters Only $49.50," *CRGB* 2, no. 4 (July 1933): 9; "Fruits and Vegetables— How to Eat Them Without Being Poisoned," *CRB* 1, no. 1 (November 1934): 17–21; Sanders, "Hocus-Pocus in the New Cosmetics," 3.

30. "Outside White Paint," *CR* 0.15 (May 1930): 6; "Rubber Hot Water Bottles," *CRGB* 4, no. 1 (November 1934): 8; "Twenty-Six Makes of Sheets Tested," *CRB* 1, no. 5 (March 1935): 23–24; "Needed: Standardized Sizes for Cotton Wash Dresses," *CRB* 1, no. 8 (June 1935): 3–4; "A Study of Men's One-Piece Cotton Underwear," *CR* 2, no. 75 (November 1932): 4.

31. See Gordon S. Thompson to Eleanor S. Loeb, August 5, 1933, Loeb to Thompson, August 25, 1933, and Evelyn H. Roberts to Thompson, September 19, 1933, all in Box 953, File 648.2255-7-33, CRP.

32. See D. H. Palmer to M. B. Howarth, November 1, 1933, December 8, 1933, and Howarth to Palmer, February 27, 1934, all in Box 953, File 646.465-12.33, CRP. The actual report was published as "Report on CR Test of Shoes," *CRB* 1, no. 4 (February 1935): 15–19.

33. "The 'Low-Down' on Our Recommendations," *Consumers' Club Bulletin* 102 (April 1929): 2, Box 11, CRP; F. R. Hoisington Jr., "Domestic Heating," *Consumers' Club* 102 (April 1929): 5; "Automobiles," *CR* 0.15 (May 1930): 1; "Preserves," *CR* 0.23 (September 1930): 4; "A Comparative Study of Canned Apricots," *CR* 1, no. 6 (January 1931): 3; "A Comparative Study of String Beans," *CR* 1, no. 6 (January 1931): 4; "A Comparative Study of Canned Pears," *CR* 1, no. 6 (January 1931): 8; "A Study of Vacuum Cleaners," *CR* 1, no. 28 (July 1931): 4. On the cost of using goods, see "Preliminary Report of CR Refrigeration Tests," *CR* 2, no. 75 (October 1932): 7–8; "Electric Kitchen Appliances," *CR* 1, no. 12 (April 1931): 5–6; Frederick H. Dutcher, "Why Do We Burn So Much Gasoline?" *CRGB* 1, no. 3 (September 1932): 10–11; "Are You Planning to Install an Electric Range?" *CRB* 1, no. 2 (December 1934): 6–7; "Relative Costs of Operation for Kerosene and Electric Refrigerators," *CRB* 1, no. 5 (March 1935): 11–12; "Automobiles of 1935," *CRB* 1, no. 7 (May 1935): 6; and "Utilize Your Electric Meter to Determine the Cost of Operating Any Electric Appliance," *CRB* 1, no. 8 (June 1935): 22–23.

34. Martha Olney conducted a sampling of durable goods advertisements in the *LHJ* from 1901 to 1941 and found that relatively few actually listed the price, and the practice actually decreased in the 1920s and especially in the early Depression, exactly when CR was making its criticisms, after 1920. Author's estimates derived from tables in Olney, *Buy Now, Pay Later*, 338–67.

35. "Off the Editors' Chest," *CRB* 1, no. 3 (January 1935): 2. The "expert closer" referred

to the salesmen usually charged with follow-up calls to close a deal with consumers who were hesitant or having second thoughts.

36. See, for example, "A Consumer's Study of Lubricating Oils," *CR* 2, no. 2 (January 1932): 1–2; "Sanitary Napkins," *CR* 2, no. 2 (January 1932): 4; "Automobiles of 1932," *CR* 2, no. 13 (April 1932): 4–8; "Three Studies of Canned Foods," *CR* 2, no. 75 (October 1932): 4–7; "Ordinary Bar Laundry Soap," *CRGB* 1, no. 3 (September 1932), 13; and "Canned Sardines," *CRGB* 2, no. 1 (October 1932): 12.

37. See, for example, "Sliced Bread," *CR* 0.23 (September 1930): 3; "Analyses of Astringent Lotions," *CRGB* 2, no. 1 (October 1932): 15; "Liquid Antiseptics—Zonite and Chlorox," *CRGB* 2, no. 2 (January 1933): 7–8; and "Household Ammonia," *CRGB* 2, no. 4 (July 1933): 13–14.

38. See "Food and Beverages," *Consumers' Club Commodity List*, October 1927, 9, Box 11, "Consumers' Clubs, 1928–29" File, CRP.

39. "An Error Corrected," *CRGB* 2, no. 2 (January 1933): 2; "Banking 'Cost Analysis,'" *CRGB* 3, no. 2 (January 1934): 19–20. See also "Special and Accessories—Some Cost Questions," *CR* 1, no. 20 (May 1931): 3–4.

40. For packaging techniques see Franken and Larrabee, *Packages That Sell*.

41. "Weights and Measures," *CR* 0.15 (May 1930): 3–4; "The Skilled Art of Deceiving the Consumer—Technically Known as Repackaging," *CRGB* 3, no. 3 (April 1934): 11; Matthews, *Guinea Pigs No More*, 107–18.

42. "Skilled Art of Deceiving the Consumer," 11; "CR and Packaged Goods," *Introduction to Consumers' Research*, 23.

43. Matthews, *Guinea Pigs No More*, 93–95.

44. "Automobile of 1932," *CR* 2, no. 13 (April 1932): 2.

45. Updegraff, *Sixth Prune*; Kendall, *New American Tempo*; Calkins, *Business, the Civilizer*, 12–14; Joseph French Johnson, "Making People Want More—The Basis of Civilization," *PI* 111, no. 11 (June 10, 1920): 19; Goode, *How to Turn People into Gold*; Phelps, *Our Biggest Customer*; Frederick, *Philosophy of Production*; J. B. Matthews, "Sweet Land of Gadgetry," *CRB* 1, no. 1 (November 1934): 3–4; C. M. Smith, "The Dial Phone—An Imposition on the Consumer," *CRGB* 3, no. 2 (April 1934): 20.

46. "Food Mixers," *CRB* 1, no. 3 (January 1935): 10. See also "Aerial Eliminators," *CRB* 1, no. 4 (February 1935): 8–9; "Another Way to Save Electricity—Don't Buy Electrical Appliances and Gadgets," *CRGB* 3, no. 1 (October 1933): 21–22; and "Modern Gas Stoves," *CRGB* 4, no. 1 (October 1934): 17–18.

47. "CR's Attitude to Luxury Goods," *Introduction to Consumers' Research*, 7.

48. M. C. Phillips, "Hold Your Man with Hand Lotions," *CRB* 1, no. 6 (April 1935): 14.

49. CR Special Bulletin on "Furs," Special Bulletin Binder, Box 11, CRP.

50. CR Special Bulletins on "The Buick 6" and "Cameras," Special Bulletin Binder, Box 11, CRP.

51. Link, *New Psychology of Selling and Advertising*. See also Lears, "Some Versions of Fantasy"; Lears, *Fables of Abundance*, 137–234; Pope, *Making of Modern Advertising*, 112–83; and Marchand, *Advertising the American Dream*.

52. See previous note, and Lears, "Ad Man and the Grand Inquisitor."

53. Leiss, Kline, and Jhally, *Social Communication in Advertising*, is a helpful survey of the

ways in which advertising places products continually as an element of human relationships; see also Miller, *Material Culture and Mass Consumption.*

54. FJS to Margaret Franklin, June 28, 1930, Box 501, File 12, CRP.

55. FJS to John C. Lober, January 28, 1936, General File, CRP.

56. *Introduction to Consumers' Research,* 5; "Another Way to Save Electricity," 21–22; Sterling W. Edwards, "The Buying and Restoration of Old Furniture," *CRGB* 3, no. 2 (January 1934): 12–14.

57. M. B. Howarth, "Shoe Project—Summary of Women's Shoes," March 31, 1934, D. H. Palmer to M. B. Howarth, November 1 , 1933, and December 8, 1933, all in Box 953, File 646.465–12.33, CRP.

58. See *Scientific Buying* (1929), esp. 4–7, 27–35, Box 11, "Consumer Clubs, 1928–29" File, CRP.

59. Schlink, "Bear Oil."

60. Ibid., 279; Kallet, *Counterfeit,* 48–50; Mary Kay [M. C. Phillips], "Discredited Magic," *Christian Century,* April 6, 1932, 444–45.

61. "If You Believe Advertising, Remember Advertisers Don't," *CR* 1.28 (July 1931): 7–8.

62. See "CR and Packaged Goods," *Introduction to Consumers' Research,* 23; "An Economist's Opinion of Advertising," *CRGB* 1, no. 3 (September 1932): 5–6; and FJS to Armand Kelly, November 10, 1933, Box 501, File 12, CRP.

63. An Engineer Subscriber, "Cost and Prices of Refrigerators for the TVA," *CRGB* 4, no. 1 (October 1934): 14 (quotation); An Engineer Subscriber, "The High Cost of Advertising," *CRGB* 3, no. 4 (July 1934): 7. See also Wilcox, "Brand Names, Quality, and Price."

64. "The 'Low-Down' on Our Recommendations," *The Consumers' Club* 102 (April 1929): 2. On the vast price differences between unadvertised and trademarked advertised goods, see "Trade-Marked Articles Held Back in General Lowering of Price Level," *CR* 1, no. 12 (April 1931): 4; and "Significant Data on Branded Goods in Senate Hearings," *CRGB* 1, no. 3 (September 1932): 6.

65. Rachel Lynn Palmer, "Have You Dentifrice Delusions?" *CRB,* n.s., 1, no. 3 (January 1935): 3–5; "The Educational Value of Advertisements," *CR* 2, no. 2 (January 1932): 4; "Once a Costly Ingredient—Now Potassium Chlorate," *CRGB* 2, no. 4 (July 1933): 9.

66. Phillips, "Hold Your Man with Hand Lotions," 13–15.

67. FJS to Henry Harap, February 5, 1930, Box 514, File 31.63, CRP. Harap was the author of *The Education of the Consumer,* a book that influenced Chase in his writings.

68. *Introduction to Consumers' Research,* 3.

69. Ibid.; "By-Laws of Consumers' Research," 1931, Article VIII, and "By-Laws of Consumers' Research, Inc.," January 1935, Article I, CRP.

70. *Introduction to Consumers' Research,* 3; "An Old Problem Restated," *CR* 1, no. 12 (April 1931): n.p.

71. *Introduction to Consumers' Research,* 3, 1. For more on the incompatibility of CR's approach with advertising, see "Ethics of Advertising Agencies," *CRGB* 1, no. 2 (May 1932): 2.

72. "Racket Rumor," *CRGB,* 1, no. 2 (May 1932): 7 (quotation); FJS to Theodore Kain, September 11, 1934, Box 341, File 31.1, CRP.

73. "To Buy or Not to Buy," *CRGB* 1, no. 3 (September 1932): 2. See also "Producers Organize—Consumers Must," *CRGB* 1, no. 3 (September 1932): 2.

74. McKown and Throop, "How Not to Buy," 12–16.

75. See, for example, FJS to Dr. Louise Stanley, November 2, 1929, Box 911, File 643.37, CRP.

76. For similar criticisms, see Seldes, *Lords of the Press*; and Matthews and Shallcross, *Partners in Plunder*, 354–65.

77. Rachel Lynn Palmer, "*Good Housekeeping* Helps the Canners against the Consumers," *CRB*, n.s., 1, no. 1 (November 1934): 7–9; "*Skin Deep*, a Book on Cosmetics Available in a Special Edition for *CR* Subscribers," *CRB*, n.s., 1, no. 1 (November 1934): 21–22.

78. "The 'Low-Down' on Our Recommendations," *Consumers' Club* 102 (April 1929): 2; see also "Whose Bread I Eat, His Song I Sing," *CRGB* 1, no. 1 (September 1931): 11–12; and FJS to Dr. Louise Stanley, November 2, 1929, Box 911, File 643.37, CRP.

79. "An Economist's Opinion of Advertising," *CRGB* 1, no. 3 (September 1932): 5–6; "Whose Bread I Eat, His Song I Sing," 2.

80. "'Harper's' and 'Time' Refuse CR's Advertising," *CRGB* 1, no. 2 (May 1932): 6.

81. "More on 'Time's' Refusal of CR's Advertising," *CR* 2.90a (November 1932): 6–7.

82. See I. Van Meter to Theodore S. Borrell, April 12, 1934, Box 871, File 65.21, CRP.

83. "*Time* and *Newsweek* Can't Afford to Print CR's Advertising," *CRB*, n.s., 1, no. 3 (January 1935): 18–20.

84. M. C. Phillips, "Memo," November 27, 1934, Box 871, File 65.21TH, CRP.

85. "Report of a Conversation Between S, MCP, and Franklin Spier, November 5, 1934," Box 871, File 65.21TH, CRP.

86. See n. 85, and Mathilde Hader to Loring Schuler [editor of *LHJ*], February 6, 1934, Photostat no. 1113, Box 732, File 339.41HE, CRP; *Annual Report of Consumers' Research, Inc. for the Fiscal Year Ending September 30, 1934*, 16, Box 11, CRP.

87. See "Report of Consumers' Research Inc: Fiscal Year Ending September 30, 1932," Appendix K; "Annual Report of Consumers' Research Inc," (1934), 14–15; FJS, "The Consumer—Shall He have Rights . . . ?"; and "Using CR Material in College and High School Classes," *CRGB* 1, no. 3 (September 1932): 5.

88. Schlink, "Responsibility of the Home Economist," 24; FJS, "The Consumer—Shall He Have Rights in the Schools?" December 1933, Box 733, Progressive Education File, CRP; Matthews and Shallcross, *Partners in Plunder*, 342–54; Dewey H. Palmer, "Consider the Consumer," *Journal of Adult Education*, January 1933, reprint, CRP. For the business attempts to place material in schools, see Stark, *How Schools Use Advertising Material*. The study, Stark's doctoral work at Columbia University Teachers College, was funded by the Association of National Advertisers.

89. "Especially Worth Reading," *CRGB* 2, no. 1 (October 1932): 7; see also James F. Corbett, "When Teachers Tell Pupils How to Buy," *CRGB* 2, no. 2 (January 1933): 10–11; "Business Gets Help from the World of Scholarship," *CR* 1, no. 28 (July 1931): n.p.

90. FJS to Elizabeth E. Hoyt, December 11, 1934, Box 732, File 339.41HE, CRP; see also Mathilde Hader to Alice Edwards, June 6, 1934, Box 732, File 339.41HE, CRP.

91. Susman, *Culture as History*, 271–85; Riesman, *Lonely Crowd*; Shi, *Simple Life*; Lears, "From Salvation to Self-Realization: Advertising and the Therapeutic Roots of Consumer Culture, 1880–1930," in *Culture of Consumption*, ed. Fox and Lears, 1–38.

92. John Hader, "Memorandum of Group Discussion, December 21, 1933," Box 501, File 12.2, CRP.

93. Lears, *No Place of Grace*, is the classic account of the accommodationist nostalgia of late nineteenth-century elites who accepted modernity by immersing themselves in cultural alternatives to their own time.

94. On CR's unwillingness to make politics its central focus, see, for example, FJS to Phelps Putnam, January 14, 1935, Box 501, File 12.2, CRP. See also FJS to Roy Veatch, October 11, 1933, 2–3, Box 501, File, 12.2, CRP.

95. Chase, *Tragedy of Waste* ; Chase, *Mexico*; Andrews, *Economics of the Household*; Lynd and Lynd, *Middletown*; Lynd with Hanson, "People as Consumers," esp. 864–71; Hoyt, *Consumption of Wealth*.

96. Schlink, *Eat, Drink, and Be Wary*, 198–201, 277–311.

97. *Introduction to Consumers' Research*, 6–7; FJS to Elizabeth Ellis Hoyt, December 11, 1934, 1, Box 732, File 339.41HE, CRP; FJS to Lynd, June 2, 1935, File NRA 312, CRP; Cherington, *Consumer Looks at Advertising*, 12–13, 72–73.

98. M. C. Phillips to Gretchen Flower, January 11, 1934, Box 73, File 339.41HE, CRP; FJS to SC, May 23, 1932, Box 516, File 51.2, CRP.

99. *Introduction to Consumers' Research*, 5–6.

100. Also hailing from semirural backgrounds was CR staffer Dewey Palmer, from Tennessee; Stuart Chase claimed a spiritual Yankee background, the simple life of New England villages, even though he was originally from Boston. See interviews with Palmer, Chase, and Warne, Oral History Collection, CSCM.

101. Schlink was living in the suburbs of White Plains, New York, before starting up CR, and he associated the city with interruptions and distractions from his work. See Warne interview, Oral History Collection, CSCM. For general animus against the city, see White and White, *Intellectual Versus the City*; and Lynch, *Image of the City*.

102. See Schlink, *Eat, Drink, and Be Wary*; "Country Quarters Wanted for CR," *CRGB* 1, no. 2 (May 1932): 7; FJS to Howard Armbruster, May 19, 1933, Box 340, File S300.212, CRP; FJS, "Things I Remember," speech given at CR Fortieth Anniversary Dinner, Easton Pa., October 12, 1967, 3–4, Box 746, CRP.

103. See Kallet and Schlink, *100,000,000 Guinea Pigs*; Schlink, *Eat, Drink, and Be Wary*; Schlink and Phillips, *Meat Three Times a Day*; and virtually every CR bulletin.

104. Schlink, *Eat, Drink and Be Wary*, 1–296; M. C. Phillips to Mathilde Hader, August 15, 1934, Box 530, File 89, CRP.

105. *Introduction to Consumers' Research*, 1–2; "Producers Organize—Consumers Must."

106. See Breen, *Marketplace of Revolution*; Frank, *Buy American!*

107. *Introduction to Consumers' Research*, 6–7.

108. See FJS to Elizabeth Ellis Hoyt, December 11, 1934, Box 732, File 339.41HE, CRP; FJS to John Dewey, February 24, 1932, Box 501, File 12.2, CRP.

109. Here the group echoed the ideas of Lippmann, *Drift and Mastery*; and Weyl, *New Democracy*, among others.

110. The closest were Phillips, *Skin Deep*, which by its contents was explicitly addressed to women, and an unfinished picture book for children that taught basic principles of wise spending.

111. See, for example, "If You Believe Advertising, Remember Advertisers Don't."

112. FJS to SC, May 23, 1932, Box 516, File 51.2, CRP; M. C. Phillips to Margaret Meyer,

November 8, 1933, Box 725, File 342.3231, CRP; FJS to Otis Pease, January 7, 1958, Box 437, CRP.

113. *Introduction to Consumers' Research* is a good example.

114. FJS to W. Cleveland Runyon, June 3, 1935, General File, CRP; M. C. Phillips to Gretchen Flower, January 11, 1934, Box 732, File 449.41HE, CRP.

115. FJS to Howard K. Bassett, February 5, 1932, Box 501, File 12, CRP.

116. M. C. Phillips to Armand Kelly, November 6, 1933, Box 501, File 12, CRP.

117. M. C. Phillips to Margaret Meyer, November 8, 1933, Box 725, File 342.3231, CRP.

118. M. C. Phillips to J. B. Matthews, February 8, 1934, Box 726, File 342.32311, CRP.

119. *Introduction to Consumers' Research*, 6–7.

120. See, for example, Schlink's description of *CR* subscribers in his letter to P. H. Good, July 10, 1944, Box 501, File 09.3, CRP.

121. See "Ethics of Advertising Agencies," *CRGB* 1, no. 2 (May 1932): 2; M. C. Phillips to Aina Ebbesen, March 1932, and correspondence between J. M. Robb and Eleanor S. Loeb, March 1932, Box 911, File 75, CRP.

122. "CR Relations with Schools," *Report of Consumers' Research: Fiscal Year Ending September 30, 1932*, Appendix K, K-1, CRP; "Course in Consumers' Problems," *CR* 2.77a (November 1932), Box 11, Special Bulletin File, CRP; *Consumers' Research Test Manual* 7.42a (April 1937), Box 11, CRP; Palmer and Schlink, "Education and the Consumer."

123. Schlink, "Bear Oil"; "Buyers' Baedecker," *New Republic*, November 26, 1930, 32–33; "In the Driftway," *The Nation*, April 8, 1931, 380–81; Schlink, "Government Bureaus for Private Profit"; Schlink, "Government Takes in Washing."

124. FJS interview with author.

125. *Introduction to Consumers' Research*, 9, 16; correspondence between E. S. Loeb and W. J. Robb, Box 911, File 75, CRP.

126. May Wood Wigginton to Consumers' Research, February 2, 1932, Box 501, File 12.2, CRP.

127. FJS to SC, May 17, 1932, Box 502, File 13, CRP; FJS to Mr. Hutter, February 27, 1935, Box 531, File 89, CRP.

128. The confidential pledge was dropped by the end of World War II, but by then, Schlink was no longer interested in expanding the organization past 100,000 members.

129. See Mathilde Hader to Loring Schuler, Box 732, File 339.41HE, CRP.

130. M. C. Phillips to Mathilde Hader, November 2, 1934, Box 530, File 89, CRP.

131. Phillips, *Skin Deep*.

132. See FJS, "Can One Buy Intelligently in the Modern Market?"

133. See "Furs" and McKown and Throop, "How Not to Buy," for two examples.

134. *Introduction to Consumers' Research*, 8; FJS to Francis Henson, October 14, 1932, Box 509, File 13.92, CRP.

135. Silber, *Test and Protest*, chap. 2; Katz, "Consumer's Union"; Arthur Kallet interview with Sybil Schwartz, December 7, 1970, 7, CSCM. Kallet recalled that Schlink "was very definitely pro-labor."

136. FJS to Mark Starr, February 22, 1932, Box 509, File 13.92, CRP.

137. Matthews, *Guinea Pigs No More*, 32–72.

138. See Kallet interview with Sybil Schwartz, December 7, 1970, 7, CSCM; and FJS interview with author, August 1984.

139. Rosenzweig, *Eight Hours for What We Will*; Peiss, *Cheap Amusements*; Kasson, *Amusing the Million*; Cohen, *Making a New Deal*.

140. See, for example, Helen Hall, talk at Stephens College, April 3, 1939, 1–2, Box 20, File 305, Helen Hall Papers, Social Welfare History Archives, University of Minnesota, Minneapolis, Minn. See also Caroline F. Ware to Helen Hall, February 6, 1940, Box 15, File 295, Hall Papers.

CHAPTER SEVEN

1. Weyl, *New Democracy*, 251.

2. John Shannon to Consumers' Research, November 28, 1933, Box 726, File 342. 323111, CRP.

3. Lynd, "Family Members as Consumers," 89.

4. White, *Alice through the Cellophane*.

5. On economic policy regarding consumers and purchasing power in the Depression, see Hawley, *New Deal and the Problem of Monopoly*; Stein, *Fiscal Revolution in America*; May, *From New Deal to New Economics*; Brinkley, " New Deal and the Idea of the State"; Brinkley, *End of Reform*, 65–85; Bernstein, *Great Depression*; Barber, *Designs within Disorder*; and Meg Jacobs, " 'Democracy's Third Estate.' "

6. See Lynd, "Democracy's Third Estate"; Lynd, "Consumer Becomes a 'Problem' "; and Schlink, "Safeguarding the Consumer's Interest." The May 1934 issue of the *Annals of the American Academy of Political and Social Science* was dedicated to the consumer as a public policy issue. It was reissued as Brainerd, *Ultimate Consumer*. For a representative sampling of works on consumption and the economy, see Chase, *A New Deal*; Chase, *Economy of Abundance*; Lamb, *Government and the Consumer*; Reid, *Consumers and the Market*; and Waite and Cassidy, *Consumer and the Economic Order*. On credit and income see Clark, *Financing the Consumer*; Leven, Moulton, and Warburton, *America's Capacity to Consume*; Kneeland, *Consumer Incomes in the United States*; Holthausen, with Merriam and Nugent, *Volume of Consumer Installment Credit*; Douglass, *Consumer Credit*; and Calder, *Financing the American Dream*, 211–90.

7. There is no good, in-depth, modern history of the consumer "movement" during the Depression. The movement in reality was several loose coalitions allied for different purposes. For a brief account see Mayer, *Consumer Movement*. Sorenson, *Consumer Movement in the United States*, is the best contemporary account, along with the more specialized focus of Lynd, "Consumer Becomes a 'Problem,' " and Campbell, *Consumer Representation in the New Deal*. See also Katz, "Consumers Union"; and Glickman, " Strike in the Temple of Consumption."

8. For useful frameworks for understanding hegemony in history, see Lears, "Antonio Gramsci's Concept of Hegemony"; and Denning, *Cultural Front*.

9. Cohen, *Making a New Deal*; Denning, *Cultural Front*; Glickman, *Living Wage*; Storrs, *Civilizing Capitalism*; Susman, *Culture as History*; May, *Big Tomorrow*; Erenberg, *Swingin' the Dream*; Stowe, *Swing Changes*; Giovacchini, *Hollywood Modernism*.

10. The best account of this is Marchand, *Advertising the American Dream*, 285–333; see also Fox, *Mirror Makers*, 118–74. Rorty, *Our Master's Voice*, 332–40, 346–53, offers some firsthand insight on the effects of the Depression on ad men.

11. Lears, *Fables of Abundance*, 235–47.

12. O'Dea, *Preface to Advertising*; Gundlach, *Facts and Fetishes in Advertising*; "What Groucho Says," *PI* 153, no. 1 (October 2, 1930): 95; "National Advertisers Put Advertising on Trial," *PI* 157, no. 8 (November 26, 1931): 33–34; "How Has the Depression Affected Agency-Client Relations?" *PI* 157, no. 6 (November 5, 1931): 3–6.

13. No hard data are available about the frequency with which accounts changed hands, but the concern for such changes became a fixture among agents, whereas throughout the advertising press in the 1920s there was virtual silence on this issue. See, for example, "How Has the Depression Affected Agency-Client Relations?"; "How the Depression Has Affected Advertising Agency Overhead," *PI* 157, no. 7 (November 12, 1931): 17–20; and Paul B. West, "A.N.A. President Challenges Advertising Costs," *PI* 174, no. 5 (January 30, 1936): 7–16. See also the sources cited in note 16.

14. On account switching see "Agencies Hold War Council," *PI* 154, no. 3 (April 21, 1932): 43; An Advertising Manager, "Another Advertising Agency Goes after Our Account," *PI* 153, no. 11 (December 11, 1930): 49–52; T. Harry Thompson, "Advertising Agency," *PI* 163, no. 5 (May 4, 1933): 4, 65; "What Groucho Says," *PI* 151, no. 5 (May 1, 1930): 84; "What Groucho Says," *PI* 151, no. 7 (May 15, 1930): 120; and Kenneth M. Goode, "Joe's Place," *Advertising and Selling* 15, no. 13 (October 29, 1930): 19.

15. On agency profits see "Not So Fast, Mr. Sloan," *PI* 160, no. 1 (July 7, 1932): 82. It is worth noting that *PI* did not represent simply the agency perspective in its editorials and articles. The figure might mean that agencies hid their profits in their compensation, but it seems equally likely that 1931 represented a cutthroat year.

16. Young, *Advertising Agency Compensation*, defended the agency system and its rates. The Association of National Advertisers commissioned a series of studies of agency services, media rates, and circulation that caused squabbling among corporate advertisers, agencies, and the media. See Haase, *Analysis of a Report Called "Advertising Agency Compensation in Relation to the Total Cost of Advertising"*; Haase and Locksley, with Digges, *Advertising Agency Compensation*; and [Association of National Advertisers], *Analysis of 285 National Advertising Budgets*. For the agencies' response to Haase's rebuttal, see Benson, *Analysis and Criticism*.

17. Raymond Rubicam, "What the Agency Gives Publisher and Advertiser," *PI* 161, no. 4 (October 27, 1932): 28–31; Young, *Advertising Agency Compensation*; "Agencies Hold War Council," 41–52; "Young Report Favors Present Agency Commission," *PI* 163, no. 7 (May 18, 1933): 3–5; "What the A.N.A. Really Thinks of Young Report," *PI* 164, no. 2 (July 13, 1933): 45–46; "A.N.A.'s Position on Agency Compensation," *PI* 167, no. 5 (May 3, 1934): 65–72; Bernard A. Grimes, "Agency System Too Rigid, Says A.N.A. Report," *PI* 169, no. 7 (November 15, 1934): 41–55; Lee H. Bristol, "Why A.N.A. Solidly Backs Agency Report," *PI* 169, no. 9 (November 29, 1934): 53–63; "Agents Answer A.N.A. Study on Compensation," *PI* 170, no. 10 (March 7, 1935): 21–28.

18. Ruthrauff and Ryan, "Now Is the Time for Advertising to Sell!" *PI* 154, no. 4 (January 22, 1931): 102–3; *Fortune* 3 (June 1931): 11. See also "Business as Usual!" *PI* 162, no. 10 (March 9, 1933): 3; "Optimism, Pessimism and Common Sense," *PI* 149, no. 8 (November 29, 1929): 178; Aesop Glim, "Ultra-Sophisticates of Modern Advertising," *PI* 153, no. 5 (October 30, 1930): 71–80; BBDO, "It's Your Honor!" *PI* 158, no. 4 (January 28, 1932): 54–55; "Drifting Leaves," *Wedge* 31, no. 11 (1931), and "1929 Was a Tough Year," *Wedge*, 31, no.

14 (1931), in BBDO; and Amos Bradbury, "A Prosperity Suggestion for Advertisers," *PI* 152, no. 2 (July 10, 1930): 105–8.

19. "The Stimulus of Adversity," *PI* 150, no. 7 (February 13, 1930): 209–10; John H. Dunham, "Advertising Now Sets Out to Do Its Biggest Job," *PI* 150, no. 6 (February 6, 1930): 138–48. See also "Jumping Sheep," *Wedge* 31, no. 2 (1931), in BBDO; Bradbury, "Prosperity Suggestion to Advertisers," 105; and "Out of the Cyclone Cellar," *PI* 152, no. 2 (July 10, 1930): 154.

20. JWT Representatives' Meeting, June 11, 1930, 11, RG 2, Box 3, JWTA.

21. "People Are Still People," 1932, N. W. Ayer House Advertising Files, Ayer Archives, New York, N.Y.; D. M. Hubbard, "Are We Licked in Advance as Buying Power Decreases?" *PI* 157, no. 12 (December 17, 1931): 42. See also Roy Dickinson, "Advertising and the New Economics," *PI* 164, no. 1 (July 6, 1933): 3–6; Roy Dickinson, "Weathering the Depression," *PI* 153, no. 4 (October 23, 1930): 3–8; "Old Clothes," *PI* 153, no. 9 (November 27, 1930): 33–34; and "Dam of Repressed Buying Is Sure to Break One of These Days," *PI* 157, no. 14 (December 31, 1931): 80.

22. JWT Creative Staff Meeting, May 4, 1932, 7, RG 2, Box 5, File 3, JWTA; Herman A. Groth, "To Advertisers: Revert," *PI* 164, no. 13 (March 29, 1934): 17. See also Ruthrauff and Ryan, *Slow Down the Band-Wagon*; Marchand, *Advertising the American Dream*, 300–306; and Gordon, *Comic Strips and Consumer Culture*, 85–105. For a sample of the commentary within the profession on these developments, see "The Little Schoolmaster's Classroom," *PI* 168, no. 11 (September 13, 1934): 122; Marsh K. Powers, "Can Advertising Offend and Still Be Effective?" *PI* 157, no. 11 (December 10, 1931): 3–4; Ben Dean, "Advertising Isn't Going to the Devil," *PI* 158, no. 2 (January 14, 1932): 33–36; and Burford Lorimer, "The American Home Is Doomed," *Advertising and Selling*, March 2, 1932, 24–25.

23. William Day, "Fundamentals and Decadence," *PI* 174, no. 10 (March 5, 1936): 22; Ruthrauff and Ryan, "Now Is the Time for Advertising to Sell!" 102–3; Glim, "Ultra-Sophisticates of Modern Advertising," 70–79; Don Francisco, "Informative Advertising Needed Now, More than Ever," *PI* 158, no. 5 (February 4, 1932): 3–6; Goode, *Modern Advertising Makes Money!*

24. See, for example, Samuel Jaros, "Barnumizing Advertising," *PI* 37, no. 5 (October 30, 1901), 10–11; "The Clown's Competition," *PI* 72, no. 10 (March 1, 1923): 8–9; "Up from Barnum," *Judicious Advertising* 21 (May 1923): 74–75; Harriet Anderson, "The End of the Era of 'Humbug,'" *J. Walter Thompson News Bulletin* 100 (July 1923): 7–13; Forum, "P. T. Barnum and His White Elephant," *PI* 137, no. 10 (December 9, 1926): 173; Hugh Brennan, "Advertising's Retreat to the Barnum Era," *PI* 142, no. 11 (March 15, 1928): 81–88; Presbrey, *History and Development of Advertising*, 211–26; Marchand, *Advertising the American Dream*, 7–9; and "'One Night Stands'" in N. W. Ayer, *Advertising Advertising 1930 (General Magazines)* (Philadelphia, 1930), Series 16, Box 20, File 8, AC.

25. The best overall study of Barnum, which discusses the evolution of his showmanship, remains Harris, *Humbug*. Lears, *Fables of Abundance*, 40–101, stresses the centrality of Barnum's practices to advertising's long history. Wicke, *Advertising Fictions*, 54–86, discusses Barnum's career and advertising. Insightful specialized studies include Reiss, *Showman and the Slave*; Cook, *Arts of Deception*, 73–118; and Adams, *E Pluribus Barnum*.

26. "Put on a Good Show," *Wedge* 33, no. 2 (June 1933), BBDO Archives. See also

"Millennium?" in Ruthrauff and Ryan, *18 Shorts on Advertising*, 19–20; H. E. Lesan, "Is Advertising Going 'Entertainment?'" *PI* 154, no. 11 (March 12, 1931): 3–8; H. S. Gardner, "National Advertisers, Inc.," *PI* 154, no. 13 (March 26, 1931): 17–20; Leon Kelley, "To Entertain or to Sell?" *PI* 155, no. 1 (April 2, 1931): 33; and John J. McCarthy, "Barnum Salesmen," *PI* 170, no. 8 (February 21, 1935): 41–48.

27. "Minutes of Creative Staff Meeting," November 2, 1932, 3–8, JWTA. See, in general, the transcripts of the Monday Night Meetings, RG 3, JWTA.

28. Such interests, ironically, paralleled those of Frankfurt's Institute for Social Research, some of whose members, affiliates, and acquaintances, including Paul Lazarsfeld and Theodor Adorno, worked in advertising or media when they came to the United States and whose visions of consumers' capacities were remarkably similar. Wiggershaus, *Frankfurt School*; Douglas, *Listening In*, 124–31, 138–60.

29. Roy Dickinson, "Shirt-Sleeve Advertising," *PI* 154, no. 6 (February 5, 1931): 77–87; John J. McCarthy, "Shirt-Sleeve Executives," *PI* 143, no. 11 (March 12, 1931): 58–67; "Advertising as Seen Through a Flannel Shirt," *PI* 165, no. 11 (December 14, 1934): 41.

30. Nancy Naghten, "Hail the Male!" *Advertising and Selling* 20, no. 7 (February 2, 1933): 20. See also Russell P. Askue, "Are Motor Cars Becoming Over-Feminized?" *Advertising and Selling* 24, no. 7 (January 22, 1930): 21–22; Ruthrauff and Ryan, *It Isn't Raining Everywhere!* 6–9; Ben Flood, "Advertising to Women," *Advertising and Selling* 15, no. 13 (October 29, 1930): 53; JWT Creative Staff Meeting," March 1, 1933, 12, JWTA; and Day, "Fundamentals and Decadence." For male resentment right at the outset of the Depression, see Phyllis V. Keyes, "Come to Papa," *PI* 149, no. 8 (November 21, 1929): 85–97; and G. S. Cox, "'Come to Papa?' Good Heavens, Phyllis!" *PI* 149, no. 11 (December 12, 1929): 204.

31. H. S. Gardner, "National Advertisers, Inc.," *PI* 154, no. 13 (March 26, 1931): 17.

32. The campaign was visible in national and local media. Ayer collected and published the ads in volumes for prospective clients. See, for representative samples, "Sign of Progress" and "Our Advertising," in N. W. Ayer, *Advertising Advertising 1930 (General Magazines)* (Philadelphia, 1930), Series 16, Box 20, File 8, AC; "A Trustworthy Business Associate," in N. W. Ayer, *Advertising Advertising 1930 (Newspapers)* (Philadelphia, 1930), Series 16, Box 20, File 6, AC; "'I Never Read the Advertisements,'" "Guide . . . Counselor . . . Friend," and "Take a Broom to the Cobwebs," in N. W. Ayer, *Advertising Advertising 1931 (Newspapers)* (Philadelphia, 1931), Series 16, Box 20, File 9, AC; "To Be Taken at Face Value" and "Armchair Shoppers," in N. W. Ayer, *Advertising Advertising 1932 (General Magazines)* (Philadelphia, 1932), Series 16, Box 21, File 3, AC; and "Partners in Purchasing," in N. W. Ayer, *Advertising Advertising 1934 (General Magazines)* (Philadelphia, 1934), Series 16, Box 21, File 8, AC.

33. See, for example, "'Public Masking Permitted from 6 A.M. to 6 p.m.,'" *Woman's Home Companion* 58, no. 7 (July 1931): 2; "Nothing Up the Sleeve," *Woman's Home Companion* 58, no. 10 (October 1931): 2; "Purchase Peace," *Woman's Home Companion* 59, no. 7 (July 1932): 2; Grace McIlrath Ellis, "Every Package Tells a Story," *Better Homes and Gardens* 10, no. 11 (July 1932): 9, 28; "Crying 'Wolf!' at the Beauty Counter," *GH* 93, no. 3 (September 1931): 182; and "What Is 'Best'?" *GH* 93, no. 3 (September 1931): 250.

34. "No Sale," *Woman's Home Companion* 57, no. 7 (July 1930): 2; "Secret Service," *Woman's Home Companion* 57, no. 8 (August 1930): 2; "The Kitchen Library," *Woman's Home Companion* 57, no. 9 (September 1990): 2; Mrs. R. A. Powell, "What's in a Label?"

Woman's Home Companion 57, no. 10 (October 1930): 2; Mrs. D. V. Palmiter, "References," Woman's Home Companion 58, no. 1 (January 1931): 2. See also " 'Who Goes There?' says the Wise Shopper," in N. W. Ayer, Advertising Advertising 1932 (Newspapers) (Philadelphia, 1932), Series 16, Box 21, File 2, AC; and "Shopping with Yourself," in N. W. Ayer, Advertising Advertising 1933 (Newspapers) (Philadelphia, 1933), Series 16, Box 21, File 5, AC.

35. Thompson's literature representing these beliefs is voluminous; the point of view is apparent in almost all of the agency's public and private material of the period. See, for instance, Research Section—J. Walter Thompson Company, Finger-Tip Touch with Consumers (1924), JWTA; "Guiding Human Decisions," (from PI 113, no. 10 [December 9, 1920]), House Ads File, RG 3, JWTA; Margaret Weishaar, " 'Psych-ing Mrs. Smith," People, October 1937, 5–27; Stanley Resor, "What Do These Changes Mean?" J. Walter Thompson News Bulletin 104 (December 1923): 1–17; Thompson, Retail Shopping Areas; Thompson, Population and Its Distribution; and Thompson, Report on Work of Committee on Standardization. The Thompson approach to overall advertising, marketing, and client relationships is outlined in Kreshel, "Toward a Cultural History of Advertising Research."

36. "Taxation without Representation Is Tyranny!" PI 168, no. 11 (September 13, 1934): 8–9; "All Men Are Created Equal," Fortune, October 1935, 95; ". . . Entangling Alliances with NONE," PI 172, no. 11 (September 12, 1935): 8–9; "Go West Young Man" PI 170, no. 5 (January 31, 1935): 8–9; "Votes for Women!" PI 173, no. 7 (November 21, 1935): 8–9. One advertisement, "The Constitution," put it best: "The physical United States—3,000 miles of forests, plains, deserts, and mountains, was and is a great product. But it took a mental concept of this product's relation to the needs of men and women—the Constitution—to give it pre-eminence among similar products. The value of this property today is the result of idea advertising." PI 172, no. 1 (July 4, 1935): 8–9.

37. "The Gettysburg Address," Fortune, December 1935, 123. See also Fortune, January 1935, 77.

38. Paul S. McElroy, "Tune In: Hear General Motors' New Radio Program 'The Parade of the States,' " BBDO Newsletter, October 9, 1931, 9–10, BBDO Archives. The idea behind the program was not limited to the private sector; the Works Progress Administration guides to the states in the mid-1930s offered similar fare. See Shaffer, See America First. NBC had previously entertained a similar idea for a program, "Fording America First," in which a typical American family toured the nation by Model A, visited historical and cultural landmarks, and witnessed the far-flung Ford empire at work. Chas. A Schuldt to John F. Royal, July 14, 1931, Box 3, File 41, NBC Collection, SHSW. See also plans for "Buick on the Air," Box 7, File 24, NBC Collection, SHSW.

39. Barton, with Garrett, Parade of the States, 78; see also especially 41–42, 49–50, 66–67, 73–74, 85–90, 102, 157–58, 197–98. On the origins of the program and authorship of the volume, see Merlin Aylesworth to Bruce Barton, December 5, 1932, and Barton to Aylesworth, December 6, 1932, Box 6, File 56, NBC Collection, SHSW.

40. See also the plans and initial copy for the Lucky Strike Hour to broadcast Republican and Democratic leaders giving political talks, much to NBC's discomfort: Thomas McAvity to John Royal, February 25, 1932, Merlin Aylesworth to Lord, Thomas & Logan, February 26, 1932, and Ralph Solitt to Merlin Aylesworth, February 27, 1932, all in Box 6, File 16, NBC Collection, SHSW.

41. Alfred P. Sloan Jr., "Foreword," in Barton, with Garrett, Parade of the States, v.

42. McElroy, "Tune In: Hear General Motors' New Radio Program," 9; "Parade of the States Going Strong," *BBDO News Letter*, December 24, 1931, 3, BBDO. A rival agency executive jealously sniped at the broadcasts, "If you ask anyone about the performance, you're likely to find that in spite of Bruce Barton's panting panegyrics, it's the program that nobody knows." JWT Staff Meeting, February 2, 1932, 6, RG 2, Box 4, File 9, JWTA. Bird, *"Better Living,"* 29–36, discusses the origins of the program in a different context. See also Marchand, *Creating the Corporate Soul*, 230–31.

43. "Radio and Celebrities" in "BBDO: A Short History" typescript, p. 14, BBDO.

44. [Buick Hall of Fame], 1932, Box 7, File 24, NBC Collection, SHSW.

45. Sheldon and Arens, *Consumer Engineering*, 19. Arens had been a founding editor of *The New Masses*.

46. Although it is unlikely that they read the American trade papers of this time, the scholars at Frankfurt's Institute for Social Research came to the same Veblenian insight. Horkheimer and Adorno, *Dialectic of Enlightenment*, 120–77.

47. Franken and Larrabee, *Packages That Sell*; Phelps, *Tomorrow's Advertisers*; Link, *New Psychology of Selling and Advertising*; Laird, *What Makes People Buy*.

48. Earnest Elmo Calkins, "Consumptionism," *PI* 151, no. 8 (May 22, 1930): 50; Earnest Elmo Calkins, "The New Consumption Engineer and the Artist," in *Philosophy of Production*, ed. Frederick, 107–31. See also Charles F. Abbott, "Obsolescence and the Passing of High-Pressure Salesmanship," in *Philosophy of Production*, ed. Frederick, 155–73.

49. Meikle, *Twentieth Century Limited*.

50. Goode, *How to Turn People into Gold*; Goode, *Modern Advertising Makes Money*; "Needed: Consumption Engineers," *PI* 160, no. 7 (August 18, 1932): 82–83.

51. I explore this in depth in "The People Who Buy Toothpaste: American Advertisers and the Radio Audience, 1920–1940," unpublished paper. See Lears, *Fables of Abundance*; and Lears, "Ad Man and the Grand Inquisitor."

52. JWT Forum, December 7, 1937, 5, RG 2, Box 7, File 4, JWTA; William Esty quoted in JWT Group Meeting, September 9, 1930, 4, RG 2, Box 3, File 1, JWTA.

53. William Day, "Importance of Strategy in Copy," JWT Staff Meeting, June 6, 1930, 16, RG 2, Box 2, File 5, JWTA.

54. "Markets Are PEOPLE," House Ads File, Ayer Archives; "Where Do They Get Their Ideas," *Fortune*, March 1931, 105; *SEP*, May 5, 1934, 115 [Commercial Credit Company]; *Collier's* 87, no. 11 (September 13, 1930): 3 [Westclox].

55. William Day, "The Two Billion" [draft], 6, William Day Speeches and Writings File, JWTA; "Lecture Given by William Day to Standard Brands Sales Class," May 1, 1931, 11–12, Day Speeches and Writings File, JWTA; Day, " Importance of Strategy in Copy," 14–15.

56. See *Tide* 11, no. 1 (January 1, 1937): 1; *PI* 177, no. 8 (November 19, 1936): 56–58; and *PI* 177, no. 13 (December 31, 1936): 33–35, for examples of "Buy-ological Urge" copy; *Fortune*, June 1930, 117.

57. "The Squire on Replacement," *PI* 165, no. 8 (November 23, 1933): 87–88.

58. "A Dollar for Dole—or an Hour of Work?" *Literary Digest* 110, no. 11 (September 12, 1931): 4; "Buy Now," *Literary Digest* 107, no. 6 (November 8, 1930): 9–10; "Buy Now, If You Can," *New Republic* (November 12, 1930): 335–36; "Business Watches Spread of 'Buy Now Campaigns," *Business Week*, November 19, 1930, 11–12; C. G. Muller, "Put a Practical Idea Behind the Buy Now Plan: The American Molasses Company," *PI* 154, no. 7 (February 12,

1931): 10–13; Roy Dickinson, "The Muncie Plan Grows," *PI* 155, no. 13 (June 25, 1931): 25–28. On "Buy American" campaigns see "'Buy American,'" *PI* 161, no. 10 (December 8, 1932): 96–97; "Patriotism and Economics" *PI* 162, no. 4 (January 26, 1933): 80; "Sell American," *PI* 162, no. 6 (February 9, 1933): 91–92. The Packard Company created similar advertising.

59. "'Buy Something from Somebody!'" *PI* 152, no. 4 (June 24, 1930): 84–85; "The Little Schoolmaster's Classroom," *PI* 154, no. 10 (June 9, 1932): 110.

60. T. Harry Thompson, "Let's Be Extravagant!" *PI* 169, no. 13 (December 27, 1934): 19–20; Frank, *Buy American!*, 56; Franklin Roosevelt, *On Our Way* (New York, 1934).

61. "This Week," *PI* 166, no. 11 (March 15, 1934): 3 (emphasis added). See also "Vermilion Tricycle vs. Old Debts," *PI* 167, no. 10 (June 7, 1934): 56–57; "To L. E. McGivena," *PI* 168, no. 3 (July 19, 1934): 21–25; and L. E. McGivena, "Was I Surprised!" *PI* 168, no. 4 (July 26, 1934): 31–37.

62. Quoted in G. F. Earnshaw "Trade Up!" *PI* 153, no. 6 (November 6, 1930): 126. See also "People Are Still PEOPLE!" *Literary Digest* 113, no. 4 (April 23, 1932): 33.

63. "Pocketbook Patriotism," *LHJ* 49, no. 2 (February 1932): 3. See also "It's Up to the Women: An Editorial," *LHJ* 49, no. 1 (January 1932): 3; "It's Up to the Women," *LHJ* 49, no. 4 (April 1932): 12, and Samuel Crowther, "What You Can Do," *LHJ* 49, no. 3 (March 1932): 3, 120. The almost exact same sentiments were voiced by the *New York Daily News* in its long-running campaign: see *Advertising and Selling*, April 4, 1932, 36–37.

64. Chevrolet's "71 Days of Work" made the similar point: each new Chevy represented that much work for its employees and those of its suppliers and clients, with thousands of dollars added to the economy. "The Little Schoolmaster's Classroom," *PI* 159, no. 10 (June 9, 1932): 110.

65. "Pocketbook Patriotism," 3; Crowther, "What You Can Do," 3, 126; "It's Up to the Women: An Editorial," *LHJ* 49, no. 1 (January 1932): 3. For a more expansive interpretation of the political potential for women at this moment, see Eleanor Roosevelt, *It's Up to the Women!*

66. "It's Up to the Women!" *LHJ* 49, no. 2 (February 1932): 6–7.

67. *LHJ* 49, no. 2 (February 1932): cover.

68. "After All, Does She Really Shop Alone?" *New York Times*, September 11, 1930, 16; [American Magazine], microfilm reel 6, JWTA.

69. *PI* 163, no. 10 (June 8, 1933): 42–43; *PI* 162, no. 13 (March 30, 1933): 34–35; *PI* 160, no. 12 (September 22, 1932): 66–67. See also *PI* 159, no. 13 (June 30, 1932): 30–31; *PI* 160, no. 4 (July 28, 1932): 30–31; *PI* 160, no. 8 (August 25, 1932): 46–47; *PI* 161, no. 9 (December 1, 1932): 38–39; *PI* 162, no. 4 (January 26, 1933): 38–39; *Advertising and Selling* 21, no. 2 (May 25, 1933): 7.

70. *Tide* 11, no. 8 (April 15, 1937): 64–65; *Tide* 11, no. 10 (May 15, 1937): 4–5.

71. *PI* 177, no. 7 (November 12, 1936): 82–83.

72. See, for some examples, *Better Homes and Gardens*, October 1934, 59 [Ford]; *Better Homes and Gardens*, June 1935, 3; *GH* 99, no. 2 (August 1934): cover II [Shredded Wheat]; *GH* 105, no. 3 (September 1937): 150 [Estate Gas Ranges]; *SEP*, May 27, 1933, 51 [Hupmobile]; *SEP*, June 8, 1935, 25 [Campbell's]; and *Collier's* 106, no. 17 (October 26, 1940): 25 [Birdseye].

73. Granville Toogood, "To the Ladies," *PI* 161, no. 11 (December 15, 1931): 27.

74. Atwan, McQuade, and Wright, *Edsels, Luckies, and Frigidaires*, 204; Lynd with Hanson, "People as Consumers," 881–88; Harap, *Education of the Consumer*; Norman Kirchbaum, "Eve Gets the Razzle-Dazzle," *Advertising and Selling*, September 24, 1936, 27–29.

75. Pitkin, *The Consumer*, 279–312 (quotations on 279, 312). See Huyssen, "Mass Culture as Modernism's Other."

76. Pitkin, *The Consumer*, 281, 298–302.

77. *Woman's Home Companion* 57, no. 7 (July 1930): 79 [Cleanliness Institute]; *Better Homes and Gardens* June 1932, cover III [Bon Ami]; *GH* 93, no. 1 (July 1931): 171 [Grape Nuts]; *GH* 103, no. 6 (December 1936): 146 [S.O.S.].

78. J. D. Tarcher, "The Serious Side of the Comic-Strip," *PI* 159, no. 4 (April 28, 1932): 3–6, briefly summarizes and comments on the Gallup survey; JWT Staff Meeting, March 12, 1932, 8, RG 2, Box 5, File 1, JWTA. See also Tax Cumings, "Who's Got a Job for a Comic?" *BBDO Newsletter*, July 15, 1931, 15–17, BBDO; "Comic Strip Advertising Doesn't Have to Be Funny," *PI* 160, no. 5 (August 4, 1932): 41–45; James S. Tyler, "Comics," *Advertising and Selling* 31, no. 4 (April 1938): 21–24; and Gordon, *Comic Strips and Consumer Culture*, 85–94.

79. "The Little Schoolmaster's Classroom," *PI* 160, no. 10 (September 8, 1932): 115.

80. Kenneth Groesbeck, "This Dangerous Business of Kidding the Public," *PI* 165, no. 7 (November 16, 1933): 6–8.

81. Ruthrauff and Ryan, *It Isn't Raining Everywhere!* 11.

82. Jacobson, "Manly Boys and Enterprising Dreamers." See also Jacobson, *Raising Consumers*.

83. JWT Creative Staff Meeting, March 1, 1933, 13, JWTA; "Jones Never Reads the Ads," *PI* 182, no. 12 (March 24, 1938): 8–9. See also " 'Gimme!' " *Advertising and Selling* 20, no. 5 (January 5, 1933): 31 [Young & Rubicam].

84. J. L. Sowers, " 'Pre-viewing' MIDDLETOWN," *Printers' Ink Monthly* 35, no. 3 (August 1937): 64.

85. "Million Club Members Buy This Product Every Week," *PI* 159, no. 9 (June 2, 1932): 33–34; "If It's Free the Kids Will Like It," *PI* 162, no. 1 (January 5, 1933): 68–71; "Post Toasties Puts Cutout Toys on Its Package," *PI* 163 (May 11, 1933): 68; "Children Are Joiners," *PI* 160, no. 7 (August 18, 1932): 68–69; "Advertising the Child to Reach the Parent," *PI* 165, no. 2 (October 12, 1933): 70–72; Grumbine, *Reaching Juvenile Markets*. See also Luke, *Constructing the Child Viewer*.

86. "No Penalty for Clipping," *PI* 154, no. 8 (February 19, 1931): 7 [American Boy]; "For the Young Collector," *PI* 168, no. 8 (August 23, 1934): 24; "If It's Free the Kids Will Like It"; "Technique of Radio Offers," *Printers' Ink Monthly* 35, no. 7 (December 1937): 17–20; Grumbine, *Reaching Juvenile Markets*, 69–117, 196–230; Longstaff, "Effectiveness of Children's Radio Programs."

87. See Palmer and Alpher, *40,000,000 Guinea Pig Children*, esp. 110–35; Morell, *Poisons, Potions, and Profits*, 105–43; Brindze, *Not to Be Broadcast*, 215–36.

88. Gruenberg, *Radio and Children*; Eisenberg, *Children and Radio Programs*, 146–73; Herzog, *Survey of Research on Children's Radio Listening*.

89. The most useful accounts of Depression culture are Denning, *Cultural Front*; Pells, *Radical Visions and American Dreams*, esp. 65–237; "The Culture of the Thirties," in Susman, *Culture as History*, 150–85; Rabinowitz, *Labor and Desire*; Wald, *Writing from the Left*;

and Maxwell, *New Negro, Old Left.* Useful reportage and journalistic assessments of the Depression include Wilson, *American Jitters*; Wilson, *Travels in Two Democracies*; Seldes, *Years of the Locust*; Rorty, *Where Life Is Better*; and Caldwell and Bourke-White, *You Have Seen Their Faces.* See Stott, *Documentary Expression and Thirties America*; and Aaron, *Writers on the Left.* For fiction see Dahlberg, *Bottom Dogs*; Kromer, *Waiting for Nothing*; McCoy, *They Shoot Horses, Don't They?*; Dos Passos, *1919*; and Dos Passos, *Big Money.*

90. Borsodi, *This Ugly Civilization*; Twelve Southerners, *I'll Take My Stand*; Agar and Tate, *Who Owns America?*

91. Bent, *Ballyhoo*; Merz, *Great American Band Wagon.* These insights would be extended more famously in the American context by Boorstin, *The Image.*

92. "The Alphabet of Ballyhoo," *Ballyhoo* 4, no. 3 (April 1933): 14–15; "Zilch's Soliloquy," *Ballyhoo* 4, no. 4 (May 1933): 22. Zilch was echoed in part by the long-running cartoon strip "The Timid Soul," whose meek character often endured consumers' inconveniences and difficulties. Webster, *Timid Soul.*

93. "Ballyhoo's Radio Log," *Ballyhoo* 3, no. 1 (August 1932): 23. The magazine's whole approach to advertising and business resembled the humor that made *Mad* magazine—like *Ballyhoo*, lacking advertising—a success in the 1950s. Zilch was a forerunner of Alfred E. Neuman. See Reidelbach, *Completely Mad.*

94. Rorty, *Our Master's Voice*, 382–84.

95. Angly, *Oh Yeah?*; H. A. Batten, "Advertising and Hard Times: A Challenge to Business," *PI* 161, no. 7 (November 17, 1932): 2–6, 86; W. C. D'Arcy, "A Warning to Advertisers, a Call to Action," *PI* 167, no. 9 (May 31, 1934): 32–34.

96. McChesney, *Telecommunications, Mass Media, and Democracy*; Smulyan, *Selling Radio.*

97. Howard Angus, "Preparation of Commercial Copy Is Hardest Task of Radio Advertiser," *Broadcast Advertising* 4 (December 1931): 8; Marchand, *Advertising the American Dream*, 108–10.

98. "We Want Cantor—Not Commercials," *Advertising and Selling*, August 30, 1934, 46.

99. McChesney, *Telecommunications, Mass Media, and Democracy*; Barnouw, *Tower in Babel*; Barnouw, *Golden Web*, 22–27.

100. William Orton, "Unscrambling the Ether," *Education by Radio* 1, no. 10 (April 16, 1931): 37–40; "Commercialized Radio to Be Investigated," *Education by Radio*, 2, no. 3 (January 21, 1932): 9; Rorty, *Our Master's Voice*, 265–75; Joy Elmer Morgan, "States Rights in Radio," address to Annual Assembly of the National Advisory Council on Radio in Education, May 22, 1931, 1–4, Container 39, Payne Fund Inc. Collection, Western Reserve Historical Society, Cleveland, Ohio; *Constitution and By-Laws, American Listeners Society, Incorporated*, Container 47, File 913, Payne Fund Inc. Collection; Rorty, *Order on the Air!*; Davis, *Capitalism and Its Culture*, 315–34; Brindze, *Not to Be Broadcast.* See also Newman, "Poisons, Potions, and Profits," 161–65.

101. On Rorty's career see Pope, "His Master's Voice"; Newman, "Poisons, Potions, and Profits"; and Newman, *Radio Active*, 53–77.

102. Rorty, *Our Master's Voice*, 333.

103. Ibid., 16, 18.

104. Ibid., 381; James Rorty, "Advertising's Role in This Transitional Period," *PI* 166, no. 7 (February 13, 1934): 13.

105. "Roy Durstine on Reading Jim Rorty," *Advertising and Selling*, May 10, 1934, 26, 69; "Comrade Rorty Lifts the Lid," *PI* 167, no. 6 (May 10, 1934): 89–92; Shaw Newton, "Open Letter to Jim Rorty," *PI* 166, no. 9 (March 9, 1934): 57–58.

106. Rorty corresponded with CR and even wrote some advertising for the fledgling organization, publicizing their *Buying Guides*. Rorty to FJS, August 5, 1932, Box 871, File 62.5, CRP; Rorty to FJS, September 15, 1932, Box 503, File 13.2, CRP.

107. "Biennial Report of Consumers' Research, Inc., for the Two-Year Period Ending September 20, 1935," E-1, CRP.

108. There is little published information on Kallet's early career, although he did a brief oral history with Sybil Schwartz, now housed in the Oral History Collection, CSCM. See Don Wharton, "Arthur Kallet: Career as Ally, Foe and Imitator of Consumers' Research," *Scribner's Magazine* 102, no. 11 (November 1937): 38–39.

109. Kallet and Schlink, *100,000,000 Guinea Pigs*, 3–96, 195–267.

110. Ibid., 276–95.

111. See James Henle, "Memorandum, March 10th [1933]," and Katherine Swan to James Henle, September 5, 1933, Box 341, Motion Picture Rights File, CRP.

112. These books were not only produced by the CR staff but also by a host of consumer sympathizers and even a few business advocates, and they addressed a host of consumer questions. See Rorty, *Our Master's Voice*; Harding, *Degradation of Science*; Harding, *Joy of Ignorance*; Phillips, *Skin Deep*; Matthews and Shallcross, *Partners in Plunder*; Kallet, *Counterfeit*; Lamb, *American Chamber of Horrors*; Schlink, *Eat, Drink, and Be Wary*; Morrell, *Poisons, Potions, and Profits*; Seldes, *Freedom of the Press*; Palmer and Greenberg, *Facts and Frauds in Women's Hygiene*; Palmer and Alpher, *40,000,000 Guinea Pig Children*; Brindze, *How to Spend Money*; Brindze, *Not to Be Broadcast*; Matthews, *Guinea Pigs No More*; Palmer, *Paying through the Teeth*; Solomon, *Traffic in Health*; Brindze, *Johnny Get Your Money's Worth*; Palmer and Crooks, *Millions on Wheels*; and Hawes, *Fashion Is Spinach*. See also C. B. Larrabee, "Guinea Pig Books," *PI* 175, no. 3 (April 16, 1936): 70–76.

113. Raymond Pearl, "The Way of the Reformer," *The Nation*, May 24, 1933, 588–89; Harding, "Food and Drugs," 402. The selection of *American Mercury* contributor Pearl to review the book prompted a protest from liberal Harry Elmer Barnes to *Nation* editor Oswald Garrison Villard: "I hold no brief for Schlink, but he is doing good work . . . then his book is handed to one of the most notoriously prejudiced men in the United States who gives his life to discrediting everything *The Nation* stands for." Barnes to Villard, June 1, 1933, Box 341, *Nation* Review File, CRP. See also Harding, "Are We Being Poisoned?" 6–7.

114. Lynd, "Must Every Issue Have Its Soapbox?" 225; James Rorty, "Poison for Profit," *New Republic*, February 15, 1933, 23–24.

115. C. B. Larrabee, "Mr. Schlink," *PI* 166, no. 2 (January 11, 1934): 10–13; "Those Guinea Pig Engineers," *PI* 166, no. 5 (February 1, 1934): 37–40; "How Secret are Consumer Research Bulletins?" *PI* 168, no. 8 (August 23, 1934): 41–48; Amos Bradbury, "Getting Offensive," *PI* 171, no. 6 (May 9, 1935): 7–8.

116. *Tide*, February 1933, 20–21; see also Dexter Masters to F. J. Schlink, Box 341, *Tide* Review File, CRP.

117. See FJS to R. G. Tugwell, February 26, 1933, File S300.3924, and FJS to Tugwell, March 7, 1933, File S335, both Box 739, CRP; Arthur Kallet interview with Sybil Schwartz,

December 7, 1970, 14, CSCM; SC to Rexford Tugwell, October 11, 1933, Stuart Chase Papers, Manuscript Division, Library of Congress, Washington, D.C.

118. Jackson, *Food and Drug Legislation in the New Deal*, is the standard history of the food and drug legislative and regulatory activity of the New Deal. Jackson scarcely acknowledges CR, but the correspondence between Schlink and Tugwell makes clear the connection between the organization and food and drug reform. See also Rexford G. Tugwell, "The 'Tugwell Bill' Becomes Un-American," Diary, June 1933–34, 74–83, Box 16, Rexford G. Tugwell Papers, Franklin D. Roosevelt Library, Hyde Park, N.Y.

119. Pease, *Responsibilities of American Advertising*, 115–47. See, for example, "The Case Against the Tugwell Bill," *Advertising and Selling* 27, no. 1 (November 9, 1933): 12, 14, 48–52.

120. Campbell, *Consumer Representation in the New Deal*, 27–80, 111–93, is the standard account. See also Lizabeth Cohen, "The New Deal State and the Making of Citizen Consumers," in *Getting and Spending*, ed. Strasser, McGovern, and Judt, 117–22; and Jacobs, "'Democracy's Third Estate,'" 37–44.

121. Schlink, "What Government Does and Might Do for the Consumer."

122. See, for example, CR Board of Directors Minutes, April 21, 1933, 17–21, Draft 1, Box 1024, CRP; Robert Brady to FJS, April 12, 1934, and FJS to Robert Brady, April 17, 1934, Box 725, File NRA3177, CRP.

123. Hawley, *New Deal and the Problem of Monopoly*, 19–143.

124. Schlink, "Safeguarding the Consumer's Interest," 115.

125. FJS to Robert Brady, February 15, 1934, and February 27, 1934, both Box 725, File 3178, CRP; Schlink, "How the Consumer Was Betrayed"; *CR* reprint, September 14, 1934, Box 734, FJS—Papers and Talks File, CRP. See also FJS to Robert S. Lynd, April 11, 1934, Box 737, File 31294, CRP.

126. Robert Brady to FJS, February 20, 1934, Box 739, File xGWP412321B Robert Brady, CRP.

127. Jackson, *Food and Drug Legislation in the New Deal*. Robins, *Copeland's Cure*, which appeared as this book was going to press, treats Copeland's life and work.

128. See JWT Representatives' Meeting, July 18, 1928, 2–5, RG 2, JWTA. On the lengths Thompson went to cover up the fact that the American Medical Association (AMA) would not permit American doctors to endorse products, and to counterattack the AMA's opposition to the Fleischmann campaigns, see letter to Thomas Greer, New York Office [Copy], July 12, 1933, 1–4, "Fleischmann Controversy—Inactive Accounts" File, JWTA.

129. Arthur Kallet, "No New Deal on Food, Drugs and Cosmetics," *CRGB* 4, no. 1 (October 1934): 1–3; Kallet interview with Sybil Schwartz, December 7, 1970, 8, CSCM. Lydia Pinkham was a successful nineteenth-century patent medicine manufacturer, whose products addressed "women's complaints" and whose company had been targeted by respectable publications.

130. Campbell, *Consumer Representation in the New Deal*, 60–67; Hawley, *New Deal and the Problem of Monopoly*, 77.

131. FJS, "Criticism of the Consumers' Advisory Board Report," and FJS, "The New Deal and the Consumer," address given at the University of Virginia, Charlottesville, July 12, 1934, Box 733, "U of Va Roundtable" File, CRP; Schlink, "100,000,000 Step-Children"; Hawley, *New Deal and the Problem of Monopoly*, 134–36, 199–203.

132. "A Proposed Act to Establish a Federal Department of the Consumer," March 1935, Box 725, File 342.3231, CRP; Phillips and Schlink, *Discovering Consumers*, 22–31; Matthews, *Guinea Pigs No More*, 259–311. Colston Warne remembered suggesting the idea to Schlink during their attendance at the Washington Emergency Conference of Consumer Organizations meeting in December 1933. Warne, *Consumer Movement Lectures*, 40, n. 55. See also "The NRA's Teaparty for Consumers," *CRB*, January 1934, 12–14.

133. Schlink, "How the Consumer Was Betrayed." The piece was also reprinted in slightly expanded and unedited form with the same title. See Box 733, "Common Sense" File, CRP; and FJS to Robert S. Lynd, April 10, 1934, and FJS to George Soule, October 2, 1934, both Box 737, File NRA31293, CRP.

134. FJS to Alfred Bingham, August 1, 1934, Box 733, "Common Sense" File, CRP; FJS to Robert S. Lynd, October 17, 1934, S—Liberals File, CRP.

135. Schlink, "How the Consumer Was Betrayed"; FJS to Robert S. Lynd, October 17, 1934, S—Liberals File, CRP; FJS, "The New Deal and the Consumer," press summary of address, Institute of Public Relations, University of Virginia, July 12, 1934, Box 734, FJS—Papers and Talks File, CRP. See also Schlink to CR counsel Oscar Cox, April 19, 1934, Box 501, CRP.

136. Matthews and Shallcross, *Partners in Plunder*, esp. 383–404; Matthews, *Guinea Pigs No More*.

137. Jacobs, " 'Democracy's Third Estate'"; Cohen, *Consumers' Republic*, 24, 28–31. Alan Brinkley takes an even dimmer view of the halting achievements of the New Deal regarding consumption and consumers in *End of Reform*, 69–72.

138. For underconsumption see Foster and Catchings, *Business without a Buyer*; Foster and Catchings, *Profits*; Foster and Catchings, *Road to Plenty*; and Chase, *Economy of Abundance*. For brief discussions of the limitations and appeal of this theory, see Calder, *Financing the American Dream*, 271–74; Brinkley, *End of Reform*, 70, 75–77; and Jacobs, " 'Democracy's Third Estate.' " On consumer fear see Roy S. Durstine, "Advertising—Its Proper and Necessary Function," address to the United States Chamber of Commerce annual meeting, May 1, 1935, 1, 17, Durstine Speeches and Writings File, BBDO.

139. D'Arcy, "Warning to Advertisers," 32–34. See also Durstine, "Advertising—Its Proper and Necessary Function," 9–10; Roy Durstine, notes for speech to Advertising Federation of America, June 18, 1934, 4–6, Durstine Speeches and Writings File, BBDO; *BBDO Newsletter*, June 23, 1934, 5, BBDO.

140. See John Dough, "Consumer Research Is the Pet Hate of This Householder," *PI* 165, no. 12 (December 21, 1933): 53–54; Frank R. Coutant, "Mr. Dough, Your Neighbors Like Consumer Surveys," *PI* 165, no. 13 (December 28, 1933): 42–44; "Research Man, Mad as Can Be, Challenges Mr. Dough," *PI* 166, no. 4 (January 25, 1934): 64–66; John Dough, "Mr. Dough Sums Up," *PI* 166, no. 9 (March 5, 1934): 65–66; Groesbeck, "This Dangerous Business of Kidding the Public," 6–8; "Consumer Disbelief," *PI* 167, no. 4 (April 26, 1934): 75–76.

141. Campbell, *Consumer Representation in the New Deal*; Robert S. Lynd, "Why Consumers Want Quality Standards," *Advertising and Selling*, January 4, 1934, 15; James Rorty, "Call for Mr. Throttlebottom," *The Nation*, January 10, 1934, 37–39; Schlink and Brady, "Standards and Specifications"; Edwards, "Standardization in the Household"; FJS, "How Specifications Bring Savings," paper read before the National Association of Purchasing

Agents, Buffalo, N.Y., June 5, 1929, Box 731, FJS—Papers and Talks File, CRP; Agnew, "Movement for Standards for Consumer Goods"; Coles, *Standardization of Consumers' Goods.*

142. Virginia Hintz, "Study of Labels on Canned Goods," *JHE* 26 (November 1934): 551–53; George B. Hotchkiss, "Will Standards of Quality Help Consumers?" *Advertising and Selling,* September 27, 1934, 29; Coles, *Standardization of Consumers' Goods;* Lynd, "Democracy's Third Estate"; Campbell, *Consumer Representation in the New Deal;* Ruth O'Brien, "An Argument for Consumer Goods Standards," *PI* 168, no. 13 (September 27, 1934): 63–65; Robert Lynd, "New Deal Consumer: A Study at Close Range," *PI* 166, no. 12 (March 22, 1934): 41–45.

143. Lynd, "Why Consumers Want Quality Standards," 15.

144. Advertising response to New Deal regulatory legislation can only be briefly outlined here but see Jackson, *Food and Drug Legislation in the New Deal;* Young, *Medical Messiahs;* Pease, *Responsibilities of American Advertising;* Kay, "Healthy Public Relations"; and most comprehensively, Stole, "Selling Advertising"; and Stole, "Consumer Protection in Historical Perspective."

145. Roy Dickinson, "Running Wild," *PI* 165, no. 12 (December 21, 1933): 6, 10, 82–83; Roy Dickinson, "Call for Mr. Rorty," *PI* 166, no. 3 (January 18, 1934): 29–34; Robert B. Palmer, "Grading? It's Here Already" *PI* 167, no. 4 (April 26, 1934): 17–21; C. B. Larrabee, "This Consumer Revolt and How to Meet It," *PI* 167, no. 3 (April 19, 1934): 7–12.

146. Larrabee, "Mr. Schlink," 10–13; "Those Guinea Pig Engineers," *PI* 166, no. 5 (February 1, 1934): 37–40. Between 1933 and 1936 the advertising and trade press mentioned Schlink and Consumers' Research frequently, at times weekly. In that sense, the organization's influence was perhaps disproportionate on Madison Avenue and not, as advertisers charged, on consumers themselves.

147. C. R. Palmer, "Why Buying by Brand Is Better Than Buying by Specification," *PI* 166, no. 3 (January 18, 1934): 7–12, 72; Nell B. Nichols, "Women Want Descriptive, not ABC Labels," *PI* 171, no. 1 (April 4, 1935): 7–8, 90–92.

148. Roy S. Durstine, "A Nation without Trademarks," *Nation's Business,* April 1934, 39–40; Amos Bradbury, "Getting Offensive," *PI* 171, no. 6 (May 9, 1935): 7–8; Larrabee, "This Consumer Revolt," 12. See also Carpenter, *Dollars and Sense;* and O'Sullivan, *Poison Pen of New Jersey.*

149. Palmer, "Why Buying by Brand Is Better," 7–12, 72; Allyn B. McIntyre, "Why Consumer Buying by U.S. Edict Won't Work," *PI* 166, no. 6 (February 8, 1934): 74–80; Durstine, "Nation without Trademarks;" Paul S. Willis, "Why Industry Fights A-B-C Labeling," *PI* 170, no. 5 (January 31, 1935): 69–72.

150. Christine M. Frederick, "Why Women Won't Buy by Specification," *PI* 166, no. 8 (February 22, 1934): 7–10; Anna Steese Richardson, "How Women Can Be Won to Belief in Advertising," *PI* 167, no. 12 (June 21, 1934): 7–11; "Let's Face the Music," *PI* 166, no. 10 (March 8, 1934): 104–5.

151. Frederick, "Why Women Will Not Buy by Specification;" Ernest C. Morse, "Women Won't Buy by the Government Yardstick," *PI* 166, no. 1 (January 4, 1934), 37.

152. Committee on Consumer Standards of the Consumers' Advisory Board, "Proposal to Develop Standards for Consumer Goods by Establishing a Consumer Standards Board and Funds for Basic Testing," December 1, 1933, National Recovery Administration, Con-

sumers' Advisory Board Records, RG 9, National Archives, Washington, D.C.; Lynd, "New Deal Consumer;" Jackson, *Food and Drug Legislation in the New Deal*; Wilcox, "Brand Names, Quality, and Price," 85.

153. O'Dea, *Preface to Advertising*; Roy S. Durstine, "Why Advertising Is an Economic Tool," *PI* 169, no. 7 (November 19, 1934): 93; Palmer, "Why Buying by Brand Is Better," 7–12.

154. Palmer, "Why Buying by Brand Is Better"; Larrabee, "This Consumer Revolt."

155. Pease, *Responsibilities of American Advertising*, 138–66; *Nation's Business* 24 (March 1936): 92–93; *Nation's Business* 23 (January 1935): 82.

156. Pease, *Responsibilities of American Advertising*, 148–51.

157. Roy S. Durstine, "Advertising a Vital Tool in Modern Business," address before Associated Grocery Manufacturers of America, New York City, [1934], Durstine Speeches and Writing File, BBDO.

158. Kenner, *Fight for Truth in Advertising*.

159. Durstine, "Why Advertising Is an Economic Tool," 93; Batten, *Written Word*.

160. Bradbury, "Getting Offensive," 7; "Congratulate the Consumer," *PI* 162, no. 2 (January 12, 1933): 90–91. For more of such "humor," see Larrabee, "Mr. Schlink," 10–13.

CHAPTER EIGHT

1. Charles D. Ammon, "Here the Boss Rebels," *PI* 183, no. 13 (June 30, 1938): 21, 23.

2. Paul W. Garrett quoted in Walker and Sklar, *Business Finds Its Voice*, 7.

3. "Business and Consumers," *Business Week*, June 10, 1939, 27.

4. C. B. Larrabee, "This Consumer Revolt and How to Meet It," *PI* 167, no. 3 (April 19, 1934): 10.

5. Marchand, *Creating the Corporate Soul*; Ewen, *PR!*; Miller, *Voice of Business*; Harris, *Right to Manage*; Fones-Wolf, *Selling Free Enterprise*.

6. See Leuchtenburg, *Franklin D. Roosevelt and the New Deal*, 146–68, 176–77. Schlesinger, *Age of Roosevelt*, 2:471, dates the business break with Roosevelt from early 1934. Hawley, *New Deal and the Problem of Monopoly*, 149–68, sees the break as decisive in the National Association of Manufacturers split in March 1935.

7. Tedlow, *Keeping the Corporate Image*; Galambos, *Public Image of Big Business*; Raucher, *Public Relations and Business*.

8. Barton, *Man Nobody Knows*.

9. On Barton see Marchand, *Creating the Corporate Soul*, 130–63; Bird, *"Better Living"*, 10–101; Susman, *Culture as History*, 122–49; Ribuffo, "Jesus Christ as Business Statesman"; and Montgomery, "Bruce Barton and the Twentieth Century Menace of Unreality." On Barton and Coolidge see Buckley, "President for the 'Great Silent Majority.'" On Barton and corporate public relations see Marchand, "Corporation Nobody Knew." Amazingly, Barton has only now received a full biography: Fried, *Man Everybody Knew*, which appeared as this book was going to press.

10. Bruce Barton, "The Public," speech before the Congress of American Industry, in conjunction with the annual convention of the National Association of Manufacturers, December 4, 1935, Barton File, BBDO. The speech in edited form appeared as "Business Can Win Public from Politician," *PI* 173, no. 11 (December 12, 1935): 17–24; and as "The Public," *Vital Speeches* 2, no. 6 (December 16, 1935): 174–77. In 1938 Barton spoke even

more candidly, arguing that the Republican losses to Roosevelt resulted from the candidates' complete loss of contact with popular concerns and everyday life. See "Barton Sees Crisis for Middle Class," *New York Times*, June 26, 1938, 3.

11. Barton, "The Public." See also William J. Enright, "Moley Sees Trend to 'Conservatism,'" *New York Times*, July 2, 1936, 7.

12. See Arnold, *Folklore of Capitalism*, 165–206.

13. "The Forgotten Man," *Fortune*, July 1934, 111; *PI* 167, no. 4 (April 26, 1934): 8–9. Sumner was JWT president Stanley Resor's intellectual mentor, and his works were required reading in training courses at JWT. See Sumner, *Forgotten Man*. Sumner's connection to the New Deal is outlined in Donald Fleming, "Social Darwinism," in *Paths of American Thought*, ed. Schlesinger and White, 146.

14. Goode, *Modern Advertising Makes Money*, 30. Barton's partner Roy S. Durstine made essentially the same statement in "Advertising as a Vital Tool in Modern Business," address before the Associated Grocery Manufacturers of America, New York City [1934], Durstine Speeches and Writings File, BBDO.

15. Barton served from 1938 to 1940, before losing a Senate bid. He entertained some presidential ambitions as well. In Congress he was an unwavering opponent of the Roosevelt administration. He campaigned on promises to repeal as many laws as possible, opposed every administration initiative in his one term, and frequently called for one hundred businessmen to join him as Republicans in Congress. See "Candidate Prepares to Be 'Great Repealer,'" *New York Times*, October 15, 1937, 25; and "Business Men Urged to Get into Politics," *New York Times*, October 22, 1937, 12.

16. Commercial literature of the late 1930s is filled with calls for public relations as the cure for business's difficulties. In addition to Barton, "The Public," among the most relevant for the analysis presented here are Donald D. Davis, "Public Must Be Given Facts about Big Business," *PI* 173, no. 5 (October 31, 1935): 29–30; Arthur H. Little, "Industry Writes Its Story," *PI* 173, no. 12 (December 19, 1935): 7–8; "Chester Points the Way," *Business Week*, March 7, 1936, 12–16; Arthur H. Little, "Industry Speaks," *PI* 177, no. 2 (October 8, 1936): 6–8; Arthur H. Little, "Let Industry Speak," *PI* 175, no. 5 (April 30, 1936): 7–8; Arthur H. Little, "N.I.A.A. to Sell America," *PI* 177, no. 3 (October 15, 1936): 49–56; Don Francisco, "Business Must Make Friends," *Advertising and Selling*, July 15, 1937, 22; Howard Wood, "Business Must 'Sell' Itself," *Nation's Business*, January 1938, 27–29, 88–89; Glen Griswold, "The Advertising Agency's Function in Public Relations," *Advertising and Selling*, October 1938, 40–42; Roy Dickinson, "Six Things to Consider in Setting Up Public Relations Policies," *PI* 185, no. 6 (November 10, 1938): 19–22; H. A. Batten, *Public Relations* (Philadelphia, 1937), N. W. Ayer Archives, New York, N.Y.; Walker and Sklar, *Business Finds Its Voice*, 1–27; and Wright, *Public Relations for Business*, 35–70.

17. The best cultural histories of these overlapping efforts are Marchand, *Creating the Corporate Soul*, 202–356; and Bird, *"Better Living."* But also see Fones-Wolf, "Creating a Favorable Business Climate"; and Fones-Wolf, *Selling Free Enterprise*, which picks up the story from the end of World War II.

18. Walker and Sklar, *Business Finds Its Voice*.

19. Tedlow, *Keeping the Corporate Image*; Marchand, *Creating the Corporate Soul*, 246–48, 375–63; Bird, *"Better Living"*; Stole, "Selling Advertising," 181–469.

20. Walker and Sklar, *Business Finds Its Voice*, 8–9 (emphasis in original).

21. "What a Country!" *Wedge* 34, no. 1 (1934), BBDO. Pamela Walker Laird's compendious *Advertising Progress*, esp. 249–303, argues that up through World War I, advertisers adopted the theme of consumption as progress largely as a process of legitimizing the profession, an interpretation in agreement with the material presented here in earlier chapters. Such an account, however, does not take into consideration the insistent nationalism that repeatedly engaged advertisers and reemerged as a cliché in the Depression.

22. General Motors, *Proving Ground of Public Opinion*; Roland Marchand, "Customer Research as Public Relations: General Motors in the 1930s," in *Getting and Spending*, ed. Strasser, McGovern, and Judt, 85–109.

23. *SEP*, October 28, 1936, 48–49.

24. *SEP*, November 7, 1936, 34–35; *Nation's Business* 25 (April 1937): 50–51. For other examples see, among others, *SEP*, September 26, 1936, 28–29; *SEP*, December 26, 1936, 42–43; *Nation's Business* 24 (August 1936): 50–51; *Nation's Business* 24 (September 1936): 66–67; *Nation's Business* 25 (February 1937): 82–83. See also Roy S. Durstine, "The Place of Advertising in Recovery," speech before Advertising Federation of America, Boston, Mass., November 4, 1935, 6–7, Durstine Speeches and Writings File, BBDO; Walker and Sklar, *Business Finds Its Voice*, 17.

25. The Graybar Building and vicinity were home to numerous advertising agencies, including Thompson. Independence Square hosted the headquarters of both Curtis Publishing and N. W. Ayer.

26. J. L. Sowers, "The Substance That Makes America," *Printers' Ink Monthly* 35, no. 5 (October 1937): 72, 75–76, 80.

27. Robinson, *Measure of Democracy*. For an early advertisement extolling the typical American, see *Literary Digest*, 117, no. 16 (April 21, 1934): 47. Berolzheimer, "Nation of Consumers," discusses academic community studies and government budget studies. See also Holli, *Wizard of Washington*.

28. Susman, *Culture and Commitment*, 187–88; Zunz, *Why the American Century?* 47–69 (quotation on 67); Igo, "America Surveyed"; Bruce Barton, "Winning Public Approval," speech before the Illinois Manufacturers' Association, Chicago, May 12, 1936, 4–9, Barton Speeches and Writings File, BBDO (emphasis added).

29. See Richard W. Fox, "Epitaph for Middletown: Robert S. Lynd and the Analysis of Consumer Culture," in *Culture of Consumption*, ed. Fox and Lears, 129–36; Smith, "Robert Lynd and Consumerism in the 1930s." The interest in Muncie survives to this day, thanks in no small part to the enduring quality of the Lynds' studies.

30. Lynd and Lynd, *Middletown in Transition*, 489–90. For a nuanced account of the connections between Lynd's consumer activism and his work in Muncie, see Smith, *Social Science in the Crucible*, 144–52.

31. "*Sales Management's* Public Relations Index to 90 Large Corporations," *Sales Management* 42, no. 10 (May 1, 1938): 18–20, 66–67; "Who Thinks What," *Tide* 12, no. 10 (May 15, 1938): 14; Sowers, "Substance That Makes America," 72. For a brief discussion see Igo, "America Surveyed," 141–44.

32. Sowers, "Substance That Makes America," 76 (quotation); "Middletown in Transition," *Tide* 11, no. 9 (May 1, 1937): 14–15. Harry R. Tosdal, "A Study of Consumer Demand in Relation to Capitalistic Society," in *Business and Modern Society*, ed. McNair and Lewis, 340, commended the Lynd study to both academic and business researchers.

33. "Executive's Bookshelf: Guinea Pig Revisited," *Wall Street Journal*, June 9, 1937, 6.

34. Lynd and Lynd, *Middletown in Transition*, 361, 498 n. 6.

35. J. L. Sowers, "'Pre-viewing' MIDDLETOWN," *Printers' Ink Monthly* 35, no. 3 (August 1937): 62–64.

36. Stott, *Documentary Expression and Thirties America*;. Daniel et al., *Official Images*; Bezner, *Photography and Politics*; Fleischauer and Brannan, *Documenting America, 1935–1943*. All trace the development of the documentary style among government and leftist organizations.

37. *Printers' Ink Monthly* 35, no. 4 (September 1937): 76–77. See also *Printers' Ink Monthly* 35, no. 5 (November 1937): 44–45; *Printers' Ink Monthly* 36, no. 3 (March 1938): 32–33; and *Printers' Ink Monthly* 36, no. 6 (June 1938): 34–35.

38. Advertiser Thomas Brophy quoted in Marchand, *Creating the Corporate Soul*, 350. See also "In a Way We Were Like Columbus," *Printers' Ink Monthly* 35, no. 4 (September 1937): 76.

39. Sara Hamilton Birchall, "Selling Mom and Sis and Bud and Pop," *Advertising and Selling*, June 8, 1936, 27, 58–60.

40. *SEP*, January 6, 1940, 75; *LHJ* 57, no. 2 (February 1940): 47. See also *SEP*, January 13, 1940, 66–67. The articles were published in a truncated form as Furnas, *How America Lives*. One short study that came to my attention too late to be considered for this discussion is Walker, "*Ladies' Home Journal*, 'How America Lives,' and the Limits of Cultural Diversity."

41. "Elected to Represent," *LHJ* 57, no. 2 (February 1940): 47. Supervising editor Mary Carson Cookman confessed that when she rang the bell of a Fuller Brush salesman, he sold her a brush. Furnas, *How America Lives*, 9.

42. Ibid., 8, 276–77.

43. Ibid., 18–19.

44. "How America Lives," *LHJ* 57, no. 2 (February 1940): 47, 50, 52.

45. Furnas, *How America Lives*, 81–85, 157, 6–7.

46. *PI* 177, no. 9 (November 26, 1936): 22–23; *PI* 175, no. 7 (May 14, 1936): 22–23, *Advertising and Selling*, December 20, 1934, 32–33. For earlier visions of Sweeney as the mass man, see *PI* 129, no. 8 (November 20, 1924): 81–83; *Advertising Fortnightly* 2, no. 1 (November 7, 1923): 29; *Advertising Fortnightly* 2, no. 7 (January 30, 1924): 43; *Advertising and Selling Fortnightly* 4, no. 12 (April 8, 1925): 43.

47. Fred Smith, "To Sell the Small Town, Sell 'Carrie Staunton' First," *Advertising and Selling*, December 1938, 11–12. See also *Advertising and Selling*, January 1939, 57.

48. Kline, *Consumers in the Country*, 1–214; Jellison, *Entitled to Power*; Tobey, *Technology as Freedom*.

49. Charles Morrow Wilson, "The New Farm Language," *Advertising and Selling*, August 1938, 32–33.

50. "Who Is Grace Ellis?" *BBDO Newsletter*, October 9, 1931, 14, BBDO. The language and arguments strikingly resemble the promotional copy that would be used in "How America Lives."

51. [CBS], "*What Does Jake Think?*" (New York, 1935), n.p., CBS Pamphlets File, LAB.

52. "Retailers Select Typical Consumer," *New York Times*, January 14, 1939, 20; "Found! The Typical Consumer: And Retail Stores Honor Her," *Christian Science Monitor*, Janu-

ary 14, 1939, 1; " 'Mrs. Typical Consumer' Pulls No Punches in Criticizing the Stores for the Executives," *New York Times*, January 18, 1939, 38. The Powells had enjoyed a much higher income before the Depression had reversed their fortunes and Mr. Powell came to be a bank clerk. Still, those days had left Mrs. Powell "all the normal labor saving household equipment," including a washing machine, refrigerator, and smaller appliances. "Housekeeper Faces Shopmen with Windtight Budget Plan," *Christian Science Monitor*, February 20, 1939, 5.

53. "Consumer," *Tide* 13, no. 3 (February 1, 1939): 8.

54. Susman, *Culture a History*, 164; Igo, "America Surveyed," 87–88.

55. For an examination of the defense of free enterprise through radio, print, and live entertainment in the Depression, see Bird, *"Better Living."* See also Bird, "Order, Efficiency, and Control," 62–77. Fones-Wolf, *Selling Free Enterprise*, continues the story in detail after World War II.

56. See N. W. Ayer & Son, *In Behalf of Management*; H. A. Batten, *Public Relations* (Philadelphia, 1937), Ayer Archives; and O'Dea, *Preface to Advertising*.

57. Walker and Sklar, *Business Finds Its Voice*, 24–58; Wright, *Public Relations for Business*, 107–71. The trade associations included the National Association of Manufacturers, the United States Chamber of Commerce, and the National Association of Industrial Advertisers.

58. Soglow, *Little King*. As early as 1933, Soglow was using the king figure in advertising for Royal Crown Gasoline. In an odd twist, the cartoon became a part of King Features syndicate, whose *Puck the Comic Weekly* became an important advertising medium. The Little King appeared in campaigns showing advertisers how to increase their sales through *Puck*. See "A King Goes to Work," *PI* 164, no. 9 (August 31, 1933): 11–12; and *Tide* 13, no. 2 (February 1, 1939): 2.

59. Thompson, *Primer of Capitalism*, 10. See also *PI* 181, no. 1 (October 7, 1937): 10–11; and William C. McKeehan Jr., "Industry Speaks Up," *People: The Monthly Bulletin of the J. Walter Thompson Company*, August 1937, 20–23, JWTA.

60. Thompson, *Primer of Capitalism*, 16–18. See also Walker and Sklar, *Business Finds Its Voice*, 11–13.

61. Thompson, *Primer of Capitalism*; Pitkin, *Let's Get What We Want!* 74–83; Wright, *Public Relations for Business*, 172–221; Cameron, *Voice of a Business: A Series of Radio Talks*; Cameron, *Series of Talks*, 53–60. See also Ward, *Ourselves*.

62. Pitkin, *Let's Get What We Want!* 39; see also Pitkin, *Capitalism Carries On*.

63. "Old Fashioned Simplicity" (1936), "It Belongs to Main Street," File 2 (1937), and "A Democracy in Industry" (1932), all Series 3, Book 466, AC; "Stockholders Are People," *Printers' Ink Monthly* 38, no. 3 (March 1939): 10–11. For the classic statement of the corporation's significance in the American economy, along with a strong defense of the divorce of management and financial control, see Berle and Means, *Modern Corporation and Private Property*.

64. *Nation's Business* 24 (September 1936): 96–97.

65. *Nation's Business* 25 (November 1937): 3; see also *Nation's Business* 24 (October 1936): 99.

66. Hubert Kelly, "America's No. 1 Communist," *American Magazine* 126 (February 1936): 29, 111.

67. *Advertising and Selling* 31, no. 11 (November 1938): 17 (quotation); *Collier's* 26, no. 19 (November 8, 1940): 61; "Near to People's Hearts," *Printers' Ink Monthly* 39, no. 4 (October 1939): 34.

68. N. W. Ayer, "Joe and the Corporate Surplus," Ayer Archives; *Nation's Business* 27 (March 1939): 46–47.

69. Walker and Sklar, *Business Finds Its Voice*, 43; Bird, "Enterprise and Meaning"; Smith, "Jam Handy Company and the Discussional Filmstrip"; "Commercial Films," *Tide* 10, no. 12 (November 1, 1936): 10–11; *Tide* 11, no. 20 (October 12, 1937): 12–13; "Good Will Film," *Printers' Ink Monthly* 26, no. 2 (February 1938): 14–15. These public relations films blurred easily with other industrial films that were publicizing a specific product or industry. See "Reaching the Consumer with Films," *Printers' Ink Monthly* 37, no. 7 (July 1938): 19–22, 60–73; and "Film Front," *Tide* 13, no. 4 (February 15, 1939): 20–21.

70. *From Dawn to Sunset* (Jam Handy Corporation, 1937). My thanks to Rick Prelinger for making this film available and discussing it with me. It is also available on CD-ROM: Prelinger, *Capitalist Realism*; and online at <http://www.archive.org/details/FromDawn 1937> (October 17, 2005). For accounts of other sponsored films, see Bird, *"Better Living,"* 120–81.

71. "Propaganda," *Tide* 13, no. 14 (July 15, 1938): 23; see also Walker and Sklar, *Business Finds Its Voice*.

72. Bird, "Enterprise and Meaning"; "American Way," *Tide* 13, no. 7 (April 1, 1939): 9–11.

73. "The Weapons of Democracy," *Business Week*, July 1, 1939, cover II.

74. Advertising and Selling, *Annual Advertising Awards, 1938*, 67.

75. *Tide* 13, no. 7 (April 1, 1939): 1. The piece originally ran in the *New York World Telegram*, February 28, 1939.

76. "New York Fair," *Tide* 13, no. 9 (May 1, 1939): 20.

77. "Build-Up," *Tide* 13, no. 5 (March 1, 1939): 9–10; Cohen, Heller, and Chwast, *Trylon and Perisphere*, 65; Bird, "Enterprise and Meaning"; Roland Marchand, "4 Industrial Aesthetics of Worlds Fair Displays," unpublished manuscript, reworked as "The Corporations Go to the Fair," in *Creating the Corporate Soul*, 249–311; Zim, Lerner, and Rolfes, *World of Tomorrow*; Harrison, *Dawn of New Day*.

78. See "On Location," *Advertising and Selling* 32, no. 7 (July 1939): 34–35. *The Middleton Family at the New York World's Fair* can occasionally be found in and out of print and at a handful of U.S. research libraries. The out-of-copyright movie is available through Moviecraft Home Video, P.O. Box 438, Orland Park, IL 60462.

79. Babs indeed was a future Mrs. Consumer. She was played by Marjorie Lord, who had a long-running role as a TV homemaker on the *Make Room for Daddy* series between 1957 and 1964. For discussion of the film see Marchand, *Creating the Corporate Soul*, 295–98; and Bird, *"Better Living,"* 140–43.

80. Corn and Horrigan, *Yesterday's Tomorrows*; "The People's Fair," in Susman, *Culture as History*, 211–29; Smith, *Making the Modern*, 405–21.

81. Marquis, *Hopes and Ashes*, 210.

82. My thanks to Rick Prelinger who made the film from Futurama, *To New Horizons*, available to me. It is now accessible on the Prelinger Archives website: <http://www. archive.org/details/ToNewHor1940> (October 17, 2005). Futurama is also discussed in

Bird, *"Better Living,"* 133–37; Marchand, *Creating the Corporate Soul*, 301–311; Rydell, *World of Fairs*, 133–35; and Marquis, *Hopes and Ashes*, 202–4. Thanks here, as so often, to Larry Bird, who generously shared his own world's fair insights and passions.

83. "21 Fair Advisers on Consumer Quit," *New York Times*, February 28, 1939, 1, 21; "A Letter to Mr. Whalen," *Consumers Union Reports* 4 (March 1939): 31 (a reprint of the resignation letter); "Resignation," *Tide* 12, no. 6 (March 15, 1939): 26–27; "Drops Fashion Hall Plan," *New York Times*, April 6, 1939, 42; "Split Fair Group Replies to Critics," *New York Times*, April 9, 1939, G5; Kathleen McLaughlin, "Consumer Exhibits Give Many Lessons," *New York Times*, May 4, 1939, 21; "The Consumer Movement," *Business Week*, April 22, 1939, 52. On Consumers Union, see chapter 9.

84. *Consumers Union Reports* 4 (August 1939): 16.

CHAPTER NINE

1. Raymond Rubicam, "Consumer Advertising Must Be Factual, Yes; But It Needs Drama and Interest Too," *PI* 191, no. 8 (May 24, 1940): 74.

2. Henry Luce to Bruce Barton, April 26, 1942, Box 1, "AFA" File, Bruce Barton Papers, SHSW.

3. *Woman's Home Companion* 67, no. 11 (November 1940): 2 (emphasis in original).

4. Walter D. Fuller, "How Advertising Helped Prepare America to Do Its War Job Superbly Well," *PI* 198, no. 4 (January 23, 1942): 34, 60.

5. Ware, *Consumer Goes to War*, 262.

6. For transcripts of town meetings see Box 911, File 021.621, CRP; Phillips and Schlink, *Discovering Consumers*, 22–30. A brief account of the later campaign for a consumer cabinet post is told in Cohen, *Consumers' Republic*, 361–63.

7. Matthews, *Odyssey of a Fellow Traveler*, traces his life up through his conversion to anticommunism and rejection of leftist politics; see also, for a short sketch, Goodman, *The Committee*, 35–42.

8. Warne, *Consumer Movement Lectures*, 48–59 (greatly revised from Colston E. Warne, "The Genesis of the Consumer Movement: The Ideological Roots of Consumerism," lecture delivered at Kansas State University, January 24, 1977, 7–11, Warne Papers, CSCM), provides a sympathetic but critical narrative of the general origins and effects of the strike by a close observer. Glickman, "Strike in the Temple of Consumption," presents a thoughtful and persuasive account of the strike's significance in assessing the fissures and continuities of consumer activism and politics.

9. The number of strikers who were bona fide employees was one of the innumerable points of contention between the union and CR, and the figures have been reported from forty to seventy. I use a figure referred to by both sides, confirmed as the union's estimate of the strikers two weeks into the dispute. CR claimed that the organization employed 102 workers (over twenty were contract laborers working on a new building). It seems fair to conclude that some forty out of eighty total workers who were involved in daily operations were on strike, quite a substantial proportion in any case. "The Strike at Consumers' Research: The Union's Reply to the Management's Statement," Strike Materials File, CUA; "Kallet vs. Schlink," *Business Week*, September 7, 1935, 8; Technical, Editorial, and Office Assistants' Union, American Federation of Labor Local 20055, "Facts in Brief of the Strike at Consumers' Research," September 5, 1935, Strike Materials File, CUA.

10. The summary dismissal of Palmer from the board inflamed tensions among the strikers, who quickly added (then retracted) his reinstatement to their demands.

11. Warne, "Genesis of the Consumer Movement," 9–10; Colston E. Warne interview with Sybil Schwartz, April 6, 1971, 4–5, CUA; E. J. [Jack] Lever interview with Colston Warne and Sybil Schwartz, July 31, 1971, 2, CUA.

12. Warne, *Consumer Movement Lectures*, 48–49.

13. For a sample of such rhetoric, near the end of a staff meeting of August 29, which was set to air the grievances and to discuss union recognition, Matthews said, "CR has not been cowed by the biggest industrialists and financiers in America and we shall not be cowed. We cannot be cowed by the potentially weak and despicably contemptible group that employs trade union tactics. . . . [W]e know exactly what we have to go through in order to stand on the principle that members of the organization must be of known integrity." Such ad hominem attacks applied to coworkers in the name of "integrity" were not atypical of Matthews's style. "Stenog Record Staff Mtg," August 29, 1935, Strike Files, CRP.

14. See "Excerpts from Letters Written by Consumers' Research in January and February 1936 to a Clergyman [Robert Weston] Critic of Its Labor Policy and its Management Apropos of the 'Strike' at CR Which Occurred September 4, 1935," Strike Files, Box 727, CRP.

15. Alexander Crosby interview with Norman Katz, November 19, 1974, 2, CUA; Lever interview with Warne and Schwartz, 2–3; Glickman, "Strike in the Temple of Consumption," 120–28.

16. J. B. Matthews, sworn statement of October 10, 1935, State of New Jersey, Warren County, made before Alvin Sloan, 5, Strike Files, Box 727, CRP. This July meeting included Palmer, Kallet, Susan Jenkins, Dexter Masters and Mildred Edie of *Tide* magazine, and Rose Nelson, a consumer activist and organizer of a New York meat strike. The Wyand statement is found in "JB's Notes of a Conversation with Wyand, November 20, 1935, corrected by Wyand, December 5, 1935," Strike Files, Box 727, CRP. Judging by the date, apparently Wyand did not inform his friends about the meetings he witnessed for some time either.

17. "Statement by Consumers' Research to Its Patrons," *Washington [N.J.] Star*, September 20, 1935, 1-1, 2-1; "The Strike at Consumers' Research," *CR* Reprint, Strike Files, Box 727, CRP. See also the union rebuttal, "Union Replies to Consumers' Research Board Statement," *Washington Star*, September 27, 1935, Strike Files, Box 727, CRP.

18. Strike song to the tune of "Gallagher and Shean," Strike Songs, File 5.5, Strike Materials, CUA.

19. Arnold Black and Kate Leers Black interview with Sybil Schwartz, April 19, 1974, 19, CUA; Crosby interview with Katz, 2.

20. See "Report of the Investigating Committee in the strike at the plant of Consumers' Research, Washington, New Jersey," November 16, 1935, typescript, Box 727, "JBM Strike File," CRP.

21. "The Strike at Consumers' Research," *New Republic*, October 9, 1935, 230–31; A. L. Crosby, "Consumers' Research Fights the Union," *The Nation*, September 25, 1935, 356–57; "The C. R. Strike," *The Nation*, December 4, 1935, 637; Kallet, "Partners in Strike Breaking," 22–23.

22. See James Gilman, letter to *Consumers' Research* Subscribers, October 20, 1935, Box 727, Strike File Consodine (1935), CRP. Gilman was the head of the association of sub-

scribers and was an organizer of Consumers Union. See Katz, "Consumers Union," 78–83.

23. "A White Collar Strike," *PI* 172, no. 12 (September 19, 1935): 37–47; "Kallet vs. Schlink," *Business Week*, September 7, 1935, 8; "CR: Comedy Relief," *Business Week*, October 12, 1935, 31; "The CR Strike," *PI* 173, no. 2 (October 10, 1935): 94; "Light from Washington, N.J." *PI* 173, no. 7 (November 14, 1935): 114.

24. See Rorty, "What's Wrong with Consumers' Research?" 5–6, 15.

25. "A Discussion of Misrepresentation and False Statements in the *New Republic*'s Editorial on 'The Strike at Consumers' Research' in Its Issue of October 9, 1935," 2, Box 727, JBM Strike File,CRP.

26. "CR Strike Over, But—," *PI* 174, no. 3 (January 16, 1936): 16.

27. Katz, "Consumers Union," 102–3; Silber, *Test and Protest*.

28. Katz, "Consumers Union," 107.

29. These issues are laid out in the early numbers of *Consumers Union Reports*. See also Katz, "Consumers Union," 85–144; and Silber, *Test and Protest*.

30. *Consumers Union Reports* 1, no. 1 (May 1936): 2, 24. Often, the articles on labor within a given industry were printed as sidebars or stand-alone features in the magazine near the articles on products.

31. *Consumers Union Reports* 4, no. 6 (June 1939): 10. Kallet reported that by April 1939 Consumers Union had 85,000 members of which 71,000 were full—not limited—subscribers.

32. See " 'Consumers Union Reports—,' " *PI* 175, no. 9 (May 28, 1936): 64–66.

33. On redistributing wealth see Schlink, "Safeguarding the Consumer's Interest," 114–15; on class-conscious consumers and on fundamental economic conflict, see Schlink, "How the Consumer Was Betrayed," 3. See also Arthur Kallet interview with Sybil Schwartz, December 7, 1970, 7, CUA.

34. "Consumers' Red Network," *Business Week*, December 16, 1939, 17–18; Kallet interview with Schwartz, December 7, 1970; Dewey Palmer interview with Colston E. Warne and Sybil Schwartz, April 26, 1970, 14, CUA; Stanley High, "Guinea Pigs, Left March," *Forum*, October 1939, 153–57; George H. Tichenor, "War on Consumers," *Forum*, February 1940, 28–31; Don Wharton, "Arthur Kallet: Career as Ally, Foe and Imitator of Consumers' Research," *Scribner's Magazine* 102, no. 11 (November 1937): 38–39; John MacCormac, "Henderson, Aides Accused of Links to Reds," *New York Times*, September 8, 1941, 1, 8; "Dies Says M'Leish Hired 'Communist,' " *New York Times*, January 16, 1942, 15.

35. J. B. Matthews, and F. J. Schlink, "A Consumers' Program for Congress." *Consumers' Digest* 5 (February 1938): 2–13 (quotation on 7–8). *Nation's Business*, among industry journals in particular, recognized the extent of Schlink's new economic orthodoxy. See Fred DeArmond, "Consumer Clans are Gathering," *Nation's Business*, January 1938, 44.

36. Glickman, "Strike in the Temple of Consumption."

37. Schlink, "How the Consumer Was Betrayed"; Schlink, "Government Bureaus for Private Profit."

38. Schlink, "100,000,000 Step-Children," 29.

39. Phillips and Schlink, *Discovering Consumers*, 11–12.

40. Ibid., 7–8, 28–30.

41. FJS to E. Pendleton Herring, May 21, 1935, Box 725, File 342.11, CRP.

42. FJS to L. Belassa, April 23, 1936, Strike Files, CRP. Like many people, Schlink recreated his memories to square with his evolving beliefs. Mindful of his past leftist sympathies and his 1928 support for socialist presidential candidate Norman Thomas, I asked him in one conversation whom he voted for in 1928. Schlink replied, "Hoover." My point here is not his faulty memory but rather that so strong was the trauma of the strike and his break with liberals, he remembered himself as having been more conservative than the record showed. See FJS to Bruce Bliven, September 19, 1928, Box 1044, Personal Items File, CRP.

43. A brief chronicle of these movements against the grassroots consumer movement by business is found in Sorenson, *Consumer Movement in the United States*, 154–78.

44. "Reply," *Tide* 9, no. 10 (May 15, 1939): 15.

45. "Cassandra," *Tide* 11, no. 24 (November 15, 1937): 22–23 (quotation); *Advertising and the Consumer Movement*, 5; Anna Steese Richardson, "An Advertising Odyssey," *Advertising and Selling* April 1935, copy in Box 512, File 16.34, CRP; "The Consumer Menace," *PI* 181, no. 5 (November 4, 1937): 96.

46. Richardson, *Consumer Relations*, 1.

47. "Institute," *Tide* 13, no. 16 (August 15, 1939): 17–8; "Wooing Consumers," *Business Week*, November 15, 1937, 38–39; "Approach," *Tide* 13, no. 7 (April 1, 1939): 32; "Ayer's Laird," *Tide* 13, no. 3 (February 1, 1939): 24; "Testing Lab," *Tide* 13, no. 24 (November 15, 1939): 22; "The Attacking Stage," *Consumers Union Reports* 2, no. 10 (December 1937): 2.

48. "Air Advice," *Tide* 12, no. 4 (February 15, 1938): 22–23.

49. "At Long Last," *Tide* 12, no. 10 (May 15, 1938): 16.

50. "A Warning to Consumers," *Consumers Union Reports* 2, no. 6 (July 1937): 2, 31; " 'Golden Cord,' " *Consumers Union Reports* 2, no. 7 (August 1937): 2; "A Bad Start," *Consumers Union Reports* 2, no. 9 (November 1937): 2; Sorenson, *Consumer Movement in the United States*, 168–70; *Consumers Union Reports* 4, no. 3 (March 1939): 6; "Silver Lining," *PI* 180, no. 11 (September 9, 1937): 107; "C.U. Inc., Objects," *PI* 181, no. 8 (November 25, 1937): 92; "One Big Union," *Tide* 12, no. 2 (January 15, 1938): 16–17. Foster briefly hooked up with Crump Smith's *National Consumer News*, which attempted to unite business and consumers; Smith's soft-pedaling of business criticism, his dependence on large advertising, and his service to retailers under the guise of disinterested consumer reporting made his publication anathema to independent consumer organizations. See, for example, "Consumer Portrait," *Tide* 11, no. 22 (October 15, 1937): 21.

51. Robert S. Lynd, "Consumer Groups at Critical Stage," *New York Times*, May 16, 1937, 57; Percy S. Straus, "Straus Backs Lynd on Consumer Units," *New York Times*, May 23, 1937, 57; "Committee Upholds Advertising Role," *New York Times*, May 12, 1939, 12.

52. *Cosmopolitan* 105, no. 5 (November 1938): 103. This series of ads ran throughout 1939. See, for examples, *Cosmopolitan* 106, no. 1 (January 1939): 71; *Cosmopolitan* 106, no. 2 (February 1939): 17; *Cosmopolitan* 106, no. 5 (May 1939); *Cosmopolitan* 107, no. 2 (August 1939): cover III. CR took notice of it quickly: "Are You a Guinea Pig?" *Consumers' Digest*, November 1938, 44–49.

53. The campaign ran in *Cosmopolitan, American Druggist,* and the Hearst newspapers. See "Fight Consumer Propaganda," *PI* 184, no. 5 (August 4, 1938): 63.

54. *Woman's Home Companion* 66, no. 6 (June 1939): 96; *Collier's* 104, no. 3 (July 22, 1939): 50. See also Verna Springer, "Me and the Consumer Movement," *Nation's Business*, March 1941, 44, 46, 64–65.

55. "The Good Housekeeping Institute," *Consumers Union Reports* 1, no. 3 (July 1936): 2, 24. See also Ayres, "Private Organizations Working for the Consumer," 158–60.

56. "Hearst Magazines Accused by F.T.C.," *New York Times*, August 21, 1939, 22; "Good Housekeeping Owners Defy F.T.C. on Ad 'Guaranties,'" *Washington Post*, August 21, 1939, 2; "Good Housekeeping Denies Trade Commission Charges," *Christian Science Monitor*, August 22, 1939, 16; "Seal of Disapproval," *Business Week*, August 26, 1939, 20–22; "Good Housekeeping Stands Indicted," *Consumers Union Reports* 4, no. 11 (September 1939): 3; "The Case against Good Housekeeping," *Consumers Union Reports* 5, no. 1 (January 1940): 26–27; "The Good Housekeeping Seals of Approval," *Consumers' Digest* 6, no. 5 (November 1939): 40–44.

57. Berlin quoted in "Good House," *Tide* 13, no. 5 (September 1, 1939): 36; "Hearst Magazines Accused by F.T.C."; "Good House II," *Tide* 13, no. 18 (September 15, 1939): 22–23; "Good Housekeeping, Refusing to Sign F.T.C. Stipulation, Will Fight Charges," *PI* 188, no. 8 (August 25, 1939): 68–71. For a discussion of the Federal Trade Commission's proceedings against Hearst, see Pease, *Responsibilities of American Advertising*, 128–31.

58. Christopher Brooks, "What Every Consumer Needs," *GH* 108, no. 2 (February 1939): 159. See also these other rebuttal pieces by Brooks: "The Romans Had Two Words for It," *GH* 108, no. 2 (February 1939): 14; "The Promise Performed," *GH* 108, no. 3 (March 1939): 14; "When 15 Minutes Equals 200 Hours," *GH* 108, no. 6 (June 1939): 16; and "Freedom of the Seals," *GH* 107, no. 1 (July 1939): 8. See also George W. Alder, "Testing Standards? Of Course!" *GH* 108, no. 1 (January 1939): 82–83.

59. "Institute," *Tide* 13, no. 16 (August 15, 1939): 18.

60. Mary Hornaday, "The Certified Product's Role in Truthful Advertising," *Christian Science Monitor*, October 18, 1939, 16. For Hearst counterpublicity see, for example, "1 Out of 4 Gets Turned Down," *Tide* 13, no. 11 (June 1, 1939): 4–5.

61. "Good House III," *Tide* 14, no. 22 (November 15, 1939): 20–21.

62. "Dies Investigator Says Reds Utilize Consumer Groups," *New York Times*, December 11, 1939, 1; "Consumer Group Heads Deny Red Tinge Charge," *Christian Science Monitor*, December 11, 1939, 2; "Consumers' Group Called Tool of Reds," *Washington Post*, December 11, 1939, 1. Among the major groups named by Matthews were the Consumers National Federation, Consumers Union, League of Women Shoppers, the Milk Consumers' Protective Committee, the Consumer-Farmer Milk Cooperative, the New York Consumers' Council, and the Committee for Boycott Against Japanese Aggression. The report, according to *PI*, was dated December 3, but not released until December 11. "Dies Report Charges Communist Influence in Consumer Groups," *PI* 190, no. 11 (December 15, 1939): 15–16, 84.

63. "Consumers' Red Network," *Business Week*, December 16, 1939, 17–18.

64. Ibid.; "Dies Report Charges Communist Influence," 15–16, 84.

65. "Mr. Berlin's Telegram," *PI* 189, no. 11 (December 15, 1939): 96; "Good House V," *Tide* 14, no. 12 (December 15, 1939): 14–15; Goodman, *The Committee*, 83–85.

66. "Only Dies Herring Is Red, Consumers Say," *Christian Science Monitor*, Decem-

ber 13, 1939, 7; "'Report' by Mr. Matthews," *Consumers Union Reports* 5, no. 1 (January 1940): 24–25; "Consumers' Red Network," 17–18; *Space and Time: Newsletter of Advertising* 137 (December 18, 1939): 1–2, and *Space and Time: Newsletter of Advertising* 152 (April 1, 1940): 1–3, both clipped in Good Housekeeping File 339.41GHI, CRP; "Deny Matthews Charges," *PI* 189, no. 11 (December 15, 1939): 93–96. See also "Dies vs. Consumers," *Business Week*, November 11, 1939, 44; and "The Way It Looks to Us . . . ," *Consumers Union Reports* 4, no. 11 (November 1939): 32, which saw the forthcoming fights between the House Un-American Activities Committee and the consumer movement as a means of stimulating publicity and gaining business support for the committee. The first historian to study this episode, Pease, *Responsibilities of American Advertising*, 153–58, essentially concludes the same thing.

67. "Voorhis Attacks Dies, Matthews," *New York Times*, December 12, 1939, 22; "Mr. Barton vs. the Truth," *Consumers Union Reports* 5, no. 3 (March 1940): 3; "Dies Rebuked by Associate," *Los Angeles Times*, December 12, 1939, 8; "Voorhis Scores Dies Attack on Consumers," *Washington Post*, December 12, 1939, 2; "Matthews Meets Denials, Attacks," *New York Times*, December 11, 1939, 14; "Red Charges Denied by Consumer Group," *New York Times*, December 13, 1939, 19; "Warne Defends Research Union," *Christian Science Monitor*, December 13, 1939, 14; "Un-American Activities," *Washington Post*, December 13, 1939; "'Report' by Mr. Matthews," 24.

68. "President Scores Dies," *Los Angeles Times*, December 13, 1939, 13; "Dies Report Scored by Mrs. Roosevelt," *New York Times*, December 14, 1939, 19.

69. Katz, "Consumers Union"; Colston Warne to Martin Dies, April 15, 1940, Warne Papers, CSCM.

70. "Matthews Lifts a Lid," *PI* 189, no. 11 (December 15, 1939): 101–2; "Willis Defends Consumer," *PI* 189, no. 12 (December 22, 1939): 65; C. B. Larrabee, "Teachers Not Anti-Advertising, Nor Red, or Even Pink, Business-Baiters," *PI* 191, no. 6 (May 10, 1940): 15–16, 78–79; G. A. Nichol, "Rough Stuff," *PI* 189, no. 12 (December 22, 1939): 15–16, 74–75; "Bigger Than Hearst," *PI* 189, no. 13 (December 29, 1939): 70–71; "Getting Cold?" *PI* 190, no. 8 (February 16, 1940): 89.

71. "A.N.P.A., on Press Freedom Issue, Would Intervene in Good House Case," *PI* 191, no. 9 (May 31, 1940): 93–94.

72. "Hearst Magazine Is Curbed on Use of Advertising Seals," *Christian Science Monitor*, May 23, 1941, 3.

73. Sokolsky, *American Way of Life*, 121, vii–viii (quotations); "Defense," *Tide* 12, no. 21 (November 1, 1938): 26; ". . . to the Editor," *Advertising and Selling* 32, no. 8 (August 1939): 12, 66. For other examples of business attacks on consumer material in schools, see "School Book," *Tide* 13, no. 12 (June 15, 1939): 22–23; Walker and Sklar, *Business Finds Its Voice*, 22–23.

74. "Magazine Movies," *Tide* 13, no. 6 (March 15, 1939): 54, 56.

75. "Meeting," *Tide* 13, no. 13 (July 1, 1939): 30.

76. "Fleischmann," *Tide* 12, no. 16 (August 15, 1938): 24–25.

77. Hawley, *New Deal and the Problem of Monopoly*, 404–71; Arnold, *Folklore of Capitalism*; "Mr. Arnold on Advertising," *Tide* 12, no. 22 (November 15, 1938): 25, 28; "Add Arnold," *Tide* 12, no. 23 (December 1, 1938): 20; Harold Fleming, "Wall Street Comment

Sardonic about Monopoly Inquiry," *Christian Science Monitor*, December 7, 1938, 19; "All Competitive Advertising Hit by New Deal Move," *Wall Street Journal*, November 9, 1938, 1; "Advertiser's Use of Power Hit by Arnold," *Christian Science Monitor*, October 28, 1940, 16; "On Record," *Tide* 13, no. 11 (June 1, 1939): 33–34.

78. "O'Mahoney Disowns Arnold Advertising Attack as Committee Agenda," *PI* 185, no. 8 (November 24, 1938): 11–12, 62; H. A. Batten "These Economic Facts Smash Arnold Theory," *PI* 185, no. 8 (November 24, 1938): 13–16, 66–67; "Committee Upholds Advertising Role," *New York Times*, May 12, 1939, 4; "Mr. Arnold and a Free Press," *Wall Street Journal*, November 10, 1938, 6; Bernard Kilgore, "Arnold Modifies General Stand on Advertising," *Wall Street Journal*, November 16, 1938, 1, 3; "On Record," *Tide* 13, no. 11 (June 1, 1939): 33–34; "Advertising Criticism by Arnold Held Step to Regimented Press," *Wall Street Journal*, December 15, 1938, 7.

79. "The Consumer Movement," *Business Week*, April 22, 1939, 39–52; "Business and Consumers," *Business Week*, June 10, 1939, 27–28; Verna Springer, "Me and the Consumer Movement," *Nation's Business*, March 1941, 44–45, 61.

80. "The Consumer Movement," *Business Week*, April 22, 1939, 42–43.

81. Ibid., 44; Gabler, *Labeling the Consumer Movement*.

82. The best surveys of those movements remain contemporary accounts: Sorenson, *Consumer Movement in the United States*; and Dameron, "Consumer Movement."

83. See "Institute for Consumer Education" (Ann Arbor, 1938), typescript, Baker Library, Harvard Business School, Harvard University; [National Conference on Consumer Education], *Next Steps in Consumer Education* (Los Angeles, 1939); "The Consumer Movement," *Business Week*, April 22, 1939, 52.

84. Fred DeArmond, "Consumer Clans Are Gathering," *Nation's Business*, January 1938, 44; "The Consumer Movement," *Business Week*, April 22, 1939, 48–50; "Selling Machine," *Tide* 13, no. 4 (February 15, 1939): 26–27.

85. "Editor Asserts Radicals Strive to Fetter Press," *New York Times*, May 18, 1940, 10; "Woman Editor Honored," *New York Times*, April 6, 1940, 19; "Free Press Foes Pack New Deal, Says Barton," *New York Times*, February 16, 1940, 3; "Barton Warns on Ads Attack," *Los Angeles Times*, February 16, 1940, 29; Katherine Clayberger, "Education of Consumer Held to Be Vital in Defense of Free Enterprise System," *PI* 195, no. 2 (April 11, 1941): 23–28.

86. "Advertising Issue Denied by Arnold," *New York Times*, October 28, 1940, 6; "Arnold Reassures Ad Men on Policy," *New York Times*, October 8, 1941, 34; Ernest K. Lindley, "The New 'Conspiracy,'" *Washington Post*, February 23, 1940, 11; "Advertising and Morale: Roosevelt Stresses Links between Them," *Washington Post*, May 27, 1941, 36.

87. Sorenson, *Consumer Movement in the United States*, 222, 224–35, lists, as of 1940, over one hundred local and national groups with substantial connections to consumers and their interests.

88. *Consumers Union Reports* 1, no. 1 (May 1936): 2, 24; Sorenson, *Consumer Movement in the United States*, 111–15.

89. Dunbar, "Advertising from the Consumers' Point of View," Consumers Union Papers, CUA; Sorenson, *Consumer Movement in the United States*, 183–95.

90. "Business and Consumers," *Business Week*, June 10, 1939, 27–28; "What Con-

sumers Told TNEC," *Business Week*, May 20, 1939, 44–45; "On Record," *Tide* 13, no. 11 (June 1, 1939): 33–34; Sorenson, *Consumer Movement in the United States*, 154–65.

91. "Business and Consumers," *Business Week*, June 10, 1939, 27.

92. Dunbar, "Advertising from the Consumers' Point of View."

93. Rubicam, "Consumer Advertising Must Be Factual, Yes But It Needs Drama and Interest, Too," 74.

94. Westbrook, *Why We Fought*, 38–56. Westbrook engages Michael Walzer's "The Obligation to Die for the State," from *Obligations*, 77–98.

95. Westbrook, *Why We Fought*, 40. This is not to suggest that the New Deal died simply through political theory, lived or otherwise. The alliance of anti-Roosevelt forces in Congress with business opponents, along with war exigencies, halted New Deal programs. But Westbrook helps us see that the wartime aura of sacrifice and dedication to home and family, especially as Americans lived with difficulties of government planning and control in a wartime state, was of a piece with the concurrent rejection of state-sanctioned obligation as embodied in the New Deal. For some important literature on the limits and undoing of the New Deal, see Patterson, *Congressional Conservatism and the New Deal*; Karl, *Uneasy State*; and Brinkley, *End of Reform*, 137–271.

96. Terkel, *"The Good War"*; Hoopes, *Americans Remember the Home Front*; Yellin, *Our Mothers' War*. Such evidence is borne out as well in material, cultural, and pictorial accounts such as Cohen, *V for Victory*.

97. Childs, *This Is Your War!* 62.

98. For a detailed overview of the principal wartime and permanent government agencies responsible for regulating consumption, see Canoyer, "Government Agencies and the Consumer in Wartime." For rationing and the home front see Lingeman, *Don't You Know There's a War On?* esp. 234–70. General accounts of the U.S. home front that make some mention of rationing and shortages include Polenberg, *War and Society*; Blum, *V Was for Victory*; Perret, *Days of Sadness, Years of Triumph*; Winkler, *Home Front U.S.A.*; and Jeffries, *Wartime America*, esp. 16–92. On the other hand, David Kennedy's recent massive account, *Freedom from Fear*, devotes only three pages, 644–47, to the home-front domestic economy, out of nearly three hundred concerning World War II.

99. Perret, *Days of Sadness, Years of Triumph*, 233–34; Lloyd Norman, "Scrap Roundup Tonnage Rises, Says Director," *Chicago Daily Tribune*, September 24, 1942, 10; Laura Haddock, "Millions of Children Mobilizing for Scrap Drive in Bay State," *Christian Science Monitor*, September 29, 1942, 1; "Richmond Leads in Scrap Campaign," *New York Times*, October 7, 1942, 1, 31; "City's 300,000 School Children to Open Scrap Drive," *Los Angeles Times*, October 18, 1942, A1.

100. From a large literature on entertainment that aided in the war effort, see, in particular, Basinger, *World War II Combat Film*; Doherty, *Projections of War*; Koppes and Black, *Hollywood Goes to War*; and Fyne, *Hollywood Propaganda of World War II*. On radio and broadcasting see Horten, *Radio Goes to War*; Blue, *Words at War*; Hilmes, *Radio Voices*, 230–70; Sweeney, *Secrets of Victory*; Smith, *God Bless America*; Malone, *Country Music U.S.A.*, 177–97; Erenberg, *Swingin' the Dream*, 181–210; Tucker, *Swing Shift*; Stowe, *Swing Changes*, 141–79; and Anderson, *Songwriter Goes to War*. In addition, see Winkler, *Politics of Propaganda*; and Short, *Film and Radio Propaganda in World War II*.

101. Gordon, *Consumers in Wartime*, 7–8.

102. Ware, *Consumer Goes to War*, 1–2. See also Coles, *Consumers Can Help Win the War*, 1–48.

103. Ware, *Consumer Goes to War*, 2–3 (emphasis added), 194–99.

104. Ibid., 220–22. In this sense Ware extended her other observations of culture as a driving force in history, and her quick, synoptic observations on the distinctiveness of American culture were akin to the study of cultural nationalism by contemporary Margaret Mead. Ware, *Cultural Approach to History*; Mead, *And Keep Your Powder Dry*. For Ware and Mead in context see Fitzpatrick, *History's Memory*; and Hegeman, *Patterns for America*.

105. Ware, *Consumer Goes to War*, 262.

106. Childs, *This Is Your War!* 146–47.

107. Jacobs, " 'How About Some Meat?' "; Cohen, *Consumers' Republic*, 62–109.

108. For a sample of public evidence of the mass interest and organization, see "Housewife Letters Flood Washington," *New York Times*, February 28, 1942, 9; "Home-Makers Get Call to Defense," *New York Times*, March 4, 1942, 16;"Consumer Education Planned by the CDVO [Civilian Defense Volunteer Organization]," *New York Times*, August 2, 1942, F5; "CDVO to Improve Information Units," *New York Times*, December 9, 1942, 35; Lucy Greenbaum, "Consumer Q's and A's: Consumer Information Centers Kept Busy Answering Point-Rationing Questions," *New York Times*, February 28, 1943, X13; Anne Hagner, "Price Charges Bring Action by OPA Here," *Washington Post*, June 27, 1943, M11; "CDVO Plans a Survey of Local Shop Prices," *New York Times*, May 18, 1945, 16; "Project for Consumer," *Consumers Union Reports* 8, no. 4 (April 1942): 105–7.

109. Brinkley, *End of Reform*, 147.

110. Cohen, *Consumers' Republic*, 100–109; Jacobs, " 'How About Some Meat?' "

111. "Consumer's Union Pledge to the Nation," *Consumers Union Reports* 7, no. 1 (January 1942): cover II.

112. Fox, *Madison Avenue Goes to War*; Marchand, *Creating the Corporate Soul*, 312–56; Fones-Wolf, *Selling Free Enterprise*, 15–31; Charles F. McGovern, "Selling the American Way," unpublished paper in possession of the author; Robert Westbrook, "Fighting for the American Family: Private Interests and Political Obligation in World War II," in *Power of Culture*, ed. Fox and Lears, 194–221; Stole, " 'Salesmanship of Sacrifice' "; Stole, "Selling Advertising," 366–405.

113. L. D. H. Weld, "$5 Million Campaign Suggested to Educate Public about Advertising," *PI* 196, no. 3 (July 18, 1941): 59–64.

114. E. B. Weiss, "Propaganda Idea," *PI* 194, no. 3 (January 17, 1941): 37.

115. Young, *Full Corn in the Ear*; Young, *Advertising Agency Compensation*.

116. Young quoted in C. B. Larrabee, "If You Looked for a Miracle," *PI* 197, no. 8 (November 21, 1941): 14–15.

117. Young, *Pills for the Angels*; Larrabee, "If You Looked for a Miracle"; "Two Challenges for Advertisers," *PI* 197, no. 8 (November 21, 1941): 88; A National Advertiser, "In Advertising's Own Back Yard!" *PI* 197, no. 11 (December 12, 1941): 55–61.

118. Fox, *Madison Avenue Goes to War*, 49–55; Griffith, "Selling of America"; Winkler, *Politics of Propaganda*.

119. Stole, " 'Salesmanship of Sacrifice' "; Weinberg, "What to Tell America"; Jones, "U.S. Office of War Information and American Public Opinion."

120. Maxon's tenure was marked by his determined attempt to stifle the consumer movement for grade labeling in canned goods, while Bowles proved more adept at mediating consumer regulatory demands and business opposition.

121. W. J. Weir, "How Business Can Sell War to People, *and Why It Must*," *PI* 199, no. 7 (May 15, 1942): 67. See also W. J. Weir, "Opportunity!" *PI* 199, no. 2 (April 10, 1942): 13–14; Emil Scram, "If American Business Wants to Run Its Own Show When This War Is Over . . . ," *PI* 198, no. 3 (January 16, 1942): 17, 38–45.

122. Edward H. Gardner, "Mischievous Economic Heresies Smashed by Harvard Study," *PI* 199, no. 1 (April 3, 1942): 19.

123. Fuller, "How Advertising Helped Prepare America to Do Its War Job Superbly Well," 34, 60.

124. "The Fight for Free Enterprise," *PI* 197, no. 11 (December 12, 1941): 80–81.

125. Bruce Barton, "This War Is a Revolution, But It Will Not End in the Clouds or in the Ditch . . . ," *PI* 199, no. 13 (June 26, 1942): 21, 62.

126. For example, see Lou Maxon to Bruce Barton, August 23, 1943, and E. P. H. James to Bruce Barton, April 21, 1942, both Box 1, "AFA" File, Barton Papers, SHSW.

127. Gardner, "Mischievous Economic Heresies," 19–31; "Teaching Consumers Economics of Advertising" *PI* 199, no. 1 (April 3, 1942): 35; L. D. H. Weld, "Harvard Looks at Advertising," *PI* 198, no. 1 (January 3, 1942): 27–28, 78–80.

128. But see as well, "Ralph Starr Butler Calls for an Intelligent Approach to Justifying Advertising," *PI* 198, no. 11 (March 13, 1942): 13–14, 61. Butler, a veteran executive at General Foods, took a more nuanced approach toward this defense, arguing that the Borden tome was not a quick, short answer to advertising critics and that indeed no such answer was possible. In general, other practitioners' enthusiasm for defending advertising overpowered Butler's caution against "unproved generalizations and unrepresentative figures" most often used to defend advertising. See also "Teaching Consumers Economics of Advertising," 35–36; and Roy F. Irvin, "An Open Letter to the Advertising Agencies of America," *PI* 196, no. 11 (September 12, 1941): 24–29.

129. Fox, *Madison Avenue Goes to War*, 10–22, 69–98; Marchand, *Creating the Corporate Soul*, 321–30, 336–40.

130. "Editorial," *PI* 196, no. 10 (June 3, 1942): 68.

131. Fuller, "How Advertising Helped Prepare America to Do Its War Job Superbly Well," 60.

132. *Life*, February 1, 1943, 70; *SEP*, March 17, 1940, 91. See also Ballantine advertising in *Life*, November 2, 1942, 10; *Life*, November 9, 1942, 9; *Life*, January 4, 1943, 46; and *Life*, February 1, 1943, 70.

133. *SEP*, March 9, 1940, cover II; *SEP*, January 31, 1943, 85; *SEP*, February 28, 1942, 77. See also *Life*, April 28, 1941, 17; *Life*, June 12, 1944, 24; *Life*, January 11, 1943, 69; and *Life*, November 9, 1942, 101.

134. *Life*, January 14, 1946, cover IV [Coca-Cola]; *SEP*, November 4, 1944, 73 [airlines]. See also the advertising for Stetson, *Life*, September 28, 1942, 116.

135. "United We March," *PI* 197, no. 11 (December 12, 1941): 11–12.

136. "Constructive Consumer Help Is Wartime Copy Theme," *PI* 199, no. 2 (April 10, 1942): 15–20, 76; "World's Greatest System of Mass Communication Is at the Call of U.S.

Government," *PI* 199, no. 2 (April 10, 1942): 33–38; "Strange But True," *PI* 199, no. 3 (April 17, 1942): 11.

137. *Life*, October 12, 1942, 63. See also *Life*, November 2, 1942, 41.

138. *SEP*, December 13, 1943, 43. See also "What We Are Fighting For," *PI* 200, no. 1 (July 3, 1942): 11–12; Virginia Herrod, "After Hours," *PI* 200, no. 6 (August 7, 1942): 62; and Larry D'Aloise, "I'm Not Mad—or Scared," *PI* 201, no. 8 (November 20, 1942): 92.

139. *PI* 201, no. 13 (December 25, 1942): 12.

140. Henry C. Link, "Brands, A Major Contribution to Social Progress and World Harmony," in *Proceedings: Wartime Conference of Members: Association of National Advertisers, Inc., June 2, 3, 4, 1943* (New York, 1943), 8–10, Series 2, Box 1, File 3, Gordon Cole Papers, Archives Center, National Museum of American History, Smithsonian Institution, Washington, D.C.

141. *SEP*, October 14, 1944, 48.

142. *SEP*, May 9, 1942, 7; *Life*, October 5, 1942, 58; *SEP*, February 14, 1944, 101. See also Charles B. Brown, "Four Freedoms in Sixty Seconds," *PI* 201, no. 2 (October 9, 1942): 52.

143. *SEP*, February 27, 1943, 63.

144. *Life*, June 5, 1944, 61.

145. *SEP*, April 25, 1942, 73.

146. *Life*, May 15, 1944, 119; *SEP*, October 21, 1944, 86; *Life*, October 19, 1942, 46; *Life*, September 14, 1942, 56. Some advertisers also saw the war as an opportunity to educate women in brand loyalty and introduce them to basic economic propaganda for the free enterprise system. See Denny Griswold, "After Hours," *PI* 199, no. 12 (June 19, 1942): 72; and P. H. Erbes Jr., "The Women Take Over," *PI* 196, no. 7 (August 15, 1941): 9–11, 68–70; Elsie Johns, "3 Million Women Will Punch War Factory Time Clocks," *PI* 199, no. 6 (May 8, 1942): 15–17, 60; and Elsie Johns, "Lady in Coveralls Wooed By Sellers," *PI* 201, no. 3 (October 16, 1942): 21–23, 54–56.

147. Series 3, Box 312, File 2, "Ladies' Home Journal," 1942–1944, AC (emphasis in original); *PI* 200, no. 4 (July 24, 1942): 29; Frank R. Coutant, "Women Now Read Advertising More Eagerly Than Ever," *PI* 199, no. 13 (June 26, 1942): 14.

148. Childs, *This Is Your War!* 5.

149. *Life*, May 11, 1942, 10.

150. See, for example, *Life*, February 7, 1944, 47; and *Life*, September 13, 1943, 24.

151. Lichtenstein, *Labor's War at Home*; Lingeman, *Don't You Know There's a War On?*; Lipsitz, *Rainbow at Midnight*.

152. *Life*, April 14, 1941, 85; "Design for a Democracy," Series 3, Box 312, File 2, "Ladies' Home Journal, 1942–1944," AC. See as well "Reaching a Cross-Section of America," ". . . by the people," and "Builders of Democracy," all in same file. Wartime Advertising Council advertisement found in *Life*, May 8, 1944, 79.

153. *Life*, November 2, 1942, 85; *Life*, February 15, 1943, 7. See also *Life*, June 19, 1944, 101.

154. *SEP*, October 7, 1944, 73; *SEP*, August 12, 1944, 73. See also "The Fight for Free Enterprise," *PI* 197, no. 11 (December 12, 1941): 80; Monroe Worthington, "Let's Not War on Wealth," *PI* 201, no. 6 (November 6, 1942): 90.

155. Walter D. Fuller, "We Can Have Guns and Butter: We Can Have Buying and Selling

without Being Unpatriotic," *PI* 195, no. 13 (June 27, 1941): 11–14, 88–92; Howard Dickinson, "What Is Leadership?" *PI* 200, no. 9 (August 28, 1942): 68.

156. *Life*, February 14, 1944, cover II. See also *Life*, September 20, 1943, 44; *Life*, January 24, 1944, cover II; and *Life*, June 26, 1944, 41.

157. *SEP*, May 1, 1943, 57 (ellipses in the original).

158. Sydney Hunt, "After Hours," *PI* 198, no. 9 (February 27, 1942): 72; Fred Bohen, "Sell Tomorrow Today!" *PI* 200, no. 4 (July 24, 1942): 13–14, 34; John H. Van Devanter, "Selling What You've Got—*when you haven't got it*," *PI* 199, no. 3 (April 17, 1942): 17–18, 65–68; Russell T. Sanford, "Fishing Tackle," *PI* 201, no. 4 (October 23, 1942): 76; John L. Love, "Can Advertising Sell Hair Shirts," *PI* 200, no. 11 (September 11, 1942): 90.

159. G. A. Nichols, "Post-War Selling Offers Dazzling Opportunity," *PI* 201, no. 13 (December 25, 1942): 13–15, 54–55; L. D. H. Weld, "Heavy Advertising Volume Sure to Follow This War," *PI* 200, no. 6 (August 7, 1942); 26–32; Everett R. Smith, "What of 1946?" *PI* 196, no. 10 (September 5, 1941): 15–18.

160. See, for example, *Life*, July 10, 1944, 40–41; *Life*, February 14, 1944, 72; "Prophetic of Things to Come," *PI* 200, no. 8 (August 21, 1942): 18–19; and James O'Shaughnessy, "A Great Day Coming," *PI* 201, no. 2 (October 9, 1942): 84.

161. Series 3, Box 239, Drawer 331 (1942), AC. See also *Life*, September 13, 1943, 10. For a feature story see Waldemar Kaempffert, "Tomorrow Has Arrived," *American Magazine* 131 (March 1941): 45, 69–71.

162. *Life*, June 26, 1944, 41; *SEP*, October 24, 1942, cover II.

163. *Life*, September 25, 1944, 57 [Westinghouse]; *Life*, October 19, 1944, 109 [Revere].

164. G. H. Smith [with P. H. Erbes Jr.], "Promotes Savings in a War to Pave Way for Postwar Sales," *PI* 200, no. 10 (September 4, 1942): 15–17; " 'Buy Bonds Now for Product Later,' " *PI* 201, no. 9 (November 27, 1942): 13, 51–53; Weld, "Heavy Advertising Sure to Follow," 26.

165. Van Devanter, "Selling What You've Got—*when you haven't got it*," 66.

166. Series 3, Box 245, Drawer 303, File 1943–47, AC.

167. Cohen, *Consumers' Republic*, 112–91.

168. From *Yank*, December 1944, quoted in *Bread and Butter* 14, no. 51 (December 16, 1944): 3.

169. Haddow, *Pavilions of Plenty*; Colomina, Brennan, and Kim, *Cold War Hothouses*; May, *Homeward Bound*; Wagenleitner, *Coca-Colonization and the Cold War*; Collins, *More*; Cross, *All-Consuming Century*, 82–109.

170. Henry Luce, "The American Century," *Life*, February 7, 1941, reprinted in Luce, *Ideas of Henry Luce*; Wallace, *Century of the Common Man*; and Willkie, *One World*.

171. *In the Suburbs* (Redbook Publishing, 1957). Thanks to Rick Prelinger for making this film available to me. It is available online at <http://www.archive.org/details/Inthe Sub1957> (October 15, 2005); and on CD-ROM: Prelinger, *Uncharted Landscape*.

172. Jacobs, " 'How About Some Meat?' " 933–41.

173. Cohen, *Consumers' Republic*, 347–87.

174. Hodgson, *America in Our Time*; Galbraith, *American Capitalism*; Rostow, *Stages of Economic Growth*.

175. Horowitz, *Anxieties of Affluence*.

176. See, most recently, Frank and Weiland, *Commodify Your Dissent!*

EPILOGUE

1. Davies, *Miracle on 34th Street*. Davies first wrote the screenplay for the film and subsequently the novel. Quotations are taken from the 1947 film.

2. Hawken, *Ecology of Commerce*; Papanek, *Green Imperative*; Princen, Maniates, and Conca, *Confronting Consumption*; Greider, *Soul of Capitalism*.

3. Lasn, *Culture Jam*; Klein, *No Logo*; De Graaf, Wann, and Naylor, *Affluenza*; Frank, *One Market under God*; Schor, *Overspent American*; Schor, *Born to Buy*.

4. National advertisers regularly participate in public service campaigns, but the overall percentage of such messages is minuscule when compared with the sheer volume of commercial messages that reach consumers every day.

5. Rodgers, *Contested Truths*, 216.

6. Smith, *Civic Ideals*.

7. The literature of American empire and exceptionalism is voluminous, much of it debating questions of when or whether the United States truly was an empire. These works have figured in those debates but have also chafed against pat questions of definition or periodization. Instead, they have asked more far-reaching questions that reflect the impact on the United States of its imperial projects from a variety of perspectives. Ferguson, *Colossus*; Noble, *Death of a Nation*; Kaplan, *Anarchy of Empire*; Hunt, *Ideology and U.S. Foreign Policy*; Gardner, LaFeber, and McCormick, *Creation of the American Empire*; Williams, *Tragedy of American Diplomacy*. See also Adas, *Dominance by Design*.

8. Louis Uchitelle, "We Pledge Allegiance to the Mall," *New York Times*, December 6, 2004. Uchitelle's title for the story only reinforces the long-term associations of consumption and nationality that this book has traced.

9. Lears, *Fables of Abundance*; Shank, *Token of My Affection*.

10. Miller, *Material Culture and Mass Consumption*; Miller, *Dialectics of Shopping*. See also Graeber, *Toward an Anthropological Theory of Value*.

11. Douglas and Isherwood, *World of Goods*, 41; Brown, *Sense of Things*; Bill Brown, "Science Fiction, the World's Fair, and the Prosthetics of Empire, 1910–1915," in *Cultures of United States Imperialism*, ed. Kaplan and Pease, 129–63; Landsberg, *Prosthetic Memory*.

12. For a representative sampling see Lichtenstein, *Wal-Mart*; Dicker, *United States of Wal-Mart*; Vance and Scott, *Wal-Mart*; and Quinn, *How Wal-Mart Is Destroying America*.

13. Zunz, *Why the American Century?* 111.

14. Appadurai, *Modernity at Large*; Ong, *Flexible Citizenship*; Canclini, *Consumers and Citizens*; Yúdice, *Expediency of Culture*.

BIBLIOGRAPHY

MANUSCRIPT COLLECTIONS
Boston, Mass.
    Baker Library, Harvard Business School
Cambridge, Mass.
    Schlesinger Library, Radcliffe Institute for Advanced Study, Harvard University
        Christine M. Frederick Papers
Cleveland, Ohio
    Western Reserve Historical Society
        Payne Fund Inc. Collection
College Park, Md.
    Library of American Broadcasting, University of Maryland
Durham, N.C.
    John W. Hartman Center for Sales, Advertising, and Marketing History, Duke
        University
        J. Walter Thompson Archives
            Paul Cherington Papers
            Howard Henderson Papers
            Inactive Accounts Files
            In-House Advertising and Publications
            J. Walter Thompson Newsletter
            Arno Johnson Papers
            Monday Night Meetings
            Staff Meeting Records
            James Webb Young Papers
Hyde Park, N.Y.
    Franklin D. Roosevelt Library
        Rexford G. Tugwell Papers
Madison, Wisc.
    State Historical Society of Wisconsin
        Bruce Barton Papers
        E. P. H. James Papers
        Edgar Kobak Papers
        NBC Collection
Minneapolis, Minn.
    Social Welfare History Archives, University of Minnesota
        Helen Hall Papers
New Brunswick, N.J.
    Special Collections, Alexander Library, Rutgers University
        Consumers' Research Papers [*Note*: the collection was totally unprocessed when I
            first began working in it. CR's own internal organization, based on the Dewey

classification system and characterized by extensive cross-referencing, was byzantine. Citations and locations used throughout the book are as specific as possible, but the collection's reorganization no doubt has moved items, as well as greatly facilitated access. Portions of the collection are soon to be microfilmed as well.]

New York, N.Y.

    N. W. Ayer Archives, N. W. Ayer, Inc.

    BBDO Archives, BBDO Inc.

        Bruce Barton, Speeches and Writings

        BBDO Newsletter

        Roy S. Durstine, Speeches and Writings

        The Wedge

Washington, D.C.

    Manuscript Division, Library of Congress

        Edward Bernays Papers

        Stuart Chase Papers

    Archives Center, National Museum of American History, Smithsonian Institution

        N. W. Ayer Collection

        John Caples Papers

        Sheldon Claire Collection

        George Clark Collection of Radioana

        Gordon Cole Papers

        Hills Brothers Collection

        Edward Orth World's Fair Collection

        Warshaw Collection of Business Americana

Yonkers, N.Y.

    Center for the Study of the Consumer Movement, Consumers Union, Inc.

        Consumers' Research Strike Files

        Consumers Union Papers

        Oral History Collection

        Colston E. Warne Papers

PERIODICALS

Ad-Art
Advertising and Selling Fortnightly
American Home
American Magazine
ASA Bulletin
Ballyhoo
Better Homes and Gardens
Bread and Butter
Broadcast Advertising
Business Week
Century
Chicago Tribune

Christian Century
Christian Science Monitor
Circular of the Bureau of Standards
Collier's
Consumers' Club
Consumers' Digest
Consumers' Research
Consumers' Research Bulletin
Consumers' Research General Bulletin
Consumers Union Reports
Cosmopolitan
Education by Radio

Everybody's Magazine
Fame
Fortune
Forum
Good Housekeeping
Harper's New Monthly Magazine
Journal of Home Economics
Judicious Advertising and Advertising
    Experience
Ladies' Home Journal
Life
Light
Literary Digest
Mahin's Magazine
McClure's Magazine
Munsey's Magazine

The Nation
National Advertising Records
Nation's Business
New Republic
New York Times
Pictorial Review
Printers' Ink
Printers' Ink Monthly
Profitable Advertising
Sales Management
Saturday Evening Post
Scribner's
Tide
Wall Street Journal
Washington Post
Woman's Home Companion

BOOKS, ARTICLES, AND DISSERTATIONS

Primary Sources

Abell, Edith. "Do Advertisements Educate the Consumer?" *Journal of Home Economics* 22 (June 1930): 475–77.

Adams, Henry Foster. *Advertising and Its Mental Laws.* New York: Macmillan, 1916.

Addams, Jane. *Twenty Years at Hull House.* 1910; New York: New American Library, 1961.

Advertising and the Consumer Movement: Digest of a Survey on Consumer Activities. New York: Crowell Publishing Company, 1937.

Advertising and Selling. *Annual Advertising Awards, 1938.* New York: Advertising and Selling, 1938.

Agar, Herbert, and Allen Tate. *Who Owns America? A New Declaration of Independence.* Boston: Houghton Mifflin, 1936.

Agnew, Hugh E., and George B. Hotchkiss. *Advertising Principles.* New York: Alexander Hamilton Institute, 1930.

Agnew, Paul G. "The Movement for Standards for Consumer Goods." *Annals of the American Academy of Political and Social Science* 173 (May 1934): 60–69.

——. "Standardization—A Woman's Problem." *Journal of the American Association of University Women* 23 (June 1930): 183–86.

——. "Technical Standards for Consumer Goods—A Five-Year Plan?" *Journal of Home Economics* 23 (December 1931): 1095–102.

——. "Work of the American Engineering Standards Committee." *Annals of the American Academy of Political and Social Science* 137 (May 1928): 13–16.

Agnew, Paul G., and J. W. McNair. "Certification and Labeling Activities in 60 Commodity Fields." *American Standards Association Bulletin* 3 (January 1932): 1–23.

Allen, Frederick J. *Advertising as a Vocation.* New York: Macmillan, 1919.

[American Home Economics Association]. *Home Economists.* Baltimore: American Home Economics Association, 1929.

American Home Economics Association. Committee on Standardization of Consumers'

Goods. *Scientific Consumer Purchasing: A Study Outline Covering Some Recent Developments in Production and Distribution Which Effect the Consumer.* Washington, D.C.: American Home Economics Association, 1932.

Andrews, Benjamin R. *Economics of the Household.* New York: Macmillan, 1923.

Angly, Edward. *Oh Yeah? Compiled from Newspapers and Public Records.* New York: Vanguard Press, 1931.

Arnold, Frank A. *Broadcast Advertising: The Fourth Dimension.* New York: J. Wiley and Sons, 1931.

Arnold, Thurman. *The Folklore of Capitalism.* New Haven, Conn.: Yale University Press, 1937.

Associated Advertising Clubs of America. *Proceedings of the Eighth Annual Convention.* Dallas: n.p., 1912.

[Association of National Advertisers]. *An Analysis of 285 National Advertising Budgets, 1932– 1933, Including a Comparison with Budget Figures for the Years 1929 and 1930.* New York: Association of National Advertisers, Inc., 1933.

Atkins, Willard E., Robert A. Brady, Corwin D. Edwards, A. Anton Friedrich, Donald McConnell, and Louis S. Reed. *The Economics of Modern Life.* New York: Robert Lee Fisher, 1928.

Atkins, Willard E., et al. *Economic Behavior: An Institutional Approach.* 2 vols. Boston: Houghton Mifflin, 1931.

N. W. Ayer & Son. *The Ayer Idea in Advertising.* Philadelphia: N. W. Ayer & Son, 1912.

——. *Better Business.* Philadelphia: N. W. Ayer & Son, 1914.

——. *The Book of the Golden Celebration.* Philadelphia: N. W. Ayer & Son, 1919.

——. *Fortune Follows Fashion.* Philadelphia: N. W. Ayer & Son, n.d.

——. *In Behalf of Advertising.* Philadelphia: N. W. Ayer & Son, 1929.

——. *Forty Years of Advertising.* Philadelphia: N. W. Ayer & Son, 1909.

——. *Memorial Booklet Issued in Commemoration of the Centennial of Lincoln's Birthday.* Philadelphia: N. W. Ayer & Son, 1909.

——. *Our Great Commander.* Philadelphia: N. W. Ayer & Son, 1910.

——. *The Story of the States.* Philadelphia: N. W. Ayer & Son, 1916.

——. *What about Radio?* New York: N. W. Ayer & Son, 1931.

Aylesworth, Merlin H. *The Modern Stentor: Radio Broadcasting in the United States.* Princeton, N.J.: n.p., 1928.

Ayres, Edith. "Private Organizations Working for the Consumer." *Annals of the American Academy of Political and Social Science* 173 (May 1934): 158–65.

Balmer, Edwin. *The Science of Advertising: The Force of Advertising as a Business Influence, Its Place in the National Development, and the Public Result of Its Practical Operation.* Chicago: Wallace Press, 1909.

Barnes, Harry Elmer, and Oreen M. Ruedi. *The American Way of Life: An Introduction to the Study of Contemporary Society.* 2d ed. 1950; Westport, Conn.: Greenwood Press, 1971.

Barnouw, Erik. *Handbook of Radio Writing.* Rev. ed. Boston: Little, Brown and Company, 1947.

Barton, Bruce. "Advertising as an Incentive to Human Progress." In *The New American Tempo,* edited by Frederick Kendall. New York: Advertising and Selling, 1927.

——. *The Man Nobody Knows: A Discovery of Jesus.* Indianapolis: Bobbs-Merrill, 1925.

Barton, Bruce, with Paul Garrett. *The Parade of the States.* Garden City, N.Y.: Doubleday, Doran, 1932.

Baruch, Bernard. *American Industry in the War: A Report of the War Industries Board.* Washington, D.C.: Government Printing Office, 1921.

Bates, Charles Austin. *Good Advertising.* New York: Holmes Publishing Company, 1896.

———. *Short Talks on Advertising.* New York: Charles Austin Bates, 1895.

Batten, H. A. *The Written Word.* Philadelphia: N. W. Ayer, 1936.

Bellamy, Francis, ed. *Effective Magazine Advertising: 508 Essays about 111 Advertisements.* New York: Mitchell Kennerley, 1909.

Bennett, Harry. *More for Your Money: A Buyer's Guide.* London: E. and F. N. Spon, 1937.

Benson, John. *Analysis and Criticism of a Study Entitled Advertising Agency Compensation: Theory, Law, Practice.* New York: [American Association of Advertising Agencies], 1935.

Bent, Silas. *Ballyhoo: The Voice of the Press.* New York: Boni and Liveright, 1927.

Berle, Adolph A., and Gardiner C. Means. *The Modern Corporation and Private Property.* New York: Macmillan, 1933.

Bernays, Edward L. *Crystallizing Public Opinion.* New York: Boni and Liveright, 1923.

———. *Propaganda.* New York: Horace Liveright, 1928.

Beville, H. M., Jr. *The Social Stratification of the Radio Audience: A Study Made for the Princeton Radio Research Project.* Princeton, N.J.: n.p., 1939.

Black, William H. *The Family Income.* New York: Butterick, 1907.

Boice, H. K. *Radio: A Discussion for Executives "Who Already Know the ABC's of Radio".* New York: CBS, 1937.

Bok, Edward. *The Americanization of Edward Bok: The Autobiography of a Dutch Boy Fifty Years After.* New York: Scribner, 1923.

Borden, Neil H. *The Economic Effects of Advertising.* Chicago: Richard D. Irwin, Inc., 1942.

Borsodi, Ralph. *Advertising vs. National Prosperity.* New York: Arcadia Press, 1923.

———. *The Distribution Age.* New York: D. Appleton and Company, 1927.

———. *Flight from the City.* New York: Harper and Brothers, 1933.

———. *This Ugly Civilization.* New York: Simon and Schuster, 1929.

Bourne, Randolph. *The Radical Will: Selected Writings, 1911–1918.* Edited by Olaf Hansen. New York: Urizen, 1977.

———. "Trans-National America." In *War and the Intellectuals: Essays, 1915–1919,* edited by Carl Resek, 107–23. New York: Harper and Row, 1964.

Brady, Robert A. "How Government Standards Affect the Ultimate Consumer." *Annals of the American Academy of Political and Social Science* 137 (May 1928): 247–52.

[———]. *Industrial Standardization.* Washington, D.C.: National Industrial Conference Board, 1929.

Brainerd, J. G., ed. *The Ultimate Consumer: A Study in Economic Illiteracy.* Philadelphia: American Academy of Political and Social Science, 1934.

Breitwieser, J. V. *Psychological Advertising.* Colorado Springs, Colo.: Apex Book Company, 1915.

Brindze, Ruth. *How to Spend Money: Everybody's Practical Guide to Buying.* New York: Vanguard Press, 1935.

———. *Johnny Get Your Money's Worth (and Jane Too!).* New York: Vanguard Press, 1938.

———. *Not to Be Broadcast: The Truth about Radio.* New York: Vanguard Press, 1937.

Brisbane, Arthur. *The Brisbane Advertising Philosophy.* Edited by Emil J. Steinheuser. New York: The Advertising Almanac, no date.

Brokenshire, Norman. *This Is Norman Brokenshire: An Unvarnished Self-Portrait.* New York: David McKay, 1954.

Brooks, Van Wyck. *Van Wyck Brooks, the Early Years : A Selection from His Works, 1908–1925.* Edited by Claire Sprague. Rev ed. Boston: Northeastern University Press, 1993.

Brown, L. Ames. "Broadcast Advertising—Its Possibilities and Limitations." *Broadcast Advertising* 1 (April 1929): 22–24.

Bruére, Martha B., and Robert W. Bruére. *Increasing Home Efficiency.* New York: Macmillan, 1912.

Buchler, E. C., and Martin Maloney. *You Sell with Your Voice.* New York: Ronald Press, 1939.

Burnes, C. Delisle. *Leisure in the Modern World.* New York: Century Company, 1932.

——. *Modern Civilization on Trial.* New York: Macmillan, 1931.

Butler, Ellis Parker. *Perkins of Portland.* Boston: Herbert B. Turner and Company, 1906.

Butler, Ralph Starr. "What the Advertiser Owes the Public." In *Ethical Problems of Modern Advertising,* 27–53. New York: Ronald Press, 1931.

Butterick Publishing Company. *Butterick Goodwill Advertisements.* New York: Butterick Publishing Company, 1922.

——. *Mrs. John Doe.* New York: Butterick Publishing Company, 1918.

Cahan, Abraham. *The Rise of David Levinsky.* 1917; New York: Harper and Row, 1960.

Caldwell, Erskine, and Margaret Bourke-White. *You Have Seen Their Faces.* New York: Viking Press, 1937.

Calkins, Earnest Elmo. *"And Hearing Not"—Annals of an Adman.* New York: Charles Scribner's Sons, 1946.

——. *The Business of Advertising.* New York: D. Appleton and Company, 1921.

——. *Business, the Civilizer.* Boston: Little, Brown and Company, 1928.

Calkins, Earnest Elmo, and Ralph Holden. *Modern Advertising.* New York: D. Appleton and Company, 1905.

Cameron, W. J. *The Ford Sunday Evening Hour Talks.* Fourth Series, 1937–38. Dearborn, Mich.: Ford Motor Company, 1938.

——. *A Series of Talks Given on the Ford Sunday Evening Hour.* Dearborn, Mich.: Ford Motor Company, 1936.

——. *The Voice of a Business: A Series of Radio Talks.* Philadelphia: Ayer Press, 1935.

Campbell, Persia Crawford. *Consumer Representation in the New Deal.* New York: Columbia University Press, 1940.

Canoyer, Helen G. "Government Agencies and the Consumer in Wartime." In *Consumer Problems in Wartime,* ed. Kenneth Dameron, 293–316. New York: McGraw-Hill, 1944.

Cantril, Hadley, and Gordon W. Allport. *The Psychology of Radio.* New York: Harper and Brothers, 1935.

Capra, Frank. *The Name above the Title: An Autobiography.* New York: Macmillan, 1971.

Carpenter, Charles E. *Dollars and Sense.* Garden City, N.Y.: Doubleday, Doran and Company, 1928.

Carroll, Carroll. *None of Your Business: Or My Life with J. Walter Thompson (Confessions of a Renegade Radio Writer).* New York: Cowles Book Company, 1970.

Chapman, Clowry. *How Advertisements Defeat Their Own Ends.* New York: Prentice-Hall, 1931.

Chase, Margaret, and Stuart Chase. *A Honeymoon Experiment.* Boston and New York: Houghton Mifflin, 1916.

Chase, Stuart. *The Economy of Abundance.* New York: Macmillan, 1934.

——. *Government in Business.* New York: Macmillan, 1937.

——. "The Luxury of Integrity." *Harper's Monthly Magazine* 161 (August 1930): 336–44.

——. *Men and Machines.* New York: Macmillan, 1929.

——. *Mexico: A Study of Two Americas.* New York: Macmillan, 1931.

——. *The Nemesis of American Business.* New York: Macmillan, 1931.

——. *A New Deal.* New York: Macmillan, 1932.

——. *Poor Old Competition.* New York: League for Industrial Democracy, 1931.

——. *Prosperity: Fact or Myth?* New York: Charles Borak, 1929.

——. "Six Cylinder Ethics." *Forum* 79 (January 1928): 26–28.

——. *The Tragedy of Waste.* New York: Macmillan, 1925.

Chase, Stuart, and F. J. Schlink. *Your Money's Worth: A Study in the Waste of the Consumer's Dollar.* New York: Macmillan, 1927.

Cherington, Paul T. *Advertising as a Business Force.* Garden City, N.Y.: Doubleday, Page and Company, 1913.

——. *The Advertising Book 1916.* Garden City, N.Y.: Doubleday, Page and Company, 1916.

——. *The Consumer Looks at Advertising.* New York: Harper and Brothers, 1928.

——. *People's Wants and How to Satisfy Them.* New York: Harper and Brothers, 1935.

Childs, Marquis. *This Is Your War!* Boston: Little, Brown, 1942.

Clair, Blanche, and Dorothy Dignam. *Advertising Careers for Women.* New York: Harper and Brothers, 1939.

Clark, Evans. *Financing the Consumer.* New York: Harper and Brothers, 1930.

Codel, Martin, ed. *Radio and Its Future.* New York: Harper Brothers, 1930.

Coles, Jessie V. *The Consumer-Buyer and the Market.* New York: J. Wiley and Sons, 1938.

——. *Consumers Can Help Win the War.* Berkeley: University of California Press, 1943.

——. *Standardization of Consumers' Goods: An Aid to Consumer Buying.* New York: Ronald Press, 1932.

Columbia Broadcasting System. *4 Hours and 28 Minutes by the Kitchen Clock at the Clancy's . . . 4 Hours and 16 Minutes by the Telechron at the Delancey's.* [New York: CBS, November 1934].

——. *An Analysis of Radio Listening in Autos.* New York: CBS, 1936.

——. *Broadcast Advertising—the Sales Voice of America.* New York: CBS, 1929.

——. *Broadcasting and the American Public.* New York: CBS, 1936.

——. *Ears and Incomes: A Study of Four Radio Programs.* New York: CBS, 1934.

——. *Radio in 1936.* New York: CBS, 1937.

——. *A Study of Consumer Response to 40 CBS Sponsored Programs.* [New York: CBS, n.d.].

——. *Two Letters That Took Ten Years to Write.* [New York: CBS, 1941].

——. *A Vertical Study of Radio Ownership (1930–33).* New York: CBS, 1933.

——. *What Does Jake Think?* New York: CBS, [1935].

Committee on the Elimination of Waste in Industry of the Federated American Engineering Societies. *Waste in Industry.* New York: McGraw-Hill, 1921.

Cone, Fairfax. *With All Its Faults: A Candid Account of Forty Years in Advertising.* Boston: Little, Brown, 1969.

Connah, Douglas Duff. *How to Build the Radio Audience.* New York: Harper and Brothers, 1938.

"The Consumers' Club." *Journal of Home Economics* 20 (September 1928): 659–60.

"The Consumer in the Saddle." *Literary Digest* 100 (March 9, 1929): 74–75.

"Consumers' Research Grows Big—Almost Without Advertising." *Sales Management* 30 (April 16, 1932): 70.

Cook, Rosamond. "Problems in Household Buying." *Journal of Home Economics* 21 (February 1929): 92–94.

——. "Standardization or Taking the Guesswork Out of Buying." *Journal of Home Economics* 20. (March 1928): 164–66.

Cooley, Charles Horton. *Human Nature and the Social Order.* New York: C. Scribner's Sons, 1902.

——. *Social Organization: A Study of the Larger Mind.* New York: C. Scribner's Sons, 1909.

Cramp, Arthur J. *Nostrums and Quackery: Articles on the Nostrum Evil and Quackery.* 3 vols. Chicago: Press of the American Medical Association, 1911–36.

Creel, George. *How We Advertised America.* New York: Harper and Brothers, 1920.

Crosby, Bing, and Pete Martin. *Call Me Lucky.* New York: Simon and Schuster, 1953.

[Crossley, Inc.]. *The Invisible Audience: First Comprehensive Four Month Report of a Nation-Wide Recording of Listening Habits.* Princeton/New York: Crossley/ANA, n.d. [ca. 1929–30].

Crowell Publishing Company. *These Merchandising Changes and the National Magazine.* New York: Crowell Publishing Company, 1929.

Crowell-Collier Publishing Company. *The Story of Selling: Yesterday, Today and Tomorrow.* New York: Crowell-Collier Publishing Company, 1946.

Crowell-Collier Research Department. *Homemaking and Appliances: A Psychological Survey.* New York: Crowell-Collier Publishing Company, 1945.

Cullinan, Howell. *Pardon My Accent.* Norwood, Mass.: Plympton Press, 1934.

Curtis Publishing Company. *An Advertising Campaign.* Philadelphia: Curtis Publishing Company, 1915.

——. *Advertising in Ladies' Home Journal and Other Women's Publications, 1927.* Philadelphia: Curtis Publishing Company, 1928.

——. *Advertising in Women's Publications, 1926.* Philadelphia: Curtis Publishing Company, 1927.

——. *Dominance.* Philadelphia: Curtis Publishing Company, n.d.

——. *National Advertising—The Modern Selling Force.* Philadelphia: Curtis Publishing Company, 1911.

——. *National Magazine Advertising.* Philadelphia: Curtis Publishing Company, 1928.

——. *The Saturday Evening Post, 1929.* Philadelphia: Curtis Publishing Company, 1929.

——. *A Short History of "The Saturday Evening Post."* Philadelphia: Curtis Publishing Company, 1936.

Dahlberg, Edward. *Bottom Dogs.* New York: Simon and Schuster, 1930.

Dameron, Kenneth. "The Consumer Movement." *Harvard Business Review* 17 (Spring 1939): 271–89.

——, ed. *Consumer Problems in Wartime*. New York: McGraw-Hill, 1944.

Davies, Valentine. *Miracle on 34th Street*. New York: Harcourt, Brace, 1947.

Davis, Jerome. *Capitalism and Its Culture*. New York: Farrar and Rinehart, 1935.

deBower, Herbert F. *Advertising Principles*. New York: Hamilton Institute, 1919.

de Tarde, Gabriel. *Social Laws*. 1899; New York: Arno Press, 1974.

——. *Underground Man*. 1905; Westport, Conn.: Hyperion Press, 1974.

DeWeese, Truman A. *Keeping a Dollar at Work: Fifty 'Talks' on Newspaper Advertising Written for the New York Evening Post*. New York: New York Evening Post, 1915.

——. *The Principles of Practical Publicity*. Buffalo, N.Y.: Matthews-Northrup Works, 1906.

Dewey, John. *The Public and Its Problems*. New York: Henry Holt and Company, 1927.

Dies, Martin. *The Trojan Horse in America*. 1940; New York: Arno Press, 1977.

Dilling, Elizabeth. *The Red Network*. 1934; New York: Arno Press, 1977.

Dixon, Peter. *Radio Writing*. New York: Century Company, 1931.

Donham, S. Agnes. "Controlling Expense by Standards." *Journal of Home Economics* 19 (January 1927): 1–7.

——. "The Outlook for Teaching Thrift." *Journal of Home Economics* 20 (January 1928): 13–16.

Donovan, H. M. *Advertising Response: A Research into Influences That Increase Sales*. Philadelphia: J. B. Lippincott, 1924.

Dos Passos, John. *1919*. New York: Harcourt, Brace and Company, 1932.

——. *The Big Money*. New York: Harcourt, Brace and Company, 1936.

Douglas, Paul H. *Wages and the Family*. Chicago: University of Chicago Press, 1927.

——. *Real Wages in the United States, 1890–1926*. Boston: Houghton Mifflin, 1930.

Douglass, Paul F. *Consumer Credit*. Philadelphia: American Academy of Political and Social Science, 1938.

Dunbar, Mrs. Sadie Orr. "Advertising from the Consumers' Point of View." Paper presented at the annual dinner meeting of the National Consumer-Retailer Council, New York City, October 24, 1939.

Dunlap, Orrin E., Jr. *Advertising by Radio*. New York: Ronald Press, 1929.

——. *Radio in Advertising*. New York: Harper and Brothers, 1931.

——. *Talking on the Radio: A Practical Guide for Writing and Broadcasting a Speech*. New York: Greenberg, 1936.

Durstine, Roy S. "An Advertising Man's View." *American Review of Reviews* 126 (September 1927): 305.

——. *Making Advertisements and Making Them Pay*. New York: Charles Scribner's Sons, 1920.

——. *This Advertising Business*. New York: Charles Scribner's Sons, 1928.

Dygert, Warren B. *Radio as an Advertising Medium*. New York: McGraw-Hill, 1939.

Edwards, Alice L. "Standardization in the Household." *Annals of the American Academy of Political and Social Science* 137 (May 1928): 213–19.

Eisenberg, Azriel L. *Children and Radio Programs: A Study of More Than Three Thousand Children in the New York Metropolitan Area*. New York: Columbia University Press, 1936.

Elder, Robert. *Does Radio Sell Goods?* New York: CBS, 1931.

Eldridge, Harold F. *Making Advertising Pay*. Columbia, S.C.: The State, 1917.

Eliot, Thomas D., ed. *American Standards and Planes of Living: Readings in the Social Economics of Consumption*. Boston: Ginn and Company, 1931.

Encyclopaedia of the Social Sciences. 15 vols. New York: Macmillan, 1930–35.

Erkel, Agnes M., and Sylvia R. Shiras. *Mrs. Consumer's Dollar: An Aid in Consumer Education*. Minneapolis, Minn.: Burgess Publishing Company, 1935.

Eskew, G. L. *Guinea Pigs and Bug Bears*. Chicago: Research Press, 1938.

Ethical Problems of Modern Advertising: Lectures Delivered in 1930 on the William A. Vawter Foundation on Business Ethics, Northwestern University School of Commerce. New York: Ronald Press, 1931.

Exact Measurement of the Spoken Word. New York: CBS, 1936.

Farrington, Frank. *Talks by the Old Storekeeper*. Delhi, N.Y.: Merchants' Helps Publishing Company, 1906.

Felix, Edgar H. *Using Radio in Sales Promotion*. New York: McGraw-Hill, 1927.

[Field, Charles Kellogg]. *The Story of Cheerio*. Garden City, N.Y.: Garden City Publishing Company, 1936.

Filene, Edward A. *Speaking of Change: A Selection of Speeches and Articles*. New York: n.p., 1939.

——. *The Way Out: A Forecast of Coming Changes in American Business and Industry*. Garden City, N.Y.: Doubleday, Page and Company, 1925.

Filene, Edward A., with Charles W. Wood. *Successful Living in This Machine Age*. New York: Simon and Schuster, 1932.

Fitz-Gibbon, Bernice. *Macy's, Gimbel's and Me*. New York: Simon and Schuster, 1967.

Floherty, John J. *Behind the Microphone*. Philadelphia: J. B. Lippincott, 1944.

Foster, William Trufant, and Waddill Catchings. *Business without a Buyer*. Boston: Houghton Mifflin, 1927.

——. *Money*. Boston: Houghton Mifflin, 1924.

——. *Profits*. Boston: Houghton Mifflin, 1925.

——. *The Road to Plenty*. Boston: Houghton Mifflin, 1928.

Fowler, Bertram B. *Consumer Cooperation in America: Democracy's Way Out*. New York: Vanguard Press, 1936.

Frank, Waldo. *Our America*. New York: Boni and Liveright, 1919.

Franken, Richard B., and Carroll B. Larrabee. *Packages That Sell*. New York: Harper and Brothers, 1928.

Frederick, Christine. *Household Engineering: Scientific Management in the Home*. Chicago: American School of Home Economics, 1919.

——. *The New Housekeeping*. Garden City, N.Y.: Doubleday, Page and Company, 1912.

——. "New Wealth, New Standards of Living, and Changed Family Budgets." *Annals of the American Academy of Political and Social Science* 115 (September 1924): 74–82.

——. *Selling Mrs. Consumer*. New York: Business Bourse, 1929.

Frederick, J. George. "Is Progressive Obsolescence the Path Toward Increased Consumption?" *Advertising and Selling* 11 (September 5, 1928).

——, ed. *Masters of Advertising Copy*. New York: Frank-Maurice, 1925.

——, ed. *A Philosophy of Production*. New York: Business Bourse, 1930.

Freeman, William C. *One Hundred Advertising Talks*. Edited by George French. New York: Winthrop Press, 1912.

French, George. *The Art and Science of Advertising.* Boston: Sherman, French and Company, 1909.

——. *Advertising: The Social and Economic Problem.* Ronald Press, 1915.

——. *How to Advertise: A Guide to Designing, Laying Out and Composing Advertisements.* Garden City, N.Y.: Doubleday, Page and Company, 1917.

Fuller, Henry Blake. *With the Procession.* New York: Harper and Brothers, 1895.

Furnas, J. C. *How America Lives.* New York: Henry Holt and Company, 1941.

Gabler, Werner Karl. *Labeling the Consumer Movement: An Analysis from the Retailers' Point of View of Organizations and Agencies Engaged in Consumer Activities.* Washington, D.C.: American Retail Federation, 1939.

Gaer, Joseph. *Consumers All: The Problem of Consumer Protection.* New York: Harcourt Brace, 1940.

General Motors. *The Proving Ground of Public Opinion.* Detroit, Mich.: General Motors, 1933.

Gilbert, Douglas. *Floyd Gibbons: Knight of the Air.* New York: Robert M. Bride and Company, 1930.

Gilbreth, Lillian M. *The Homemaker and Her Job.* New York: D. Appleton and Company, 1927.

Gilman, Charlotte Perkins Stetson. *Women and Economics* 1898; New York: Harper and Row, 1979.

Goldsmith, Alfred N., and Austin C. Lescaboura. *This Thing Called Broadcasting.* New York: Henry Holt and Company, 1930.

Goode, Kenneth. *How to Turn People into Gold.* New York: Harper and Brothers, 1929.

——. *Modern Advertising Makes Money!* New York: Harper and Brothers, 1934.

——. *What about Radio?* New York: Harper and Brothers, 1937.

Gordon, Leland. *Consumers in Wartime.* New York: Harper and Brothers, 1943.

Gruenberg, Sidonie M. *Radio and Children.* New York: Radio Institute of the Audible Arts, 1935.

Gruenberg, Sidonie M., and Benjamin C. Gruenberg. *Parents, Children and Money: Learning to Spend, Save, and Earn.* New York: Viking Press, 1933.

Grumbine, E. Evalyn. *Reaching Juvenile Markets.* New York: McGraw-Hill, 1938.

Gundlach, E. T. *Facts and Fetishes in Advertising.* Chicago: Consolidated Book Publishers, 1931.

——. *Old Sox on Trumpeting.* Chicago: Consolidated Press, 1927.

Haase, Albert E. *An Analysis of a Report Called "Advertising Agency Compensation in Relation to the Total Cost of Advertising."* New York: Association of National Advertisers, Inc., 1933.

Haase, Albert E., and Lawrence Campbell Locksley, with Isaac Watlington Digges. *Advertising Agency Compensation: Theory, Law, Practice.* New York: National Process Company, 1934.

Hader, Mathilde C. "Consumers' Research and the Home Economist." *Journal of Home Economics* 22 (April 1930):292–94.

Hall, S. Roland. *Writing an Advertisement.* Boston: Houghton Mifflin, 1915.

Hamilton, Walton H. "The Ancient Maxim Caveat Emptor." *Yale Law Journal* 40 (June 1931): 1133–87.

——. "The Institutional Approach to Economic Theory." *American Economic Review* 9, Suppl. (March 1919): 309–18.

Harap, Henry. *The Education of the Consumer.* New York: Macmillan, 1924.

Harding, T. Swann. "Are We Being Poisoned?" *Modern Living,* June 1933, 6–7.

——. *The Degradation of Science.* New York: Farrar and Rinehart, 1931.

——. "Food and Drugs." *Saturday Review of Literature,* January 28, 1933, 402.

——. *The Joy of Ignorance.* New York: W. Godwin, 1932.

——. *The Popular Practice of Fraud.* New York: Longmans, Green and Company, 1935.

Harris, Credo Fitch. *Microphone Memoirs of the Horse and Buggy Days of Radio.* Indianapolis, Ind.: Bobbs-Merrill, 1937.

Hawes, Elizabeth. *Fashion Is Spinach.* New York: Randon House, 1938.

Hawley, Raymond, and James Barton Zabin. *Understanding Advertising.* New York: Gregg Publishing Company, 1931.

Herzog, Herta. *Survey of Research on Children's Radio Listening.* New York: Columbia University, Office of Radio Research, 1941.

Heseltine, Marjorie M. "The Preparation and Distribution of Commercial Educational Material Used by Home Economists." *Journal of Home Economics* 21 (June 1929): 412–23.

Hess, Herbert W. *Advertising: Its Economics, Philosophy and Technique.* Philadelphia: J. B. Lippincott, 1931.

Hettinger, Herman S. *A Decade of Radio Advertising.* Chicago: University of Chicago Press, 1933.

Hettinger, Herman S., and Walter J. Neff. *Practical Radio Advertising.* New York: Prentice-Hall, 1938.

Higham, Charles F. *Scientific Distribution.* New York: Alfred A. Knopf, 1918.

Hill, Helen M. "What Advertising Has Done for Women." *Judicious Advertising* 21 (November 1923): 68–69.

Hollingworth, Harry. *Advertising and Selling: Principles of Appeals and Response.* New York: D. Appleton and Company, 1913.

Holthausen, Duncan McC., with Malcolm L. Merriam and Rolf Nugent. *The Volume of Consumer Installment Credit, 1929–1938.* New York: National Bureau of Economic Research, 1938.

Homan, Paul T. *Contemporary Economic Thought.* New York: Harper and Brothers, 1927.

Hopkins, Claude C. *My Life in Advertising.* New York: Harper and Brothers, 1927.

——. *Scientific Advertising.* 1923; New York: H. B. Moore, 1952.

Hotchkiss, George Burton. *Advertising Copy.* Rev. ed. New York: Harper and Brothers, 1936.

——. "An Economic Defence of Advertising." *American Economic Review* 15, Suppl. (March 1925): 14–22.

——. *Milestones of Marketing: A Brief History of the Evolution of Market Distribution.* New York: Macmillan, 1938.

Hotchkiss, George Burton, and Richard B. Franken. *The Leadership of Advertised Brands: A Study of 100 Representative Commodities Showing the Names and Brands That Are Most Familiar to the Public.* Garden City, N.Y.: Doubleday, Page and Company, 1923.

Hoyt, Elizabeth Ellis. *Consumption in Our Society.* New York: McGraw-Hill, 1938.

——. *The Consumption of Wealth*. New York: Macmillan, 1928.

Hudson, Ray M. "Organized Effort in Simplification." *Annals of the Academy of Political and Social Science* 137 (May 1928): 1–8.

[Hunt, Edward Eyre, ed.] *Recent Economic Changes in the United States: Report of the Committee on Recent Economic Changes of the President's Conference on Unemployment.* New York: McGraw-Hill, 1929.

Hurley, Edward N. *Awakening of Business*. Garden City, N.Y.: Doubleday, Page and Company, 1916.

Johnston, Alva. "Testimonials C.O.D." *Outlook and Independent* 157 (March 18, 1931): 398–99.

Jones, Arthur C. *Piggly Wiggly Store Management*. Los Angeles: n.p., 1927.

Kallen, Horace M. *A Free Society*. New York: Robert O. Ballou, 1934.

Kallet, Arthur. *Counterfeit: Not Your Money But What It Buys*. New York: Vanguard Press, 1934.

——. "Partners in Strike Breaking." *Common Sense*, October 1935, 22–23.

Kallet, Arthur, and F. J. Schlink. *100,000,000 Guinea Pigs: Dangers in Everyday Foods, Drugs and Cosmetics*. New York: Vanguard Press, 1932.

Kendall, Frederick C., ed. *The New American Tempo: And Other Articles on Modern Advertising and Selling Practice*. New York: Advertising and Selling, 1927.

[Kennedy, John E.] *The Book of Advertising Tests*. Chicago: Lord & Thomas, 1911.

Kenner, Hugh. *The Fight for Truth in Advertising*. New York: Round Table Press, 1936.

[Kesten, Paul]. *You Do What You're Told!* New York: CBS, 1935.

Kidd, Bj [Elizabeth]. *Just Like a Woman!: How to Tell the Girls*. New York: Appleton-Century, 1945.

Kitson, Harry Dexter. "Understanding the Consumer's Mind." *Annals of the American Academy of Political and Social Science* 110 (November 1923): 132–37.

Kneeland, Hildegarde. *Consumer Incomes in the United States: Their Distribution in 1935–1936*. Washington, D.C.: Government Printing Office, 1938.

Knight, Frank H. *Freedom and Reform: Essays in Economics and Social Philosophy*. 1947; Indianapolis, Ind.: Liberty Press, 1982.

——. *Risk, Uncertainty, and Profit*. Boston: Houghton Mifflin, 1921.

Knight, Ruth Adams. *Stand for the Ladies!* New York: Coward-McCann, 1939.

Kromer, Tom. *Waiting for Nothing*. New York: Alfred A. Knopf, 1935.

Kyrk, Hazel. *The Consumption of Wealth*. Boston: Houghton Mifflin, 1923.

——. *Economic Problems of the Family*. New York: Harper and Brothers, 1933.

——. *A Theory of Consumption*. Boston: Houghton Mifflin, 1923.

Laird, Donald M. *What Makes People Buy*. New York: McGraw-Hill, 1935.

Lamb, Beatrice Pitney. *Government and the Consumer*. Washington, D.C.: National League of Women Voters, 1935.

Lamb, Ruth deForest. *American Chamber of Horrors: The Truth about Food and Drugs*. New York: Farrar and Rinehart, 1936.

Larkin, Brand. *Learn to Croon*. London: W. Foulsham and Company, 1936.

Lasker, Albert D. *The Lasker Story: As He Told It*. Chicago: Advertising Publications, Inc., 1963.

Lazarsfeld, Paul. *Radio and the Printed Page: An Introduction to the Study of Radio and Its Role in the Communication of Ideas.* New York: Duell, Sloan and Pearce, 1940.

Le Bon, Gustave. *The Crowd: A Study of the Popular Mind.* London: T. F. Unwin, 1897.

Lee, Gerald Stanley. *Crowds: A Moving-Picture of Democracy.* Garden City, N.Y.: Doubleday, Page and Company, 1913.

——. *We.* Garden City, N.Y.: Doubleday, Page and Company, 1916.

Lerner, Max. "Book Notes" [review of *Your Money's Worth*, by Stuart Chase and F. J. Schlink]. *Political Science Quarterly* 43 (June 1928): 306–7.

Lestico, H. H. *Building the Story of Piggly Wiggly: A Practical System of Piggly Wiggly Advertising Used by Prominent Operators Throughout the United States in Selling the Piggly Wiggly Story to the Consuming Public.* Los Angeles: H. H. Lestico, 1926.

Leven, Maurice, Harold G. Moulton, and Clark Warburton. *America's Capacity to Consume.* Washington, D.C.: Brookings Institution, 1934.

Lewis, Sinclair. *Babbitt.* New York: Harcourt, Brace and Company, 1922.

Lichtenberg, Bernard, with Bruce Barton. *Advertising Campaigns.* New York: Alexander Hamilton Institute, 1930.

Link, Henry C. *The New Psychology of Selling and Advertising.* New York: Macmillan, 1932.

Lippmann, Walter. *Drift and Mastery: An Attempt to Diagnose the Current Unrest.* 1914; Madison: University of Wisconsin Press, 1985.

——. *Public Opinion.* 1922; New York: Free Press, 1965.

Longstaff, H. P. "Effectiveness of Children's Radio Programs." *Journal of Applied Psychology* 20 (April 1936): 208–19.

Looker, Earl. *The American Way: Franklin Roosevelt in Action.* New York: John Day, 1933.

Lord & Thomas. *Concerning a Literature That Compels Action: Altruism in Advertising.* Chicago: Lord & Thomas, 1911.

——. *The New Way in Advertising.* New York and Chicago: Lord & Thomas, n.d.

Lowell, Maurice. *Listen In: An American Manual of Radio.* New York: Dodge, 1937.

Lownds, William, Edward D. Chenery, and George J. Wiltshire. *Advertising and Selling Digest.* New York: Advertising Club of New York, 1926.

Lucas, D. B., and C. E. Benson. *Psychology for Advertisers.* New York: Harper and Brothers, 1930.

Luce, Henry R. *The Ideas of Henry Luce.* Edited by John K. Jessup. New York: Atheneum, 1969.

Lumley, Frederick H. *Measurement in Radio.* Columbus: Ohio State University Press, 1934.

Lynd, Robert S. "The Consumer Becomes a 'Problem.'" *Annals of the American Academy of Political and Social Science* 173 (May 1934): 1–6.

——. "Democracy's Third Estate: The Consumer." *Political Science Quarterly* 51 (December 1936): 481–515.

——. "Family Members as Consumers." *Annals of the American Academy of Political and Social Science* 160 (March 1932): 86–93.

——. "Must Every Issue Have Its Soapbox?" *Survey Graphic* 22 (April 1933): 225.

Lynd, Robert S., with Alice Hanson. "The People as Consumers." In *Recent Social Trends in the United States: Report of the President's Research Committee on Social Trends*, edited by Wesley C. Mitchell, 857–911. New York: McGraw-Hill.

Lynd, Robert S., and Helen Merrell Lynd. *Middletown: A Study in Modern American Culture.* New York: Harcourt, Brace and World, 1929.

———. *Middletown in Transition: A Study in Cultural Conflicts.* New York: Harcourt, Brace and Company, 1937.

Lyons, Eugene. *The Red Decade.* 1941; New York: Arlington House, 1970.

MacManus, Theodore F. *"Stupid" Genius That Makes Millions.* Detroit, Mich.: MacManus, Inc., 1923.

———. *The Sword Arm of Business.* New York: Devin-Adair, 1927.

Mahin, John Lee. *Advertising: Selling the Consumer.* Garden City, N.Y.: Doubleday, Page and Company, 1914.

———. *Lectures on Advertising.* Chicago: n.p., 1915.

Mann, George Carlisle. *Bibliography on Consumer Education.* New York: Harper and Brothers, 1939.

Matlack, Mary E., and William H. Matlack. "The Feminine Appeal in Advertising." *American Gas Journal*, October 16, 1922, 316–17.

Matthews, J. B. *Guinea Pigs No More.* New York: Covici-Friede Publishers, 1936.

———. *Odyssey of a Fellow Traveler.* New York: Mount Vernon Publishers, 1938.

Matthews, J. B., and R. E. Shallcross. *Partners in Plunder: The Cost of Business Dictatorship.* New York: Covici-Friede Publishers, 1935.

Mazur, Paul. *American Prosperity: Its Causes and Consequences.* New York: Harper and Brothers, 1928.

McCoy, Horace. *They Shoot Horses, Don't They?* New York: Simon and Schuster, 1935.

McDougall, William. *Is America Safe for Democracy?* New York: C. Scribner's Sons, 1921.

McNair, Malcolm, and Howard T. Lewis, eds. *Business and Modern Society.* Cambridge, Mass.: Harvard University Press, 1938.

McNamee, Graham, with Robert Gordon Anderson. *You're on the Air.* New York: Harper and Brothers, 1926.

Mead, George Herbert. *Mind, Self, and Society from the Standpoint of a Social Behaviorist.* Chicago: University of Chicago Press, 1933.

———. *On Social Psychology.* Edited by Anselm Strauss. Chicago: University of Chicago Press, 1977.

Mead, Margaret. *And Keep Your Powder Dry: An Anthropologist Looks at America.* New York: W. Morrow and Company, 1942.

Mencken, H. L. *Prejudices: A Selection.* Baltimore, Md.: Johns Hopkins University Press, 1996.

Merton, Robert. *Mass Persuasion: The Social Psychology of a War Bond Drive.* New York: Harper and Brothers, 1946.

Merz, Charles. *The Great American Band Wagon.* New York: John Day Company, 1928.

Mitchell, Lucy Sprague. *Two Lives: The Story of Wesley Clair Mitchell and Myself.* New York: Simon and Schuster, 1953.

Mitchell, Wesley Clair. "The Backward Art of Spending Money." *American Economic Review* 2 (June 1912): 269–81.

———. *The Backward Art of Spending Money and Other Essays.* Edited by Joseph Dorfman. New York: McGraw-Hill, 1937:

——. *Business Cycles*. Berkeley: University of California Press, 1913.

——. *Business Cycles: The Problem and Its Setting*. New York: National Bureau of Economic Research, 1927.

——. "Human Behavior and Economics: A Review of Recent Literature." *Quarterly Journal of Economics* 29 (November 1914): 1–47.

——, ed. *Recent Social Trends in the United States: Report of the President's Research Committee on Social Trends*. New York: McGraw-Hill, 1933.

Monroe, Day. "A Conference on the Problems of the Household Buyer." *Journal of Home Economics* 20 (February 1928): 95–97.

Morell, Peter. *Poisons, Potions, and Profits: The Antidote to Radio Advertising*. New York: Knight Publishers, 1937.

Mumford, Lewis. *The Golden Day: A Study in American Experience and Culture*. New York: Boni and Liveright, 1926.

——. *Technics and Civilization*. New York: Harcourt, Brace and Company, 1934.

Munsterberg, Hugo. *American Problems: From the Point of View of a Psychologist*. New York: Moffat, Yard and Company, 1910.

Naether, Carl. *Advertising to Women*. New York: Prentice-Hall, 1928.

National Broadcasting Company. *Alice in Sponsor-Land*. New York: NBC, 1941.

——. *Broadcasting in the Public Interest*. New York: NBC, 1940.

——. *The Colonel's Lady an' Judy O'Grady*. New York: NBC, [1941].

——. "The History of Advertising." A Broadcast by NBC, Dedicated to Advertising. New York: NBC, 1933.

——. *Improving the Smiles of a Nation! Advertising Has Worked for the Makers of Ipana Tooth Paste*. New York: NBC, 1928.

——. *It's Not Done with Mirrors*. New York: NBC, 1940.

——. *Let's Look at Radio Together*. New York: NBC, 1936.

——. *NBC Daytime Hours: Effective Advertising at Low Cost*. New York: NBC, 1934.

——. *Straight Across the Board*. New York: NBC, 1936.

——. *35 Hours of Joy!* New York: NBC, 1937.

[National Bureau of Standards]. *Standards Yearbook, 1927*. Washington, D.C.: Government Printing Office, 1927.

National Conference on Consumer Education. *Next Steps in Consumer Education*. Los Angeles: Ward Ritchie Press, 1939.

——. *Proceedings*. Vols. 1–3. Columbia, Mo.: Institute for Consumer Education, Stephens College, 1939–41.

Neil, Marion Harris. *The Story of Crisco*. Cincinnati, Ohio: McDonald Printing Company, 1915.

Nelson, Mariana T. "What Consumers Learned about Purchasing Household Goods." *Journal of Home Economics* 24 (June 1932): 519–20.

New York News. *Tell It to Sweeney!* New York: New York News, n.d.

Norris, James. *Radio Entertaining*. San Francisco: Gillett Publishing Company, 1930.

Norris, Ruby T. *The Theory of Consumers' Demand*. New Haven, Conn.: Yale University Press, 1941.

Nystrom, Paul H. *Economic Principles of Consumption*. New York: Ronald Press, 1929.

O'Dea, Mark. *A Preface to Advertising*. New York: Whittlesey House, 1937.

Ogburn, William F. *Social Change, with Respect to Culture and Original Nature*. New York: B. W. Huebsch, 1922.

Ogilvy, David. *Confessions of an Advertising Man*. New York: Atheneum, 1963.

O'Neill, Neville. *The Advertising Agency Looks at Radio*. New York: D. Appleton and Company, 1932.

Opdycke, John B. *The Language of Advertising*. New York: Isaac Pilman and Sons, 1925.

O'Sullivan, Frank Dalton. *The Poison Pen of Jersey*. Chicago: O'Sullivan Publishing House, 1936.

O'Toole, John. *The Trouble with Advertising*. New York: Chelsea House, 1981.

Palmer, Bissell B. *Paying through the Teeth*. New York: Vanguard Press, 1935.

Palmer, Dewey H. "Mechanical and Electrical Goods for the Consumer." *Annals of the American Academy of Political and Social Science* 173 (May 1934): 43–52.

Palmer, Dewey H., and Lawrence H. Crooks. *Millions on Wheels*. New York: Vanguard Press, 1938.

Palmer, Dewey H., and Frederick J. Schlink. "Education and the Consumer." *Annals of the American Academy of Political and Social Science* 173 (May 1934): 188–99.

Palmer, Rachel Lynn, and Isidore M. Alpher. *40,000,000 Guinea Pig Children*. New York: Vanguard Press, 1937.

Palmer, Rachel Lynn, and Sarah Greenberg. *Facts and Frauds in Women's Hygiene*. New York: Vanguard Press, 1936.

Park, Robert, *The Crowd and the Public and Other Essays*. Edited by Harry Elsner Jr. Chicago: University of Chicago Press, 1972.

Parlin, Charles Coolidge. *The Merchandising of Automobiles*. Philadelphia: Curtis Publishing Company, 1915.

——. *The Merchandising of Textiles*. Philadelphia: Curtis Publishing Company, n.d.

Patten, Simon N. *The New Basis of Civilization*. 1907; Cambridge, Mass.: Harvard University Press, 1967.

——. *Product and Climax*. New York: B. W. Huebsch, 1909.

Phelps, George Harrison. *Our Biggest Customer*. New York: Harper and Brothers, 1929.

——. *Tomorrow's Advertisers and Their Advertising Agencies*. New York: Harper and Brothers, 1929.

Phillips, M. C. *More Than Skin Deep*. New York: Richard Smith, 1948.

——. *Skin Deep: The Truth about Beauty Aids—Safe and Harmful*. New York: Vanguard Press, 1934.

Phillips, M. C., and F. J. Schlink. *Discovering Consumers*. New York: John Day Company, 1934.

Phillips, Wilbur C. *The Social Unit*. New York: Social Unit Press, 1929.

Photoplay Magazine. *The Age Factor in Selling and Advertising: A Study in a New Phase of Advertising*. Chicago and New York: Photoplay Magazine, 1922.

Pitkin, Walter B. *Capitalism Carries On*. New York: Whittlesey House, 1935.

——. *The Consumer: His Nature and His Changing Habits*. New York: McGraw-Hill, 1932.

——. *Let's Get What We Want: A Primer in a Sadly Neglected Art*. New York: Simon and Schuster, 1935.

——. *Life Begins at 40*. New York: Whittlesey House, 1932.

Poffenberger, Albert. *The Psychology of Advertising*. Chicago: A. W. Shaw Company, 1925.

Presbrey, Frank M. *The History and Development of Advertising.* Garden City, N.Y.: Doubleday, Doran, 1929.

"Progress in Standardization." *Journal of Home Economics* 19 (November 1927): 634–35.

Purcell, Madeline Kelly. "Why Otherwise Good Copy Fails in the Eyes of Women—the Eighty-Five Percent Buyers." *Inland Printer* 44 (December 1924): 162–64.

Ramsaye, Terry. *One Million and One Nights: A History of Motion Pictures to 1926.* New York: Simon and Schuster, 1926.

Reid, Margaret Gilpin. *Consumers and the Market.* New York: F. S. Crofts and Company, 1938.

Rheinstrom, Carroll. *Psyching the Ads: The Case Book of Advertising.* New York: Covici-Friede, 1929.

Richards, Ellen H. *The Cost of Living as Modified by Sanitary Science.* 3d ed. New York: J. Wiley and Sons, 1905.

Richardson, Anna Steese. *Adventures in Thrift.* Indianapolis, Ind.: Bobbs-Merrill, 1916.

——. *Consumer Relations: A Study Course Compiled for the Consumer Division of the Crowell Publishing Company.* New York: Crowell Publishing Company, 1938.

Richardson, Bertha June. *The Woman Who Spends: A Study of Her Economic Functions.* Boston: Whitcomb and Barrows, 1904.

Roosevelt, Eleanor. *It's Up to the Women!* New York: Frederick A. Stokes Company, 1933.

Rorty, James. *Order on the Air!* New York: John Day Company, 1934.

——. *Our Master's Voice: Advertising.* New York: John Day Company, 1934.

——. "What's Wrong with Consumers' Research?" *Consumers Defender,* October 1935, 5–6, 15.

——. *Where Life Is Better: An Unsentimental American Journey.* New York: Reynal and Hitchcock, 1936.

Rourke, Constance. *American Humor: A Study of the National Character.* New York: Harcourt, Brace and Company, 1931.

Rowell, George Presbury. *Forty Years an Advertising Agent, 1865–1905.* New York: Printers' Ink Publishing Company, 1906.

Ruskin, John. *"Unto This Last:" Four Essays on the First Principles of Political Economy.* 1862; Lincoln: University of Nebraska Press, 1967.

Ruthrauff and Ryan, Inc. *18 Shorts on Advertising.* New York: Ruthrauff and Ryan, Inc., 1931.

——. *It Isn't Raining Everywhere!* New York: Ruthrauff and Ryan, Inc. 1931.

——. *People Are Funny That Way.* New York: Ruthrauff and Ryan, Inc., 1930.

——. *Slow Down the Band-Wagon: The Elephants Can't Keep Up.* New York: Ruthrauff and Ryan, Inc., 1930.

Sandage, C. H., ed. *The Promise of Advertising.* Homewood, Ill.: Richard D. Irwin, Inc., 1961.

Saunders, Clarence. *The National Standard for Piggly Wiggly Store Conduct and Maintenance.* Memphis, Tenn.: Piggly Wiggly Home Office, 1919.

——. *Piggly Wiggly: A System of Selling Merchandise* Memphis, Tenn.: n.p., 1917.

Schlink, Frederick J. "100,000,000 Step-Children." *Executive Purchaser,* March 1934, 11–29.

——. "Advantages of Standardization." *Purchasing Agent* 14 (January 1925): 33, 70–71.

——. "Bear Oil: Old Magic for New Times." *New Republic*, July 31, 1929, 277–79.
——. "Classification of Engineering and Industrial Standards." *Mechanical Engineering* 47 (February 1925): 119–22.
——. "The Consumer Must Decide." *Ladies' Home Journal* 46 (October 1929): 104, 137.
——. *Eat, Drink, and Be Wary.* New York: Covici-Friede, 1935.
——. "Government Bureaus for Private Profit." *The Nation*, November 11, 1931, 508–11.
——. "Government Takes in Washing." *The Nation*, June 1, 1932, 620–21.
——. "How the Consumer Was Betrayed." *Common Sense*, September 1934.
——. "Improving Purchasing Methods through Specifications." *American City* 42 (April 1930).
——. "The Responsibility of the Home Economist as a Consumer." *Omicron Nu*, Fall 1930, 24.
——. "Safeguarding the Consumer's Interest: An Essential Element in National Recovery," *Annals of the American Academy of Political and Social Science* 172 (March 1934): 113–22.
——. "Tests and Specifications for the Household." *Journal of Home Economics* 19 (April 1927): 181–84.
——. "What Government Does and Might Do for the Consumer." *Annals of the American Academy of Political and Social Science* 173 (May 1934): 125–43.
Schlink, F. J., and Robert A. Brady. "Standards and Specifications from the Standpoint of the Ultimate Consumer." *Annals of the American Academy of Political and Social Science* 137 (May 1928): 231–39.
Schlink, F. J., and M. C. Phillips. *Meat Three Times a Day.* New York: R. R. Smith, 1946.
Scott, Walter Dill. *The Psychology of Advertising: A Simple Exposition of the Principles of Psychology in Their Relation to Advertising.* Boston: Small, Maynard and Company, 1908.
——. *The Theory of Advertising: A Simple Exposition of the Principles of Psychology in Their Relation to Successful Advertising.* Boston: Small, Maynard and Company, 1903.
Seldes, George. *Freedom of the Press.* New York: Bobbs-Merrill Company, 1935.
——. *Lords of the Press.* New York: J. Messner, 1938.
Seldes, Gilbert. *The Years of the Locust: America, 1929–1932.* Boston: Little, Brown and Company, 1933.
Seymour, Katherine, and J. T. W. Martin. *How to Write for Radio.* New York: Longmans, Green, 1931.
Shaw, Arch. "Some Problems of Market Distribution." *Quarterly Review of Economics* 26 (August 1912): 703–65.
Sheldon, Roy, and Egmont Arens. *Consumer Engineering: A New Technique for Prosperity.* New York: Harper and Brothers, 1932.
Sherman, Caroline B. "The Consumer and Standardization in Food Products." *Journal of Home Economics* 20 (November 1928): 801–3.
Siegfried, Andre. *America Comes of Age.* New York: Harcourt, Brace and Company, 1927.
Simmel, Georg. *The Philosophy of Money* [1907]. Translated by Tom Bottomore and David Frisby. 2d ed. New York: Routledge, 1990.
Sinclair, Upton. *The Brass Check: A Study of American Journalism.* Pasadena, Calif.: Upton Sinclair, 1919.
Sioussat, Helen. *Mikes Don't Bite!* New York: L. B. Fischer, 1943.

Slichter, Sumner H. *Modern Economic Society*. Boston: Little, Brown and Company, 1928.

Soglow, Otto. *The Little King*. New York: Farrar and Rinehart, 1933.

Sokolsky, George E. *The American Way of Life*. New York: Farrar and Rinehart, 1939.

Solomon, Charles. *The Traffic in Health*. New York: Navarre Publishing, 1937.

Sorenson, Helen L. *The Consumer Movement in the United States: What It is and What It Means*. New York: Harper and Brothers, 1941.

"Standard and Substandard Goods." *Journal of Home Economics* 23 (March 1931): 259–61.

Stanton, Frank N. "A Critique of Present Methods and a New Plan for Studying Present Listener Behavior." Ph.D. diss., Ohio State University, 1936.

———. *Memory for Advertising Copy Presented Visually vs. Orally*. Columbus, Ohio: n.p., 1933.

Starch, Daniel. *300 Effective Advertisements*. New York: Daniel Starch, 1930.

———. *An Analysis of Over 3,000,000 Inquiries Received by 98 Firms from 2,339 Magazine Advertisements*. Cambridge, Mass.: Daniel Starch, 1937.

———. *An Analysis of 5,000,000 Inquiries*. New York: Daniel Starch, 1930.

———. *Buying Power of the American Market*. Cambridge, Mass.: n.p., 1931.

———. *A Study of Radio Broadcasting Based Exclusively on Personal Interviews with Families in the United States East of the Rocky Mountains*. Cambridge, Mass.: n.p., [1929].

Stark, Saidee E. *How Schools Use Advertising Material: A Study of the Use of Advertising Material by Teachers in Schools and Colleges and by Home Economics Workers*. New York: Association of National Advertisers, Inc., 1930.

Stearns, Harold, ed. *Civilization in the United States: An Inquiry by Thirty Americans*. New York: Harcourt, Brace and Company, 1922.

Sumner, William Graham. *Folkways: A Study of the Sociological Importance of Usages, Manners, Customs, Mores, and Morals*. Boston: Ginn, 1907.

———. *The Forgotten Man*. New Haven, Conn.: Yale University Press, 1918.

Switzer, Maurice. *Who Pays the Advertising Bills?* New York: n.p., 1915.

Tawney, R. H. *The Acquisitive Society*. New York: Harcourt, Brace, and Howe, 1920.

Taylor, Frederick W. *Principles of Scientific Management*. New York: Harper and Brothers, 1915.

Terman, Louis M. *The Measurement of Intelligence*. Boston: Houghton Mifflin, 1916.

Thompson, J. Walter. *A Primer of Capitalism Illustrated*. New York: J. Walter Thompson, 1937.

———. *Population and Its Distribution*. New York: J. Walter Thompson, 1912.

———. *Report on Work of Committee on Standardization*. New York: J. Walter Thompson, 1919.

———. *Retail Shopping Areas*. New York: J. Walter Thompson, 1927.

———. *Things to Know about Trade-Marks: A Manual of Trade-Mark Information*. New York: J. Walter Thompson Company, 1911.

Tipper, Harry. *The New Business*. Garden City, N.Y.: Doubleday, Page and Company, 1914.

Tipper, Harry, with Harry J. Hollingworth, George Burton Hotchkiss, and Frank Alvah Parsons. *Advertising: Its Principles and Practice*. New York: Ronald Press, 1915.

[True Story Magazine]. *The American Economic Evolution* New York: True Story Magazine, 1930.

Tucker, Robert C., ed. *The Marx-Engels Reader*. New York: W. W. Norton, 1972.

Tugwell, Rexford G.. *The Battle for Democracy*. New York: Columbia University Press, 1935.

———. "Contemporary Buncombe." *Saturday Review of Literature* 3, no. 50 (July 9, 1927): 958.

Tugwell, Rexford G., Thomas Munro, and Roy E. Stryker. *American Economic Life and the Means of Its Improvement*. 3d ed. New York: Harcourt, Brace and Company, 1930.

Twelve Southerners. *I'll Take My Stand: The South and the Agrarian Tradition*. New York: Harper, 1930.

Tyler, Poyntz, ed. *Advertising in America*. New York: H. W. Wilson, 1959.

Ulanov, Barry. *The Incredible Crosby*. New York: Whittlesey House, 1948.

Updegraff, Robert R. *Obvious Adams: The Story of a Successful Business Man*. New York: Harper and Brothers, 1916.

———. *Old Specification*. Chicago: A. W. Shaw Company, 1929.

———. *The Sixth Prune*. Chicago: A. W. Shaw Company, 1929.

U.S. Bureau of the Census. *Historical Statistics of the United States, Colonial Times to 1970*. Washington, D.C.: Census Bureau, 1976.

U.S. Department of Commerce. *Simplified Practice: What It Is and What It Offers* [1928 edition]. Washington, D.C.: Government Printing Office, 1929.

Vallee, Rudy. *Vagabond Dreams Come True*. New York: E. P. Dutton, 1930.

Veblen, Thorstein. *Absentee Ownership and Business Enterprise in Recent Times*. New York: B. W. Huebsch, 1923.

———. *The Engineers and the Price System*. 1921; New York: Harcourt, Brace and World, 1963.

———. *Essays in Our Changing Order*. Edited by Leon Ardzrooni. New York: Viking Press, 1934.

———. *The Instinct of Workmanship and the State of the Industrial Arts*. New York: Macmillan, 1914.

———. *The Place of Science in Modern Civilization*. New York: B. W. Huebsch, 1919.

———. *The Theory of Business Enterprise*. New York: Charles Scribner's Sons, 1904.

———. *The Theory of the Leisure Class*. New York: Macmillan, 1899; New York: New American Library, 1953.

———. *The Vested Interests and the Common Man*. New York: B. W. Huebsch, 1919.

Waite, Warren C., and Ralph Cassidy. *Consumers and the Economic Order*. New York: McGraw-Hill, 1939.

Wakeman, Frederick. *The Hucksters*. New York: Rinehart and Company, 1946.

Walker, S. H., and Paul Sklar. *Business Finds Its Voice: Management's Effort to Sell the Business Idea to the Public*. New York: Harper and Brothers, 1938.

Wallace, Henry A. *The Century of the Common Man*. Edited by Russell Lord. New York: Reynal and Hitchcock, 1943.

Walsh, Richard J., for the Curtis Publishing Company. *Selling Forces*. Philadelphia: Curtis Publishing Company, 1913.

Warbasse, James P. *Cooperative Democracy*. New York: Harper and Brothers, 1936.

Ward, Leo R. *Ourselves, Inc.: The Story of Consumer Free Enterprise*. New York: Harper and Brothers, 1945.

Ware, Caroline F. *The Consumer Goes to War: A Guide to Victory on the Home Front*. New York: Funk and Wagnalls, 1942.

——, ed. *The Cultural Approach to History: Edited for the American Historical Association.* New York: Columbia University Press, 1940.

Watson, J. B. "Psychology as the Behaviorist Views It." *Psychological Review* 20 (March 1913): 158–77.

Weber, Max. "On Bureaucracy." In *From Max Weber*, edited by Hans Gerth and C. Wright Mills, 196–252. New York: Oxford University Press, 1946.

——. *The Protestant Ethic and the Spirit of Capitalism* [1904]. Translated by Talcott Parsons. New York: Charles Scribner's Sons, 1960.

Webster, Harold Tucker. *The Timid Soul: A Pictorial Account of the Life and Times of Caspar Milquetoast.* New York: Simon and Schuster, 1931.

West, Robert. *The Rape of Radio.* New York: Rodin, 1941.

——. *So-o-o-o You're Going on the Air! and the Radio Speech Primer.* New York: Rodin, 1934.

Weyl, Walter. *The New Democracy: An Essay on Certain Political and Economic Tendencies in the United States.* 1912; New York: Harper Torchbooks, 1964.

White, E. B. *Alice through the Cellophane.* New York: John Day Company, 1933.

Wilcox, Clair. "Brand Names, Quality, and Price." *Annals of the American Academy of Political and Social Science* 173 (May 1934): 80–85.

Wiley, Harvey Washington. *The History of a Crime against the Food Law.* Washington, D.C.: H. W. Wiley, 1929.

Willkie, Wendell L. *One World.* New York: Simon and Schuster, 1943.

Williams, Faith M. "Purchasing Problems of the Household Buyer." *Journal of Home Economics* 21 (October 1929): 724–30.

Wilson, Edmund. *The American Jitters.* New York: C. Scribner's Sons, 1932.

——. *Travels in Two Democracies.* New York: Harcourt, Brace and Company, 1936.

Woodward, Helen. *It's an Art!* New York: Harcourt, Brace and Company, 1938.

——. *Through Many Windows.* New York: Harper and Brothers, 1926.

Wright, Milton. *Public Relations for Business.* New York: Whittlesea House, 1939.

Wyand, Charles S. *The Economics of Consumption.* New York: Macmillan, 1937.

Yerkes, Robert M. *Psychological Examining in the United States Army.* Vol. 15 of *Memoirs of the National Academy of Sciences.* Washington, D.C.: Government Printing Office, 1921.

——. "Report of the Psychology Committee of the National Research Council." *Psychological Review* 26 (1919): 83–149.

Yerkes, Robert M., James W. Bridges, and Rose S. Hardwick. *A Point Scale for Measuring Mental Ability.* Baltimore, Md.: Warwick and York, 1915.

Yoakum, Clarence S., and Robert M. Yerkes, eds. *Army Mental Tests.* New York: Henry Holt and Company, 1920.

Young, James Webb. *Advertising Agency Compensation in Relation to the Total Cost of Advertising.* Chicago: University of Chicago Press, 1933.

——. *Diary of an Ad Man: The War Years, June 1, 1942, December 41, 1943.* Chicago: Advertising Publications, Inc., 1944.

——. *Full Corn in the Ear.* Coapa, N.M.: Pinon Press, 1959.

——. *Pills for the Angels.* Coapa, N.M.: Pinon Press, 1952.

Zu Tavern, A. B., and A. E. Bullock. *The Consumer Investigates.* South Pasadena, Calif.: Commercial Textbook Company, 1938.

Secondary Sources

Aaron, Daniel. *Writers on the Left: Episodes in Literary Communism*. New York: Harcourt, Brace and World, 1961.

Abbott, Andrew D. *The System of Professions: An Essay on the Division of Expert Labor*. Chicago: University of Chicago Press, 1988.

Adams, Bluford. *E Pluribus Barnum: The Great Showman and the Making of U.S. Popular Culture*. Minneapolis: University of Minnesota Press, 1997.

Adams, Russell B., Jr. *King C. Gillette: The Man and His Wonderful Shaving Device*. Boston: Little, Brown, 1978.

Adas, Michael. *Dominance by Design: Technological Imperatives and America's Civilizing Mission*. Cambridge, Mass.: Belknap Press of Harvard University Press, 2005.

Adorno, T. W. "Veblen's Attack on Culture." *Studies in Philosophy and Social Science* 9 (1941): 389–413.

Agnew, Jean-Christophe. "Coming Up for Air: Consumer Culture in Historical Perspective." *Intellectual History Newsletter* 12 (1990): 3–23.

——. *Worlds Apart: The Market and the Theater in Anglo-American Thought, 1550–1750*. Cambridge, U.K.: Cambridge University Press, 1986.

Aguilhon, Maurice. *Marianne into Battle: Republican Imagery and Symbolism in France, 1789–1880*. Cambridge, U.K.: Cambridge University Press, 1981.

Aitken, Hugh G. J. *Scientific Management in Action: Taylorism at the Watertown Arsenal, 1908–1915*. Princeton, N.J.: Princeton University Press, 1973.

Akin, William E. *Technocracy and the American Dream*. Berkeley: University of California Press, 1982.

Alchon, Guy. *The Invisible Hand of Planning: Capitalism, Social Science, and the State in the 1920s*. Princeton, N.J.: Princeton University Press, 1985.

Alexander, Charles C. *Here the Country Lies: Nationalism and the Arts*. Bloomington: Indiana University Press, 1981.

Allen, Craig. *Eisenhower and the Mass Media: Peace, Prosperity, and Prime-Time TV*. Chapel Hill: University of North Carolina Press, 1993.

Allen, Frederick Lewis. *The Big Change: America Transforms Itself, 1900–1950*. New York: Harper, 1952.

——. *Only Yesterday: An Informal History of the Nineteen-Twenties*. New York: Harper and Brothers, 1931.

——. *Since Yesterday: The Nineteen-Thirties in America, September 3, 1929–September 3, 1939*. New York: Harper and Brothers, 1940.

Althusser, Louis. "Ideology and Ideological State Apparatuses." In *Lenin and Philosophy and Other Essays*, translated by Ben Brewster, 127–86. New York: Monthly Review Press, 1971.

Ames, Kenneth L. "Meaning in Artifacts: Hall Furnishings in Victorian America." *Journal of Interdisciplinary History* 9 (Summer 1978): 19–46.

Anderson, Alan. *The Songwriter Goes to War: The Story of Irving Berlin's World War II All-Army Production of "This Is the Army."* Pompton Plains, N.J.: Limelight Editions, 2004.

Anderson, Benedict. *Imagined Communities: Reflections on the Origin and Spread of Nationalism*. London: Verso, 1983.

Anderson, Oscar. *The Health of a Nation: Harvey W. Wiley and the Fight for Pure Food.* Chicago: University of Chicago Press, 1958.

Appadurai, Arjun. *Modernity at Large: Cultural Dimensions of Globalization.* Minneapolis: University of Minnesota Press, 1996.

——, ed. *The Social Life of Things: Commodities in Cultural Perspective.* Cambridge, U.K.: Cambridge University Press, 1986.

Appleby, Joyce. *Capitalism and a New Social Order.* New York: New York University Press, 1984.

Atwan, Robert, Donald McQuade, and John W. Wright, eds. *Edsels, Luckies, and Frigidaires: Advertising the American Way.* New York: Delacorte Press, 1979.

Auslander, Leora. *Taste and Power: Furnishing Modern France.* Berkeley: University of California Press, 1996.

Avila, Eric. *Popular Culture in an Age of White Flight: Fear and Fantasy in Suburban Los Angeles.* Berkeley: University of California Press, 2004.

Bailyn, Bernard. *The Ideological Origins of the American Revolution.* Cambridge, Mass.: Harvard University Press, 1967.

Baker, Lee D. *From Savage to Negro: Anthropology and the Construction of Race, 1896–1954.* Berkeley: University of California Press, 1998.

Bakhtin, Mikhail. *The Dialogic Imagination: Four Essays.* Edited by Michael Holquist, and translated by Caryl Emerson and Michael Holquist. Austin: University of Texas Press, 1981.

Bannister, Robert C. *Sociology and Scientism: The American Quest for Objectivity, 1880–1940.* Chapel Hill: University of North Carolina Press, 1987.

Banta, Martha. *Imaging American Women: Idea and Ideals in Cultural History.* New York: Columbia University Press, 1987.

——. *Taylored Lives: Narrative Productions in the Age of Taylor, Veblen, and Ford.* Chicago: University of Chicago Press, 1993.

Barbalet, J. M. *Citizenship.* Minneapolis: University of Minnesota Press, 1988.

Barber, Benjamin R. *Jihad vs. McWorld.* New York: Times Books, 1995.

Barber, William J. *Designs within Disorder: Franklin D. Roosevelt, the Economists, and the Shaping of American Economic Policy, 1933–1945.* New York: Cambridge University Press, 1996.

——. *From New Era to New Deal: Herbert Hoover, the Economists, and American Economic Policy, 1921–1933.* New York: Cambridge University Press, 1985.

Baritz, Loren. *The Good Life: The Meaning of Success for the American Middle Class.* New York: Knopf, 1988.

——. *The Servants of Power: A History of the Use of Social Science in Industry.* Middletown, Conn.: Wesleyan University Press, 1960.

Barnouw, Erik. *The Golden Web: A History of Broadcasting in the United States, 1933–1953.* New York: Oxford University Press, 1968.

——. *A Tower in Babel: A History of Broadcasting in the United States, to 1933.* New York: Oxford University Press, 1966.

Bartels, Robert. *The History of Marketing Thought.* 3d ed. Columbus, Ohio: Publishing Horizons, 1988.

Barth, Gunther. *City People: The Rise of Modern City Culture in Nineteenth-Century America.* New York: Oxford University Press, 1980.

Bartholdi, Frederic Auguste. *The Statue of Liberty Enlightening the World.* 1885; New York: New York Bound, 1984.

Basinger, Jeanine. *The World War II Combat Film: Anatomy of a Genre.* New York: Columbia University Press, 1986.

Basinger, Jeanine, with the Trustees of the Frank Capra Archives. *The "It's a Wonderful Life" Book.* New York: Knopf, 1986.

Baumgarten, Linda. *What Clothes Reveal: The Language of Clothing in Colonial and Federal America.* New Haven, Conn.: Yale University Press, 2002.

Baxandall, Rosalyn, and Elizabeth Ewen. *Picture Windows: How the Suburbs Happened.* New York: Basic Books, 2000.

Beard, Charles A., and Mary R. Beard. *The Rise of American Civilization.* 2 vols. New York: Macmillan, 1927.

Becker, Gary. *The Economic Approach to Human Behavior.* Chicago: University of Chicago Press, 1976.

Bederman, Gail. *Manliness and Civilization: A Cultural History of Gender and Race in the United States, 1880–1917.* Chicago: University of Chicago Press, 1995.

Bell, Daniel. *The Cultural Contradictions of Capitalism.* New York: Basic Books, 1976.

———. *The Winding Passage: Essays and Sociological Journeys, 1960–1980.* New York: Basic Books, 1980.

Bellomy, Donald C. "Social Darwinism Revisited." *Perspectives in American History,* n.s., 1 (1984): 1–129.

Belmonte, Laura A. *Selling America: Propaganda, National Identity, and the Cold War, 1945–1959.* Philadelphia: University of Pennsylvania Press, forthcoming.

———. "Selling Capitalism: Modernization and U.S. Overseas Propaganda, 1945–1959." In *Staging Growth: Modernization, Development, and the Global Cold War,* edited by David C. Engerman, Nils Gilman, Mark Haefele, and Michael E. Latham, 107–28. Amherst: University of Massachusetts Press, 2003.

Bender, Thomas. *Community and Social Change in America.* New Brunswick, N.J.: Rutgers University Press, 1978.

Bensel, Richard Franklin. *Yankee Leviathan: The Origins of Central State Authority in America, 1859–1877.* New York: Cambridge University Press, 1990.

Benson, Lee. *Turner and Beard: American Historical Writing Reconsidered.* Glencoe, Ill.: Free Press, 1960.

Benson, Susan Porter. *Counter Cultures: Saleswomen, Managers, and Customers in American Department Stores, 1890–1940.* Urbana: University of Illinois Press, 1986.

Berger, Peter, and Thomas Luckmann. *The Social Construction of Reality: A Treatise in the Sociology of Knowledge.* Garden City, N.Y.: Doubleday, 1966.

Bermingham, Ann, and John Brewer, eds. *The Consumption of Culture, 1600–1800: Image, Object, Text.* New York: Routledge, 1995.

Bernstein, Michael A. *The Great Depression : Delayed Recovery and Economic Change in America, 1929–1939.* Cambridge, U.K.: Cambridge University Press, 1987.

———. *A Perilous Progress: Economists and Public Purpose in Twentieth-Century America.* Princeton, N.J.: Princeton University Press, 2001.

Berolzheimer, Alan Roy. "A Nation of Consumers: Mass Consumption, Middle-Class Standards of Living, and American National Identity, 1910–1950." Ph.D. diss., University of Virginia, 1996.

Bezner, Lili Corbus. *Photography and Politics in America: From the New Deal into the Cold War*. Baltimore, Md.: Johns Hopkins University Press, 1999.

Bird, William L., Jr. *"Better Living": Advertising, Media, and the New Vocabulary of Business Leadership, 1935–1955*. Evanston, Ill.: Northwestern University Press, 1999.

——. "Enterprise and Meaning: Sponsored Film, 1939–1949." *History Today* 39 (December 1989): 24–30.

——. "Order, Efficiency, and Control: The Evolution of the Political Spot Advertisement, 1936–1956." Ph.D. diss., Georgetown University, 1985.

Birken, Lawrence. *Consuming Desire: Sexual Science and the Emergence of a Culture of Abundance, 1871–1914*. Ithaca, N.Y.: Cornell University Press, 1988.

Black, Edwin. *War against the Weak: Eugenics and America's Campaign to Create a Master Race*. New York: Four Walls Eight Windows, 2003.

Black, Max. *Models and Metaphors: Studies in Language and Philosophy*. Ithaca, N.Y.: Cornell University Press, 1962.

Blake, Casey Nelson. *Beloved Community: The Cultural Criticism of Randolph Bourne, Van Wyck Brooks, Waldo Frank, and Lewis Mumford*. Chapel Hill: University of North Carolina Press, 1990.

Blaszczyk, Regina Lee. *Imagining Consumers: Design and Innovation from Wedgwood to Corning*. Baltimore, Md.: Johns Hopkins University Press, 2000.

Block, N. J., and Gerald Dworkin, eds. *The IQ Controversy: Critical Readings*. New York: Pantheon, 1976.

Blue, Howard. *Words at War: World War II Era Radio Drama and the Postwar Broadcasting Industry Blacklist*. Lanham, Md.: Scarecrow Press, 2002.

Blum, John Morton. *V Was for Victory: Politics and American Culture during World War II*. New York: Harcourt Brace Jovanovich, 1976.

Boardwell, David, Kristin Thompson, and Janet Staiger. *The Classical Hollywood Cinema: Film Style and Mode of Production to 1960*. New York: Columbia University Press, 1985.

Bodnar, John. *Remaking America: Public Memory, Commemoration, and Patriotism in the Twentieth Century*. Princeton, N.J.: Princeton University Press, 1991.

Bogart, Michele H. *Artists, Advertising, and the Borders of Art*. Chicago: University of Chicago Press, 1995.

Boorstin, Daniel J. *The Americans: The Colonial Experience*. New York: Random House, 1958.

——. *The Americans: The Democratic Experience*. New York: Random House, 1973.

——. *The Americans: The National Experience*. New York: Random House, 1965.

——. *The Genius of American Politics*. New York: Random House, 1952.

——. *The Image: or What Happened to the American Dream?* New York: Atheneum, 1961.

Boris, Eileen. *Art and Labor: Ruskin, Morris, and the Craftsman Ideal in America*. Philadelphia: Temple University Press, 1986.

Bourdieu, Pierre. *Distinction: A Social Critique of the Judgement of Taste*, translated by Richard Nice. Cambridge, Mass.: Harvard University Press, 1984.

———. *The Field of Cultural Production: Essays on Art and Literature*. New York: Columbia University Press, 1993.

———. *Language and Symbolic Power*. Edited by John B. Thompson, translated by Gino Raymond and Matthew Adamson. Cambridge, Mass.: Harvard University Press, 1991.

Bowlby, Rachel. *Carried Away: The Invention of Modern Shopping*. New York: Columbia University Press, 2001.

Bowser, Eileen. *The Transformation of Cinema, 1907–1915*. New York: Scribner, 1990.

Boyer, Paul S. *Urban Masses and Moral Order in America, 1820–1920*. Cambridge, Mass.: Harvard University Press, 1978.

Bradley, Linda J., and Barbara D. Merino. "Stuart Chase: A Radical CPA and the Meat Packing Investigation, 1917–1918." *Business and Economic History* 23 (Fall 1994): 190–200.

Brantlinger, Patrick. *Bread and Circuses: Theories of Mass Culture as Social Decay*. Ithaca, N.Y.: Cornell University Press, 1983.

Braverman, Harry. *Labor and Monopoly Capital: The Degradation of Work in the Twentieth Century*. New York: Monthly Review Press, 1974.

Breen, T. H. *The Marketplace of Revolution: How Consumer Politics Shaped American Independence*. New York: Oxford University Press, 2004.

Brewer, John, and Roy Porter, eds. *Consumption and the World of Goods*. New York: Routledge, 1993.

Brinkley, Alan. *The End of Reform: New Deal Liberalism in Recession and War*. New York: Alfred A. Knopf, 1995.

———. "The New Deal and the Idea of the State." In *The Rise and Fall of the New Deal Order, 1930–1980*, edited by Steve Fraser and Gary Gerstle, 85–122. Princeton, N.J.: Princeton University Press, 1989.

Brinkley, Douglas. *Wheels for the World: Henry Ford, His Company, and a Century of Progress, 1903–2003*. New York: Viking, 2003.

Bronner, Simon, ed. *Consuming Visions: Accumulation and Display of Goods in America, 1880–1920*. New York: W. W. Norton, 1989.

Brooks, David. *Bobos in Paradise: The New Upper Class and How They Got There*. New York: Simon and Schuster, 2000.

Brown, Bill. *A Sense of Things: The Object Matter of American Literature*. Chicago: University of Chicago Press, 2004.

Brown, Elspeth H. *The Corporate Eye: Photography and the Rationalization of American Commercial Culture, 1884–1929*. Baltimore, Md.: Johns Hopkins University Press, 2005.

Brown, JoAnne. *The Definition of a Profession: The Authority of Metaphor in the History of Intelligence Testing, 1890–1930*. Princeton, N.J.: Princeton University Press, 1992.

———. "Professional Language: Words that Succeed." *Radical History Review* 34 (1986): 33–51.

Brown, Lester. *Plan B: Rescuing a Planet under Stress and a Civilization in Trouble*. New York: W. W. Norton, 2003.

Buckley, Kerry W. "A President for the 'Great Silent Majority': Bruce Barton's Construction of Calvin Coolidge." *New England Quarterly* 76, no. 4 (2003): 593–626.

Buddenseig, Tilmann, et al. *Industrielkultur: Peter Behrens and the AEG, 1907–1914.* Translated by Ian Boyd White. Cambridge, Mass.: MIT Press, 1984.

Burke, Kenneth. *Language as Symbolic Action: Essays on Life, Literature, and Method.* Berkeley: University of California Press, 1966.

Burns, Arthur T., ed. *Wesley Clair Mitchell: The Economic Scientist.* New York: National Bureau of Economic Research, 1952.

Bush, Gregory Wallace. *Lord of Attention: Gerald Stanley Lee and the Crowd Metaphor in Industrializing America.* Amherst: University of Massachusetts Press, 1991.

Butsch, Richard, ed. *For Fun and Profit: The Transformation of Leisure into Consumption.* Philadelphia: Temple University Press, 1990.

——. *The Making of American Audiences: From Stage to Television, 1750–1990.* Cambridge, U.K.: Cambridge University Press, 2000.

Calder, Lendol. *Financing the American Dream: A Cultural History of Consumer Credit.* Princeton, N.J.: Princeton University Press, 1999.

Calhoun, Craig, ed. *Habermas and the Public Sphere.* Cambridge, Mass.: MIT Press, 1992.

Campbell, Colin. *The Romantic Ethic and the Spirit of Modern Consumerism.* Oxford, U.K.: Basil Blackwell, 1987.

Canclini, Néstor García. *Consumers and Citizens: Globalization and Multicultural Conflicts.* Minneapolis: University of Minnesota Press, 2001.

Carey, James W. *Communication as Culture: Essays on Media and Society.* Boston: Unwin Hyman, 1989.

Carney, Ray. *American Vision: The Films of Frank Capra.* New York: Cambridge University Press, 1986.

Carpenter, Daniel P. *The Forging of Bureaucratic Autonomy: Reputations, Networks, and Policy Innovation in Executive Agencies, 1862–1928.* Princeton, N.J.: Princeton University Press, 2001.

Carson, Cary, Ronald Hoffman, and Peter J. Albert, eds. *Of Consuming Interests: The Style of Life in the Eighteenth Century.* Charlottesville: University Press of Virginia, 1994.

Carson, Mina. *Settlement Folk: Social Thought and the American Settlement Movement, 1885–1930.* Chicago: University of Chicago Press, 1990.

Chambers, John Whiteclay, II. *The Tyranny of Change: American in the Progressive Era, 1890–1920.* 2d ed. New Brunswick, N.J.: Rutgers University Press, 2000.

Chandler, Alfred D., Jr., *The Visible Hand: The Managerial Revolution in American Business.* Cambridge, Mass.: Harvard University Press, 1977.

Chapman, Paul D. *Schools as Sorters: Lewis M. Terman and the Intelligence Testing Movement.* New York: New York University Press, 1988.

Chen, Aric. *Campbell Kids: A Souper Century.* New York: Harry N. Abrams, 2004.

Cheng, Ann Anling. *The Melancholy of Race: Psychoanalysis, Assimilation, and Hidden Grief.* New York: Oxford University Press, 2000.

Chua, Amy. *World on Fire: How Exporting Free Market Democracy Breeds Ethnic Hatred and Global Instability.* New York: Doubleday, 2002.

Clark, Clifford E., Jr. *The American Family Home, 1800–1960.* Chapel Hill: University of North Carolina Press, 1986.

Cobb, Lawrence. "Patriotic Themes in Advertising." Ph.D. diss., Emory University, 1981.

Cochrane, Rexmond A. *Measures for Progress: A History of the National Bureau of Standards.* Washington, D.C.: National Bureau of Standards, 1965.

Cohen, Barbara, Steven Heller, and Seymour Chwast. *Trylon and Perisphere: The 1939 New York World's Fair.* New York: Abrams, 1989.

Cohen, Lizabeth. *A Consumers' Republic: The Politics of Mass Consumption in Postwar America.* New York: Alfred A. Knopf, 2003.

——. "Encountering Mass Culture at the Grassroots: The Experience of Chicago Workers in the 1920s." *American Quarterly* 41 (March 1989): 6–33.

——. "From Town Center to Shopping Center: The Reconfiguration of Community Marketplaces in Postwar America." *American Historical Review* 101 (October 1996): 1050–81.

——. *Making a New Deal: Industrial Workers in Chicago, 1919–1939.* New York: Cambridge University Press, 1990.

Cohen, Nancy. *The Reconstruction of American Liberalism, 1865–1914.* Chapel Hill: University of North Carolina Press, 2002.

Cohen, Stan. *V for Victory: America's Home Front during World War II.* Missoula, Mont.: Pictorial Histories Publishing Company, 1991.

Cohn, Jan. *Creating America: George Horace Lorimer and "The Saturday Evening Post."* Pittsburgh, Pa.: University of Pittsburgh Press, 1988.

Collins, Robert. *More: The Politics of Economic Growth in Postwar America.* New York: Oxford University Press, 2000.

Colomina, Beatriz, Annmarie Brennan, and Jeannie Kim. *Cold War Hothouses: Inventing Postwar Culture, from Cockpit to Playboy.* Princeton, N.J.: Princeton University Press, 2004.

Connolly-Smith, Peter. *Translating America: An Immigrant Press Visualizes American Popular Culture, 1890–1918.* Washington, D.C.: Smithsonian Books, 2004.

Cook, James W. *The Arts of Deception: Playing with Fraud in the Age of Barnum.* Cambridge, Mass.: Harvard University Press, 2001.

Corn, Joseph J., and Brian Horrigan. *Yesterday's Tomorrows: Past Visions of the Future.* 1984; Baltimore: Johns Hopkins University Press, 1996.

Cott, Nancy. *The Grounding of Modern Feminism.* New Haven, Conn.: Yale University Press, 1987.

Couvares, Francis G. *The Remaking of Pittsburgh: Class and Culture in an Industrializing City, 1877–1919.* Albany: State University of New York Press, 1984.

Cowan, Ruth Schwartz. *More Work for Mother: Ironies of Household Technology from the Open Hearth to the Microwave.* New York: Basic Books, 1983.

Craig, Robert Leo. "The Changing Communicative Structure of Advertisements, 1850–1930." Ph.D. diss., University of Iowa, 1986.

Creighton, Lucy Black. *Pretenders to the Throne: The Consumer Movement in the United States.* Lexington, Mass.: D. C. Heath and Company, 1976.

Cronin, Anne M. *Advertising Myths: The Strange Half-Lives of Images and Commodities.* New York: Routledge, 2004.

Cross, Gary S. *An All-Consuming Century: Why Commercialism Won in Modern America.* New York: Columbia University Press, 2000.

———. *Kids' Stuff: Toys and the Changing World of American Childhood*. Cambridge, Mass.: Harvard University Press, 1997.

———. *Time and Money: The Making of Consumer Culture*. New York: Routledge, 1993.

Cuff, Robert D. *The War Industries Board: Business-Government Relations during World War I*. Baltimore, Md.: Johns Hopkins University Press, 1973.

Cullen, Jim. *The American Dream: The Short History of an Idea that Shaped a Nation*. New York: Oxford University Press, 2003.

Cutlip, Scott. *The Unseen Power: Public Relations—A History*. Hillsdale, N.J.: Erlbaum, 1994.

Czitrom, Daniel. *Media and the American Mind: From Morse to McLuhan*. Chapel Hill: University of North Carolina Press, 1982.

Daniel, Pete, et al. *Official Images: New Deal Photography*. Washington, D.C.: Smithsonian Institution Press, 1987.

Daniels, Roger. *Guarding the Golden Door: American Immigration Policy and Immigrants Since 1882*. New York: Hill and Wang, 2004.

Dant, Tim. *Material Culture in the Social World: Values, Activities, Lifestyle*. Buckingham, Pa.: Open University Press, 1999.

Daunton, Martin, and Matthew Hilton, eds. *The Politics of Consumption: Material Culture and Citizenship in Europe and America*. Oxford, U.K.: Berg, 2001.

Davis, Janet. *The Circus Age: Culture and Society under the American Big Top*. Chapel Hill: University of North Carolina Press, 2002.

De Cordova, Richard. *Picture Personalities: The Emergence of the Star System in America*. Urbana: University of Illinois Press, 1990.

De Graaf, John, David Wann, and Thomas H. Naylor. *Affluenza: The All-Consuming Epidemic*. San Francisco, Calif.: Berrett-Koehler Publishers, 2001.

De Grazia, Victoria. *Irresistible Empire: America's Advance through Twentieth-Century Europe*. Cambridge, Mass.: Harvard University Press, 2005.

De Grazia, Victoria, and Ellen Furlough, eds. *The Sex of Things: Gender and Consumption in Historical Perspective*. Berkeley: University of California Press, 1996.

Denning, Michael. *The Cultural Front: The Laboring of American Culture in the Twentieth Century*. New York: Verso, 1997.

———. *Mechanic Accents: Dime Novels and Working-Class Culture in America*. London: Verso, 1987.

Desai, Meghnad. *Marx's Revenge: The Resurgence of Capitalism and the Death of Statist Socialism*. New York: Verso, 2002.

Dicker, John. *The United States of Wal-Mart*. New York: Tarcher-Penguing, 2005.

Diggins, John P. *The Bard of Savagery: Thorstein Veblen and Modern Social Theory*. New York: Seabury Press, 1978.

———. *The Lost Soul of American Politics: Virtue, Self-Interest, and the Foundations of Liberalism*. New York: Basic Books, 1985.

Dirks, Jacqueline K. "Righteous Goods: Women's Production, Reform Publicity, and the National Consumers' League, 1891–1919." Ph.D. diss., Yale University, 1996.

Doherty, Thomas M. *Projections of War: Hollywood, American Culture, and World War II*. New York: Columbia University Press, 1993.

Donohue, Kathleen G. *Freedom from Want: American Liberalism and the Idea of the Consumer.* Baltimore, Md.: Johns Hopkins University Press, 2003.

Dorfman, Joseph. *The Economic Mind in American Civilization.* 5 vols. New York: Viking Press, 1946–59.

———. *Thorstein Veblen and His America.* New York: Viking Press, 1934.

Douglas, Mary, and Baron Isherwood. *The World of Goods: Toward an Anthropology of Consumption.* Rev. ed. New York: Routledge, 1996.

Douglas, Susan J. "Amateur Operators and American Broadcasting: Shaping the Future of Radio." In *Imagining Tomorrow: History, Technology, and the American Future,* edited by Joseph J. Corn, 35–56. Cambridge, Mass.: MIT Press, 1985.

———. *Inventing American Broadcasting, 1899–1922.* Baltimore, Md.: Johns Hopkins University Press, 1987.

———. *Listening In: Radio and the American Imagination from "Amos 'n' Andy" and Edward R. Murrow to Wolfman Jack and Howard Stern.* New York: Times Books, 1999.

Dowd, Douglas F. "Thorstein Veblen: The Evolution of Capitalism from Economic and Political to Social Dominance; Economics as its Faithful Servant." In *Understanding Capitalism: Critical Analysis from Karl Marx to Amartya Sen,* edited by Douglas Dowd, 37–56. London: 2002.

Drinkwater, John. *The Life and Adventures of Carl Laemmle.* 1931; New York: Arno Press, 1978.

Dubofsky, Melvin. *The State and Labor in Modern America.* Chapel Hill: University of North Carolina Press, 1994.

Edelman, Murray J. *Political Language: Words That Succeed and Policies That Fail.* New York: Academic Press, 1977.

———. *Politics as Symbolic Action: Mass Arousal and Quiescence.* Chicago: Markham Publishing, 1971.

———. *The Symbolic Uses of Politics.* 1964; Urbana: University of Illinois Press, 1985.

Edgell, Stephen. *Veblen in Perspective: His Life and Thought.* Armonk, N.Y.: M. E. Sharpe, 2001.

Ehrenreich, Barbara. *Nickel and Dimed: On (Not) Getting by in America.* New York: Metropolitan Books, 2001.

Elster, Jon. *An Introduction to Karl Marx.* Cambridge, U.K.: Cambridge University Press, 1986.

Ely, Melvin Patrick. *The Adventures of Amos 'n' Andy: A Social History of an American Phenomenon.* New York: Free Press, 1991.

Emmet, Boris, and Robert Jouck. *Catalogs and Counters: A History of Sears Roebuck and Company.* Chicago: University of Chicago Press, 1950.

Enstad, Nan. *Ladies of Labor, Girls of Adventure: Working Women, Popular Culture, and Labor Politics at the Turn of the Century.* New York: Columbia University Press, 2000.

Erenberg, Lewis A. *Swingin' the Dream: Big Band Jazz and the Rebirth of American Culture.* Chicago: University of Chicago Press, 1998.

Ewen, Elizabeth. *Immigrant Women in the Land of Dollars: Life and Culture on the Lower East Side, 1890–1925.* New York: Monthly Review Press, 1985.

Ewen, Stuart. *Captains of Consciousness: Advertising and the Social Roots of the Consumer Culture.* New York: McGraw-Hill, 1976.

———. *PR!: A Social History of Spin*. New York: Basic Books, 1996.

Fabian, Johannes. *Time and the Other: How Anthropology Makes Its Object*. New York: Columbia University Press, 1983.

Ferguson, Niall. *Colossus: The Price of America's Empire*. New York: Penguin Press, 2004.

Fernandez, James. *Persuasions and Performances: The Play of Tropes in Culture*. Bloomington: Indiana University Press, 1986.

Finnegan, Margaret. *Selling Suffrage: Consumer Culture and Votes for Women*. New York: Columbia University Press, 1999.

Fischer, Claude S. *America Calling: A Social History of the Telephone to 1940*. Berkeley: University of California Press, 1992.

Fitzpatrick, Ellen. *Endless Crusade: Women Social Scientists and Progressive Reform*. New York: Oxford University Press, 1990.

———. *History's Memory: Writing America's Past, 1880–1980*. Cambridge, Mass.: Harvard University Press, 2002.

Fleischauer, Carl, and Beverly Brannan, eds. *Documenting America, 1935–1943*. Berkeley: University of California Press, 1988.

Fleming, Donald. "Attitude: The History of a Concept." *Perspectives in American History* 1 (1967): 287–365.

Foner, Eric. *Free Soil, Free Labor, Free Men: The Ideology of the Republican Party before the Civil War*. New York: Oxford University Press, 1970.

Fones-Wolf, Elizabeth. "Creating a Favorable Business Climate: Corporations and Radio Broadcasting, 1934 to 1954." *Business History Review* 73, no. 2 (1999): 221–55.

———. *Selling Free Enterprise: The Business Assault on Labor and Liberalism, 1945–1960*. Urbana: University of Illinois Press, 1994.

Forty, Adrian. *Objects of Desire: Design and Society from Wedgwood to IBM*. New York: Pantheon, 1986.

Fox, Daniel M. *The Discovery of Abundance: Simon N. Patten and the Transformation of Social Theory*. Ithaca, N.Y.: Cornell University Press, 1967.

Fox, Frank. *Madison Avenue Goes to War: The Strange Military Career of American Advertising*. Provo: University of Utah Press, 1975.

Fox, Richard Wightman, and T. J. Jackson Lears, eds. *The Culture of Consumption: Critical Essays in American History, 1880–1980*. New York: Pantheon Books, 1983.

———. *The Power of Culture: Critical Essays in American History*. New York: Pantheon, 1993.

Fox, Stephen R. *The Mirror Makers: A History of American Advertising and Its Creators*. New York: William Morrow, 1984.

Frank, Dana. *Buy American! The Untold Story of Economic Nationalism*. Boston: Beacon Press, 1999.

———. *Purchasing Power: Consumer Organizing, Gender, and the Seattle Labor Movement, 1919–1929*. New York: Cambridge University Press, 1994.

Frank, Robert H. *Luxury Fever: Money and Happiness in an Age of Excess*. Princeton, N.J.: Princeton University Press, 2000.

Frank, Thomas. *The Conquest of Cool: Business Culture, Counterculture, and the Rise of Consumerism*. Chicago: University of Chicago Press, 1997.

———. *One Market under God: Extreme Capitalism, Market Populism, and the End of Economic Democracy*. New York: Doubleday, 2000.

Frank, Thomas, and Matt Weiland, eds. *Commodify Your Dissent! Salvos from The Baffler*. New York: W. W. Norton, 1997.

Fraser, Steve, and Gary Gerstle, eds. *The Rise and Fall of the New Deal Order, 1933–1980*. Princeton, N.J.: Princeton University Press, 1989.

Freeman, Mike. "Clarence Saunders, the Piggly Wiggly Man." M.S. thesis, Memphis State University, 1988.

Fried, Richard M. *The Man Everybody Knew: Bruce Barton and the Making of Modern America*. Chicago: Ivan R. Dee, 2005.

Friedman, Milton. *Free to Choose: A Personal Statement*. New York: Harcourt Brace Jovanovich, 1980.

Friedman, Walter. *Birth of a Salesman: The Transformation of Selling in America*. Cambridge, Mass.: Harvard University Press, 2004.

Fuller, Wayne E. *The American Mail: Enlarger of the Common Life*. Chicago: University of Chicago Press, 1972.

Fyne, Robert. *The Hollywood Propaganda of World War II*. Metuchen, N.J.: Scarecrow Press, 1994.

Galambos, Louis. *The Public Image of Big Business in America, 1880–1940*. Baltimore, Md.: Johns Hopkins University Press, 1975.

Galbraith, John Kenneth. *The Affluent Society*. 3d ed., rev. New York: Mentor, 1976.

——. *American Capitalism: The Concept of Countervailing Power*. Boston: Houghton Mifflin, 1952.

——. *The New Industrial State*. Boston: Houghton Mifflin, 1967.

Gardner, Lloyd C., Walter F. LaFeber, and Thomas J. McCormick. *Creation of the American Empire*. 2 vols. Chicago: Rand McNally, 1976.

Garvey, Ellen Gruber. *The Adman in the Parlor: Magazines and the Gendering of Consumer Culture, 1880s to 1910s*. New York: Oxford University Press, 1996.

Gelatt, Roland. *The Fabulous Phonograph, 1877–1977*. 2d rev. ed. New York: Macmillan, 1977.

Gellner, Ernest. *Nations and Nationalism*. Ithaca, N.Y.: Cornell University Press, 1983.

Gerstle, Gary. *American Crucible: Race and Nation in the Twentieth Century*. Princeton, N.J.: Princeton University Press, 2001.

Geertz, Clifford. *The Interpretation of Cultures*. New York: Basic Books, 1973.

Giddens, Gary. *Riding on a Blue Note: Jazz and American Pop*. New York: Oxford University Press, 1981.

Giedion, Siegfried. *Mechanization Takes Command: A Contribution to Anonymous History*. 1948; New York: W. W. Norton, 1975.

Gilbert, James. *Designing the Industrial State: The Intellectual Pursuit of Collectivism in America, 1880–1940*. Chicago: Quadrangle, 1972.

——. *Perfect Cities: Chicago's Utopias of 1893*. Chicago: University of Chicago Press, 1991.

Gilkeson, John S. *Middle-Class Providence, 1820–1940*. Princeton, N.J.: Princeton University Press, 1986.

Gilman, Nils. *Mandarins of the Future: Modernization Theory in Cold War America*. Baltimore, Md.: Johns Hopkins University Press, 2003.

Giovacchini, Saverio. *Hollywood Modernism: Film and Politics in the Age of the New Deal*. Philadelphia: Temple University Press, 2001.

Girgus, Sam B. *The American Self: Myth, Ideology, and Popular Culture.* Albuquerque: University of New Mexico Press, 1981.

Gleason, Philip. "American Identity and Americanization." In *Concepts of Ethnicity,* edited by William Petersen, Michael Novak, and Philip Gleason, 57–143. Cambridge, Mass.: Belknap Press, 1982.

Glenn, Evelyn Nakano. *Unequal Freedom: How Race and Gender Shaped American Citizenship and Labor.* Cambridge, Mass.: Harvard University Press, 2002.

Glickman, Lawrence B. *A Living Wage: American Workers and the Making of Consumer Society.* Ithaca, N.Y.: Cornell University Press, 1997.

———. "The Strike in the Temple of Consumption: Consumer Activism and Twentieth-Century American Political Culture." *Journal of American History* 88 (June 2001): 99–128.

———, ed. *Consumer Society in American History: A Reader.* Ithaca, N.Y.: Cornell University Press, 1999.

Goffman, Erving. *The Presentation of Self in Everyday Life.* Garden City, N.Y.: Doubleday, 1959.

Goldstein, Carolyn. "Mediating Consumption: Home Economics and American Consumers, 1900–1940." Ph.D. diss., University of Delaware, 1994.

Gomery, Douglas. *The Hollywood Studio System.* New York: St. Martin's Press, 1986.

Goodman, Walter. *The Committee: The Extraordinary Career of the House Committee on Un-American Activities.* New York: Farrar, Straus, and Giroux, 1968.

Goodwyn, Lawrence. *The Populist Moment: A Short History of the Agrarian Revolt in America.* New York: Oxford University Press, 1978.

Gordon, Colin. *New Deals: Business, Labor, and Politics in America, 1920–1935.* Cambridge, U.K.: Cambridge University Press, 1994.

Gordon, Ian L. *Comic Strips and Consumer Culture, 1890–1945.* Washington, D.C.: Smithsonian Institution Press, 1999.

[Gordon, Nightingale]. *WNEW: Where the Melody Lingers On.* New York, 1984.

Gorman, Paul R. *Left Intellectuals and Popular Culture in Twentieth-Century America.* Chapel Hill: University of North Carolina Press, 1996.

Graeber, David. *Toward an Anthropological Theory of Value: The False Coin of Our Own Dreams.* New York: Palgrave, 2001.

Graham, Otis P. *An Encore for Reform: The Old Progressives and the New Deal.* New York: Oxford University Press, 1967.

Greider, William. *One World, Ready or Not: The Manic Logic of Global Capitalism.* New York: Simon and Schuster, 1997.

———. *The Soul of Capitalism: Opening Paths to a Moral Economy.* New York: Simon and Schuster, 2003.

Grier, Katherine C. *Culture and Comfort: People, Parlors, and Upholstery, 1870–1930.* Amherst: University of Massachusetts Press, 1988.

Griffith, Robert. "The Selling of America: The Advertising Council and American Politics, 1942–1960." *Business History Review* 57 (Autumn 1983): 388–412.

Gudis, Catherine. *Buyways: Billboards, Automobiles, and the American Landscape.* New York: Routledge, 2004.

Gunther, John. *Inside U.S.A.* New York: Harper and Brothers, 1947.

——. *Taken at the Flood: The Story of Albert D. Lasker.* New York: Harper, 1960.

Guterl, Matthew Pratt. *The Color of Race in America, 1900–1940.* Cambridge, Mass.: Harvard University Press, 2001.

Gutman, Herbert. *Work, Culture, and Society in Industrializing America: Essays in American Working Class and Social History.* New York: Alfred A. Knopf, 1976.

Haber, Samuel. *The Quest for Authority and Honor in the American Professions, 1750–1900.* Chicago: University of Chicago Press, 1991.

Habermas, Jurgen. *The Structural Transformation of the Public Sphere: An Inquiry into a Category of Bourgeois Society,* translated by Thomas Burger, assisted by Frederick Lawrence. Cambridge, Mass.: MIT Press, 1989.

Haddow, Robert. *Pavilions of Plenty: Exhibiting American Culture Abroad in the 1950s.* Washington, D.C.: Smithsonian Institution Press, 1997.

Hahn, Steven. *The Roots of Southern Populism: Yeoman Farmers and the Transformation of the Georgia Upcountry, 1850–1890.* New York: Oxford University Press, 1983.

Halttunen, Karen. *Confidence Men and Painted Women: A Study of Middle-Class Culture in America, 1830–1870.* New Haven, Conn.: Yale University Press, 1982.

Hamm, Charles. *Irving Berlin: Songs from the Melting Pot—The Formative Years, 1907–1914.* New York: Oxford University Press, 1997.

Hansen, Jonathan M. *The Lost Promise of American Patriotism: Debating American Identity, 1890–1920.* Chicago: University of Chicago Press, 2003.

Hardt, Michael, and Antonio Negri. *Empire.* Cambridge, Mass.: Harvard University Press, 2000.

Hardwick, M. Jeffrey. *Mall Maker: Victor Gruen, Architect of an American Dream.* Philadelphia: University of Pennsylvania Press, 2003.

Harper, F. J. " 'A New Battle on Evolution': The Anti-Chain Store Trade-at-Home Agitation of 1929–1930." *American Studies* 16, no. 3 (1982): 407–26.

Harris, Howell John. *The Right to Manage: Industrial Relations Policies of American Business in the 1940s.* Madison: University of Wisconsin Press, 1982.

Harris, Neil. *Humbug: The Art of P. T. Barnum.* Boston: Little, Brown, 1973.

Harrison, Helen A., ed. *Dawn of a New Day: The New York World's Fair, 1939/40.* Flushing, N.Y.: Queens Museum, 1980.

Hartz, Louis. *The Liberal Tradition in America: An Interpretation of American Political Thought Since the Revolution.* New York: Harcourt, Brace and World, 1955.

Haskell, Thomas, ed. *The Authority of Experts: Studies in History and Theory.* Bloomington: Indiana University Press, 1984.

——. *The Emergence of Professional Social Science: The American Social Science Association and the Nineteenth-Century Crisis of Authority.* Urbana: University of Illinois Press, 1977.

Haug, W. F. *Critique of Commodity Aesthetics: Appearance, Sexuality, and Advertising in Capitalist Society.* Translated by Robert Bock. Minneapolis: University of Minnesota Press, 1986.

Hawken, Paul. *The Ecology of Commerce: A Declaration of Sustainability.* New York: Harper Business, 1993.

Hawley, Ellis W. *The Great War and the Search for a Modern Order in America: A History of the American People and Their Institutions, 1917–1933.* 2d ed. New York: St. Martin's Press, 1992.

——. "Herbert Hoover, the Commerce Secretariat, and the Vision of an Associative State." *Journal of American History* 61 (June 1974): 116–40.

——. *The New Deal and the Problem of Monopoly: A Study in Economic Ambivalence.* Princeton, N.J.: Princeton University Press, 1966.

Hayden, Dolores. *The Grand Domestic Revolution: A History of Feminist Designs for American Homes, Neighborhoods, and Cities.* Cambridge: MIT Press, 1981.

Hegeman, Susan. *Patterns for America: Modernism and the Concept of Culture.* Princeton, N.J.: Princeton University Press, 1999.

Heinze, Andrew R. *Adapting to Abundance: Jewish Immigrants, Mass Consumption, and the Search for American Identity.* New York: Columbia University Press, 1990.

Henderson, Amy. *On the Air: Pioneers of American Broadcasting.* Washington, D.C.: Smithsonian Institution Press, 1988.

Hertz, Noreena. *Silent Takeover: Global Capitalism and the Death of Democracy.* New York: Free Press, 2003.

Hessler, Julie. *A Social History of Soviet Trade: Trade Policy, Retail Practices, and Consumption, 1917–1953.* Princeton, N.J.: Princeton University Press, 2004.

Higham, John. *Send These to Me: Immigrants in Urban America.* Rev. ed. Baltimore, Md.: Johns Hopkins University Press, 1984.

——. *Strangers in the Land: Patterns of American Nativism, 1860–1925.* 1955; New York: Atheneum, 1963.

Hilmes, Michele. *Hollywood and Broadcasting: From Radio to Cable.* Urbana: University of Illinois Press, 1990.

——. *Radio Voices: American Broadcasting, 1922–1952.* Minneapolis: University of Minnesota Press, 1997.

Hine, Thomas. *The Total Package: The Evolution and Secret Meanings of Boxes, Bottles, Cans, and Tubes.* Boston: Little, Brown, 1995.

Hirschman, Albert O. *Exit, Voice, and Loyalty: Responses to Declines in Firms, Organizations, and States.* Cambridge, Mass.: Harvard University Press, 1970.

——. *The Passions and the Interests: Political Arguments for Capitalism before Its Triumph.* Princeton, N.J.: Princeton University Press, 1977.

Hobsbawm, Eric. *Nations and Nationalism Since 1780: Programme, Myth, Reality.* Cambridge, U.K.: Cambridge University Press, 1990.

Hochschild, Arlie. *The Managed Heart: The Commercialization of Human Feeling.* Berkeley: University of California Press, 1983.

Hodgson, Geoffrey. *The Evolution of Institutional Economics: Agency Structure and Darwinism in Institutional Economics.* New York: Routledge, 2004.

Hodgson, Godfrey. *America in Our Time.* Garden City, N.Y.: Doubleday, 1976.

Hofstadter, Richard. *The Age of Reform: From Bryan to F. D. R.* New York: Random House, 1955.

——. *The Progressive Historians: Turner, Beard, Parrington.* New York: Alfred A, Knopf, 1968.

Holli, Melvin G. *The Wizard of Washington: Emil Hurja, Franklin Roosevelt, and the Birth of Public Opinion Polling.* New York: Palgrave, 2002.

Hollitz, John. "The Challenge of Abundance: Reactions to the Development of a Consumer Economy, 1890–1920." Ph.D. diss., University of Wisconsin–Madison, 1981.

Hoopes, Roy. *Americans Remember the Home Front: An Oral Narrative of the World War II Years in America.* New York: Berkley Books, 2002.

Horkheimer, Max, and Theodor Adorno. *The Dialectic of Enlightenment.* Translated by John Cumming. New York: Seabury Press, 1972.

Horowitz, Daniel. *Anxieties of Affluence: Critiques of American Consumer Culture, 1939–1979.* Amherst: University of Massachusetts Press, 2004.

———. *The Morality of Spending: Attitudes toward the Consumer Society in America, 1875–1940.* Baltimore, Md.: Johns Hopkins University Press, 1985.

———. "Periodization, Hegemony, and Method in the History of American Consumer Culture." *Maryland Historian* 19 (1988): 59–62.

Horowitz, Irving Louis, ed. *Veblen's Century: A Collective Portrait.* New Brunswick, N.J.: Transaction Publishers, 2002.

Horten, Gerd. *Radio Goes to War: The Cultural Politics of Propaganda during World War II.* Berkeley: University of California Press, 2002.

Horwitz, Morton. *The Transformation of American Law, 1870–1960: The Crisis of Legal Orthodoxy.* New York: Oxford University Press, 1992.

Hounshell, David. *From the American System to Mass Production, 1800–1932: The Development of American Manufacturing Technology.* Baltimore, Md.: Johns Hopkins University Press, 1984.

Hower, Ralph M. *The History of an Advertising Agency: N. W. Ayer & Son at Work, 1869–1939.* Cambridge, Mass.: Harvard University Press, 1939.

Howey, Richard S. *The Rise of the Marginal Utility School, 1870–1889.* Lawrence: University of Kansas Press, 1960.

Hunt, Michael. *Ideology and U.S. Foreign Policy.* New Haven, Conn.: Yale University Press, 1987.

Hurley, Andrew. *Diners, Bowling Alleys, and Trailer Parks: Chasing the American Dream in the Postwar Consumer Culture.* New York: Basic Books, 2001.

Hutchison, T. W. *A Review of Economic Doctrines, 1870–1929.* Oxford, U.K.: Clarendon Press, 1953.

Huyssen, Andreas. "Mass Culture as Modernism's Other." In *After the Great Divide: Modernism, Mass Culture, Postmodernism,* 44–64. Bloomington: Indiana University Press, 1986.

Igo, Sarah E. "America Surveyed: The Making of a Social Scientific Public, 1920–1960." Ph.D. diss., Princeton University, 2001.

Isin, Engin F., and Bryan S. Turner, eds. *Handbook of Citizenship Studies.* London: Sage, 2002.

Jackall, Robert, and Janice M. Hirota. *Image Makers: Advertising, Public Relations, and the Ethos of Advocacy.* Chicago: University of Chicago Press, 2000.

Jackson, Charles O. *Food and Drug Legislation in the New Deal.* Princeton, N.J.: Princeton University Press, 1970.

Jacobs, Meg. "'Democracy's Third Estate': New Deal Politics and the Construction of a 'Consuming Public.'" *International Labor and Working Class History* 55 (April 1999): 27–51.

———. "'How About Some Meat?': The Office of Price Administration, Consumption Politics, and State Building from the Bottom Up, 1941–1946." *Journal of American History* 84 (December 1997): 910–41.

———. *Pocketbook Politics: Economic Citizenship in Twentieth Century America*. Princeton, N.J.: Princeton University Press, 2004.

Jacobson, Jacob Zavel. *Scott of Northwestern: The Life Story of a Pioneer in Psychology and Education*. Chicago: L. Mariano, 1951.

Jacobson, Lisa. "Manly Boys and Enterprising Dreamers: Business Ideology and the Construction of the Boy Consumer, 1910–1930." *Enterprise and Society* 2 (2001): 225–58.

———. *Raising Consumers: Children and the American Mass Market in the Early Twentieth Century*. New York: Columbia University Press, 2004.

Jacobson, Matthew Frye. *Barbarian Virtues: The United States Encounters Foreign Peoples at Home and Abroad*. New York: Hill and Wang, 2001.

———. *Whiteness of a Different Color: European Immigrants and the Alchemy of Race*. Cambridge, Mass.: Harvard University Press, 1998.

Jameson, Fredric. *The Political Unconscious: Narrative as a Socially Symbolic Act*. Ithaca, N.Y.: Cornell University Press, 1981.

———. *Postmodernism: or, The Cultural Logic of Late Capitalism*. Durham, N.C.: Duke University Press, 1991.

———. "Reification and Utopia in Mass Culture." *Social Text* 1 (1979): 130–48.

Jamieson, Kathleen Hall. *Packaging the Presidency: A History and Criticism of Presidential Campaign Advertising*. 3d ed. New York: Oxford University Press, 1996.

Jeffries, John W. *Wartime America: The World War II Home Front*. Chicago: Ivan R. Dee, 1990.

Jellison, Katherine. *Entitled to Power: Farm Women and Technology, 1913–1963*. Chapel Hill: University of North Carolina Press, 1993.

Jhally, Sut. *The Codes of Advertising: Fetishism and the Political Economy of Meaning in the Consumer Society*. New York: St. Martin's Press, 1987.

Johnston, Robert D. *The Radical Middle Class: Populist Democracy and the Question of Capitalism in Progressive Era Portland, Oregon*. Princeton, N.J.: Princeton University Press, 2003.

Jones, David Lloyd. "The U.S. Office of War Information and American Public Opinion during World War II, 1939–1945." Ph.D. diss., State University of New York, Binghamton, 1976.

Kammen, Michael G. *American Culture, American Tastes: Social Change and the 20th Century*. New York: Knopf, 1999.

———. *Spheres of Liberty: Changing Perceptions of Liberty in American Culture*. Madison: University of Wisconsin Press, 1986.

Kaplan, Amy. *The Anarchy of Empire in the Making of U.S. Culture*. Cambridge, Mass.: Harvard University Press, 2002.

Kaplan, Amy, and Donald Pease, eds. *Cultures of United States Imperialism*. Durham, N.C.: Duke University Press, 1994.

Karl, Barry D. "Presidential Planning and Social Science Research: Mr. Hoover's Experts." *Perspectives in American History* 3 (1969): 347–409.

———. *The Uneasy State: The United States from 1915 to 1945*. Chicago: University of Chicago Press, 1983.

Kasson, John S. *Amusing the Million: Coney Island at the Turn of the Century*. New York: Hill and Wang, 1978.

———. *Houdini, Tarzan, and the Perfect Man: The White Male Body and the Challenge of Modernity in America*. New York: Hill and Wang, 2001.

Kasson, Joy. *Buffalo Bill's Wild West: Celebrity, Memory, and Popular History*. New York: Hill and Wang, 2000.

Katz, Norman D. "Consumers Union: The Movement and the Magazine, 1936–1957." Ph.D. diss., Rutgers University,1977.

Kay, Gwen. "Healthy Public Relations: The FDA's 1930s Legislative Campaigns." *Bulletin of the History of Medicine* 75 (Fall 2001): 446–87.

Keller, Morton. *Affairs of State: Public Life in Late Nineteenth-Century America*. Cambridge, Mass.: Harvard University Press, 1979.

Kelley, Robin D. G. *Race Rebels: Culture, Politics and the Black Working Class*. New York: Free Press, 1994.

Kennedy, David. *Freedom from Fear: The American People in Depression and War, 1929–1945*. New York: Oxford University Press, 1999.

———. *Over Here: The First World War and American Society*. New York: Oxford University Press, 1980.

Kenney, William Howland. *Recorded Music in American Life: The Phonograph and Popular Memory, 1890–1945*. New York: Oxford University Press, 1999.

Kern, Stephen. *The Culture of Time and Space, 1880–1918*. Cambridge, Mass.: Harvard University Press, 1983.

Kern-Foxworth, Marilyn. *Aunt Jemima, Uncle Ben, and Rastus: Blacks in Advertising, Yesterday, Today, and Tomorrow*. Westport, Conn.: Greenwood Press, 1994.

Kessler-Harris, Alice. *In Pursuit of Equity: Women, Men, and the Quest for Economic Citizenship in Twentieth-Century America*. New York: Oxford University Press, 2001.

Kettner, James H. *The Development of American Citizenship, 1608–1870*. Chapel Hill: University of North Carolina Press, 1980.

Kilbourne, Jean. *Can't Buy My Love: How Advertising Changes the Way We Think and Feel*. New York: Simon and Schuster, 2000.

Kitch, Carolyn. *The Girl on the Magazine Cover: The Origins of Visual Stereotypes*. Chapel Hill: University of North Carolina Press, 2001.

Klein, Naomi. *No Logo: Taking Aim at the Brand Bullies*. New York: Picador, 2000.

Kline, Ronald R. *Consumers in the Country: Technology and Social Change in Rural America*. Baltimore, Md.: Johns Hopkins University Press, 2002.

Kloppenberg, James T. *The Virtues of Liberalism*. New York: Oxford University Press, 1998.

Koppes, Clayton R., and Gregory D. Black. *Hollywood Goes to War: How Politics, Profits, and Propaganda Shaped World War II Movies*. New York: Free Press, 1987.

Kouwenhoven, John. *The Beer Can by the Highway: Essays on What's American about America*. Garden City, N.Y.: Doubleday, 1961.

Krause, Elliott A. *The Death of the Guilds: Professions, States, and the Advance of Capitalism, 1930 to the Present*. New Haven, Conn.: Yale University Press, 1996.

Kreshel, Peggy Jean. "Toward a Cultural History of Advertising Research: A Case Study of J. Walter Thompson, 1908–1925." Ph.D. diss., University of Illinois, 1989.

Kroes, Rob. *If You've Seen One, You've Seen the Mall: Europeans and American Mass Culture*. Urbana: University of Illinois Press, 1996.

Kuisel, Richard F. *Seducing the French: The Dilemmas of Americanization*. Berkeley: University of California Press, 1993.

Kuna, David P. "The Concept of Suggestion in the Early History of Advertising Psychology." *Journal of the History of the Behavioral Sciences* 12 (1976): 347–53.

———. "The Psychology of Advertising, 1896–1916." Ph.D. diss., University of New Hampshire, 1976.

Kuttner, Robert. *Everything for Sale: The Virtues and Limits of Markets*. New York: Alfred A. Knopf, 1997.

Laird, Pamela Walker. *Advertising Progress: American Business and the Rise of Consumer Marketing*. Baltimore, Md.: Johns Hopkins University Press, 1998.

Lakoff, George, and Mark Johnson. *Metaphors We Live By*. Chicago: University of Chicago Press, 1980.

Lakoff, Robin Tolmack. *Talking Power: The Politics of Language in Our Lives*. New York: Basic Books, 1990.

Lamoreaux, Naomi. *The Great Merger Movement in American Business, 1895–1904*. Cambridge, U.K.: Cambridge University Press, 1985.

Landes, David. *Unbound Prometheus: Technological Change and Industrial Development in Western Europe from 1750 to the Present*. Cambridge, Mass.: Harvard University Press, 1977.

Landsberg, Alison. *Prosthetic Memory: The Transformation of American Remembrance in an Age of Mass Culture*. New York: Columbia University Press, 2004.

Lang, Robert, ed. *Birth of a Nation: D. W. Griffith, Director*. New Brunswick, N.J.: Rutgers University Press, 1994.

Larson, Erik. *The Naked Consumer: How Our Private Lives Become Public Commodities*. New York: Henry Holt, 1992.

Larson, Magali Sarfatti. *The Rise of Professionalism: A Sociological Analysis*. Berkeley: University of California Press, 1977.

Lasch, Christopher. *The New Radicalism in America: The Intellectual as Social Type, 1889–1963*. New York: Knopf, 1965.

Lasn, Kalle. *Culture Jam: The Uncooling of America*. New York: Eagle Brook, 1999.

Latham, Michael E. *Modernization as Ideology: American Social Science and "Nation-Building" in the Kennedy Era*. Chapel Hill: University of North Carolina Press, 2000.

Laurie, Bruce. *The Working People of Philadelphia, 1800–1850*. Philadelphia: Temple University Press, 1980.

Lawson, R. Alan. *The Failure of Independent Liberalism, 1930–41*. New York: Putnam, 1971.

Layton, Edwin T. *The Revolt of the Engineers: Social Responsibility and the American Engineering Profession*. 1971; Baltimore, Md.: Johns Hopkins University Press, 1986.

——. "Veblen and the Engineers." *American Quarterly* 14 (Spring 1962): 64–72.

Leach, Eugene E. "Mastering the Crowd: Collective Behavior and Mass Society in American Social Thought, 1917–1933." *American Studies* 27 (Spring 1986): 99–114.

Leach, William R. *Land of Desire: Merchants, Power, and the Rise of a New American Culture.* New York: Pantheon, 1993.

——. "Transformations in a Culture of Consumption: Women and Department Stores, 1890–1925." *Journal of American History* 71 (September 1984): 319–42.

Lears, T. J. Jackson. "The Ad Man and the Grand Inquisitor." In *Constructions of the Self,* edited by George Levine, 107–42. New Brunswick, N.J.: Rutgers University Press, 1992.

——. "Antonio Gramsci's Concept of Hegemony: Some Problems and Possibilities." *American Historical Review* 90 (June 1985): 567–93.

——. "Beyond Veblen: Rethinking Consumer Culture in America." In *Consuming Visions: Accumulation and Display of Goods in America, 1880–1920,* edited by Simon Bronner, 73–98. New York: W. W. Norton, 1989.

——. *Fables of Abundance: A Cultural History of Advertising in America.* New York: Basic Books, 1994.

——. *No Place of Grace: Antimodernism and the Transformation of American Culture, 1880–1920.* New York: Pantheon, 1981.

——. "Packaging the Folk: Tradition and Amnesia in American Advertising, 1880–1940." In *Folk Roots, New Roots: Folklore in American Life,* edited by Jane S. Becker and Barbara Franco, 103–40. Lexington, Mass.: Museum of Our National Heritage, 1988.

——. "Some Versions of Fantasy: Toward a Cultural History of Advertising, 1880–1930." *Prospects* 9 (1984): 349–409.

Lebergott, Stanley. *Pursuing Happiness: American Consumers in the Twentieth Century.* Princeton, N.J.: Princeton University Press, 1993.

Lebhar, Godfrey M. *Chain Stores in America, 1859–1950.* New York: Chain Store Publishing Corporation, 1952.

Leff, Mark H. *The Limits of Symbolic Reform: The New Deal and Taxation, 1933–1939.* New York: Cambridge University Press, 1984.

——. "The Politics of Sacrifice on the American Home Front in World War II." *Journal of American History* 77 (March 1991): 1296–318.

Leiss, William, Stephen Kline, and Sut Jhally. *Social Communication in Advertising: Persons, Products, and Images of Well-Being.* Toronto: Methuen, 1986.

Lekachman, Robert. *A History of Economic Ideas.* New York: Harper and Brothers, 1959.

Lerner, Max, ed. *The Portable Veblen.* New York: Viking Press, 1948.

Leuchtenburg, William E. *Franklin D. Roosevelt and the New Deal, 1932–1940.* New York: Harper and Row, 1963.

——. *The Perils of Prosperity, 1914–32.* Chicago: University of Chicago Press, 1958.

Levine, Lawrence W. *Highbrow/Lowbrow: The Emergence of Cultural Hierarchy in America.* Cambridge, Mass.: Harvard University Press, 1987.

——. *The Unpredictable Past: Explorations in American Cultural History.* New York: Oxford University Press, 1993.

Lewis, David L. *The Public Image of Henry Ford: An American Folk Hero and His Company.* Detroit, Mich.: Wayne State University Press, 1976.

Leymore, Varda Langholz. *Hidden Myth: Structure and Symbolism in Advertising.* New York: Basic Books, 1975.

Lichtenstein, Nelson. *Labor's War at Home: The CIO in World War II.* New York: Cambridge University Press, 1982.

———, ed. *Wal-Mart: A Field Guide to America's Largest Company and the World's Largest Employer.* New York: New Press, 2006.

Lienesch, Michael. *New Order of the Ages: Time, the Constitution, and the Making of Modern American Political Thought.* Princeton, N.J.: Princeton University Press, 1988.

Lindblom, Charles. *The Market System: What It Is, How It Works, and What to Make of It.* New Haven, Conn.: Yale University Press, 2001.

Lingeman, Richard. *Don't You Know There's a War On? The American Home Front, 1941–1945.* 1970; New York: Thunder's Mouth Press, 2003.

Lippard, Lucy. *The Lure of the Local: Senses of Place in a Multicentered Society.* New York: New Press, 1997.

Lipset, Seymour Martin. *American Exceptionalism: A Double Edged Sword.* New York: W. W. Norton, 1996.

Lipsitz, George. "Consumer Spending as State Project." In *Getting and Spending: Twentieth-Century European and American Consumer Societies,* edited by Susan Strasser, Charles F. McGovern, and Mattias Judt, 127–47. Cambridge, U.K.: Cambridge University Press, 1998.

———. "In the Sweet Buy and Buy: Consumer Culture and American Studies." In *American Studies in a Moment of Danger,* 235–69. Minneapolis: University of Minnesota Press, 2001.

———. *Rainbow at Midnight: Labor and Culture in the 1940s.* Urbana: University of Illinois Press, 1994.

Livingston, James. *The Origins of the Federal Reserve System: Money, Class and Corporate Capitalism.* Ithaca, N.Y.: Cornell University Press, 1986.

———. *Pragmatism and the Political Economy of Cultural Revolution, 1850–1940.* Chapel Hill: University of North Carolina Press, 1994.

———. *Pragmatism, Feminism, and Democracy: Rethinking the Politics of American History.* New York: Routledge, 2001.

———. "The Social Analysis of Economic History and Theory: Conjectures on Late Nineteenth-Century American Development." *American Historical Review* 92 (February 1987): 69–95.

Lloyd, David, and Paul Thomas. *Culture and the State.* New York: Routledge, 1998.

Loeb, Lori Anne. *Consuming Angels: Advertising and Victorian Women.* New York: Oxford University Press, 1994.

Longstreth, Richard. *The Drive-In, the Supermarket, and the Transformation of Commercial Space in Los Angeles, 1919–1941.* Cambridge, Mass.: MIT Press, 1999.

Loviglio, Jason William. *Radio's Intimate Public: National Broadcasting and Mass Mediated Democracy.* Minneapolis: University of Minnesota Press, 2005.

Lowe, Lisa. *Immigrant Acts: On Asian American Cultural Politics.* Durham, N.C.: Duke University Press, 1996.

Luke, Carmen. *Constructing the Child Viewer.* New York: Praeger, 1990.

Lustig, R. Jeffrey. *Corporate Liberalism: The Origins of Modern American Political Theory, 1890–1920*. Berkeley: University of California Press, 1982.

Lynch, Edmund C. "Walter Dill Scott: Pioneering Industrial Psychologist." *Business History Review* 42 (Summer 1968): 149–70.

Lynch, Kevin. *The Image of the City*. Cambridge, Mass.: MIT Press, 1960.

Lynes, Russell. *The Tastemakers*. New York: Harper, 1954.

Madsen, Deborah L. *American Exceptionalism*. Jackson, Miss.: University Press of Mississippi, 1998.

Maland, Charles. *Chaplin and American Culture: Evolution of a Star Image*. Princeton, N.J.: Princeton University Press, 1989.

Malone, Bill. *Country Music U.S.A.* Austin: University of Texas Press, 1985.

Manring, M. M. *Slave in a Box: The Strange Career of Aunt Jemima*. Charlottesville: University Press of Virginia, 1998.

Marchand, Roland. *Advertising the American Dream: Making Way for Modernity, 1920–1940*. Berkeley: University of California Press, 1985.

——. "The Corporation Nobody Knew: Bruce Barton, Alfred Sloan, and the Founding of the General Motors 'Family.' " *Business History Review* 64 (Winter 1991): 825–75.

——. *Creating the Corporate Soul: The Rise of Public Relations and of Corporate Imagery in American Big Business*. Berkeley: University of California Press, 1998.

——. "The Fitful Career of Advocacy Advertising: Political Protection, Client Cultivation, and Corporate Morale." *California Management Review* 39 (Winter 1987): 128–56.

Marcus, George E., and Michael M. J. Fischer. *Anthropology as Cultural Critique: An Experimental Movement in the Human Sciences*. Chicago: University of Chicago Press, 1986.

Marquis, Alice G. *Hopes and Ashes: The Birth of Modern Times, 1929–1939*. New York: Free Press, 1986.

Marshall, T. H. *Citizenship and Social Class and Other Essays*. Cambridge, U.K.: Cambridge University Press, 1950.

Martinson, Tom. *American Dreamscape: The Pursuit of Happiness in Postwar Suburbia*. New York: Carroll and Graf, 2000.

Matthews, Glenna. *"Just a Housewife": The Rise and Fall of Domesticity in America*. New York: Oxford University Press, 1987.

Mátyás, Antal. *History of Modern Non-Marxian Economics: From Marginalist Revolution through the Keynesian Revolution to Contemporary Monetarist Counter-Revolution*. 2d ed. New York: St. Martin's Press, 1985.

Maxwell, William J. *New Negro, Old Left: African American Writing and Communism between the Wars*. New York: Columbia University Press, 1999.

May, Dean L. *From New Deal to New Economics: The Liberal Response to the Recession*. New York: Garland, 1981.

May, Elaine. *Homeward Bound: American Families in the Cold War Era*. New York: Basic Books, 1988.

May, Lary. *The Big Tomorrow: Hollywood and the Politics of the American Way*. Chicago: University of Chicago Press, 2000.

——. *Screening Out the Past: The Birth of Mass Culture and the Motion Picture Industry*. New York: Oxford University Press, 1980.

Mayer, Robert N. *The Consumer Movement: Guardians of the Marketplace.* Boston: Twayne, 1989.

McChesney, Robert W. *Telecommunications, Mass Media, and Democracy: The Battle for Control of U.S. Broadcasting, 1928–1934.* New York: Oxford University Press, 1993.

McCoy, Drew R. *The Elusive Republic: Political Economy in Jeffersonian America.* Chapel Hill: University of North Carolina Press, 1980.

McCracken, Grant. *Culture and Consumption: Essays in Theory.* Indianapolis: Indiana University Press, 1987.

McCraw, Thomas K. *Prophets of Regulation: Charles Francis Adams, Louis D. Brandeis, James M. Landis, Alfred E. Kahn* Cambridge, Mass.: Belknap Press of Harvard University Press, 1984.

McDannell, Colleen. *The Christian Home in Victorian America, 1840–1890.* Bloomington: Indiana University Press, 1986.

McGerr, Michael E. *The Decline of Popular Politics: The American North, 1865–1928.* New York: Oxford University Press, 1986.

McGovern, Charles F. "Consumption." In *A Companion to 20th-Century America*, edited by Stephen J. Whitfield, 336–57. Malden, Mass.: Blackwell, 2004.

——. "Consumption and Citizenship in the United States, 1900–1940." In *Getting and Spending: European and American Consumer Societies in the Twentieth Century*, edited by Susan Strasser, Charles F. McGovern, and Mattias Judt, 37–58. Cambridge, U.K.: Cambridge University Press, 1998.

McKendrick, Neil, John Brewer, and J. H. Plumb. *The Birth of a Consumer Society: The Commercialization of Eighteenth-Century England.* Bloomington: Indiana University Press, 1982.

Meikle, Jeffrey M. *Twentieth Century Limited: Industrial Design in America, 1925–1939.* Philadelphia: Temple University Press, 1979.

Melnick, Jeffrey. *A Right to Sing the Blues: Blacks, Jews and American Popular Song.* Cambridge, Mass.: Harvard University Press, 1999.

Mendenhall, John. *Character Trademarks.* San Francisco: Chronicle Books, 1990.

Merish, Lori. *Sentimental Materialism: Gender, Commodity Culture, and Nineteenth-Century American Literature.* Durham, N.C.: Duke University Press, 2000.

Meštrović, Stjepan Gabriel. *Thorstein Veblen on Culture and Society.* London: Sage, 2003.

Meyer, Stephen. *The Five Dollar Day: Labor Management and Social Control in the Ford Motor Company, 1908–1921.* Albany: State University of New York Press, 1981.

Michaels, Walter Benn. *Our America: Nativism, Modernism, and Pluralism.* Durham, N.C.: Duke University Press, 1995.

Micklethwait, John, and Adrian Wooldridge. *The Company: A Short History of a Revolutionary Idea.* New York: Modern Library, 2003.

Millard, Andre. *America on Record: A History of Recorded Sound.* New York: Cambridge University Press, 1995.

Miller, Daniel. *The Dialectics of Shopping.* Chicago: University of Chicago Press, 2001.

——. *Material Culture and Mass Consumption.* Oxford, U.K.: Basil Blackwell, 1987.

——, ed. *Acknowledging Consumption: A Review of New Studies.* New York: Routledge, 1995.

Miller, Karen S. *The Voice of Business: Hill & Knowlton and Postwar Public Relations.* Chapel Hill: University of North Carolina Press, 1999.

Miller, Karl Hagstrom. "Segregating Sound: Folklore, Phonographs, and the
    Transformation of Southern Music, 1888–1935." Ph.D. diss., New York University,
    2002.

Mills, C. Wright. *White Collar: The American Middle Classes*. New York: Oxford University
    Press, 1951.

Minton, Henry L. *Lewis M. Terman, Pioneer in Psychological Testing*. New York: New York
    University Press, 1988.

Mitchell, Wesley Clair, ed. *What Veblen Taught*. New York: Viking Press, 1936.

Montgomery, David. *The Fall of the House of Labor: The Workplace, the State, and American
    Labor Activism, 1865–1925*. New York: Cambridge University Press, 1987.

——. *Workers' Control in America: Studies in the History of Work, Technology, and Labor
    Struggles*. Cambridge, U.K.: Cambridge University Press, 1976.

Montgomery, Edrene Stephens. "Bruce Barton and the Twentieth-Century Menace of
    Unreality." Ph.D. diss., University of Arkansas, 1984.

Morello, John A. *Selling the President, 1920: Albert D. Lasker, Advertising, and the Election of
    Warren G. Harding*. Westport, Conn.: Praeger, 2001.

Mukerji, Chandra. *From Graven Images: Patterns of Modern Materialism*. New York:
    Columbia University Press, 1983.

Musser, Charles S. *The Emergence of Cinema: The American Screen to 1907*. New York:
    Scribner, 1990.

Nasaw, David. *Going Out: The Rise and Fall of Public Amusements*. New York: Basic Books,
    1993.

Nash, George H. *The Life of Herbert Hoover*. Vol. 3: *Master of Emergencies, 1917–1918*. New
    York: W. W. Norton, 1996.

Nelson, Daniel. *Managers and Workers: Origins of the Twentieth-Century Factory System in
    the United States*. 2d ed. Madison: University of Wisconsin Press, 1995.

Nelson, Elizabeth White. *Market Sentiments: Middle-Class Market Culture in Nineteenth-
    Century America*. Washington, D.C.: Smithsonian Books, 2004.

Nelson, John, Jr. *Liberty and Property: Political Economy and Policy-Making in the New
    Nation, 1789–1812*. Baltimore, Md.: Johns Hopkins University Press, 1987.

Newman, Kathy M. "Poisons, Potions, and Profits: Radio Rebels and the Origins of the
    Consumer Movement." In *Radio Reader: Essays in the Cultural History of Radio*, ed.
    Michele Hilmes and Jason Loviglio, 157–81. New York: Routledge, 2002.

——. *Radio Active: Advertising and Consumer Activism, 1935–1947*. Berkeley: University of
    California Press, 2004.

Ngai, Mae. *Impossible Subjects: Illegal Aliens and the Making of Modern America*. Princeton,
    N.J.: Princeton University Press, 2003.

Nickles, Shelley. "More Is Better: Mass Consumption, Gender, and Class Identity in
    Postwar America." *American Quarterly* 54 (December 2002): 581–622.

——. "Object Lessons: Household Appliance Design and the American Middle Class,
    1920–1960." Ph.D. diss., University of Virginia, 1999.

Noble, David F. *America by Design: Science, Technology, and the Rise of Corporate Capitalism*.
    New York: Oxford University Press, 1977.

Noble, David W. *Death of a Nation: American Culture and the End of Exceptionalism*.
    Minneapolis: University of Minnesota Press, 2002.

——. *The End of American History: Democracy, Capitalism, and the Metaphor of Two Worlds in Anglo-American Historical Writing, 1880–1980.* Minneapolis: University of Minnesota Press, 1985.

Novick, Peter. *That Noble Dream: The "Objectivity Question" and the American Historical Profession.* New York: Cambridge University Press, 1988.

Nye, David E. *Electrifying America: Social Meanings of a New Technology.* Cambridge, Mass.: MIT Press, 1990.

——. *Image Worlds: Corporate Identities at General Electric.* Cambridge, Mass.: MIT Press, 1985.

——. *The Invented Self: An Antibiography from Documents of Thomas A. Edison.* Odense, Denmark: Odense University Press, 1983.

O'Donnell, John. *The Origins of Behaviorism: American Psychology, 1870–1920.* New York: New York University Press, 1985.

Ogren, Kathy. *The Jazz Revolution: Twenties America and the Meaning of Jazz.* New York: Oxford University Press, 1989.

Ohmann, Richard M. *Selling Culture: Magazines, Markets, and Class at the Turn of the Century.* New York: Verso, 1996.

Okun, Mitchell. *Fair Play in the Marketplace: The First Battle for Pure Food and Drugs.* DeKalb: Northern Illinois University Press, 1986.

O'Leary, Cecelia Elizabeth. *To Die For: The Paradox of American Patriotism.* Princeton, N.J.: Princeton University Press, 1999.

Ollman, Bertell. *Alienation: Marx's Conception of Man in a Capitalist Society.* 2d ed. New York: Cambridge University Press, 1976.

Olney, Martha. *Buy Now, Pay Later: Advertising, Credit, and Consumer Durables in the 1920s.* Chapel Hill: University of North Carolina Press, 1991.

Ong, Aihwa. *Flexible Citizenship: The Cultural Logics of Transnationality.* Durham, N.C.: Duke University Press, 1999.

Oriard, Michael. *Reading Football: How the Popular Press Created an American Spectacle.* Chapel Hill: University of North Carolina Press, 1998.

Orleck, Annelise. *Common Sense and a Little Fire: Women and Working-Class Politics in the United States, 1900–1965.* Chapel Hill: University of North Carolina Press, 1995.

Ortony, Andrew. *Metaphor and Thought.* New York: Cambridge University Press, 1979.

Ownby, Ted. *American Dreams in Mississippi: Consumers, Poverty, and Culture, 1830–1998.* Chapel Hill: University of North Carolina Press, 1999.

Packard, Vance. *The Waste Makers.* New York: D. McKay Company, 1960.

Papanek, Victor. *The Green Imperative: Natural Design for the Real World.* New York: Thames and Hudson, 1995.

Parrington, Vernon L. *Main Currents in American Thought: An Interpretation of American Literature from the Beginnings to 1920.* 3 vols. New York: Harcourt, Brace and Company, 1927–30.

Parson, Don. *Making a Better World: Public Housing, the Red Scare, and the Direction of Modern Los Angeles.* Minneapolis: University of Minnesota Press, 2005.

Passman, Arnold. *The Deejays.* New York: Macmillan, 1971.

Patterson, James T. *Congressional Conservatism and the New Deal: The Growth of the*

Conservative Coalition in Congress, 1933–1939. Lexington: University of Kentucky Press, 1967.

Patterson, Mark R. *Authority, Autonomy, and Representation in American Literature, 1776–1865*. Princeton, N.J.: Princeton University Press, 1988.

Pease, Otis. *Responsibilities of American Advertising: Private Control and Public Influence, 1920–1940*. New Haven, Conn.: Yale University Press, 1958.

Peiss, Kathy. *Cheap Amusements: Working Women and Leisure in Turn-of-the-Century New York*. Philadelphia: Temple University Press, 1986.

———. *Hope in a Jar: The Making of American Beauty Culture*. New York: Metropolitan Books, 1998.

Pells, Richard. *Not Like Us: How Europeans Have Loved, Hated, and Transformed American Culture Since World War II*. New York: Basic Books, 1997.

———. *Radical Visions and American Dreams: Culture and Social Thought in the Depression Years*. New York: Harper and Row, 1973.

Penz, G. Peter. *Consumer Sovereignty and Human Interests*. Cambridge, U.K.: Cambridge University Press, 1986.

Perrow, Charles. *Organizing America: Wealth, Power, and the Origins of Corporate Capitalism*. Princeton, N.J.: Princeton University Press, 2002.

Perret, Geoffrey. *Days of Sadness, Years of Triumph: The American People, 1939–1945*. New York: Coward, McCann, and Geoghegan, 1973.

Pertschuk, Michael. *Revolt against Regulation: The Rise and Pause of the Consumer Movement*. Berkeley: University of California Press, 1983.

Pleasants, Henry. *The Great American Popular Singers*. New York: Simon and Schuster, 1974.

Pocock, J. G. A. *The Machiavellian Moment: Florentine Political Thought and the Atlantic Republican Tradition*. Princeton, N.J.: Princeton University Press, 1975.

———. *Politics, Language, and Time: Essays on Political Thought and History*. New York: Atheneum, 1971.

Polan, Dana B. *Power and Paranoia: History, Narrative, and the American Cinema, 1940–1950*. New York: Columbia University Press, 1986.

Polanyi, Karl. *The Great Transformation*. New York: Farrar and Rinehart, 1944.

Polenberg, Richard A. *War and Society: The United States, 1941–1945*. Philadelphia: Lippincott, 1972.

Pollack, Norman. *The Just Polity: Populism, Law, and Human Welfare*. Urbana: University of Illinois Press, 1987.

Ponce de Leon, Charles. *Self-Exposure: Human-Interest Journalism and the Emergence of Celebrity in America, 1890–1940*. Chapel Hill: University of North Carolina Press, 2002.

Pope, Daniel. "American Economists and the High Cost of Living: The Late Progressive Era." *Journal of the History of the Behavioral Sciences* 17, no. 1 (1981): 75–87.

———. "His Master's Voice: James Rorty and the Critique of Advertising." *Maryland Historian* 19 (1988): 5–16.

———. *The Making of Modern Advertising*. New York: Basic Books, 1983.

Potter, David M. *People of Plenty: Economic Abundance and the American Character*. Chicago: University of Chicago Press, 1954.

Prelinger, Rick. *Capitalist Realism*. Vol. 2 of *Our Secret Century: Archival Films from the Darker Side of the American Dream*. CD-ROM; Los Angeles: Voyager, 1996.

———. *The Uncharted Landscape*. Vol. 6 of *Our Secret Century: Archival Films from the Darker Side of the American Dream*. CD-ROM; Los Angeles: Voyager, 1996.

Princen, Thomas, Michael Maniates, and Ken Conca, eds. *Confronting Consumption*. Cambridge, Mass.: MIT Press, 2002.

Prothro, James W. *The Dollar Decade: Business Ideas in the 1920s*. Baton Rouge: Louisiana State University, 1954.

Purcell, Edward A., Jr. *The Crisis of Democratic Theory: Scientific Naturalism and the Problem of Value*. Lexington: University Press of Kentucky, 1973.

Quinn, Bill. *How Wal-Mart Is Destroying America and What You Can Do about It*. Berkeley: Ten Speed Press, 1998.

Rabinovitz, Lauren. *For the Love of Pleasure: Women, Movies, and Culture in Turn-of-the-Century Chicago*. New Brunswick, N.J.: Rutgers University Press, 1998.

Rabinowitz, Paula. *Labor and Desire: Women's Revolutionary Fiction in Depression America*. Chapel Hill: University of North Carolina Press, 1991.

Radway, Janice. *A Feeling for Books: The Book-of-the-Month Club, Literary Taste, and Middle-Class Desire*. Chapel Hill: University of North Carolina Press, 1997.

Rappaport, Erika. *Shopping for Pleasure: Women in the Making of London's West End*. Princeton, N.J.: Princeton University Press, 1999.

Raucher, Alan. *Public Relations and Business, 1900–1929*. Baltimore, Md.: Johns Hopkins University Press, 1968.

Ray, Robert B. *A Certain Tendency of the Hollywood Cinema, 1930–1980*. Princeton, N.J.: Princeton University Press, 1985.

Razlogova, Elena. "Voice of the Listener: Americans and the Radio Industry, 1930–1950." Ph.D. diss., George Mason University, 2003.

Reagan, Patrick D. *Designing a New America: The Origins of New Deal Planning, 1890–1943*. Amherst: University of Massachusetts Press, 2000.

Reddin, Paul. *Wild West Shows*. Urbana: University of Illinois Press, 1999.

Register, Woody. *The Kid of Coney Island: Fred Thompson and the Rise of American Amusements*. New York: Oxford University Press, 2001.

Reidelbach, Maria. *Completely Mad: A History of the Comic Book and Magazine*. Boston: Little, Brown, 1991.

Reiss, Benjamin. *The Showman and the Slave: Race, Death, and Memory in Barnum's America*. Cambridge, Mass.: Harvard University Press, 2001.

Reiss, Stephen A. *Touching Base: Professional Baseball and American Culture in the Progressive Era*. Rev. ed. Urbana: University of Illinois Press, 1999.

Ribuffo, Leo. "Jesus Christ as Business Statesman: Bruce Barton and the Selling of American Corporate Capitalism." *American Quarterly* 33 (Summer 1981): 206–31.

Riesman, David, with Reuel Denney and Nathan Glazer. *The Lonely Crowd: A Study of the Changing American Character*. New Haven, Conn.: Yale University Press, 1950.

Riggs, Thomas. *Encyclopedia of Major Marketing Campaigns*. Detroit, Mich.: Gale Group, 2000.

Robbins, Bruce. *Secular Vocations: Intellectuals, Professionalism, Culture*. New York: Verso, 1993.

——, ed. *The Phantom Public Sphere*. Minneapolis: University of Minnesota Press, 1993.

Robins, Natalie. *Copeland's Cure: Homeopathy and the War between Conventional and Alternative Medicine*. New York: Knopf, 2005.

Robinson, Daniel J. *The Measure of Democracy: Polling, Market Research, and Public Life, 1930–1945*. Toronto: University of Toronto Press, 1999.

Rochberg-Halton, Eugene. *Meaning and Modernity: Social Theory in the Pragmatic Attitude*. Chicago: University of Chicago Press, 1986.

Rochberg-Halton, Eugene, and Mihaly Csikszentmihalyi. *The Meaning of Things: Domestic Symbols and the Self*. Cambridge, U.K.: Cambridge University Press, 1984.

Roche, Daniel. *A History of Everyday Things: The Birth of Consumption in France 1600–1800*. Translated by Brian Pearce. New York: Cambridge University Press, 2000.

Rodgers, Daniel T. *Contested Truths: Keywords in American Politics Since Independence*. New York: Basic Books, 1987.

——. "In Search of Progressivism." *Reviews in American History* 10 (December 1982): 113–32.

——. *The Work Ethic in Industrial America, 1865–1920*. Chicago: University of Chicago Press, 1978.

Rogin, Michael. *Blackface, White Noise: Jewish Immigrants in the Hollywood Melting Pot*. Berkeley: University of California Press, 1996.

Rosenzweig, Roy S. *Eight Hours for What We Will: Workers and Leisure in an Industrial City, 1870–1920*. New York: Cambridge University Press, 1983.

Ross, Dorothy. "The Liberal Tradition Revisited and the Republican Tradition Addressed." In *New Directions in Intellectual History*, edited by John Higham and Paul Conkin, 116–31. Baltimore, Md.: Johns Hopkins University Press, 1979.

——. *The Origins of American Social Science*. New York: Cambridge University Press, 1991.

——. "Socialism and American Liberalism: Academic Social Thought in the 1880s." *Perspectives in American History* 11 (1977–78): 5–79.

Rostow, W. W. *The Stages of Economic Growth: A Non-Communist Manifesto*. Cambridge, U.K.: Cambridge University Press, 1960.

Roy, William G. *Socializing Capital: The Rise of the Large Industrial Corporation in America*. Princeton, N.J.: Princeton University Press, 1997.

Rubin, Joan Shelley. *Constance Rourke and American Culture*. Chapel Hill: University of North Carolina Press, 1980.

——. *The Making of Middlebrow Culture*. Chapel Hill: University of North Carolina Press, 1992.

Russo, Alexander Todd. "Roots of Radio's Rebirth: Audiences, Aesthetics, Economics, and Technologies of American Broadcasting, 1926–1951." Ph.D. diss., Brown University, 2004.

Rydell, Robert W. *World of Fairs: The Century-of-Progress Expositions*. Chicago: University of Chicago Press, 1993.

Samson, Peter. "The Emergence of a Consumer Interest in America, 1870–1930." Ph.D. diss., University of Chicago, 1980.

Samuels, Warren J., ed. *The Founding of Institutional Economics: The Leisure Class and Sovereignty*. New York: Routledge, 1998.

Samuels, Warren J., and Arthur S. Miller. *Corporations and Society: Power and Responsibility*. New York: Greenwood Press, 1987.

Samuelson, Robert. *The Good Life and Its Discontents: The American Dream in the Age of Entitlement, 1945–1995*. New York: Times Books, 1995.

Sandel, Michael. *Democracy's Discontent: America In Search of a Public Philosophy*. Cambridge, Mass.: Belknap Press of Harvard University Press, 1996.

Sapir, J. David, and J. Christopher Crocker, eds. *The Social Use of Metaphor: Essays on the Anthropology of Rhetoric*. Philadelphia: University of Pennsylvania Press, 1977.

Scanlon, Jennifer. *Inarticulate Longings: The Ladies' Home Journal, Gender, and the Promises of Consumer Culture*. New York: Routledge, 1995.

——, ed. *The Gender and Consumer Culture Reader*. New York: New York University Press, 2000.

Schainwald, Sybil Schwartz. "The Genesis and Growth of the First Consumer Testing Organization." M.A. thesis, Columbia University, 1971.

Schama, Simon. *An Embarrassment of Riches: Dutch Culture in the Seventeenth Century*. New York: Alfred A. Knopf, 1987.

Schatz, Thomas. *The Genius of the System: Hollywood Filmmaking in the Studio Era*. New York: Pantheon, 1988.

Schivelbusch, Wolfgang. *Disenchanted Night: The Industrialization of Light in the Nineteenth Century*. Berkeley: University of California Press, 1988.

——. *The Railway Journey: The Industrialization of Time and Space in the Nineteenth Century*. Berkeley: University of California Press, 1985.

Schlereth, Thomas J. *Victorian America: Transformations in Everyday Life, 1876–1915*. New York: HarperCollins, 1991.

Schlesinger, Arthur M., Jr. *The Age of Roosevelt*. 3 vols. Boston: Houghton Mifflin, 1957–1960.

Schlesinger, Arthur M., Jr., and Morton White, eds. *Paths of American Thought*. Boston: Houghton Mifflin, 1963.

Schmidt, Leigh Eric. *Consumer Rites: The Buying and Selling of American Holidays*. Princeton, N.J.: Princeton University Press, 1995.

Schor, Juliet B. *Born to Buy: The Commercialized Child and the New Consumer Culture*. New York: Scribner, 2004.

——. *The Overspent American: Upscaling, Downshifting, and the New Consumer*. New York: Basic Books, 1998.

Schudson, Michael. *Advertising, the Uneasy Persuasion: Its Dubious Impact on American Society*. New York: Basic Books, 1984.

Schultze, Quentin James. "Advertising, Science, and Professionalism, 1885–1917." Ph.D. diss., University of Illinois, 1976.

Schumpeter, Joseph A. *Capitalism, Socialism and Democracy*. New York: Harper and Brothers, 1942.

Schwartz, Barry. *The Costs of Living: How Market Freedom Erodes the Best Things in Life*. New York: W. W. Norton, 1994.

——. *The Paradox of Choice: Why More Is Less*. New York: Ecco, 2004.

Schwartz, Vanessa. *Spectacular Realities: Early Mass Culture in Fin-de-Siècle Paris*. Berkeley: University of California Press, 1998.

Scott, Joan Wallach. *Gender and the Politics of History*. New York: Columbia University Press, 1988.

Scranton, Philip D. *Endless Novelty: Specialty Production and American Industrialization, 1865–1925*. Princeton, N.J.: Princeton University Press, 1997.

Segal, Howard P. *Technological Utopianism in American Culture*. Chicago: University of Chicago Press, 1984.

Seth, Andrew, and Geoffrey Randall. *The Grocers: The Rise and Rise of the Supermarket Chains*. London: Kogan Page, 2000.

Shaffer, Marguerite S. *See America First: Tourism and National Identity, 1880–1940*. Washington, D.C.: Smithsonian Institution Press, 2001.

Shank, Barry. "Pierre Bourdieu and the Field of Cultural History." *Intellectual History Newsletter* 23 (2001).

———. *A Token of My Affection: Greeting Cards and American Business Culture*. New York: Columbia University Press, 2004.

Shannon, Christopher. *Conspicuous Criticism: Tradition, the Individual, and Culture in American Social Thought, from Veblen to Mills*. Baltimore, Md.: Johns Hopkins University Press, 1996.

Shi, David E. *The Simple Life: Plain Living and High Thinking in American Culture*. New York: Oxford University Press, 1985.

Shklar, Judith N. *American Citizenship: The Quest for Inclusion*. Cambridge, Mass.: Harvard University Press, 1991.

Short, K. R. M., ed. *Film and Radio Propaganda in World War II*. Knoxville: University of Tennessee Press, 1983.

Silber, Norman Isaac. *Test and Protest: The Influence of Consumers Union*. New York: Holmes and Meier, 1983.

Silva, Jonathan. "The Development of American Marketing Thought and Practice, 1902–1940." Ph.D. diss., Ohio State University, 1998.

Singer, Ben. *Melodrama and Modernity: Early Sensational Cinema and Its Contexts*. New York: Columbia University Press, 2001.

Skinner, Quentin. "Meaning and Understanding in the History of Ideas." *History and Theory* 8, no. 1 (1969): 3–53.

Sklar, Katherine Kish. *Catherine Beecher: A Study in American Domesticity*. New York: W. W. Norton, 1976.

———. *Florence Kelley and the Nation's Work*. New Haven, Conn.: Yale University Press, 1995.

Sklar, Martin. *The Corporate Reconstruction of American Capitalism, 1890–1916: The Market, the Law, and Politics*. New York: Cambridge University Press, 1988.

Sklar, Robert. *Movie-Made America: A Cultural History of American Movies*. New York: Vintage Books, 1975.

Skowronek, Stephen. *Building a New American State: The Expansion of National Administrative Capacities, 1877–1920*. New York: Cambridge University, 1982.

Slater, Don. *Consumer Culture and Modernity*. Cambridge, U.K.: Polity Press, 1997.

Slide, Anthony. *American Racist: The Life and Films of Thomas Dixon*. Lexington: University Press of Kentucky, 2004.

Sokal, Michael M., ed. *Psychological Testing and American Society, 1890–1920*. New Brunswick, N.J.: Rutgers University Press, 1987.

Small, Christopher. *Music of the Common Tongue: Survival and Celebration in Afro-American Music*. New York: Riverrun Press, 1987.

Smith, Anthony D. *Nationalism: Theory, Ideology, History*. Malden, Mass.: Polity Press, 2001.

Smith, David Dion. "The Jam Handy Company and the Discussional Filmstrip." Ph.D. diss., Wayne State University, 1975.

Smith, Kathleen E. R. *God Bless America: Tin Pan Alley Goes to War*. Lexington: University Press of Kentucky, 2003.

Smith, Mark C. *Social Science in the Crucible: The American Debate over Objectivity and Purpose, 1918–1941*. Durham, N.C.: Duke University Press, 1994.

———. "Robert Lynd and Consumerism in the 1930s." *Journal of the History of Sociology* 2 (Fall–Winter 1979–80): 99–119.

Smith, Rogers M. *Civic Ideals: Conflicting Visions of Citizenship in U.S. History*. New Haven, Conn.: Yale University Press, 1997.

Smith, Steven. "Personalities in the Crowd: The Idea of the 'Masses' in American Popular Culture." *Prospects* 19 (1994): 225–87.

Smith, Terry. *Making the Modern: Industry, Art, and Design in America*. Chicago: University of Chicago Press, 1993.

Smith, Woodruff D. *Consumption and the Making of Respectability, 1600–1800*. New York: Routledge, 2002.

Smoodin, Eric. *Regarding Frank Capra: Audience, Celebrity, and American Film Studies, 1930–1960*. Durham, N.C.: Duke University Press, 2004.

Smulyan, Susan R. *Selling Radio: The Commercialization of American Broadcasting, 1820–1932*. Washington, D.C.: Smithsonian Institution Press, 1994.

Smythe, Dallas W. *Dependency Road: Communications, Capitalism, Consciousness, and Canada*. Norwood, N.J.: Ablex Publishing, 1981.

Socolow, Michael J. "To Network a Nation: N.B.C., C.B.S., and the Development of National Network Radio in the United States, 1925–1950." Ph.D. diss., Georgetown University, 2001.

Sokal, Michael M., ed. *Psychological Testing and American Society, 1890–1930*. New Brunswick, N.J.: Rutgers University Press, 1987.

Sollers, Werner. *Beyond Ethnicity: Consent and Descent in American Culture*. New York: Oxford University Press, 1986.

Spears, Timothy B. *100 Years on the Road: The Traveling Salesman in American Culture*. New Haven, Conn.: Yale University Press, 1995.

Spindler, Michael. *Veblen and Modern America: Revolutionary Iconoclast*. London: Pluto Press, 2002.

Spitzer, Leo. *Essays on English and American Literature*. Princeton, N.J.: Princeton University Press, 1962.

Spurgeon, Anne M. "Marketing the Unmentionable: Wallace Meyer and the Introduction of Kotex." *Maryland Historian* 19 (Spring/Summer 1988): 17–30.

Stage, Sarah, and Virginia B. Vicenti, eds. *Rethinking Home Economics: Women and the History of a Profession*. Ithaca, N.Y.: Cornell University Press, 1997.

Starr, Paul. *The Creation of the Media: Political Origins of Modern Communications*. New York: Basic Books, 2004.

——. *The Social Transformation of American Medicine*. New York: Basic Books, 1982.

Steel, Ronald. *Walter Lippmann and the American Century*. Boston: Little, Brown, 1980.

Stein, Herbert L. *The Fiscal Revolution in America*. Chicago: University of Chicago Press, 1969.

Stein, Roger. *John Ruskin and Aesthetic Thought in America, 1840–1900*. Cambridge, Mass.: Harvard University Press, 1967.

Steinberg, Salme Hadju. *Reformer in the Marketplace: Edward W. Bok and the Ladies' Home Journal*. Baton Rouge: Louisiana State University Press, 1974.

Stevenson, Nick. *Cultural Citizenship: Cosmopolitan Questions*. Berkshire, Eng.: Open University Press, 2003.

——, ed. *Culture and Citizenship*. Thousand Oaks, Calif.: Sage, 2001.

Stocking, George W., Jr., *Race, Culture, and Evolution: Essays in the History of Anthropology*. Chicago: University of Chicago Press, 1982.

——. *Romantic Motives: Essays on Anthropological Sensibility*. Madison: University of Wisconsin Press, 1989.

Stole, Inger L. "Consumer Protection in Historical Perspective: The Five-Year Battle over Federal Regulation of Advertising, 1933 to 1938." *Mass Communication and Society* 3, no. 4 (2000): 351–72.

——. "The 'Salesmanship of Sacrifice': The Advertising Industry's Use of Public Relations during the Second World War." *Advertising and Society Review* 2, no. 2 (2001), <http://muse.jhu.edu/journals/advertising—and—society— review/voo2/2.stole.htm> (accessed October 17, 2005).

——. "Selling Advertising: The U.S. Advertising Industry and Its Public Relations Activities, 1932–1946." Ph.D. diss., University of Wisconsin, 1998.

Storrs, Landon R. Y. *Civilizing Capitalism: The National Consumers' League, Women's Activism, and Labor Standards in the New Deal Era*. Chapel Hill: University of North Carolina Press, 2000.

Stott, William. *Documentary Expression and Thirties America*. New York: Oxford University Press, 1973.

Stowe, David M. *Swing Changes: Big-Band Jazz in New Deal America*. Cambridge, Mass.: Harvard University Press, 1994.

Strasser, Susan. *Never Done: A History of American Housework*. New York: Pantheon, 1982.

——. *Satisfaction Guaranteed: The Making of the American Mass Market*. New York: Pantheon, 1989.

——, ed. *Commodifying Everything: Relationships of the Market*. New York: Routledge, 2003.

Strasser, Susan, Charles F. McGovern, and Mattias Judt, eds. *Getting and Spending: European and American Consumer Societies in the Twentieth Century*. Cambridge, U.K.: Cambridge University Press, 1998.

Sugrue, Thomas J. *Origins of the Urban Crisis: Race and Inequality in Postwar Detroit*. Princeton, N.J.: Princeton University Press, 1996.

Suisman, David. "The Sound of Money: Music, Machines, and Markets, 1890–1925." Ph.D. diss., Columbia University, 2002.

Susman, Warren I. *Culture and Commitment, 1929–1945*. New York: George Braziller, 1973.

———. *Culture as History: The Transformation of American Society in the Twentieth Century.* New York: Pantheon, 1984.

Sweeney, Michael J. *Secrets of Victory: The Office of Censorship and the American Press and Radio during World War II.* Chapel Hill: University of North Carolina Press, 2001.

Symes, Colin. *Setting the Record Straight: A Material History of Classical Recording.* Middletown, Conn.: Wesleyan University Press, 2004.

Tedlow, Richard S. "From Competitor to Consumer: The Changing Focus of Federal Regulation of Advertising, 1914–1938." *Business History Review* 60 (Spring 1981): 35–58.

———. *Keeping the Corporate Image: Public Relations and Big Business.* Greenwich, Conn.: JAI Press, 1979.

———. *New and Improved: The Story of Mass Marketing in America.* New York: Basic Books, 1990.

Terkel, Studs. *"The Good War": An Oral History of World War II.* New York: Pantheon, 1984.

———. *Hard Times: An Oral History of the Great Depression.* New York: Washington Square Press, 1978.

Thelen, David. *The New Citizenship: Origins of Progressivism in Wisconsin, 1885–1900.* Columbia: University of Missouri Press, 1972.

———. *Paths of Resistance: Tradition and Dignity in Industrializing Missouri.* New York: Oxford University Press, 1986.

———. "Patterns of Consumer Consciousness in the Progressive Movement: Robert M. LaFollette, the Antitrust Persuasion, and Labor Legislation." In *The Quest for Social Justice: The Morris Fromkin Memorial Lectures, 1970–1980,* edited by Ralph M. Aderman, 19–47. Madison: University of Wisconsin Press, 1983.

Thomas, John. *Alternative America: Henry George, Edward Bellamy, Henry Demarest Lloyd, and the Adversary Tradition.* Cambridge, Mass.: Harvard University Press, 1983.

Thompson, Emily. *The Soundscape of Modernity: Architectural Acoustics and the Culture of Listening in America, 1900–1933.* Cambridge, Mass.: MIT Press, 2002.

Tichi, Cecilia. *Shifting Gears: Technology, Literature, Culture in Modernist America.* Chapel Hill: University of North Carolina Press, 1987.

Tiersten, Lisa. *Marianne in the Market: Envisioning Consumer Society in Fin-de-Siècle France.* Berkeley: University of California Press, 2001.

Tilman, Rick, ed. *The Legacy of Thorstein Veblen.* Northampton, Mass.: Edward Elgar, 2003.

Tobey, Ronald C. *Technology as Freedom: The New Deal and the Electrical Modernization of the American Home.* Berkeley: University of California Press, 1996.

Tomes, Nancy. "Merchants of Health: Medicine and Consumer Culture in the United States, 1900–1940." *Journal of American History* 88 (June 2001): 519–47.

Tomlins, Christopher L. *The State and the Unions: Labor Relations, Law, and the Organized Labor Movement in America, 1880–1960.* Cambridge, U.K.: Cambridge University Press, 1985.

Trachtenberg, Alan. *The Incorporation of America: Culture and Society in the Gilded Age.* New York: Hill and Wang, 1982.

Trachtenberg, Marvin. *The Statue of Liberty.* Rev. ed. New York: Penguin Books, 1986.

Tucker, Sherrie. *Swing Shift: "All-Girl" Bands of the 1940s.* Durham, N.C.: Duke University Press, 2000.

Turner, Frederick Jackson. *The Frontier in American History.* New York: Henry Holt and Company, 1920.

Turow, Joseph. *Breaking Up America: Advertisers and the New Media World.* Chicago: University of Chicago Press, 1997.

Tuttle, William M. Jr. *Daddy's Gone to War: The Second World War in the Lives of America's Children.* New York: Oxford University Press, 1993.

Tye, Larry. *Edward L. Bernays and the Birth of Public Relations.* New York: Crown, 1998.

Vance, Sandra Stringer, and Roy V. Scott. *Wal-Mart: A History of Sam Walton's Retail Phenomenon.* New York: Twayne Publishers, 1994.

Vaughn, Stephen. *Holding Fast the Inner Lines: Democracy, Nationalism, and the Committee on Public Information.* Chapel Hill: University of North Carolina Press, 1980.

Venturi, Robert, Denise Scott Brown, and Steven Izenour. *Learning from Las Vegas: The Forgotten Symbolism of Architectural Form.* Cambridge, Mass.: MIT Press, 1972.

Veysey, Lawrence. "The Autonomy of American History Reconsidered." *American Quarterly* 31 (Autumn 1979): 455–77.

———. *The Emergence of the American University.* Chicago: University of Chicago Press, 1965.

Voloshinov, V. N. [Mikhail Bakhtin]. *Marxism and the Philosophy of Language.* Translated by Ladislav Matejha and I. R. Titunik. Cambridge, Mass.: Harvard University Press, 1986.

Wachhorst, Wyn. *Thomas Alva Edison: An American Myth.* Cambridge, Mass.: MIT Press, 1981.

Wagenleitner, Reinhold. *Coca-Colonization and the Cold War: The Cultural Mission of the United States in Austria after the Second World War.* Chapel Hill: University of North Carolina Press, 1994.

Wald, Alan M. *Writing from the Left: New Essays on Radical Culture and Politics.* New York: Verso, 1994.

Walker, Nancy. *"The Ladies' Home Journal,* 'How America Lives,' and the Limits of Cultural Diversity." *Media History* 6, no. 2 (2000): 129–38.

———. *Shaping Our Mothers' World: American Women's Magazines.* Jackson, Miss.: University Press of Mississippi, 2000.

Waller, Mary Ellen. "Popular Women's Magazines, 1890–1917." Ph.D. diss., Columbia University, 1987.

Walsh, Lorena S. "Urban Amenities and Rural Sufficiency: Living Standards and Consumer Behavior in the Colonial Chesapeake, 1643–1777." *Journal of Economic History* 43 (March 1983): 109–17.

Walzer, Michael. *Obligations: Essays on Disobedience, War, and Citizenship.* Cambridge, Mass.: Harvard University Press, 1970.

———. *Spheres of Justice: A Defense of Pluralism and Equality.* New York: Basic Books, 1983.

Ward, Barbara McLean, ed. *Produce and Conserve, Share and Play Square: The Grocer and Consumer on the Home-Front Battlefield during World War II.* Portsmouth, N.H.: Strawberry Banke Museum, 1994.

Ward, Douglas B. "Tracking the Culture of Consumption: Curtis Publishing Company,

Charles Coolidge Parlin, and the Origins of Market Research, 1911–1930." Ph.D. diss., University of Maryland, 1998.

Ware, Susan M. *Beyond Suffrage: Women in the New Deal*. Cambridge, Mass.: Harvard University Press, 1981.

Warne, Colston E. *The Consumer Movement Lectures*. Edited by Richard L. D. Morse, assisted by Florence E. Snyder. Manhattan, Kans.: Family Economics Trust Press, 1993.

Watts, Steven. *The People's Tycoon: Henry Ford and the American Century*. New York: Knopf, 2005.

———. *The Republic Reborn: War and the Making of Liberal America, 1790–1820*. Baltimore, Md.: Johns Hopkins University Press, 1987.

Weems, Robert E., Jr. *Desegregating the Dollar: African American Consumerism in the Twentieth Century*. New York: New York University Press, 1998.

Weigley, Emma S. "It Might Have Been Euthenics: The Lake Placid Conferences and the Home Economics Movement." *American Quarterly* 26 (March 1974): 79–96.

Weinberg, Sidney. "What to Tell America: The Writers' Quarrel in the Office of War Information." *Journal of American History* 55 (June 1968): 73–89.

Weiss, Michael J. *The Clustered World: How We Live, What We Buy, and What It All Means about Who We Are*. Boston: Little, Brown, 2000.

Wells, Coleman Harwell. "Remapping America: Market Research and American Society, 1900–1940." Ph.D. diss., University of Virginia, 1999.

Westbrook, David A. *City of Gold: An Apology for Global Capitalism in a Time of Discontent*. New York: 2004.

Westbrook, Robert B. *John Dewey and American Democracy*. Ithaca, N.Y.: Cornell University Press, 1991.

Westbrook, Robert B. "Tribune of the Technostructure: The Popular Economics of Stuart Chase." *American Quarterly* 32 (Fall 1980): 387–408.

———. *Why We Fought: Forging American Obligations in World War II*. Washington, D.C.: Smithsonian Books, 2004.

White, G. Edward. *Creating the National Pastime: Baseball Transforms Itself, 1903–1953*. Princeton, N.J.: Princeton University Press, 1996.

White, Morton. *Social Thought in America: The Revolt Against Formalism*. Rev. ed. Boston: Beacon Press, 1957.

White, Morton, and Lucia White. *The Intellectual Versus the City, from Thomas Jefferson to Frank Lloyd Wright*. New York: Oxford University Press, 1962.

Wicke, Jennifer A. *Advertising Fictions: Literature, Advertising, and Social Reading*. New York: Columbia University Press, 1988.

Wiebe, Robert. *The Search for Order, 1877–1920*. New York: Hill and Wang, 1969.

Wiedenhoft, Wendy Ann. "The Politics of Consumption: A Comparative Study of the American Federation of Labor and the National Consumers' League during the Progressive Era." Ph.D. diss., University of Maryland, 2002.

Wiggershaus, Rolf. *The Frankfurt School: Its History, Theories, and Political Significance*. Translated by Michael Robertson. Cambridge, Mass.: MIT Press, 1994.

Wilentz, Sean. *Chants Democratic: New York City and the Rise of the American Working Class, 1788–1850*. New York: Oxford University Press, 1984.

Williams, Raymond. "Advertising: The Magic System." In *Problems in Materialism and Culture*, 170–95. London: Verso, 1980.

———. *Keywords: A Vocabulary of Culture and Society*. Rev ed. New York: Oxford University Press, 1983.

Williams, Rosalind H. *Dream Worlds: Mass Consumption in Late Nineteenth-Century France*. Berkeley: University of California Press, 1982.

Williams, William Appleman. *The Tragedy of American Diplomacy*. 1959; New York: W. W. Norton, 1988.

Wilson, Richard Guy, Dianne H. Pilgrim, and Dickran Tashjian. *The Machine Age in America, 1918–1941*. New York: Brooklyn Museum, 1986.

Winkler, Allan M. *Home Front U.S.A.: America during World War II*. 2d ed. Wheeling, Ill.: Harlan Davidson, 2000.

———. *The Politics of Propaganda: The Office of War Information, 1942–1945*. New Haven, Conn.: Yale University Press, 1978.

Wolfe, Allis R. "Women, Consumerism, and the National Consumers' League in the Progressive Era, 1900–1923." *Labor History* 16 (Summer 1975): 378–92.

Wood, Ellen Meiksins. *Empire of Capital*. New York: Verso, 2003.

Wood, Gordon S. *The Creation of the American Republic, 1776–1789*. Chapel Hill: University of North Carolina Press, 1969.

Wright, Gwendolyn. *Moralism and the Model Home: Domestic Architecture and Cultural Conflict in Chicago, 1873–1913*. Chicago: University of Chicago Press, 1980.

Yates, JoAnne. *Control through Communication: The Rise of System in American Capitalism*. Baltimore, Md.: Johns Hopkins University Press, 1989.

Yellin, Emily. *Our Mothers' War: American Women at Home and at the Front during World War II*. New York: Free Press, 2004.

Young, James Harvey. *The Medical Messiahs: A Social History of Health Quackery in Twentieth-Century America*. Princeton, N.J.: Princeton University Press, 1967.

———. *Pure Food: Securing the Federal Food and Drugs Act of 1906*. Princeton, N.J.: Princeton University Press, 1989.

———. *The Toadstool Millionaires: A Social History of Patent Medicines in the Era before Regulation*. Princeton, N.J.: Princeton University Press, 1961.

Yúdice, George. *The Expediency of Culture: The Uses of Culture in the Global Era*. Durham, N.C.: Duke University Press, 2003.

Zelinsky, Wilbur. *Nation into State: The Shifting Symbolic Foundations of American Nationalism*. Chapel Hill: University of North Carolina Press, 1988.

Zelizer, Viviana. *Pricing the Priceless Child: The Changing Social Value of Children*. New York: Basic Books, 1985.

———. *The Social Meaning of Money: Paychecks, Pin Money, Poor Relief, and Other Currencies*. New York: Basic Books, 1994.

Zim, Larry, Mel Lerner, and Herbert Rolfes. *The World of Tomorrow: The 1939 New York World's Fair*. New York: Harper and Row, 1988.

Zunz, Olivier. *Making America Corporate, 1870–1929*. Chicago: University of Chicago Press, 1990.

———. *Why the American Century?* Chicago: University of Chicago Press, 1999.

INDEX

Page numbers in italics refer to illustrations.

A&P grocery stores, 50
Abundance, 19, *337*, 344, 347, *370*, *374*
Adams, Samuel Hopkins, 148
Ad-Busters, *370*
Adorno, Theodor, 144
Advertisements: as political documents, 24, 67; reason-why copy style, 38–39
Advertisers: and professionalism, 5, 23, 25, 65; contempt of consumers, 8, 34, 51–53, 56–58, 180, 229–30; claim to power, 17, 67, 91–93, 242, 294; distance from consumers, 33–36, 56–60, 130, 229–30, 238–41, 270–84; and women consumers, 36–48, 79–88, 226, 232–38, 344; political language of, 62, 67–92, 130, 226–27, *369*, 371; compare themselves to politicians, 65–66, 73–74; equate market choice with political freedom, 68–75, 130, 285; equate consuming with democracy, 75–77, 270–80; resist consumer sovereignty, 76–77; and social inequality, 96–103, 194–95; and distinct American culture, 103–30; defend selling, 178–82; enemies of CR defend advertising, 178–82, 257–60, 263, 334–35, 338; critique *Your Money's Worth*, 179–82; clash with consumerists, 222, 253–60, 261, 327; defend capitalism, 222, 284–300, 319–23; against New Deal, 223, 253–60, 262–70, 284–90; in Depression, 223–41; and children, 238–41; against Food and Drug Bill, 255–60; and public relations, 265–60, 334; and rural consumers, 280; charge consumerists with communism, 319–23, 324;

private war against government, 334–40; in World War II, 334–53; selling postwar abundance, 350–53, 361–63. *See also* Advertising; Advertising agencies; Copywriters; Madison Avenue
Advertising: and identity, 23; influence on modernity, 23–31; history of, 23–36; service of corporations, 23–36, 88–94, 131, 262–300; depictions of American society in, 24–25, 270–84; and consumer demand, 26–29; and national progress, 27–31, 266–67; as anthropologists, 29–31; as sociologists, 31–36, 58–59, 270–84; in radio, 49–53, 241, 243; oral vs. print, 51–53; corporate imagery, 89–94, 125; corporate executives as elected rulers, 91–93; and upper-class consumers, 96–97; depictions of American history, 124–40, 227–28, 266; Veblen on, 146–48; misleading and false, 172–73, 196–97; wasteful, 172–74; testimonial, 173; monopolistic, 173–74; unscientific, 197; and showmanship, 225–26, 229; comic-strip, 237, 238; to children, 241; backlash against, 241–45; political economy and, 284–300; American exceptionalism in, 294–300, 338–41, *370*; free press guaranteed by, 320; in World War II, 338–53, 361–64. *See also* Advertisers; Advertising agencies; Copywriters; Madison Avenue
Advertising agencies: and service, 25–27; development of marketing in, 26–27, 32–34, 119; in radio, 50–59; and commission system, 224, 335
Advertising and Selling, 247
Advertising Federation of America, 322, 337

Food, Drug and Cosmetic Act (1938), 248; reform of, 251
Ford, Henry, 89, 92
The Ford Hour, 291
Ford Motor Company, 291, 298, *298*
Foster, William T., 254, 315
Four Freedoms, 343, 361
Fox, Frank, 334
Fox, Richard, 11
France, 103
Frank, Dana, 232
Frank, Thomas, 370
Frank, Waldo, 119
Franklin, Benjamin, 267
Frederick, Christine M., 39, 42, 45, 68, 69, 81, 122, 127–28, 180, 257
Frederick, J. George, 32, 65
Freedom of choice, 48, 81, 130, 156–58, 285, 300, 329, 342, 371
Free enterprise, 284–300, 328, 336, 337–38, 342, 347, 350, 362, 370
Friedan, Betty, 365, 372
From Dawn to Sunset, 290–91, *292–93*
Fuller, Walter H., 337, 339
Functionality, 140–41, 149, 153
Furnas, J. C., 277, 279
Futurama, 298, *299*
F. W. Woolworth Company, 89

Gainaday Electric Washer, 83
Gallup, George, 238
Gardiner, Edward H., 337
Gellner, Ernest, 105–6
General Electric Corporation, 83, 84, 89, 256, 263, 265, 290, 352, 353; *G-E Circle*, 281
General Federation of Women's Clubs, 325, 326, 332
General Foods Corporation, 294
General Motors Corporation (GM), 89, 227–28, 256, 263, 265, 266–67, *268–69*, 279; strikes at, 279, 290, 298, *299*, 350
Generation of Vipers, 238
George Batten Agency, 90–91

Germany, 103
Gerstle, Gary, 104–5
Gettysburg Address, 227
Gillette, King, 91–92, 98–99, *99*, 126
Gillies Coffee, 81
Gilman, Charlotte Perkins, 151
Glickman, Lawrence, 12, 311
Globalism, 370, 372–75
Gold Cross shoes, 343
Gold Dust soap, 88
Golden Gate International Exposition, 295
Goode, Kenneth, 56–57, 179, 181, 264
Good Housekeeping, 201, 226, 316, 319–20, 321, 322
Good Housekeeping Institute, 316, 319–20
Gordon, Leland, 329
"Grace Ellis," 280–81
Graybar Building, 270
Griffith, Bill, 370
Griswold, Kate, 40
Groesbeck, Kenneth, 338
Guisewite, Cathy, 370

Habermas, Jurgen, 18
Hader, Mathilde, 189, 214
Hall, S. Roland, 37
Happiness Candy, 50
Harap, Harry, 179, 198
Harding, T. Swann, 247
Harper's, 201, 211
Harrington, Michael, 365, 372
Hayek, Friedrich, 309
Hearst Corporation, 316–17, 320, 321, 324
Heasty, John, 305
Heinz, 339, 345
Henderson, Leon, 251, 336
Herring, E. Pendleton, 312
Hill, George Washington, 50
Hires Root Beer, 107
Hobsbawm, Eric, 9
Holmes, Mildred, 41, 180
Home economics, 152–54, 155, 179, 202
Home economists, 5, 154, 179, 189, 214, 254
Hoosier Kitchen Cabinets, 42, 81